R. Gupta's®

POPULAR MASTER GUIDE

Health Inspector Malaria Inspector

Recruitment Exam

ALSO USEFUL FOR

Sanitary Inspector • Paramedical Staff

CONDUCTED BY:

Railway Recruitment Boards (RRBs), DSSSB, MCD, NDMC, BMC, Cantonment Boards and Other Hospitals

Ravindra Pandey

B.Sc., Dip. in Sanitary Inspector

&

RPH Editorial Board

2027 EDITION

RAMESH PUBLISHING HOUSE, NEW DELHI

Published by
O.P. Gupta *for* Ramesh Publishing House

Admin. Office
12-H, New Daryaganj Road, Opp. Officers' Mess,
New Delhi-110002 ✆ 23275224, 23245124

E-mail: info@rameshpublishinghouse.com
For Online Shopping: www.rameshpublishinghouse.com

Showroom
● Balaji Market, Nai Sarak, Delhi-110006 ✆ 23282525 📱 9354373464
● 4457, Nai Sarak, Delhi-110006

Book Code: R-948

ISBN: 978-93-87604-07-0

Price: ₹ 440

Printed at: Deepak Offset, Delhi

CONTENTS

Previous Years' Paper

RRB–Health and Malaria Inspector (Grade-III)

Recruitment Exam, 2025

(Exam held on 28-04-2025)

1. What is the work done in moving a charge of 10C between two points with a potential difference of 14 V?

1. 10 J 2. 140 J
3. 1.4 J 4. 14 J

2. The Dachigam Sanctuary, located in Jammu and Kashmir in India, is home to which of the following species?

1. Indian bison
2. Snow leopard
3. Hippopotamus
4. One-horned rhinoceros

3. Who was sworn in as the Chief Minister of Maharashtra on 5 December 2024, following the state assembly elections?

1. Uddhav Thackeray
2. Eknath Shinde
3. Devendra Fadnavis
4. Ajit Pawar

4. Identify the element whose given valency does not match its typical valency.

Element	Atomic Number	Given valency
Be	4	2
Ne	10	0
Al	13	3
F	9	7

1. Be 2. F
3. Ne 4. Al

5. Which constitutional amendment to the Indian Constitution introduced a Legislative Assembly for the Union Territory of Delhi?

1. 74th Amendment 2. 61st Amendment
3. 42nd Amendment 4. 69th Amendment

6. Which transformative reform was introduced in 2016, aiming to create 'one nation, one tax and one market' in India?

1. Nationalisation of state banks
2. Revision of the Customs Act for certain goods
3. Introduction of the Direct Tax Code
4. Implementation of the Goods and Services Tax

7. Bleaching powder is a white solid with a strong chlorine smell. It is commonly used in:

1. disinfecting water and bleaching fabrics
2. preserving food and softening water
3. manufacturing cement and glass
4. making fertilisers and plastics

8. Which of the following correctly lists the sections of the Western Coastal Plains in India?

1. Konkan Coast, Karnataka Coast and Malabar Coast
2. Northern Circar Coast, Malabar Coast and Coromandel Coast
3. Konkan Coast, Coromandal Coast and Vembanad Coast
4. Karnataka Coast, Eastern Coast and Malabar Coast

1. 2	**2.** 2	**3.** 3	**4.** 2	**5.** 4	**6.** 4	**7.** 1	**8.** 1

9. Read the given statements and conclusions carefully. Assuming that the information given in the statements is true, even if it appears to be at variance with commonly known facts, decide which of the given conclusions logically follow(s) from the statements.

Statements:

All piles are quantities.

All stores are quantities.

Conclusions:

I. Some piles are stores.

II. Some quantities are stores.

1. Neither conclusion (I) nor (II) follows
2. Only conclusion (II) follows
3. Only conclusion (I) follows
4. Both conclusions (I) and (II) follow

10. Which of the following statements about sensitivity in plants is INCORRECT?

1. Plants have specialized nervous tissues for conducting information.
2. Plants exhibit phototropism by growing towards the light source.
3. Thigmotropism is the response of plants to touch or physical contact.
4. Chemotropism is the growth response of plants to chemical stimuli in their environment.

11. Which of the following sexual maturation changes occur in females?

1. Narrowing of hips
2. The breasts begin to grow
3. Skin decreased oil production
4. Stop of the menstrual cycle

12. A and B can together completes a piece of work in 25 days. They worked together for 20 days and then B left. After another 10 days, A completed the remaining work. In how many days can A complete the entire work alone?

1. 54 2. 60
3. 50 4. 40

13. The value of $\left(\frac{4}{7}\right) \times \left(\frac{21}{20}\right) + \left(\frac{6}{5} - 9\right)$ is:

1. $-\frac{36}{5}$
2. $-\frac{39}{8}$
3. $-\frac{29}{3}$
4. $-\frac{35}{9}$

14. Which of the following sacrificed their lives for the protection of Khejri trees?

1. Amrita Devi Bishnoi
2. Sunita Devi
3. Sunita Willium
4. Savita Devi Bishnoi

15. The Indian government launched a new digital health initiative in 2025, to improve healthcare accessibility and interoperability of medical data. What is the name of this initiative?

1. Ayushman Bharat Digital Mission 2.0
2. Bharat AI Health Grid
3. Digital India Healthcare 2025
4. National Health Stack Expansion

16. Based on the English alphabetical order, three of the following four letter-clusters are alike in a certain way and thus form a group. Which letter-cluster DOES NOT belong to that group?

(Note: The odd one out is not based on the number of consonants/vowels or their position in the letter-cluster.)

1. NPO 2. FHG
3. JLK 4. RTU

9. 2	**10.** 1	**11.** 2	**12.** 3	**13.** 1	**14.** 1	**15.** 1	**16.** 4

17. For image formation by a concave mirror, which of the following statements is true?

1. The size of the image is enlarged when the object is placed at infinity.
2. The nature of the image is real and erect when the object is at the centre of curvature.
3. An object placed at the focus forms a highly diminished image.
4. At the centre of curvature, the size of the image is the same as the size of the object.

18. Which of the following is correct regarding complex permanent tissue of plants?

1. Xylem is responsible for transporting organic nutrients
2. These tissues are plant tissues that consist of one type of cell
3. These tissues are essential for the plant's transport system
4. Phloem is responsible for transporting water

19. Who among the following social reformers worked to promote widow remarriage during the Indian National Movement?

1. EV Ramaswamy Naicker
2. Swami Vivekananda
3. Ishwarchandra Vidyasagar
4. Jyotirao Phule

20. 18 is related to 107 following a certain logic. Following the same logic, 21 is related to 125. To which of the given options is 14 related, following the same logic?
(Note: Operations should be performed on the whole numbers, without breaking down the numbers into their constituent digits. E.g., 13 – Operations on 13 such as adding/subtracting/multiplying to 13 can be performed. Breaking down 13 into 1 and 3 and then performing mathematical operations on 1 and 3 is not allowed.)

1. 95   2. 91
3. 83   4. 87

21. Find the circumference (in m) of the largest circle that can be inscribed in a rectangle whose dimensions are given as 49 m and 94 m. (take $\pi = 22/7$).

1. 159   2. 149
3. 154   4. 163

22. Under Article 74 of the Indian Constitution, the Union Council of Ministers is mandated to aid and advise which authority?

1. The President of India
2. The Lok Sabha Speaker
3. The Supreme Court of India
4. The Prime Minister of India

23. Which of the following options is true about carbon compound combustion?

1. Burns without oxygen
2. Never produces water
3. Always forms carbon monoxide
4. Needs more oxygen for complete combustion

24. Six boxes A, B, C, D, E and F are kept one over the other but not necessarily in the same order. B is kept second from the bottom. Only one box is kept between B and F. Only three boxes are kept between C and D. D is kept immediately below B. Only two boxes are kept between A and E. A is kept immediately above C. Which box is third from the bottom?

1. E   2. A
3. F   4. C

25. Harish and Vineet move towards town B starting from town A, at a speed of 35 km/h and 36 km/h respectively. If Vineet reaches town B 40 minutes earlier than Harish, what is the distance between towns A and B?

1. 834 km   2. 838 km
3. 840 km   4. 841 km

17. 4	**18.** 3	**19.** 3	**20.** 3	**21.** 3	**22.** 1	**23.** 4	**24.** 1	**25.** 3

26. A vendor sold 20 chocolates for a rupee, thereby gaining 35%. How many did he buy for a rupee?

1. 33
2. 31
3. 27
4. 29

27. Which one of the following monuments, constructed during the Mughal rule, is situated on the bank of river Yamuna?

1. Panch Mahal
2. Jama Masjid
3. Akbar's Tomb
4. Taj Mahal

28. Who among the following was posthumously awarded the Padma Vibhushan in January 2025 for his or her contributions to literature and education?

1. Kumudini Lakhia
2. Sharda Sinha
3. MT Vasudevan Nair
4. Osamu Suzuki

29. The angle of deviation for a ray of light after passing through a prism is _____.

1. the angle between the emergent ray and incident ray
2. indeterminate
3. the angle of the prism
4. the angle between the incident ray and one of the sides of the prism

30. Based on the English alphabetical order, three of the following four letter cluster pairs are alike in a certain way and thus form a group. Which is the one that DOES NOT belong to that group?
(Note: The odd one out is not based on the number of consonants/vowels or their position in the letter-cluster.)

1. ZS – EN
2. EA – JV
3. CO – HJ
4. MQ – RK

31. Which is an environmental consideration when using larvicides?

1. Increase in adult mosquito population
2. Residual effect on soil nutrients
3. Toxicity to non-target aquatic organisms
4. Attraction of more larvae

32. What does the 'Iceberg Phenomenon' of disease primarily represent?

1. The effect of antibiotics on disease progression
2. The cost of healthcare in chronic diseases
3. A small visible portion of disease cases with a larger hidden component
4. Genetic mutations below the surface

33. Which of the following is the correct sequence for removing personal protective equipment (PPE) after contact precautions?

1. Mask → Gloves → Hand hygiene
2. Gown → Gloves → Mask
3. Gloves → Mask → Gown
4. Gloves → Gown → Hand hygiene

34. The purpose of contact tracing in communicable disease control is to:

1. Identify and treat individuals exposed to the infection
2. Determine patient recovery time
3. Analyze mortality rates
4. Monitor vaccine effectiveness

35. Which of the following represents the most accurate sequence of stages in the natural history of a communicable disease?

1. Exposure → Incubation → Clinical disease → Recovery/disability/death
2. Exposure → Symptom onset → Pre-pathogenesis → Mortality
3. Carrier state → Pathogenesis → Recovery → Immunity
4. Incubation → Pathogenesis → Resolution → Latent phase

26. 3	**27.** 4	**28.** 1	**29.** 1	**30.** 4	**31.** 3	**32.** 3	**33.** 4	**34.** 1	**35.** 1

36. Which of the following best explains the primary public health impact of improved sanitation in healthcare settings?
1. Minimises the risk of healthcare-associated infections
2. Enhances the visual appeal of healthcare facilities
3. Reduces patient waiting time in outpatient departments
4. Increases patient compliance with medication

37. Which of the following is the most appropriate method for health education delivery in rural areas through Primary Health Centres?
1. Interactive group discussions using local language
2. Mass media advertisements
3. Health articles in scientific journals
4. Online webinars and mobile applications

38. What does the Air Quality Index (AQI) primarily indicate?
1. The overall air temperature
2. The level of humidity in the air
3. The concentration of air pollutants
4. The level of oxygen in the environment

39. Which of the following is not typically included in the Demographic and Health Survey (DHS)?
1. Fertility rates
2. Infant and child mortality
3. Contraceptive use
4. National GDP statistics

40. Which of the following is the most appropriate method for preventing eye strain while using digital devices?
1. Blinking frequently and resting the eyes every 20 minutes
2. Keeping the screen at a very close distance
3. Wearing sunglasses indoors to reduce glare
4. Using a high brightness setting for the screen at all times

41. Which of the following is a major barrier in implementing effective nutrition education programmes in underserved populations?
1. Access to multiple sources for information
2. Overuse of modern communication technology
3. Abundance of nutritious food
4. Cultural food taboos and low literacy

42. Which of the following is not true regarding Oral Polio Vaccine?
1. It is prepared from live organisms
2. It is less potent immunizing agent than killed vaccines
3. It engages intestinal mucosa of the body
4. The organisms lose their capacity to induce full blown disease

43. How does census data most directly support health policy planning?
1. By estimating hospital infection rates
2. By identifying specific pathogens causing outbreaks
3. By tracking the number of medical professionals in each hospital
4. By providing population data to allocate health resources

44. Cross ventilation in housing refers to:
1. allowing air to pass through only one window
2. using air conditioners only
3. blocking all air entry points
4. air entering from one side and exiting through the opposite side

45. Which of the following is a biological method of vector control?
1. Using insect repellents
2. Eliminating breeding grounds
3. Using chemical larvicides
4. Introducing fish that eat mosquito larvae

36. 1	**37.** 1	**38.** 3	**39.** 4	**40.** 1	**41.** 4	**42.** 2	**43.** 4	**44.** 4	**45.** 4

46. Which of the following is the most accurate test for detecting coronary artery blockages?

1. Cardiac biomarker testing
2. Coronary angiography
3. Electrocardiogram (ECG)
4. Exercise stress test

47. In septic tank systems, which component ensures partial treatment of liquid waste before it reaches the soil?

1. Soak pit or leach field
2. UV sterilizer
3. Chlorine tank
4. Incinerator

48. Which of the following characteristics define infectious diseases?

1. They cannot be transmitted from person to person.
2. They always lead to chronic illness.
3. They are inherited from parents.
4. They are caused by infectious agents and may spread through direct or indirect contact.

49. According to the Food Safety and Standards Authority of India (FSSAI), which of the following is mandatory for licensing a food handling establishment?

1. Providing valet parking
2. Regular health check-ups of food handlers
3. Availability of an in-house dietitian
4. Serving organic produce

50. Which of the following bag is used for segregating discarded or expired medicines as per BMWM guidelines 2016?

1. Yellow bag 2. Red bag
3. Blue bag 4. White bag

51. Which of the following types of Viral Hepatitis is primarily transmitted through blood and other bodily fluids?

1. Hepatitis E 2. Hepatitis B
3. Hepatitis A 4. Hepatitis C

52. Which of the following is a statutory responsibility of a Sanitary Health Inspector under municipal health regulations?

1. Performing vector-borne disease diagnosis
2. Administering vaccines in rural areas
3. Licensing and inspection of food establishments
4. Conducting pathological lab tests

53. What does prevalence measure in public health?

1. The rate at which a disease causes death in a population
2. The number of people at risk for developing a disease
3. The total number of cases (new and existing) of a disease in a population at a given time
4. The number of new cases of a disease during a specific time period

54. Which of the following is a major environmental determinant of health in urban populations?

1. Family history of chronic diseases
2. Availability of clean drinking water
3. Education level
4. Consumption of fruits and vegetables

55. Which of the following infection control practices is most supported by evidence in reducing the transmission of healthcare-associated infections?

1. Routine administration of antibiotics to all hospitalised patients
2. Regular hand hygiene and the use of alcohol-based hand rubs
3. Frequent fumigation of healthcare facilities
4. Mandatory use of surgical masks for all healthcare workers at all times

46. 2 **47.** 1 **48.** 4 **49.** 2 **50.** 1 **51.** 2 **52.** 3 **53.** 3 **54.** 2 **55.** 2

56. Which of the following pathogens is most commonly associated with foodborne illness in poorly maintained food handling establishments?

1. Mycobacterium tuberculosis
2. Neisseria gonorrhoeae
3. Salmonella enterica
4. Clostridium tetani

57. Which of the following lipid parameters is most closely associated with an increased risk of Coronary Heart Disease (CHD)?

1. Total cholesterol
2. High-density lipoprotein (HDL) cholesterol
3. Low-density lipoprotein (LDL) cholesterol
4. Triglycerides

58. The permissible concentration of methane gas generated at land fill site is:

1. Not exceeding 25 percent of lower explosive limit
2. Not exceeding 10 percent of upper explosive limit
3. Not exceeding 25 percent of upper explosive limit
4. Not exceeding 10 percent of lower explosive limit

59. Which of the following best defines the incubation period of an infectious disease?

1. Time from infection to development of immunity
2. Time during which the disease is most contagious
3. Time between symptom onset and full recovery
4. Time from exposure to the appearance of first symptoms

60. The biomedical waste generated from a hospital must be segregated:

1. At the point of generation
2. After collecting them from all sources
3. Once it reaches the area of disposal
4. Only at the end of the day

61. Which of the following is a key consideration when using a digital scale for measuring body weight?

1. Weigh the individual without shoes only
2. Measure weight at different times during the day
3. Avoid using the scale if the individual is wearing any clothing
4. Ensure the scale is calibrated regularly

62. In the assessment of respiration in an emergency, which finding suggests impending respiratory failure?

1. Shallow breathing with $PaCO_2$ > 50 mm Hg
2. Respiratory rate of 14/min with clear breath sounds
3. Respiratory rate of 20/min with accessory muscle use
4. Mild cyanosis of fingertips during cold exposure

63. In what situation is assent from a child required in addition to parental consent?

1. If the child undergoes surgery
2. If the child is over the age of 7
3. If the child is physically injured
4. If the child is accompanied by a sibling

64. Which category of biomedical waste poses the highest risk of transmitting infectious diseases?

1. Expired pharmaceuticals
2. Sharps (needles, blades, etc.)
3. Radioactive waste
4. General non-hazardous waste

65. Which of the following is considered a social determinant of health that significantly affects hygiene practices in a community?

1. Access to internet
2. Cultural beliefs
3. Availability of clean drinking water
4. Transportation facility

56. 3	**57.** 3	**58.** 1	**59.** 4	**60.** 1	**61.** 4	**62.** 1	**63.** 2	**64.** 2	**65.** 2

66. Which of the following strategies contributed most to the success of the Pulse Polio programme in India?

1. Synchronised National Immunization Days (NIDs) targeting all children under five
2. Vaccine administration only in high-risk states
3. Introduction of polio booster at school entry
4. Use of inactivated polio vaccine (IPV)

67. Which of the following is considered a major air pollutant?

1. Nitrogen 2. Water molecules
3. Oxygen 4. Carbon monoxide

68. Biomedical waste is a waste generated during:

1. Housekeeping functions of hospital
2. Diagnosis, treatment or immunization of human beings
3. Administrative functions of hospital
4. Maintenance of health care premises

69. Annual Day for Home Guards and Civil Defence is celebrated on ______.

1. 6th December 2. 10th November
3. 10th December 4. 6th November

70. In the event of a power outage, which equipment ensures the longest duration of safe vaccine storage without external power supply?

1. Standard refrigerator
2. Domestic deep freezer
3. Ice-lined refrigerator
4. Cold box

71. The Vaccine Vial Monitor (VVM) typically changes colour when:

1. The vaccine is nearing its expiration date
2. The vial is opened
3. The vaccine has been exposed to sunlight
4. The temperature exceeds the safe level for the vaccine

72. Which of the following is a common long-term complication of poorly controlled type 1 diabetes mellitus?

1. Hypertension
2. Diabetic neuropathy
3. Hypoglycaemia
4. Diabetic Ketoacidosis

73. Under the National Rabies Control Programme (NRCP), which of the following is a key strategy for controlling rabies?

1. Immunisation of humans against rabies
2. Only treating human cases
3. Treating infected animals
4. Mass dog vaccination and stray dog population control

74. Which mosquito species is the primary vector for Japanese Encephalitis?

1. Culex mosquitoes
2. Anopheles mosquitoes
3. Aedes mosquitoes
4. Haemagogus mosquitoes

75. Which of the following components is essential for an effective infection control programme in a healthcare setting?

1. Use of antibiotics for all admitted patients
2. Continuous surveillance and staff training
3. Isolated interventions during outbreaks only
4. Reliance solely on post-exposure prophylaxis

76. Treatment of vaginitis as per syndromic management includes all the following drugs, EXCEPT:

1. Secnidazole 2. Amikacin
3. Fluconazole 4. Tinidazole

66. 1	**67.** 4	**68.** 2	**69.** 1	**70.** 3	**71.** 4
72. 2	**73.** 4	**74.** 1	**75.** 2	**76.** 2	

77. Which of the following is a key strategy used under National Vector Borne Disease Control Programme for malaria control?

1. Immunization
2. Indoor residual spraying (IRS) and use of insecticide-treated nets (ITNs)
3. Mass chemotherapy
4. Water purification

78. What evidence-based practice is recommended for preventing the spread of respiratory infections in healthcare facilities?

1. Educating healthcare workers and patients on proper cough etiquette and respiratory hygiene
2. Use of surgical masks for all patients, regardless of symptoms
3. Isolation of patients with respiratory symptoms in separate rooms at all times
4. Routine administration of antiviral medications for all patients with flu-like symptoms

79. In patients with Rheumatic Heart Disease, which heart valve is most commonly affected, potentially increasing the risk of stroke?

1. Pulmonary valve 2. Tricuspid valve
3. Aortic valve 4. Mitral valve

80. The primary goal of the Swachh Bharat Abhiyan is:

1. promote industrial growth
2. increase forest cover
3. achieve universal healthcare
4. eliminate open defecation and improve sanitation

81. Which of the following health habits is most influenced by local customs and social conditioning rather than scientific reasoning?

1. Handwashing with soap after defecation
2. Avoidance of certain foods during menstruation
3. Use of oral rehydration solution during diarrhea
4. Immunisation of children under 5 years

82. In the context of hygiene education, which of the following strategies is most effective in sustaining long-term hygiene behaviour change in low-resource communities?

1. Implementing strict penalties for unhygienic practices
2. Providing one-time distribution of hygiene kits
3. Conducting awareness campaigns via radio advertisements
4. Integrating hygiene promotion into community-based participatory programmes

83. Which of the following best demonstrates the effective utilisation of community resources in planning a nutrition education campaign in a rural community?

1. Using printed materials distributed by pharmaceutical companies
2. Collaborating with Anganwadi workers for cooking demonstrations
3. Organising TV ads featuring celebrities
4. Hiring external dietitians from urban hospitals

84. Which of the following public health interventions is most effective in preventing dental caries at the community level?

1. Free toothbrush distribution
2. Mandatory dental insurance
3. Annual dental camps in schools
4. Water fluoridation

85. Which of the following best reflects a functional approach to family health assessment?

1. Recording the family's socioeconomic status
2. Evaluating family roles, communication and decision-making
3. Measuring BMI of all family members
4. Mapping the geographic location of the household

77. 2	**78.** 1	**79.** 4	**80.** 4	**81.** 2	**82.** 4	**83.** 2	**84.** 4	**85.** 2

86. Which of the following is a classic symptom of pertussis?

1. Persistent coughing followed by a "whooping" sound
2. Painless blisters on the skin
3. High fever and body rash
4. Sudden severe headache

87. The antibiotic of choice for trachoma is:

1. Clofazimine
2. 4% of opthalmic ointment of neomycin
3. Erythromycin
4. 1% ophthalmic ointment of tetracycline

88. Which of the following is the most critical first step in planning a community-based health education activity?

1. Scheduling dates for the activity
2. Assessing the health needs of the target population
3. Preparing audiovisual materials
4. Setting learning objectives

89. The CD4 count in a person with AIDS is typically:

1. 2000 cells/mm^3 or higher
2. Less than 200 cells/mm^3
3. Between 500 and 800 cells/mm^3
4. Greater than 1000 cells/mm^3

90. What is the main difference between disinfectants and pesticides?

1. Pesticides are safer than disinfectants
2. Disinfectants are used only outdoors
3. Pesticides are used on humans
4. Disinfectants target microorganisms; pesticides target pests like insects and rodents

91. Which of the following diseases is most commonly associated with exposure to untreated sewage?

1. Asthma
2. Skin cancer
3. Vomiting
4. Typhoid

92. Which of the following is a type of natural ventilation?

1. Cross ventilation using windows and vents
2. Air purifiers
3. Ceiling fans
4. Mechanical exhaust systems

93. Arrange the following according to the recommended steps of hand washing. Select the right order from the options given.

S.No.	Steps of hand washing
1.	Wet your hands with clean running water.
2.	Rinse your hands and wrists under clean and running water.
3.	Use a towel to turn off the faucet.
4.	Lather and rub your hands together briskly and thoroughly, make sure to scrub all surfaces of your hands, fingertips, fingernails and wrist.
5.	Apply enough soap to cover all surfaces of your hands and wrist.
6.	Dry your hands and wrists with a clean towel or let them air dry.
7.	Scrub your hands and wrists for at least 20 seconds.

1. 1, 5, 4, 7, 2, 6, 3
2. 2, 4, 5, 6, 7, 1, 3
3. 4, 2, 3, 1, 5, 6, 7
4. 4, 3, 2, 6, 7, 1, 5

94. In a school-based health education programme, which of the following is the most appropriate opportunity to promote healthy behaviours among adolescents?

1. Conducting final exams on public health topics
2. Incorporating health modules in the life skills curriculum
3. Organising health talks once a year
4. Posting health statistics on the school notice board

86. 1	**87.** 4	**88.** 2	**89.** 2	**90.** 4	**91.** 4	**92.** 1	**93.** 1	**94.** 2

95. Which of the following is an example of biodegradable solid waste?

1. Vegetable peels
2. Aluminum cans
3. Glass jars
4. Plastic bottles

96. Which of the following Sexually Transmitted Diseases can lead to cervical cancer, if left untreated?

1. Syphilis
2. Gonorrhoea
3. Human Papillomavirus (HPV) infection
4. AIDS

97. Increased rate of respiration above 20 breaths per minutes is called:

1. Hyperventilation
2. Tachypnea
3. Apnea
4. Bradypnea

98. What is the primary risk of using open-air burning or incineration without proper controls for biomedical waste?

1. Release of toxic pollutants
2. Reduced waste volume
3. Increased recycling rate
4. Efficient waste segregation

99. Rubella is commonly known as:

1. Chickenpox 2. Scarlet fever
3. Whooping cough 4. German measles

100. Why is segregation at the point of generation crucial in biomedical waste management?

1. It reduces the risk to waste handlers and ensures appropriate treatment
2. It prevents hospital staff from touching waste
3. It increases the amount of recyclable waste
4. It eliminates the need for transportation

EXPLANATORY ANSWERS

1. (2): Work done (W) in moving a charge is given by the formula:

$$W = q \times V,$$

where q is the charge in coulombs and V is the potential difference in volts.

Substituting the values:

$$W = 10\text{ C} \times 14\text{ V} = 140\text{ J}.$$

Thus, 140 joules of work is done in moving a 10C charge across a 14V potential difference.

2. (2): Dachigam Sanctuary in Jammu and Kashmir is located in a high-altitude Himalayan region. The snow leopard, a rare and endangered species adapted to cold mountainous terrain, inhabits this sanctuary. Other animals like Indian bison, hippopotamus, and one-horned rhinoceros are not found in this region.

3. (3): On 5 December 2024, Devendra Fadnavis was sworn in again as the Chief Minister of Maharashtra. He is a senior BJP leader and had previously served as CM from 2014 to 2019. His party emerged victorious in the 2024 state assembly elections.

4. (2): Fluorine (atomic number 9) has 7 electrons in its outer shell, so its normal valency is 1. It gains one electron to complete its octet. The given valency of 7 is incorrect, as fluorine does not lose 7 electrons in chemical reactions.

5. (4): The 69th Constitutional Amendment Act of 1991 introduced a Legislative Assembly for Delhi. It granted Delhi partial statehood and added Article 239AA, giving it special powers while keeping police, land, and public order with the Centre.

6. (4): The Goods and Services Tax (GST), introduced in 2016 and implemented in 2017, aimed to unify India's indirect tax structure under

95. 1	**96.** 3	**97.** 2	**98.** 1	**99.** 4	**100.** 1

a single system. It replaced multiple cascading taxes levied by the Centre and States, creating a single national market.

7. (1): Bleaching powder ($CaOCl_2$) is widely used as a disinfectant and bleaching agent. Its strong chlorine content helps kill bacteria and purify water. It is also used to bleach cotton and linen in the textile industry, making it effective for sanitation and whitening.

8. (1): The Western Coastal Plains of India are divided into three sections from north to south: Konkan Coast (Maharashtra and Goa), Karnataka Coast (Karnataka), and Malabar Coast (Kerala). These coastal regions lie between the Western Ghats and the Arabian Sea.

9. (2): From given statements

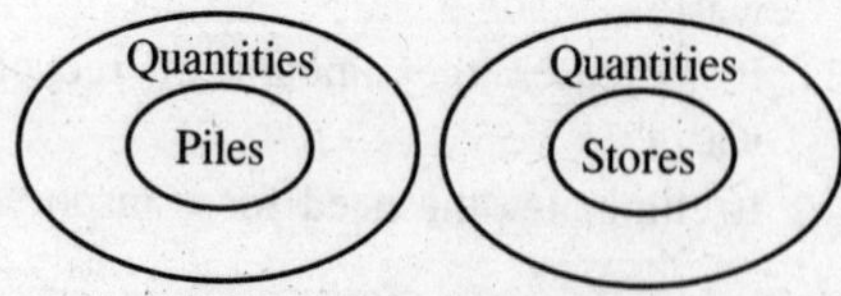

Conclusions:

I. Some piles are stores. (False)

II. Some quantities are stores. (True)

Here, only conclusion (II) follows

10. (1): Plants do not have specialized nervous tissues like animals; they rely on hormones and chemical signals to respond to stimuli. This makes statement 1 incorrect. On the other hand, phototropism, thigmotropism, and chemotropism are all correct examples of plant sensitivity responses.

11. (2): In females, puberty leads to the development of breasts due to rising estrogen levels. This is a primary sexual characteristic indicating maturation. Other signs include the start of menstruation and widening of hips. Narrowing of hips and decreased oil production are incorrect changes.

12. (3): Let A and B can complete a piece of work in x days and y days

Then, $25\left(\frac{1}{x}+\frac{1}{y}\right) = 20\left(\frac{1}{x}+\frac{1}{y}\right)+\frac{10}{x}$

$\Rightarrow \quad 5\left(\frac{1}{x}+\frac{1}{y}\right) = \frac{10}{x}$

$\Rightarrow \quad \frac{5}{y} = \frac{5}{x} \Rightarrow x = y \quad \ldots(i)$

Now, (A + B)'s 1 day's work $= \frac{1}{25}$

$\Rightarrow \quad \frac{1}{x}+\frac{1}{y} = \frac{1}{25} \quad \ldots(ii)$

From (*i*) and (*ii*), we get

$\frac{1}{x}+\frac{1}{x} = \frac{1}{25} \Rightarrow \frac{2}{x} = \frac{1}{25}$

$\Rightarrow \quad x = 50$

∴ A can complete the entire work alone in 50 days.

13. (1): $\left(\frac{4}{7}\right)\times\left(\frac{21}{20}\right)+\left(\frac{6}{5}-9\right)$

$= \frac{4}{7}\times\frac{21}{20}+\frac{6-45}{5}$

$= \frac{4}{7}\times\frac{21}{20}+\frac{-39}{5}$

$= \frac{3}{5}-\frac{39}{5} = -\frac{36}{5}.$

14. (1): Amrita Devi Bishnoi sacrificed her life in 1730 along with over 360 other Bishnois to protect Khejri trees from being cut by royal soldiers. This act of environmental bravery in Rajasthan inspired the Chipko Movement centuries later.

15. (1): In 2025, the Indian government launched Ayushman Bharat Digital Mission 2.0 to improve digital healthcare infrastructure. It aims to create a seamless and unified health record system for all citizens. This upgraded version enhances data interoperability and accessibility across health services.

16. (4):

1. N P O (N +1 → O; P −1 → O)
2. F H G (F +1 → G; H −1 → G)
3. J L K (J +1 → K; L −1 → K)
4. R T U (R +3 → U; T +1 → U)

Here, option (4) does not belong the group.

17. (4): When an object is placed at the centre of curvature (C) of a concave mirror, the image is formed at C itself. The image is real, inverted, and of the same size as the object. This is a standard result from mirror ray diagrams based on concave mirror properties.

18. (3): Complex permanent tissues like xylem and phloem are vital for transport in plants. Xylem carries water and minerals from roots to other parts, while phloem transports organic nutrients.

19. (3): Ishwarchandra Vidyasagar was a key 19th-century reformer who actively promoted widow remarriage in India. He persuaded the British government to pass the Widow Remarriage Act of 1856. His efforts challenged orthodox Hindu norms and helped improve women's rights during the colonial era.

20. (3): Given, 18 is related to 107

$\Rightarrow \quad 18 \times 6 - 1 = 108 - 1 = 107$

21 is related to 125

$\Rightarrow \quad 21 \times 6 - 1 = 126 - 1 = 125$

Similarly,

$14 \times 6 - 1 = 84 - 1 = 83$

$\therefore$ In the same logic, 14 is related to 83.

21. (3): Given, Dimensions of a rectangle are 49 m and 94 m

$\because$ the largest circle inscribed in a rectangle

$\therefore$ diameter of circle = 49 m

$\Rightarrow \quad 2r = 49$ m

$\Rightarrow \quad r = \frac{49}{2}$ m

$\therefore$ The circumference of the largest circle $= 2\pi r$

$$= 2 \times \frac{22}{7} \times \frac{49}{2}$$

$$= 22 \times 7 \Rightarrow 154 \text{ m.}$$

22. (1): According to Article 74 of the Indian Constitution, the Council of Ministers, headed by the Prime Minister, is constitutionally required to aid and advise the President of India in the exercise of their functions. The President acts on this advice in most cases, making it a key element of India's parliamentary system.

23. (4): For complete combustion of carbon compounds (like hydrocarbons), a sufficient supply of oxygen is necessary. This process produces carbon dioxide and water. If oxygen is insufficient, incomplete combustion occurs, forming carbon monoxide or soot instead.

24. (1): Six boxes are kept one over the other.

Order	Box
6	A
5	C
4	F
3	E
2	B
1	D

Here, Box E is third from the bottom.

25. (3): Let the distance between towns A and B be d km

Then, $\frac{d}{35} - \frac{d}{36} = \frac{40}{60}$

$\Rightarrow \quad \frac{36d - 35d}{35 \times 36} = \frac{2}{3}$

$\Rightarrow \quad \frac{d}{35 \times 36} = \frac{2}{3}$

$\Rightarrow \quad d = \frac{2}{3} \times 35 \times 36$

$\Rightarrow \quad d = 2 \times 35 \times 12$

$\Rightarrow \quad d = 840$ km

$\therefore$ Required distance between towns A and B is 840 km.

26. (3): $\because$ S.P. of 20 chocolates

$= ₹\ 1 = 100$ paise

$\therefore$ C.P. of 20 chocolate $= 100 \times \frac{100}{135}$ paise

$= \frac{2000}{27}$ paise

$\because \quad \frac{2000}{27}$ paise $= 20$ chocolates

$\therefore \quad ₹\ 1 = 100$ paise $= \frac{20 \times 27}{2000} \times 100$

$= 27$ chocolates

$\therefore$ He buy 27 chocolates for ₹ 1.

27. (4): The Taj Mahal, built by Mughal emperor Shah Jahan in memory of his wife Mumtaz Mahal, is located in Agra on the banks of the Yamuna River. Its strategic riverside location enhances its reflection and beauty. None of the other listed monuments are directly situated on the bank of the Yamuna.

28. (1): Kumudini Lakhia, a legendary Kathak dancer and choreographer, was posthumously awarded the Padma Vibhushan in January 2025. She was known for revolutionizing Kathak by blending traditional techniques with modern themes. Her contribution to performing arts and education spanned decades.

29. (1): The angle of deviation in a prism is defined as the angle between the direction of the incident ray and the emergent ray after refraction through the prism. It varies with the angle of incidence and the material of the prism. This angle represents how much the ray bends from its original path.

30. (4):

1. Z S – E N (S → N: –5; S → E: +5)
2. E A – J V (A → V: –5; A → J: +5)
3. C O – H J (O → J: –5; O → H: +5)
4. M Q – R K (Q → K: –6; Q → R: +5)

Here, option (4) does not belong to the group.

31. (3): While larvicides target mosquito larvae in water bodies, they can also harm non-target aquatic organisms like fish, amphibians, or beneficial insect larvae. This ecological impact is a major environmental concern when using chemical larvicides. Therefore, environmental safety and selectivity are critical in larvicide application.

32. (3): The Iceberg Phenomenon illustrates that only a small fraction of disease cases (like those showing symptoms) are visible. The larger portion remains hidden, including asymptomatic, undiagnosed, or subclinical cases. It emphasizes the need for surveillance and screening to detect the full burden of a disease.

33. (4): The correct sequence for removing PPE under contact precautions is: First gloves, as they are most contaminated, then the gown, followed by hand hygiene to prevent contamination during removal. Mask is removed later in other contexts like droplet or airborne precautions.

34. (1): Contact tracing helps in controlling communicable diseases by identifying people who have come in contact with an infected person. These individuals are then monitored or treated to prevent further spread. It is a vital public health tool during outbreaks and epidemics.

35. (1): This is the standard sequence in the natural history of a communicable disease. Exposure is followed by the incubation period, then the clinical stage when symptoms appear, and finally either recovery, disability, or death, depending on the case outcome.

36. (1): Improved sanitation in healthcare settings significantly reduces the spread of healthcare-associated infections (HAIs). It prevents contamination of surfaces, equipment, and patient-care areas, protecting both patients and staff.

37. (1): For effective health education in rural areas, interactive group discussions in the local language ensure better understanding and participation. This method respects cultural contexts and promotes two-way communication, especially where literacy levels may be low.

38. (3): The Air Quality Index (AQI) indicates the level of air pollutants such as $PM_{2.5}$, PM_{10}, ozone, carbon monoxide, sulfur dioxide, and nitrogen dioxide. It is a composite measure used to assess how polluted or clean the air is. AQI values help the public understand health risks from air pollution.

39. (4): The Demographic and Health Survey (DHS) focuses on health and population indicators like fertility, mortality, nutrition, and contraceptive use. It does not include economic metrics like Gross Domestic Product (GDP), which are covered by economic surveys. Thus, GDP statistics are not part of DHS data.

40. (1): To prevent digital eye strain, the 20-20-20 rule is recommended: every 20 minutes, look at something 20 feet away for 20 seconds. Frequent blinking keeps the eyes moist and reduces dryness.

41. (4): Cultural food taboos may prevent the acceptance of certain nutritious foods, even when they are available. Low literacy levels hinder understanding of nutritional messages and limit the effectiveness of educational materials. These are major barriers in delivering successful nutrition education in underserved populations.

42. (2): This statement is incorrect. Oral Polio Vaccine (OPV) is generally more effective in providing gut immunity and community protection due to its live attenuated virus. It is more potent in endemic areas compared to inactivated (killed) polio vaccine.

43. (4): Census data offers detailed information about population size, density, age distribution, and other demographics. This helps health planners allocate resources such as hospitals, health workers, and vaccination centers according to community needs. It forms the foundation for evidence-based health policy.

44. (4): Cross ventilation involves air movement across a room or building, from openings like windows or vents on one side to those on the opposite side. It promotes fresh air circulation, reduces indoor pollutants, and maintains thermal comfort in homes.

45. (4): A biological method of vector control involves using larvivorous fish, like Gambusia, which feed on mosquito larvae in water bodies. This reduces mosquito breeding without chemicals and is environmentally friendly. It is especially useful in stagnant water sources like ponds and tanks.

46. (2): Coronary angiography is the most accurate and definitive test to detect blockages in coronary arteries. It involves injecting a contrast dye into the coronary arteries and taking X-ray images to visualize narrowing or obstructions.

47. (1): A soak pit or leach field allows partially treated wastewater from a septic tank to percolate into the soil. This process enables further natural filtration and breakdown of contaminants by soil microbes. It is a critical component in rural sanitation systems for safe disposal of liquid waste.

48. (4): Infectious diseases are caused by pathogens like bacteria, viruses, fungi, or parasites. They can spread via direct contact (touch, droplets) or indirect routes (contaminated food, water, or surfaces). Unlike genetic disorders, they are not inherited and may be acute or chronic.

49. (2): As per FSSAI guidelines, food handlers must undergo periodic health check-ups to ensure they do not transmit infections through food. This is a mandatory condition for licensing food establishments to ensure hygiene and public safety.

50. (1): According to Biomedical Waste Management (BMWM) Rules 2016, discarded or expired medicines fall under yellow category waste. They must be segregated into yellow bags for incineration or deep burial. This ensures safe disposal of pharmaceutical waste and prevents environmental contamination.

51. (2): Hepatitis B virus (HBV) is primarily transmitted through blood and body fluids, including via unprotected sex, sharing needles, or from mother to child during childbirth. It can cause both acute and chronic liver disease.

52. (3): A Sanitary Health Inspector is statutorily responsible for enforcing public health laws, which includes inspecting food establishments, ensuring hygienic practices, and issuing licenses. Their role is regulatory and preventive, not diagnostic or clinical.

53. (3): Prevalence measures the burden of a disease in a population at a specific point or period. It includes both new and existing cases, unlike incidence, which only counts new cases. Prevalence helps in resource allocation and assessing the need for health services.

54. (2): Access to safe and clean drinking water is a crucial environmental determinant of health, especially in urban areas with high population density. It prevents waterborne diseases and improves overall health outcomes.

55. (2): Evidence strongly supports that hand hygiene is the most effective method to reduce healthcare-associated infections (HAIs). Alcohol-based hand rubs are quick, effective, and widely recommended in clinical settings.

56. (3): Salmonella enterica is one of the most common pathogens responsible for foodborne illnesses, especially in establishments with poor hygiene and food storage practices. It is transmitted via contaminated food such as undercooked meat, eggs, or dairy. Symptoms include diarrhea, fever, and abdominal cramps.

57. (3): LDL cholesterol, often called "bad cholesterol", is strongly associated with an increased risk of Coronary Heart Disease (CHD). High levels of LDL lead to plaque formation in arteries, reducing blood flow and increasing the risk of heart attacks. In contrast, HDL is protective and total cholesterol includes both.

58. (1): Methane gas at landfill sites is flammable and poses explosion risk. Regulations require its concentration to be kept below 25% of the lower explosive limit (LEL) for safety. Monitoring and venting are necessary to prevent gas buildup in and around landfill zones.

59. (4): The incubation period refers to the time between initial exposure to a pathogen and the onset of clinical symptoms. This period varies by disease and helps in determining quarantine duration and contact tracing.

60. (1): According to Biomedical Waste Management Rules, waste must be segregated at the source, i.e., where it is generated (like patient rooms or labs). Proper segregation ensures safe handling, transportation, and disposal, and reduces the risk of infection and environmental contamination.

61. (4): Accurate body weight measurement requires regular calibration of digital scales to eliminate errors due to mechanical or electronic drift. Calibration ensures consistency, especially in clinical settings where small differences can influence medical decisions.

62. (1): A $PaCO_2$ above 50 mm Hg with shallow breathing suggests hypoventilation and impending respiratory failure. It indicates inadequate CO_2 elimination and poor gas exchange, requiring urgent intervention. Such findings reflect worsening respiratory mechanics and compromised ventilation.

63. (2): Assent is ethically required from children typically over the age of 7 who are capable of understanding the nature of the procedure. While parental consent is legally mandatory, assent ensures the child's voluntary agreement, respecting their autonomy in healthcare decisions.

64. (2): Sharps pose the highest risk for disease transmission, especially of bloodborne infections like HIV, HBV, and HCV. They can cause needlestick injuries and must be handled and disposed of in puncture-proof containers. They require strict protocols due to high infection risk.

65. (2): Cultural beliefs significantly influence hygiene practices like handwashing, use of toilets, and menstrual hygiene. In many communities, traditional norms can hinder or promote certain hygienic behaviours. Addressing these beliefs is key to implementing effective public health interventions.

66. (1): India's Pulse Polio Programme achieved success through synchronised NIDs, ensuring every child under five was vaccinated regardless of prior status. This mass strategy interrupted transmission cycles and helped India achieve polio-free status.

67. (4): Carbon monoxide (CO) is a major air pollutant, primarily produced by incomplete combustion of fossil fuels. It is colorless, odorless, and highly toxic, impairing oxygen delivery in the body. High CO levels pose serious health hazards, particularly in urban areas with heavy traffic.

68. (2): Biomedical waste includes all waste generated during diagnosis, treatment, or immunization processes in healthcare facilities. This covers materials like syringes, dressings, blood products, and lab waste. Proper segregation and disposal are essential to prevent infections and environmental harm.

69. (1): Home Guards and Civil Defence Annual Day is celebrated on 6th December to recognize the contributions of volunteer forces in maintaining internal security and disaster response. It honours their dedication to public service during emergencies and national events.

70. (3): An Ice-Lined Refrigerator (ILR) maintains stable temperatures for vaccine storage during power outages by using ice packs lining its walls. It provides long-duration cold storage and is more reliable than standard or domestic refrigerators in immunization programs.

71. (4): The Vaccine Vial Monitor (VVM) is a heat-sensitive label that changes colour when the vaccine has been exposed to temperatures above the recommended safe limit for a cumulative period. This ensures the vaccine's potency hasn't been compromised during storage or transport. It helps healthcare workers identify and discard heat-damaged vaccines.

72. (2): Diabetic neuropathy is a common long-term complication of poorly controlled type 1 diabetes. It results from prolonged high blood sugar damaging peripheral nerves, leading to symptoms like numbness, pain, or tingling—especially in the feet.

73. (4): The correct and most effective strategy under the National Rabies Control Programme (NRCP) is mass vaccination of dogs and stray dog population control. Since over 95% of human rabies cases in India are caused by dog bites, controlling rabies in dogs is the primary preventive measure.

74. (1): Japanese Encephalitis (JE) is primarily transmitted by Culex mosquitoes, particularly Culex tritaeniorhynchus. These mosquitoes breed in rice fields and stagnant water and feed on pigs and wading birds, which act as amplifying hosts.

75. (2): An effective infection control programme requires ongoing surveillance of infection rates and regular training of healthcare staff in best practices. This proactive approach helps in early detection, prevention, and management of healthcare-associated infections (HAIs).

76. (2): Amikacin, an aminoglycoside antibiotic, is not included in the syndromic management of vaginitis, which typically covers bacterial vaginosis, trichomoniasis, and candidiasis. Standard treatment includes Secnidazole or Tinidazole (for protozoal infections) and Fluconazole (for fungal infections).

77. (2): The National Vector Borne Disease Control Programme (NVBDCP) uses IRS and ITNs as key vector control strategies to reduce malaria transmission. These methods target Anopheles mosquitoes, the vectors of malaria, by killing or repelling them, especially in high-risk areas.

78. (1): Respiratory hygiene and cough etiquette are evidence-based infection control practices that significantly reduce respiratory infection transmission. These include covering the mouth/nose when coughing, using tissues or elbows, and disposing of tissues properly. Education reinforces adherence and complements other infection prevention measures.

79. (4): In Rheumatic Heart Disease (RHD), the mitral valve is most commonly affected due to autoimmune inflammation following streptococcal infection. Mitral stenosis or regurgitation can lead to atrial fibrillation, which increases the risk of embolism and stroke.

80. (4): The Swachh Bharat Abhiyan, launched in 2014, aims to eliminate open defecation, promote the construction of toilets, and improve sanitation and hygiene practices. It seeks to ensure a cleaner India and reduce the spread of diseases related to poor sanitation.

81. (2): Avoiding specific foods during menstruation is primarily driven by cultural beliefs and social conditioning, not scientific evidence. Such practices vary across regions and are often rooted in taboos or myths. In contrast, handwashing, ORS use, and immunisation are backed by public health research and guidelines.

82. (4): Sustained hygiene behaviour change is best achieved by involving the community directly through participatory programmes. This approach builds ownership, respects local practices, and reinforces consistent messaging. One-time distributions or media campaigns are less effective in creating long-term change in low-resource settings.

83. (2): Anganwadi workers are trusted local figures in rural communities and can effectively demonstrate nutrition practices using local resources. This approach utilizes existing community structures for meaningful and relatable education. It is more impactful than relying on external materials or urban professionals unfamiliar with local context.

84. **(4):** Water fluoridation is a well-established and cost-effective public health intervention to prevent dental caries at the community level. It ensures consistent fluoride exposure, which strengthens enamel and reduces cavity risk across all age groups. Individual methods like toothbrush distribution have limited reach and compliance.

85. **(2):** A functional approach to family health assesses how the family operates, including decision-making, role distribution, emotional support, and communication patterns. This helps identify strengths and dysfunctions that affect health behaviours. Purely structural data like BMI or income provide limited insight into functional dynamics.

86. **(1):** Pertussis (whooping cough) is a bacterial respiratory infection caused by Bordetella pertussis. A classic symptom is severe bouts of coughing, often ending in a high-pitched "whoop" during the next breath. It is highly contagious and particularly dangerous for infants and unvaccinated individuals.

87. **(4):** Trachoma, a chronic eye infection caused by Chlamydia trachomatis, is treated effectively with 1% tetracycline eye ointment, applied topically. It is part of the WHO's SAFE strategy (Surgery, Antibiotics, Facial cleanliness, Environmental improvement) for trachoma control. Oral azithromycin is also used in mass drug administration.

88. **(2):** Before planning any community health education activity, it is essential to assess the community's health needs. This ensures the activity is relevant, focused, and addresses real issues faced by the target group.

89. **(2):** In individuals with AIDS, the CD4 T-cell count typically falls below 200 cells/mm^3, indicating severe immune suppression. This threshold marks progression from HIV infection to AIDS, increasing vulnerability to opportunistic infections. Monitoring CD4 count helps guide treatment and prophylaxis.

90. **(4):** Disinfectants are chemicals used to eliminate or reduce microorganisms on surfaces and objects. Pesticides, on the other hand, are designed to kill or repel pests like insects, rodents, or weeds. They serve different purposes in public health and environmental management.

91. **(4):** Typhoid fever, caused by Salmonella typhi, is commonly spread through ingestion of food or water contaminated with untreated sewage. Poor sanitation and unsafe drinking water significantly increase the risk of transmission. It is a classic example of a waterborne disease linked to fecal contamination.

92. **(1):** Natural ventilation occurs through openings like windows, doors, and vents, allowing fresh air to replace indoor air without mechanical aid. Cross ventilation, where air enters from one side and exits from the opposite, enhances airflow and indoor air quality. Other options involve mechanical or artificial ventilation methods.

93. **(1):** This is the correct recommended sequence for proper hand washing:

1. Wet your hands with clean running water.
5. Apply soap to cover all surfaces of hands and wrists.
4. Lather and rub hands thoroughly, including fingertips, nails, and wrists.
7. Scrub for at least 20 seconds to ensure removal of microbes.
2. Rinse thoroughly under running water.
6. Dry with a clean towel or air dry.
3. Use a towel to turn off the faucet to avoid recontamination.

94. **(2):** Integrating health education into the life skills curriculum ensures regular, age-appropriate exposure to health topics. This approach encourages sustained behavioural change by teaching adolescents decision-making, emotional management, and health-promoting habits as part of their routine learning.

95. **(1):** Vegetable peels are an example of biodegradable solid waste, meaning they can decompose naturally by microorganisms. They can be composted and returned to the soil, making them environmentally friendly. In contrast, aluminum, glass, and plastic are non-biodegradable and persist in the environment unless recycled.

96. **(3):** HPV infection, especially with high-risk strains like HPV-16 and HPV-18, is the primary cause of cervical cancer. If left untreated, persistent HPV infection can lead to abnormal cell changes and eventually cancer of the cervix.

97. (2): Tachypnea refers to an abnormally increased respiratory rate, typically defined as more than 20 breaths per minute in adults. It is often a response to fever, anxiety, lung disease, or metabolic imbalances. It is distinct from hyperventilation, which involves rapid and deep breathing.

98. (1): Open-air burning or uncontrolled incineration of biomedical waste releases toxic substances like dioxins, furans, and heavy metals into the air. These pollutants are harmful to human health and the environment. Controlled and regulated incineration with pollution control devices is essential for safe disposal.

99. (4): Rubella is commonly known as German measles, a mild viral infection that causes fever and rash. However, if contracted during pregnancy, especially the first trimester, it can lead to congenital rubella syndrome (CRS), causing birth defects.

100. (1): Segregation at the point of generation ensures biomedical waste is categorized correctly—infectious, sharps, general, etc.—before mixing with other waste. This protects waste handlers from injury and infection, and facilitates safe, compliant disposal according to category-specific treatment protocols.

YOUR SPACE

Previous Years' Paper

HEALTH & SANITARY INSPECTOR

Recruitment Exam, 2023

1. Disinfectant action of sunlight is due to:
A. UV Rays
B. Infrared Rays
C. Heating effect
D. None of these

2. Which of the following is the standard for biomedical waste disposal?
A. Agmark B. FSSAI
C. BIS D. NIKSHAY

3. Stomach poison amongst insecticides is:
A. Paris green
B. Pyrethrum
C. Lindane
D. Chlorthione

4. Horrock's apparatus is used for estimating
A. Free chlorine
B. Combined chlorine
C. (A) and (B) both
D. Chlorine demand

5. Which of the following bacteria is not seen in faecal contamination?
A. Staphylococcus
B. Streptococcus
C. E. Coli
D. Clostridium perfringence

6. Waste water from kitchen is known as:
A. Refuse
B. Sullage
C. Garbage
D. Sewage

7. Which of the following method is used for the removal of fluoride from drinking water?
A. Bangalore method
B. Indore method
C. Mangalore method
D. Nalgonda method

8. Which of the following is the major reason for 'Algal Bloom'?
A. Presence of heavy metals in water
B. Contamination of pathogens in water
C. Eutrophication
D. Soil erosion

9. In soft water, concentration of $CaCO_3$ is ______.
A. zero
B. 30-60 mg/litre
C. 61-90 mg/litre
D. 91-120 mg/litre

10. Which of the following techniques is used to determine the concentration of odour compounds in the given water sample?
A. Settling
B. Flushing
C. Stripping process
D. Chlorination

11. The surface of filter in the Katadyn filter is coated with which of the following catalyst?
A. Potassium permanganate
B. Silver
C. Halogen
D. Nitrite

1. A	2. C	3. A	4. D	5. A	6. B	7. D	8. C	9. B	10. C	11. B

12. Permanent hardness of water is caused by _____ of calcium and magnesium.
A. Carbonate and bicarbonate
B. Bicarbonate and nitrate
C. Carbonate and nitrate
D. Chloride and sulphate

13. What is measured by the Nephelometer in the polluted water?
A. Colour
B. Odour
C. Suspended particles
D. Gases

14. Relative humidity is determined by:
A. Kata thermometer
B. Anemometer
C. Sling psychrometer
D. Guard band apparatus

15. Following are indicators for measuring air pollution except:
A. Soiling index
B. Mc Ardle's index
C. Suspended particle count
D. SO_2 concentration

16. Which of the following is not a source of Indoor Air Pollution?
A. Carbon monoxide
B. Nitrogen dioxide
C. Radon
D. Mercury vapour

17. Simultaneous warming of one part of the world and the cooling of another is called as:
A. Green House effect
B. Differential Green House effect
C. Earth warming
D. Ocean warming

18. Air borne particulate matter consists of both solids and liquid particles, their size ranges from:
A. 0.01 micron to 20 microns
B. 0.1 micron to 10 microns
C. 0.001 micron to 1 micron
D. 1 micron to 10 microns

19. Which radiations are absorbed by carbon dioxide?
A. X-ray radiations
B. Ultra violet radiations
C. Infrared radiations
D. Visible spectrum

20. The bio-amplification of mercury in organisms is by mobilization and accumulation of it at higher levels in food webs is mediated by _____.
A. Planktons B. Beetles
C. Viruses D. Bacteria

21. Read the following statements carefully and choose the correct answer:
1. Primary pollutants are those that are emitted directly from source.
2. Secondary pollutants are those that are permanently present in the atmosphere.
A. Statement 1 is correct only.
B. Statements 1 and 2 are correct.
C. Statement 2 is correct only.
D. None is correct

22. Where was photochemical smog first observed?
A. San Francisco
B. Los Angeles
C. London
D. Paris

23. Which of the following gases has the maximum Global Warming Potential (GWP)?
A. Methane
B. Carbon monoxide
C. Carbon dioxide
D. Nitrous oxide

12. D **13.** C **14.** C **15.** B **16.** D **17.** B **18.** A **19.** C **20.** D **21.** A **22.** B **23.** D

24. Whispering produces a sound of
A. 20-30 dB B. 40-50 dB
C. 50-60 dB D. 60-70 dB

25. _____ unit is used to measure the frequency of sound.
A. Pascal B. Watt
C. Hertz D. Decibel

26. Maximum noise limits (dB) in residential area during day time is:
A. 55 decibel B. 40 decibel
C. 60 decibel D. 70 decibel

27. A 30 dB increase in noise pollution level represents:
A. 30 fold increase in sound intensity
B. 100 fold increase in sound intensity
C. 15 fold increase in sound intensity
D. 1000 fold increase in sound intensity

28. 'Green Muffler' is related to:
A. Soil pollution B. Air pollution
C. Noise pollution D. Water pollution

29. What is the primary purpose of maintaining sanitation at fairs and festivals?
A. To increase ticket sale.
B. To promote healthy and safe environment.
C. To generate revenue for the event.
D. To showcase cultural diversity.

30. If proper sanitation is not maintained during fairs and festivals the chances of the following disease are more:
A. Cancer B. Cholera
C. Pneumonia D. Dropsy

31. The effective temperature of 'comfort zone' is:
A. 69-76°F B. 77-80°F
C. 81-85°F D. 86-90°F

32. Which Indian city has continuous & uninterrupted water supply?
A. Delhi B. Kota
C. Guwahati D. Puri

33. Which of the following is not a criterion for 'healthy housing'?
A. It provides physical protection and shelter.
B. It provides adequate space for cooking and eating.
C. It provides adequate space for excretory functioning.
D. It does not provide protection from hazards of noise pollution.

34. What are the proportions of protein and calories in mid-day meal?
A. 1/2 protein and 1/2 calories
B. 1/2 protein and 1/4 calories
C. 1/2 protein and 1/3 calories
D. 2/3 protein and 1/3 calories

35. What is the recommended frequency for regular dental checkup and cleaning for most adults?
A. Every six months
B. Every two years
C. Every five years
D. Every month

36. The toilet shared between a group of households in a single building or plot is known as:
A. Community toilet
B. Personal toilet
C. Shared toilet
D. Western toilet

37. Which of the following disease is not associated with smoking?
A. Diphtheria B. Cancer of lungs
C. Bronchitis D. Cancer of mouth

38. Which of the following is the most sensitive indicator of environmental iodine deficiency?
A. Serum T_3 levels
B. Serum T_4 levels
C. Neonatal hypothyroidism
D. Urine Iodine excretion

24. A	**25.** C	**26.** A	**27.** D	**28.** C	**29.** B	**30.** B	**31.** B
32. B	**33.** D	**34.** C	**35.** A	**36.** C	**37.** A	**38.** C	

39. Females need more _____ due to blood loss during menstruation.
A. Calcium B. Iron
C. Sodium D. Zinc

40. Which of the following toxins is responsible for epidemic dropsy?
A. Ergot toxins B. Sanguinarine
C. BOAA D. Aflatoxins

41. Which ancient civilization is known for using a method of preservation involving mummification?
A. Greek B. Roman
C. Egyptian D. Chinese

42. What are the health hazards associated with unsanitary disposal of dead body?
A. Increase risk of disease transmission
B. Occurrence of cancer
C. Hypocalcemia among population
D. Increase risk of diabetes

43. Which of the following methods is associated with cremation?
A. Immersing the body in a preserving solution.
B. Placing the body in a sealed bag.
C. Reducing the body to ashes through high temperature combustion.
D. Submerging the body in a preservation tank.

44. Following diseases are transmitted through contaminated water with faecal origin except
A. Hepatitis A B. Hepatitis C
C. Hepatitis E D. Typhoid

45. Minimum floor area of a living room for a single person should be
A. 50 square feet to 70 square feet
B. 70 square feet to 90 square feet
C. 90 square feet to 100 square feet
D. 100 square feet to 110 square feet

46. Kala-Azar has been declared as notifiable disease in the state of:
A. Punjab B. Uttar Pradesh
C. Bihar D. Madhya Pradesh

47. Which of the following is an indirect method of disease transmission?
A. Direct contact or touching
B. Droplets of saliva
C. Contact with soil
D. Using other person's towel

48. Occurrence of disease in haphazard and irregular pattern is known as
A. Endemic B. Epidemic
C. Sporadic D. Pandemic

49. In the National Immunization Schedule, measles vaccine is given at the age of:
A. Birth B. 6 months
C. 9 months D. 5 years

50. Total number of serotypes of dengue virus is:
A. 1 B. 2
C. 3 D. 4

51. Last case of polio in the country was reported in year
A. 2009 B. 2010
C. 2011 D. 2014

52. For production of BCG vaccine, BCG laboratory at Chennai is using strain _____.
A. 1133 B. 1113
C. 1331 D. 1311

53. Koplik's spots are found in the disease
A. Measles B. Chicken-pox
C. Monkey-pox D. German Measles

54. Ty 21a vaccine is given to prevent which disease?
A. Measles B. Rotavirus diarrhoea
C. Typhoid D. Diphtheria

39. B	**40.** B	**41.** C	**42.** A	**43.** C	**44.** B	**45.** B	**46.** C
47. D	**48.** C	**49.** C	**50.** D	**51.** C	**52.** C	**53.** A	**54.** C

55. Aedes aegypti index should not be more than _____ in towns.
A. 1 B. 2
C. 5 D. 10

56. Aldehyde test of Napier has been used for the diagnosis of:
A. Malaria B. Dengue
C. Filaria D. Leishmaniasis

57. Match List 'A' with List 'B'.

'A'	'B'
(*a*) Syphilis	(*i*) K. grannulomatis
(*b*) Gonorrhoea	(*ii*) H. ducreyi
(*c*) Chancroid	(*iii*) N. gonorrhoeae
(*d*) Donovanosis	(*iv*) T. Pallidum

	(*a*)	(*b*)	(*c*)	(*d*)
A.	(*iv*)	(*i*)	(*ii*)	(*iii*)
B.	(*iii*)	(*i*)	(*iv*)	(*ii*)
C.	(*iv*)	(*iii*)	(*ii*)	(*i*)
D.	(*ii*)	(*iii*)	(*iv*)	(*i*)

58. Which of the following statements is incorrect?
A. Malaria is a vector borne disease.
B. Plasmodium is a protozoa.
C. Malaria spread by the bite of male anopheles mosquito.
D. Malaria spread by the bite of female anopheles mosquito.

59. The most common cancer worldwide affecting both male and female
A. Cancer of Pancreas
B. Buccal mucosa cancer
C. Lung cancer
D. Colorectal cancer

60. The type of Ultraviolet Radiation (UV) that is known to induce skin cancer is:
A. Ultraviolet Radiation – E
B. Ultraviolet Radiation – B
C. Ultraviolet Radiation – C
D. Ultraviolet Radiation – D

61. Which one of the following is not the measure of primary prevention of hypertension?
A. Weight reduction
B. Exercise promotion
C. Reduction of salt intake
D. Early diagnosis of hypertension

62. What is the definition of blindness under National Programme for Control of Blindness and Visual Impairment (NPCBVI)?
A. 3/60 B. 6/60
C. 3/18 D. 6/18

63. Which amongst the following will be considered as the most important factor of diabetes mellitus?
A. Residence
B. Male Gender
C. Gestational diabetes in mother
D. Presence of HLA-DR3

64. Which Index of obesity does not include height?
A. BMI B. Ponderal index
C. Broca's index D. Corpulence index

65. How many stages are there in demographic cycle?
A. 3 B. 2
C. 5 D. 6

66. Vital statistics in a population is depicted by which one of the following?
A. Sex ratio
B. Birth rate
C. Age composition
D. Dependency ratio

67. Which parameter is taken into account in calculating literacy rate?
A. Schooling upto 10th class
B. Age above 7 years
C. Whole population
D. Schooling upto 15 years

68. India is in which stage of demographic cycle?
A. Late expanding B. Early expanding
C. High expanding D. Low expanding

55. A	**56.** D	**57.** C	**58.** C	**59.** C	**60.** B	**61.** D
62. A	**63.** D	**64.** D	**65.** C	**66.** B	**67.** B	**68.** A

69. Best representation of population with age variation is done by
A. Life table
B. Correlation coefficient
C. Population pyramid
D. Bar chart

70. The most common cause of maternal mortality in India is:
A. Anaemia
B. Hemorrhage
C. Abortion
D. Obstructal labour

71. According to Plastic Waste Management Rule (Amendment 2021) the carry bags made up of plastic should not be less than _____ in thickness after December 31, 2022.
A. 30 micron
B. 50 micron
C. 90 micron
D. 120 micron

72. As per Environment Protection Rules, 1999 the permitted noise level generated by firecrackers is:
A. 125 dB B. 120 dB
C. 100 dB D. 70 dB

73. According to Solid Waste Management Rules, 2016 the post closure care of land-fill site should be conducted for at least ____ years.
A. 5 B. 10
C. 15 D. 20

74. According to the Medical Termination of Pregnancy (MTP) Act, 1971 medical termination of pregnancy is considered safe upto _____ weeks of pregnancy.
A. 4 B. 8
C. 10 D. 12

75. According to the Factories Act, 1948 the space for every worker employed in the factory should be _____ cubic meters after the commencement of this Act.
A. 4.2 B. 6.3
C. 8.7 D. 14.2

76. According to the Immoral Traffic (Prevention) Act, 1956, child means a person who has not completed the age of _____ years.
A. 8 B. 12
C. 16 D. 18

77. According to the Food Safety and Standards Act, 2006, any material which is or could be used for making the food unsafe or sub-standard is known as _____.
A. Adulterant
B. Contaminant
C. Food additive
D. Secondary food

78. The Central Pollution Control Board (CPCB) was established under which Section of the Water (Prevention and Control of Pollution) Act, 1974?
A. Section 3 B. Section 18
C. Section 25 D. Section 57

79. Section 39 of the Air (Prevention and Control of Pollution) Act, 1981 provide _______.
A. Powers to declare air pollution control areas
B. Powers to entry and inspection
C. Penalty for contravention of certain provisions of this Act
D. Dissolution of State Boards

80. According to the Prevention of Food Adulteration Act, 1954, which of the following is an example of "Primary Food"?
A. Produce of agriculture in natural form
B. Packaged water bottle
C. Cooked rice
D. Soft drinks

69. C **70.** B **71.** D **72.** A **73.** C **74.** D **75.** D **76.** C **77.** A **78.** A **79.** C **80.** A

81. Maternity benefit allowed under the ESI Act are:
A. 7/12 of daily wages
B. Half wages
C. Quarter wages
D. Full wages

82. Byssinosis occurs due to inhalation of _____.
A. Silica B. Cotton fibre
C. Sugarcane dust D. Coal dust

83. The Constitution prohibits employment of children in factories below which age?
A. 12 years B. 14 years
C. 16 years D. 18 years

84. Silicosis, an occupational disease that is significant contributor to permanent disability and mortality is primarily caused by
A. Inhaling dust containing silica or silicon
B. Inhaling cotton fibre dust
C. Inhaling sugarcane dust
D. Radiations

85. Ergonomics deals with
A. People's efficiency at workplace
B. Risk assessment at workplace
C. Sanitation at workplace
D. Air quality at workplace

86. Chairman of the Employees State Insurance (ESI) Scheme is:
A. Union Minister of Health & Family Welfare
B. Union Minister of Social Justice & Empowerment
C. Union Minister of Labour
D. Secretary, Ministry of Health

87. Micropolyspora faeni is the main cause of:
A. Bagassosis B. Byssinosis
C. Farmer's Lung D. Anthracosis

88. Vaccination is which level of prevention?
A. Primary prevention
B. Secondary prevention
C. Tertiary prevention
D. Primordial prevention

89. Which of the following statement is not true about didactic method?
A. Knowledge imposed
B. No feedback
C. Active learning
D. Does not influence human behaviour

90. Which of the following is not a cultural barrier of communication?
A. Illiteracy B. Noise
C. Attitude D. Knowledge

91. Which of the following is not a principle of Health Education?
A. Acculturation B. Credibility
C. Interest D. Participation

92. For effective group discussion the group should comprise not less than 6 and not more than _____ persons.
A. 16 B. 9
C. 12 D. 15

93. Which of the following is not a method of mass approach in Health Education?
A. Television B. Role Play
C. Health Museum D. Internet

94. Which of the following is not a method used in group approach in Health Education?
A. Lectures B. Panel discussion
C. Symposium D. Personal contact

95. Which of the following compounds is used as larvicide in mosquito control?
A. Mineral oil B. DDT
C. Pyrethrum D. Lindane

96. The number of holes in one square inch of mosquito net is generally:
A. 50 B. 100
C. 150 D. 200

81. D	**82.** B	**83.** B	**84.** A	**85.** A	**86.** C	**87.** C	**88.** A
89. C	**90.** B	**91.** A	**92.** C	**93.** B	**94.** D	**95.** A	**96.** C

97. Under the World Health Organisation's International Health Regulations (IHR), all international airports and sea ports are kept free from all types of mosquitos for a distance of:

A. 100 meters B. 400 meters
C. 500 meters D. 1000 meters

98. Which one of the following is not behavioural development?

A. Motor development
B. Sensory development
C. Adaptive development
D. Language development

99. A person may get the infestation if he walk bare feet:

A. Fasciolosis B. Pinworm
C. Hook worm D. Tape worm

100. The main principle of public participation is ________.

A. Openness and adaptability
B. Enhancing employability
C. Poverty eradication
D. Enhancing subsidy

101. Exposure with sun light increases utilization ability of which vitamin?

A. Vitamin D B. Vitamin A
C. Vitamin B1 D. Vitamin C

102. The Chipko Movement had a focus to protect:

A. Forests B. Grasslands
C. Deserts D. Wetlands

103. What does 'E' stand for in ABCDE method of first aid?

A. Exposure B. Expression
C. Experience D. Examination

104. Which one of the following is not the characteristic of Ideal dressing (wound)?

A. Should keep the wound moist.
B. Should limit bacterial overgrowth.
C. Keep odour to a minimum.
D. Dressing should be extremely tight around the wound.

105. Which one of the following is not the type of disinfection?

A. Concurrent disinfection
B. Recurrent disinfection
C. Terminal disinfection
D. Pre-current disinfection

106. Golden period for treatment of open wound is:

A. 10 hours B. 6 hours
C. 12 hours D. 24 hours

107. Which is the first and the most important measure in the management of severely injured patient?

A. To maintain airway
B. Arrest Bleeding
C. Start IV fluids
D. Splinting Fractures

108. In an emergency which of the following blood groups can be transfused without crossmatching?

A. B Positive B. AB Positive
C. O Positive D. O Negative

109. Mid-day meal scheme was launched on

A. 15 August, 1995
B. 05 September, 1990
C. 02 November, 1998
D. 08 December, 1999

110. Which of the following is not related to dimensions of health?

A. Physical dimensions
B. Mental dimensions
C. Primary dimensions
D. Social dimensions

97. B	**98.** C	**99.** A	**100.** A	**101.** A	**102.** A	**103.** A
104. D	**105.** B	**106.** B	**107.** A	**108.** D	**109.** A	**110.** C

111. The aim of 'Mission Indradhanush' launched by Ministry of Health and Family Welfare is:
A. Fully immunize 90% of children, who are either unvaccinated or partially vaccinated.
B. Fully immunize 80% of children, who are either unvaccinated or partially vaccinated.
C. Fully immunize 70% of children, who are either unvaccinated or partially vaccinated.
D. Fully immunize 50% of children, who are either unvaccinated or partially vaccinated.

112. Which parameter is not required in calculation of infant mortality rate?
A. Early neonatal death
B. Still birth
C. Late neonatal death
D. Post natal death

113. Primary health care was first proposed by which committee?
A. Chaddha Committee
B. Bhore Committee
C. Mukherjee Committee
D. Shrivastav Committee

114. Ottawa Charter 1986 is related to
A. Reproductive health
B. Health promotion
C. Primary health care
D. Population development

115. Which one of the following is not the principle component of avalanches?
A. Beginning zone B. Avalanche track
C. End zone D. Runout zone

116. Sentinel surveillance is used to
A. Know the total number of affected people.
B. Know the hidden cases in the community.
C. Compare the incidence.
D. Measure incidence and prevalence.

117. Which of the following is not a principle of primary healthcare?
A. Community participation
B. Appropriate technology
C. Intersectoral coordination
D. Provision of essential drugs

118. The Kayakalp scheme is aimed at:
A. Providing physical aids and devices to senior citizens.
B. Delivering government sponsored health insurance in India.
C. Initiating a clean hospital program.
D. Establishing an integrated health information system.

119. The International Agency providing assistance in the National Program for Control of Blindness in India is:
A. SIDA B. DANIDA
C. Ford Foundation D. CARE

120. In Hilly areas, a health subcentre is recommended for a population of:
A. 1000 B. 3000
C. 5000 D. 20000

121. The Nitrogen requirement of the human body is supplied by which nutrient?
A. Triacyl glycerol B. Protein
C. Glucose D. Lipids

122. The daily requirement of protein for the adult human is:
A. 6 grams B. 60 grams
C. 120 grams D. 250 grams

123. High content of cholesterol is present in which food content of the following?
A. Coconut oil
B. Egg yolk
C. Hydrogenated fat
D. Unsaturated ghee

111. A	**112.** B	**113.** B	**114.** C	**115.** C	**116.** B	**117.** D
118. C	**119.** B	**120.** B	**121.** B	**122.** B	**123.** B	

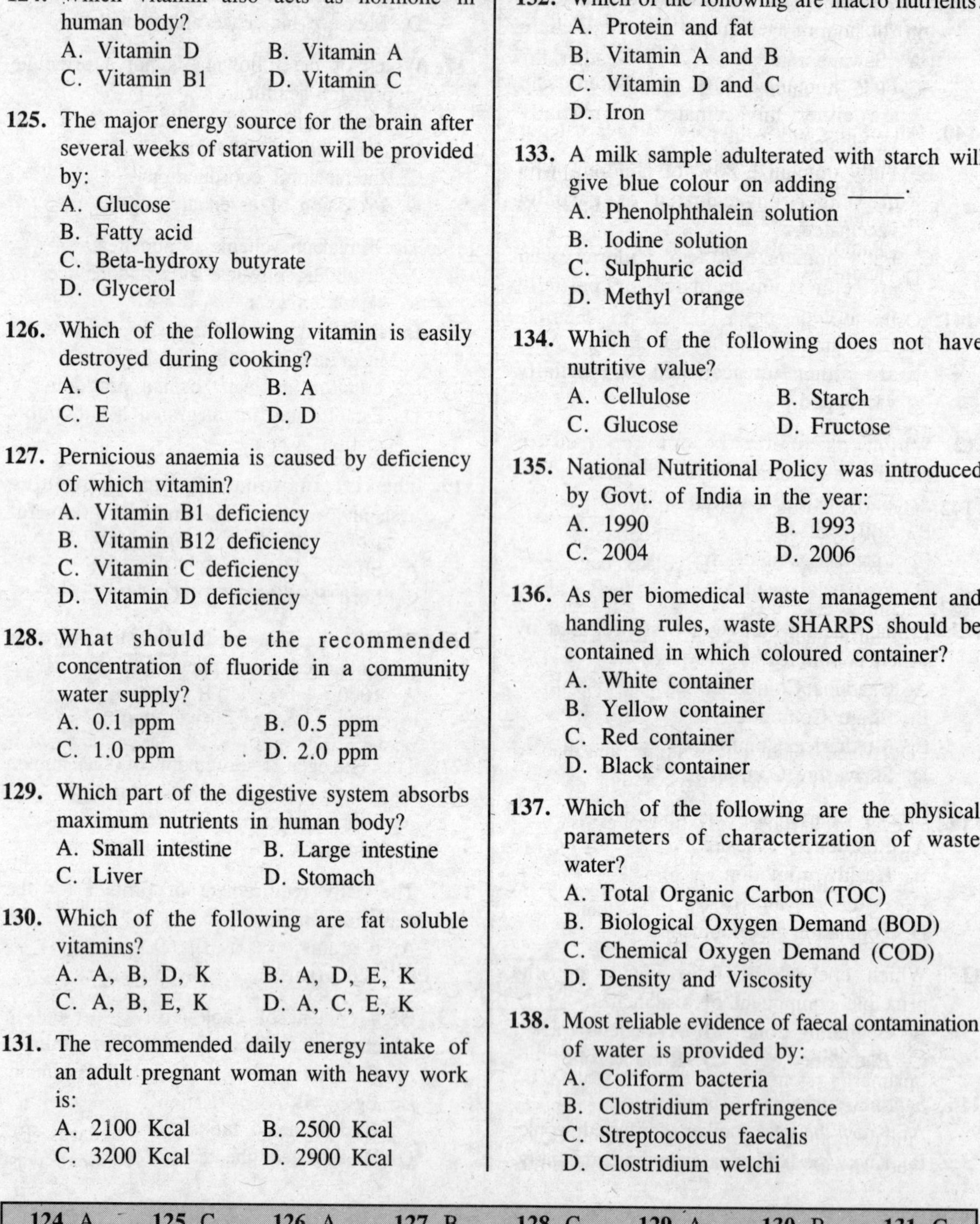

124. Which vitamin also acts as hormone in human body?
A. Vitamin D B. Vitamin A
C. Vitamin B1 D. Vitamin C

125. The major energy source for the brain after several weeks of starvation will be provided by:
A. Glucose
B. Fatty acid
C. Beta-hydroxy butyrate
D. Glycerol

126. Which of the following vitamin is easily destroyed during cooking?
A. C B. A
C. E D. D

127. Pernicious anaemia is caused by deficiency of which vitamin?
A. Vitamin B1 deficiency
B. Vitamin B12 deficiency
C. Vitamin C deficiency
D. Vitamin D deficiency

128. What should be the recommended concentration of fluoride in a community water supply?
A. 0.1 ppm B. 0.5 ppm
C. 1.0 ppm D. 2.0 ppm

129. Which part of the digestive system absorbs maximum nutrients in human body?
A. Small intestine B. Large intestine
C. Liver D. Stomach

130. Which of the following are fat soluble vitamins?
A. A, B, D, K B. A, D, E, K
C. A, B, E, K D. A, C, E, K

131. The recommended daily energy intake of an adult pregnant woman with heavy work is:
A. 2100 Kcal B. 2500 Kcal
C. 3200 Kcal D. 2900 Kcal

132. Which of the following are macro nutrients?
A. Protein and fat
B. Vitamin A and B
C. Vitamin D and C
D. Iron

133. A milk sample adulterated with starch will give blue colour on adding _____.
A. Phenolphthalein solution
B. Iodine solution
C. Sulphuric acid
D. Methyl orange

134. Which of the following does not have nutritive value?
A. Cellulose B. Starch
C. Glucose D. Fructose

135. National Nutritional Policy was introduced by Govt. of India in the year:
A. 1990 B. 1993
C. 2004 D. 2006

136. As per biomedical waste management and handling rules, waste SHARPS should be contained in which coloured container?
A. White container
B. Yellow container
C. Red container
D. Black container

137. Which of the following are the physical parameters of characterization of waste water?
A. Total Organic Carbon (TOC)
B. Biological Oxygen Demand (BOD)
C. Chemical Oxygen Demand (COD)
D. Density and Viscosity

138. Most reliable evidence of faecal contamination of water is provided by:
A. Coliform bacteria
B. Clostridium perfringence
C. Streptococcus faecalis
D. Clostridium welchi

124. A	**125.** C	**126.** A	**127.** B	**128.** C	**129.** A	**130.** B	**131.** C
132. A	**133.** B	**134.** A	**135.** B	**136.** A	**137.** D	**138.** A	

139. The amount of sewage flowing in a system in 24 hours is called:
A. Sewage rate B. Dry weather flow
C. R.C.A. Index D. Sludge

140. All of the following come under category of health care waste, except one:
A. SHARPS
B. Chemical waste
C. Pathological waste
D. Night soil

141. Ortho-toulidine test is used to determine _____.
A. Free and combined chlorides in water
B. Nitrites in water
C. Nitrates in water
D. Ammonia content in water

142. Cytotoxic drug is disposed in _____.
A. Yellow bag B. Red bag
C. Blue bag D. Black bag

143. Schmitzdecke layer refers to the following:
A. Suspended matter in drinking water
B. Algae in drinking water
C. Alum flacculate on surface of sand bed filter
D. Algae, plankton, diatoms and bacteria on surface of sand bed filter

144. Level of hardness of soft water is _____ mEq/litre.
A. less than 1 B. 2-3
C. 3-6 D. more than 6

145. United Nations International Children's Emergency Fund (UNICEF) provides fund for all except one.
A. Child nutrition
B. Child health education
C. Immunisation
D. Family planning

146. What is the colour coding of bag in hospital to dispose off human anatomical waste?
A. Yellow B. Black
C. Red D. Blue

147. Most satisfactory method of refuse disposal is:
A. Dumping
B. Manure pits
C. Incineration
D. Controlled tipping

148. In triage, black colour denotes:
A. Death B. Transfer
C. High priority D. Low priority

149. According to WHO, which of the following aspect/s is/are included in water quality standards for drinking water?
A. Radioactivity
B. Microbiological
C. (A) and (B) both
D. None of these

150. All mosquito pupa have long siphon except:
A. Culex B. Anopheles
C. Aedes D. Mansonia

ANSWERS

1. (A): The disinfectant action of sunlight primarily stems from its ultraviolet (UV) rays. When UV rays from the sun penetrate microorganisms such as bacteria and viruses, they disrupt the DNA or RNA within these pathogens, interfering with their ability to replicate and causing damage that ultimately leads to their inactivation.

2. (C): The Bureau of Indian Standards (BIS) sets the standard for biomedical waste

139. B	**140.** D	**141.** A	**142.** D	**143.** D	**144.** A
145. D	**146.** A	**147.** D	**148.** A	**149.** C	**150.** A

disposal in India. These standards outline the proper procedures and protocols for the safe and environment friendly disposal of biomedical waste, which includes waste generated from healthcare facilities such as hospitals, clinics, and laboratories.

3. **(A):** Paris green, a copper acetoarsenite compound, was a historically significant stomach poison insecticide. Paris green is extremely toxic due to the presence of arsenic. Side effects of exposure to Paris green can include severe abdominal pain and vomiting, convulsions, heart disruption, organ failure, and hemorrhages.

4. **(D):** Horrock's apparatus is used for estimating chlorine demand in water treatment. Chlorine demand refers to the amount of chlorine required to oxidize all the reducing substances present in the water. This process helps in determining the appropriate amount of chlorine needed for effective disinfection without over-chlorinating the water, which can lead to taste and odor issues as well as potential health risks.

5. **(A):** Staphylococcus bacteria are not typically associated with fecal contamination. While Staphylococcus species can be found in various environments, including on human skin and in the respiratory tract, they are not commonly found in fecal matter. Instead, bacteria such as Escherichia coli (E. coli), Streptococcus, and Clostridium perfringens are more frequently associated with fecal contamination, as they are part of the natural flora of the gastrointestinal tract and are excreted in feces.

6. **(B):** Wastewater from the kitchen, which typically includes water used for washing dishes, cooking, and other kitchen activities, is known as sullage. Sullage contains organic matter, grease, and food particles, making it distinct from sewage, which primarily consists of human waste and wastewater from toilets. Proper management of sullage is essential to prevent environmental pollution and ensure the efficient treatment of wastewater.

7. **(D):** The Nalgonda technique, also known as the Nalgonda method, is employed for the removal of fluoride from drinking water. This method involves adsorption of fluoride ions onto activated alumina, a porous material with a high surface area. The Nalgonda method is a simple and cost-effective approach widely used in areas with high fluoride content in groundwater, helping to mitigate the adverse health effects associated with excessive fluoride consumption, such as dental and skeletal fluorosis.

8. **(C):** Eutrophication occurs when excessive nutrients, such as nitrogen and phosphorus, enter water bodies, often from sources like agricultural runoff or sewage discharge. These nutrients promote the rapid growth of algae, leading to a dense and visible accumulation of algae known as algal bloom. As the algae multiply, they can deplete oxygen levels in the water, disrupt aquatic ecosystems, produce toxins harmful to humans and animals, and cause aesthetic issues such as foul odors and discoloration of water.

9. **(B):** In soft water, the concentration of CaCO3 (calcium carbonate) typically ranges from 30-60 mg/litre. This level of calcium carbonate concentration characterizes water as being soft, as it indicates a relatively low concentration of dissolved calcium and carbonate ions, resulting in fewer issues related to scaling and soap scum formation compared to hard water.

10. **(C):** The stripping process is used to determine the concentration of odor

compounds in a given water sample. In this technique, the water sample is aerated or passed through a stripping tower where air or an inert gas is bubbled through the water. Odor compounds, which are volatile, transfer from the water phase to the gas phase due to the increased surface area and contact with the stripping gas. The gas phase is then analyzed using techniques such as gas chromatography to quantify the concentration of odor compounds present in the water sample.

11. **(B):** The surface of the filter in the Katadyn filter is coated with silver as a catalyst. Silver has long been recognized for its antimicrobial properties, effectively inhibiting the growth of bacteria and other microorganisms. In the Katadyn filter, the silver coating serves to kill or inhibit the growth of bacteria and pathogens that may be present in the water being filtered. This additional layer of protection helps ensure that the filtered water is safe for consumption by reducing the risk of waterborne illnesses.

12. **(D):** Permanent hardness arises from dissolved calcium and magnesium salts, specifically chlorides and sulphates (e.g., calcium chloride, magnesium sulfate). Boiling doesn't affect these salts, making the hardness permanent. This is because the chemical bonds between the calcium/magnesium cations and the chloride/sulfate anions are strong enough to withstand the increased temperature. As a result, permanent hardness persists in the water.

13. **(C):** A nephelometer is a device used to measure the concentration of suspended particles in water. In polluted water, suspended particles can include various contaminants such as sediment, organic matter, and pollutants. The nephelometer works by shining a light source into the water sample and measuring the amount of light scattered by the suspended particles. The degree of light scattering is directly proportional to the concentration of suspended particles in the water.

14. **(C):** Relative humidity is determined using a sling psychrometer. This instrument consists of two thermometers mounted on a handle, one of which has a wet bulb covered with a moistened wick. To measure relative humidity, the psychrometer is whirled around in the air, causing the water on the wet bulb to evaporate. As the water evaporates, it cools the wet bulb thermometer. The rate of evaporation and the extent of cooling depend on the moisture content of the air.

15. **(B):** McArdle's index is not typically used as an indicator for measuring air pollution. Instead, it is an index commonly employed in exercise physiology to estimate an individual's aerobic capacity. On the other hand, the other options listed are indeed indicators for measuring air pollution.

16. **(D):** Mercury vapor is not typically considered a common source of indoor air pollution. While mercury vapor can be released indoors from certain sources like broken compact fluorescent lamps (CFLs) or mercury-containing products, such occurrences are relatively rare compared to other indoor air pollutants. Carbon monoxide, nitrogen dioxide, and radon, on the other hand, are recognized as significant sources of indoor air pollution.

17. **(B):** The simultaneous warming of one part of the world and the cooling of another is termed as the "Differential Greenhouse Effect." This phenomenon occurs when changes in atmospheric circulation patterns redistribute heat unevenly across the Earth's surface. Certain regions may experience

intensified warming due to factors such as increased greenhouse gas concentrations or altered atmospheric circulation patterns, while other areas may undergo cooling due to shifts in ocean currents, changes in land surface properties, or variations in cloud cover.

18. (A): Airborne particulate matter consists of both solid and liquid particles, with sizes ranging from approximately 0.01 micron to 20 microns. These particles can originate from various sources such as combustion processes, industrial activities, vehicle emissions, and natural sources like dust and pollen. Particles within this size range are capable of being suspended in the air for extended periods and can have significant impacts on human health and the environment, depending on their composition and size distribution.

19. (C): Carbon dioxide absorbs infrared radiation. When infrared radiation interacts with carbon dioxide molecules in the Earth's atmosphere, the molecules absorb some of the energy, causing them to vibrate. This absorption and subsequent re-emission of infrared radiation contribute to the greenhouse effect, where certain gases, including carbon dioxide, trap heat in the Earth's atmosphere, leading to warming of the planet.

20. (D): Specific types of bacteria in aquatic environments can methylate mercury, converting it into methylmercury. Methylmercury is a highly bioavailable form that is easily absorbed by organisms at the beginning of the food chain. As these organisms are consumed by predators higher up the food chain, the methylmercury bioaccumulates and reaches much higher concentrations in the tissues of top predators like fish, birds, and mammals.

21. (A):

1. Primary pollutants are those that are emitted directly from source. This statement is correct. Primary pollutants come directly from identifiable sources like factories, cars, volcanoes, etc.
2. Secondary pollutants are those that are permanently present in the atmosphere. This statement is incorrect. Secondary pollutants are not always present in the atmosphere. They form through reactions between primary pollutants and other atmospheric components like sunlight.

22. (B): Photochemical smog was first observed in Los Angeles. This type of smog is characterized by high levels of ozone and other secondary pollutants formed through complex chemical reactions involving sunlight, nitrogen oxides, and volatile organic compounds emitted by vehicles, industrial activities, and other sources. Los Angeles, with its high population density, automobile usage, and geographical features that trap pollutants, provided ideal conditions for the formation of photochemical smog.

23. (D): Nitrous oxide has the highest Global Warming Potential (GWP) among the gases listed. Despite being less abundant in the atmosphere compared to carbon dioxide, nitrous oxide has a much greater ability to trap heat. It has a GWP that is approximately 298 times greater than that of carbon dioxide over a 100-year period. Nitrous oxide is emitted from various human activities, including agricultural practices, industrial processes, and combustion of fossil fuels.

24. (A): Whispering produces a relatively soft sound, typically falling within the range of 20-30 decibels (dB) when measured. This low level of sound intensity is due to the minimal vibration of vocal cords and the gentle airflow during whispering. As a result, whispering is quieter compared to normal speech or other louder sounds.

25. (C): The unit used to measure the frequency of sound is Hertz (Hz). Frequency refers to the number of cycles or vibrations per second of a sound wave and is measured in Hertz. For example, if a sound wave completes 440 cycles per second, it has a frequency of 440 Hz.

26. (A): In many residential areas, the maximum noise limit during the daytime indeed falls within the range of 55 decibels. This limit is often set by local regulations or guidelines to ensure a suitable environment for residents. Nighttime noise limits in residential areas are typically even lower than daytime limits.

27. (D): A 30 dB increase in noise pollution level represents a 1000-fold increase in sound intensity.

The decibel (dB) scale is logarithmic, not linear. This means that an increase of 10 dB corresponds to a 10-fold increase in sound intensity, not a simple addition. So:

A 10 dB increase = $10x$ sound intensity

A 20 dB increase = $(10x) \times (10x) = 100x$ sound intensity (100-fold increase)

A 30 dB increase = $(10x) \times (10x) \times (10x) = 1000x$ sound intensity (1000-fold increase)

28. (C): The term "Green Muffler" is related to noise pollution. It refers to the concept of using vegetation, such as trees and bushes, as a natural barrier or buffer to reduce the transmission of noise from one area to another. Vegetation can absorb and scatter sound waves, thereby attenuating the noise and creating a quieter environment behind it. This approach is often employed in urban areas to mitigate the impact of noise pollution from sources such as roads, highways, and industrial facilities.

29. (B): The primary purpose of maintaining sanitation at fairs and festivals is to promote a healthy and safe environment for attendees. Sanitation practices such as proper waste management, clean water supply, and hygienic facilities help prevent the spread of diseases and ensure the well-being of participants. By maintaining cleanliness and sanitation standards, organizers can minimize health risks, protect public health, and enhance the overall experience of attendees.

30. (B): If proper sanitation is not maintained during fairs and festivals, the chances of diseases such as cholera are more likely to increase. Cholera is a bacterial infection caused by ingesting contaminated food or water, particularly water. In environments where sanitation is lacking, such as crowded fairs and festivals with inadequate waste disposal and hygiene facilities, there is a higher risk of fecal contamination of water sources and the spread of cholera.

31. (B): The effective temperature of the "comfort zone" typically falls within the range of 77-80°F (25-27°C). This range represents the temperature range at which most people feel comfortable and are least likely to experience discomfort due to thermal conditions. It's considered an optimal range for indoor environments to ensure occupant comfort and productivity.

32. (B): Kota in Rajasthan is known for having continuous and uninterrupted water supply. This achievement is largely attributed to the city's innovative water management systems, including efficient water distribution networks and advanced infrastructure.

33. (D): The absence of protection from noise pollution is not considered a criterion for healthy housing. Noise pollution can have adverse effects on physical and mental health, including sleep disturbances, increased stress levels, and hearing impairment. Therefore, healthy housing should ideally include measures to mitigate noise pollution, such as soundproofing, adequate distance from noisy areas, or urban planning strategies to reduce noise levels in residential areas.

34. (C): In the mid-day meal program, the nutritional content is structured to provide essential nutrients while also meeting caloric needs. The proportions typically follow a ratio of 1/2 protein to 1/3 calories. This means that about half of the nutritional content is allocated to protein, which is crucial for growth and development, while the remaining third is dedicated to providing calories, which serve as energy sources for daily activities.

35. (A): For most adults, the recommended frequency for regular dental checkups and cleanings is every six months. These biannual visits to the dentist allow for the early detection and treatment of dental issues such as cavities, gum disease, and oral infections. Additionally, professional dental cleanings help remove plaque and tartar buildup that cannot be adequately addressed through brushing and flossing alone, thus reducing the risk of dental problems.

36. (C): The toilet shared between a group of households in a single building or plot is known as a shared toilet. These toilets are commonly found in settings where multiple households share sanitation facilities due to space constraints or lack of individual facilities.

37. (A): Diphtheria is not directly associated with smoking. It is a bacterial infection caused by Corynebacterium diphtheriae, typically transmitted through respiratory droplets from an infected person or contact with contaminated surfaces. On the other hand, cancers of the lungs and mouth, as well as bronchitis, are well-established health risks associated with smoking due to the carcinogens and toxins present in tobacco smoke.

38. (C): Neonatal hypothyroidism is the most sensitive indicator of environmental iodine deficiency. Iodine is essential for the production of thyroid hormones, particularly thyroxine (T_4) and triiodothyronine (T_3). Inadequate iodine intake during pregnancy can lead to insufficient thyroid hormone production in the fetus, resulting in neonatal hypothyroidism.

39. (B): Females need more iron due to blood loss during menstruation. Menstruation involves the shedding of the uterine lining, which contains blood. As a result, females lose a certain amount of blood each month during their menstrual cycles. Iron is an essential mineral for the production of hemoglobin, the protein in red blood cells that carries oxygen from the lungs to the rest of the body.

40. (B): Sanguinarine is a toxic alkaloid found in the seeds of the Mexican prickly poppy (Argemone mexicana). When mustard oil, common cooking oil in some regions, is adulterated with Argemone mexicana oil, either deliberately or accidentally, and consumed, the sanguinarine in the Argemone mexicana oil can cause epidemic dropsy. Sanguinarine disrupts normal function in the body by interfering with cellular processes and damaging capillary walls.

41. (C): The ancient civilization known for using the method of preservation involving mummification is the Egyptian civilization. Mummification was a process used by the ancient Egyptians to preserve the bodies of the deceased for the afterlife. It involved removing internal organs, treating the body with preservatives like natron, and wrapping it in layers of linen bandages.

42. (A): The unsanitary disposal of dead bodies can increase the risk of disease transmission. When bodies are not disposed of properly, there is a heightened risk of pathogens spreading to living populations through contact with contaminated soil, water, or air. Diseases such as cholera, typhoid fever, dysentery, and viral infections can result from the improper disposal of dead bodies, posing significant public health risks.

43. (C): Cremation is the method associated with reducing the body to ashes through high temperature combustion. During cremation, the deceased body is placed in a cremation chamber, where it is subjected to intense heat, typically between 760 to 982 degrees Celsius. This high temperature reduces the body to bone fragments and ultimately to ashes.

44. (B): Hepatitis C is not typically transmitted through contaminated water with fecal origin. Hepatitis A, Hepatitis E, and Typhoid are diseases that can be transmitted through water contaminated with fecal matter, as they are caused by viruses or bacteria that can survive in water contaminated with human or animal feces. However, Hepatitis C is primarily transmitted through blood-to-blood contact, such as sharing needles or receiving blood transfusions from an infected individual.

45. (B): The minimum floor area of a living room for a single person should typically be within the range of 70 square feet to 90 square feet. This range ensures adequate space for comfortable living and movement within the room.

46. (C): Kala-Azar, also known as visceral leishmaniasis, has been declared as a notifiable disease in the state of Bihar. This means that health authorities in Bihar are required to report all cases of Kala-Azar to the appropriate health department for monitoring and control purposes.

47. (D): Using another person's towel is an example of indirect disease transmission. It involves the transfer of pathogens from one person to another through contaminated objects or surfaces, rather than through direct contact with an infected individual.

48. (C): Sporadic occurrence of a disease refers to its random and irregular pattern of occurrence, with isolated cases or small clusters appearing unpredictably over time. Unlike endemic diseases, which are consistently present within a particular population or geographic area, sporadic diseases do not follow a predictable pattern of occurrence. Instead, they may occur infrequently and without a clear pattern, making them more challenging to anticipate and control.

49. (C): In the National Immunization Schedule, the measles vaccine is typically given at the age of 9 months. This timing is strategic as it helps provide protection against measles, a highly contagious viral disease, at an early age when infants are most vulnerable to severe complications from the infection.

50. (D): The total number of serotypes of the dengue virus is 4. Dengue virus exists in four distinct serotypes: DEN-1, DEN-2, DEN-3, and DEN-4. These serotypes are genetically related but distinct enough to elicit separate immune responses in infected individuals. Dengue fever can be caused by any of these serotypes, and individuals who have been infected with one serotype are not necessarily immune to infection with the other serotypes.

51. (C): The last case of polio in India was reported in 2011. This marked a significant milestone in the country's decades-long fight to eradicate the crippling disease. India's polio eradication efforts began in the 1990s with nationwide vaccination campaigns and a focus on improving surveillance. The last case in 2011 served as a crucial turning point, and India officially received polio-free certification from the World Health Organization (WHO) in 2014.

52. **(C):** The BCG laboratory at Chennai is using the strain 1331 for the production of the BCG vaccine. This strain has been widely used in BCG vaccine production due to its effectiveness in inducing immunity against tuberculosis.

53. **(A):** Koplik's spots are small white spots surrounded by a red halo that appear on the inside lining of the mouth, particularly on the cheeks. They are a characteristic feature of measles, a highly contagious viral infection caused by the measles virus. Koplik's spots typically develop a few days before the onset of the measles rash and are considered a diagnostic sign of the disease.

54. **(C):** The Ty 21a vaccine is administered to prevent typhoid fever, a bacterial infection caused by Salmonella Typhi bacteria. This vaccine contains a weakened strain of Salmonella Typhi known as Ty 21a, which stimulates the immune system to produce protection against the bacteria without causing the disease itself.

55. **(A):** The Aedes aegypti index should not be more than 1 in towns. This index is a measure used by health authorities to assess the risk of dengue fever transmission in an area. It represents the percentage of houses with mosquito breeding sites, particularly those of the Aedes aegypti mosquito, which is the primary vector for dengue virus transmission. Keeping the Aedes aegypti index below 1 indicates effective vector control measures and reduces the likelihood of dengue transmission within the community.

56. **(D):** The Aldehyde test, or Napier's aldehyde test, is a simple and rapid test used to diagnose visceral leishmaniasis, also known as kala-azar. The test works by detecting the presence of globulin proteins in the patient's serum, which increase in response to Leishmania parasite infection. When formalin is added to the serum, it reacts with these globulins, causing a gel-like formation if leishmaniasis is present.

57. **(C):**

(*a*) **Syphilis:** Caused by the bacterium Treponema pallidum, a spiral-shaped bacterium that can cause a wide range of symptoms depending on the stage of infection. Early symptoms may include a painless sore at the infection site, while later stages can affect the nervous system, cardiovascular system, and other organs.

(*b*) **Gonorrhoea:** Caused by the bacterium Neisseria gonorrhoeae, which infects the mucous membranes of the genitals, rectum, and throat. Symptoms can include burning sensation during urination, discharge from the penis or vagina, and pain in the lower abdomen.

(*c*) **Chancroid:** Caused by the bacterium Haemophilus ducreyi, which leads to the formation of one or more painful, open sores (chancres) on the genitals.

(*d*) **Donovanosis:** Caused by the bacterium Klebsiella granulomatis, which primarily affects the skin and mucous membranes of the genitals and groin. It can cause painless, red bumps that eventually ulcerate and spread.

58. **(C):** Malaria spread by the bite of male Anopheles mosquito. In reality, malaria is spread by the bite of female Anopheles mosquitoes. Female mosquitoes require a blood meal to nourish their eggs, and when they feed on an individual infected with the malaria parasite (Plasmodium), they can transmit the parasite to other humans through subsequent bites.

59. **(C):** The most common cancer worldwide affecting both males and females is lung cancer. It is a type of cancer that starts in the lungs and is often associated with smoking, although non-smokers can also develop lung cancer due to other factors such as exposure to secondhand smoke, radon gas, asbestos, and air pollution.

60. **(B):** The type of ultraviolet radiation (UV) known to induce skin cancer is Ultraviolet Radiation – B (UVB). UVB radiation penetrates the outermost layer of the skin (epidermis) and is primarily responsible for sunburn and the development of skin cancers such as basal cell carcinoma, squamous cell carcinoma, and melanoma. Prolonged exposure to UVB radiation damages the DNA in skin cells, leading to mutations that can trigger the uncontrolled growth of cancerous cells.

61. **(D):** Measures such as weight reduction, exercise promotion, and reduction of salt intake are examples of primary prevention measures for hypertension, targeting modifiable risk factors to reduce the likelihood of developing high blood pressure. On the other hand, early diagnosis of hypertension is crucial for timely management and treatment to prevent complications and further progression of the condition, making it a key aspect of secondary prevention efforts.

62. **(A):** The definition of blindness under the National Programme for Control of Blindness and Visual Impairment (NPCBVI) is 3/60. This definition signifies that a person with visual acuity less than 3/60 in the better eye after best correction, or a visual field less than 10 degrees from the point of fixation, is considered blind according to the NPCBVI.

63. **(D):** The presence of HLA-DR3 is considered one of the most important factors in diabetes mellitus. HLA-DR3 is a specific human leukocyte antigen (HLA) genotype that is associated with an increased risk of developing type 1 diabetes mellitus. HLA genes play a critical role in the immune system and are involved in regulating the body's immune response.

64. **(D):** The corpulence index does not include height in its calculation. It's a relatively obscure measure and not widely used in modern clinical practice. The formula for corpulence index is weight in kilograms divided by height in meters cubed (kg/m^3). While it might seem like height is included because it's in the denominator, the fact that it's cubed makes its influence minimal compared to weight. So, for all practical purposes, corpulence index focuses solely on weight.

65. **(C):** The demographic cycle typically consists of five stages. These stages represent the pattern of population growth and decline experienced by societies over time. The stages are: (1) high stationary, (2) early expanding, (3) late expanding, (4) low stationary, and (5) declining.

66. **(B):** Vital statistics in a population are primarily depicted by the birth rate. The birth rate refers to the number of live births per 1,000 individuals in a population over a specific period, usually one year. It is a key indicator of population dynamics and is used to assess population growth or decline. A high birth rate typically indicates a growing population, while a low birth rate suggests a declining or stable population.

67. **(B):** The parameter taken into account in calculating the literacy rate is Age above 7 years. Literacy rate is typically calculated by assessing the proportion of individuals aged 7 years and above who can read and write a simple message in any language. This age threshold is commonly used because it is assumed that by the age of 7, individuals have had sufficient opportunity for basic education and should be able to acquire basic literacy skills.

68. (A): India is indeed in the stage of demographic cycle known as late expanding. In this stage, birth rates begin to decline, but they are still higher than death rates, leading to continued population growth. This stage is characterized by a decrease in the proportion of young people and an increase in the proportion of working-age individuals.

69. (C): Population pyramid is the best representation of population with age variation. It is a graphical illustration that shows the distribution of various age groups in a population, typically divided by gender. The pyramid shape is formed by plotting the percentage or number of individuals in each age group along the horizontal axis, with the youngest age groups at the base and the oldest age groups at the top.

70. (B): The most common cause of maternal mortality in India is hemorrhage. Hemorrhage refers to excessive bleeding, typically during childbirth or immediately after delivery. It can occur due to various factors such as uterine atony (failure of the uterus to contract after childbirth), placental abnormalities, and trauma during delivery or complications from cesarean section.

71. (D): The Plastic Waste Management Rules (Amendment) 2021 stipulate that carry bags made of plastic must meet a minimum thickness requirement after December 31, 2022. The minimum thickness specified is 120 microns. This requirement aims to address concerns related to the environmental impact of single-use plastic bags by promoting the use of thicker bags that are more durable and less likely to contribute to litter and pollution.

72. (A): The Environment Protection Rules, 1999, set the permitted noise level generated by firecrackers at 125 dB. This regulation aims to control and mitigate the adverse effects of noise pollution resulting from the use of firecrackers, particularly during festivals and celebrations.

73. (C): According to the Solid Waste Management Rules, 2016, the post-closure care of a landfill site should be conducted for at least 15 years. This duration ensures proper monitoring and maintenance of the landfill site after its closure to prevent environmental contamination and other risks associated with landfill operations.

74. (D): Under the Medical Termination of Pregnancy (MTP) Act, 1971, medical termination of pregnancy is considered safe up to 12 weeks of pregnancy. Beyond 12 weeks, termination of pregnancy may be allowed in certain exceptional circumstances, such as when there is a risk to the life or health of the pregnant woman or if there is substantial fetal abnormality.

75. (D): According to the Factories Act, 1948, each worker employed in a factory should have a minimum space of 14.2 cubic meters. This provision ensures adequate working conditions for employees, including sufficient space to move around comfortably and perform their duties safely.

76. (C): According to the Immoral Traffic (Prevention) Act, 1956, a child is defined as a person who has not completed the age of 16 years. This legal definition is crucial in the context of preventing immoral trafficking and protecting children from exploitation and abuse. By setting the age limit at 16 years, the Act aims to safeguard the rights and well-being of minors, ensuring that they are not subjected to activities related to immoral trafficking or forced into prostitution.

77. (A): Adulterants are substances that are added intentionally or unintentionally to food products, leading to a decrease in their quality, safety, or nutritional value. These substances may include chemicals, toxins, or other foreign materials that contaminate food during processing, storage, or handling. Detecting and preventing the presence of adulterants in food is essential for ensuring food safety and protecting public health.

78. (A): The Central Pollution Control Board (CPCB) was established under Section 3 of the Water (Prevention and Control of Pollution) Act, 1974. This section empowers the central government to constitute a Central Pollution Control Board to prevent and control water pollution effectively. The CPCB plays a crucial role in coordinating and implementing pollution control measures at the national level.

79. (C): Section 39 of the Air (Prevention and Control of Pollution) Act, 1981, deals with the penalty for contravention of certain provisions of the Act. This section outlines the consequences for individuals or entities that violate the regulations set forth in the Act. It specifies the penalties or fines that may be imposed upon those found guilty of contravening the provisions aimed at preventing and controlling air pollution.

80. (A): "Primary Food" under the Prevention of Food Adulteration Act, 1954, refers to the produce of agriculture in its natural form. This includes fruits, vegetables, grains, and other agricultural products that are consumed without undergoing significant processing or modification. These foods are typically consumed in their natural state and are considered essential components of a healthy diet.

81. (D): Under the Employees' State Insurance (ESI) Act, maternity benefits provide for full wages to eligible employees during the period of maternity leave. This means that the employee receives their entire wage during the maternity leave period, ensuring financial support during this crucial time. The provision aims to promote the well-being of female employees and encourage their participation in the workforce by providing adequate maternity benefits.

82. (B): When cotton fibres are processed, they release fine dust particles into the air, which can be inhaled by workers. Prolonged exposure to this dust can lead to respiratory symptoms such as coughing, wheezing, chest tightness, and shortness of breath. Byssinosis is a type of occupational lung disease and is also known as "brown lung disease" or "Monday fever" due to its association with symptoms that often worsen at the beginning of the workweek.

83. (B): The Constitution prohibits the employment of children in factories below the age of 14 years. This provision aims to protect the rights and well-being of children by ensuring that they are not engaged in hazardous or exploitative work environments. By setting a minimum age for employment in factories, the Constitution seeks to promote the physical, mental, and social development of children and safeguard their right to education, health, and a safe childhood.

84. (A): Silicosis, a debilitating occupational lung disease, primarily results from the inhalation of dust containing silica or silicon particles. When silica dust is inhaled, it can cause inflammation and scarring of the lung tissue over time, leading to respiratory symptoms such as coughing, shortness of breath, and chest pain. In severe cases, silicosis can progress to respiratory failure and death.

85. (A): Ergonomics focuses on optimizing the interaction between people and their work environment to enhance efficiency, productivity, and well-being. It involves designing tasks, tools, equipment, and workspaces in a way that minimizes physical and mental strain on workers while maximizing performance. By considering factors such as posture, movement, workspace layout, and equipment design, ergonomics aims to prevent work-related injuries and musculoskeletal disorders, improve comfort and satisfaction, and promote overall health and productivity in the workplace.

86. **(C):** The Chairman of the Employees State Insurance (ESI) Scheme is the Union Minister of Labour. As the head of the Ministry responsible for labor welfare and social security initiatives, the Union Minister of Labour oversees the implementation and administration of the ESI Scheme. This scheme provides medical and cash benefits to employees and their dependents in case of sickness, maternity, disablement, or death due to employment injury.

87. **(C):** Farmer's Lung is a type of hypersensitivity pneumonitis caused by the inhalation of organic dust containing fungal spores, particularly from moldy hay or grain. Micropolyspora faeni is a thermophilic actinomycete fungus found in the dust of moldy hay and straw, and it is a significant antigen responsible for triggering the immune response in Farmer's Lung.

88. **(A):** Vaccination is categorized as a form of primary prevention because it aims to prevent the onset of disease by boosting the body's immune response against specific pathogens. By administering vaccines, individuals develop immunity to infectious diseases, thereby reducing the risk of contracting and spreading the illness. This proactive approach helps to protect individuals and communities from the initial occurrence of the targeted diseases.

89. **(C):** The didactic method typically involves the transmission of knowledge from the teacher to the students through lectures, presentations, or demonstrations. It is characterized by a one-way flow of information, where the teacher imparts knowledge to the students without active participation or engagement from the learners. Therefore, the statement "Active learning" being associated with the didactic method is not true, as it usually lacks interactive and participatory elements commonly found in active learning approaches.

90. **(B):** While noise can indeed disrupt communication, it is not typically categorized as a cultural barrier. Cultural barriers of communication, such as illiteracy, attitude, and knowledge, are related to differences in cultural backgrounds, beliefs, values, and perspectives that can hinder effective communication between individuals or groups from different cultures. Noise, on the other hand, refers to external disturbances or interference that can affect the transmission or reception of messages but is not inherently tied to cultural differences.

91. **(A):** Acculturation in health education refers to the process of individuals from various cultural backgrounds adopting new health-related beliefs and practices. It involves recognizing cultural diversity, understanding how cultural factors influence health behaviors, and tailoring health education strategies accordingly.

92. **(C):** For effective group discussion, it's ideal to have a group size ranging from 6 to 12 persons. This range ensures a balance between having enough participants to generate diverse perspectives and ideas, while also preventing the group from becoming too large and unwieldy, which can lead to difficulties in managing the discussion and ensuring active participation from all members.

93. **(B):** Role play is not a method of mass approach in health education, as it typically involves smaller groups or individuals acting out scenarios to simulate real-life situations. In contrast, mass approaches in health education aim to reach a wide audience simultaneously. Methods such as television, health museums, and the internet are examples of mass approaches because they have the capacity to disseminate health information to large numbers of people at once, whether through broadcasting, exhibitions, or online platforms.

94. (D): Personal contact is not typically considered a method used in group approaches in health education. Instead, it often falls under individual or interpersonal approaches. In group approaches, methods such as lectures, panel discussions, and symposiums are more commonly utilized to disseminate health information and facilitate discussions among multiple participants simultaneously.

95. (A): Mineral oil is commonly used as a larvicide in mosquito control due to its ability to form a thin film on the surface of standing water, effectively suffocating mosquito larvae and preventing them from breathing. This method disrupts the mosquito life cycle by targeting the immature stages in their development, reducing the population of adult mosquitoes that can transmit diseases such as malaria, dengue fever, and Zika virus.

96. (C): Mosquito nets typically have around 150 holes per square inch, serving as a physical barrier to prevent mosquitoes from entering and biting individuals sleeping under the net. This density of holes is carefully designed to be small enough to block mosquitoes while still allowing airflow for comfort.

97. (B): International Health Regulations aim to prevent the spread of diseases. Mosquitoes can transmit various diseases, so keeping them away from airports and seaports is crucial. According to research on mosquito control in airports, a 400-meter radius around these areas is targeted for mosquito elimination.

100. (A): The main principle of public participation is openness and adaptability, emphasizing transparency, inclusivity, and flexibility in decision-making processes involving the public. This principle underscores the importance of providing accessible information, opportunities for meaningful engagement, and mechanisms for feedback and dialogue to ensure that diverse perspectives are considered and integrated into policies, programs, and projects.

101. (A): Exposure to sunlight increases the utilization ability of Vitamin D in the body. When the skin is exposed to ultraviolet B (UVB) radiation from sunlight, a chemical reaction occurs that enables the synthesis of Vitamin D in the skin. Vitamin D plays a crucial role in maintaining bone health, regulating calcium and phosphorus levels in the body, supporting immune function, and reducing the risk of various diseases.

102. (A): The Chipko Movement, originating in India in the 1970s, had a primary focus on protecting forests. The movement aimed to raise awareness about the ecological significance of forests and the detrimental impact of deforestation on local communities, biodiversity, and the environment.

103. (A): In the ABCDE method of first aid, 'E' stands for Exposure. This step involves exposing the patient's body to assess for any additional injuries or medical conditions that may be present but not immediately obvious. It includes removing clothing or other obstructions that may hinder examination and treatment.

104. (D): Ideal wound dressing should maintain a moist environment, control bacterial growth, and minimize odor while promoting healing. However, it's vital to avoid excessively tight dressing as it can impair blood flow, damage tissues, and lead to complications. Instead, dressings should offer gentle yet secure coverage, allowing for proper airflow and drainage to facilitate the healing process effectively.

105. (B): Recurrent disinfection is not a recognized type of disinfection. Disinfection typically involves the use of chemical or physical agents to eliminate or reduce the number of microorganisms on surfaces or objects to prevent the spread of infectious diseases.

106. (B): The golden period for treating an open wound is typically within 6 hours of the injury occurring. During this critical window, prompt medical attention can significantly reduce the risk of infection and complications, enhance wound healing, and improve overall outcomes.

107. (A): The first and most crucial measure in managing a severely injured patient is to ensure the maintenance of the airway. This involves assessing the patient's airway for any obstructions or compromise and taking immediate steps to establish and maintain a clear and patent airway to facilitate adequate breathing.

108. (D): In emergency situations, O Negative blood can be transfused without cross matching. O Negative blood is often referred to as the "universal donor" blood type because it lacks both A and B antigens on the surface of red blood cells, making it compatible with individuals of any blood type.

109. (A): The Mid-day meal scheme, officially launched on India's Independence Day, August 15, 1995, was initially called the National Programme of Nutritional Support to Primary Education (NP-NSPE). This program aimed to improve the nutritional status of children in primary school and boost school enrollment rates, particularly for girls.

110. (C): Dimensions of health typically include physical, mental, and social aspects, but "primary dimensions" is not commonly recognized as a category in health dimensions. Instead, health dimensions refer to various facets that contribute to overall well-being, such as physical health, which encompasses bodily functions and fitness; mental health, which involves emotional and psychological well-being; and social health, which involves interactions with others and community engagement.

111. (A): Mission Indradhanush, initiated by the Ministry of Health and Family Welfare, aims to fully immunize 90% of children who are either unvaccinated or partially vaccinated. Through intensified immunization drives and focused efforts, Mission Indradhanush strives to protect children from vaccine-preventable diseases, reduce morbidity and mortality rates, and achieve significant progress towards public health goals.

112. (B): In the calculation of infant mortality rate (IMR), the parameter not required is stillbirth. IMR specifically measures the number of deaths of infants under one year of age per 1,000 live births. It focuses solely on infant deaths that occur after live births, encompassing early neonatal deaths (within the first week of life), late neonatal deaths (from 7 to 28 days after birth), and postnatal deaths (from 29 days to one year of age).

113. (B): The Bhore Committee, also known as the Health Survey and Development Committee, was established in 1943 under the chairmanship of Sir Joseph Bhore. This committee played a pivotal role in shaping India's healthcare system. Among its significant contributions was the proposal for a primary healthcare system that focused on preventive and promotive care at the community level.

115. (C): Avalanches typically consist of three primary components: the starting zone, avalanche track, and runout zone. The end zone is not a commonly recognized component of avalanches and is therefore not typically considered as a principle component.

116. (B): Sentinel surveillance doesn't aim to capture every single case of a disease. It focuses on collecting data from a representative sample, like specific hospitals or clinics, to identify trends and potential outbreaks. Hidden cases, which might not be reported through standard channels, can be identified through sentinel surveillance by observing a rise in cases at reporting facilities.

117. (D): There are five principles of primary health care—Accessibility, Public participation, Health promotion, Appropriate skills and technology, and Intersectoral cooperation—it does not explicitly include the provision of essential drugs as one of those principles. However, it's important to note that the provision of essential drugs is often considered an essential component, integral to ensuring access to necessary medications for the population.

118. (C): The Kayakalp scheme is primarily focused on initiating a clean hospital program. It aims to promote cleanliness, hygiene, and infection control practices within healthcare facilities across India. Through this scheme, hospitals are encouraged to adopt and implement best practices in sanitation, waste management, and overall cleanliness to create a safe and hygienic environment for patients, visitors, and healthcare workers.

119. (B): The international agency providing assistance in the National Program for Control of Blindness in India is DANIDA (Danish International Development Agency). DANIDA collaborates with the Indian government to support initiatives aimed at preventing and controlling blindness. These initiatives include providing eye care services, conducting vision screenings, distributing spectacles, and performing surgeries to treat preventable causes of blindness.

120. (B): A health subcenter is recommended for a population of 3,000 in hilly areas. According to the Government of India, a subcenter is recommended for a population of 5,000 in plain areas, and 3,000 in hilly and tribal areas. Each subcenter is required to have at least one Auxiliary Nurse Midwife (ANM) or Female Health Worker.

121. (B): Protein is the nutrient that supplies the nitrogen requirement of the human body. Proteins are macromolecules composed of amino acids, and nitrogen is an essential component of amino acids. When proteins are broken down during digestion, the nitrogen in the amino acids is released and utilized by the body for various physiological functions, including building and repairing tissues, synthesizing hormones and enzymes, and supporting immune function.

122. (B): The daily requirement of protein for the adult human is approximately 60 grams. Proteins are essential macronutrients that play vital roles in the body, including building and repairing tissues, supporting immune function, and producing enzymes and hormones.

123. (B): Egg yolk is known to contain a high content of cholesterol. Cholesterol is a type of fat found in animal-based foods, and egg yolks are particularly rich in this nutrient. While eggs are a nutritious source of protein and essential vitamins and minerals, including vitamin D and choline, they also contain cholesterol. A single large egg yolk may contain around 186 milligrams of cholesterol, which is predominantly found in the yolk portion.

124. (A): Vitamin D is unique among vitamins in that it also functions as a hormone in the human body. In its hormonal role, vitamin D binds to specific receptors in cells throughout the body, affecting gene expression and signaling pathways. This dual role as both a vitamin and a hormone underscores the importance of vitamin D in various physiological processes and highlights its significance for overall health and well-being.

125. **(C):** After several weeks of starvation, when glucose stores become depleted, the major energy source for the brain shifts to ketone bodies, primarily beta-hydroxybutyrate. During prolonged fasting or starvation, the body begins breaking down stored fat to produce ketone bodies through a process called ketogenesis. These ketone bodies, including beta-hydroxybutyrate, can cross the blood-brain barrier and serve as an alternative fuel source for the brain.

126. **(A):** Vitamin C is water-soluble and sensitive to heat. This means that it can dissolve easily in water and is broken down by high temperatures. Cooking methods that involve high heat and long durations, such as boiling, roasting, or stewing, can significantly reduce the vitamin C content of foods. Additionally, exposure to air can also contribute to vitamin C loss.

127. **(B):** Pernicious anemia is primarily caused by a deficiency of vitamin B12. This condition occurs when the body is unable to properly absorb vitamin B12 from the gastrointestinal tract, often due to autoimmune destruction of the cells in the stomach that produce intrinsic factor, a protein necessary for vitamin B12 absorption. Deficiency of this vitamin leads to pernicious anemia, which can cause a variety of symptoms, including fatigue, weakness, pale skin, shortness of breath, and cognitive problems.

128. **(C):** The recommended concentration of fluoride in a community water supply is generally around 1.0 parts per million (ppm). Fluoride is added to water supplies as a public health measure to help prevent dental cavities and promote dental health. At this concentration, fluoride can effectively strengthen tooth enamel and reduce the risk of tooth decay without causing adverse effects such as dental fluorosis.

129. **(A):** The small intestine is the primary site for the absorption of nutrients in the human digestive system. This long, coiled tube, comprising the duodenum, jejunum, and ileum, is lined with millions of tiny finger-like projections called villi and microvilli, which greatly increase the surface area available for nutrient absorption.

130. **(B):** Fat-soluble vitamins are those that can dissolve in fat and are absorbed along with dietary fats in the intestine. Among the options listed, vitamins A, D, E, and K are fat-soluble. Vitamin A supports vision, immune function, and cell growth. Vitamin D is crucial for calcium absorption and bone health. Vitamin E acts as an antioxidant, protecting cells from damage caused by free radicals. Vitamin K is necessary for blood clotting and bone metabolism.

132. **(A):** Among the options provided, proteins and fats are classified as macronutrients. Proteins serve as the building blocks of tissues and organs, playing crucial roles in muscle development, immune function, enzyme production, and hormone regulation. Fats, also known as lipids, provide a concentrated source of energy and play vital roles in cell structure, hormone synthesis, and the absorption of fat-soluble vitamins.

133. **(B):** When a milk sample is adulterated with starch, the addition of iodine solution will result in a blue color. Iodine solution reacts with starch to form a blue-colored complex. This reaction is used as a test to detect the presence of starch in various substances, including milk.

134. **(A):** Among the options provided, cellulose is the component that does not have nutritive value. Cellulose is a complex carbohydrate found in the cell walls of plants and is considered a dietary fiber. While it is a major structural component of plant cell walls and provides structural support to plants, cellulose cannot be digested by humans due to the lack of the necessary enzymes in the human digestive system.

135. (B): The Government of India adopted the National Nutrition Policy (NNP) in 1993. The policy is under the Department of Women and Child Development. It's a multi-sectoral strategy to eliminate malnutrition and achieve optimum nutrition for all. The NNP recognizes the extent of under-nutrition in the country. The NNP has been a prime subject of various five-year plans. The policy covers all areas and aspects that affect nutrition.

136. (A): According to the Biomedical Waste Management (BMW) Rules, white sharps waste, including needles, syringes, scalpels, blades, and more, should be contained in white or translucent containers. These containers should be puncture, leak, and tamper proof.

137. (D): The physical parameters used for the characterization of wastewater include density and viscosity. Density refers to the mass per unit volume of the wastewater, providing information about its concentration and composition. Viscosity, on the other hand, measures the resistance of the wastewater to flow and indicates its fluidity or thickness.

138. (A): Coliform bacteria, particularly Escherichia coli (E. coli), serve as the most reliable evidence of fecal contamination in water. These bacteria are commonly found in the intestines of warm-blooded animals, including humans, and their presence in water indicates recent fecal contamination. E. coli is specifically used as an indicator organism for assessing water quality and determining the potential presence of harmful pathogens associated with fecal matter.

139. (B): Dry weather flow refers to the volume of sewage or wastewater that flows through a system during a 24-hour period under normal weather conditions, excluding any inflow from precipitation. This measurement is essential for assessing the capacity and performance of sewage treatment systems and designing infrastructure to manage wastewater effectively.

140. (D): Night soil, which refers to human feces collected for use as fertilizer, does not fall under the category of healthcare waste. While improper disposal of night soil can pose sanitation and environmental concerns, it is not directly generated from healthcare facilities or activities. Healthcare waste encompasses various types of waste generated from healthcare activities, including SHARPS (such as needles and syringes), chemical waste, and pathological waste.

141. (A): The ortho-toulidine test, also known as the ortho-toluidine test, is used to determine the amount of residual chlorine in water, including free and combined chlorine. The test uses a reagent made of analytical grade ortho-toulidine dissolved in a 10% solution of hydrochloric acid (HCl). When the reagent is added to water containing chlorine, it turns yellow, and the intensity of the yellow color is proportional to the concentration of chlorine.

143. (D): The "Schmutzdecke layer" is a microbial layer that forms on the surface of a sand bed filter used in water treatment processes. It consists of a complex mixture of algae, plankton, diatoms, and bacteria, which develop and thrive in the upper layer of the filter media. This layer plays a crucial role in the filtration process by trapping and removing suspended particles, pathogens, and organic matter from the water as it passes through the filter.

144. (A): Soft water is characterized by a low level of hardness, typically containing less than 1 milliequivalent per liter (mEq/L) of dissolved minerals, such as calcium and magnesium ions. This minimal concentration of hardness ions results in water that feels smooth and does not leave scale deposits or soap scum residues.

145. (D): UNICEF focuses on a wide range of programs to address child health and development; it typically does not directly provide funding for family planning initiatives, which are often managed by other organizations and agencies specializing in reproductive health and population control efforts.

147. (D): Controlled tipping is a method involves disposing of waste in a designated area with proper engineering controls to minimize environmental impact. Modern sanitary landfills are lined to prevent contamination of soil and groundwater. They also have methane gas capture systems to reduce greenhouse gas emissions. Controlled tipping offers a more balanced approach to waste disposal compared to the other options listed.

148. (A): In triage, the black color denotes Death. In triage, the black color tag signifies the highest priority, which is assigned to individuals who are deemed deceased or beyond medical assistance. This categorization helps medical personnel focus their attention on individuals who have the highest chance of survival and require immediate medical intervention.

149. (C):

A. Radioactivity: This aspect refers to the presence of radioactive substances in drinking water. Radioactive elements such as radium, uranium, and radon can naturally occur in groundwater sources or may be introduced through human activities such as mining and nuclear accidents.

B. Microbiological: This aspect focuses on the presence of microorganisms in drinking water, particularly harmful pathogens such as bacteria, viruses, and protozoa. Contamination of water sources with fecal matter or other sources of microbial contamination can lead to waterborne diseases such as cholera, typhoid fever, and gastroenteritis.

Previous Paper (Solved)

HEALTH & SANITARY INSPECTOR

Recruitment Exam, 2021*

Part-A

1. Minimum illumination required for Operation Theatre (OT) and Labour room should be:

A. 100 lux B. 150 lux
C. 200 lux D. 300 lux

2. How many times the hospital corrdors should be cleaned in a day?

A. At least once B. At least twice
C. At least thrice D. Not required at all

3. Wards should be cleaned in a day with wet mop:

A. At least once B. At least twice
C. At least thrice D. Not required at all

4. Which of the following Ministry of Govt. of India notified 'Bio-Medical Waste Management Rules, 2016'?

A. Ministry of Health & Family Welfare
B. Ministry of Environment, Forest and Climate Change
C. Ministry of Food Processing Industries
D. Ministry of Drinking Water and Sanitation

5. 'Bio-Medical Waste Management Rules, 2016' also cover the:

A. Radioactive wastes as covered under provisions of the Atomic Energy Act 1962 (33 of 1962) and the rules made under the Act.
B. Solid wastes covered under the Municipal Solid Waste (Management and Handling) Rules, 2000 made under the Act.
C. Hazardous micro-organisms, genetically engineered micro-organisms and cells covered under the manufacture, use, import, export and storage of hazardous micro-organisms, genetically engineered micro-organisms or cells Rules, 1989 made under the Act.
D. None of the above

6. In 2011, the number of females per thousand male in Haryana State was:

A. 876 B. 818
C. 879 D. 868

7. In 2011, the number of females per thousand males in India was:

A. 958 B. 973
C. 943 D. 996

8. In 2011, the number of females per thousand males exceeded in the states:

A. Tamil Nadu & Kerala
B. Tamil Nadu & Chhattisgarh
C. Tamil Nadu & Puducherry
D. Kerala & Puducherry

9. In 2011, the highest population density was of the state/UT:

A. Chandigarh B. Uttar Pradesh
C. NCT, Delhi D. Bihar

10. In 2011, the highest decadal growth rate was of the state/UT:

A. Haryana
B. Andaman & Nicobar Islands
C. Lakshadweep
D. Dadra & Nagar Haveli

11. The Infant Mortality Rate of India in 2013 was:

A. 40 B. 54
C. 50 D. 12

* Held on 27-12-2021.

12. In 2013, the death rate in Haryana state was:
A. 6.20 B. 4.00
C. 6.30 D. 4.10

13. The highest population of the state resides below poverty line:
A. Uttarakhand B. Bihar
C. West Bengal D. Uttar Pradesh

14. In 2014, Net availability of cereals & pulses per capita per day in India was:
A. 491.30 gm B. 400.00 gm
C. 450.30 gm D. 416.20 gm

15. Which districts of Haryana state are with fluoride affected rural inhabitations with excess fluoride quantity in drinking water as on 1st April, 2015?
A. Faridabad & Sonepat
B. Faridabad & Sirsa
C. Faridabad & Mahendragarh
D. Sirsa & Mahendragarh

16. As per 2011 records, per cent houses do not have household latrine and practice open defecation:
A. 33.10 B. 34.80
C. 29.80 D. 3.20

17. Which statement hold true for Non-communicable diseases dealt under NPCDCS?
A. Diabetes, dengue, kala-azar & stroke
B. Diabetes, cancer, chikungunya & stroke
C. Diabetes, cancer, cardiovascular disease & stroke
D. Diabetes, cancer, cholera & stroke

18. Which state reported highest number of encephalitis cases & deaths in 2014?
A. Bihar B. Odisha
C. Haryana D. Uttar Pradesh

19. Which state reported highest number of chickenpox cases & deaths in 2015?
A. Bihar B. Odisha
C. West Bengal D. Delhi

20. The highly kala-azar affected states of India are:
A. Bihar, Delhi, Jharkhand & Uttar Pradesh
B. Bihar, Jharkhand, Uttar Pradesh & West Bengal
C. Bihar, Jharkhand, Madhya Pradesh & West Bengal
D. Bihar, Jharkhand, Assam & West Bengal

21. Which of the following is the zoonotic disease?
A. Plague B. Dengue
C. Zika D. Filaria

22. Which spray will be done to interrupt the active transmission of the disease transmitted by the mosquito?
A. Space spray according to the prevailing situations
B. Indoor Residual Spray with DDT/ Malathion/Synthetic Pyrethroids WP according to the availability
C. Larvicidal Spray in the stagnant water
D. All the above

23. Which mosquito is anthropophilic?
A. *Anopheles culicifacies*
B. *Aedes aegypti*
C. *Mansonia annulifera*
D. *Culex quinquefasciatus*

24. Which intervention measure is best for prevention & control of dengue, Chikungunya & Zika?
A. Regular Insecticidal Fogging
B. Mosquito breeding source reduction
C. Indoor Residual Spray with DDT/ Malathion/Synthetic Pyrethroids
D. Beating of Drums

25. Causative organism of plague is:
A. *Yercinia pestis*
B. *Leishmania donovani*
C. *Wuchereria bancrofti*
D. *Xenopsylla cheopsis*

26. In 2014, to total number of accidental deaths accounted in India was:
A. 400517 B. 357021
C. 451757 D. 294175

27. Urban malaria vector is:
A. *Anopheles culicifacies*
B. *Anopheles stephensi*
C. *Anopheles minimus*
D. *Anopheles fluviatilis*

28. Mosquitoes make sound with the help of:
A. Proboscis B. Legs
C. Wings D. Antenna

29. The surface/subsurface water is contaminated with:
A. Feacal coliform bacteria
B. Organic pollutants
C. Parasitic organisms/pathogens
D. All of these

30. The sanitation related diseases are:
A. Water borne (oral-fecal route: typhoid, cholera, dysentary; water based (schistosomiasis)
B. Water related (dengue, malaria, filaria, zika); excreta related (trachoma)
C. Water collection & storage related (caused improper handling of excreta containers); toxin related (by toxic bacteria in surface water-hepatic illness)
D. All the above

31. The Disability-Adjusted Life Year (DALY) stands for:
A. One lost year of "healthy life" as a result of health condition such as disease or disability
B. Total period lost of "healthy life" as a result of health condition such as disability
C. Total period lost of "healthy life" as a result of health condition such as disease
D. None of the above

32. The quality triangle concept includes:
A. Cost, time & quality on the corners of the triangle and scope in the middle/centre of the triangle
B. Cost, time & scope on the corners of the triangle and quality in the middle/centre of the triangle
C. Quality, time & scope on the corners of the triangle and Cost in the middle/centre of the triangle
D. Cost, quality & scope on the corners of the triangle and time in the middle/centre of the triangle

33. Water disinfection is done by:
A. Chlorination
B. Boiling
C. UV rays treatment
D. All of these

34. The chlorine concentration should be at the tail end of piped water supply:
A. 5 ppm B. 6 ppm
C. 4 ppm D. 1 ppm

35. The fairs, festivals and public gatherings cultural practices should be ensured:
A. Only safe drinking water supply with adequate light and air
B. Use of bio-toilets/bio-degradable devices
C. Fresh and covered eatables
D. All the above

36. Which ASQ Standard stands for Environmental management?
A. ISO 9000 ISO 9001
B. ISO 19011
C. ISO 31011
D. ISO 14000 ISO 14001

37. Which ASQ Standard stands for Food Safety?
A. ISO 9000 ISO 9001
B. ISO 22000
C. ISO 31011
D. ISO 14000 ISO 14001

38. FSSAI stands for:
A. Govt. of India body under Food safety and Standards Act, 2006 to register the food product business to manufacture, distribute and transport food products.
B. Issuance of license for a period of one to five years for local/basic, state, central level license
C. Certificate/license helps the business to grow and creates a sense of security for customers.
D. All the above

39. What intervention resulted in elimination of plague disease?
A. Co-lateral impact as a result of introduction/use of chemical insecticides both in health and agriculture after world war II.
B. Exercising indigenous practices for killing rodents
C. Both the above
D. None of the above

40. Why Japanese encephalitis is transmitted from man-to-man?
A. Peripheral viremia in man of short duration
B. Inadequate to infect
C. Mosquitoes sucks virus
D. Virus is inactivated in the man

41. Bureau of Indian Standards is National Standards Body of India for:
A. The harmonious development of the activities of Standardization, marking and quality certification of goods and matters connected therewith or incidental thereto.
B. Provides traceability and tangibility benefits to the national economy in terms of safe, reliable quality goods; minimizing health hazards to consumers; promoting exports and import substitute; control over proliferation of varieties etc. through standardization, certification & testing.
C. Both the above
D. None of the above

42. Bureau of Indian Standards specification for testing Skimmed milk powder Standard Grade is:
A. IS 13334 : Part 2 : 1992
B. IS 13334 : Part 1 : 1998
C. IS 12299 : 1998
D. IS 1166 : 1986

43. Bureau of Indian Standards specification for testing Iodized Salt is:
A. IS 1166 : 1986 B. IS 1165 : 2002
C. IS 7224 : 2006 D. IS 14433 : 2007

44. Expenditure on public health as % of GDP of south east asian countries was highest of the country in 2013:
A. Bhutan B. Nepal
C. Maldives D. India

45. National Nutrition week is observed every year from:
A. 1-7 September B. 1-7 August
C. 1-7 April D. 1-7 November

46. Anti-Dengue Month is observed every year in the month of:
A. June B. August
C. September D. July

47. Japanese encephalitis vaccine SA 14-14-2 has been administerd in children age group of the country:
A. 1-15 years B. 2-15 years
C. 3-15 years D. None of these

48. NABH is the constituent board of:
A. Medical Council of India (MCI)
B. Quality Council of India (QCI)
C. Pharmacy Council of India (PCI)
D. None of the above

49. NABH stands for:
A. National Accreditation Board for Hospitals only
B. National Accreditation Board for Healthcare providers only
C. National Accreditation Board for Hospitals & Healthcare providers
D. None of the above

50. NABL 120 offers services in the field of:
A. Guidance for classification of Product Groups in Testing & Calibration
B. Guidance for classification of Product Groups in Testing only
C. Guidance for classification of Product Groups in calibration only
D. None of the above

51. NABL 180 offers services in the field of:
A. Application Form for Proficiency Testing Providers only
B. Application Form for Reference Material Producers Accreditation only
C. Both the above
D. None of the above

52. NABL 190 offers services in the field of:
A. Application Form for Proficiency Testing Providers only
B. Application Form for Reference Material Producers Accreditation only
C. Both the above
D. None of the above

53. Junior Chamber International (JCI) is:
A. Non-profit International Government Organization of young people
B. Non-profit International Non-Governmental Organization of young people

C. Both the above
D. None of the above

54. Members of JCI are benefitted by:
A. Expansion of network of friends and business contacts locally and across the globe.
B. Getting chance to give back to community and effect positive change.
C. Developing leadership and management skills and personal development opportunities.
D. All the above

55. The extra-cellular disease causing parasite is:
A. *Plasmodium vivax*
B. *Wuchereria bancrofti*
C. *Leishmania donovani*
D. None of the above

56. Infective stage of malaria parasite is:
A. Trophozoite B. Sporozoite
C. Gametocyte D. All of these stages

57. The pyrethrum insecticide is natural extract of a plant:
A. *Azadirachta indica*
B. *Artimisia annua*
C. *Chrysanthemum* sp
D. *Ocimum sanctum*

58. DDT insecticide is a:
A. Organophosphorus compound
B. Synthetic pyrethroid compound
C. Chlorinated hydrocarbon compound
D. None of these compounds

59. Which plant deter the growth of mosquito larvae in the water?
A. *Jatropha curcas* B. *Brassica campestris*
C. *Sonchus asper* D. *Cynodon dactylon*

60. Disinfection of water is done by release of nascent gas in piped water:
A. Oxygen B. Chlorine
C. Hydrogen D. Nitrogen

61. Environmental engineering methods for antimosquito measures include:
A. deweeding and desilting from drains/water bodies
B. maintaining gradient in drains for swift flow of water
C. dressing and filling of low lands/pits/drain margins
D. All the above

62. Home based morbidity management & disability prevention is practiced in:
A. Malaria & Filaria patients
B. Filaria & leprosy patients
C. Dengue & Filaria patients
D. None of these

63. Leprosy is caused by:
A. Protozoan parasite B. Virus
C. Bacteria D. Worm

64. Disease is caused by virus:
A. Dengue B. Chikungunya
C. Zika D. All of these diseases

65. Vector borne diseases proposed for elimination in India are:
A. Malaria, Filaria & Kala-azar
B. Malaria, Dengue & Kala-azar
C. Chikungunya, Filaria & Kala-azar
D. Japanese Encephalitis, Filaria & Kala-azar

66. Vector borne disease proposed for elimination by 2030 in India is:
A. Dengue B. Chikungunya
C. Malaria D. All of these diseases

67. Annual Parasitic Index (API) denotes malaria infection in the community:
A. per hundred of population
B. per thousand of population
C. per lac of population
D. None of these

68. How index is determined?
A. When numerator and denominator are of same unit
B. When numerator and denominator are of different units
C. Units have to do nothing with the index
D. None of the above

69. Pupal stage of mosquito is:
A. Herbivorous B. Carnivorous
C. Omnivorous D. Not feed at all

70. The BIS specification for mosquito net is:
A. IS 1166 : 1986 B. IS 9886 : 1990
C. IS 12299 : 1998 D. None of these

Part-B

71. Which Ministry has launched 'Vikas Portal' on 16 December 2021?
A. Ministry of Rural Development
B. Ministry of Agriculture and Farmers Welfare
C. Ministry of Health and Family Welfare
D. Ministry of Labour and Employment

72. When was the State of Haryana formed?
A. 1st November, 1966
B. 10th December, 1966
C. 2nd January, 1967
D. 4th March, 1967

73. Which of the following geographical term related to the "piece of sub-continental land that is surrounded by water"?
A. Peninsula B. Gulf
C. Strait D. Island

74. Consider the following statements about Unified Payments Interface (UPI):
1. It seeks to promote cashless economy in the country
2. It has been developed by National Payments Corporation of India (NPCI)
3. It facilitates the user to have a single virtual address for multiple bank accounts

Which of the above statements is/are correct?
A. Only 1 B. Only 1 and 2
C. All of above D. None of above

75. The first-ever Haryana Sahitya Sangam has started in which city?
A. Faridabad B. Panchkula
C. Gurgaon D. Karnal

76. Which of the following Articles promote the idea of equal justice and to provide free legal aid to the poor?
A. Article 38 B. Article 39
C. Article 39 A D. Article 41

77. The sum of three consecutive numbers is 87. The middle number is?
A. 30 B. 27
C. 29 D. 28

78. A man saves ₹ 200 at the end of each year and lends the money at 5% compound interest. How much will it become at the end of 3 years.
A. ₹ 662 B. ₹ 662.01
C. ₹ 662.02 D. ₹ 662.03

79. Ramesh sold a statue for a price 25% higher than the original price of the statue. He had however bought the statue at 20% discount on the original price. With the profit of ₹ 2025, find the original price of the statue.
A. ₹ 6000 B. ₹ 7500
C. ₹ 3500 D. ₹ 4500

80. Surendra covers a distance by cycle at 18 km/h. He returns to the starting point in a bus at a speed of 45 km/h. Find the average speed for the entire journey.
A. 27.39 km/hr B. 25.71 km/hr
C. 27 km/hr D. 31.5 km/hr

81. What will be value of (74.6 – 38.9 – 5.7)/(26.4 – 18.9)?
A. 3.5 B. 2.25
C. 2.0 D. 4.0

82. If $a * b = 2a + 3b$, then the value of $2 * 3 + 3 * 4$ is?
A. 24 B. 31
C. 32 D. 34

83. A good judge never gropes ______ the conclusion.
A. for B. to
C. at D. on

84. Talk ______ now. The music is ______ so people will be disturbed.
A. Softly, softly B. Soft, soft
C. Softly, soft D. Soft, softly

85. Which tense is used to express an action completed in the immediate past?
A. Past indefinite tense
B. Present indefinite tense
C. Present perfect tense
D. Past perfect tense

86. What's the synonym of MENDACIOUS?
A. untruthful B. irritating
C. provocative D. misleading

87. The indirect form of the sentence "Everybody said, "How well she sings!", is:
A. Everybody exclaimed that she sang very well.
B. Everybody told us that how she sang very well.
C. Everybody exclaimed that she sings very well.
D. Everybody told us that she sings very well.

88. The officer asked the peon ________ why he was late.
A. that B. if
C. but D. No word needed

89. Which number comes next in the series
1536, 384, 96, ___?
A. 23 B. 24
C. 28 D. 18

90. Raman says "Anuj's mother is the only daughter of my mother." How is Anuj related to Raman?
A. Brother B. Nephew
C. Father D. None of the above

91. What comes next in the series
ATNHG, DKCMB, CVPJI, GNFPE, EXRLK, JQISH, GZTNM, ______
A. MTLVK B. PQMTH
C. RIJTU D. HSKUJ

92. If PINK is coded as 1691411, then RED will be coded as?
A. 1963 B. 1854
C. 1853 D. 1954

93. Which of the following pairs of words are differently related?
A. Kind : Cruel B. Slow : Sluggish
C. Stale : Fresh D. Truth : Lie

94. **Statement:** Should schools in India have only one board of education?
Arguments:
I. Yes, it will create uniformity and equality in education.
II. No, it will reduce chances of either quality education or/and may affect literacy rate.
A. Only argument I is strong
B. Only argument II is strong correct
C. Either argument I or II is strong wrong
D. Neither argument I nor II is strong

95. Find the number of triangles in the given figure.

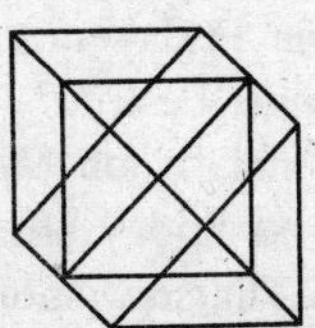

A. 18 B. 20
C. 24 D. 27

96. What is the number of straight lines and the number of triangles in the given figure.

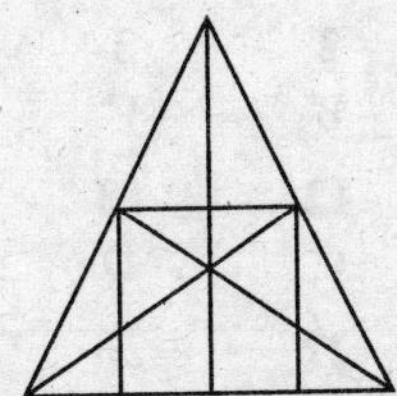

A. 10 straight lines and 34 triangles
B. 9 straight lines and 34 triangles
C. 9 straight lines and 36 triangles
D. 10 straight lines and 36 triangles

Direction (Qs. No. 97-100): *The supervisor of a commuter airline is scheduling pilots to fly the round-trip from City X to City Y....*

The supervisor of a commuter airline is scheduling pilots to fly the round-trip from City X to City Y. The trip takes only two hours, and the airline has one round-trip flight in the morning and one round-trip flight in the afternoon, each day, Monday through Friday. Pilots must be scheduled in accordance with the following rules:

Only W, X, and Y can fly the morning flight.

Only V, X, and Z can fly the afternoon flight.

No pilot may fly twice on the same day.

No pilot may fly on two consecutive days.

X must fly the Wednesday morning flight.

Z must fly the Tuesday afternoon flight.

97. Which of the following must be true?
- A. W flies the Monday morning flight
- B. X flies the Monday afternoon flight
- C. Y flies the Tuesday morning flight
- D. Z flies the Thursday afternoon flight

98. If X flies on Friday morning, which of the following must be true?
- A. X does not fly on Monday afternoon
- B. V flies on Friday afternoon
- C. W flies Thursday morning
- D. Y flies Thursday morning

99. If X flies only one morning flight during the week, which of the following must be true?
- A. W flies exactly two days during the week
- B. X flies exactly three days during the week
- C. Y flies only one day during the week
- D. Z flies Monday afternoon and Friday afternoon

100. If W is not scheduled to fly at all during the week, all of the following must be true EXCEPT:
- A. X flies on Monday morning
- B. V flies on Monday afternoon
- C. Y flies on Thursday morning
- D. Z flies on Friday afternoon

ANSWERS

1	2	3	4	5	6	7	8	9	10
D	B	C	B	D	C	C	D	C	D
11	**12**	**13**	**14**	**15**	**16**	**17**	**18**	**19**	**20**
A	C	D	A	D	C	C	D	C	B
21	**22**	**23**	**24**	**25**	**26**	**27**	**28**	**29**	**30**
A	A	B	B	A	C	B	C	D	D
31	**32**	**33**	**34**	**35**	**36**	**37**	**38**	**39**	**40**
A	B	D	D	D	D	B	D	A	A
41	**42**	**43**	**44**	**45**	**46**	**47**	**48**	**49**	**50**
C	B	C	C	A	D	A	B	C	A
51	**52**	**53**	**54**	**55**	**56**	**57**	**58**	**59**	**60**
A	B	B	D	B	B	C	C	A	B
61	**62**	**63**	**64**	**65**	**66**	**67**	**68**	**69**	**70**
D	B	C	D	A	C	B	B	D	B
71	**72**	**73**	**74**	**75**	**76**	**77**	**78**	**79**	**80**
A	A	D	B	B	C	C	C	D	B
81	**82**	**83**	**84**	**85**	**86**	**87**	**88**	**89**	**90**
D	B	A	C	D	A	A	D	B	B
91	**92**	**93**	**94**	**95**	**96**	**97**	**98**	**99**	**100**
A	B	B	B	C	C	D	B	A	D

Previous Paper (Solved)

HEALTH & MALARIA INSPECTOR Recruitment Exam 2019*

1. The Lodh Waterfalls is located in which of the following States?
A. Uttarakhand B. Odisha
C. Jharkhand D. Chhattisgarh

2. Above 40 kg/m^2 of BMI indicates:
A. Underweight
B. Overweight
C. Morbid obesity
D. Class 1 Obesity

3. Which vitamin is essential for Calcium Absorption?
A. Vitamin D B. Vitamin A
C. Vitamin K D. Vitamin B_{12}

4. Who is the guarantor of the fundamental rights of the Indian citizens?
A. The Governor
B. The Prime Minister
C. The Supreme Court
D. The President

5. Two bells ring at intervals of 57 seconds and 68 seconds. If they both ring at 10 O'clock in the morning together, after how many seconds will they ring together again?
A. 3776 B. 3976
C. 3676 D. 3876

6. Identify the fiber-rich food group.
A. Vegetables and green leafy vegetables
B. Oils and fats
C. Meat and fish
D. Sugar and honey

7. World Health Day falls on ....
A. July 7th B. May 31st
C. April 7th D. March 27th

8. What is a major health problem that occurs due to inadequate/poor housing?
A. Kidney disease
B. Respiratory disease
C. Heart disease
D. Skin cancer

9. Which food stuff contains saturated fat?
A. Potatoes B. Coconuts
C. Wheat D. Apples

10. The term 'Environmental Sanitation' is now being replaced by ....
A. Public Health
B. Environmental Health
C. Both I and II
D. None of the above

11. Cooking with excess quantities of water causes food to be deprived of ....
A. Vitamin K B. Vitamin A
C. Vitamin C D. Vitamin E

12. Which of the following is NOT a risk factor for stroke?
A. Alcohol and smoking
B. Intake of oral contraceptive pills
C. Diabetes and Hypertension
D. Diet regulation

13. In a certain code language, if BASIC is coded as CDUEK, then how is FORCE coded in that language?
A. HFURI B. QHTGE
C. ULIXV D. HQTEG

14. The City of Harappa is situated on the banks of which river?
A. Indus B. Saraswati
C. Luni D. Ravi

15. What is the motto of Olympic Games?
A. Integrity - Fraternity - Agility
B. Do or Die
C. Faster - Higher - Stronger
D. Promote fighting spirit

* Held on 19/07/2019; Conducted by RRB.

16. When an epidemic has already broken out, which of the following is most important in Chikungunya fever control?

A. Keeping water storage container free of mosquito breeding.
B. Sources reduction
C. Larvicide
D. Anti adult measures

17. What is the concentration of oxygen present in air?

A. 20.9% B. 27.8%
C. 25% D. 24%

18. Which of the following is also called Quick lime?

A. Calcium oxide (Chosen option)
B. Sodium oxide
C. Calcium bicarbonate
D. Nitrous oxide

19. Which food group yields more protein?

A. Cereals and millets
B. Vegetables
C. Meat and fish
D. Fruits

20. Which of the following is NOT a preventive and control measure against hypertension?

A. Treatment with anti-hypertensive drugs
B. Weight reduction and exercise
C. Avoiding fatty foods
D. Reducing intake of food

21. A boy started to walk 3 km in East direction. He then took a right turn and walked 4 km and took a left turn and walked 3 km. He took a right turn and walked 3 km before taking another right turn to cover 6 km. In which direction is the starting point from the ending point?

A. East B. South
C. West D. North

22. Which of the following is the meaning of 'Sanitation Barrier'?

A. Segregation of faeces
B. Personal hygiene
C. Water pollution
D. Elimination of flies

23. Fruits like amla are rich in ....

A. Vitamin C
B. Vitamin D
C. Vitamin folic acid
D. Vitamin K

24. What is the main source of energy?

A. Vitamins B. Iron
C. Water D. Fats

25. What is the disability caused by diabetes?

A. Blindness B. Dementia
C. Deafness D. Paralysis

26. What kind of nutritive foodstuff will reduce Type 2 Diabetes?

A. Vitamin content
B. Mineral content
C. Protein content
D. Fibre content

27. How much energy does a pregnant women need per day?

A. 3200 Calories
B. 2000 Calories
C. 1500 Calories
D. 2500 Calories

28. Which one of these is NOT a criterion for the consumption of safe water?

A. Free from harmful chemical substances
B. Free from odour and colour
C. Free from pathogens
D. Adding agents for extra taste

29. The bio-toilet used in trains function based on which of the following principles?

A. Aerobic process
B. Anaerobic process
C. Both I and II
D. None of the above

30. Which one of the following is a type of combustible rubbish?

A. Crockery B. Cans
C. Cardboards D. Metal

31. Raised Body Mass Index (BMI) will not lead to ....

A. Stroke B. Heart disease
C. Jaundice D. Diabetes

32. Which one of the following is NOT the control measures for viral hepatitis 'B'?
A. Immunization against Hepatitis 'B'
B. Avoiding touching the infected person
C. Precautions with blood and body fluids
D. Using condoms

33. Which of the following is NOT a symptom or sign of poliomyelitis?
A. Paralysis
B. Severe chest pain
C. Pain in the neck & back
D. Diarrhoea and vomiting

34. In domestic water sewage, which of the following things is/are not a part of 'Suspended solids'?
A. Clay B. Sand
C. Silt D. Paper Fibres

35. Night blindness is caused by the deficiency of ....
A. Zinc B. Vitamin K
C. Vitamin A D. Folic Acids

36. The 'Great Sanitary Awakening' took place in:
A. India B. England
C. USA D. Germany

37. Which is known as the sunshine vitamin?
A. Vitamin D B. Vitamin K
C. Vitamin A D. Vitamin C

38. Which of the following is a clear liquid diet?
A. Milk
B. Lassi
C. Tender coconut water
D. Thick vegetable soup

39. Find the next number in the series.

6, 7, 9, 13, 21, ?
A. 43 B. 29
C. 37 D. 35

40. The major signs for diagnosis of AIDS
A. Weight loss more than or equal to 10% of the body weight
B. Chronic diarrhoea for more than one month
C. Prolonged fever for more than one month
D. All of the above

41. Which of the following is NOT an arthropod-borne disease?
A. Hookworm B. Malaria
C. Plague D. Filaria

42. A material which gets decomposed through natural processes is called ....
A. biodegradable material
B. non-biodegradable material
C. thermal material
D. fissile material

43. Which of the following is called a millet?
A. Rice B. Corn
C. Wheat D. Bajra

44. 17 D vaccine is used to control ....
A. Chikungunya fever
B. Yellow fever
C. Typhoid fever
D. Q fever

45. The 19th Asian Games will be held in which of the following countries?
A. Australia B. India
C. Brazil D. China

46. Which of the following is NOT a prevention and control measure against Sexually Transmitted Infections?
A. Using disposable syringes and needles
B. Screening of blood and organ donors
C. Using condoms
D. Encouraging promiscuous sexual act

47. By selling a CPU for ₹ 7705, a man makes a profit of 15%. At what price should he sell it to make a profit of 25%? (in ₹)
A. 8375 B. 8275
C. 8575 D. 8475

48. Which one of the following is NOT spread by aedes mosquitos?
A. Chickungunya
B. Dengue
C. Yellow fever
D. Japanese encephalitis

49. Of the following which one is the normal level of oxygen present in the blood?

A. 70 to 74 mmHg
B. 75 to 100 mmHg
C. 60 to 72 mmHg
D. 55 to 60 mmHg

50. The environmental control measure of Leptospirosis ....
A. All are correct
B. Preventing exposure to potentially contaminated water
C. Rodent control measures
D. Proper disposal of waste and health education

51. The allocation of seats in Rajya Sabha is made on the basis of .... of each State/ Union Territory
A. Population
B. Area
C. Number of constituencies
D. GDP

52. Which one of the following diseases is caused by culex mosquitos?
A. Malaria B. Cholera
C. Plague D. Filaria

53. What is the daily protein requirement of male workers doing moderate work?
A. 55 gm B. 65 gm
C. 40 gm D. 30 gm

54. Preterm babies are those whose gestational age is between ....
A. 38 to 40 weeks
B. 40 to 42 weeks
C. 39 to 42 weeks
D. 34 to 37 weeks

55. 2350 boys and 1400 girls are examined in a test; 42% of the boys and 36% of the girls pass the test. The percentage of the total who failed is:
A. 60.24 B. 63.24
C. 62.24 D. 61.24

56. What is CPI, which is used to measure inflation?
A. Consumer Pay Index
B. Caller Price Index
C. Consumer Price Index
D. Caller Pay Index

57. What is the full form of ORS?
A. Oral Rejuvenate Solution
B. Oral Rehydration Salt
C. Oral Rejuvenate Salt
D. Oral Repair Solution

58. Which one is NOT a sign and symptom of hypoglycemia?
A. Confusion B. Sweating
C. Shivering D. Trembling

59. On dividing a number by 469, we get 66 as remainder. On dividing the same number by 67, what will be the remainder?
A. 36 B. 56
C. 66 D. 46

60. Which of the following appliances works according to the principle of heating effect of electric current?
A. Electric heater
B. Refrigerator
C. Fan
D. Television

61. Which waste material is utilized in the production of electricity?
A. Jute waste
B. Garbage
C. Sugarcane waste
D. Plastic

62. Which of the following methods is used for the estimation of chlorine demand of water?
A. Chlorometer
B. Berkefeld Filter
C. Horrock's Apparatus
D. Double Pot Method

63. Which one of the following is a type of propagation of microfilaria in culex mosquito?
A. Propagative
B. Cyclodevelopmental
C. Cyclical
D. Cyclopropagative

64. Which oil contains more unsaturated fatty acids?
A. Groundnut oil
B. Coconut oil
C. Sunflower oil
D. Palm oil

65. The bending ability of an optical medium is measured by its ....

A. diffusion index

B. refractive index

C. dispersion index

D. compression index

66. Who among the following is the author of the famous story book 'Panchatantra'?

A. Mahavastu B. Naladiyar

C. Vishnu Sharma D. Dipavamsa

67. What is the substitute for milk in case of lactose intolerance?

A. Cow milk B. Soy milk

C. Buffalo milk D. Curd

68. Malaria is a .... disease caused by mosquito bite

A. Protozoal B. Bacterial

C. Viral D. Worms

69. The ratio of number of girls to boys in a school of 4320 students is 47:49. How many more girls should be admitted to make the ratio 1:1?

A. 86 B. 92

C. 90 D. 88

70. Which of these is NOT among the food sanitation best practices?

A. Regular examination of food handlers

B. Personal hygiene of cooks and food handlers

C. Reusing food kept in a refrigerator

D. Pasteurisation of milk

71. In this question, relationship between different elements is shown in the statement. This statement is followed by three conclusions. Assume the given statement to be true and choose the answer from the given options:

Statement: W = O > R . I > E < D

Conclusions: (*i*) R > D

(*ii*) D > O

(*iii*) W > R

A. Only (*i*) and (*ii*) follow

B. Only (*iii*) follows

C. Only (*ii*) and (*iii*) follow

D. All follow

72. Which is at the heart of a slow sand filter?

A. Vital layer B. Brick layer

C. Water level D. Sand bed

73. The waste water which does not contain human excreta is called ....

A. Sewage B. Sewer

C. Sullage D. All of the above

74. Which is the disaccharide present in milk?

A. Maltose B. Starch

C. Sucrose D. Lactose

75. What is the main function of dietary protein?

A. Promoting bone growth

B. Body building

C. Increasing bowel movements

D. Promoting iron absorption

76. In Urban Leprosy control programme, the population size should be more than ....

A. 50000 B. 100000

C. 70000 D. 75000

77. Which force will be experienced by an object when it is immersed in water?

A. Force of repulsion

B. Force of attraction

C. Force of Buoyancy

D. Force of gravity

78. Dengue syndrome is a/an .... kind of infection

A. Respiratory

B. Intestinal

C. Arthropod-borne

D. None of the above

79. Which one of the following is an aquatic disaster?

A. Avalanches B. Blizzards

C. Hailstorm D. Storm Surge

80. A train passes a station platform in 63 seconds and a man standing on the platform in 47 seconds. If the speed of the train is 29 m/s, what is the length of the platform?(meter)

A. 474 B. 484

C. 494 D. 464

81. Which nutrient deficiency causes the disease 'Pellagra'?
A. Nicotinic acid B. Calcium
C. Iron D. Vitamin K

82. Which of the following is not a method of screening for breast cancer?
A. Ultrasonogram
B. Breast self-examination
C. Mammography
D. Clinical breast examination

83. Who discovered electrons?
A. James Chadwick
B. Eugen Goldstein
C. Philip Warren Anderson
D. J.J. Thomson

84. Scrub typhus is transmitted by:
A. Flea B. Louse
C. Tick D. Larval mite

85. How many rooms are required for a house with five people?
A. 3 B. 2
C. 5 D. 4

86. Where are the nitrogenous wastes in humans such as urea or uric acid removed?
A. Lungs B. Aorta
C. Kidney D. Blood vessels

87. How much energy does 1 gram of fat provide?
A. 9 cal B. 5 cal
C. 12 cal D. 7 cal

88. What is the main clinical manifestation of rabies?
A. Photophobia B. Hydrophobia
C. Claustrophobia D. Agarophobia

89. Pituitary gland is attached to ....
A. thyroid glands B. lungs
C. pancreas D. brain

90. What is the unit of energy called?
A. Pound B. Calorie
C. Gram D. Ml

91. What is the incubation period for polio myelitis?
A. 7 to 14 days B. 4 to 5 days
C. 1 to 3 days D. 20 to 30 days

92. What type of organism is Candida Albicans?
A. Ectoparasites
B. Fungal agent
C. Viral agent
D. Protozoal agent

93. The deficiency of which of the following is the causative factor for microcytic anemia?
A. Phosphorus B. Iodine
C. Iron D. Calcium

94. Which of the following diseases is not caused by bacteria?
A. Tuberculosis B. Hepatitis-A
C. Cholera D. Typhoid

95. Which of the following is NOT a mosquito control measure?
A. Reduction of mosquito breeding sites
B. Fogging/spraying DDT
C. Oil on stagnant water
D. Drinking hot water

96. Which foodstuff contains a high biological value of protein?
A. Oats B. Pulses
C. Egg D. Cabbage

97. .... is a severe form of Dengue Fever.
A. Haemorrhagic fever
B. Undifferentiated fever
C. Isolated organopathy
D. None of the above

98. For what purpose the VVM label is put on a vaccine vial?
A. Test for vaccine potency
B. Test for vaccine contamination
C. Test for correct proportion
D. Measurement of dosage

99. What is the symbol of the element Xenon?
A. Xe B. Xo
C. Xn D. X

100. What is the incubation period of typhoid?
A. 5 to 7 days
B. 20 to 25 days
C. 18 to 24 days
D. 10 to 14 days

ANSWERS

1	2	3	4	5	6	7	8	9	10
C	C	A	C	D	A	C	B	B	B
11	**12**	**13**	**14**	**15**	**16**	**17**	**18**	**19**	**20**
C	D	B	D	C	D	A	A	C	D
21	**22**	**23**	**24**	**25**	**26**	**27**	**28**	**29**	**30**
D	A	A	D	A	D	D	D	B	C
31	**32**	**33**	**34**	**35**	**36**	**37**	**38**	**39**	**40**
C	B	B	D	C	B	A	C	C	D
41	**42**	**43**	**44**	**45**	**46**	**47**	**48**	**49**	**50**
A	A	D	B	D	D	A	D	B	A
51	**52**	**53**	**54**	**55**	**56**	**57**	**58**	**59**	**60**
A	D	A	D	A	C	B	C	C	A
61	**62**	**63**	**64**	**65**	**66**	**67**	**68**	**69**	**70**
C	C	B	C	B	C	B	A	C	C
71	**72**	**73**	**74**	**75**	**76**	**77**	**78**	**79**	**80**
B	A	C	D	B	B	C	C	D	D
81	**82**	**83**	**84**	**85**	**86**	**87**	**88**	**89**	**90**
A	A	D	D	A	C	A	B	D	B
91	**92**	**93**	**94**	**95**	**96**	**97**	**98**	**99**	**100**
A	B	C	B	D	C	A	A	A	D

Previous Paper (Solved)

JUNIOR HEALTH INSPECTOR Recruitment Exam 2018*

1. Who wrote the famous article 'Poura Samatva Vadam' in 1918 for promoting civic rights agitation in Travancore?
A. K.Kelappan
B. T.K. Madhavan
C. Muhammed Yusuf Thangal
D. John Nidhiri

2. Which among the social reformer had introduced holy bath in the well called 'Muttiripatham'?
A. Vaikunda Swamikal
B. Thycaud Aiya
C. Ramana Maharshi
D. Ayyankali

3. Who wrote the Vayalar Award (2017) winning novel 'Sugandhi Enna Andal Devanayaki' ?
A. T.D. Ramakrishnana
B. K.P. Ramanunni
C. Benyamin
D. Punathil Kunhabdulla

4. Who was the first Anglo Indian Adhikari at Thangasseri during the British period?
A. John D'costa
B. Dr. Bishop Jerome
C. John Neves Fernandez
D. Richard Netto Franky

5. Which among the following was a street play?
A. Thadankal Palayam
B. Nadugadhika
C. Devadasi
D. Althara

6. Which Christian Missionary was responsible for the establishment of CMS press at Kottayam?
A. Benjamin Bailey
B. Samuel Mateer
C. Herman Gundert
D. Charles Mead

7. Who was the father of Renaissance Movement in Kerala?
A. Sree Narayana Guru
B. Chattambi Swamikal
C. Vakkom Abdul Qadhir Moulavi
D. Ram Mohan Roy

8. Who wrote the poem, "Veenapoovu"?
A. Kumaranasan
B. O.N.V. Kurup
C. Changampuzha Krishna Pillai
D. Vayalar Rama Varma

9. Who wrote the book 'Unhappy India'?
A. C. Rajagopalachari
B. Bal Gangadhar Tilak
C. Jawahar Lal Nehru
D. Lala Lajpat Rai

10. Which Indian Viceroy said, "Judge me by my acts and not my words"?
A. Lord Curzon
B. Lord Lytton
C. Lord Mayo
D. Lord Rippon

11. "No Caste, No Religion, No God for Man" was the slogan of:
A. Vaikunda Swamikal
B. Thykattu Ayya Swami
C. K. Ayyappan
D. Sree Narayan Guru

12. Which among the following was known as the 'Magna Carta of English Education in India'?

* Held on 11/09/2018; Conducted by Kerala PSC.

A. Minutes of Macaulay
B. Wood's Despatch
C. Sadler Commission
D. Hunter Commission

13. Rajagopalachari Formula was in:
A. 1929 B. 1934
C. 1944 D. 1943

14. Manjampothikkunnu is situated in:
A. Payyannor
B. Kanhangad
C. Wynad
D. Thenmala

15. Who was known as 'the faint-hearted moderate'?
A. Dadabai Nauroji
B. Firoz Shah Mehta
C. Gopala Krishna Gokhale
D. Surendranath Banerjee

16. 'Theory of Safety Valve' was associated with:
A. INA B. IUML
C. INC D. SUCI

17. The first Indian to win the Pritzker prize in 2018:
A. Nagaraja Chettiyar
B. Arunachalam Pandhyan
C. Kanakraj Malhotra
D. Balakrishna Doshi

18. Who was the winner of the Australian Grand Prix-2018?
A. Raphel Nadal
B. Sebastian Vettel
C. Gagan Narang
D. George Woodcock

19. The athlete who enter into the 400 meters final in the Commonwealth Games after Milkha Singh in 1958:
A. Ranjit Maheswari
B. K.T. lrfan
C. Deen Dayal Pandey
D. Mohammed Anas Yahiya

20. Karattu Govinda Menon was popularly known as:
A. Chinmayananda Swami
B. Vagbhadanandan
C. Ananda Theerthan
D. Brahmananda Sivayogi

21. In optical fibre cables the transmission of light is by the process of:
A. Polarisation
B. Total internal reflection
C. Diffraction
D. Refraction

22. Who invented thermometer?
A. Galilio Galili
B. Albert Einstein
C. Kelvin
D. James Watt

23. Before the main shock of earthquake animals appear to be irritated. This is due to a special type of sound waves produced at that time. Such waves are:
A. Ultrasonic waves
B. Audible sound waves
C. Infrasonic waves
D. None of the above

24. Which is the strongest force in nature?
A. Magnetic force
B. Electric force
C. Nuclear force
D. Gravitational force

25. Which one of the following electronic component is the essential part of a voltage regulator?
A. Zener diode B. LED
C. LCD D. Transistor

26. Find the odd one out.
A. Force B. Mass
C. Time D. Temperature

27. The electromagnetic radiations emitted from mobile phones are:
A. X-ray
B. Radio frequency wave
C. 'gamma' ray
D. None of the above

28. If raw egg among with a shell is placed in a microwave oven which among the following is most likely happen?

A. The egg shell changes in colour
B. The egg will get cooked slowly as usual
C. The egg will not get warmed
D. The egg shell will explode

29. The three states of water are ice, water and water vapour. Which one of them has lowest density?

A. Ice
B. Water
C. Water vapour
D. All of them have same density

30. Joule/second is nothing but

A. Ampere B. Coulomb
C. Calory D. Watt

31. The United Nations General Assembly declared the year 2010 as the International year for conservation of:

A. Soil B. Water
C. Biodiversity D. Agriculture

32. Name the vector that transmit the disease Malaria

A. Female anopheles mosquito
B. Aedes
C. Female culex mosquito
D. Male anopheles mosquito

33. In India which state's High Court declared the holy rivers Ganga and Yamuna having same status of a legal person wilh all corresponding rights, duties and liabilities of a living person?

A. Andhra Pradesh
B. Madhya Pradesh
C. Uttarakhand
D. Sikkim

34. World Day of Migratory Birds:

A. April 30 B. May 12
C. April 18 D. May 11

35. Which of the following is not a primary green house gas present in Earth's atmosphere?

A. Water vapour
B. Nitrous oxide
C. Carbon monoxide
D. Carbon dioxide

36. Dolphins breath by swimming on the surface of water and inhaling fresh air. Name the respiratory organ of Dolphin.

A. Lungs B. Skin
C. Gills D. Gill slits

37. India's first organic state:

A. Andhra Pradesh
B. West Bengal
C. Karnataka
D. Sikkim

38. The bacteria Rhizobium found in root nodules of legumes to fix atmospheric:

A. Nitrogen
B. Oxygen
C. Carbon dioxide
D. Phosphorus

39. Which of the following is a Vitamin deficiency disease?

A. Acromegaly B. Dwarfism
C. Beriberi D. Goitre

40. Among the following hormones find out the plant hormone.

A. Melatonin
B. Gibberellin
C. Thymosin
D. Glucagon

41. If a child has to be immunised with two live vaccines:

A. It should be given at an interval of 3 weeks
B. It should be given in the same hand
C. It should be mixed in a syringe and given
D. It should be at an interval of 1 week

42. Aim of Swachchh Bharat Abhiyan:

A. Eradication of poverty by 2019
B. Eradication of open defecation by 2019
C. Eradication of poverty by 2018
D. Eradication of open defecation by 2018

43. Purest water in nature:
A. Ground water
B. Surface water
C. Rain
D. Stream

44. Sanitary well should be:
A. Located not less than 15 metres from source of contamination
B. Located 50 metres away from source of contamination
C. Located 50 feet away from source of contamination
D. Located 15 feet away from source of contamination

45. This year's World Health Day theme is:
A. Depressionlet's talk
B. Universal health coverage
C. Beat plastic pollution
D. Wanted leaders for a TB free world

46. Diseases which are naturally transmitted between vertebrate animals and man is called:
A. Epidemic
B. Zoonosis
C. Endemic
D. Nosocomial infection

47. According to census 2011, definition of urban area include all except:
A. A minimum population of 5000
B. At least 75% of males engaged in non-agricultural work
C. Density of population is at least 400 persons per sq.km.
D. A minimum population of 3000

48. Open Vial Policy is applicable to all except
A. DPT
B. TT
C. BCG
D. Pentavalent vaccine

49. Which country is hosting World Environment Day 2018?
A. India
B. Brazil
C. Russia
D. Australia

50. Under Acute Flaccid Paralysis (AFP) surveillance stool samples should be collected within:
A. 24-48 hours
B. Within 24 hours
C. Within 72 hours
D. Within 2 days

51. The minimum recommended concentration of free residual chlorine is:
A. 1 mg/*l* for one hour
B. 0.5 mg/*l* for half hour
C. 1 mg/*l* for half hour
D. 0.5 mg/*l* for one hour

52. All are correct about boiling of water except:
A. Rolling boil for 10-20 minutes
B. Removes temporary hardness
C. Taste of water altered
D. It offers residual protection

53. All are true about zero dose OPV except:
A. Two drops of OPV is given
B. Can be given within the first 15 days
C. It is given orally
D. OPV is given after diluting with sterile water

54. Concurrent disinfection is:
A. Application of disinfective measures as soon as infectious material discharged from the body
B. Applicaiton of disinfective measures after patient is removed
C. Application of prophylactic disinfection of water
D. Application of sterilization procedure

55. The most common greenhouse gas which is contributing to global warming is:
A. Methane
B. Carbon dioxide
C. Fluorocarbons
D. Nitrous oxide

56. Soiling index is used to measure:
A. Radioactive pollution
B. Soil pollution

C. Air pollution
D. Water pollution

57. Exclusive breast feeding should be given:
A. Upto 4 months
B. Upto 6 months
C. Upto 1 year
D. Upto 8 months

58. Supplementary nutrition provided by anganwadi for a 1 year old child is:
A. 500 calories and 12-15 gm protein
B. 800 calories and 20-25 gm protein
C. 600 calories and 18-20 gm protein
D. 400 calories and 16-18 gm protein

59. How many days anganwadi provide supplementary nutrition in a year?
A. 100 B. 200
C. 365 D. 300

60. As per national programme, pregnant women should get iron and folic acid tablet for how many days?
A. 70 B. 200
C. 100 D. 90

61. Till what age can a child be given OPV?
A. 3 yrs. B. 5 yrs.
C. 1½ yrs. D. 2 yrs.

62. In case of malaria surveillance, annual blood examination should be:
A. 5% of the population/year
B. 10% of the population/year
C. 2% of the population/year
D. 15% of the population/year

63. Local wound treatment in animal bite cases can reduce chances of developing rabies by up to:
A. 50% B. 80%
C. 100% D. 60%

64. What percentage of under five mortality is constituted by measles?
A. 5% B. 10%
C. 2% D. 4%

65. All are correct about AFP (Acute Falccid Paralysis) except:
A. Finding and reporting children with AFP under 15 yrs
B. Two specimens of stool taken should reach the lab within 72 hrs
C. Identify which of the three serotypes
D. Mapping the virus to identify source of importation

66. Following are correct about *Aedes aegypti* except:
A. Highly domesticated and strongly anthropophilic
B. Nervous feeder
C. Able to replicate the virus and transmit the virus to another host
D. Concordant species

67. Chlorine acts best as a disinfectant when pH of water is around:
A. 7 B. 8
C. 6 D. 9

68. A plague outbreak can occur when the cheopis index is:
A. >1 B. <1
C. >10 D. >50

69. All are true about scrub typhus except:
A. Causative agent is rickettsia tsutsugamushi
B. Reservoir is trombiculid mite
C. Weil Felix reaction is confirmatory
D. Typical feature is eschar

70. Following diseases makes largest contribution towards mortality and morbidity due to non-communicable diseases except:
A. Diabetes
B. Chronic liver diseases
C. Cancer
D. Cardiovascular disease

71. All the following diseases are considered as iceberg disease except:
A. Hypertension
B. Diabetes

C. Anaemia
D. Kidney disease

72. Body mass index is calculated by:
A. Weight (kg)/height (cm)
B. Weight (kg)/height (m)
C. Weight (kg)/height^2 m
D. Weight (kg)/height^2 cm

73. All are critical determinants of an FRU (First Referral Unit) except:
A. Availability of surgical intervention
B. New born care
C. Blood storage facility
D. Safe abortion services

74. Instrument used to measure chlorine demand of well water is:
A. Berkefeld
B. Horrock's
C. Pasteurchamberland
D. Katadyn

75. What is early registration of pregnancy?
A. Registering before 20 weeks
B. Before 6 weeks
C. Before 24 weeks
D. Before 12 weeks

76. Which gas is known as swamp gas?
A. Chlorofluorocarbons
B. Nitrous oxide
C. Carbon dioxide
D. Methane

77. Under PFA Act at production level, iodine content of salt should be:
A. 10 ppm
B. 50 ppm
C. 30 ppm
D. 15 ppm

78. The process of preventing nutrient lose from rice is:
A. Puffing
B. Parboiling
C. Germinating
D. Sprouting

79. Global hand washing day is celebrated on:
A. Oct. 15th
B. Nov. 15th
C. June 5th
D. June 14th

80. Satisfactory water is which contain:
A. 1-3 coliform/100 cc water
B. No coliform/100 cc
C. 4-10 coliform/100 cc
D. >10 coliform/100 cc

81. To disinfect 1000 litres of water bleaching powder required is:
A. 1.5 gm
B. 3.5 gm
C. 2.5 gm
D. 5 gm

82. All are names of biological method of composting except:
A. Bangalore method
B. Anaerobic method
C. Aerobic method
D. Hot fermentation method

83. 'Hidden hunger' is:
A. Micronutrient deficiency
B. Protein malnutrition
C. Energy malnutrition
D. Vitamin B_1 deficiency

84. For drinking purpose the water required/day is
A. 2 litre/day
B. 5 litre/day
C. 1 litre/day
D. 2.5 litre/day

85. The normal dose of chlorine does not affect which of the following organism?
A. HIV
B. Salmonella
C. Polio
D. Shigella

86. Nov. 19th is celebrated as:
A. World Toilet Day
B. World Water Day
C. World Health Day
D. World Diabetes Day

87. In India, food standards are based on:
A. The Agmark Standards
B. PFA Standards
C. Standards of Codex Alimentaries
D. Bureau of Indian Standards

88. The Sun Protection Factor (SPF) which should be present in a good sunscreen ointment is:
A. 10
B. 15
C. 20
D. 25

89. The sequence of steps to be followed in a cardiac emergency:
A. Airway-breathing-circulation
B. Breathing-airway-circulation
C. Circulation-breathing-airway
D. Circulation-airway-breathing

90. Ortho-toluidine arsenate test is used to determine:
A. Iron in water
B. Free and combined chlorine
C. Nitrites
D. Manganese

91. What is the depth of compression while doing CPR (Cardiopulmonary Resuscitation)?
A. 5 cm
B. 4 cm
C. 4.5 cm
D. 3.5 cm

92. Which organisms causes sleeping sickness?
A. Lice
B. Rat flea
C. Black fly
D. Tsetse fly

93. All are true in case of 'problem village' except:
A. Water at a distance of 1.6 kilometers
B. Water is exposed to risk of cholera
C. Water available at a depth of more than 10 metres
D. Water has excess iron and heavy metals

94. All are true about biological oxygen demand except:
A. Temperature should be 20°C
B. Most important test on sewage
C. It takes 5 days for the test
D. Value ranges between 300-400 mg/*l*

95. The modern method of sewage purification is:
A. Activated sludge process
B. Trickling filter process
C. Sludge digestion chamber process
D. Grit chamber process

96. Chlorine will not kill all the following organisms except:
A. Polio
B. Viral hepatitis
C. Spore
D. E.Coli

97. Name the disease which is 100% fatal but 100% preventable:
A. HIV
B. Rabies
C. Malaria
D. Measles

98. All are true about measles vaccine except:
A. Live attenuated vaccine
B. Reconstituted vaccine should be stored at 2-8°
C. Diluent also should be frozen
D. Reconstituted vaccine should be used within 4 hours

99. Endemic fluorous can occur when fluorine content of drinking water is:
A. > 3-5 mg/L
B. 0.5-0.8 mg/L
C. < 0.5-0.8 mg/L
D. < 3-5 mg/L

100. National Deworming Day is on:
A. Dec. 1st
B. Feb. 10th
C. Nov. 1st
D. Aug. 1st

ANSWERS

1	2	3	4	5	6	7	8	9	10
B	A	A	C	B	A	A	A	D	D
11	**12**	**13**	**14**	**15**	**16**	**17**	**18**	**19**	**20**
C	B	C	B	C	C	D	B	D	D
21	**22**	**23**	**24**	**25**	**26**	**27**	**28**	**29**	**30**
B	A	C	C	A	A	B	D	C	D
31	**32**	**33**	**34**	**35**	**36**	**37**	**38**	**39**	**40**
C	A	C	B	C	A	D	A	C	B
41	**42**	**43**	**44**	**45**	**46**	**47**	**48**	**49**	**50**
A	B	C	A	B	B	D	C	A	A
51	**52**	**53**	**54**	**55**	**56**	**57**	**58**	**59**	**60**
D	D	D	A	B	C	B	A	D	C
61	**62**	**63**	**64**	**65**	**66**	**67**	**68**	**69**	**70**
B	B	B	C	C	D	A	A	C	B
71	**72**	**73**	**74**	**75**	**76**	**77**	**78**	**79**	**80**
D	C	D	B	D	D	C	B	A	A
81	**82**	**83**	**84**	**85**	**86**	**87**	**88**	**89**	**90**
C	C	A	A	C	A	C	B	D	B
91	**92**	**93**	**94**	**95**	**96**	**97**	**98**	**99**	**100**
A	D	C	D	A	D	B	C	D	B

Previous Paper (Solved)

Assistant Sanitary Inspector Recruitment Exam, 2017*

1. According to Biomedical Waste Management Rules, wastes generated from disposable items such as tubing, bottles, intravenous tubes are collected in one of the following bag:
A. yellow B. red
C. white D. blue

2. How much of the general health waste is generated in total biomedical waste?
A. 15% B. 1%
C. 3% D. 80%

3. The function of the vertebral column is protection of:
A. spinal cord
B. thoracic organs
C. abdominal organs
D. brain

4. The lacrimal glands of eyes secrete:
A. saliva B. tears
C. mucus D. cells

5. The energy produced in the body may be measured and expressed in units of heat *i.e.,*
A. Joule B. Celsius
C. Kilocalories D. Fahrenheit

6. From poorly managed infectious wastes and sharp instruments, one of the following infections may be transmitted
A. Cancer B. HIV
C. Malaria D. Dengue

7. If there is sprain in a límb of a person, then one of the following measures should be done:
A. rest and support the injured in the most comfortable position
B. make the injured lying
C. make the injured sleep on abdomen
D. make the injured stand

8. The rate of chest compressions to breath in children during CPR is:
A. 15 compressions and 2 breathing
B. 15 compressions and 1 breathing
C. 30 compressions and 2 breathing
D. 30 compressions and 1 breathing

9. A superficial wound with peeling of skin is known as:
A. cut B. torn
C. puncture D. abrasion

10. To protect water from being contaminated, Parliament enacted the first Water (Prevention and Control of Pollution) Act in the year of:
A. 1974 B. 1984
C. 1994 D. 2004

11. Optimum period of storage of river water is considered to be of:
A. 5-7 days B. 10-14 days
C. 15-20 days D. 21-30 days

12. The components of a typical water purification system on large scale comprises of one of the following measures:
A. storage, filtration and disinfection
B. chemical, physical and mechanical
C. surveillance
D. survey

13. How much approximate percent of available chlorine does the bleaching powder contain?
A. 10 B. 20
C. 33 D. 50

*Conducted by Haryana SSC on 28/10/17.

14. How much ppm of available chlorine does the sodium hypochlorite contain?
A. 80,000 to 1,80,000 ppm
B. 10,000 to 25,000 ppm
C. 30,000 to 55,000 ppm
D. 60,000 to 80,000 ppm

15. Formaldehyde is more commonly known as:
A. Savlon B. Dettol
C. Formalin D. Alcohol

16. Dental caries can be occurred more frequently if the excessive intake of one of the following is there:
A. sugar and refined carbohydrates
B. fruits and vegetables
C. water
D. home-made food

17. The conditions resulting from infection of the eye are:
A. eye strain and cataract
B. conjunctivitis and trachoma
C. cataract and trachoma
D. glaucoma and trachoma

18. The amino acids which cannot be synthesized in the body are called:
A. essential amino acids
B. non-essential amino acids
C. complete proteins
D. protein quality

19. From the following, this is a water soluble vitamin:
A. Vitamin A B. Vitamin B complex
C. Vitamin E D. Vitamin D

20. The daily requirement of sodium chloride of human should be:
A. 1-10 gm B. 1-06 gm
C. 20-30 gm D. 30-50 gm

21. The determinants of health include all of the following, except:
A. aging of the population
B. health system
C. equity and social justice
D. quality of life

22. A diseased condition can be explained as:
A. physiological/psychological dysfunction
B. a subjective state of person who feels aware of not being well
C. social dysfunction
D. absence of health

23. The epidemiological triad includes the factors of:
A. agent and host
B. agent and environment
C. host and environment
D. agent, host and environment

24. Waste water from a community, containing solid and liquid excreta, derived from houses, street and industries is called:
A. sewage
B. sewerage system
C. sewer appurtenances
D. sullage

25. The medical model of health education is primarily interested in:
A. translate health information into the desired health action
B. recognition and treatment of disease
C. combination of all models
D. activation of group participation

26. From the following, these all can be included in the health education, except:
A. human biology B. nutrition
C. hygiene D. entertainment

27. Waste water which does not contain human excreta, *e.g.*, waste water from kitchens is called:
A. sewage
B. sewerage system
C. sewer appurtenances
D. sullage

28. The point at which the residual chlorine appears and when all combined chlorine have been completely destroyed is called:
A. corresponding dosage
B. breakpoint dosage
C. breakpoint chlorination
D. superchlorination

29. The most effective and cheapest method of disinfecting wells is:
A. bleaching powder
B. potassium permanganate
C. ozonation
D. ultraviolet irradiation

30. Measles can be transmitted by the:
A. contact
B. droplet infection
C. blood contact
D. nosocomial infection

31. The non-suppurative enlargement and tenderness of one or both the parotid glands are known as the disease of:
A. cancer B. rubella
C. mumps D. chicken-pox

32. For immunization against the diphtheria, the vaccine of choice is:
A. tuberculine vaccine
B. DPT vaccine
C. Hepatitis vaccine
D. oral drops of polio

33. In child guidance clinic for psychotherapy, following methods are employed, except:
A. play therapy
B. counselling
C. reconstruction of parental attitudes
D. scolding

34. For remedial measure and follow up, special clinics should be conducted exclusively for school children in the rural area at the:
A. child guidance clinic
B. community health centres
C. primary health centres
D. dispensaries

35. From the following this is the physical method of the barrier methods for contraception:
A. sterilization B. foam tablets
C. condoms D. contraceptive pills

36. The aim of barrier methods of the contraception is:
A. to kill sperms
B. to prevent the formation of sperm
C. to prevent live sperms from meeting the ovum
D. to release hormone

37. The non-medicated or inert IUDs are often referred as:
A. first generation IUDs
B. second generation IUDs
C. third generation IUDs
D. fourth generation IUDs

38. The neonatal tetanus in new born can be prevented by vaccination of:
A. adults B. children
C. pregnant women D. healthy baby

39. From the following this is the genetic abnormality found in the neonates:
A. low birth weight B. tetanus
C. HIV infection D. Phenylketonuria

40. The monetary limits of the compensation that can be granted by the District Consumer Court is:
A. upto ₹ 20 lacs
B. ₹ 20 lacs to ₹ 40 lacs
C. ₹ 40 lacs to ₹ 80 lacs
D. ₹ 80 lacs to ₹ 1 crore

41. The time limit for registering the event of birth is:
A. 7 days B. 14 days
C. 21 days D. 28 days

42. The sub-centre provides interface with the community at the:
A. grass root level B. primary level
C. secondary level D. tertiary level

43. The maternal health care of sub-centre includes:
A. minimum three antenatal check-ups
B. every month antenatal check-ups
C. deliveries at sub-centre
D. treatment of high risk pregnancies

44. The best approach to achieve goal of health for all is by providing:
A. prmary health care
B. secondary health care

C. tertiary health care
D. hospice care

45. The first level of contact of individuals, the family and community with the national health system, where the care is provided is called:
A. primary care level
B. secondary care level
C. tertiary care level
D. referral system

46. From the following infections, this is the important bacterial cause of acute watery diarrhoea:
A. *E. histolytica* B. *Giardia intestine*
C. *Trichuris* D. *Escherichia coli*

47. The anopheles lays her eggs in the quantity of:
A. in cluster B. 100-250 eggs
C. 50-100 eggs D. singly

48. The *Aedes egypti* bite at the time of:
A. day B. night
C. evening D. 24 hours

49. The DMC in RNTCP stands for:
A. Designated Microscopy Centres
B. Designed Microscopy Centres
C. Divisional Microscopy Centres
D. Depositional Microscopy Centres

50. Anti-malaria month campaign is observed every year in the month of:
A. February B. March
C. April D. June

51. President of India has appointed whom as India's first full time woman Defence Minister?
A. Nirmala Sitharaman
B. Najma Heptullah
C. Smriti Irani
D. Sushma Swaraj

52. Nicolas Copernicus was:
A. Astronomer B. Economist
C. Sociologist D. Philosopher

53. Light-year is the unit of:
A. Power B. Volume
C. Time D. Distance

54. Minakshi temple is located in:
A. Ahmedabad B. Mumbai
C. Madurai D. Delhi

55. Choose the odd one from the following:
A. Calendar B. Minute
C. Hour D. Second

56. If we arrange all the words (given in the option) alphabetically, which word would be last in the arrangement?
A. Shovel B. Shoes
C. Shower D. Shout

57. In the product of 3759 × 9573, the sum of tens' digit and units' digit is:
A. 9 B. 16
C. 0 D. 7

58. If $a - b = 3$ and $a^2 + b^2 = 29$, find the value of ab.
A. 10 B. 12
C. 15 D. 18

59. The value of:

$$\frac{(0.96)^3 - (0.1)^3}{.96^2 + (.96 \times 0.1) + 0.1^2} \text{ is:}$$

A. 0.86 B. 0.95
C. 0.97 D. 1.06

60. The average monthly income of P and Q is ₹ 5,050. The average monthly income of Q and R is ₹ 6,250 and the average monthly income of P and R is ₹ 5,200. The monthly income of P is:
A. ₹ 3,500 B. ₹ 4,000
C. ₹ 4,050 D. ₹ 5,000

61. Which of the following is the least heavy metal?
A. Mercury B. Silver
C. Iron D. Gold

62. Leprosy bacillus was invented by:
A. Koch B. Hansen
C. Fleming D. Harvey

63. Name the unit in which noise of sound is measured.

A. Ampere B. Hertz
C. Cycles D. Decibel

64. Choose one option that expresses the meaning of the sentence:

A person who does not believe in the existence of god.

A. Theist B. Atheist
C. Ascetic D. Agnostic

65. Choose one option that expresses the most appropriate meaning for the idiom out of four options:

To take a thing lying down

A. to beg
B. to submit without resistance
C. to disregard
D. to avoid

66. Choose the most appropriate preposition out of four options:

Reena was invited his friends .... dinner.

A. for B. to
C. with D. over

67. For blank space, choose the proper article:

I waited for .... hour.

A. a B. an
C. no article D. the

68. Choose the pair of words that best expresses a relationship similar to that expressed in the pair of words in capital.

AIRPLANE : HANGER

A. automobile : garage
B. ship : seaport
C. train : station
D. bus : bus stop

69. The National Cancer Control Programme includes the scheme which is one of the following:

A. Oncology wing development programme
B. Maternal and child health
C. ICTS
D. Janani Suraksha Yojana

70. The National Water Supply and Sanitation Programme was initiated with the object of:

A. for rural electrification
B. for starting accelerated rural water supply
C. for rural health
D. providing safe water supply and adequate drainage facilities

71. Under the Accelerated Rural Water Supply Programme, the "problem village" is defined as:

A. one where there is shortage of safe water
B. one where there is no source of safe water available within a distance of 1.6 km
C. one where there is no source of safe water available within a distance of 100 km
D. one where there is no river as source of water

72. According to Child Labour Act, no child should be employed or permitted to work in following occupations, except:

A. bidi making
B. domiciliary work
C. construction site
D. work relating to the construction of railway station

73. The first line of treatment of malaria is:

A. Chloroquine B. ART
C. Sulphamides D. Penicillin

74. The first line of treatment in Chloroquine resistant cases is:

A. Anti-Retroviral therapy
B. Anti-dots therapy
C. Artesunate combination therapy
D. Anti-malarial therapy

75. According to WHO/UNICEF definition, an attack of sudden onset which usually lasts 3 to 14 days, is called:

A. Diarrhoea
B. Acute diarrhoea
C. Chronic diarrhoea
D. Food poisoning

76. The first clinical management of acute diarrhoea is:

A. intravenous rehydration
B. maintenance therapy
C. chemotherapy
D. oral rehydration salt

77. From following, this is the one of the principles of primary health care:
A. tertiary prevention
B. establishing the superspecialty hospital
C. equitable distribution
D. establishing referral system

78. According to concept and definitions of Millennium Development Goals indicators, those are drugs that satisfy the health care needs of the majority of the population is called:
A. emergency drugs B. cytotoxic drugs
C. ART drugs D. essential drugs

79. The family planning and contraception care of sub-center includes the insertion of IUD where:
A. the ANM is trained for IUD insertion
B. gynaecologists are available
C. facility for calling the gynaecologist
D. 24 hours services of normal delivery is available

80. The sub-center provides one of the following facilities for the Revised National Tuberculosis Control programme:
A. microscopy centre
B. ICTC centre
C. providing DOTS
D. diagnostic procedures

81. From following, this is the warning signs of pregnancy that should be informed to pregnant woman:
A. malaise
B. nausea and vomiting
C. tiredness
D. blurring of the vision

82. From following tests, the test done on infants of all Rh negative mothers is:
A. ELISA test B. Widal test
C. Coomb's test D. Weston bot test

83. Abortion is theoretically defined as termination of pregnancy:
A. before the full term
B. before the foetus become viable
C. before the first stage of labour
D. before the second stage of labour

84. Male sterilization is known as:
A. tubectomy B. vasectomy
C. cholecystectomy D. appendectomy

85. To achieve the objective of good nutrition, the mid-day meal should provide minimum of:
A. 100 calories and 1-4 gms of protein
B. 150 calories and 4-6 gms of protein
C. 200 calories and 6-8 gms of protein
D. 300 calories and 8-12 gms of protein

86. According to school health committee for primary school there should be the provision of land of:
A. 2 acres B. 3 acres
C. 4 acres D. 5 acres

87. The hepatitis B is an acute systemic infection transmitted usually by the:
A. orofecal route B. naso-pharynx route
C. parenteral route D. oral route

88. Following of the supplement when given during an episode of acute diarrhoea, reduces the episode duration and severity of diarrhoea:
A. Magnesium B. Potassium
C. Sodium D. Zinc

89. The severe form of dengue, caused by infection with more than one dengue virus is called:
A. Break bone fever
B. Dengue hemorrhagic fever
C. Disseminated intravascular coagulation
D. Dengue shock syndrome

90. By the method of group discussion, health education can be given best on one of the following topics:
A. construction of sanitary latrine
B. installation of hand pump

C. reduction of obesity
D. personal hygiene

91. The non-projected visual aid used during health education is:
A. television B. earphones
C. posters D. slides

92. The projected visual aid used for health education aids used during health education is:
A. television B. earphones
C. posters D. slides

93. Except the high doses, the chlorine has no effect on pathogens like:
A. bacteria B. fungi
C. water turbidity D. spores

94. The device used for measuring, regulating and administering gaseous chlorine to water supplies is:
A. Horrock's apparatus
B. Paterson's chloronome
C. Sphygmomanometer
D. Orthotolidine

95. The disposal of liquid waste into water sources such as rivers and streams is called:
A. oxidation ditches
B. oxidation pond
C. disposal by dilution
D. sewage farming

96. Choose one option that expresses the meaning of the sentence:
A general pardon granted by the government to political offenders.
A. Amnesty B. Alimony
C. Diplomacy D. Armistice

97. Choose one option that expresses the most appropriate meaning for the idiom out of four options:
To change colour
A. to cheat someone
B. to blush or grow pale
C. politician
D. unfriendly

98. Choose the most appropriate preposition out of four options:
There is an exception .... every rule.
A. to B. in
C. for D. with

99. For blank space, choose the proper article:
Bring .... umbrella. It is going to rain
A. a B. an
C. no article D. the

100. Choose the option that expresses the meaning of the given word:
DICEY
A. bold B. risky
C. happiness D. skilled

ANSWERS

1	2	3	4	5	6	7	8	9	10
B	D	A	B	C	B	A	A	D	A
11	**12**	**13**	**14**	**15**	**16**	**17**	**18**	**19**	**20**
B	A	C	A	C	A	B	A	B	B
21	**22**	**23**	**24**	**25**	**26**	**27**	**28**	**29**	**30**
D	A	D	A	B	D	D	C	A	B
31	**32**	**33**	**34**	**35**	**36**	**37**	**38**	**39**	**40**
C	B	D	C	C	C	A	C	D	A
41	**42**	**43**	**44**	**45**	**46**	**47**	**48**	**49**	**50**
C	A	A	A	A	D	D	A	A	D

51	52	53	54	55	56	57	58	59	60
A	A	D	C	A	C	D	A	A	B
61	**62**	**63**	**64**	**65**	**66**	**67**	**68**	**69**	**70**
C	B	D	B	B	B	B	A	A	D
71	**72**	**73**	**74**	**75**	**76**	**77**	**78**	**79**	**80**
D	B	A	C	B	D	C	D	A	C
81	**82**	**83**	**84**	**85**	**86**	**87**	**88**	**89**	**90**
D	C	B	B	D	D	C	D	B	C
91	**92**	**93**	**94**	**95**	**96**	**97**	**98**	**99**	**100**
C	D	D	B	C	A	B	A	B	B

EXPLANATORY ANSWERS

57.

$$\begin{array}{r} 3759 \\ 9573 \\ \hline 11277 \\ 26313 \\ 18795 \\ 33831 \\ \hline 35984907 \end{array}$$

The sum of ten's digit and unit's digit

$= 0 + 7 = 7$

58. $\because \quad a - b = 3$

Squaring both sides

$$(a - b)^2 = (3)^2$$

$\Rightarrow a^2 + b^2 - 2ab = 9$

$\Rightarrow 29 - 2ab = 9$

$\Rightarrow 2ab = 20$

$\Rightarrow ab = 10$

59. $$\frac{(0.96)^3 - (0.1)^3}{.96^3 + (.96 \times 0.1) + 0.1^2}$$

Let, $0.96 = a$ and $0.1 = b$

$\therefore$ The given expression

$$= \frac{a^3 - b^3}{a^2 + ab + b^2} = \frac{(a-b)(a^2+ab+b^2)}{(a^2+ab+b^2)}$$

$= a - b$

$= 0.96 - 0.1 = .86$

Hence, required value = 0.86

60. (P + Q)'s income = 5050 × 2 = 10100 ...(*i*)

(Q + R)'s income = 6250 × 2 = 12500 ...(*ii*)

(P + R)'s income = 5200 × 2 = 10400...(*iii*)

From (*i*) and (*ii*),

$$\begin{array}{l} R - P = 2400 \\ \underline{\overset{-}{R} + \overset{-}{P} = \overset{-}{10400}} \\ 2P = 8000 \\ P = 4000 \end{array}$$

Hence, monthly income of P = ₹ 4000

Previous Paper (Solved)

RRB—HEALTH & MALARIA INSPECTOR RECRUITMENT EXAM 2015*

1. What is Gout?
   A. A degenerative disorder
   B. A vascular disorder
   C. A renal disorder
   D. A metabolic disorder
2. The Civil Disobedience Movement was started in the year:
   A. 1905 AD B. 1920 AD
   C. 1930 AD D. 1942 AD
3. If 1st April, 2014 is Tuesday, then 1st June, 2014 will be :
   A. Thursday B. Friday
   C. Saturday D. Sunday
4. The currency of Japan is:
   A. Yen B. Pound
   C. Yuan D. Peso
5. In a certain code language, 'mink yang pe' means 'fruits are ripe'; 'pe lao may mink' means 'oranges are not ripe' and 'may pe nue mink' means 'mangoes are not ripe'. Which word in that language means 'mangoes'?
   A. may B. pe
   C. nue D. mink
6. The product of two numbers is 7. One of the numbers is $\frac{3}{2}$. Find the sum of these two numbers.
   A. $8\frac{1}{2}$ B. $5\frac{1}{2}$
   C. $7\frac{1}{7}$ D. $6\frac{1}{6}$
7. The light of which colour is used to treat neonatal jaundice?
   A. Red Light B. Yellow Light
   C. Orange Light D. Blue Light
8. There are 40 boys in a row. Ramesh is fourteenth from the right end of the row. What is his position from the left end of the row?
   A. 27th B. 26th
   C. 25th D. 24th
9. Identify the part of Human Stomach which connects/joins with Oesophagus:
   A. Fundus B. Cardia
   C. Body D. Pylorus
10. Which one of the following is infectious Hepatitis?
    A. Hepatitis A B. Hepatitis B
    C. Hepatitis C D. Hepatitis D
11. Internationally, the Nursing Day is observed on :
    A. May, 12 B. Nov, 14
    C. Oct, 24 D. Dec, 22
12. Which one of the following vaccinations is necessary for pregnant lady?
    A. Tetanus B. BCG
    C. Rubella D. DPT
13. What is the chemical name of Aspirin (ASA)?
    A. Acetic Salicyclic Acid
    B. Acetyl Salicyclic Acid
    C. Acetone Salicyclic Acid
    D. Amide Salicyclic Acid
14. Indian Standard Time (I.S.T.) refers to the local time of which one of the following places in India?
    A. Delhi B. Kolkata
    C. Allahabad D. Jaipur
15. The first stool of neonate is called:
    A. Sebum B. Lenugo
    C. Meconium D. Vernix Caseosa
16. Mohan and Sohan, together can do a job in 12 days. Sohan alone can do this job in 28 days. In how many days can Mohan alone do this job?
    A. 21 days B. 16 days
    C. 24 days D. 20 days

* Held on 08/02/2015.

17. Which one of the following is known as Poor Man's meat?
A. Milk B. Fish
C. Pulses D. Chicken

18. Rajan is sixth from the left end and Vinay is tenth from the right end in a row of boys. If there are eight boys between Rajan and Vinay, how many boys are there in the row?
A. 23 B. 24
C. 25 D. 26

19. Which of the following tests is used to detect Typhoid bacillus?
A. VDRL B. WIDAL
C. BCG D. UDRL

20. Find the 21st term of the following series : 3, 9, 15, 21, ...
A. 123 B. 129
C. 117 D. 135

21. Thalessemia is a congenital :
A. Defect in bones B. Blood disorder
C. Neural defect D. Muscular defect

22. Rice Water Stool is a symptom of:
A. Dengue B. Malaria
C. Cholera D. Typhoid

23. Which of the following is a Presentation Graphics Software?
A. MS Windows B. MS Word
C. MS Excel D. MS Power Point

24. Who built 'Red Fort' at Delhi?
A. Akbar B. Shahjahan
C. Jehangir D. Aurangzeb

25. Wilm's tumour affects which of the following?
A. Liver B. Kidney
C. Uterus D. Skin

26. In a certain code, DOG is written as GRJ, then how will CAT be written in that code?
A. FEW B. FEV
C. FDW D. EDV

27. Which one of the following blood group is universal recipient?
A. A B. O
C. AB D. B

28. Bulimia Nervosa and Anorexia Nervosa are:
A. Sleep disorder B. Eating disorder
C. Nervous disorder D. None of these

29. Which city will host Olympic Games, 2020?
A. Madrid B. Istanbul
C. Rio de Janeiro D. Tokyo

30. One side of a rectangle is 40 metres and its diagonal is 50 metres. Find the perimeter of this rectangle.
A. 180 m B. 140 m
C. 70 m D. 90 m

31. What does an electronic spread sheet consist of ?
A. Rows B. Columns
C. Cells D. All of these

32. The general side effect of Penicillin is:
A. Rashes with itching
B. Fever
C. Renal Calculi
D. Gastro Intestinal disturbances

33. Complete the series:
21, 47, 23, 49, 25, 51, 27, ...
A. 29 B. 53
C. 31 D. 55

34. Snellen chart is used for measuring ......?
A. Vision B. Hearing
C. Smell D. Touch

35. Which is the largest Nerve in human body?
A. Femoral Nerve B. Sciatic Nerve
C. Pudendal Nerve D. Thoracic Nerve

36. A person spends $\frac{1}{4}$th part of his salary on food; $\frac{3}{8}$th part of his salary on house rent. He is now left with ₹ 4,800. Find his total salary.
A. ₹ 7,680 B. ₹ 15,600
C. ₹ 9,600 D. ₹ 12,800

37. Which one of the following ion helps in blood clotting?
A. Ca^{+2} B. Mn^{+2}
C. K^{+} D. PO_4^{-2}

38. The weight of an infant baby becomes twice the birth weight at the age of:
A. 6 months B. 1 year
C. 2 years D. 3 years

39. Angiography is X-ray visualization of :
A. Heart B. Lungs
C. Blood clots D. Blood vessels

40. MMR vaccination is done for protection against:
A. Measles; Mumps; Rubella
B. Measles; Mumps; Rabies
C. Measles; Malaria; Rabies
D. Meningitis; Mumps; Rubella

41. Find the simple interest amount if ₹ 1,500 is lent out at the rate of 9% per annum simple interest for 6 years.
A. ₹ 810 B. ₹ 900
C. ₹ 1,350 D. ₹ 675

42. Find the compound interest if ₹ 2,000 is lent out at the rate of 10% per annum, (compounded yearly) for 3 years.
A. ₹ 600 B. ₹ 200
D. ₹ 662 D. ₹ 680

43. Which one of the following a test for Diptheria?
A. Mantoux test B. Schick test
C. WIDAL test D. VDRL test

44. When we open an internet site, we see 'www'. What is the full form of 'www'?
A. World Wide Web B. World Wide Word
C. Words Wise Web D. None of these

45. The number of chromosomes in normal human cell is:
A. 46 B. 48
C. 50 D. 52

46. Which extension is given to word document by default?
A. COM B. EXT
C. DOC D. None of these

47. Who was called as the 'Grand old man of India'?
A. Dadabhai Naoroji
B. G. K. Gokhale
C. Mahatma Gandhi
D. Rabindranath Tagore

48. Find the value of $(128)^{\frac{-2}{7}}$.
A. 4 B. $\frac{1}{4}$
C. 24 D. $\frac{1}{16}$

49. Paracetamol is not given to those patients who are already suffering from:
A. Liver disorder B. Kidney disorder
C. Lung disorder D. G.I.T. disorder

50. Who is known as 'Lady with the Lamp'?
A. Mother Teresa
B. Sarojini Naidu
C. Florence Nightingale
D. None of these

51. Which is the most effective method of disposal of hospital waste?
A. By Recycling B. By Composting
C. Dumping D. Incineration

52. Pointing to an old man, Kunal said, "His son is my son's uncle." How is the old man related to Kunal?
A. Brother B. Grandfather
C. Father D. Brother-in-law

53. What is the basic functional unit of kidney?
A. Renal cortex B. Nephron
C. Glomerulus D. Renal Medulla

54. The difference between the circumference and the diameter of a circle is 30 cms. The area of this circle is :
A. 154 cm^2 B. 616 cm^2
C. 308 cm^2 D. 462 cm^2

55. The disorder that affects the memory and cognitive function in older persons is called:
A. Insomnia B. Paranoia
C. Aphasia D. Dementia

56. Who gave the slogan 'Swaraj is my birth right and I shall have it'?
A. Mahatma Gandhi
B. Pandit Nehru
C. Subhash Chandra Bose
D. Bal Gangadhar Tilak

57. Primary storage in computer terminology refers to:
A. Hard Disc Drive
B. Random Access Memory (RAM)
C. Read Only Memory (ROM)
D. None of these

58. Find the greatest 4-digit number which is exactly divisible by 13.
A. 9991 B. 9997
C. 9996 D. 9993

59. If a 13 m long iron rod weighs 24.7 kg, then what will be the weight of 6 m long iron rod?

A. 1.9 kg
B. 11.4 kg
C. 10.8 kg
D. 11.9 kg

60. Which one of the following Cancer is associated with High Fat diet?
A. Ovary Cancer
B. Lung Cancer
C. Colon Cancer
D. Liver Cancer

61. At present Reena is twice as old as Sunita. Three years ago, Reena was three times as old as Sunita was. How old is Reena now?
A. 6 years
B. 8 years
C. 10 years
D. 12 years

62. Insulin is not administered through oral route because:
A. It causes GIT bleeding
B. It causes Nausea and Vomiting
C. It is destroyed by GIT
D. None of these

63. In which of the following states is 'Kakrapar Nuclear Power Station' located?
A. Karnataka
B. Tamil Nadu
C. Maharashtra
D. Gujarat

64. Manoj walks 40 metres towards North. Then he takes left turn and walks 20 metres. He again takes left turn and walks 40 metres. How far and in which direction is he from the starting point?
A. 100 m, North
B. 80 m, East
C. 60 m, West
D. 20 m, West

65. Green leafy vegetables are rich source of:
A. Vitamin A
B. Vitamin B
C. Vitamin C
D. Vitamin D

66. Find the LCM (Lowest Common Multiple) of 15, 21 and 30.
A. 210
B. 3
C. 630
D. 105

67. The full form of "AMBU" bag is:
A. Artificial Mouth Breathing Unit
B. Artificial Manual Breathing Unit
C. Airway Mouth Breathing Unit
D. None of these

68. The heart beat rate of new born babies is generally:
A. 75 beats per minute
B. 80 beats per minute
C. 90 beats per minute
D. 120 - 140 beats per minute

69. A boat takes 10 hours to travel 100 km downstream. It takes 15 hours to travel 75 km upstream. Then the speed of the boat in still water is:
A. 10 km/h
B. 5 km/h
C. $2\frac{1}{2}$ km/h
D. $7\frac{1}{2}$ km/h

70. Disulfiram is a drug used in treatment of:
A. Malaria
B. AIDS
C. Alcoholism
D. Mania

71. Fertilization process takes place in:
A. Ovary
B. Fallopian tube
C. Uterus
D. Vagina

72. Hair colour in Humans turn white due to absence of which of the following pigments?
A. Melanin
B. Melatonin
C. Bilirubin
D. Biliverdin

73. Identify the Winner(s) of Nobel Peace Prize, 2014:
A. Kailash Satyarthi and Malala Yousafzai
B. B. Obama
C. V. Putin
D. Jean Tirole

74. Express 0.7% in terms of fraction.
A. $\frac{7}{10}$
B. $\frac{7}{100}$
C. $\frac{7}{1000}$
D. $\frac{7}{10000}$

75. The State of Jammu and Kashmir was accorded special status under:
A. Article 360 of constitution
B. Article 370 of constitution
C. Article 380 of constitution
D. Article 356 of constitution

76. Which one of the following is due to deficiency of Vitamin 'D'?
A. Night Blindness
B. Pellagra
C. Rickets
D. Kwashiorkor

77. 18th SAARC Summit was recently held in November 2014 at:
A. Thimpu
B. Dhaka
C. Kathamandu
D. New Delhi

78. Complete the series:
6, 11, 21, 36, ...?.... 81, 111.

A. 46 B. 51
C. 56 D. 71

79. The White Lines formed in the lower part of abdomen during pregnancy are called:
A. Pregnancy Mask
B. Linea Nigra
C. Striae Gravidarum
D. None of these

80. Arrange the following fractions in descending order:

$\frac{1}{2}, \frac{3}{5}, \frac{3}{10}, \frac{21}{50}$

A. $\frac{3}{5} > \frac{1}{2} > \frac{21}{50} > \frac{3}{10}$ B. $\frac{21}{50} > \frac{3}{5} > \frac{3}{10} > \frac{1}{2}$
C. $\frac{1}{2} > \frac{3}{5} > \frac{3}{10} > \frac{21}{50}$ D. $\frac{3}{10} > \frac{21}{50} > \frac{3}{5} > \frac{1}{2}$

81. In which of the following years did the Right to Information Act come into force?
A. 2002 AD B. 2003 AD
C. 2004 AD D. 2005 AD

82. Which one of the following is called the 'Power House' of the cell?
A. Nucleus B. Ribosome
C. Lysosome D. Mitochondria

83. A man is walking at a speed of 3.5 kmph. Find the distance covered by him in 15 minutes.
A. 875 m B. 525 m
C. 850 m D. 675 m

84. The main symptom of Pemphigus is:
A. Red Spots B. Bluish Spots
C. Small Vesicles D. Large Vesicles

85. The normal blood pressure of an Adult is:
A. 120/80 B. 120/100
C. 150/100 D. 150/60

86. If the Cost Price is ₹ 120 and Selling Price is ₹ 90, then find the loss percentage.
A. 30% B. $33\frac{1}{3}\%$
D. 25% D. 75%

87. HCF and LCM of two numbers are 8 and 320 respectively. If one of the numbers is 64, find the other number.
A. 40 B. 80
C. 32 D. 48

88. The average salary of 15 teachers is ₹ 4,500 per month, 5 teachers now leave the school. The average salary of remaining 10 teachers now is ₹ 4,200 per month. Find the total salary per month of the 5 teachers who left the school.
A. ₹ 24,000 B. ₹ 25,000
C. ₹ 27,000 D. ₹ 25,500

89. Chicken Pox is caused due to infection by :
A. Fungi B. Bacteria
C. Virus D. Protozoa

90. Which one of the following Teeth are used for crushing and grinding of food?
A. Canine B. Incisor
C. Molar D. Premolar

91. If L stands for (+); M stands for (–) ; N stands for (×) and P stands for (÷); then find the value of:
14 N 10 L 42 P 2 M 8 = ?
A. 153 B. 216
C. 248 D. 251

92. The feeling of fetus movement by mother is known as:
A. Ballottement B. Palmar Sign
C. Hegar Sign D. Quickening

93. Which one of the following is known as the "Great Circle"?
A. Equator B. Arctic Circle
C. Tropic of Cancer D. Tropic of Capricorn

94. Who is called the "Indian Napoleon"?
A. Samudragupta B. Chandragupta II
C. Ashoka D. Skandagupta

95. Find the sum of squares of first 8 natural numbers *i.e.* $(1^2 + 2^2 + 3^2 + \ldots\ldots + 8^2)$
A. 184 B. 194
C. 204 D. 72

96. Choose the correct alternative to complete the following series:
a _ ba _ b _ b _ a _ b
A. abaab B. abbab
C. aabba D. bbabb

97. Who is Defence Minister of India? (As on 01.12.2014)

A. Rajnath Singh B. Manohar Parrikar
C. Arun Jaitley D. Smriti Irani

98. Complete the series:
1, 4, 27, 16, ...?...., 36, 343.
A. 25 B. 120
C. 125 D. 81

99. A man is facing East. He turns 100° in the clockwise direction and then turns 145° in the anti-clockwise direction. Which direction is he facing now?
A. East B. North - East
C. North D. South - West

100. If 1000 men can do a job in 12 days, in how many days will 1200 men do this job?
A. 6 days B. 8 days
C. 9 days D. 10 days

ANSWERS

1	2	3	4	5	6	7	8	9	10
D	C	D	A	C	D	D	A	B	A
11	**12**	**13**	**14**	**15**	**16**	**17**	**18**	**19**	**20**
A	A	B	C	C	A	C	B	B	A
21	**22**	**23**	**24**	**25**	**26**	**27**	**28**	**29**	**30**
B	C	D	B	B	C	C	B	D	B
31	**32**	**33**	**34**	**35**	**36**	**37**	**38**	**39**	**40**
D	A	B	A	B	D	A	A	D	A
41	**42**	**43**	**44**	**45**	**46**	**47**	**48**	**49**	**50**
A	C	B	A	A	C	A	B	A	C
51	**52**	**53**	**54**	**55**	**56**	**57**	**58**	**59**	**60**
D	C	B	A	D	D	B	B	B	C
61	**62**	**63**	**64**	**65**	**66**	**67**	**68**	**69**	**70**
D	C	D	D	A	A	B	D	D	C
71	**72**	**73**	**74**	**75**	**76**	**77**	**78**	**79**	**80**
B	A	A	C	B	C	C	C	C	A
81	**82**	**83**	**84**	**85**	**86**	**87**	**88**	**89**	**90**
D	D	A	D	A	C	A	D	C	C
91	**92**	**93**	**94**	**95**	**96**	**97**	**98**	**99**	**100**
A	D	A	A	C	D	B	C	B	D

SOME SELECTED EXPLANATORY ANSWERS

5. mink yang pe — fruits are ripe
pe lao may mink — oranges are not ripe
may pe **nue** mink — **mangoes** are not ripe
Hence, Code for mangoes is **nue**.

6. Let one number is x, from question,

$$\frac{3}{2}x = 7 \Rightarrow x = \frac{14}{3}$$

Hence, Sum of two numbers

$$= x + \frac{3}{2} = \frac{14}{3} + \frac{3}{2} = \frac{37}{6} = 6\frac{1}{6}.$$

8. Position from left end = 40 – 14 + 1 = 27th.

16. In 1 day Mohan and Sohan together can do $\frac{1}{12}$ work

In one day Sohan alone can do $\frac{1}{28}$ work.

Number of days in which Mohan alone do this job

$$= \frac{1}{12} - \frac{1}{28} = \frac{7-3}{84} = \frac{4}{84} = \frac{1}{21}$$

Hence, Mohan alone can do this work in 21 days.

18. Number of boys in the row

$= 6 + 8 + 10 = 24.$

20. 3, 9, 15, 21

Given series is in A.P.

First term, $a = 3$

Common difference, $d = 6$.

$$t_n = a + (n - 1).d$$
$$t_{21} = 3 + (21 - 1).6$$
$$= 3 + 20 \times 6 = 123.$$

26. D O G → G R J (+3, +3, +3)

Similarly,

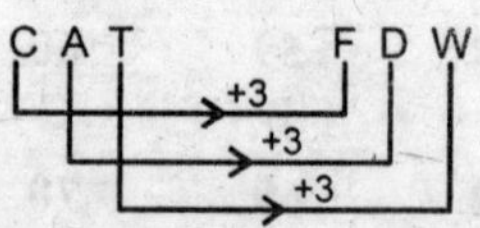

30. From ΔABC,

D, C, A, B; 50 m; 40 m

$$BC = \sqrt{(AC)^2 - (AB)^2}$$
$$= \sqrt{(50)^2 - (40)^2}$$
$$= 30$$

Perimeter of the rectagle

$= 2(AB + BC)$

$= 2(40 + 30) = 140$ m.

33. 21 47 23 49 25 51 27 53 (+2, +2, +2, +2, +2, +2)

36. Let, total Salary of the person is x.

then, $\frac{x}{4} + \frac{3}{8}x + 4800 = x$

$$\frac{5x}{8} + 4800 = x$$
$$x - \frac{5x}{8} = 4800$$
$$\frac{3x}{8} = 4800$$
$$x = \frac{4800 \times 8}{3} = 12800.$$

41. $S.I. = \frac{PRT}{100} = \frac{1500 \times 6 \times 9}{100} =$ ₹ 810.

42. Compound Interest (C.I.)

$$= 2000 \times \left(1 + \frac{10}{100}\right)^3 - 2000$$
$$= 2000 \times \frac{11 \times 11 \times 11}{1000} - 2000$$
$$= 2662 - 2000$$

= ₹ 662.

44. www is acronym for world wide web.

48. $(128)^{-\frac{2}{7}} = \frac{1}{(128)^{\frac{2}{7}}}$

$$= \frac{1}{(2^7)^{\frac{2}{7}}} = \frac{1}{2^{7 \times \frac{2}{7}}} = \frac{1}{2^2} = \frac{1}{4}.$$

54. Let, diameter of the circle is d cm.

then, Perimeter of the circle $= \pi.d$.

from question,

$$\pi d - d = 30$$
$$(\pi - 1)d = 30$$
$$\left(\frac{22}{7} - 1\right)d = 30$$
$$\frac{15}{7} \cdot d = 30 \Rightarrow d = 14 \text{ cm}$$

Area of the circle $A = \frac{\pi \cdot d^2}{4} = \frac{\pi \cdot (14)^2}{4}$

$$= \frac{22}{7} \times \frac{14 \times 14}{4}$$
$$= 154 \text{ cm}^2.$$

59. Weight per unit length = $\frac{24.7}{13}$ kg/m

Weight of 6 m long iron rod

$$= \frac{24.7}{13} \times 6 = 11.4.$$

61. Let Sunita's age is x year, then Reena's age $= 2x$ years.

From question, their age's before 3 years

$$2x - 3 = 3(x - 3)$$
$$2x - 3 = 3x - 9$$
$$3x - 2x = 9 - 3$$
$$x = 6$$

Hence, Reena's Present age = $2x$ = 12 years.

64. Distance from starting point = 20 m and He is in the west direction w.r.t. starting point.

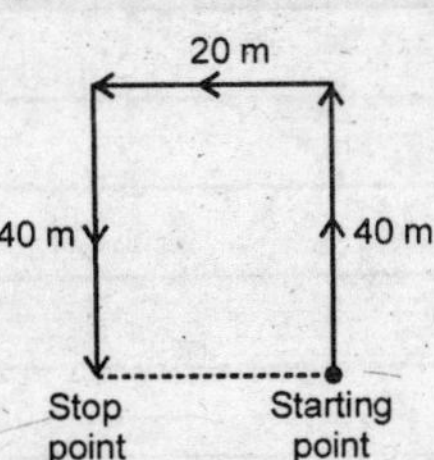

66.

3	15, 21, 30
5	5, 7, 10
	1, 7, 2

L.C.M. = 3 × 5 × 7 × 2 = 210.

69. Let, speed of boat in the still water is x km/hr and speed of current is y km/hr.

Downstream speed = $(x + y)$ km/hr.

Upsteam speed = $(x - y)$ km/hr.

From question,

$$(x + y) = \frac{100}{10}$$

$$x + y = 10 \quad ...(i)$$

and $$x - y = \frac{75}{15}$$

$$x - y = 5 \quad ...(ii)$$

from (*i*) and (*ii*), we get

$$x = 7\frac{1}{2} \text{ km/hr}$$

Hence, speed of boat in still water

$$= 7\frac{1}{2} \text{ km/hr.}$$

74. $0.7\% = \frac{0.7 \times 1}{100} = \frac{7}{1000}.$

78. 6 → 11 → 21 → 36 → 56 → 81 → 111 (+5, +10, +15, +20, +25, +30)

86. Loss = Cost price – selling price

$$= 120 - 90 = 30$$

$$\text{Loss\%} = \frac{\text{Loss}}{\text{Cost Price}} \times 100$$

$$= \frac{30}{120} \times 100 = 25\%$$

87. Product of two numbers

= L.C.M. × H.C.F.

Let the required numbers is x.

then, $64 \times x = 8 \times 320$

$$x = \frac{8 \times 320}{64} = 40.$$

88. Total monthly salary of 15 teachers

= 4500 × 15

Total monthly salary of 10 teachers

= 4200 × 10 = 42000

Hence, total monthly salary of 5 teachers who left the school

= 67500 – 42000 = 25500.

95. Sum of the square of 1st n natural numbers

$$= \frac{n(n+1)(2n+1)}{6}$$

$$= \frac{8 \times (8+1)(2 \times 8+1)}{6}$$

$$= \frac{8 \times 9 \times 17}{6} = 204.$$

98.

1	4	27	16	125	36	343
↓	↓	↓	↓	↓	↓	↓
1^3	2^2	3^3	4^2	5^3	6^2	7^3

100. 1 man can complete a job in 12 × 1000 days.

∴ 1200 men can complete a job in

$$\frac{12 \times 1000}{1200} = 10 \text{ days.}$$

YOUR SPACE

Health Awareness

1

Health and Diseases

INTRODUCTION

Health is a common theme in most cultures. In fact, all communities have their concept of health, as part of their culture. Probably the oldest definitions still used, is that health is the "absence of disease". In some cultures, health and harmony are considered equivalent, harmony being defined as "being at peace with the self, the community, god and cosmos". The ancient Indians and Greeks shared this concept and attributed disease to disturbances in bodily equilibrium of what they called "humors".

"Health" is one of these terms which most people find it difficult to define although they are confident of its meaning. Therefore, many definitions of health have been offered from time to time, including the following:

"A state of relative equilibrium of body form and function which result from its successful dynamic adjusment to forces tending to disturb it. It is not passive interplay between body substance and forces impinging upon it but an active response of body forces working toward readjustment" (*Perkins*) .

VARIABLES OF HEALTH

Health has multifactorial influence. The factors which influence health lie both within the individual and externally in the society in which he or she lives. These factors interact among themselves may be health–promoting or deleterious. Thus conceptionally, the health of individuals and whole communities may be considered to be the result of many interactions.

Some of the most important determinats or variables are given below:

1. Heredity
2. Environment
3. Life-Style
4. Socio-economic conditions
5. Health and family Welfare Services
6. Other factors

1. Heredity

The physical and mental status of every human being are to some extent determined by the nature of his genes at the moment of conception. The genetic make-up is unique in that it cannot be altered after conceptions. A number of diseases are now know to be of genetic origin due to, chromosomal anomalies, mutation etc. The state of health, therefore depends partially on the genetic constitution of man.

2. Environment

It was Hipppocrates who first related disease to environment, *e.g.*, climate, water, air, *etc.* Centuries later, Pettenkofer in Germany revived the concept of disease environment association.

Environment is classified as "internal" and "external". The internal environment of man pertains to "each and every component part, every tissue, organ and organ-system and their harmonious functioning within the system." Internal environment is the domain of internal medicine. The external or macro-environment consists of those things to which man is exposed. It is defined as "all that which is external to the individual human."

3. Life-Style

The term "lifestyle" is rather a diffuse concept often used to denote "the way people live", reflecting a whole range of social values, altitude and activities. It is composed of cultural and behavioural patterns and lifelong personal habits (*e.g.*, smoking, alcoholism) that have developed through processes of socialization. Lifestyle are learnt through social interaction with parents, peer groups, friends and siblings and through school and mass media.

4. Socio-Economic Conditions

Socio-economic conditions have long been known to influence human health. For the majority of the world's people, health status is determined primarily by their level of Socio-economic development, *e.g.*, per capita G.N.P., education nutrition, employment, housing, the political system of the country, *etc.*

5. Health Services

The term health and family welfare services cover a wide spectrum of personal and community services for treatment of disease, prevention of illness and promotion of health. The purpose of health services is to improve the health status of population. For example, immunization of children can influence the incidence/prevalence of particular disease. Provision of safe water can prevent mortality and morbidity from water-borne diseases. In case of pregnant women and children would contribute to the reduction of maternal and child morbidity and mortality. To be effective, the health services must reach the social periphery equitably distributed, accessible at a cost the country and community can afford and Socially acceptable. All these are ingredients of what is now termed "primary health care", which is seen as the way to better health.

Health services can also be seen as essential for social and economic development. It is well to remind ourselves that "health care does not produce good health". Whereas, there is a strong co-relation between GNP and expectation of life at birth, there is no significant cor-relation between medical density and expectation of life at birth. The most we can expect from an effective health service is good care. The epidemiological perspective emphasizes that health services, no matter how technically elegant or cost-effective, are ultimately pertinent only if they improve health.

6. Other Factors

Other contributions to the health of a population is derive from systems outside the formal health care system, or health related system (*e.g.*, food and agriculture, education, industry, social welfare, rural development) as well as adoption of policies in the economic and social fields that would assist in raising the standards of living. This would include employment opportunities, increased wages, prepaid medical programmes and family support systems.

INDICATORS OF HEALTH

Indicators are required not only to measure the health status of a community, but also to compare the health status of one country with that of another; for assessment of health care needs, for allocation of health resources; and for monitoring and evaluation of health services, activities and programmes. Indicators help to measure the extent to which the objectives and targets of a programme are being attained.

Characteristics of Indicators

Indicators have been given scientific respectability. Examples ideal indicators:

(a) **Should be valid,** *i.e.,* they should actually measure what they are supposed to measure;

(b) **Should be reliable and objective,** *i.e.*, the answers should be the same if measured by different people in similar circumstances;
(c) **Should be sensitive;** *i.e.,* they should be sensitive to changes in the situation concerned, and;
(d) **Should be specific,** *i.e.*, they should, reflect changes only in the situation concerned.

Our understanding of health therefore cannot be in terms of a single indicators; it must be conceived in terms of a profile employing many indicators, which may be classified as:

1. Mortality indicators
2. Morbidity indicators
3. Disability rates
4. Nutritional status indicators
5. Health care delivery indicators
6. Utilization rates
7. Indicators of social and mental health
8. Environmental indicators
9. Socio-economic indicators
10. Health policy indicators
11. Indicators of quality of life

HEALTH CONDITION IN INDIA

1. Demographic Profile

A major cancern today is population explosion. The demographic profile is characterised by:

(a) large population base
(b) high fertility both in terms of birth rate and family size
(c) low or declining mortality.
(d) "young" population (about 40 per cent of the population) is below the age of 15 years.
(e) the proportion of illiterate population is close to 48 per cent: this explains why the decline in birth-rate has been so slow.
(f) dependency ratio of 0.9; that is every economically productive member has to support almost one dependent

2. Mortality Profile

During the last few decades, there has been a notable improvement in the health status of the population. The death rate has steadily declined from 10 (1994) to 5.2 (2004).

3. Morbidity Profile

Morbidity is dominated by communicable diseases. According to one estimate, about 17.2 per cent of all deaths and about 20.8 per cent of all illnesses are due to communicable diseases in India. The major problems continue to be tuberculosis, filariasis, leprosy, malaria, diarrhoeal and malnutrition. Among viral diseases smallpox was eradicated in 1980. In bacterial diseases meningococcal meningitis has shows a substantial increase. Cholera has significantly declined, but the other water-borne diseases (*e.g.,* acute diarrhoea, dysentery and enteric fever) have not abated. Half the world's tuberculosis patients are in India accounting for 14 million cases of which approximately 3.5 million are infectious cases.

HEALTH CARE

Health care is an expression of concern for fellow human beings. It is defined as a "multitude of services rendered to individuals, families or communities by the agents of the health services or professions, for the purpose of promoting, maintaining, monitoring or restoring health". Such services might be staffed, organized, administered and financed in every imaginable way, but they all have one thing in common: People are being "served", that is: diagnosed, helped, cured, educated and habilitated by health personnel.

Health Care has many characteriestics. They include:

(i) *appropriateness (relevance)*, *i.e.*, whether the services is needed at all in relation to essential human needs, priorities and policies;
(ii) *comprehensiveness*, *i.e.*, whether there is an optimum mix of preventive, curative and promotional services;
(iii) *adequacy, i.e.*, if the services is proportionate to requirement;
(iv) *availability*, *i.e.*, ratio between population of an administrative unit and the health

facility (*e.g.* population per centre; doctor-population ratio); and

(v) *affordability, i.e.*, the cost of health care should be within the means of the individual and the state.

CONCEPT OF DISEASE

There have been many attempts to define disease. Webster defines disease as "a condition in which body health is impaired; a departure from a state of health, an alteration of the human body interrupting the performance of vital fuctions". The Oxford English Dictionary defines discase as "a condition of the body or some part or organ of the body in which its functions are disrupted or deranged". The term " disease" literally means "without ease" (uneasiness) – disease, the opposite of ease when something is wrong with body functioning. "Illness" refers not only to the presence of a specific disease, but also to the individual's perceptions and behaviour in response to the disease, as well as the impact of the disease on the psychosocial environment. "Sickness" refers to a state of social dysfunction. Susser has suggested the following usage:-

Disease is a physiological/psychological dysfuntion;

Illness is a subjective state of the person who feels aware of not being well.

Sickness is a state of social dysfunction, *i.e.*, a role that the individual assumes when ill ("sickness role").

Natural History Of Disease

The term natural history of disease is a key concept in epidemiology. It signifies the way in which a disease evolves over time from the earliest stage of its prepathogenesis phase to its termination as recovery, disability or death, in the absence of treatment or prevention. Let us consider the events that take place in the natural history of disease using infections disease as a principal model:

1. **Prepathogenesis Phase :** This refers to the period preliminary to the onset of disease in man. The disease agent has not yet entered man, but the factors which favour its interaction with the human host are already existing in the environment. This situation is frequently referred to as "man in the midst of disease" or "man exposed to the risk of disease".

2. **Pathogenesis Phase :** The pathogonesis phase begins with the entry of the disease "agent" in the susceptible human host. The further events in the pathogenesis phase are clear cut in infectious disease, *i.e.*, the disease agent multiplies and induces tissue to a physiologic changes. The final outcome of the disease may be recovery, disability or death. The pathogenesis phase may be modified by intervention measures such as immunization and chemotherapy. In chronic diseases (*e.g.*, coronary heart disease, hypertension, cancer), the early pathogenesis phase is less dramatic, thus phase in chronic disease is refrerred to as presymptomatic phase. During the presymptomatic stage, there is no manifest disease. The pathological changes are essentially below the level of the "Clinical horizon."

Agent Factors

The "*agent*" in concept of disease is defined as a substance, living or non-living or a force, tangible or intangible, the excessive presence or relative lack of which may initiate or perpetuate a disease process.

Disease agents may be classified broadly into the following groups:

1. **Biological Agents :** These are living agents of disease, *viz*, viruses, rickettsiae, fungi, bacteria, protozoa and metazoa. These agents exhibit certain "host-related" biological properties such as:

   (i) ***Infectivity:*** This is the ability of an infectious agent to invade and multiply (produce infection) in a host;

   (ii) ***Pathogenecity:*** This is the ability to induce clinically apparent illness.

(iii) ***Virulence:*** This is defined as the proportion of clinical cases resulting in severe clinical manifestations (including sequelae).

2. **Nutrient Agents :** These can be proteins, fats, carbohydrate, vitamins, minerals and water.
3. **Physical Agents :** Exposure to excessive heat, cold, humidity, pressure, radiation, electricity, sound, *etc.*, may result in illness.
4. **Chemical Agents :**
   (i) ***Endogenous:*** Some of the chemicals may be produced in the body as a result of derangement of function, *e.g.*, urea (uraemia), serum bilirubin (jaundice), ketones (ketosis), uric acid (gout), Calcium Carbonate (kidney stones) *etc.*
   (ii) ***Exogenous:*** Agents arising outside of human host, *e.g.*, allergens, metals, fumes, dust, gases, insecticides, *etc.*
5. **Mechanical Agents :** Exposure to chronic friction and other mechanical forces may result in crushing, tearing, sprains, dislocations and even death.
6. **Social Agents :** It is also necessary to consider social agents of disease. These are poverty, smoking, abuse of drugs and alcohol, unhealthy lifestyles, social isolation maternal deprivation, *etc.*

Intrinsic Factors

The host factors may be classified as: *(i)* Demographic Characteristics such as age, sex, ethnicity, *(ii)* Biological characteristics such as genetic factors; biochemical levels of the blood (*e.g.*, cholesterol); blood groups and enzymes; cellular constituents of the blood; immunological factors; and physiological function of different organ systems of the body (*e.g.*, blood pressure, forced expiratory ventilation) *etc.* *(iii)* Social and economic characteristics such as socio-economic status, education, occupation, stress, marital status, housing, *etc.*

Extrinsic Factors

The study of disease is really the study of man and his environment. Hundreds of millions of people are affected by preventable diseases originating in the environment in which they live. The external or macro-environment is defined as "all that which external to the individual human host, living and non-living, and with which he is in constant interaction". This includes all of man's external surroundings such as air, water, food, housing *etc.*

CONCEPTS OF CONTROL

Disease Control

The term "disease control" describes ongoing operations aimed at reducing:

(i) the incidence of disease
(ii) the duration of disease, and consequently the risk of transmission
(iii) the effects of infection, including both the physical and psychosocial complications; and
(iv) the financial burden to the community.

DISEASE ERADICATION

Eradication literally means to "tear out by roots". Eradication of disease implies termination of all transmission of infection by extermination of the infectious agents. As the name implies, eradication is an absolute process, and not a relative goal. It is "all or none phenomenon". The word eradication and disease from the whole world.

MONITORING AND SURVEILLANCE

Monitoring

Monitoring is "the performance and analysis of routine measurements, aimed at detecting changes in the environment or health status of populations". Thus, we have monitoring of air pollution, water quality, growth and nutritional status, *etc.* It also refers to ongoing measurement of performance of a health service or a health professionals the extent to which patients comply with or adhere to advice of health professionals.

Surveillance

Surveillance is defined in many ways. According to one interpretation surveillance means to watch over with great attention, authority and often with suspicion. According to another, surveillance is defined as "the continuous scrutiny of the factors that determine the occurrence and distribution of disease and other conditions of ill-health".

MODES OF INTERVENTION

"Intervention" can be defined as any attempt to intervene or interrupt the usual sequence in the development of disease in man. This may be by the provision of treatment, education, help or social support. Five modes of intervention have been described which form a continuum corresponding to the natural history of any disease, which are as follows:—

1. Health Promotion

Health promotion is "the process of enabling people to increase control over and to improve health". The well-known interventions in this area are:

(i) health education
(ii) environmental modifications
(iii) nutritional interventions
(iv) lifestyle and behavioural changes.

2. Specific Protection

The following are some of the currently available intervention aimed at specific protection. (a) immunization (b) use of specific nutrients (c) chemoprophylaxis (d) protection against occupational hazards (e) protection against accidents (f) protection from carcinogens (g) avoidance of allergens.

3. Early Diagnosis and Treatment

A WHO Expert Committee defined early detection of health impairment as "the detection of disturbances of homoeostatic and compensatory mechanise while biochemical, morphological, and functional changes are still reversible." Thus, in order to prevent disease, the criteria of diagnosis should , if possible, be based on early biochemical, morphological and functional changes that precede the occurrence of manifest signs and symptoms. This is of particular importance in chronic disease.

4. Disability Limitation

When a patient reports late in the pathogenesis phase, the mode of intervention is disability limitation. The objective of this intervention is to prevent or halt the transition of the disease process from impairment to handicap.

5. Rehabilitation

Rehabilitation has been defined as "the combined and coordinated use of medical, social, education and vocational measures for training and retraining the individual to the highest possible level of functional ability". It includes all measures aimed at reducing the impact of disabling and handicapping conditions and enabling the disabled and handicapped to achieve social integration.

POPULATION MEDICINE

Population medicine is referred to as hygiene, public health, preventive medicine social medicine or community medicine. All these share common ground in their concern for promotion of health and prevention of disease.

Hygiene

The world "hygiene" is derived from Hygeia, the goddess of health in Greek mythology. She is represented as a beautiful woman holding in her hand a bowl from which a serpent is drinking. In Greek, mythology, the serpent testified the art of healing whose symbol is retaines even today. Hygiene is defined as "the science of health and embraces all factors which contribute to healthful living."

Public Health

The term "Public Health" came into general use around 1840. It arose from the need to protect "the public" from the spread of communicable diseases. Later it appeared in

1848 in the name of the law, the Public Health Act in England to crystallise the efforts organized by society to protect, promote and restore the people's health. Public health, in its present form, is a combination of scientific disciplines (*e.g.*, epidemiology, biostatistics, laboratory science, social sciences, demography) and skills and strategies (*e.g.*, epidemiological investigations, planning and management, interventions, surveillance, evaluation) that are directed to the maintenance & improvement of the health of the people.

LATIN ABBREVIATIONS

Abbreviation	*Derivation (Latin)*	*Meaning*
a.c.	Ante cibum	Before meal
a.e.d. (T.D.S.)	Ter die sumendus	Three times a day
a.i.d	quarter in die	Four times a day
a.m.	Ante meridiem	Before noon
alt. die	Alternus diebus	Alternate days
b.d. (b.i.d.)	bis die	Two times a day
c.m.	cras mane	Tomorrow morning
h.	Hora	Hour per hour
h.n.	Hac nocte	Today night
h.s.	Hora somni	Bed time
o.d.	Omni die	Once a day
o.m.	Omni mane	Every morning
o.n.	Omni nocte	Every night
p.c.	Post cibum	After meal
p.m.	Post meridiem	After noon
p.r.n.	Pro-re-nata	As per required
q.	quaque	Each
rep	repetatur	Repeat again
s.o.s.	Si opus sit	As per required in emergency
stat	statim	At once

ABBREVIATIONS

ABG	Artial Blood Gas
AFB	Acid Fast Bacilli
AFP	Alfa Fetoprotein
AHF	Antihemophilic Factor
AHG	Antihemophilic Globulin
AIDS	Acquired Immune Deficiency Syndrome
ASD	Atrial Septal Defect
ASD	Atrial Septal Defect
ASOT	Antistreptolysin O titer
AST	Aspartate Aminotransferase
ATTK	Anti Tubercular Treatment Kits
BBB	Bundle Branch Block
BMI	Body Mass Index
BMR	Basal Metabolic Rate
BMT	Bone Marrow Transplantation
CABG	Coronary Artery bypass Graft

CAG	Coronary Angiography
CAT/CT	Computerised Axial Tomography/Computerised Tomography
CHD	Congenital Heart Disease
CHF	Congestive Heart Failure
CPK	Creatine Phsophokinase
CSOM	Chronic Suppurative Otitis Media
CSP	Cerebro Spinal Fluid
CSSD	Centrise Sterile Supply Department
CSSM	Child Servival and Safe Motherhood
DES	Deithyle Stilbestrol
DPT	Diphtheria Pertussis Tetanus
DVT	Deep Veins Thrombosis
ECG	Electrocardiogram
ECT	Electroconvulsive Therapy
EEG	Electroencephalogram
ELISA	Enzyme Linked Immuno Sorbent Assay
EPS	Extrapyramidal Syndroms
ERCP	Endoscopic Retrograde Cholangio Pancreatography
ESRD	End stage Renal disease
ESWL	Extracorporeal Shock Wave Lithotripsy
ESWL	Extracorporeal Shock Wave Lithotripsy
ETT	Endotracheal Tube
FBS	Fasting Blood Sugar
GTT	Glucose Tolerance Test
HCG	Human Chorionic Gonadotrapic
IABP	Intra Aortic Ballon Pump
ICDS	Integrated Child Development Service
ICP	Intracranial Pressure
ICU	Intensive Care Unit
IHD	Ischemic Heart Disease
IOP	Intraocular Pressure
IPPB	Intermitted Positive Pressure Breathing
IQ	Intelligence Quotients
IVP	Intra Venous Pyelogram
IVU	Intravenous Urogram
KUB	Kidney Uterus Bladder
MAOI	Monoamine Oxidase Inhibitor
MMR	Measles Mumps Rubella
MOPP	Mechlorethamine Oncovin Procarbazine Prednisone
MRI	Magnetic Resonance Imaging
NACO	National Aids Control Organisation
NFCP	National Filaria Control Programme
NSAIDS	Nonsteroidal Anti Inflammatory Drug
OCD	Obessive Compulsive Disorder
ORS	Oral Rehydration Solution
PDA	Patent Ductus Arteriosus
PET	Positron Emission Tomography
PID	Pelvic Inflammatory Disease
PID	Prolapsed Intravertibrae Disk
PND	Paroxysmal Noetural Dyspnea
PR	Per Rectum
PSA	Prostate Specific Antigen
PTCA	Percutaneous Transluminal Coronay Angioplasty
PVT	Proxysmal Ventricular Trachycardia
RBS	Random Blood Sugar
RCH	Reproduction and Child Health
RDS	Respiratory Distress Syndrome
REM	Rapid Eye Movement
ROM	Range of Motion
RPLND	Retroperitoneal Lymph Node Dissection
SGOT	Serum Glutamic Oxalocetic Transaminase
SGPT	Serum Glutamic Pyruvic Transaminase
SMR	Submuscous Resection
SVPB	Supraventricular Premature Beat
SVT	Supraventricular Trachycardia
TAO	Thrombo Angitis Obliterans
TCA	Tricyclic Antidepressants
TPN	Total Parental Nutrition
TURP	Trans Urethral Resection of Prostate
UNICEF	United Nations International Children's Emergency Fund (United Nations Children's Funds)
VVF	Vesicovaginal Fustula

OBJECTIVE QUESTIONS

1. One of the following is *not true* international classification of disease (ICD):
(*a*) It is revised once in 10 years
(*b*) It was devised by UNICEF
(*c*) The 10th revision consists of 21 major chapters
(*d*) It provides the basis for use in other health fields.
(*e*) It is accepted for National and International use.

2. The concept of social Medicine was first introduced by:
(*a*) Neumann and virchow
(*b*) Robert Gritjahn
(*c*) John Ryle
(*d*) Rene Sand
(*e*) Crew

3. Prophylactic administration of vitamin A in a child is:
(*a*) Health promotion
(*b*) Treatment
(*c*) Specific protection
(*d*) Rehabilitation

4. The restoration of body function is known as:
(*a*) Vocational rehabilitation
(*b*) Primary prevention
(*c*) Social rehabilitation
(*d*) None of these

5. *False* about primary prevention is:
(*a*) Early diagnosis and treatment
(*b*) Environmental sanitation
(*c*) Vaccination
(*d*) Health promotion

6. About community diagnosis all are *true* except:
(*a*) Virtual statistics taken
(*b*) Age and sex distribution statistics needed
(*c*) Age specific, death rate needed
(*d*) Incidence of important diseases taken

7. Administration of oral polio vaccine to the children is a measure of:
(*a*) Health promotion
(*b*) Specific protection
(*c*) Treatment
(*d*) Rehabilitation

8. Which of the following constitutes specific protection?
(*a*) Immunization
(*b*) Aviodance of allergens
(*c*) Healthy environment
(*d*) Chemoprophylaxis

9. Which of the following is tertiary level of prevention?
(*a*) Health promotion
(*b*) Specific protection
(*c*) Early diagnosis and treatment
(*d*) Disability limitation

10. Screening for carcinoma cervix is:
(*a*) Health promotion
(*b*) Specific protection
(*c*) Early diagnosis and treatment
(*d*) Disability limitation

11. Iron and folic acid supple-mentation is type of:
(*a*) Specific protection
(*b*) Health promotion
(*c*) Health education
(*d*) Primordial protection

12. The current concept of health promotion and the related activities lead to:
(*a*) Better treatment of a problem
(*b*) Critical awareness and lifestyle changes
(*c*) Adoption of prophylactic services
(*d*) Better health services usage

13. The best method of promoting healthy lifestyle in children:
(*a*) Primordial prevention
(*b*) Specific protection
(*c*) Secondary prevention
(*d*) High risk strategy

14. All are health promotion activities *except*:
(*a*) Better treatment of a problem
(*b*) Critical awareness and lifestyle changes
(*c*) Adoption of prophylactic services
(*d*) Better health services and usage

15. Primary aim of sentinel surveil-lance is:
(*a*) To know total number of disease patient
(*b*) To know trend of disease
(*c*) To decide mode of treatment
(*d*) Notification

16. Primordial prevention is applied when:
(*a*) Risk factors appear before disease
(*b*) After risk factors appear
(*c*) Prevalence of disease is low
(*d*) No disease and no risk factors

17. *False* about primary prevention is:
(*a*) Early diagnosis and treatment
(*b*) Environmental sanitation
(*c*) Vaccination
(*d*) Health promotion

18. Which type of prevention used in change of smoking habit?
(*a*) Primordial prevention
(*b*) Population (mass) strategy
(*c*) High risk strategy
(*d*) Secondary prevention

19. Tertiary level of prevention is:
(*a*) Health promotion
(*b*) Chemoprophylaxis
(*c*) Rehabilitation
(*d*) Early diagnosis and treatment

20. Sentinel surveillance is done for all *except*:
(*a*) HIV
(*b*) Diarrohea
(*c*) Acute flaccid paralysis
(*d*) Per capita income

21. A concept directed against prevention of risk factors of CAD is:
(*a*) Primordial prevention
(*b*) Secondary prevention
(*c*) Health education
(*d*) Primary prevention

22. Total morbidity is determined by:
(*a*) Active surveillance
(*b*) Passive surveillance
(*c*) Sentinel surveillance
(*d*) Annual survey

23. Pap smear is an example of:
(*a*) Primary level of prevention
(*b*) Secondary level of prevention
(*c*) Tertiary level of prevention
(*d*) None of above

24. Keeping the frequency of illness within acceptable limits is best described as disease:
(*a*) Control
(*b*) Prevention
(*c*) Eradication
(*d*) Surveillance
(*e*) Treatment

25. Match List I (*activities*) with List II (*levels of prevention*) and select the correct answer using the codes given below the lists:

List-I
A. Post exposure prophylaxis with rabies vaccine
B. Screening for hypertension
C. Surgical intervention for claw hand in leprosy
D. Preventing emergencey of high prevalence of obesity in the population

List-II
1. Secondary level prevention
2. Tertiary level prevention
3. Primordial prevention
4 Primary level prevention

Codes:

	(A)	(B)	(C)	(D)
(*a*)	4	3	2	1
(*b*)	4	1	2	3
(*c*)	2	1	3	4
(*d*)	1	2	4	3

26. Main purpose of sentinel surveillance is:
(*a*) To find out total number of cases
(*b*) For intervention of thera-peutics
(*c*) To depict natural history of disease
(*d*) Prevention of sentinel piles

27. Which *one* of the following is not a socio-economic indicator?
(*a*) Literacy rate
(*b*) Family size
(*c*) Housing
(*d*) Life expectancy at birth

28. The measure used to express the global burden of disease *i.e.*, how a healthy life is affected by disease, is:

(*a*) Disability-adjusted life year
(*b*) Case fatality rate
(*c*) Life expectancy
(*d*) Age-specific incidence rate

29. Most important epidemiological tool used for assessing disability in children is:
(*a*) Activities of daily living (ADL) scale
(*b*) Wing's handicaps, behaviour and skills (HBS) schedule
(*c*) Binet and Simon IQ tests
(*d*) Physical quality of life index (PQLI)

30. The burden of disease is best represented by:
(*a*) Infant mortality rate
(*b*) DALY's
(*c*) PQLI
(*d*) Case fatality

31. Infant mortality rate in Kerala is:
(*a*) 38 (*b*) 30
(*c*) 26 (*d*) 16

32. Objectives of the health services include each of the following except:
(*a*) Delivery of curative care only
(*b*) Health promotion
(*c*) Prevention control, or eradication of disease
(*d*) Treatment and rehabilitation

33. PQLI includes all except:
(*a*) Per capita income
(*b*) Life expectancy at age 1 year
(*c*) Literacy
(*d*) Infant mortality

34. Physical quality of life in India is:
(*a*) 31 (*b*) 43
(*c*) 50 (*d*) 61

ANSWERS

1	2	3	4	5	6	7	8	9	10
(*b*)	(*a*)	(*c*)	(*a*)	(*a*)	(*c*)	(*b*)	(*a*)	(*a*)	(*c*)
11	**12**	**13**	**14**	**15**	**16**	**17**	**18**	**19**	**20**
(*a*)	(*b*)	(*a*)	(*b*)	(*d*)	(*a*)	(*a*)	(*a*)	(*c*)	(*b*)
21	**22**	**23**	**24**	**25**	**26**	**27**	**28**	**29**	**30**
(*a*)	(*c*)	(*b*)	(*a*)	(*c*)	(*a*)	(*d*)	(*a*)	(*b*)	(*b*)
31	**32**	**33**	**34**						
(*d*)	(*a*)	(*a*)	(*b*)						

Basic Physiology

1. **Anatomy** describes the internal structures of the different part of the body. *Physiology* describes the functions of the different structures of the body.
2. **Cell:** A cell is a unit of living matter. It has a cell membrane and the living matter called protoplasm. The protoplasm has a denser part called nucleus and a lighter part called cytoplasm. The nucleus controls the activities of the cell.
3. **Amoeboid Movement:** Some type of cells can move. They have no cell wall. They are amoeba cells, white blood cell *etc*. At first such cell puts out a projection and then the whole protoplasm flows in that direction. Such movement is called amoeboid movement.
4. **Phagocytosis:** The process of engulfing solid particles is phagocytosis. In the cells, exchange of food and gases occur by a process known as osmosis. Selective osmosis occurs frequently.
5. **Tissue:** A tissue is a group of similar type of cells bound together *i.e.*, tissue of skin, tissue of bone, tissue of muscle *etc*.
6. **Organ:** An organ is a group of tissues, which can carry out some special type of work. Heart is an organ which pumps the blood, an artery is an organ which carries blood to different parts of the body, eye is an organ of sight *etc.*
7. **System:** A system is a group of organs carrying out some special type of work.
8. **The Bony System:** The bony or the skeletal system forms the frame work of the body. There are 206 bones in our body. The bones are joined together by fibrous capsules with thickend bands called ligaments. In some cases bones are fused together and do not have any movement. The skull, sacrum, pelvis etc. are of this type.

Functions of the Bones

(i) Bones give shape and firmness to the body.

(ii) They protect the delicate organs and soft parts of the body.

(iii) They give attachment to the muscles so that the muscles contract. The bones move about the joint.

(iv) The bones manufacture red blood cells and some white blood cells.

(a) The skull consists of a large hollow cavity called the cranial cavity. In it lies the brain. Skull is fused mass of bone including the face bones. 32 teeth are fixed in the gum. A tooth has an enamel dentine and the tooth pulp. The tooth enamel is the hardest bone in the body.

(b) The spinal column consists of 33 vertebrae.

(c) Thorax is the upper portion of the trunk. It consists of a bony cage with 12 vertebrae at the back.

The Bones of the Upper Limbs are: *1.* clavicle or collar bone, *2.* scapula or shoulder blade, *3.* humerus on the bone of arm, *4.* radius and ulna or the bones of fare arm, *5.* 8 corpal bones of wrist, *6.* metacarpal bones of palm and, 7. 14 phalanges.

The Bones of the Lower Limbs are: *1.* the hip bone, *2.* the femur or the thigh bone, *3.* tibia and fibula or the leg bones, *4.* 7 Tarsal bones of the ankle, *5.* 5 meta tarsal bonc of thc foot, *6.* 14 phalanges or the bones of the fingers of leg, *7.* In addition 'Patella' or the knee pan is a small flat bone in front of the knee joint. It protects the knee joint. It is a ball and socket joint.

Fracture: In fracture the bone is cracked or broken. In dislocation the capsule of the joint is torn and bone comes out of the joint.

9. The Abdomen: The abdomen is the lower part of the trunk. The diaphragm forms the roof of the abdomen.

Organs in the Abdominal Cavity are: 1. liver, 2. spleen, 3. stomach, 4. small and large intestines, 5. pancreas, 6. two kidneys, 7. urinary bladder. In females there are two ovaries and the uterus.

10. Muscular System: There are over 580 muscles in our body. The function of the muscles are: 1. They give shape to the body, 2. Muscle are attached to the bone and when such muscle contracts the bones move so that body movement is effected, 3. They protect the internal organs. All muscles act in co-ordination. Thus when the extensor muscles contract, the flexor muscles relax, or when the intestinal muscle contracts the intestinal sphincter muscle relaxes.

11. Digestive System: The digestive system starts at the cavity of mouth and ends at the anus.

At the entrance to the stomach there is a ring muscle called 'the cardiac sphincter'. It prevents food from going back to oesophagus on the other end is 'the pyloric sphincter'. It allows the food to pass to duodenum only after digestion in stomach is complete. Food remains in stomach for 2 to 3 hours.

Amylase digests carbohydrates to glucose. Trypin digests protein to peptide and amino acid. Liapase breaks up the emulsified fat to fatty acids and glycerol.

Villi are minute finger like projection from the wall of the small intestine. They are in millions. Each vilrus contains lymphatic capillaries called lacteals and the blood capillaries. The lacteals absorb fatty acid and glycerol. The blood capillaries absorb amino acid, glucose, vitamins and various salts *etc.*

The Digestive gland: The glandular systems are different types of glands. The glands of the digestive system are:

(a) Salivary gland: There are a pair of parotid gland, a pair of submaxillary gland and a pair of sublingual gland. They secrete saliva. Saliva contains "Ptyalin" which digests starch to maltose.

(b) Glands on the wall of the stomach produce Gastric juice. It contains hydrochloric acid, renin and pepsin. Hydrochloric acid curdles milk and kills some types of germs.

(c) Liver is the largest gland in the body. It is in the upper part of the abdomen on the right side. Liver manufactures bile from the broken down R.B.Cs. Hence bile is the product of excretion of R.B.Cs bile is stored in the gall bladder and passes to the duodenum through the bile duct. Bile emulsifies fat and helps digestion of fat, so bile is also a secretion. Bile duct joins pancreatic duct and open into duodenum. The functions of the liver are:

  (i) It produces bile
  (ii) It changes glucose to glycogen and store glycogen.
  (iii) Poisonous matter in blood are changed to harmless product
  (iv) It stores fat, soluble vitamin *i.e.*, A, D and K.

(d) Pancreas is situated between duodenum and spleen and is behind the stomach. It secretes.

  (i) Trypsin which digests protein to peptones and amino acid.

(ii) Amylase which digests starch and other sugar to glucose

(iii) Liapase digests emulsified fat to fatty acid and glycerol. Pancreas also produces an internal secretion called insulin.

The spleen: It is on the left upper portion of the abdomen. It has no duct. It is not known if spleen produces any internal secretion or not. The spleen destroys the worn out R.B.Cs and produces W.B.Cs.

12. Respiratory System: The respiratory system consists of nasal passage, pharynx, larynx, trachea, bronchi and its division and subdivisions each of which finally ends in an air-sac called alveolus.

When the diaphragm contracts the air goes in the chest. It is called inspiration when diaphragm relaxes and we breathe out, it is called expiration. Inspiration and expiration is respiration.

When blood passes through capillaries the red blood cells give out CO_2 in the alveolus. This is called external respiration. In case of internal respiration the red blood cells give out O_2 to the tissue cells and take in CO_2 from the tissue cell.

Normally, a person breathes 18 times a minute. When we breathe in the oxygen is 20.95% and carbon dioxide is 0.4% and when we breathe out the oxygen becomes 16.5% and carbon dioxide increases to 4.5%

13. Circulatory System: The circulatory system consists of the heart, the arteries, the capillaries and the veins.

The Red Blood Cells (R.B.C.) are tiny discs of 7 microns. They contain haemoglobin which takes up oxygen from the lung alveolus and give out in the tissue cells. They take up carbon dioxide from the tissue cells and give out in the alveolus of the lung. Normally there are 5 millions R.B.Cs in one ml. of blood.

The White Blood Cells (W.B.C.) are bigger than R.B.Cs and are about 5,000 per ml. There are variety of W.B.Cs. They have nuclei and can multiply. They are also produced in the spleen and in the lymphatic glands.

The antibodies are defensive proteins in our body. They are present in as gamma globulin in blood.

The Platelets are smaller than the R.B.C. Their function is to bring about the clotting of the blood. When blood is flow from injury, the platelets break down. This causes the soluble fibrinogen in blood to become insoluble fibrin or threads. The R.B.Cs are caught up by the fibrins as the fibrin contract and then the clot is formed. The W.B.C. escape from the clot by their amoeboid movement.

14. Heart: The heart is hollow muscular organ on the left side of the chest. There is a complete muscular organ partitioned the heart to left and right sides. The left side has an upper chamber called left *auricle* and a lower chamber called left *ventricle*. The right side has also an upper and a lower chamber called right auricle and right ventricle respectively.

Blood Vessels: Blood vessels mean arteries, capillaries and veins.

Arteries: Arteries carry blood from the heart to the different parts of the body. Except pulmonary arteries all other arteries carry oxygenated blood. Except pulmonary vein all other vein carries the deoxygenated blood. The arteries have a thick fibrous coat, a thick muscular coat and a layer of cells forming the inner coat called endothelium. Arteries are always full of blood and produce a pressure is called diastolic pressure. Normally the diastolic pressure is about 80 mm of Hg. When the heart contracts and forces more blood into the arteries, the blood pressure increases. This is called systolic pressure. Normally the systolic pressure varies from 120 to 160 mm of Hg. If it is more, then the person has high blood pressure.

The **plasma** together with the W.B.C. is called "lymph".

The capillaries are minute veins which join together to form large veins.

Types of Circulation:

(i) The pulmonary circulation means the flow of blood from the right ventricle to pulmonary arteries-capillaries around the alveolus of the lungs-pulmonary veins and then to the left auricle.

(ii) The systemic circulation means the flow of blood from the left ventricle-Aorta-Arteries to all over the body-capillaries-veins, and then to the right auricle.

Portal Circulation: The veins of stomach, the small and large intestines, spleen and pancreas join together and form the portal vein. The blood from the portal vein and hepatic artery enters the liver. Hence the hepatic vein has the blood from the hepatic artery as well as the blood from the portal vein.

15. The Excretory System: The excretory system throws away the waste product from the body. The waste products are formed due to catabolic process in the body cells.

Excretory system consists of the two kidneys, the skin, the lungs and the large intestine.

Urine contains:

(a) water 96%

(b) urea uric acid *etc.*

(c) certain poisonous materials and other material that are not necessary for the body

(d) certain mineral salts that are in excess in the body or not required by the body.

Functional units of a kidneys are *Nephrons*.

The lungs remove CO_2 and water vapour. Kidneys remove waste matters like urea uric acid, salt *etc.*

16. The Nervous System: The nervous system consists of:

(a) The central nervous system consisting of the brain, the spinal cord and the nerves.

(b) The autonomic nervous system consisting of the sympathetic and the parasympathetic nerves.

Largest cell of human body is *Neuron*.
Largest gland of human body is *Liver*.
The brain consists of 1. cerebrum 2. cerebellum 3. Pons and 4. medulla oblongata. The medulla oblongata continues below as the spinal cord.

The medulla oblongata is the expanded upper portion of the spinal cord. At its lower ends fibres from the cerebrum cross to the other side. It regulates breathing and heart beat and controls the blood pressure and the body temperature. Injury to medulla oblongata causes instant death.

Reflex Action: The entire impulse circuit of a reflex response—

receptors → CNS → effectors

is called reflex arc. It is spontaneous without involving spinal cord.

17. The Reproductive System: Unlike other systems, the reproductive system of males and the females are quite different.

The Reproductive System in males consist of:

(a) The *testes* where sperms are manufactured.

(b) The *vas deferens* through which the sperms pass.

(c) The *seminal vesicle* where sperms are stored.

(d) The *ejaculatory duct*, through which the sperms are spurted out into the *urethra* and finally get discharged through the *penis*.

Reproductive System in Females: In females, the reproductive system consists of:

(a) The *two ovaries* in the lower part of the abdomen.

(b) The ovum passes through the *fallopian tube* to the *uterus*.

(c) If the ovum is fertilized by the sperm then the fertilized ovum enters the wall of the uterus and pregnancy occurs.

(*d*) Otherwise, the unfertilized ovum, together with the blood *etc.* from the wall of the uterus is thrown out through the *vaginal canal* as *menstruation*.

Ovums are discharged from any of the two ovaries after every 28 days. Hence the menstrual cycle occurs after every 28 days.

Tubectomy is the cutting of the fallopian tube. It is a permanent method of birth control in females. This operation is more difficult than *Vasectomy* in males. The ovaries also produce an internal secretion which develop the formal sexual characters.

OBJECTIVE QUESTIONS

1. Person living at high altitude will have:
(*a*) High alveolar capacity
(*b*) More erythrocytes
(*c*) Haemoglobin curve shifted toward right
(*d*) All of these

2. Carbon dioxide is carried in the blood:
(*a*) As dissolved gas
(*b*) As bicarbonates
(*c*) In combination with haemoglobin
(*d*) All of these

3. The largest quantity of air that can be expired after a maximum inspiratory effort is:
(*a*) Residual volume
(*b*) Tidal volume
(*c*) Vital capacity
(*d*) Total lung volume

4. The exchange of gases in the alveoli of the lungs takes place by:
(*a*) Osmosis
(*b*) Simple diffusion
(*c*) Passive transport
(*d*) Active transport

5. Lungs are enclosed in:
(*a*) Pericardium
(*b*) Pleura
(*c*) Peritoneum
(*d*) Perichondrium

6. Artificial respiration at the rate of 10-15 times per minute is being given to a man saved from drowing. This is because:
(*a*) Water in respiratory passage is cleared fast at this rate
(*b*) Chocking is least at this rate
(*c*) It is normal rate of respiration
(*d*) Lungs are ventilated best at this rate

7. Pasteurization of milk means that:
(*a*) All bacteria are killed
(*b*) Pathogenic bacteria are killed
(*c*) Milk is enriched with vitamins
(*d*) Milk casein is partially digested.

8. Dissociation curve is connected with:
(*a*) Oxygen
(*b*) Oxyhaemoglobin
(*c*) Carbon dioxide
(*d*) Carbonic anhydrate

9. What would happen if human body becomes acidic (low pH)?
(*a*) Oxygen carrying capacity of haemoglobin increases
(*b*) Oxygen carrying capacity of haemoglobin decreases
(*c*) RBC count increases
(*d*) RBC count decreases

10. Haemoglobin-oxygen dissociation curve is:
(*a*) Hyperbolic (*b*) Sigmoid
(*c*) Straight (*d*) Constant

11. Epithelial linning the alveoli of the frog's lung facing cavity is:
(*a*) Squamous and ciliated
(*b*) Columnar and ciliated
(*c*) Columnar and non-ciliated
(*d*) Squamous and non-ciliated.

12. Oxygen dissociation curve of haemoglobin is
(*a*) Sigmoid (*b*) Slope
(*c*) Straight line (*d*) Parabola

13. Air bladder or swim bladder in fishes is associated with
(*a*) Hydrostatic
(*b*) Sound production
(*c*) Gaseous exchange
(*d*) All of these

14. Arytenoid cartilage occurs in
(*a*) Nose (*b*) Larynx
(*c*) Hyoid (*d*) Sternum

15. Respiratory Quotient (RQ) is less than one for
(*a*) Banana (*b*) Potato
(*c*) Citrus fruits (*d*) Castor seeds

16. Oxygen carrier or the respiratory pigment in the blood of frog and other vertebrates is
(*a*) Haemocyanin (*b*) Cytochrome
(*c*) Haemoglobin (*d*) None of these

17. In an organism utilising carbohydrates as a source of energy anaerobically, RQ is likely to be
(*a*) 0.7 (*b*) 1.0
(*c*) 0.9 (*d*) Infinity

18. The state during which are respiratory centre is inhibited is termed
(*a*) Asphyxia (*b*) Chocking
(*c*) Anoxia (*d*) Suffocation

19. Which of the following are respiratory organs of scorpion?
(*a*) Lungs (*b*) Book-lungs
(*c*) Gills (*d*) Ctenidia

20. Bohr effect is related with
(*a*) Reduced oxygen level in haemoglobin
(*b*) Reduced CO_2 level in blood
(*c*) Reduced carbon level in lymph
(*d*) Oxidised phosphorus level in blood

21. Stimulation of heart during stress condition by sympathetic nerve is result of
(*a*) Release of acetyl choline
(*b*) Release of adrenalin
(*c*) Inhibition of acetylcholine
(*d*) Inhibition of adrenalin

22. Shape of an eye is maintained by
(*a*) Aqueous humour
(*b*) Vitreous humour
(*c*) Conjunctiva
(*d*) All of these

23. Eyelashes are lubricated by
(*a*) Ceruminous glands
(*b*) Meibomian glands
(*c*) Lacrymal glands
(*d*) All of these

24. Main function of semicircular canals is
(*a*) Perceive and transmit sound vibrations
(*b*) Direct the animal towards the source of sound
(*c*) Perceive sound vibrations
(*d*) Perceive the motion of head

25. Organs of Ruffini are receptors of
(*a*) Cold (*b*) Pressure
(*c*) Heat (*d*) Touch

26. Broca's area and Wernicke centre of association area of cerebrum are connected with
(*a*) Memory (*b*) Voluntary action
(*c*) Blind spot (*d*) Both (a) and (b)

27. Structure connected with vision in rabbit is
(*a*) Corpus callosum
(*b*) Corpora quadrigeuina
(*c*) Corpus albicans
(*d*) Hippocampus

28. The depression in the retina of one eye which lodges only the cones is called
(*a*) Blind spot (*b*) Fovea centralis
(*c*) Fenestra rotunda (*d*) Red nuclei

29. For sound (good) reflex actions we require intact
(*a*) Spinal cord
(*b*) Cerebellum
(*c*) Hypothalamus
(*d*) Medulla oblongata

30. Which of the following cranial nerves of man are both sensory or motor?
(*a*) Optic (*b*) Vagus
(*c*) Olfactory (*d*) Trigeminal

31. Preganglionic sympathetic fibres are
(*a*) Adrenergic (*b*) Cholinergic
(*c*) Synergic (*d*) Hypergonic

32. Atoconium is found in
(*a*) Perilymph
(*b*) Haemolymph
(*c*) Synovial fluid
(*d*) Otolith membrane

33. When the direction of nerve impulse is reversed, the condition is called
(*a*) Axo-axonic
(*b*) Axo-dendritic
(*c*) Axo-axon dendritic
(*d*) None of the above

34. Ora serrata is
(*a*) Oral cavity of protochordates
(*b*) Anterior edge of sensory part of retina
(*c*) Gland present in oral cavity of frog
(*d*) A part of utriculus of ear

35. Arbor vitae is mainly composed of
(*a*) Gray matter (*b*) Neuroglial cells
(*c*) White matter (*d*) All of these

36. Secretion of which of the following is under neuro-secretory nerve axons?
(*a*) Pineal
(*b*) Adrenal cortex
(*c*) Anterior pituitary
(*d*) Posterior pituitary

37. Sympathetic nervous in mammals arise from
(*a*) Sacral region
(*b*) Cervical region
(*c*) Thoraco-lumbar region
(*d*) 3rd, 7th, 9th 10th cranial

38. Pacinial corpuscles in the skin of mammals aries from
(*a*) Type of gland
(*b*) Pain receptors
(*c*) Naked tactilereceptors
(*d*) Encapsulated pressure receptor

39. Sensation of stomach pain is due to
(*a*) Interoreceptors (*b*) Exteroreceptors
(*c*) Proprioreceptors (*d*) Teloreceptors

40. Blood dust present in the blood plasma is known as
(*a*) Blood platelets (*b*) Chylomicrons
(*c*) Haemoconia (*d*) Chyluria

41. Cardiac cycle in man takes about
(*a*) 0.5 seconds (*b*) 1.0 seconds
(*c*) 1.2 seconds (*d*) 0.8 seconds

42. The movement of neutrophils to site of inflammation is due to
(*a*) Release of hormone
(*b*) Chemotaxis
(*c*) Activity of antigens
(*d*) Activations of antigens

43. RBCs are generally destroyed in the liver, while WBCs are destroyed in
(*a*) Plasma
(*b*) Lymph
(*c*) Inside various cells of body
(*d*) Out side the blood stream

44. With increasing distance from heart, the elasticity as well as magnitude of muscular layer of arteries would
(*a*) Decreases
(*b*) Remains constant
(*c*) Slightly decrease
(*d*) Increase

45. Pulse pressure is difference of diastole and systole and is equal to ——— mm Hg.
(*a*) 40 (*b*) 30
(*c*) 10 (*d*) 80

46. Pacemaker is implanted when one of these is defective
(*a*) SA node (*b*) AV node
(*c*) Purkinje fibres (*d*) Bundle of lines

47. Thromboplastin is secreted by
(*a*) Platelets (*b*) Lymphoaytes
(*c*) Helper T cells (*d*) Mast cells

48. Circulation of blood was discovered by
(*a*) Darwin (*b*) Harvey
(*c*) Aristotle (*d*) Pasteur

49. RBCs in mammals have no nucleus because
(*a*) It has degenerated during development
(*b*) They do not have nucleus since early
(*c*) Nucleus is harmful for RBC
(*d*) Nucleus decreases surface area.

50. Hepatic portal system starts from
(*a*) Digestive system to liver
(*b*) Kidney to liver
(*c*) Liver to heart
(*d*) Liver to Kidney

51. The number of hormones secreted by anterior pituitary is
(*a*) 3 (*b*) 4
(*c*) 6 (*d*) 8

52. The reabsorption of water in the kidneys is under the control of hormone
(*a*) LH (*b*) ADH
(*c*) STH (*d*) ACTH

53. Parathormone is secreted by
(*a*) Parathyroid (*b*) Liver
(*c*) Pituitary (*d*) Hypothalamus

54. The calcium level in blood can be increased by administration of
(*a*) Glucagon (*b*) Thyroxine
(*c*) Parathormone (*d*) Calcitonin

55. The disease caused by hyposecretion of thyroxine is
(*a*) Goitre (*b*) Cretinism
(*c*) Acromegaly (*d*) Addison's disease

56. Gigantism and acromegaly result from hypersceretion of
(*a*) ADH (*b*) GH
(*c*) STH (*d*) None of these

57. Emergency gland of blood is
(*a*) Thymus (*b*) Testis
(*c*) Adrenal (*d*) Pituitary

58. Point out the odd one
(*a*) Corticotropin (*b*) Vasopressin
(*c*) Nonedrenaline (*d*) Prolactin

59. Receptors for protein hormones are located
(*a*) In cytoplasm
(*b*) On cell surface
(*c*) In nucleus
(*d*) On endoplasmic reticulum

60. Progesterone hormone is secreted by
(*a*) Corpus callosum (*b*) Corpus luteum
(*c*) Corpus albicans (*d*) Thymus

61. Secretin stimulates
(*a*) Lungs (*b*) Gall bladder
(*c*) Pancreas (*d*) Gastric glands

62. Parathormone induces
(*a*) Increase in serum calcium level
(*b*) Decrease in serum calcium level
(*c*) Increase in blood sugar level
(*d*) Decrease in blood sugar level

63. Which of the following is not a steroid hormone?
(*a*) Aldosterone (*b*) Androgen
(*c*) Estrogen (*d*) Thyroxine

64. Pituitary gland is under the control of
(*a*) Pineal gland (*b*) Thyroid gland
(*c*) Adrenal gland (*d*) Hypothalamus

65. Hormone responsible for urine concentration is
(*a*) Vasopressin (*b*) Pitocin
(*c*) Thyroxine (*d*) Renin

66. FSH is produced by
(*a*) Thyroid gland
(*b*) Posterior pituitary
(*c*) Anterior pituitary
(*d*) Gonads

67. Median eminence is a part of
(*a*) Neurohypophysis
(*b*) Pars inter media
(*c*) Adenohypophysis
(*d*) Pars distalis

68. At menopause, there is a rise in urinary excretion of
(*a*) STH (*b*) LTH
(*c*) MSH (*d*) FSH

69. The pituitary gland effect the urine formation through
(*a*) Thyroxine (*b*) ACTH
(*c*) Oxytocin (*d*) ADH

70. Disorders caused by hypersecretion of concerned hormones
(*a*) Gigantism and exophthalmic goitre
(*b*) Mongolism, and Cretinism
(*c*) Cretinism, diabetes mellitus and goitre
(*d*) Rickets and diabetes mellitus

71. Goitre is a pathological condition associated with
(*a*) Glucagon (*b*) Thyroxine
(*c*) Progesterone (*d*) Testosterone

72. Which disease is due to hyposecretion of an endocrine gland?
(*a*) Exophthalmic goitre
(*b*) Hypertension
(*c*) Gigantism
(*d*) Simple goitre

ANSWERS

1	2	3	4	5	6	7	8	9	10
(*d*)	(*d*)	(*c*)	(*b*)	(*b*)	(*d*)	(*a*)	(*b*)	(*b*)	(*b*)
11	**12**	**13**	**14**	**15**	**16**	**17**	**18**	**19**	**20**
(*d*)	(*a*)	(*d*)	(*b*)	(*d*)	(*c*)	(*d*)	(*c*)	(*b*)	(*a*)
21	**22**	**23**	**24**	**25**	**26**	**27**	**28**	**29**	**30**
(*b*)	(*b*)	(*d*)	(*d*)	(*c*)	(*d*)	(*b*)	(*b*)	(*a*)	(*b*)
31	**32**	**33**	**34**	**35**	**36**	**37**	**38**	**39**	**40**
(*b*)	(*b*)	(*a*)	(*b*)	(*c*)	(*d*)	(*c*)	(*d*)	(*a*)	(*b*)
41	**42**	**43**	**44**	**45**	**46**	**47**	**48**	**49**	**50**
(*d*)	(*c*)	(*b*)	(*b*)	(*d*)	(*a*)	(*a*)	(*b*)	(*d*)	(*b*)
51	**52**	**53**	**54**	**55**	**56**	**57**	**58**	**59**	**60**
(*c*)	(*b*)	(*a*)	(*c*)	(*b*)	(*b*)	(*c*)	(*c*)	(*b*)	(*b*)
61	**62**	**63**	**64**	**65**	**66**	**67**	**68**	**69**	**70**
(*c*)	(*a*)	(*d*)	(*d*)	(*a*)	(*c*)	(*a*)	(*d*)	(*d*)	(*a*)
71	**72**								
(*b*)	(*d*)								

First Aid and Behavioural Sciences

1. **Artificial Respiration of Resuscitation:** If a person has ceased to breath then immediately place him on his back, and press the top of head backwards so as to extend the head. Pull the chin forward to make a clear airway. If patient is still not breathing, perform mouth to mouth resuscitation immediately to saves lives.

   To do this open your mouth and take a deep breath. Close the patient's nostrils with yours fingers and then seal his mouth with your lips (keeping the head held back all the time). Blow into the patient's mouth until the chest rises, then remove your mouth and watch his chest deflate. Repeat this operation as long as is necessary at normal breath rate but give the first four blows as rapidly as possible.

2. **Bleeding:** Direct pressure on an open, clean wound will usually control the bleeding. This can be done by pressure by the fingers or hand, but if readily available use a sterile dressing with an adequate pad, and bandage firmly in position. A tourniquet should never be used.

3. **Burns:** If a limb is affected, immerse the part immediately in cold water to relieve the pain. Then cover the part (including any burned clothing) with a dry sterile dressing or freshy laundered material such as tea cloth. If burns are severe, treat for shock and get medical aid as quickly as possible. Do not use ointment or oil dressings.

4. **Choking:** This is usually caused by food or some foreign body, getting into the wind pipe and can often be cured by getting the patient to bend over and then thumping with the flat of the hand between the shoulder blades. A small child can be held upside down and thumped. If this does not work tickle the back of the throat with the finger tips in an attempt to make the patient cough or vomit. If neither method succeeds get medical help at once.

5. **Electric Shock:** If the patient is still in contact with electrical equipment and you cannot switch off the electricity, do not touch him unless protected by rubber roles or rubber gloves. Apply artificial respiration and treat for burns and shock as necessary.

6. **Poisoning:** If some one is thought to have swallowed poison, send for medical help at once, even if no effect have appeared have the poison container ready to show the doctor, corrosive acid or alkaline poison such as oceosote, ammonia, caustic soda, strong carbolic and oxalic and other acids will all burns or stain the lips and mouth. Give water at once but not an emetic.

   If the poison is known to be an acid such as oxalic, nitric or sulphuric acid, rinse the mouth with an alkali such as magnesia, chalk and water, whiting and water or even plaster from the ceiling. If the poison is an alkali such as ammonia or caustic soda, give an acid drink such as vinegar or lemon juice in water. Slow pulse, pallor, sleepiness and in some cases, pin point pupils are symptoms of an overdose of narcotics such as sleeping tablets. Give emetic and try to keep patient awake. For gas poisoning, give the patient fresh air, artificial respiration and warmth and send for doctor.

7. **Shock:** Serious burns or injury always cause shock. The patient is pale, his skins cold clammy, his breathing quick and irregular and his pulse fast. He should be lying down with head low and hips and legs raised a little, keep him warm and if he is conscious, give him a warm sweet drink but no stimulants. Keep him quiet and reassure him, shock can also occur after quite minor accidents.

8. **Foreign Bodies in the Eye:** Lifting the upper eyelid over the lower will often bring the foreign body on the lower lid from which it can be removed or making the eyes water by rubbing the other eye or blowing the nose will sometimes help. If the object is clearly visible the torn and moisturised edge of a piece of soft paper can be used to remove it. Never use tweezers and never rub the injured eye. If the object appears to be embedded in the eyeball leave it for the doctor to remove.

9. **Emetics:** If the poison taken is known to be corrosive, acid or alkaline or if there is any burning or staining of the mouth an emetics is dangerous and should not be given. For other poison give two tablespoonfuls of salt or a half tablespoonsful of mustard, in a half pint of water.

Mental Health and Drug Dependence

Mental health is an important component of health of a person. It is a balanced interaction of individual personality and emotions which help him to live happily with the society.

1. **Neuroses or Psychoneuroses:** Patient is not able to react normally to life situation. These are most common forms of psychiatric illness observed in practice. These are:

   (a) Anxiety (b) Hysteria (c) Obsession (d) Depression and Phobias

2. **Mental Handicap:** Mental subnormality is an impairment of intellectual function from birth or early age.

   Broadly it has two categories:

   (i) Mild mental retardation (I.Q. 50-70) this level is below normal (I.Q. 85 to 115) the child can be benefited by special training.

   (ii) Severe mental retardation (I.Q 49 or below) they cannot lead normal life and always require supervisons, support.

   Causes of mental retardation:

   1. Down syndrome (Mongolism)
   2. Hypothyroidism (cretins)
   3. Birth injury
   4. Infections of brain

   Warning signs of poor mental health

   1. Always worrying
   2. Inability to concentrate
   3. Losing temper easily and often
   4. Loss of sleep
   5. Wide fluctuation of mood
   6. Not happy in the company of people
   7. Phobia present (fear)
   8. Aches and pains without cause

Drug Dependence

It is the state of psychological and physical dependence on a drug with tendency to increase dose of drug *e.g.,* Heroin, morphine, L.S.D. addiction means physical dependence.

Depressants: Barbiturates, Mandrax, Heroin

Stimultants: cocaine, Amphetamine

Mood elevator (Psychedelics) Hashish, charas, Ganja

Treatment of Drug Addicts

The treatment is more successful if:

1. Person is taking less dose and only one drug.
2. Newly addicted and highly motivated addict.

3. No other stress or problem is present.
4. Good family cooperation is available.

Behavioural Sciences

1. **Family:** It is basic and most universal unit of society. Family is considered as basic unit in all health programmes and role of family in health and disease as follows:
   1. Child rearing
   2. Personality formation
   3. Socialisation
   4. Care of dependents
   5. Help in facing stress in every walk of life
   6. Genetic susceptibility to disease like haemophilia, overcrowding in family to communicable disease
2. **Role of Model Social Worker:**
   1. To assist doctor.
   2. To help patient.
   3. Guiding family members how to nurse the patient.
   4. Help in securing financial assistance from social welfare agencies.
   5. Directing community for getting better health facilities
3. **Relation of Behavioural Sciences to Medicine:** Understanding of these sciences helps health workers to add more information about causes of some diseases. For scientific treatment of patient knowledge of customs, habits, level of education, economic status, relation with members of family is necessary.
4. **Personal hygiene:** Personal hygiene is the science of preserving and promoting health mainly through individual effort. Three main points are to be observed in personal hygiene.

I. ***Temperature*****:**

1. Eating Nutrition: The diet should be adequate and balanced.
2. Personal comfort
3. Basic emotional needs
4. Clothing and shoes
5. Exercise and rest

II. Cleanliness of Body, Hair, Skin, Ears, Eyes, Nose, Teeth, Nails, Hands and feet.

Pharmacology

1. *Pharmacology* is the science which deals with sources, actions of drugs in disease and on health of living organism. A drug is defined as any substance used for diagnosis, cure or prevention of disease.
2. **Analgesics:** are drugs which decreases or eliminate pain *e.g.,* aspirin, morphine.
3. **Antiseptics and Disinfectants:** Drugs used for killing micro organisms or used to prevent growth of micro organisms on surface of body or in the environment or in articles used.
4. **Antibiotics:** Drugs are taken internally or applied locally to kill micro-organism.
5. **Anthelmintics:** They kill worm or make them loose so they do not get attached to body (piperazine, Mebendozole)
6. **Laxatives or Purgatives:** Drugs used for emptying (evacuating) bowels *e.g.,* milk of magnesia, castor oil.
7. **Expectorants:** (cough mixtures) Assist in coughing up of sputum and thereby relieve pain.
8. **Tonics:** Which are given to the patient with idea to strengthen the body and supplement deficiency of food.
9. **Forms of Drugs:** Whether drug is for internal and external use or local application. Normally used forms are:
   1. Pills, tablets, capsules, spansules (Internally).
   2. Ointment pastes, creams or jellies (externally).
   3. Liquid-mixtures (taken internally), Lotions, liniments (externally) suspension and emulsion both internally as well as externally.
   4. Injectable - powder with distilled water, liquids in ampoules and vials.
      Ampoule - usually single
      vial - single or multidose

5. Powders.
6. Enema preparation suppository per rectum.

9. Routes for administration of drugs:

Routes for Administration of Drugs

- Entral (through mouth)
  - Oral
    - Subligual
    - Swallowing tablets
- Parential (without mouth)
  - Intradermal
  - Subcutanous
  - Intra muscular
  - Intra venous
  - Intra articular

10. Major characterstic of drugs:

1. *Therapeutic effect*: This is the ability to act selectively on the part of body or disease producing agents and restore normal function.
2. *Side effects*: In addition to useful effect drug may also produce undesirable effect (oral pills cause nausea, vomitting).
3. *Allergic effect*: unexpected reaction *e.g.*, aspirin may cause asthma *etc*.

11. Habituation: There is tendency to take drug and increase dose *e.g.* smoking cigarettes psychological dependence is present.

12. Addiction: Tendency to increase dose of drug and physical and psychological dependence on effect of drug. When a person is addicted he tries to get drug by any mean and if patient does not get drug, withdrawal symptoms are produced, examples Heroin, Marphine L.S.D., Bhang, Ganja, Charas *etc*.

Nutrition and Health

Nutrition may be defined as the science of food and its relationship to health. It is concerned primarily with the part played by nutrients in body growth, development and maintenance. The word *nutrient* or "food factor" is used for specific dietary constituents such as proteins, vitamins and minerals. *Dietetics* is the practical application of the principles of nutrition means "maintaining a nutritional status that enables us to grow well and enjoy good health". The subject of nutrition is very extensive.

CLASSIFICATION OF FOODS

There are many basis of classifying foods:

(a) Classification by origin:

1. Foods of animal origin
2. Foods of vegetable origin

(b) Classification by chemical composition:

1. Proteins
2. Fats
3. Carbohydrates
4. Vitamins
5. Minerals

(c) Classification by predominant function.

1. Body **building foods** e.g., milk, meat, poultry, fish, eggs, pulses, groundnuts, etc.
2. **Energy-** giving foods, e.g. cereals, sugars, roots and tubers, fats and oils.
3. **Protective foods**, e.g., vegetables, fruits, milk.

(d) Classification by nutritive value:

1. Cereals and millets
2. Pulses (legumes)
3. Vegetables
4. Nuts and oilseeds
5. Fruits
6. Animal foods
7. Fats and oils
8. Sugar and jaggery
9. Condiments and spices
10. Miscellaneous foods.

NUTRIENTS

Nutrients are organic and inorganic complexes contained in food. There are about 50 different nutrients which are normally supplied through the foods we eat. Each nutrient has specific functions in the body. Most natural foods contain more than one nutrient. These may be divided into:

(i) Macronutrients: These are proteins, fats and carbohydrates which are often called "proximate principles" because they form the main bulk of food. In the Indian dietary, they contribute to the total energy intake in the following proportions.

Proteins	7 to 15 per cent
Fats	10 to 30 per cent
Carbohydrates	65 to 80 per cent

(ii) Micronutrients: These are vitamins and minerals. They are called micronutrients because they are required in small amounts which may vary from a fraction of a milligram to several grams.

PROTEINS

Proteins are complex organic nitrogenous compounds. They are composed of carbon, hydrogen, oxygen, nitrogen and sulphur in varying amounts. Some proteins also contain phosphorus and iron and occasionally other elements. Proteins constitute about 20 per cent of the body weight in an adult.

Essential Amino Acids

Proteins are made up of smaller units, called amino acids. Some 24 amino acids are stated to be needed by the human body, of which 9 are called "essential" because the body cannot synthesize them in amounts corresponding to its needs, and therefore, they must be obtained from dietary proteins. Non-essential amino acids include arginine, asparaginic acid, serine, glutamic acid, proline and glycine. Both essential and non- essential amino acids are needed for synthesis of tissue proteins, the former must be supplied through diet, whereas the latter can be synthesized by the body provided other building blocks are present.

Some of the essential amino acids have important biological functions, e.g. formation of niacin from tryptophan; the action of methionine as a donor of methyl groups for the synthesis of choline, folates and nucleic acids. There is evidence the cystine and tyrosine are essential for premature babies. Now tissues cannot be formed unless all the essential amino acids (EAA) are present in the diet.

Functions: Proteins are needed by the body for *(a)* body building—this component is small component is small compared with the maintenance component, except in the very young child and infant; *(b)* repair and maintenance of body tissues; *(c)* maintenance of osmotic pressure; and *(d)* synthesis of certain substances like antibodies, plasma proteins, haemoglobin, enzymes, hormones and coagulation factors. Proteins are connected with the immune mechanism of the body.

Sources: Humans obtain protein from main dietary sources; *(a) Animal sources:* Proteins of animal origin are found in milk, meat, eggs, cheese, fish and fowl. These proteins contain all the essential amino acids (EAA) in adequate amounts. Egg proteins are considered to be the best among food proteins because of their high biological value and digestibility. They are used in nutrition studies as a "reference protein" *(b) Vegetable sources:* Vegetable proteins are found in pulses (legumes), cereals, beans, nuts, oil-seed cakes, etc. They are poor in EAA. In developing countries such as India, cereals and pulses are the main sources of dietary protein because they are cheap, easily available and consumed in bulk.

FATS

Fats are solid at 20º C they contains unsaturated fatty acid. if they are liquid at that temperature they are called oil. Fats and oils are concentrated sources of energy. They are classified as:

(a) Simple lipids, e.g., triglycerides
(b) Compound lipids, e.g. phospholipids
(c) Derived lipids, e.g., cholesterol

The human body can synthesize triglycerides and cholesterol endogenously. Most of the body fat (99 per cent) in the adipose tissue is in the form of triglycerides.

Fatty acids

Fats yield fatty acids and glycerol on hydrolysis. Fatty acids are divided into **saturated** fatty acids such as lauric palmitic and steric acids, and **unsaturated** fatty acids which are further divided into monounsaturated (e.g. oleic acid) and polyunsaturated fatty acids (e.g., linoleic acid).

The polyunsaturated fatty acids are mostly found in vegetable oils, and the saturated fatty acids mainly in animal fats.

Essential fatty acids

Essential fatty acids are those that cannot be synthesized by humans. They can be derived only from food. The most important essential fatty acid (EFA) is *linoleic acid,* which serves as a basis for the production of other essential fatty acids.

Sources: The dietary sources of fats may be classified as:

(a) *Animal fats :* The major sources of animal fats are ghee, butter, milk, cheese, eggs, and fat of meat and fish. Animal fats with few exceptions like cod liver oil and sardine oil are mostly saturated fats.

(b) *Vegetable fats :* Some plants store fat in their seeds, e.g. groundnut, mustard, sesame, coconut, etc.

(c) *Other sources :* Small quantities of fat (invisible fat) are found in most other foods such as cereals, pulses, nuts and vegetables.

Functions: Fats have always been equated with calories. They are high energy foods, providing as much as 9 kcal for every gram. Fats in the body support viscera such as heart, kidney and intestine; and fat beneath the skin provides insulation against cold.

Fats and disease:

(a) *Obesity :* A diet,, rich in fat, can pose a threat to human health by encouraging obesity.

(b) *Phrenoderma :* Deficiency of essential fatty acids in the diet is associated with rough and dry skin, a condition known as phrenoderma or "toad skin".

(c) *Coronary heart disease :* High fat intake (i.e. dietary fat representing 40 per cent or over of the energy supply and containing a high proportion of saturated fats) has been identified as a major risk factor for CHD.

(d) *Cancer :* In recent years, there has been some evidence that diets high in fat increase the risk of colon cancer and breast cancer.

CARBOHYDRATE

The major component of food is carbohydrate, which is the main source of energy, providing 4 kcals per gram. Carbohydrate is also essential for the oxidation of fats and for the synthesis of certain non-essential amino acids. There are three main sources of carbohydrate, viz, starches, sugar and cellulose. *Starch* is basic to the human diet. It is found in abundance in cereals, roots and tubers. *Sugars* comprise monosaccharides (glucose, fructose and galactose) and disaccharides (Sucrose, lactose and maltoses.) *Cellulose* which is the indigestible component of carbohydrate with scarcely any nutritive value, contributes to dietary fibre.

VITAMINS

Vitamins are a class of organic compounds categorized as essential nutrients. They are required by the body in very small amounts. They fall in the category of micronutrients. Vitamins do not yield energy but enable the body to use other nutrients. Since the body is generally unable to synthesize them (at least in sufficient amounts) they must be provided by food. A well balanced diet supplies in most instances the vitamin needs of a healthy person. Vitamins are divided into two groups : *(a)* fat soluble vitamins, viz vitamins A, D, E and K, and *(b)* water soluble vitamins, viz vitamins of the B-group and vitamin C.

Vitamin A

"Vitamin A" covers both a pre-formed vitamin, retinol and a pro-*vitamin*, beta *carotene*, some of *which is converted* to *retinol in the* intestinal *mucosa*.

Functions : Vitamin *A participates in many bodily functions* :

(a) It is indispensable for normal vision. It contributes to the production of retinal pigments which are needed for vision in dim light.

(b) It is necessary for maintaining the integrity and the normal functioning of glandular and epithelial tissue which lines intestinal, respiratory and urinary tracts as well as the skin and eyes.

(c) It supports growth especially skeletal growth.

Sources: Vitamin A is widely distributed in animal and plant foods—in animal foods as pre-formed vitamin A (retinol), and in plant foods as pro-vitamins (carotenes).

(a) *Animal foods :* Foods rich in retinol are liver, eggs, butter, cheese, whole milk, fish and meat. Fish liver oils are the richest natural sources of retinol but they are generally used as nutritional supplements rather than as food sources.

(b) *Plant foods :* The cheapest source of vitamin A is green leafy vegetables such as spinach and amaranth which are found in great abundance in nature throughout the year. The darker the green leaves, the higher its carotene content.

(c) *Fortified foods :* Foods fortified with vitamin A (e.g., Vanaspati, margarine, milk) can be an important source.

Deficiency:—

(a) *Nightblindness :* It is due to Lack of vitamin A, first causes nightblindness or inability to see in dim light. Nightblindness is due to impairment in dark adaptation.

(b) *Conjunctival xerosis :* This is the first clinical sign of vitamin A deficiency. The conjuctiva becomes dry and non- wettable instead of looking smooth and shiny.

(c) *Bitot's spots :* Bitot's spots are triangular, pearly- white or yellowish, foamy spots on the bulbar conjunctiva on either side of the cornea.

(d) *Corneal xerosis :* This stage is particularly serious. The cornea appears dull, dry and non-wettable and eventually opaque.

(e) *Keralomakia :* Liquification of cornea.

(f) Extra occular manifestations.

Treatment : Vitamin A deficiency should be treated urgently. Nearly all of the early stages of xerophthalmia can be reversed by administration of a massive dose orally on two successive days.

Vitamin D

The nutritionally important forms of Vitamin D in man are Calciferol (Vitamin D_2) and Cholecalciferol (Vitamin D_3). Calciferol may be derived by irradiation of the plant sterol, ergosterol. Cholecalciferol is the naturally occurring (preformed) vitamin D which is found in animal fats and fish liver oils. 'It is also derived from exposure to UV rays of the sunlight which convert the cholesterol in the skin to vitamin D.

Major advances have been made in recent years in our understanding of the metabolism of vitamin D in the body. It has been proposed that vitamin D should be regarded as kidney hormone because it does not meet the classic definition of a vitamin, that is, a substance which must be obtained by dietary means because of a lack of capacity in the human body to synthesize it. In fact vitamin D_3 is not a dietary requirement at all in conditions of adequate sunlight. It can be synthesized in the body in adequate amounts by simple exposure to sunlight even for 5 minutes per day.

Functions: The functions of vitamin D are summarised as below.

Intestine:	Promotes intestinal absorption of calcium and phosphorus
Bone:	Stimulates normal mineralization. Enhances bone resorption. Affects collagen maturation.
Kidney:	Increases tubular reabsorption of phosphate. Variable effect on reabsorption of calcium.

Daily Requirements: Pregnancy 100 mcg. Adults-2.5 mcg, Infants-5 mcg. (mcg = microgram)

Sources: Vitamin D is unique because it is derived both from sunlight and foods.

(a) **Sunlight :** Vitamin D is synthesized by the body by the action of UV rays. Dark skinned races such as Negroes also suffer from this disadvantage because black skin can filter off

up to 95 per cent of UV rays. *(b)* **Foods** : Vitamin D occurs only in foods of animal origin. Liver, egg yolk, butter and cheese and some species of fish contain useful amounts.

Deficiency

1. Rickets : Vitamin D deficiency leads to *rickets,* which is usually observed in young children between the age of six months and two years. There is reduced calcification of growing bones, The disease is characterised by growth failure, bone deformity, muscular hypotonia, tetany and convulsions due to hypo- calcemia.
2. Osteomalacia : In adults, vitamin D deficiency may result in *osteomalacia* which occurs mainly in women, especially during pregnancy and lactation when requirements of vitamin D are increased.

Both rickets and osteomalacia are frequently reported in India, although they do not appear to be a problem of public health importance.

Prevention: Prevention measures include *(a)* educating parents to expose their children regularly to sunshine; *(b)* periodic dosing (prophylaxis) of young children with vitamin D.

Vitamin E (Tocoferol)

Vitamin E is the generic name for a group of closely related and naturally occurring fat soluble compounds, the tocopherols. Of these alpha-tocopherol is biologically the most potent. Vitamin E is widely distributed in foods. By far the richest sources are vegetable oils, cotton - seed, sunflower seed, egg yolk and butter. Foods rich in polyunsaturated fatty acids are also rich in vitamin E.

Vitamin K

Vitamin K occurs in at least two major forms- Vitamin K_1 and Vitamin K_2. Vitamin K_1 is found mainly in fresh green vegetables particularly dark green ones, and in some fruits. Vitamin K_2 is synthesized by the intestinal bacteria, which usually provide an adequate supply in man. Long term administration of antibiotic doses for more than a week may temporarily suppress the normal intestinal flora, (a source of vitamin K_2) and may cause a deficiency of vitamin K. Vitamin K is stored in the liver.

The role of vitamin K is to stimulate the production and/or the release of certain coagulation factors. In vitamin K deficiency, the prothrombin content of blood is markedly decreased and the blood clotting time is considerably prolonged.

Thiamine

Thiamine (Vitamin B_1) is a water-soluble vitamin. It is essential for the utilization of carbohydrates. In thiamine deficiency, there is accumulation of pyruvic and lactic acids in the tissues and body fluids.

Sources: Thiamine occurs in all natural foods, although in small amounts. Important sources are: whole grain cereals, wheat, gram, yeast, pulses, oilseeds and nuts, especially groundnut.

Deficiency: The two principal deficiency diseases are beriberi and Wernick's encephalopathy.

Prevention: Beriberi can be eliminated by educating people to eat well balanced, mixed diets containing thiamine-rich foods (e.g., paraboiled and undermilled rice).

Riboflavin

Riboflavin (Vitamin B_2) is a member of the B-group vitamins. It has a fundamental role in cellular oxidation. It is a co-factor in a number of enzymes involved in energy metabolism.

Sources: Its richest natural sources are milk, eggs, liver, kidney and green leafy vegetables. Meat and fish contain small amounts.

Deficiency: Deficiency of riboflavin, or ariboflavinosis is widespread in India particularly in populations where rice is the staple. The most common lesion associated with riboflavin deficiency is angular stomatitis, which occurs frequently in malnourished children and its prevalence is used as an index of the state of nutrition in the children.

Niacin

Niacin or nicotinic acid is essential for the metabolism of carbohydrate, fat and protein. It is also essential for the normal functioning of the skin, intestinal and nervous systems.

Sources: Foods rich in niacin and/or tryptophan are liver, kidney, meat, poultry, fish, legumes and ground nut.

Deficiency: Niacin deficiency results in pellagra.

Disease characterised by : *(i)* Diarrhoea, *(ii)* Dermitis, *(iii)* Dementia.

Prevention: Pellagra is preventable disease. A good mixed diet containing milk and/ or meat is universally regarded as an essential part of prevention and treatment.

Vitamin B_6

Pyridoxine (vitamin B_6) exists in three forms : pyridoxine, pyridoxal and pyridoxamine. It plays an important role in the metabolism of amino acids, fats, and carbohydrate. It is widely distributed in foods, e.g. milk, liver, meat, egg yolk, fish, whole grain cereals, legumes and vegetables.

Pantothenic Acid

There is a long standing evidence for a relation between pantothenic acid and adrenal cortical function.

Folate

The recommended name is folate, alternative name is folacin and the usual pharmaceutical preparation is folic acid.

Folic acid occurs in food in two forms : Free folates and bound folates. It is also needed for the normal development of blood cells in the marrow.

Sources: The name comes from the latin folia (=leaf) but foods such as liver, meat, dairy products, eggs, milk, fruits and cereals are as good dietary sources as leafy vegetables.

Deficiency: Folate deficiency may occur simply from a poor diet. Its deficiency is common in pregnancy and lactation.

Vitamin B_{12}

Its normal requirement in adult-1 mcg, pregnant.-1.5 mcg, and infants-2 mcg. Vitamin B_{12} is complex organometallic compound with a cobalt atom. The preparation which is therapeutically used is cyanocobalamine. Vitamin B_{12} cooperates with folate in the synthesis of DNA , so deficiency of either leads to megaloblastosis. Vitamin B_{12} has a separate biochemical role, unrelated to folate, in synthesis of fatty acids in myelin.

Sources: Good sources are liver, kidney, meat, fish, milk and cheese. Vitamin B_{12} is not found in foods of vegetable origin. It is also synthesized by bacteria in colon.

Deficiency: Vitamin B_{12} deficiency is associated with megaloblastic anaemia (pernicious anaemia), demyelinating neurological lesions in the spinal cord and infertility (in animal species). Dietary deficiency of B_{12} may arise in subjects who are strict vegetarians and eat no animal products. At the present time, there is little evidence that vitamin B_{12} deficiency anaemia represents an important public health problem.

Vitamin C

Vitamin C (ascorbic acid) is a water soluble vitamin. It is the most sensitive to heat. Man, monkey and guinea pig are perhaps the only species known to require vitamin C in their diet.

Functions: Vitamin C plays an important role in tissue oxidation. It is needed for the formation of collagen, which accounts for 25 per cent of total body protein. Collagen provides a supporting matrix for the blood vessels and connective tissue and for bones and cartilage. It inhibits nitrosamine formation by the intestinal mucosa. Other claims such as prevention of common cold and protection against infections are not substantiated.

Sources: The main dietary sources of vitamin C are fresh fruits and green leafy vegetables. Traces of vitamin C occur in fresh meat and fish but scarcely any in cereals. Germinating pulses contain good amounts. Roots and tubers contain small amounts. Amla or the Indian gooseberry is one of the richest sources of vitamin C both in the fresh as well as in the dry condition.

Deficiency: Deficiency of vitamin C results in scurvy.

MINERALS

More that 50 chemical elements are found in the human body, which are required for growth, repair and regulation of vital body functions. These can be divided into three major groups: *(a) Major minerals:* These include calcium, phosphorus, sodium, potassium and magnesium. *(b) Trace elements:* These are elements required by the body in quantities of less than a few milligrams per day e.g. iron, iodine, fluorine, zinc, copper, cobalt, chromium, manganese, molybdenum, selenium, nickel, tin, silicon and vanadium. Many more have been added to the list in the last few years. *(c) Trace contaminants with no known function:* These include lead, mercury, barium, boron and aluminium.

Calcium

Calcium is a major mineral element of the body. It constitutes 1.5 -2 per cent of the body weight of an adult human. An average adult body contains about 1200g of calcium of which over 98 per cent is found in the bones.

Functions: Ionized calcium in the plasma has many vital functions including formation of bones and teeth, coagulation of blood, contraction of muscles, cardiac action, milk production, relay of electrical and chemical messages that arrive at a cell's surface membrane to the biochemical machinery within the cell, keeping the membranes of cells intact and in the metabolism of enzymes and hormones.

Sources: The best sources of calcium are milk and milk products, eggs and fish. The cheapest dietary sources are green leafy vegetables, cereals and millets.

Deficiency: No clear-cut disease due to calcium deficiency has ever been observed, even under conditions of low intake. It has been detectable abnormalities. An intermediate stage of "latent iron deficiency" that is, iron stores are exhausted, but anaemia has not occurred as yet.

Phosphorus

Phosphorus is essential for the formation of bones and teeth. It plays an important roles in all metabolisms. An adult human body contains about 400-700 g of phosphorus as phosphates, most of this occurs in bones and teeth.

Sodium

Sodium is found in all body fluids. The adult human body contains about 100g of sodium ion. Sodium occurs in many foods, and is also added to food during cooking in the form of sodium chloride. Sodium is lost from the body through urine and sweat; that which is passed out in urine is regulated by the kidney but that which is lost by sweating is not controlled. Depletion of sodium chloride causes muscular cramps.

Potassium

The adult human body contains about 250 g of potassium. Potassium occurs widely in foodstuffs, so there is little likelihood of its deficiency. The daily requirement of potassium has not been determined accurately.

Magnesium

Magnesium is a constituent of bones, and is present in all body cells. Human adult body contains about 25g of magnesium of which about half is found in the skeleton. The principal clinical features attributed to magnesium deficiency are irritability, tetany, hyperreflexia and occasionally hyporeflexia.

Iron

Iron is of great importance in human nutrition. The adult human body contains between 3-4 g of iron, of which about 60-70 per cent present in the blood (Hb iron) as circulating iron, and the rest (1 to 1.5 g) as storage iron. Each gram of haemoglobin contains about 3.34 mg of iron.

Functions: Iron is necessary for many functions in the body including formation of haemoglobin, brain development and function, regulation of body temperature, muscle activity, and catecholamine metabolism. Lack of iron directly affects the immune system; it diminishes the number of T cells and the production of antibodies. Besides haemoglobin, iron is a component of myoglobin, the cytochromes catalase and certain enzyme systems. Iron is essential for binding oxygen to the blood cells. The central function of iron is "oxygen transport" and cell respiration.

Fluorine

Fluorine is the most abundant element in nature. Being so highly reactive, it is never found in its elemental gaseous form, but only in combined form. About 98 per cent of the fluoride in the body is found in bones and teeth. Fluorine is essential for the normal mineralization of bones and formation of dental enamel.

Sources: The principal sources of fluorine available to man are *(a) Drinking water :* The major source of fluorine to man is drinking water. In most parts of India, the fluoride content of drinking water is about 0.5 mg/L, but in fluorosis-endemic areas, it may be as high as 3 to 12 mg/L *(b) Foods :* Fluorides occur in traces in many foods, but some foods such as sea fish, cheese and tea are reported to rich in fluorides.

Deficiency/ Excess: Fluorine is often called a two edged sword. Prolonged ingestion of fluorides through drinking water in excess of the daily requirement is associated with dental and skeletal fluorosis; and inadequate intake with dental caries. The use of fluoride is recognized as the most effective means available for the prevention of dental caries.

Other Trace Elements

Zinc

Zinc is a component of many enzymes. It is active in the metabolism of glucosides and proteins, and is required for the synthesis of insulin by the pancreas and for the immunity function.

Copper

The amount of copper in an adult body is estimated to between 100-150 mg. Copper is widely distributed in nature. Even poor diets provide enough copper for human needs. Deficiency or excess of this element is very rare. Hypocupremia occurs in patients with nephrosis, Wilson's disease and protein- energy malnutrition and in infants fed for long periods exclusively on cow's milk. Neutropenia is the best documented abnormality of copper deficiency.

Cobalt

The only established function of cobalt in the human is as a part of the vitamin B_{12} molecule, which must be ingested preformed. It is suggested that cobalt may be necessary for the first stage of hormone production. i.e. capture of iodine by the gland. Cobalt may interact with iodine and affect its utilization.

Chromium

Total body content of chromium is small, less then 6 mg. Current interest in chromium is based on the occurrence of unusual glucose tolerance curves that are responsive to chromium. Thus there is suggestive evidence that chromium plays a role in relation to carbohydrate and insulin function.

NUTRITIONAL REQUIREMENTS

The science of human nutrition is mainly concerned with defining the nutritional requirements for the promotion, protection and maintenance of health in all groups of the population. Such knowledge is necessary in order to assess the nutritional adequacy of diets for growth of infants, children and adolescents, and for maintenance of health in adults of both sexes and during pregnancy and lactation in women. In this context, a variety of terms have been used to define the amount of nutrients needed by the body such as : *optimum requirements, minimum requirements, recommended intakes or allowances, and safe level of intake,* Of these, the term "recommended daily intake" or allowance (RDA) has been widely accepted.

RECOMMENDED DAILY ALLOWANCE (RDA)

The term "recommended daily intake" is defined as the amounts of nutrient sufficient for the maintenance of health in nearly all people. They are reference standards of nutritional intakes. For all nutrients, except energy, estimates of allowances are based on the defined "minimum requirement" plus a safety margin, often generous, for individual variation and stresses of everyday life. In some cases, this has entailed adding to the observed mean, twice the standard deviation of the distribution of minimum requirement for the subjects measured. This value will more than meet the requirement of 97.5 per cent of population. In fact for many individuals this level will be in excess of their needs. It is considered that such excessive consumption of nutrients is not injurious to health. It is important to emphasize that the recommended intake of nutrients represents does not apply to sick people. The recommended intake of nutrients represents value judgements based on the existing knowledge of nutritional sciences; these will be elaborated in this section.

The recommendation is estimated to meet the requirement of practically all healthy people. The recommendation is for the intake over several days.

1. ENERGY

Energy is a prime requisite for body function and growth. When a world's intake of food falls below a standard reference, growth slows, and if low levels of intake persist, adult stature will be reduced. Similarly, if adults fail to meet their food requirements they lose weight. This may lead to reduced ability to work, less resistant to infection. This underlines the need for an adequate intake of food which is the source of all energy.

Energy requirements :

Broadly, the total energy requirement of an individual is made up of three components:

(a) energy required for basal metabolism. This is about 1 kcal/ hour for every kg of body weight for an adult;

(b) energy required for daily activities such as walking, sitting, standing, dressing, climbing stairs, etc; and

(c) energy expenditure for occupational work. This is further classified as light work (an office clerk), moderate work and heavy work (manual physical labour).

The first component is nearly the same for all individuals. It is the latter two components that vary depending upon the types of activities. Procedures for calculating total energy expenditure are given in the WHO Expert Committee Report on Energy and protein Requirements.

Factors affecting energy requirement:

Energy requirements vary from one person to another depending upon inter-related variables acting in a complex way, such as age, sex, working condition, body composition, physical activity, physiological state etc. All these factors lead to differences in food intake.

Energy requirements have been laid down by various expert groups of FAO and WHO. It has becomes customary for countries to lay down their own standards. Thus there are British standards, American standards, Canadian standards, etc.

2. PROTEIN

Protein requirements vary from individual to individual. Apart from age, sex and other physiological variables, factors like infection worm infestation, emotional disturbances and stress situations can affect a person's protein requirement.

Protein: (i) Essential Amino Acids, (ii) Non-essential Amino Acids.

Assessment of Protein

(a) **Protein Quality:** The quality of a protein is assessed by comparison to the "reference protein" which is usually egg protein. Two methods of assessment of protein quality need mention :

(i) ***Amino acid score:*** It is a measure of the concentration of each essential amino acid in the test protein expressed as a percentage of that amino acid in the reference protein.

Amino acid score =

$$\frac{\text{No. of mg of one amino acid per g of protein}}{\text{No. of mg of the same amino acid per g of egg protein}} \times 100$$

The amino acid (or chemical) score is somewhere between 50 and 60 for starches, and 70 and 80 for animal foods.

(ii) ***Net protein utilization (NPU):*** It is a product of digestibility coefficient and biological value divided by 100. The NPU gives a more complete expression of protein quality than the amino acid score. It is a biological method that requires special laboratory facilities.

$$\text{NPU} = \frac{\text{Nitrogen retained by the body}}{\text{Nitrogen intake}} \times 100$$

In calculating protein quality, 1 gram of protein is assumed to be equivalent to 6.25 g of N.

The protein requirement varies with the NPU of dietary protein. If the NPU is low, the protein requirement is high and vice versa.

(b) **Protein Quantity:** The protein content of many Indian foods has been determined and published in food composition tables. One way of evaluating foods as source of protein is to determine what per cent of their energy value is supplied by their protein content. This is know as Protein -Energy Ratio (PE ratio or percentage).

$$\text{PE per cent} = \frac{\text{Energy from protein}}{\text{Total energy in diet}} \times 100$$

This concept is useful because in many population groups adequate diet is not consumed to meet energy needs, resulting in energy deficits.

Dietary intakes: It is customary to express requirement in terms of grams per kg of body weight. This principle applies to all age groups, although absolute additions in units of grams of protein per day are made for pregnancy and lactation.

3. FAT

The daily requirement of fat is not known with certainty. During infancy, fats contribute to a little over 50 per cent of the total energy intake. This scales down to about 20 per cent in adulthood. The requirement of essential fatty acids ranges from 3 per cent energy intake to 5.7 per cent of energy intake in young children.

4. CARBOHYDRATE

The recommended intake of carbohydrate in balanced diets is between 50 to 70 per cent of total energy intake.

BALANCED DIET

A diet may be defined as the kinds of food on which a person or group lives. A balanced diet is defined as one which contains a variety of foods in such quantities and proportions that the need for energy, amino acids, vitamins, minerals, fats, carbohydrate and other nutrients is adequately met for maintaining health, vitality and general well- being and also makes a small provision for extra nutrients to withstand short duration of leanness. A balanced diet has become an accepted means to safeguard a population from nutritional deficiencies.

In constructing balanced diet, the following principles should be borne in mind; *(a)* First and foremost, the daily requirement of protein should be met. This amounts to 15-20 per cent of the daily energy intake. *(b)* Next comes the fat requirement, which should be limited to 20-30 per cent of the daily energy intake *(c)* Carbohydrates rich in natural fibre should constitute the remaining food energy. The requirements of micronutrients should be met.

The dietary pattern varies widely in different parts of the world. It is generally developed on the basis of kinds of food produced (or imported) depending upon the climatic conditions of the region, economic capacity, religion, customs, taboos, tastes and habits of the people.

DIETARY GOALS

All countries should develop a national nutrition and food policy setting out "dietary goals" for achievement. The dietary goals ("prudent diet") recommended by the various Expert Committees of WHO are as below:

(a) dietary Ist should be limited to approximately 20-30 per cent of total daily intake;

(b) saturated fats should contribute no more than 10 per cent of the total energy intake; unsaturated vegetable oils should be substituted for the remaining fat requirement;

(c) excessive consumption of refined carbohydrate should be avoided; some amount of carbohydrate rich in natural fibre should be taken;

(d) sources rich in energy such as fats and alcohol should be restricted;

(e) salt intake should be reduced to an average of not more than 5 g per day; (salt intake is more in tropical countries. In India it averages 15 g per day);

(f) protein should account for approximately 15-20% of the daily intake;

(g) junk foods such as colas, ketchups and other foods that supply empty calories should be reduced.

There may be conditions under which the above recommendations for daily food intake do not apply. For example, diet should be adapted to the special needs of growth, pregnancy, lactation, physical activity, and medical disorders (e.g., diabetes).

NUTRITIONAL PROBLEMS IN PUBLIC HEALTH

There are many nutritional problems which affect vast segments of our population. The major ones which deserve special mention are highlighted:

1. Low birth weight

Low birth weight (i.e., birth weight less than 2500g) is a major public health problem in many developing countries. About 30 per cent of babies born in India are LBW as compared to 4 per cent in some developed countries. In countries where the proportion of LBW is high the majority are suffering from foetal growth retardation. In countries where the proportion of LBW infants is low, most of them are pre-term. Although we do not know all the causes of LBW, maternal malnutrition and anaemia appear to be significant risk factors in its occurrence. Among the other causes of LBW are hard physical labour during pregnancy, and illnesses especially infections. Short maternal stature, very young age, high parity, smoking, close birth intervals are all associated factors. All these factors are interrelated.

The proportion of infants born with LBW has been selected as one of the nutritional indicators for monitoring progress towards Health for All by the year 2000. The goal of the National Health Policy is to reduce the incidence of LBW infants to about 10 per cent by the year 2000.

2. Protein Energy Malnutrition (PEM)

Protein energy malnutrition (PEM) has been identified as a major health and nutrition problem in India. It occurs particularly in weaklings and children in the first years of life. It is not only an important cause of childhood morbidity and mortality, but leads also to permanent impairment of physical and possibly, of mental growth of those who survive. The current concept of PEM is that its clinical forms - Kwashiorkor and Marasmus - are two different clinical pictures at opposite poles of a single continuum.

The incidence of PEM in India in preschool age children is 1-2 per cent. The great majority of cases of PEM, nearly 80 per cent, are the "intermediate" ones, that is the mild and moderate cases which frequently go unrecognized. The problem exists in all the States and that nutritional marasmus is more frequent than kwashiorkor.

Early Detection of PEM

The first indicator of PEM is under -weight for age. The most practical method to detect this, which can be employed even by field health workers, is to maintain growth charts. These charts indicate at a glance whether the child is gaining or losing weight.

Preventive Measures: There is no simple solution to the problem of PEM. Many types of actions are necessary. The following is adapted from the 8th FAO/WHO Expert Committee on Nutrition for the prevention of PEM in the community:

(a) Health Promotion:

1. Measures directed to pregnant and lactating women (education, distribution of supplements)
2. Promotion of breast feeding.
3. Development of low cost weaning foods: the child should be made to eat more food at frequent intervals.
4. Measures to improve family diet
5. Nutrition education- Promotion of correct feeding practices.

(b) Specific Protection

1. The child's diet must contain protein and energy rich foods. Milk, eggs, fresh fruits should be given if possible.
2. Immunization
3. Food fortification

(c) Early Diagnosis and Treatment:

1. Periodic surveillance
2. Early diagnosis of any lag in growth
3. Early diagnosis and treatment of infections and diarrhoea.
4. Development of programmes for early rehydration of children with diarrhoea.
5. Development of supplementary feeding programmes during epidemics.

(d) Rehabilitation :

1. Nutritional rehabilitation services
2. Hospital treatment
3. Follow- up care

3. Xerophthalmia

Xerophthalmia (dry eye) refers to all the ocular manifestations of vitamin A deficiency in man. It is the most widespread and serious nutritional disorder leading to blindness particularly in South- East Asia.

Xerophthalmia is most common in children aged 1-3 years, and is often related to weaning. The younger the child, the more severe the disease. It is often associated with PEM. Mortality is often high in this age group. The victims belong to the poorest families. Associated risk factors include ignorance, faulty feeding practices and infection paticularly diarrhoea and measles which often precipitate xerophthalmia. In some countries, "epidemics" of xerophthalmia have occurred in association with food donation programmes involving skimmed milk, which is totally devoid of vitamin A.

The States badly affected are the southern and eastern States of India notably Andhra, Tamil Nadu, Karnataka, Bihar and West Bengal. These are predominantly rice-eating States and rice is devoid of carotene. The North Indian States have relatively few cases of xerophthalmia.

Prevention and control: Prevention and control of xerophthalmia must be an integral part of primary health care. An overall strategy can be defined according to WHO in terms of short-term, medium-term and long-term action.

(a) Short-term action: A short-term preventive approach that has already demonstrated its efficacy is the administration of large doses of vitamin A orally, in recommended does to vulnerable groups, on a periodic basis. This can be organized quickly and with a minimum of infrastructure.

(b) Medium-term action: An approach widely used to promote regular and adequate intake of vitamin A is fortification of certain foods with vitamin A. Addition of vitamin A to *dalda* in India is a typical example. Many other foods have also been considered for vitamin A fortification, viz. sugar, salt, tea, margarine and dried skimmed milk. Fortifying an appropriate food with vitamin A is a complex process. The greatest challenge to successful fortification programmes is choosing a food that is likely to be consumed in sufficient quantities by groups at risk.

(c) Long-term action: These are measures aimed at reduction or elimination of factors contributing to ocular disease, e.g. persuading people in general , and mothers in particular, to consume generously dark green leafy vegetables or other vitamin A rich foods, promotion of breast feeding for as long as possible, improvements in environmental health such as ensuring safe and adequate water supply and construction and maintenance of pit latrines.

4. Nutritional Anaemia

Nutritional anaemia is a disease syndrome caused by malnutrition in its widest sense. It has defined by WHO as "a condition in which the haemoglobin content of blood is lower than normal as a result of a deficiency of one or more essential nutrients, regardless of the cause of such deficiency." Anaemia is established if the haemoglobin is below the cut-off points recommended by WHO. By far the most frequent cause of nutritional anaemia is iron deficiency, and frequently folate or vitamin B_{12}.

THE NUTRITIONAL PROBLEM IN INDIA

Iron deficiency anaemia is a major nutrition problem in India and many other developing countries. In addition, many have iron deficiency without anaemia. The incidence of anaemia is highest among women and young children, varying between 60 to 70 per cent. Recent surveys indicate that in rural India anaemia is much more widespread than hitherto believed, even among men.

Iron deficiency can arise either due to inadequate intake or poor bioavailability of dietary iron or due to excessive losses of iron from the body. Although most habitual diets contain seemingly adequate amounts of iron, only a small amount (less than 5 per cent) is absorbed. This poor bioavailability is considered to a major reason for the widespread iron deficiency. Women lose a considerable amount of iron especially during menstruation. Some of the other factors leading to anaemia are malaria and hookworm infestations. In addition mothers who have born children at close intervals become anaemic due to the additional demands of the rapid pregnancies and the loss of blood in each delivery.

In some areas of India, it has been shown that folate deficiency anaemia affects 25 to 50 per cent of pregnant women attending hospital clinics. Present evidence suggests that a high prevalence of folate deficiency anaemia in pregnancy is a universal phenomenon and is associated unnecessarily with economically underprivileged.

Detrimental effects : The detrimental effects of anaemia can be seen in three important areas. *(a) Pregnancy :* Anaemia increases the risk of maternal and foetal mortality and morbidity. *(b) Infection :* Anaemia can be caused or aggravated by parasitic diseases, e.g. malaria, intestinal parasites. *(c) Work capacity :* Anaemia (even when mild) causes a significant impairment of maximal work capacity.

5. Goitre

The magnitude of the problem in India is far greater than what had been estimated in 1960s, when it was estimated that about 9 million persons were affected by goitre.

Goitre control: There are four essential components of national goitre control programme. These are iodized salt or oil, monitoring and surveillance, manpower training and mass communication.

Iodized Salt: The iodization of salt is now the most widely used prophylactic public health measure against endemic goitre. In India the level of iodization is fixed under the Prevention of Food Adulteration (PFA) Act and is not less than 30 ppm at the production point and not less than 15 ppm of iodine at the consumer level.

SELECTED NUTRITIONAL DISEASES

1. Cardiovascular disease

It is now generally agreed that diet governs many situations favouring the on set of "heart disease", particularly coronary heart disease (CHD). Of all the factors associated with CHD (e.g. plasma cholesterol, high blood pressure, cigarette smoking, lack of physical activity) plasma cholesterol has a very high statistical significance with the incidence of CHD. The risk of CHD appears to increase as the plasma cholesterol concentration rises.

The *lipid hypothesis*- although debated for more than 30 years- has not, in the opinion of some researchers, yet been proven. For instance, data from the Framingham Heart Study did not find significant association between dietary lipids and the risk of CHD within populations. This has been cited as evidence against diet- hear hypothesis. However, various other studies have supported the role of elevated blood levels of cholesterol and low density lipoproteins (LDL) in the development of atherosclerosis. Geographical studies have shown that there is no population in whom CHD is common that does not have a relatively high mean level of plasma total cholesterol (TC) in adults.

Cholesterol : Cholesterol occurs in all foods of animal origin. Part of it is synthesized in the body. The plasma cholesterol is determined by *(a)* the amount absorbed from food *(b)* the amount synthesized in the body *(c)* the rate of catabolism and excretion in the bile *(d)* intestinal reabsorption of bile acids, and *(e)* the equilibrium between plasma and tissues. The extent to which cholesterol intake influences total cholesterol levels is highly variable.

Fatty acids: In populations where the plasma cholesterol is high, there is also generally high consumption of saturated fats. Clinical studies on selected volunteers under well-defined conditions have clearly demonstrated that a high intake of saturated fatty acids over several weeks or months causes an increase in plasma cholesterol.

Polyunsaturated fatty acids (e.g. Linoleic and arachidonic acids) have an additional role, that is, to inhibit aggregation and thus prevent thrombus formation. Recent research indicates that arachidonic acid metabolises in the vascular endothelium to form two important metabolism namely prostacyclin and thromboxane.

It has been shown that cholesterol in blood can be reduced by controlling the amount and type of fat in the diet.

Carbohydrate: Coronary heart disease rates are lowest in population eating high carbohydrate diets. Support for the hypothesis that consumption of complex carbohydrates may decrease the risk of CHD comes from historical trends of food consumption patterns and mortality rates in India, It is generally recognized that such mortality rates were quite low until about 1920.

Salt: There are good and consistent correlations between dietary sodium intake and the incidence of hypertension. Thus the highest incidence of hypertension is found in north Japan where the sodium intake is above 400 mmol/day, while primitive societies ingesting less than 60 mmol/day have virtually no hypertension. Susceptible individuals in primitive populations who change from low to high intake of sodium have been found to develop hypertension.

2. Diabetes

In a diabetic, there is impaired metabolism of glucose in the body, which leads to excess of glucose in blood and urine. Insulin helps in checking and maintaining the level of glucose in blood. Insulin deficiency leads to accelerated utilization of energy reserves from fat stores. The fatty acids are oxidized by liver to ketone bodies. Excess of ketone bodies leads to their accumulation in urine. This condition is known as ketoacidosis and can result in diabetic coma. Due to insulin deficiency excess of fatty acids are converted to triglycerides. In diabetes these accumulate in the blood. Insulin is also important for synthesis of proteins and deficiency of insulin leads to muscle wasting.

It has been suggested that deficiencies of trace elements such as chromium, copper and zinc may play a role in the pathogenesis of diabetes mellitus, but clinical evidence is lacking.

Malnutrition-related diabetes mellitus has recently attracted attention. Protein deficiency may be involved in the pathogenesis of some forms of diabetes. Excessive consumption of alcohol can increase the risk of diabetes by damaging the pancreas and liver and by promoting obesity.

3. Obesity

In richer countries and in some developing countries, obesity is a health problem. The connection between severe obesity and premature death from diabetes, hypertension and CHD is well established. The basic cause of obesity is overnutrition. A diet containing more energy than needed may lead to prolonged post- prandial hyperlipidaemia and to deposition to triglycerides in adipose tissue resulting in obesity.

It is known that a relative insulin resistance takes place in obesity in peripheral tissues, mainly adipose tissues, while the insulin secretion is normal or increased. The demonstrated reduction in the sensitivity to insulin of the large adipocyte can be attributed to the decreased affinity of the insulin receptors or to a reduction in their number in the cell membrane, Through a feedback mechanism the insulin secretion is stepped up, thus leading to a state of hyperinsulinism.

From a practical point of view all hypotheses concerning the genesis of obesity could be put down to over-nutrition, to a hyper-energy food intake. This is a sound basis for preventive and therapeutic recommendations.

4. Cancer

It is postulated that 80 per cent of cancers may be due to environmental factors, and it is possible that some dietatic factors may be involved. Existing knowledge is reviewed briefly as below:

***(a)* Dietary fat:** Population surveys have shown a strong positive correlation between cancer colon and dietary intake of fat. It has been suggested that the high fat intake accounts for the high incidence of colon cancer in Western communities. Dietary fat is believed to increase the secretion of bile acids in the bowl which are then metabolised by bacterial flora into carcinogens or co-carcinogens.

A positive correlation between per capita consumption of dietary fat and breast cancer rates has also been noted. A reduction in dietary fat may alter the risk of breast cancer, perhaps by increasing oestrogen production or prolactin release.

***(b)* Dietary fibre:** Several studies indicate that the risk of colon cancer is inversely related to the consumption of dietary fibre, which may protect against intestinal carcinogens or precursors by dilutional or other effects. Although the available epidemiological data are not entirely consistent, the weight of evidence generally supports the hypothesis that fibre protects against colon cancer.

***(c)* Micronutrients :** Micronutrients may also have a protective influence, since cancers of the lung and several other sites have been associated with a low intake of vitamin A. The risk of stomach cancer has been related to a deficiency of vitamin C, which may act by inhibiting the formation of carcinogenic nitrosamines in the stomach. Trace elements (e.g. selenium) have also been implicated in the aetiology of cancer.

***(d)* Food additives and contaminants :** Food additives and contaminants (e.g. preservatives, artificial colours, artificial sweeteners, pesticides, flavours, anti oxidants) have always been under suspicion as possible carcinogens in their long- term effects. It is thought in some quarters that nitrosamines are responsible for certain types of gastric carcinoma.

***(e)* Alcohol:** Heavy drinking increases the risk of liver cancer. It is estimated that alcohol contributes to about 3 per cent of all cancer deaths. Some recent studies have suggested that beer consumption may be related to cancer rectum, but the association has not been confirmed.

The above review, indicates that in recent years, much evidence has accumulated to indicate that nutrition has an influence on cancer incidence and mortality. There is in this field a remarkable dearth of facts and an abundance of speculation.

HYGIENE

Pasteurization

Pasteurization is a preventive measure of public health importance and corresponds in all respects to the modern principles of supplying safe milk. Pasteurization kills nearly 90 per cent of the bacteria in milk including the more heat-resistant tubercle bacillus and the Q fever organisms. But it will not kill thermoduric bacteria nor the bacterial spores. Therefore, despite pasteurization, with subsequent rise in temperature, the bacteria are bound to multiply. In order to check the growth of microorganisms, pasteurized milk is rapidly cooled to 4 deg C. It should be kept cold until it reaches the consumer. Hygienically produced pasteurized milk has a keeping quality of not more than 8 to 12 hours at 18 deg C.

Meat Hygiene

The term "meat" includes various tissues of animal origin. The diseases which may be transmitted by eating unwholesome meat are:

1. Tape Worm Infestations: *Tinea solium, T, saginata, Trichinella spiralis and Fasciola hepatica,*
2. Bacterial Infections: Anthrax, actinomycosis, tuberculosis and food poisoning.

Meat Inspection : Animals intended for slaughter are subjected to proper antemortem and postmortem inspection by qualified veterinary staff. The principal causes of antemortem rejection of animals are emaciation, exhaustion pregnancy, sheep- pox, foot-rot, actinomycosis, brucellosis, febrile conditions, diarrhoea and other diseases of an infectious nature rendering meat unfit for human consumption. The main causes of the postmortem rejection are cysticercus bovis, liver fluke, abscesses, sarcocystis, hydatidosis septicaemia, parasitic and nodular infections of liver and lungs, tuberculosis, cysticercus cellulose, etc.

Slaughter houses : Slaughter houses are the places where animals, whose flesh is intended for human consumption are killed. The hygiene of the slaughter house is of paramount importance to prevent the contamination of meat during the process of dressing. The following minimum standards for slaughter houses have been suggested under the Model public Health Act (1955) in India.

1. *Location :* Preferably away from residential areas.
2. *Structure :* Floors and walls upto 3 feet should be impervious and easy to clean.
3. *Disposal of wastes :* Blood, offal, etc. should not be discharged into public sewers but should be collected separately.

4. *Water supply :* Should be independent, adequate and continuous.
5. *Examination of animals :* Antemortem and postmortem examination to be arranged. Animals or meat found unfit for human consumption should be destroyed or denatured.
6. *Storage of meat :* Meat should be stored in fly- proof and rat- proof rooms; for overnight storage, the temperature of the room shall be maintained below 5 deg C.
7. *Transportation of meat :* Meat shall be transported in fly- proof covered vans.
8. *Miscellaneous :* Animals other than those to be slaughtered should no be allowed inside the shed.

Fruits and Vegetables

Fruits and vegetables constitute another important source for the spread of pathogenic organisms, protozoans and helminths. These infections are a serious menace to public health where sewage used for growing vegetables. The vegetables which are consume raw in the form of salads pose a problem in food sanitation. People should be educated to wash the vegetables before eating them raw. Vegetables which are cooked are free from this danger.

Sanitation of Eating Places : Sanitation of eating establishments is a challenging problem to food sanitation. The following minimum standards have been suggested for Restaurants and Eating Houses in India under the Model Public Health Act (1955).

1. *Location :* Shall not be near any accumulation of filth or open drain, stable, manure pit and other sources of nuisances.
2. *Floors :* To be higher than the adjoining land, made with impervious material and easy to keep clean.
3. *Rooms : (a)* Rooms where meals are served shall not be less than 100 sq. feet and shall provide accommodation for a persons *(b)* Walls up to 3 feet should be smooths, corners to rounded; should be impervious and easily washable *(c)* Lighting a ventilation- ample natural lighting facilities aided by artificial light with good circulation of air are necessary
4. *Kitchen : (a)* Floor space minimum 60 sq. ft *(b)* Window opening to be 25 per cent floor area. *(c)* Floor to be impervious smooth, easy to keep clean and non-slippery *(d)* Doors and windows to be rat proof, fly proof and the self closing type *(e)* Ventilators 2 per cent of the floor area.

FOODBORNE DISEASES

The term "foodborne disease" is defined as "A disease, usually either infectious or toxic in nature, caused by agents that enter the body through the ingestion of food." With the increase in urbanization, industrialization, tourism and mass catering systems, foodborne diseases are on the increase throughout the world. Foodborne diseases may be classified as:

A. Foodborne Intoxications

1. Due to naturally occurring toxins in some foods
   (a) Lathyrism (beta oxalyl amino-alanine)
   (b) Endemic ascitis (Pyrrolozidine alkaloids)
2. Due to toxins produced by certain bacteria
   (a) Botulism
   (b) Staphyloccus poisons
3. Due to toxins produced by some fungi
   (a) Aflatoxin
   (b) Ergot
   (c) Fusarium toxins
4. Foodborne chemical poisoning
   (a) Heavy metals, e.g., mercury (usually in fish), cadmium (in certain shellfish) and lead (in canned food)
   (b) Oils, petroleum derivatives and solvents (e.g.. Trycresyn phosphate or TCP)
   (c) Migrant chemicals from package materials
   (d) Asbestos
   (e) Pesticide residues (DDT, BHC)

B. Foodborne infections

Group Examples of illness in each group

1. Bacterial diseases: Typhoid fever, paratyphoid fever, Salmonellosis,

Staphylococcal intoxication, *Cl. perfringens* illness, Botulism, *B. cereus* Food poisoning, *E. coli* diarrhoea. Non - cholera vibrio illness, *V. parahaemolyticus* infection, Streptococcal infection, Shigellosis Brucellosis

2. Viral diseases: Viral hepatitis, Gastroenteritis
3. Parasites: Taeniasis Hydatidosis, Trichinosis, Ascariasis, Amoebiasis, Oxyuriasis.

FOOD TOXICANTS

1. ***Neurolathyrism :*** The cause of neurolathyrism is a toxin, Beta oxalyl amino alanine (BOAA) which is found in the seeds of the pulse, *L. sativus* (Khesari dal). Neurolathyrism is a public health problem in certain parts of the country where this pulse is eaten.
2. ***Aflatoxins :*** Aflatoxins are a group of mycotoxins produced by certain fungi, *Aspergillus flavus* and *A. parasiticus*. These fungi infest foodgrains such as groundnut, maize, parboiled rice, sorghum, wheat, rice, cotton seed and tapioca under conditions of improper storage, and produce aflatoxins of which B_1 and G_1 are the most potent hepatotoxins, in addition to being carcinogenic.

   Control and preventive Measures: A crucial factor in the prevention of fungal contamination of foodgrains is to ensure their proper storage after drying. Moisture content should be kept below 10 per cent. If the food is contaminated, it must not be consumed. It is also essential to educate the local population on the health hazards of consuming contaminated foodgrains.
3. ***Ergot:*** Unlike Aspergillus, ergot is not a storage fungus, but a field fungus. Foodgrains such as bajra, rye, sorghum, and wheat have a tendency to get infested during the flowering stages by the ergot fungus, *Claviceps fusiformis (Claviceps purpurea)*. Fungus grows as a blackish mass and the seeds become black and irregular and are harvested along with food grains. Consumption of ergot infested grain leads to ergotism. Sporadic outbreaks of ergot poisoning in human population have been reported from time to time in areas where bajra is consumed as a staple. The symptoms are acute but rarely fatal and include nausea, repeated vomiting, giddiness and drowsiness extending sometimes for periods up to 24 to 48 hours after the ingestion of ergoty grain. Ergot-infested grains can be easily removed by floating them in 20 per cent salt water. They can also be removed by handpicking or air floatation. The upper safe limit for the ergot alkaloids has been estimated to be 0.05 mg per 100 grams of the food material.
4. ***Epidemic Dropsy :*** The symptoms of epidemic dropsy consist of sudden, non-inflammatory, bilateral swelling of legs, often associated with diarrhoea. Dyspnoea, cardiac failure and death may follow. Some patients may develop glaucoma. The disease may occur at all ages except breast-fed infants.

   The contamination of mustard or other oils with argemone oil may be accidental or deliberate. Seeds of *Argemone mexicana* (prickly poppy) closely resemble mustard seeds. The plant grows wild in India. It has prickly leaves and bright yellow flowers. Crops of mustard are gathered during March, and during this period, the seeds of argemone also mature and are likely to be harvested along with mustard seeds. Sometimes unscrupulous dealers mix argemone oil with mustard or other oils.

   The accidental contamination of mustard seeds can be prevented at the source by removing the argemone weeds growing among oil-seed crops. Unscrupulous dealers may be dealt with by the strict enforcement of the Prevention of Food Adulteration Act.

Food Fortification

Fortification of food is a public health measure aimed at reinforcing the usual dietary intake of nutrients with additional supplies to prevent/ control some nutritional disorders. WHO has defined "food fortification" as "the process whereby nutrients are added to foods (in relatively small quantities) to maintain or improve the quality of the diet of a group, a community, or a population."

Programmes of demonstrated effectiveness of fortification of food or water are: fluoridation of water as a preventive of dental caries: iodization of salt for combating the problem of endemic goitre, and food fortification (e.g., vansapathi, milk) with vitamins A and D. Recently, technology has been developed for the twin fortification of salt with iodine and iron.

In order to qualify as suitable for fortification, the vehicle and the nutrient must fulfill certain criteria:

(a) the vehicle fortified must be consumed consistently as part of the regular daily diet by the relevant sections of the population or total population;

(b) the amount of nutrient added must provide an effective supplement for low consumers of the vehicle, without contributing a hazardous excess to high consumers;

(c) the addition of the nutrient should not cause it to undergo any noticeable change in taste, smell, appearance, or consistency; and

(d) the cost of fortification must not raise the price of the food beyond the reach of the population in greatest need.

Finally, an adequate of surveillance and control is indispensable for the effectiveness of food fortification. Food fortification is a long-term measure for mitigating specific problems of malnutrition in the community.

Adulteration of foods: Adulteration of foods is an age-old problem. It consists of a large number of practices, e.g., mixing, substitution, concealing the quality, putting up decomposed foods for sale, misbranding or giving false labels and addition of toxicants. Adulteration results in two disadvantages for the consumer : first, he is paying more money for a foodstuff of lower quality; secondly, some forms of adulteration are injurious to health, even resulting in death, as for example, adulteration of mustard oil with argemone oil causing epidemic dropsy or adulteration of edible oils with trycresyn phosphate (TCP) resulting in paralysis and death.

Food adulteration practices vary from one part of the country to another, and from time to time. Our knowledge about the current practices of food adulteration is by no means complete.

Prevention of Food Adulteration Act, 1954

Enacted by the Indian Parliament in 1954, with the objective of ensuring pure and wholesome food to the consumers and to protect them from fradulent and deceptive trade practices, the Prevention of Food Adulteration (PFA) Act was amended in 1964, 1976 and lately in 1986 to make the Act more stringent.

Rules are framed which are revised from time to time by an expert body called the "Central Committee for Foods standards" which is constituted by the Central Government under the provisions of the Act. Any food that does not conform to the minimum standards is said to be adulterated. Although it is a Central Act, its implementation is largely carried out by the State Governments and local bodies in their respective areas. However, the Centre plays a vital role in proper coordination, monitoring and surveillance of the programme throughout the country. A chain of food laboratories and four regional appellate Central Food Laboratories (Calcutta, Mysore, Ghaziabad and Pune) whose report is considered to be final have been established.

Training being an important component of the programme for prevention of food adulteration, the Directorate General of Health Services organises in-service training programme for different functionaries responsible for implementation of the PFA Act. Food inspectors, analysts and the senior officers concerned with the implementation of the Act in States are provided training.

OBJECTIVE QUESTIONS

1. Bile helps in :
(*a*) producing enzymes
(*b*) esterification
(*c*) both (*a*) and (*b*)
(*d*) emulsification of fats

2. Fat soluble vitamins are :
(*a*) A, D and E. (*b*) B, C and D
(*c*) E, D and B (*d*) A, B and C

3. Synthesis of vitamin A takes place in :
(*a*) blood (*b*) spleen
(*c*) pancreas (*d*) liver

4. Vitamin-C is :
(*a*) ascorbic acid (*b*) aspartic acid
(*c*) lipoic acid (*d*) nicotinic acid

5. The deficiency of vitamin 'C' causes :
(*a*) anaemia (*b*) scurvy
(*c*) rickets (*d*) xerophthalmia

6. Earliest known vitamin is :
(*a*) Vitamin-A (*b*) Vitamin-C
(*c*) Vitamin-B_1 (*d*) Vitamin-K

7. Synthesis of vitamin D with the help of sunlight takes place by :
(*a*) skin (*b*) liver
(*c*) adipose tissue (*d*) gall bladder

8. Water-soluble vitamins are :
(*a*) A, B and C (*b*) C and D
(*c*) B and C (*d*) None of these

9. Chronic alcoholics are always short of :
(*a*) A (*b*) B
(*c*) C (*d*) D

10. Vitamin containing a cobalt cyanide linkage is :
(*a*) A (*b*) B
(*c*) B_6 (*d*) B_{12}

11. Xerophthalmia in children and Nyctalopia (night blindness) in adults is caused by deficiency of vitamin :
(*a*) A (*b*) D
(*c*) E (*d*) K

12. Scurvy is caused due to dificiency of :
(*a*) Vitamin-C (*b*) Vitamin-D
(*c*) Vitamin-K (*d*) Vitamin-A

13. Deficiency of Vitamin-K may lead to :
(*a*) failure of clotting of blood
(*b*) non-maturation of ova
(*c*) blastocyst formation in uterus
(*d*) neuritis

14. Recently discovered vitamin with anticancer properties is :
(*a*) Vit.-B_{15} (*b*) Vit.-Q
(*c*) Vit.-U (*d*) Vit.-B_{17}

15. Rickets in children and osteomalacia in adults is caused by the deficiency of :
(*a*) Vitamin-A (*b*) Vitamin-B
(*c*) Vitamin-C (*d*) Vitamin-D

16. Wound healing is enhanced by vitamin :
(*a*) A (*b*) C
(*c*) D (*d*) E

17. Pellagra is caused by the deficiency of :
(*a*) thiamine
(*b*) ascorbic acid
(*c*) nicotinic acid (Niacin)
(*d*) calciferol

18. The antihaemorrhagic vitamin is essential for coagulation of blood. It is :
(*a*) B (*b*) D
(*c*) E (*d*) K

19. Ascorbic acid is :
(*a*) Vitamin-A (*b*) Vitamin-C
(*c*) Vitamin-B (*d*) Biotin

20. The best source of vitamin A is :
(*a*) apples (*b*) carrots
(*c*) honey (*d*) pea nuts

21. Beri-beri caused by deficiency of vitamin B, was discovered by :
(*a*) Stanley (*b*) Foxon
(*c*) Funk (*d*) Fijkman

22. Vitamins are :
(*a*) inorganic substances that cannot be synthesised by animal
(*b*) inorganic substances that can be synthesised by animal
(*c*) organic substances that cannot be synthesised by animal
(*d*) organic substances that can be synthesised by animal

23. Deficiency of Vitamin D in children causes :
(*a*) beri-beri (*b*) pellagra
(*c*) rickets (*d*) osteomalacia

24. Substance required to overcome xerophthalmia derived from carrots is :
(*a*) Vitamin-A (*b*) Vitamin-D
(*c*) Proteins (*d*) Xanthophyll

25. Vitamin A was discovered by :
(*a*) Mc. Collum and Devis
(*b*) Richert and Dam
(*c*) Funk
(*d*) Ejikmann Christian

26. Riboflavin is :
(*a*) Vitamin-B_1 (*b*) Vitamin-B_2
(*c*) Vitamin-B_6 (*d*) Vitamin-B_{12}

27. Which is vital for protein synthesis?
(*a*) Thiamine (*b*) Riboflavin
(*c*) Nicotinic acid (*d*) Cyanocobalamin

28. Calciferol is :
(*a*) Vitamin-A (*c*) Vitamin-B
(*b*) Vitamin-C (*d*) Vitamin-D

29. Deficiency of thiamine causes :
(*a*) scurvy (*b*) pellagra
(*c*) osteomalacia (*d*) beri-beri

30. Certain B vitamins act as :
(*a*) enzymes
(*b*) coenzymes
(*c*) hormones
(*d*) digestive substances

31. Which is the best source of vitamin B_1?
(*a*) Cod liver oil
(*b*) Egg
(*c*) Whole wheat bread
(*d*) Curd

32. Deficiency of vitamin A causes :
(*a*) scurvy
(*b*) rickets
(*c*) xerophthalmia
(*d*) xerophthalmia and nyctalopia

33. A vitamin which is excreted in urine usually is :
(*a*) C (*b*) K
(*c*) B_1 (*d*) E

34. The enzymes responsible for the digestion of starch in food of man are present in :
(*a*) saliva and gastric juice
(*b*) salvia and pancreatic juice
(*c*) gastric and pancreatic juice
(*d*) gastric and duodenal juice

35. Vitamin B is related with :
(*a*) FMN/FAD (*b*) NAD
(*c*) NADH (*d*) ATP

36. The substrate for gastric enzymes, renin is :
(*a*) pepsin (*b*) casein of milk
(*c*) starch (*d*) lipids of milk

37. The enzymes found in the stomach of rabbit are :
(*a*) renin, pepsin, lipase
(*b*) lipase, amylase, renin
(*c*) erepsin, lipase, renin
(*d*) pepsin, amylase, lipase

38. Pepsin is an enzyme which acts in :
(*a*) alkaline medium in stomach
(*b*) alkaline medium in duodeum
(*c*) acidic medium in stomach
(*d*) acidic medium in duodenum

39. Milk protein is acted upon by an enzyme :
(*a*) renin (*b*) cassein
(*c*) caesinogen (*d*) pepsin

40. Digestion of carbohydrates is enhanced by :
(*a*) repsin (*b*) pepsin
(*c*) amylopsin (*d*) trypsin

41. Pepsin acts only in acidic medium within certain pH limits which is :
(*a*) 1.2 - 1.8 (*b*) 1.5 - 2.6
(*c*) 2 - 2.3 (*d*) 1.00 - 1.50

42. If the diet of a rabbit is deficient in vitamin A, it results in :
(*a*) darkening of skin due to reduced yellow colour
(*b*) formation of diffused images due to loss of yellow spot
(*c*) loss of vision in dim light due to insufficient rhodopsin in rods
(*d*) None of these

43. The pancreatic juice contains the enzymes :
(*a*) trypsin, amylase, lipase
(*b*) lipase, renin, ptyalin
(*c*) amylase, lipase, lactase
(*d*) pepsin, trypsin, amylase

44. Gastric gland of man in stomach produce an enzyme :
(*a*) insulin (*b*) gastrin
(*c*) pepsin (*d*) trypsin

45. Beri-beri is caused due to deficiency of :
(*a*) Vitamin-B_1 (*b*) Proteins
(*c*) Enzymes (*d*) Vitamin-B_2

46. The enzymes are chemically speaking :
(*a*) proteins (*b*) lipids
(*c*) vitamins (*d*) none of these

47. A vitamin needed for production of collagen fibres is :
(*a*) thiamine (*b*) ascorbic acid
(*c*) retinol (*d*) tocopherol

48. The total iron content of the adult body is normally :
(*a*) 1 to 3 grams (*b*) 5 to 6 grams
(*c*) 3 to 5 grams (*d*) 6 to 8 grams

49. Balanced diet should have approximately :
(*a*) 1/5 proteins, 1/4 fats and 1/4 carbohydrates
(*b*) 1/2 proteins, 3/5 fats and 1/5 carbohydrates
(*c*) 3/5 proteins, 1/5 fats and 1/5 carbohydrates
(*d*) 1/5 proteins, 1/5 fats and 3/5 carbohydrates

50. Fish liver oil is a rich source of :
(*a*) Vitamin-D and A
(*b*) Vitamin-B_6 and C
(*c*) Vitamin-K and E
(*d*) Vitamin-B_1 and B_{12}

51. The sunshine vitamin prevents the deficiency disease of :
(*a*) scurvy (*b*) pellagra
(*c*) rickets (*d*) beri-beri

52. Xerophthalmia, nyctalopia and hyper keratosis are major symptoms of the deficiency of :
(*a*) calciferol (*b*) carotene
(*c*) tocopherol (*d*) naphthoquinone

53. Which one of the following vitamins has some physiological effects similar to those of parathormone?
(*a*) Vitamin-A (*b*) Vitamin-K
(*c*) Vitamin-E (*d*) Vitamin-D

54. The vitamin which is not excreted in urine in higher vertebrates is :
(*a*) Vitamin-C (*b*) Vitamin-B_2
(*c*) Vitamin-A (*d*) Vitamin-B_1

55. Curdling of milk is caused by :
(*a*) a large variety of useful bacteria
(*b*) the action of renin
(*c*) the action of pepsin
(*d*) the high acid content in stomach

56. A person decides to live exclusively on a diet of milk, eggs and bread. He would suffer from :
(*a*) scurvy (*b*) rickets
(*c*) beri-beri (*d*) night blindness

57. Cracks in the corners of mouth, purplish colour of tongue, inflammation of eyes and loss of hair are the symptoms of the deficiency of :
(*a*) thiamine (*b*) riboflavin
(*c*) niacin (*b*) pyridoxine

58. An organ that assists in the mobilisation of energy reserves for use during periods of starvation is :
(*a*) pancreas (*b*) liver
(*c*) adipose *tissue* (*d*) lungs

59. Vitamins which are needed to be taken orally by food are :
(*a*) fat-soluble vitamins
(*b*) water-soluble vitamins
(*c*) water-soluble vitamins which can be stored in liver
(*d*) fat-soluble vitamins which can be stored in liver

60. Peyer's patches in the wall of alimentary canal are :
(*a*) group of nerve endings
(*b*) group of lymph nodes
(*c*) group of veins
(*d*) group of arteries

61. The essential mineral for the formation of body protein is :
(*a*) calcium (*b*) sodium
(*c*) magnesium (*d*) potassium

62. Anaemia is caused due to deficiency of :
(*a*) biotin (*b*) folic acid
(*c*) niacin (*d*) ascorbic acid

63. The lacteals are central lymph vessels which are found in :
(*a*) liver (*b*) pancreas
(*c*) villi (*d*) spleen

64. Pseudorumination is :
(*a*) chewing of food
(*b*) swallowing of food
(*c*) eating own faeces
(*d*) eating the skin

65. The wisdom teeth in man appear at the age of 17-25 years. It is :
(*a*) first premolar (*b*) first molar
(*c*) last premolar (*d*) last molar

66. When a man starves, he first of all consumes stored :
(*a*) fats (*b*) proteins
(*c*) glycogen (*d*) carbohydrates

67. If a child bleeds, he is prescribed by the doctor :
(*a*) Vitamin-C (*b*) Vitamin-K
(*c*) Heparin (*d*) Vitamin-D

68. A doctor advices a person to have more meat, butter, milk and eggs in his diet. The person is suffering from :
(*a*) scurvy (*b*) night blindness
(*c*) rickets (*d*) kwashiorkor

ANSWERS

1	2	3	4	5	6	7	8	9	10
(*d*)	(*a*)	(*d*)	(*a*)	(*b*)	(*c*)	(*a*)	(*c*)	(*c*)	(*d*)
11	**12**	**13**	**14**	**15**	**16**	**17**	**18**	**19**	**20**
(*a*)	(*a*)	(*a*)	(*d*)	(*d*)	(*d*)	(*c*)	(*d*)	(*b*)	(*b*)
21	**22**	**23**	**24**	**25**	**26**	**27**	**28**	**29**	**30**
(*d*)	(*b*)	(*c*)	(*a*)	(*a*)	(*b*)	(*d*)	(*d*)	(*d*)	(*b*)
31	**32**	**33**	**34**	**35**	**36**	**37**	**38**	**39**	**40**
(*c*)	(*d*)	(*a*)	(*b*)	(*a*)	(*b*)	(*a*)	(*c*)	(*a*)	(*c*)
41	**42**	**43**	**44**	**45**	**46**	**47**	**48**	**49**	**50**
(*d*)	(*c*)	(*a*)	(*c*)	(*a*)	(*a*)	(*b*)	(*c*)	(*d*)	(*a*)
51	**52**	**53**	**54**	**55**	**56**	**57**	**58**	**59**	**60**
(*c*)	(*b*)	(*d*)	(*d*)	(*b*)	(*a*)	(*b*)	(*b*)	(*d*)	(*b*)
61	**62**	**63**	**64**	**65**	**66**	**67**	**68**		
(*c*)	(*b*)	(*c*)	(*b*)	(*d*)	(*c*)	(*b*)	(*d*)		

Epidemiology

Epidemiology is the basic science of preventive and social medicine. Although of ancient lineage, it made only slow progress up to the start of this century. Epidemiology has evolved rapidly during the past three decades.

Definition

Epidemiology has been defined by John M. last in 1988 as "The study of the distribution and determinants of health-related states or events in specified populations, and the application of this study to the control of health problems.

Aims of Epidemiology

According to the International Epidemiological Association (IEA), epidemiology has three main aims:

(a) to describe the distribution and magnitude of health and disease problems in human populations.

(b) to identify etiological factors (risk factors) in the pathogenesis of disease; and

(c) to provide the data essential to the planning, implementation and evaluation of services for the prevention, control and treatment of disease and to the setting up of priorities among those services.

In order to fulfil these aims, three rather different classes of epidemidogical studies may be mentioned: descriptive studies, analytical studies, and experimental or intervention studies.

The ultimate aim of epidemiology is to lead to effective action:

(a) to eliminate or reduce the health problem or its consequence; and

(b) to promote the health and well-being of society as a whole.

Uses of Epidemiology

While the study of disease distribution and causation remains centred to epidemiology; the techniques of epidemiology have a wider application covering many more important areas relating not only to disease but also health and health services. In more utilitarian terms, epidemiology has been defined as "a means of learning, or asking questions and getting answers that lead to further questions. In this context, Morris has identified seven distinct uses of epidemiology, five of which extend epidemiology beyond the search for causes of disease and bring it closer to day-to-day concerns of modern medicine. These are:

1. **To Study Historically the Rise and Fall of Disease in the Population:** *Winston Churchill said:* "The farther back you look, the farther forward you can see! The first use of epidemiology relates to this aspect, that is, study of the history of disease in human population. It is well known that the health and disease pattern in a community is never constant. There are fluctuations both ever short and along periods of time.

2. **Community Diagnosis :** One of the uses of epidemiology is community diagnosis. Community diagnosis generally refers to the identification and quantification of health problems in a community in terms of mortality and morbidity rates and ratios, and identification of their correlates for the purpose of defining those individuals or

groups at risk or those in need of health care. By quantification of health problems, we lay down priorities in disease control and prevention.

3. **Planning and Evaluation :** *Planning* is essential for a rational allocation of the limited resources. For example in developing countries, too many hospitals have been built and equipped without knowledge of the particular disease problems in the community. Epidemiologic information about the distribution of health problems over time and place provides the fundamental basis for planning and developing the needed health services and for assessing the impact of these services on the people's problems.

   Evaluation is an equally important concern of epidemiology. Any measures taken to control or prevent a disease must be followed by an evaluation to find out whether the measures undertaken are effective in reducing the frequency of the disease. Evaluation of a control method such as hepatitis vaccine requires more than the demonstration of its effectiveness in reducing disease frequency.

4. **Evaluation of Individual's Risks and Chances :** One of the important tasks of epidemiologists is to make a statement about the degree of risk in a population. Besides the incidence rate and specific rates which are measures of absolute risk, the epidemiologists calculate relative risk and attributable risk for a factor related to or believed to be a cause of the disease.

5. **Syndrome Identification :** Medical syndromes are identified by observing frequently associated findings in individual patients. It is worth recalling that, although approximately 3000 so-called syndromes are described in the contemporary paediatric literature, a primary defect is known only in about 20 per cent of these. Epidemiological investigation can be used to define and refine syndromes. By observation of groups such studies have been able to correct misconceptions concerning many disease syndromes.

6. **Completing the Natural History of Disease :** Epidemiology is concerned with the entire spectrum of disease in a population. The picture of disease constructed on the basis of hospital patients is quite different from that found in the community. The epidemiologists by studying disease patterns in the coummunity in relation to agent, host and environmental factors is in a better position to fill up the gaps in the natural history of disease than the clinician. For example an outstanding contribution by epidemiology to the natural history of atheresclerosis in the recognition that one third to two thirds of all deaths due to ischaemic heart disease are sudden, is occur in less than one hour. Hospital studies could never have come to this conclusion, for most victims do not reach the hospital.

7. **Searching for causes and risk factors:** Epidemiology, by relating disease to interpopulation differences and other attributes of the population examined, tries to identify the causes of disease. The contribution of epidemiology have been many in this regard.

8. **Infection:** When an agent of an Infectious disease enters the body of man or animal and multiplies there it is called infection.

9. **Parasite:** Micro organism or plant or an animal which lives inside or outside the body of a person or animal and gets its nourishment for them.

10. **Infestation:** When a parasite establishes in or on the body it is called infestation.

    Contamination: When infectious agent is present in non living matter like soil, water *etc.* it is called contaimination.

11. **Contagious Disease:** Disease which spread by direct contact (skin, sexual *etc.*)
12. **Communicable Diseases:** All diseases which spread between man and man, man and animal and also from environment (air, water *etc.*). It includes all these due to infection, infestation or contagion.
13. **Endemic Disease:** Diseases which are present continuously in the community and never disappear (typhoid, malaria *etc.*). e.g., goitre in hill station.
14. **Epidemic Diseases:** Disease occuring in a community or in an area spreading from a common source and occuring above the expected limit (expected limit is decided by previous records), an endemic may become epidemic if too many cases occur. If the disease is not expected at all even few cases will be an epidemic. e.g., Plague in Surat 1994.
15. **Pandemic Disease:** Disease spreading quickly from one country to another or when it starts at the same time in many countries.
16. **Sporadic Disease:** When a few scattered cases of a disease occur in an area it is called sporadic.
17. **Immunity:** If a person has good resistance of the body he does not get the disease even if he is infected. This is called immunity and the person is immune.
18. **Incubation Period:** The period between the entry of an agent in the body of host and the appearance of manifestation (signs and symptoms) of disease.
19. **Infective Period:** Period in which the diseased person or animal can spread the disease to others.
20. **Cellular Immunity:** White blood cells in blood and some cells in tissues have the power to destroy germs. Some lymphocytes in the blood also stimulate production of antibodies, cellular immunity plays a very important part in protecting the body against infection. Both humoral and cellular immunity are necessary for body defence against infection.
21. **Natural (*innate*) Immunity:** This is acquired under natural condition. It is present at the time of birth and remain throughout life without any change. Man does not suffer from many diseases of animal even if he comes in contact. Similarly animals do not suffer from many disease of man (cholera, measles *etc.*). These are examples of innate immunity.
22. **Acquired Immunity:** Acquired immunity is either active or passive. When the antibodies are produced in a person's own body it is called active immunity. When they are supplied to the body from outside (from mother or an animal or any other person) it is passive immunity. Horse is usually the animal from whose blood antibodies are taken out. Passive immunity are necessary if a person does not have antibodies in his blood and if they are urgently required. Sometimes the body fails to produce antibodies due to the failure of the immune system. The liquid part of the blood (serum) contains the antibodies and this can be prepared from the blood.
23. **Immunization (Vaccination):** This is an artificial way of creating immunity in a person. This is one of the greatest achievements of modern medicine. When an antigen is introduced in the body antibodies are produced. Germs or their toxins are antigen. If they are introduced in the body artificially which is called 'Vaccination' antibodies are produced.
24. **Prevention and Control of Communicable Disease:** Common broad principles of prevention and control of communicable diseases are described here. Particular measure for each disease are described under each disease because they will be different according to nature of the disease. These principles are:

    1. Notification
    2. Isolation

3. Quarantine
4. Desinfection
5. Immunization
6. General measures
7. Health education.

25. Chemical disinfectants are solid, liquid and gases.
1. *Solids:* Lime (CaO), Bleaching powder ($CaOCl_2$)
2. *Liquids:* Coal Tar group, Carbonic acid (Phenol)
3. *Gases:* Formaldehyde, Ethylene oxide

OBJECTIVE QUESTIONS

1. First step in investigation of epidemic:
(*a*) Find the source
(*b*) Confirm diagnosis
(*c*) Sanitation
(*d*) Spot map

2. In fresh bleaching powder the chlorine availability is:
(*a*) 20% (*b*) 30%
(*c*) 33% (*d*) 40%

3. All of the following are *false* about bleaching powder except:
(*a*) Contains 20% available chlorine
(*b*) 20% solution used for disinfection of faeces
(*c*) Unstable compound on storage
(*d*) Not used for disinfection of faeces and urine

4. Sharp instruments may be sterilized with:
(*a*) Radiation
(*b*) Lysol
(*c*) Hot air
(*d*) Any of the above

5. Which of the following is most powerful chemical disinfectant?
(*a*) Phenol
(*b*) Lysol
(*c*) Dettol
(*d*) Potassium permangnate

6. For disposable items, the best method for sterilization is:
(*a*) Dry heat
(*b*) Incineration
(*c*) Gamma radiation
(*d*) Boiling heat

7. According to WHO, all the following diseases require surveillance except:
(*a*) Chickenpox
(*b*) Yellow fever
(*c*) Malaria
(*d*) Rabies

8. Chemoprophylaxis is given in all except
(*a*) Cholera
(*b*) Plague
(*c*) Measles
(*d*) Meningococcal meningitis

9. Surveillance by WHO is not done for:
(*a*) Polio
(*b*) Malaria
(*c*) Viral encephalitis
(*d*) Relapsing fever

10. The target by which primary immunization is to be completed under the Universal Immunization Programme is:
(*a*) 1 years (*b*) 2 years
(*c*) 3 years (*d*) 5 years

11. Vaccine which is given at earliest:
(*a*) BCG (*b*) OPV
(*c*) MMR (*d*) DPT
(*e*) DT

12. Following diseases require isolation to break transmission *except*:
(*a*) Measles (*b*) Mumps
(*c*) Chickenpox (*d*) Tetanus

13. In control of communicable diseases, the period of quarantine in respect of a disease is determined by:
(*a*) Incubation period
(*b*) Infectivity period
(*c*) Duration of illness
(*d*) Carrier state

14. Notifiable disease is:
(*a*) *Varicella* (*b*) Cholera
(*c*) Malaria (*d*) Influenza

15. The following diseases are under surveillance by WHO, *except*:
(*a*) Relapsing fever

(*b*) Plague
(*c*) Malaria
(*d*) Tuberculosis

16. Ideal temperature for DPT storage:
(*a*) Room temperature
(*b*) 4 to 8°C
(*c*) 0 to –20°C
(*d*) None of the above

17. Measles vaccine is kept in refrigerator in:
(*a*) Chilled tray
(*b*) Freezer
(*c*) Tray below the freezer
(*d*) Shelves in the door

18. Live attenuated vaccines are all *except*:
(*a*) BCG (*b*) Salk
(*c*) Sabin (*d*) Measles

19. Which one of the following is not a live vaccine?
(*a*) OPV
(*b*) BCG
(*c*) Hib vaccine
(*d*) Try 21a against typhoid

20. Live attenuated vaccines are:
(*a*) OPV
(*b*) Hepatitis
(*c*) Japanese-B-encephalitis
(*d*) Chickenpox

21. Killed bacterial vaccine is:
(*a*) BCG (*b*) Diphtheria
(*c*) Pertussis (*d*) Toxoid

22. Live attenuated vaccine used in man is:
(*a*) Influenza
(*b*) BCG
(*c*) Yellow fever
(*d*) Japanese-B-encephalitis

23. Live vaccines are all except:
(*a*) Typhoid oral (*b*) Measles
(*c*) BCG (*d*) Pertussis

24. Match List-I with List-II and select the correct answer using the codes given below in the lists:

List-I
A. Tuberculosis B. Measles
C. Diphtheria D. Whooping cough

List-II
1. Toxoids
2. Killed bacteria
3. Live attenuated viruses
4. Live attenuated bacteria

Codes:

	A	B	C	D
(*a*)	4	3	2	1
(*b*)	3	4	2	1
(*c*)	3	4	1	2
(*d*)	2	3	4	1

25. All are live vaccines except:
(*a*) Measles (*b*) BCG
(*c*) OPV (*d*) Hepatitis B

26. Secondary attack rate reflects:
(*a*) Severity
(*b*) Communicability
(*c*) Fatality
(*d*) Infectivity

27. Which does *not* have latent infection?
(*a*) Smallpox (*b*) Chickenpox
(*c*) Mumps (*d*) Malaria

28. Incubation period is helpful for all except:
(*a*) Quarantine
(*b*) Source identification
(*c*) Preventive immunization
(*d*) Isolation

29. The period after entry of the organism to produce maximum infection known as:
(*a*) Incubation period
(*b*) Generation time
(*c*) Serial interval lead
(*d*) Lead time

30. Which is most difficult to block spread of?
(*a*) Vector (*b*) Man to man
(*c*) Airborne (*d*) Waterborne

31. The cycle of yellow fever virus in *Aedes* is:
(*a*) Propagative
(*b*) Cyclopropagative
(*c*) Cyclodevelopment
(*d*) Any of the above

32. Vertical transmission is by:
(*a*) Mosquitoes (*b*) Direct contact
(*c*) Droplet (*d*) Placenta

33. Transovarian transmission of diseases includes:
(*a*) Syphilis (*b*) AIDS
(*c*) KFD (*d*) *Rubella*

34. Carrier state is important in following *except*:
(*a*) Measles (*b*) Polio
(*c*) Cholera (*d*) Typhoid

35. Carriers are not an important source of transmission in the following disease:
(*a*) Diphtheria (*b*) Measles
(*c*) Typhoid (*d*) Poliomyelitis

36. Healthy carriers are found in all *except*:
(*a*) Cholera (*b*) Diptheria
(*c*) Typhoid (*d*) Pertussis

37. Diseases which are imported into a country in which they do not otherwise occur is:
(*a*) Exotic
(*b*) Epizootic
(*c*) Endemic
(*d*) None of the above

38. Disease imported to a country *not* otherwise present:
(*a*) Exotic (*b*) Enzootic
(*c*) Epizootic (*d*) Endemic

39. Anthropozoonosis are all *except*:
(*a*) Guinea worm infestation
(*b*) Rabies
(*c*) Plague
(*d*) Hydatid cyst

40. The best criteria to judge association causes relationship is:
(*a*) Strength of association
(*b*) Consistency
(*c*) Chronological sequence of event
(*d*) Specificity

41. Prevalance of disease in a community can be found out by:
(*a*) case control study
(*b*) cohort study
(*c*) cross-sectional study
(*d*) analytical study

42. Evaluation of new antihypertens drug, test of significance is:
(*a*) Chi-square test
(*b*) Fischer F. test
(*c*) Paired t-test
(*d*) Pooled

43. Best indicator to determine maximum benefit to the community through preventive intervention strategies is:
(*a*) Relative risk
(*b*) Attributable risk
(*c*) Absolute risk
(*d*) Odd's ratio

44. As a Health Inspector, treatment plan of action you should use:
(*a*) Relative risk
(*b*) Attributable risk
(*c*) Population attributable risk
(*d*) Odd's ratio

45. Best method to calculate the incidence rate is:
(*a*) Case control study
(*b*) Sentinel surveillance
(*c*) Cohort study
(*d*) Cross sectional prevalance study

46. If you desire to study the incidence of diarrhoea in a community which study method would you like to opt for:
(*a*) Cross-sectional study
(*b*) Cohort study
(*c*) Case control study
(*d*) Double blind placebo study

47. All true about cohort studies *except*:
(*a*) Prospective
(*b*) Useful for rare diseases
(*c*) Necessary for incidence
(*d*) Costly

48. Case control study most characteristic is:
(*a*) Odd's ratio estimation
(*b*) Problem bias
(*c*) Yields incidence rate
(*d*) Expensive

49. When launching a study many respondents are invited some of whom fail to come. This is called:
(*a*) Respnse bias (*b*) Volunteer bias
(*c*) Selection bias (*d*) Berkesonian bias

50. Case control study is used for:
(*a*) Finding a rare cause
(*b*) Finding multiple risk factors
(*c*) Finding incidence rate
(*d*) Finding morbidity

51. Calculate the Odd's ratio:

Diseased	***Undiseased***
Positive	30 – 20
Negative	20 – 30

(*a*) 0.44 (*b*) 1.5
(*c*) 0.8 (*d*) 2.25

52. In a village of 1 lakh population among 20,000 exposed to smoking, 200 developed cancer and among 40,000 people unexposed, 40 developed cancer. The relative risk of smoking in the development of cancer is:
(*a*) 20 (*b*) 10
(*c*) 5 (*d*) 15

53. Relative risk can be obtained from:
(*a*) Case study
(*b*) Cohort study
(*c*) Case control study
(*d*) Experimental study

54. Incidence among exposed and nonexposed is called:
(*a*) Relative risk (*b*) Attributable risk
(*c*) Odd's ratio (*d*) Attack ratio

55. Weighting is:
(*a*) Normal variable
(*b*) Discrete variable
(*c*) Confounding variable
(*d*) Continuous Variable

56. All are true about case control study *except*:
(*a*) It is cheaper than other studies
(*b*) It is useful to investigate a rare disease
(*c*) Odd's ratio can be detected from it
(*d*) Relative risk can be detected from it

57. The process of 'matching' allows:
(*a*) The matched variables to be evaluated
(*b*) For selecting the case and control group with the same known confounding variables
(*c*) Matching of factors in doubt
(*d*) One to avoid focussing on variables desired

58. All of the following are true regarding case control study *except*:
(*a*) Relative risk can be calculated
(*b*) Less expensive
(*c*) Suitable for rare disease
(*d*) Backward study

59. All are true about case control studies *except*:
(*a*) It is easy to conduct
(*b*) It is cheaper
(*c*) Can measure attributable risk
(*d*) Those with disease are matched with those without

60. The most useful study in a hospital setting is:
(*a*) Cross-sectional
(*b*) Longitudinal
(*c*) Cohort
(*d*) Case control

61. Residents of three villagers with three different types of water supply were asked to participate in a study to identify cholera carriers. Because several cholera deaths had occured in the recent past, virtually everyone occurred in the time submitted to examination. The proportion of carriers was in each village who were carriers was computed and compared, this study is a:
(*a*) cross-sectional study
(*b*) case-control study
(*c*) concurrent cohort study
(*d*) non-concurrent

62. *False* about point source epidemic is:
(*a*) Children are more affected
(*b*) Rapid rise and fall
(*c*) All cases occur in one incubation period
(*d*) No secondary waves

63. *Bhopal gas tragedy* is an example of:
(*a*) Slow epidemic
(*b*) Continuous epidemic
(*c*) Point source epidemic
(*d*) Propagated epidemic

64. *Chernobyl tragedy* is an example of:
(*a*) Point source epidemic
(*b*) Propagated epidemic
(*c*) Modern epidemic
(*d*) Continuous epidemic

65. The three major types of epidemics would include all except:
(*a*) Common source epidemics
(*b*) Periodic epidemics
(*c*) Propagated epidemics
(*d*) Slow epidemics

ANSWERS

1	2	3	4	5	6	7	8	9	10
(*b*)	(*c*)	(*c*)	(*d*)	(*b*)	(*c*)	(*c*)	(*c*)	(*c*)	(*a*)
11	**12**	**13**	**14**	**15**	**16**	**17**	**18**	**19**	**20**
(*a*)	(*d*)	(*a*)	(*b*)	(*d*)	(*b*)	(*b*)	(*c*)	(*a*)	(*a*)
21	**22**	**23**	**24**	**25**	**26**	**27**	**28**	**29**	**30**
(*c*)	(*a*)	(*d*)	(*a*)	(*d*)	(*b*)	(*a*)	(*d*)	(*b*)	(*c*)
31	**32**	**33**	**34**	**35**	**36**	**37**	**38**	**39**	**40**
(*a*)	(*d*)	(*c*)	(*a*)	(*b*)	(*d*)	(*a*)	(*b*)	(*a*)	(*c*)
41	**42**	**43**	**44**	**45**	**46**	**47**	**48**	**49**	**50**
(*a*)	(*c*)	(*b*)	(*c*)	(*c*)	(*b*)	(*b*)	(*a*)	(*b*)	(*b*)
51	**52**	**53**	**54**	**55**	**56**	**57**	**58**	**59**	**60**
(*d*)	(*b*)	(*b*)	(*a*)	(*d*)	(*d*)	(*c*)	(*b*)	(*c*)	(*d*)
61	**62**	**63**	**64**	**65**					
(*a*)	(*a*)	(*c*)	(*a*)	(*b*)					

Communicable & Non-Communicable Diseases

Human diseases may be divide into

1. **Congenital Diseases:** Present since birth.
2. **Acquired Diseases:** Develop after birth. Acquired diseases can be grouped into:

   (a) Infections disease-caused by viruses, bacteria, protozoa, fungi and worms.

   (b) Deficiency diseases-caused by the deficiency of vitamins, minerals, carbohydrates, proteins & fat in diet.

   (c) Allergies-caused by hypersensitivity of the body like perfumes, pollen, grains etc.

   (d) Degenerative diseases-caused by malfunctioning of vital organs like heart, kidney, lungs, brain etc.

- Acquired infections diseases are communicable diseases *e.g.,* Plague, Typhoid.
- Acquired non infections disease are Non-communicable. *e.g.,* Diabetes, Night blindness, Scurvy.
- Hippocrates (B.C. 460–350) wrote detailed descriptions of disease symptoms and emphasized the need for good diet, fresh air and rest. He showed & explained that human body has self immunity power.
- Louis Pasteur and Robert Koch stated Germs theory of disease.
- Epidemology is the study which deals with the mode of transmission of diseases.
- John Snow is regarded as father of epidemology *i.e.,* the nature of the spread of communicable disease.
- Study which deals with, defence, resistant mechanism against germs called immunology.
- Edward Jenner invented small pox vaccine (1749–1823).
- Jonas Salk (1955) discovered Polio vaccine.
- Louis Pasteur in 1885 produce the first rabies vaccine. Rabbies is contagious disease which easily spread by association with infected persons *e.g.,* mumps, measles, wooping cough through cough sneezing or contact etc.
- Non-contagious diseases are spread by means of insects bites, contaminates, water and food.
- Various factors influence the infection *i.e.,* potency of organism number of organism, resistance of body and immune system.

COMMUNICABLE DISEASES

According to the nature of causative organism communicable diseases may be of following types:

1. **Bacterial Diseases:**
   1. Tuberculosis by *Mycobacterium tuberculosis.*
   2. Typhoid by *Salmonella typhi.*
   3. Leprosy by *Mycobacterium leprae.*
   4. Cholera by *Vibrio cholerae*
   5. Diptheria by *Corynebacterium diptheriae*
   6. Tetanus-by *Clostridium tetani*
   7. Plague (Gram negative) by *Yersinia pestis.*

8. Bacterial Pneumonia by *Streptococcus pneumoniae*
9. Syphilis by *Treponema pallidum*
10. Gonorrhoea by *Neisseria gonorrhoea*
11. Whooping cough - *Bordetella pertussis*

2. Viral Diseases: Chickenpox, Measles, Rabies, Influenza, Polio, AIDS.

3. Protozoans Diseases: Amoebic dysentery, balantidial dysentry, cryptosporidium diarrhoea, Giardiasis, malaria, sleeping sickness.

4. Helminths Diseases: Taeniasis, ascariasis schistomiasis, filariasis, ancylostomiasis.

5. Fungal Diseases: Due to fungal infection.

Other Classification

1. **Airborne Infection:** Disease caused by inhalation of infectious agent.
   - **Viral diseases:** chickenpox, small pox, measles, rubella (German measles mumps and influenza).
   - **Bacterial disease:** Diptheria, whooping cough (Pertusis) tuberculosis and cerebro spiral fever).
2. **Intestinal Infections:** Diseases by ingestion of infectious agent through water, food etc.
3. **Arthroprod Borne Infection:** Diseases transmitted by vectors (insects *etc.*).
4. **Surface Infections:** Disease caused by animals, bites, contact etc.

NON-COMMUNICABLE DISEASES

Non-communicable diseases (non-infectious) are (a) Deficiency diseases, (b) Degenerative diseases.

(a) Deficiency Diseases : Deficiency diseases are due to deficiency of vitamins, minerals, carbodydrates, proteins & fats, *e.g.*,

Kwashiokar - protein deficiency
Anaemia - Fe & Folic acid deficiency
Night blindness - Vit. A deficiency
Xeropthalmia - Vit. A deficiency
Beri-Beri - Vit. B_1 deficiency
Pellagra - Vit. B_3 Riboflavin deficiency
Rickets - Vit. D deficiency
Scurvy - Vit. C deficiency
Pernicious Anaemia - Vit.B_{12} deficiency
Haemorrhagic Diathesis - Vit. K

(b) Degenerative Diseases: These are associated with vital organs *e.g.* Heart, Nervous system, Lung, Kidney.

Some Common Communicable Disease

1. **Chickenpox (*Varricella*):** This is a common but mild disease found all over the world. It is highly infectious. It occurs only in human beings. The incubatim period is 2-5 weeks.
2. **Smallpox (*Variola*):** This was once a major public health problem in India. It is caused by small pox virus and used to occur at the same time with chickenpox. Vaccination against smallpox was introduced by Edward Jenner in England in 1796 and it proved to be extremely effective in preventing smallpox. World Health Organisation launched small pox eradication programme in 1967. Its transmitted through oral and nasal discharges. The incubation periods 12 days. Rashes charges to rustules finally form scales.
3. **Measles (*Rubeola*):** It is highly infectious disease occuring in children all over the world. It is severe, causes many complication and deaths particularily in very young and undernourished children. Measles is caused by RNA-virus para Myxovirus Rubeolla virus. It transmitted through the discharge from nose and throat of sick person. It has 10 days of incubation period.

   Treatment: Antibiotics are given if complications like bronchopneumonia develop. Vaccination for measles be given to every child between 9–15 months.

4. **Rubella (German Measles):** This is a disease similar to measles but caused by a different virus (rubella virus). It is spread by droplet infection and has an incubation period of 14-21 days. Period of incubation is 4-7 days. It affects children and young adults. Infected person gets the lifelong immunity.

   Low fever, sore throat and cough are early symptoms. The importance of rubella is that an attack in pregnent women is serious. If a woman develops rubella in pregnency, especially during first 3 months it may cause defect in the foetus.

   The only method of prevention of rubella is by active immunization with vaccine (freeze dried live). It is given to all children below 5 years age and in some countries it is given only to girls at the age of 10–14 years (before puberty).

5. **Mumps:** This is a mild virus disease found all over the world. Incubation periods 16-21 days. It spreed through the saliva of person. It cause the painful enlargment of parotid gland.

   Preventions and Control: Isolation does not help. But may be necessary if an outbreak occurs in hostels of children.

6. **Diphtheria:** This is an important childhood disease and is found all over the world. It is caused by bacterium *Corynebacterium diphtherae.* The incubation period is 2-5 days. Disease appears with high fever, sore throat difficulties in breathing due to choking. Disease spreed through touching, kissing, talking, coughing and use of contaminated articles.

   Treatment: Diphtheria Antitoxin is immediately given to destroy Toxin produced by *diphtheria bacilli.*

   DPT Vaccine: For immunizing infants, the preparation of choice is DPT. Firstly because, the infant can be immunized simultaneously against three diseases, viz. diphtheria, pertussis and tetanus which is a great achivement. Secondly the pretussis component in DPT vaccine enhances the potency of the diphtheria toxoid.

7. **Pertusis (whooping cough):** This is another disease affecting children. It is found all over the world though in developed countries due to active immunization it has become rare. It is caused by *Bordetella pertusis*. The incubation period of this disease is 10-16 days.

8. **Cerebrospinal Fever** (Meningococal Meningitis): C.S. fever occurs all over the world. In India it is reported in sporadic and sometimes in epidemic form.

   Treatment: Early treatment with penicillin, chloraphericol or with sulphadiazine may cure an attack. Carriers are given an antibiotic Rifampicix.

9. **Tuberculosis:** It is an serious disease and inspite of many advances in treatment. It is a major public health problem in India.

   Treatment: For effective treatment of tuberculosis following drugs are used:
   1. Streptomycin
   2. I.N.H. (Isonicotinic acid hydrazide)
   3. P.A.S. (Paraamino Salicylic acid)
   4. Thiacetazone

   DOT is effective now a days.

   B.C.G Vaccination was introduced in 1927. B.C.G (*Bacillus Calmette Guerin*) is a bovine tubercle bacillus cultured in the laboratory. In India it was prepared in Madras.

10. **Poliomyelitis:** This is an old disease but at present it become a public health problem. In India the disease has become common after 1948. It is spread through intestinal discharge, contaminated food and water. It cause inflammation of nervous system and stiffess of the neck, muscles fail to work. The incubation period of disease is 7-14 day. It is caused by RNA entrovirus. There is no drugs available for polio.

Immunization: It is the only way to prevent and control poliomyelitis.

Oral polio vaccine (sabin) was prepared in 1957. It is a live vaccine. Mostly the vaccine containing all the three types is used, doses are given (in 4th, 5th and 6th month) one booster dose is given between 18–24 months.

11. **Viral Hepatitis:** Virus infection of liver is called viral hepatitis. There are many viruses which infect liver. Two are main virus A and B are found in India but viral hepatitis A is more common. Hepatis A and E are typically caused by ingestion of contaminated food or water. Hepatitis B, C and D usually occurs as a result of parental contact with infected body fluids. Hepatitis B is also transmitted by sexual contact. The symptoms of the disease is jaundice, dark urine, extreme fatigue, nausea and abdominal pain.

    Viral Hepatitis A: Viral or Hepatitis 'A' is found all over the world. It is present in endemic form. It has incubation period of 20-35 days. It cause inflammation liver and fever.

    Treatment: There is no drug treatment for infectious hepatitis. Bed rest, vitamin B complex and high carbodydrates diet are given. Fats in diet should be reduced.

12. **Cholera:** It was known in India as 'Visuchika'. It is caused by *Vibrio cholera*. It has the incubation period of 2-3 days.

    Treatment: In the treatment of cholera, the first most important thing is to maintain the water balance of the body. This is known as rehydration. The salts which must be given are sodium & potassium chlorides and bicarbonates. Rehydration may be oral or Intravenous Readymade oral rehydration solution (ORS) contains: *Sodium chloride* (3.5 g); *Potassium chloride* (2.5g); *Sodium Biocarbonate* (1.5g) and *Glucose* (20g). In cholera 500 mg tetracyline is given every 6 hours for 3 days.

13. **Diarrhoeal Diseases:** This group of diseases includes a number of acute infections caused by viruses, bacteria etc. of which diarrhoea is the main symptom. Poverty, ignorance, poor sanitation, overcrowding are also responsible for these diseases. They are transmitted through water and food. Control of these infections is similar to control of cholera. Early treatment with oral rehydration, proper nutrition and improvement of sanitation are the main preventive control measures.

14. **Food poisoning:** Diarrhoea and vomiting due to food or drink contaminated by organisms or due to chemical poisons is known food poisoning. Food poisoning may be due to bacterial or non-bacterial organisms. The *Salmonella* food poisoning is quite common. *Staphylococcal* food poisoning is due to intake of contaminated milk.

15. **Difference Between Cholera & Food Poisoning:**

Cholera	Food Poisoning
1. Occurs in endemic or epidemic form, by spread of infection.	1. Only in persons who have taken contaminated food, does not spread
2. Incubation period is few hours to 5 days.	2. Incubation period is 1–24 hours
3. Starts with diarrhoea followed by vomiting	3. Starts with vomiting followed by diarrhoea.
4. No *nausea* or *headache*	4. *Nausea* and *Headache* present
5. Watery stools, may be *rice water*.	5. Yellow coloured stools with offensive smell.
6. Severe dehydration	6. Less dehydration
7. No fever	7. Fever present

16. **Typhoid Fever:** It is found all over the world. Causative organism: *Salmonella typhi.* Incubation period 10-15 days.

    Treatment: Chloramphemicol is given in doses of 500 mlg/ 4 hourly till fever comes down and then the dose is reduced to 4 times a day for 14 days.

17. Amoebic dysentery (Amoebiasis): It is extremely common all over the world but more in tropical countries as in Asia and Africa. In India 10–50% persons are affected. It is a chronic disease lasting for many years. It is endemic in India. Patient passes 4–5 loose motions which contain blood and mucus and brown coloured.

18. Arthropod Borne Infections:

1. *Mosquitoes:* Malaria, filariasis, yellow fever, dengue fever, virus encephalitis.
2. *Sandflies:* Leishmaniasis (Kalaazar and oriental sore)
3. *Rat fleas:* Plague, endemic typhus
4. *Lice:* Epidemic typhus, relapsing fever
5. *Ticks:* Kyasnur forest disease, relapsing fever
6. *Mites:* Scrub typhus, scabies.

19. Yellow Fever: This disease is found in some parts of Africa and South America. It has never occurred in India. Yellow fever occurs in monkeys and other wild animals and from them it spreads to villages and cities becoming urban yellow fever. It is an haemorrhagic disease. The yellow fever is transmitted by *Aedes aegypti*. In most cases it cause fever, nausea, and pain. The disease is caused by RNA virus of flaviviridae family.

20. Dengue Fever: This disease is found in all parts of India and many parts of Asia. It is caused by four closley related virus serotypes of genus flavivirus, family flaviviridae. It is also known as backbone fever. The disease is manifest as sudden on set of serve headache, muscle and joint pains, fever and rash. Transmission is by the female *Aedes aegypti* mosquito.

The virus is present in the blood of patients. It grows in the body of the mosquito for 8-14 days then becomes infective. Incubation period is 2 to 15 days. Control of mosquito *Aedes aegypti* is only control measures.

21. Japanese Encephhalitis: This is a virus disease and epidemics have been reported from Tamil Nadu, U.P., Bihar and West Bengal. Birds and animals (e.g., pigs) are reservoirs of infection. The disease is transmitted to man by a type of culex mosquito. Incubation period is 5–15 days. Fever and **encephalitis** inflammation of brain are the symptoms. Unconsciousness and death may occur in 20–40 per cent cases. There is no specific treatment for Japanese encephalitis and treatment is supportive; with assistance given for feeding, breathing or seizure control as required.

22. Kyasnur Forest Disease: This is virus disease found in Shimoga district of Karnataka. It mainly affects monkeys and many other animals e.g., cattle, rats, birds. The virus is transmitted to man by hard ticks which are present in forest. Incubation Period is about 8 days Persons in the age group 20–40 years are mainly attacked.

Fever, headache and haemorrhage are the symptoms. Death occurs in about 5 per cent cases. Treatment is symptomatic. The disease is controlled by measures against hard ticks. A killed vaccine has been developed. Gloves, boots and repellents are used to prevent bites of ticks.

23. Sandfly fever: This is a virus disease found in some parts of Asia, Africa and S. America. Some cases have been reported from India. It is transmitted by a sand fly (*Phlebotomous papatassi*) Incubation period is 3–4 days. Fever and headache are main symptoms. The disease is controlled by measure against sand flies.

24. Malaria: Malaria is one of the oldest diseases of mankinds. It has caused sickness and deaths for thousand of years and it is not yet completely under control.

In 1880, Leveran discovered the malaria parasite in the blood. Ross in 1898 showed that the disease is transmitted by mosquitoes. The disease is caused by eukaryotic protists of the genus plasmodium. There are five species of plasmodium which can infect human are *P. falciparum, P. vivax, P. ovale, and P. malariae.* Symptoms of malaria include fever, shiviring, joint pain, vomiting, renal damage and convulsions.

National Malaria Control Programme: In India the National Malaria control programme was started in 1953. By 1965 the progress of NMEP was good but after that the cases of malaria started increasing every year. Therefore, a modified plan of operation was adopted by the Government of India in 1977. Now the attacks and deaths due to Malaria are lessen but it is still a big public health problem in India. In 2009 (April) 0.27 million cases of malaria has been recorded.

In 1958 N.M.C.P. was converted into National Malaria Eradication Programme for the following reasons:

1. It was thought that with success of NMCP eradication of malaria would be possible in about 10 years.
2. There was a possibility that if DDT was used for a long time it might reult in resistance in mosquitoes.

   The aim of NMET programme was to stop spread of malaria completely by destroying the parasites and the programme was started all over the country.

25. Filariasis: This disease is caused by nematode. They are mostly found in tropical countries of Asia and Africa etc. This disease is also known as Wuchereriasis or Elephantiasis. The nomatode present in the lymphatic vessels and lumph nodes of man only. Man is primary host and mosquito is intermediate host of disease. The swelling and pain in the affected part (testis, breasts, hand, feet) is due to lymphatic obstruction by microfilariae. Diethyl carbamazine (Hetrazen) or MSb is the recommended drugs. The caustive agent of this disease is *Wucherea bancrofti.*

In India, Filariasis is major public health problem like malaria. U.P., Bihar, Andhra Pradesh, Tamil Nadu, Orissa, Kerala and Gujarat. Vidarbha and coastal region of Maharashtra are more affected regions.

26. Leishmaniasis: This is a parasitic infections caused by *Leishmania bransitiensis*. There are two types of disease in this category, they are kala azar and oriental sore. Treatment with antimony salt cures the diseases.

27. Plague: This disease is transmitted to man by rodents, rats. In the past it was one of the dangerous diseases and was responsible for many epidemics and death is Asia, Africa and South America. Europe also had epidemics of plague in the 14th century and was called "black death" In India epidemics occurred in 1612 and in 1896 it broke out in Mumbai and spread to the whole country. The disease exists in two forms "wild plague" in wild animals and "domestic plague" in man. This disease is caused by *Yersinia pestis.* Flea is a vector (*Xenopsylla cheopsis*) which feed on infected rodent and may bite man. Drugs used for the treatment are streptomycin, chloromycin and kanamycin. Tetracycline is given for 10 days and is quite effective in plague.

28. Rabies: It is a viral disease that causes acute encephalitis (inflammation of the brain) in warm-blooded animals. It is zoonotic (i.e., transmitted by animals), most commonly by a bite from an infected Rabies is almost invariably fatal if post-exposure prophylaxis is not administered prior to the onset of severe symptoms.

The rabies virus travels to the brain by following the peripheral nerves. Once the rabies virus reaches the central nervous system and symptoms begin to show, the infection is effectively untreatable and usually fatal within days.

Early-stage symptoms of rabies are malaise, headache and fever, progressing to acute pain, violent movements, uncontrolled excitement, depression, and hydrophobia. Finally, the patient may experience periods of mania and lethargy, eventually leading to coma.

The rabies virus is the type species of the Lyssavirus genus, single stranded RNA genome.

All human cases of rabies were fatal until a vaccine was developed in 1885 by Louis Pasteur and Émile Roux. The human diploid cell rabies vaccine was started in 1967; however, a new and less expensive purified chicken embryo cell vaccine and purified vero cell rabies vaccine are now available.

29. **Tetanus:** Tetanus, also called lockjaw, is a medical condition characterized by a prolonged contraction of skeletal muscle fibers. The primary symptoms are caused by tetanospasmin, a neurotoxin produced by the Gram-positive, obligate anaerobic bacterium *Clostridium tetani*. Infection generally occurs through wound contamination and often involves a cut or deep puncture wound. Mortality rates reported vary from 40% to 78%. Administration of the antibiotic metronidazole decreases the number of bacteria but has no effect on the bacterial toxin. Passive immunization with human anti-tetanospasmin immunoglobulin or tetanus immunoglobulin is crucial.

30. **Leprosy or Hansen's disease (HD):** it is named after Norwegian physician Gerhard Armauer Hansen, is a chronic disease caused by the bacteria *Mycobacterium leprae and Mycobacterium lepromatosis*. Leprosy is primarily a granulomatous disease of the peripheral nerves and mucosa of the upper respiratory tract; skin lesions are the primary external sign. The mechanism of transmission of leprosy is prolonged close contact and transmission by nasal droplet.

MDT (multidrug therapy) for multi-bacillary leprosy consists of rifampicin, dapsone, and clofazimine taken over 12 months. Single dose MDT for single lesion leprosy consists of rifampicin, ofloxacin, and minocycline.

Lepromin test: This test is done to find out the type of disease and its future progress (prognosis).

31. **Sexually transmitted disease (STD):** It is also known as sexually transmitted infection (STI) or venereal disease (VD), is an illness that has a significant probability of transmission between humans or animals by means of human sexual behaviour, including vaginal intercourse, oral sex, and anal sex. While in the past, these illnesses have mostly been referred to as STDs or VD. Some STIs can also be transmitted via the use of infected needles childbirth or breastfeeding.

Bacterial:

- Chancroid (*Haemophilus ducreyi*)
- Chlamydia (*Chlamydia trachomatis*)
- Granuloma inguinale or (*Klebsiella granulomatis*)
- Gonorrhea (*Neisseria gonorrhoeae*)
- Syphilis (*Treponema pallidum*)

Fungal

- Tinea cruris "Jock Itch"
- Candidiasis or "yeast Infection"

Viral

- Viral hepatitis (Hepatitis B virus)-saliva, venereal fluids. Hepatitis A and Hepatitis E are transmitted via the fecal-oral route;
- Herpes simplex (Herpes simplex virus)
- HIV/ AIDS (Human Immunodeficiency Virus)- venereal fluids
- HPV (Human Papilloma Virus)-skin
- *Molluscum contagiosum* (molluscum contagiosum virus MCV).

Parasites

- Crab louse, colloquially known as "crabs" (*Phthirius pubis*)
- Scabies (*Sarcoptes scabiei*)

Protozoal

- Trichomoniasis (*Trichomonas vaginalis*)

High risk exposure cases may be treated prophylacticly using antibiotic combinations such as azithromycin, cefixime, and metronidazole.

The first three (syphilis, Gonorrahoea, Chanroid) are common all over India, but Lympho granuloma Vernerum (LGV) and Donovanosis are mainly found in South India.

32. **Acquired immune deficiency syndrome or acquired immunodeficiency syndrome (AIDS):** It is a disease of the human immune system caused by the human immunodeficiency virus (HIV). AIDS was first recognized by the U.S. Centers for Disease Control and Prevention in 1981 and its cause, HIV, identified in the early 1980s. AIDS is now a pandemic. HIV is transmitted through direct contact of a mucous membrane or the bloodstream with a bodily fluid containing HIV, such as blood, semen, vaginal fluid, preseminal fluid, and breast milk. This transmission can involve anal, vaginal or oral sex, blood transfusion, contaminated hypodermic needles, exchange between mother and baby during pregnancy, childbirth, breastfeeding or other exposure to one of the above bodily fluids. There is currently no available vaccine for HIV or cure for HIV or AIDS. The only known methods of prevention are based on avoiding exposure to the virus. HIV is an uncommon type of virus called a retrovirus, and drugs developed to disrupt the action of HIV are known as antiretrovirals or ARVs.

NON-COMMUNICABLE DISEASES

This disease donot have infections agents which make them spread from one person to another. They are caused by nonreversible pathological changes due to multiple factors. They have long and variable incubation periods. These diseases are permanent and leave residual disability. These diseases require special training of patients for treatment and rehabilitation.

The diseases considered in this group are:

1. Diabetes
2. Cancer
3. Heart diseases
4. Blindness
5. Deafness
6. Obesity
7. Asthma
8. Allergies

1. **Diabetes Mellitus:** It often simply referred to as **diabetes**—is a condition in which a person has a high blood sugar (glucose) level as a result of the body either not producing enough insulin, or because body cells do not properly respond to the insulin. If the body cells do not absorb the glucose, the glucose accumulates in the blood (hyperglycemia), leading to various potential medical complications. There are many types of diabetes, the most common of which are:
   - **Type-1 diabetes:** results from the body's failure to produce insulin, therefore injection of insulin is required.
   - **Type-2 diabetes:** results from insulin resistance, a condition in which cells fail to use insulin properly. Type-2 diabetes is uncommon.
   - **Other forms of diabetes mellitus** include congenital diabetes, which is due to genetic defects of insulin secretion, cystic fibrosis-related diabetes, steroid diabetes induced by high doses of glucocorticoids, and several forms of monogenic diabetes.

Type-2 diabetes is determined primarily by lifestyle factors and genes.

Diagnotic features

- Fasting plasma glucose level at or above 7.0 mmol/L (126 mg/dL).
- Plasma glucose at or above 11.1 mmol/L (200 mg/dL) two hours after a 75 g

oral glucose load as in a glucose tolerance test.

- Symptoms of hyperglycemia and casual plasma glucose at or above 11.1 mmol/L (200 mg/dL).
- Glycated hemoglobin (hemoglobin A1C) at or above 6.5.

Treatment: Anti-diabetic drugs treat diabetes mellitus by lowering glucose levels in the blood. With the exceptions of insulin, exenatide, and pramlintide, all are administered orally and are thus also called oral hypoglycemic agents or oral antihyperglycemic agents. In Type-I diabetic Insulin is used, which must be injected or inhaled.

2. **Cancer (malignant neoplasm):** It is a class of diseases in which a group of cells display uncontrolled growth (division beyond the normal limits), invasion (intrusion on and destruction of adjacent tissues), and sometimes metastasis (spread to other locations in the body via lymph or blood).

Cancers are classified into following general categories:

- **Carcinoma:** Malignant tumors derived from epithelial cells, including the breast, prostate, lung and colon cancer.
- **Sarcoma:** Malignant tumors derived from connective tissue, or mesenchymal cells.
- **Lymphoma and leukemia:** Malignancies derived from hematopoietic (blood-forming) cells.

Cause of cancer

Cancers are caused by abnormalities in the genetic material of the transformed cells. These abnormalities may be due to the effects of carcinogens, such as *tobacco smoke, radiation, chemicals, or infectious agents*. Other cancer-promoting genetic abnormalities may randomly occur through errors in DNA replication, or are inherited, and thus present in all cells from birth. Genetic abnormalities found in cancer typically affect two general classes of genes. Cancer-promoting oncogenes are typically activated in cancer cells, and Tumor suppressor genes are then inactivated in cancer cells, resulting in the loss of normal functions in those cells.

Symptoms of cancer

Cancer symptoms can be divided into three groups:

- **Local symptoms:** unusual lumps or swelling (tumor), hemorrhage (bleeding), pain and/or ulceration. Compression of surrounding tissues may cause symptoms such as jaundice (yellowing the eyes and skin).
- **Symptoms of metastasis (spreading):** enlarged lymph nodes, cough and hemoptysis, hepatomegaly (enlarged liver), bone pain, fracture of affected bones and neurological symptoms.
- **Systemic symptoms:** weight loss, poor appetite, fatigue and cachexia (wasting), excessive sweating (night sweats), anemia and specific paraneoplastic phenomena.

Treatment: 1. Surgry, 2. Chemotherapy by drugs, 3. Radiotherapy, 4. Symptomatic in late-stages.

SOME IMPORTANT DISEASES

TUBERCULOSIS

Tuberculosis is a specific infectious disease caused by *Mycobacterium tuberculosis*. The disease primarity affects lungs. It can also affect intestine, meninges, bones and joints lymph glands, skin and other tissues of the body. The disease is usually chronic with varying clinical manifestations.

Treatment : Treatment for TB uses antibiotics to kill the bacteria. The two antibiotics most commonly used are rifampicin and isoniazid.

- **Rifampicin** (INN) or rifampin (USAN) is a bactericidal antibiotic drug of the rifamycin group
- **Isoniazid** (Laniazid, Nydrazid), also known as isonicotinylhydrazine (INH), is the first-line antituberculosis medication in prevention and treatment.

Treatment of drug-resistant TB requires a longer time and more expensive drugs as for examples;

- **Multi-drug-resistant tuberculosis (MDR-TB)** is defined as resistance to the two most effective first-line TB drugs: rifampicin and isoniazid.
- **Extensively drug-resistant TB (XDR-TB)** is also resistant to three or more of the six classes of second-line drugs.
- **DOTS (Directly Observed Treatment Short-course)** strategy of tuberculosis treatment recommended by WHO was based on clinical trials done in the 1970s by Tuberculosis Research Centre, Chennai, India.

BCG Vaccination : Ever since Koch discovered *M. tuberculosis*, attempts have been made to prepare a prophylactic vaccine against tuberculosis. Calmette and Guerin, two French scientists began attenuating a virulent strain of *M. bovis* in 1906 with a view to develop a vaccine against tuberculosis. After 230 subcultures over a period of 13 years, they were able to evolve a strain-known as Bacillus Calmette Guerin or BCG, which was avirulent for man while retaining its capacity to induce an immune response.

BCG is the only widely used live bacterial vaccine. It consists of living bacteria derived from an attenuated bovine strain of tubercle bacilli. For vaccination, the usual strength is 0.1 mg in 0.1 ml volume.

Revised National Tuberculosis Control Programme (RNTCP)

RNTCP or the Revised National Tuberculosis Control Programme is the State-run Tuberculosis Control Initiative of the Government of India. It incorporates the principles of Directly observed treatment-Shortcourse (DOTS) - the global TB control strategy of the World Health Organization. The programme provides, free of cost, quality Anti-Tubercular drugs across the country through the numerous Primary Health Centres and the growing numbers of the private-sector DOTS-providers. DOTS strategy began as a pilot in 1993 and was launched as a national program in 1997. This programme has been declared a success and India has received accolades from the world health authorities.

District Tuberculosis Programme (DTP)

The District Tuberculosis Programme (DTP) is the backbone of the national Tuberculosis Programme. It was evolved by the National Tuberculosis Institute, Bangalore, and was accepted by the Government of India for implementation which started in 1962. The District Tuberculosis Centre (DTC) is the nucleus of the DTP.The function of the DTC is to plan, organize and implement the DTP, in the entire district, in association with general health services. There are at present 390 District Tuberculosis centres provides all services to RNTCP.

POLIOMYELITIS

Poliomyelitis is an acute viral infection caused by an RNA virus. It is primarily an infection of the human alimentary tract but the virus may infect the central nervous system in a very small percentage (about 1 per cent) of cases resulting in varying degrees of paralysis.

Environmental Factors: Polio is more likely to occur during the rainy season. Approximately 60 per cent of cases recorded in India were during June to September. The environmental sources of infection are contaminated water, food and flies. Polio virus survives for a long time in a cold environment. Overcrowding and poor sanitation provide opportunities for exposure to infection.

Prevention: Immunization is the sole effective means of preventing poliomyelitis. Both killed and live attenuated vaccines are available and both are safe and effective when used correctly. It is essential to immunize all infants by 6 months of age to protect them against polio. Two types of vaccine are used throughout the world; they are:

1. Inactivated (salk) polio vaccine (IPV)
2. Oral (sabin) polio vaccine (OPV)

1. ***Inactivated (salk) Polio Vaccine (IPV):*** First deveoped by Jonas Salk and was tested in 1952. This vaccine contains all the three types of poliovirus, inactivated by formalin. It contains 20, 2, and 4 D antigen units of types 1, 2 and 3 respectively. The primary or initial course of immunization consists of 4 inoculations. The first 3 doses are given at intervals of 1–2 months and 4th dose 6–12 months after the third dose. First dose is usually given when the infant is 6 weeks old. Additional doses are recommended prior to school entry and then every 5 years untill the age of 18. Alternatively, one or two doses of live vaccine (OPV) can be given safely as boosters after an initial course of immunization with inactivated vaccine.
2. ***Oral (sabin) Polio Vaccine (OPV) :*** Developed by Albert Sabin using attenuated poliovirus. First human trial Sabin's vaccin began in 1957. Oral polio vaccine (OPV) was described by Sabin in 1957. It contains live attenuated virus (types 1, 2 and 3) grown on primary monkey kidney cells or human diploid cell cultures. Ideally each virus type should be given separately as monovalent vaccine, but for administrative convenience, rather than efficacy, it is given as trivalent oral polio vaccine (TOPV) vaccine. The vaccine contains (i) over 3,00,000 TCID 50 of type 1 poliovirus (ii) over 1,00,000 TCID 50 of type 2 virus, and (iii) over 3,00,000 TCID 50 of type 3 virus per dose. (TCID is tissue culture infection dose).

National Immunization Schedule

The WHO programme on Immunization (EPI) and the National Immunization programme in India recommend a primary course of 3 doses of OPV at one-month intervals. Commencing the first dose when infant is 6 weeks old. OPV is given concurrently with DPT; BCG can be given simultaneously with the first dose of OPV.

Pulse Polio Immunization (PPI) Programme

It is a global initiative to eradicate poliomyelitis by the end of the year 2000 is the largest international disease control effort ever. In pursuance to the World Health Assembly Resolution of 1988, in addition to administration of routine OPV through the Universal Immunization Program, the Pulse Polio Immunization (PPI) Programme was launched in 1995-96 to cover all children below the age of 3 years. In order to accelerate the pace of polio eradication, the target age group was increased from 1996-97 to all children under the age of 5 years. The number of reported cases of polio declined from 28757 during 1987 to 3265 in 1995. India is still the largest polio endemic country in the world accounting for 20% of the cases reported globally during 2000 (till July 2000) mainly on account of the situation in Uttar Pradesh and Bihar.

HEPATITIS

Hepatitis A (formerly known as "infection" hepatitis or epidemic jaundice) is an acute infectious disease caused by hepatitis A virus (HAV). The disease is heralded by non-specific symptoms such as fever, chills, headache, fatigue, generalised weakness and aches and pains followed by anorexia, nausea, vomiting, dark urine and jaundice.

Prevention

- Keeping away from contact with the blood and body fluids, including semen and vaginal secretions of infected persons.

- Avoid sharing personal items such as razors and toothbrushes with individuals who are infected with the hepatitis B virus.
- Use latex condoms to prevent getting infected through sexual contact.
- Vaccines protecting against Hepatitis B are available and should be seriously considered by people exposed to a high risk of infection such as those who receive blood transfusions, share needles for drug use or have multiple sex partners.

In India, it is estimated that at least 100,000 people die every year due to illnesses related to HBV infection. Realizing the dangers of Hepatitis B, the government expanded the Universal Immunization Programme (UIP) to include Hepatitis B vaccine in the year 2002.

CHOLERA

Cholera is an acute diarrhoeal disease caused by *Vibrio cholerae* O1 (classical or El Tor). It is now commonly due to the El Tor biotype. Cases range from symptomless to severe infections. The majority of infections are mild or asymptomatic. Typical cases are characterised by the sudden onset of profuse, effortless, watery diarrhoea followed by vomiting, rapid dehydration, musclular cramps and suppression of urine.

Pathogenesis : The main symptom of cholera is diarrhoea. Diarrhoea increases permeability of the intestinal epithelial cells, increased peristalsis, mucosal damage, an increase in mesenteric blood flow and failure of the "Sodium pump", *i.e.,* interference with the passage of sodium from the lumen to the plasma.

Control of Cholera : It is considered that the best way to control cholera is to implement a national programme for the control of all diarrhoeal diseases. Some of the control measures are given below:

1. **Verification of the diagnosis:** It is important to have confirmation of the outbreak as possible all cases of diarrhoea should be investigated even on the slightest suspicion. For the specific diagnosis of cholera, it is important to identify *V. cholera* O1 in the stools of the patient.
2. **Notification:** Cholera is a notifiable disease locally, nationally and internationally. Health workers at all levels (such as the community health workers and the multi-purpose workers) should be trained to identify and notify cases immediately to the local health authority.
3. **Establishment of Treatment Centres:** In the control of cholera, no time should be lost in providing treatment for the patients. To achieve this objective, it is necessary to establish easily accessible treatment facilities in the community. The mildly dehydrated patients (which account for over 90 per cent of cases) should be treated at home with oral rehydration fluid. Severly dehydrated patients, requiring intravenous fluids, should be transferred to the nearest treatment centre or hospital; if possible they should received oral rehydration on the way to the hospital or treatment centre.
4. **Rehydration Therapy:** The introduction of oral rehydration by WHO in 1971, has greatly simplified the treatment of cholera and other acute diarrhoeal diseases. The aim of oral fluid theraphy is to prevent dehydration and reduce mortality.

   Oral fluid therapy is based on the observation that glucose given orally enhances the intestinal absorption of salt and water and is capable of correcting the electrolyte and water deficit.
5. **Sanitation Measures:**

   (a) *Water Control:* As water is the most important vehicle of transmission of cholera, all steps must be taken to provide properly treated or safe water to the community for all purposes (drinking, washing and cooking).

   (b) *Excreta Disposal:* Provision of simple cheap and effective excreta disposal system (sanitary latrines) is a basic need of all human settlements. When cholera appears in a community, the need for these facilities become vital.

(c) *Food sanitation:* Since food may be an important vehicle of infection, steps should be taken to improve food sanitation, particulary sale of foods under hygienic conditions.

(d) *Disinfection:* Disinfection should be both concurrent and terminal. The most effective disinfectant for general use is a coal tar disinfectant with a Rideal-Walker (RW) Coefficient of 10 or more such as cresol.

6. **Vaccination:** Cholera vaccine is the only specific prophylactic available against cholera. The vaccine employed at present is a saline suspension of approximately 6,000 million each of classical Ogawa and Inaba serotypes of *V. cholerae* O1 per ml. So that each millilitre of the vaccine contains a total of 12,000 million vibrios.

7. **Health Education:** The most effective prophylactic measure is perhaps health education. It should be directed mainly to (a) the effectiveness and simplicity of oral rehydration therapy. (b) the benefits of early reporting for prompt treatment (c) food hygiene practices (d) handwashing after and before eating, and (e) the benefit of cooked, hot foods and safe water. Since cholera is mainly a disease of the poor and ignorant, these groups should be tackled first.

FOOD POISONING

Food poisoning is a common, usually mild, but sometimes deadly illness. Typical symptoms include nausea, vomiting, abdominal cramping, and diarrhea that occur suddenly (within 48 hours) after consuming a contaminated food or drink. Depending on the contaminant, fever and chills, bloody stools, dehydration, and nervous system damage may follow. These symptoms may affect one person or a group of people who ate the food.

Types of Food Poisoning : Food poisoning may be due to toxic chemical substances or pathogenic organisms.

(a) **Toxic chemical substances:** Food poisoning is due to adulteration or contamination with formaldehyde, melamine, 3-MCPD, cyanide, Lead poisoning, Mercury in fish, Sudan red dye, Aldicarb.

(b) **Pathogenic organisms:** Bacteria are a common cause of food poisoning.

(i) Most common bacterial food poisoning pathogens are: *Campylobacter jejuni, Clostridium perfringens,* Salmonella spp. *S. typhimurium, Escherichia coli.*

(ii) Other common bacterial food poisoning pathogens are: *Bacillus cereus; Salmonella; Listeria monocytogenes; Shigella* spp.; *Staphylococcus aureus* etc.

(iii) Exotoxins: Some food poisoning is caused by exotoxins which are excreted by the cell as the bacterium grows. e.g. *Clostridium botulinum* (causes deadly disease botulism), *Clostridium perfringens, Staphylococcus aureus* (causes intense vomiting) and *Bacillus cereus.*

(iv) Aflatoxins: It originated from *Aspergillus parasiticus* and *Aspergillus flavus*. Aflatoxin predominantly targets the liver, which will result in necrosis, cirrhosis, and carcinoma.

Salmonella Food Poisoning

An extremely common form of food poisoning. Five reasons have been given for increase of food poisining in recent years *(a)* an increase in contaiminated feeding *(b)* increase in international trade in human food *(c)* a higher incidence of salmonellosis in farm animals *(d)* wide distribution of "prepared food".

Perfringens Food Poisoning

Cl. perfringens (welchii) is the causative agent the organism has been found in faeces of humans and animals, and in soil, water and air. Incubation Period is 6 to 24 hours, with a peak from 10 to 14 hours.

Mechanism of Food Poisoning: The spores are able to survive cooking and if the cooked meat and poultry are not cooled enough, they will germinate. The organisms multiply between 30° and 50° C and produce a variety of toxins, *e.g.*, alpha toxin, theta toxin *etc*.

Clinical Symptoms: The most common symptoms are diarrhorea, abdominal cramps and little or no fever, occurring 8 to 24 hours after consumption of the food.

Bacillus cereus Food Poisoning

Bacillus cereus is a Gram-positive, facultatively aerobic sporeformer whose cells are large rods and whose spores do not swell the sporangium. The symptoms of *B. cereus* mimic those of *Clostridium perfringens* food poisoning. The onset of watery diarrhea, abdominal cramps, and pain occurs 6-15 hours after consumption of contaminated food. Nausea may accompany diarrhea, but vomiting (emesis) rarely occurs. Symptoms persist for 24 hours in most instances.

Prevention and Control

(i) *Meat inspection*: The food animals must be free from infection. This can be ensured by their examination by Veterinary staff both before and after slaughter.

(ii) *Personal hygiene*: A high standard of personal hygiene among individuals engaged in the handing, preparation and cooking of food is needed.

(iii) *Food handlers*: Those suffering from infected wounds, boils diarrhoea, dysentery, throat infection, *etc,* should be excluded from food handling.

(iv) *Food handling techniques*: The handling of ready to eat foods with bare hands should be reduced to a minimum.

(v) *Sanitary improvements*: Sanitization of all work surfaces, utensils and equipment must be ensured.

(vi) *Health education*: Food handlers should be educated in matters of clean habits and personal hygiene such as frequent and the rough hand washing.

ARTHROPOD-BORNE INFECTIONS

Dengue

Dengue viruses are arboviruses capable of infecting humans, and causing disease. These infections may be asymptomatic or may lead to (a) "classical" dengue fever or (b) dengue haemorrhagic fever without shock or (c) dengue haemorrhagic fever with shock.

(*a*) Classical Dengue Fever: Classical Dengue Fever or "breakbone fever" has been known in India for a very long time. It is an acute viral infection, casused by at least 4 serotypes (1, 2, 3, and 4) of dengue virus. Dengue fever can occur epidemically or endemically. Epidemics may be explosive and after start during the rainy reason when the breeding of the vector mosquitoes (*e.g. Aedes aegypti*) is genreally abundant. Temperature also plays an important role in the transmission of dengue virus by moquities. Mosquitoes kept at 26°C fail to transmit DEN-2 virus. The reservoir of infection is both man and mosquito. The transmission cycle is "Man-mosquito-Man". Aedes aegypti is the main vector. Dengue outbreaks have also been attributed to Aedes aklbopictus, Aedes polynesiensis, and several species of the Aedes scutellaris complex.

(*b*) Dengue Haemorrhagic Fever: Dengue Haemorrhagic Fever (DHF) is a severe from of dengue fever, caused by infection with more than one dengue virus. The severe illness is thought to be due to double infection with dengue viruses—the first infection probably sensitizes the patient, while the second appears to produce an immunological catastrophe.

DHF is transmitted by *A.aegypti*, epidemics of DHF have occurred in recent years in South East Asia (Burma,

Indonesia, Thailand and India) and western pacific (Malaysia, Philippines, singapore, Vietnam) regions of WHO. The disease is confined exclusively to children less than 15 years of age, with fatalities. Reports indicate that many adults are now being affected.

(c) Dengue Shock Syndrome: The clinical diagnosis is based on all the above criteria, plus Shock-manifested by rapid and weak pulse with narrowing of the pulse pressure (20 mmHg or less) or hypotension with the presence of cold. Clammy skin and restlessness.

Treatment: The management of dengue fever is symptomatic and supportive. Bed rest is advisable during the acute febrile phase. Antipyretics or sponging are required to keep the body temperature below 40°C. Aspirin should be avoided, particularly in areas where DHF is endemic, since it may be cause gestritis, bleeding and acidosis. Oral flrid and electrolyte there by is recommended for patients with excessive sweating, vomiting or diarrhoea.

In small children, five per cent dextrose in a half-strength normal saline solution (5 per cent D/1/2 NSS) is used following initial resuscitation, and 5 per cent D/1/3 NSS may be used in infants under one year of age if the serum sodium is normal. Intravenous fluid should be discontinued. When the haematocrit reading drops to around 40 per cent and vital signs are stable. A good urine flow indicates sufficient circulating renal volume.

Malaria

Malaria is a protozoal disease caused by infection with parasites of the genus Plasmosium and transmitted to man by certain species of infected female Anopheline mosquito. A typical attack comprises three distinct stages: Cold stage hot stage and sweating stage.

Malaria Control: Malaria control programmes have been defined as "an organized effort to carry out those antimalaria measures that are possible with the available resources and suitable under the prevailing epidemiological conditions, with the objective of achieving the greatest possible reduction of mortality and morbidity. National Malaria controal programme. (NMCP) was launched in India in April 1953. It was based on indoor residual spraying with DDT (1g per sq. metre in endemic areas) twice a year in endemic areas where spleen rates were over 10 per cent. The NMCP was in operation for 5 years (1953–58).

Malaria Eradication: The term "eradication" literally means "pulling out by the roots". By definition it implies an intensive short term effort for the elimination of Malaria parasites from the human population so that there is no further occurrence of Malaria even in the presence of carrier mosquitoes. In other words, Malaria eradication signifies abolition of the human reservoir of infection, and not the eradication of mosquitoes. The global programme of malaria eradication commence in 1957 under the aegis of WHO.

OBJECTIVE QUESTIONS

1. In acetone killed typhoid vaccine the immunity last for:

(*a*) 6 months (*b*) 1 year
(*c*) 2 years (*d*) 3 years

2. In salmonellosis, isolation is recommended till:

(*a*) 3 consecutive stool cultures are –ve
(*b*) Fever subsides
(*c*) widal reaction is –ve
(*d*) 72 hour after chloramphenical therapy

3. The time period is more than ______ for chronic carrier of typhoid.

(*a*) 3 months (*b*) 6 months
(*c*) 9 months (*d*) 12 months

4. Highest incidence of typhoid fever in the age group (years):
(*a*) 10–12 (*b*) 20–30
(*c*) 30–40 (*d*) 40–60

5. In typhoid, a permanent carrier is one who excretes bacilli for more than:
(*a*) 3 months (*b*) 6 months
(*c*) 1 year (*d*) 3 years

6. Only human beings are the reservoirs for:
(*a*) Pox (*b*) Influenza
(*c*) Salmonella (*d*) Rabies

7. In Salmonellosis isolation done till:
(*a*) Fever subsides
(*b*) Blood culture negative
(*c*) Spleen subsides
(*d*) Stool culture negative for three times

8. Vomiting occurs in a group of children in the night who had a meal at noon. The causative agent for food poisoning is most likely to be:
(*a*) Salmonella
(*b*) Botulism
(*c*) Staphylococcus
(*d*) Viral gastroenteritis

9. The common cause of diarrhoea in children is:
(*a*) Rota virus (*b*) Norwalk virus
(*c*) Adenovirus (*d*) Giardiasis

10. Certificate of cholera vaccination is valid after ______ days:
(*a*) 1 (*b*) 3
(*c*) 6 (*d*) 10

11. Regarding cholera vaccine all are correct except that:
(*a*) It is given at intervals of 6 months
(*b*) Long-lasting immunity
(*c*) Not useful in epidemics
(*d*) Not given orally

12. As per the latest guidelines which of the following dehydration status requires ORS prescription:
(*a*) Mild dehydration
(*b*) Moderate dehydration
(*c*) Some dehydration
(*d*) Any dehydration

13. Best prophylaxis of cholera is:
(*a*) Early case detection
(*b*) Improved water sanitation
(*c*) Chemoprophylaxis
(*d*) Check spread of epidemic

14. In a cholera epidemic, the information is to be given up to level of:
(*a*) Health ministry
(*b*) DGAFMS
(*c*) Hospital
(*d*) CMO and IMO

15. Chemoprophylaxis for cholera is by administrating:
(*a*) Doxycycline 300 mg. ounce
(*b*) Metrogyl 400 mg. 3 tablets
(*c*) Vancomycin 1 mg.
(*d*) Kannamycin 500 mg.

16. The drug of choice in cholera is:
(*a*) Tetracycline (*b*) Sulphadiazine
(*c*) Ampicillin (*d*) Streptomycin

17. Osmolality of WHO ORS is (mmol):
(*a*) 240 (*b*) 270
(*c*) 800 (*d*) 330

18. Citrate is added to conventional oral rehydration solution (ORS) in order to:
(*a*) Improve sodium chloride absorption
(*b*) Correct acidosis
(*c*) Increases its shelf-life
(*d*) Improve glucose absorption

19. Oral rehydration therapy consists of the following *except*:
(*a*) Sodium chloride
(*b*) Potassim chloride
(*c*) Magnesium sulphate
(*d*) Glucose

20. The WHO formula for ORS provides in mEqIL:
(*a*) 70 of sodium (*b*) 20 of potassium
(*c*) 30 of chloride (*d*) 80 of sodabicarb

21. Oral rehydration fluid does not contain:
(*a*) Sodium chloride
(*b*) Calcium lactate
(*c*) Bicarbonate
(*d*) Glucose

22. Which is not essential in case of cholera epidemic:
(*a*) Weekly chlorination
(*b*) Notification
(*c*) Vaccination of individuals
(*d*) Treatment with ORS and tetracycline

23. The required amount of bleaching powder necessary to disinfect choleric stools is:
(*a*) 25 gm/litre (*b*) 50 gm/litre
(*c*) 75 gm/litre (*d*) 100 gm/litre

24. The infectivity of a convalescent case of cholera lasts for:
(*a*) Less than 7 days
(*b*) 7 to 14 days
(*c*) 14 to 21 days
(*d*) 21 to 28 days

25. In a case control study of a suspected association between breast cancer and the contraceptive pill, all of the following are true statements *except*:
(*a*) The control should come from a population that has the same potential for breast cancer as the cases
(*b*) The control should exclude women known to be taking the pill at the time of the survey
(*c*) All the control needs to be healthy
(*d*) The attributable risk of breast cancer resulting from the pill may be directly measured.

26. Which one of the following is the longest carrier state found in the disease of cholera?
(*a*) 2 to 3 weeks (*b*) 1 to 5 years
(*c*) 5 to 10 years (*d*) Above 10 years

27. Of the total deaths, diarrhoea induced deaths among children below 5 years of age in India are:
(*a*) 35% to 40% (*b*) 25% to 30%
(*c*) 15% to 20% (*d*) 5% to 10%

28. Epidemiology of cholera in England was classified by:
(*a*) John Snow (*b*) Winslow
(*c*) Chadwick (*d*) Howard Hughes

29. *True* about eltor epidemiology are all except:
(*a*) Chronic carrier are common
(*b*) Asymptomatic mild cases common
(*c*) Long extraintestinal survival
(*d*) High secondary attack rate in famales

30. *True* in Eltor cholera are E:
(*a*) Infections are mild and symptomatic
(*b*) They are resistant to polymyxin-b unit disc
(*c*) Chronic carriers are common
(*d*) Secondary attacks rate high

31. About cholera *true* is:
(*a*) Eltor variety rarer than classical
(*b*) Vaccine is essential during epidemics
(*c*) Antibiotic theraphy contraindicated
(*d*) Ganglioside receptors in the intestines

32. Cholera is a vehicle transmitted disease because:
(*a*) When the vehicle is controlled the epidemic subsides
(*b*) It is always possible to isolate the organism from the vehicle
(*c*) The common source of infection is not traceable
(*d*) The organism does not travel great distances

33. Most common cause of epidemic of infective hepatitis in India is:
(*a*) HAV (*b*) HBV
(*c*) HCV (*d*) HEV

34. Maximum maternal mortality is seen in:
(*a*) Hepatitis B (*b*) Hepatitise E
(*c*) Hepatitis C (*d*) Hepatitis

35. Best method to protect newborn from HB B +ve, mother is:
(*a*) Isolation
(*b*) Stopping breastfeeding
(*c*) Hep B immunoglobulin
(*d*) Hep B-vaccine and immunoglobulin

36. *True* about viral hepatitis B is:
(*a*) Transmits by oral route
(*b*) More incubation period than viral A
(*c*) Different histopathologically from viral A hepatitis
(*d*) Can be cultured

37. Average incubation period of infectious hepatitis is:
(*a*) 7 days (*b*) 15 days
(*c*) 25 days (*d*) 50 days

38. Acute flaccid paralysis in which age group is to be reported:
(*a*) 0–5 years (*b*) 0–10 years
(*c*) 0–15 years (*d*) 0–3 years

39. All of the following feature are suggestive of asbestosis *except*:
(*a*) Occurs within five years of exposer
(*b*) The disease progress even after removal of contact
(*c*) Can lead to pleural mesothelima
(*d*) Sputum contains asbestos bodies

40. In an epidemic of poliomyelitis best to stop spread by:
(*a*) Injection of killed vaccine
(*b*) OPV drops to all children
(*c*) Isolation of the cases
(*d*) Chlorination of all the wells

41. False regarding polio vaccine:
(*a*) Helps in herd immunity
(*b*) Killed vaccine prevants paralysis
(*c*) Difficult to maintain chain
(*d*) Immunity takes a long time to develop

42. The following statements are *true* for inactivated polio vaccine *except*:
(*a*) It does not produce intestinal immunity
(*b*) It prevents paralysis
(*c*) It is contraindicated in immune deficiency disorders
(*d*) Booster doses with oral polio vaccine can be given

43. The following is *not ture* of inactivated polio vaccine:
(*a*) Induces only circulating antibodies
(*b*) Prevents both paralysis and reinfection by wild polio virus
(*c*) Does not require stringent epidemics
(*d*) Not useful in controlling epidemics

44. Least likely to diagnosed Polio is:
(*a*) Fever, malaise for 2 days
(*b*) Fever and signs of neck rigidity
(*c*) Descending symmetrical paralysis with preservation of reflexes and sensory system
(*d*) Gradual recovery of muscle function in 6 months

45. In polio transmission easy block can be applied by acting on:
(*a*) Reservoir (*b*) susceptible host
(*c*) Faecooral (*d*) Agent

46. The epidemiological trend of poliomyelitis are all *except*:
(*a*) Affects higher age groups
(*b*) Increasing in tropics
(*c*) Also cause upper limb paralysis
(*d*) Sporadic to epidemic

47. Which of the following type of polio is most common?
(*a*) Inapparent (*b*) Abortive
(*c*) Nonparalytic (*d*) Paralytic

48. *Wrong* about polio patient who had paralysis:
(*a*) Can transmit it by nasal discharge
(*b*) Subclinical infection common
(*c*) Can be given vaccine
(*d*) None of the above

49. All *true* for a polio epidemic curve in a community except:
(*a*) All cases within 7–14 days
(*b*) Orofaecal mode of transmission
(*c*) Herd immunity present
(*d*) Epidemic curve has a slow rising slope and decline

50. Number of subclinical cases for 1 paralytic polio is:
(*a*) 50 (*b*) 100
(*c*) 1,000 (*d*) 10,000

51. AIDS was first detected in India in the year:
(*a*) 1975 (*b*) 1981
(*c*) 1986 (*d*) 1991

52. All are true of BCG innoculation, except:
(*a*) Papule in 7 days
(*b*) Forms an ulcer
(*c*) Heals spontaneously
(*d*) Size of 4–8 mm in 5 weeks

53. Effectivity of BCG vaccine is:
(*a*) 80% (*b*) 60%
(*c*) 40% (*d*) Less than 40%

54. A positive Mantoux test indicates that the child:
(*a*) is suffering from active TB
(*b*) has had BCG vaccination recently
(*c*) has had tuberculosis infection
(*d*) all of the above

55. BCG is not given to patients with:
(*a*) Generalised eczema
(*b*) Infective dermatosis
(*c*) Hypogammaglobulin anaemia
(*d*) All of the above

56. In the administration of BCG vaccine, the diluent is:
(*a*) Glycerine (*b*) Glycerol
(*c*) Normal saline (*d*) Distilled water

57. The vaccine administered by subcutaneous route is:
(*a*) BCG (*b*) OPV
(*c*) Tetanus toxoid (*d*) Measles

58. The direct BCG vaccination in Inida is given up to age of:
(*a*) 10 years (*b*) 15 years
(*c*) 20 years (*d*) 25 years

59. BCG vaccine is administered to children:
(*a*) Intradermally (*b*) Subcutaneously
(*c*) Intramuscularly (*d*) Orally

60. All the following are correct regarding BCG vaccination reactions *except*:
(*a*) Ulceration with crust
(*b*) Heals within 6–19 weeks
(*c*) Maximum size of papule is reached at 5 weeks
(*d*) Suppurative lymphadenitis

61. 0.1 ml of BCG contains ______ mg. moist weight:
(*a*) 0.050 (*b*) 0.025
(*c*) 0.075 (*d*) 0.100

62. 'DOTS' indicates
(*a*) Long-term treatment under direct observation
(*b*) Short-term treatment under direct observation
(*c*) Short-term treatment without observation
(*d*) Domiciliary treatment without observation

63. Short-term antitubercular therapy is given to minimise:
(*a*) Resistance (*b*) Toxicity
(*c*) Relapse (*d*) Cost

64. To prevent emergence of resistance in TB following are done *except*:
(*a*) Multidrug regimen used
(*b*) Drug to which bacteria are sensitive is used
(*c*) Defaulter action
(*d*) Pre-treatment regular culture sensitivity

65. *True* about tuberculin test:
(*a*) Used for diagnosis of TB
(*b*) Measure incidence of disease
(*c*) More than 10 mm in 72 hr indicates positive test
(*d*) Measure immunity status

66. Tuberculin test positivity depends on:
(*a*) Erythema (*b*) Nodule formation
(*c*) Induration (*d*) Ulcerative change

67. For Mantoux test, the standard dose of tuberculin used in India is:
(*a*) 0.5 TU (*b*) 1.0 TU
(*c*) 5.0 TU (*d*) 10.0 TU

68. Tuberculin test is read after:
(*a*) 48 hours (*b*) 72 hours
(*c*) 96 hours (*d*) 24 hours

69. 'Annual infection rate' in TB is the percentage of:
(*a*) Persons converted from tuberculine negative to positive
(*b*) New cases of tuberculosis
(*c*) Sputum positive cases
(*d*) Radiological cases

70. Under the revised National Tuberculosis Control Programme, a new case is one who has never had treatment for tuberculosis or has taken anti-tubercular drugs for less than:
(*a*) 2 weeks (*b*) 4 weeks
(*c*) 6 weeks (*d*) 8 weeks

71. HIV virus can be isolated from all *except*:
(*a*) Semen (*b*) Saliva
(*c*) Blood (*d*) Skin scraping

72. A 'case' in TB is defined as:
(*a*) X-ray positive
(*b*) Culture positive
(*c*) Sputum AFB positive
(*d*) Tuberculosis positive

73. Prevalence of tuberculosis infection is measured by:
(*a*) Chest X-ray
(*b*) Sputum AFB
(*c*) Tuberculin test
(*d*) Sputum culture

74. 'Annual infection rate' in TB is the percentage of:
(*a*) Persons converted from tuberculine negative to positive
(*b*) New cases of tuberculosis
(*c*) Sputum positive cases
(*d*) Radiological cases

75. Infectious pool of tuberculosis is denoted by:
(*a*) Prevalence of sputum +ve cases
(*b*) Prevalence of X-ray +ve cases
(*c*) Clinically +ve cases
(*d*) Any of the above

76. Which is best indicator of evaluating TB and its trends in society?
(*a*) Tuberculosis conversion index
(*b*) Mortality rate
(*c*) Prevalence of infection
(*d*) New cases

77. Assessment of magnitude of TB and its trend in community is by:
(*a*) Tuberculin conversion index
(*b*) Incidence rate
(*c*) Prevalence rate
(*d*) Fatality rate

78. The drug used by health workers in the management of acute respiratory illness
(*a*) Cotrimoxazole
(*b*) Chloramphenicol
(*c*) Benzyl penicillin
(*d*) Gentamycin

79. In meningococcal meningitis:
(*a*) Fatality of typical untreated case is 10%
(*b*) Rifampicin is the drug of choice in eradicating carrier state
(*c*) Cases are the most important source of infection
(*d*) Cases start losing their infectiousness 3–4 days after starting specific anti-microbial therapy

80. The following diseases are under surveillance by WHO, *except*:
(*a*) Relapsing fever
(*b*) Plague
(*c*) Malaria
(*d*) Tuberculosis

81. In meningococcal epidemic all of the following are useful for prophylaxis except:
(*a*) Rifampicin (*b*) Sulfas
(*c*) Vaccine (*d*) Tetracycline

82. Vaccines are available against group ______ Meningococcus.
(*a*) A (*b*) B
(*c*) C (*d*) A and C

83. Which vaccine is contraindicated in pregnancy?
(*a*) Cholera vaccine
(*b*) Typhoid vaccine
(*c*) Meninggococcal vaccine
(*d*) None of above

84. Average incubation period for meningococcal meningitis is:
(*a*) 90 days (*b*) 25 days
(*c*) 10 days (*d*) 5 days

85. Which of the following is *true* about meaning ococcal meningitis?
(*a*) Case fatality less than 10% in untreated cases
(*b*) Cases are the main source of infection
(*c*) Rifampicin is the drug of choice
(*d*) Treatment in the first 2 days can save the life of 95% cases

86. *Not true* about carrier state of *N. gonorrhoeal* is:
(*a*) Carrier state remains for several months

(*b*) Organisms can be isolated from nasopharynx
(*c*) Affected 5–30% of cases during epidemics
(*d*) It is coccobacillus

87. The absolute contraindication for administration of pertussis vaccine is:
(*a*) Diarrhoea (*b*) Fever
(*c*) Malnutrition (*d*) Convulsions

88. Incubation period of pertussis is:
(*a*) 7–14 days (*b*) Less than 2 weeks
(*c*) 16–28 days (*d*) 6 weeks

89. If convulsions are present, which vaccine should not be given:
(*a*) DPT (*b*) Oral polio
(*c*) BCG (*d*) Tetanus toxoid
(*e*) Measles

90. Which one of the following doses in lethal flocculent units of diphtheria toxoid is incorporated in DPT vaccine?
(*a*) 5 (*b*) 15
(*c*) 25 (*d*) 35

91. Management of unimmunised contacts of diphtheria is:
(*a*) Antitoxins
(*b*) Immunoglobins and antitoxin
(*c*) Erythromycin
(*d*) Isolation

92. Treatment of choice for diphtheria carrier is:
(*a*) Erythromycin (*b*) Tetracycline
(*c*) Penicillin (*d*) DPT

93. A herd immunity of over ______ is considered necessary to prevent epidemic spread of diptheria:
(*a*) 50% (*b*) 55%
(*c*) 60% (*d*) 70%

94. Management of nonimmunised diphtheria contacted includes all *except*:
(*a*) Prophylactic penicillin
(*b*) Single dose of toxoid
(*c*) Daily throat examinations
(*d*) Throat swab culture

95. For which of the following diseases is the usual antibody source equine?
(*a*) Tetanus, Diphtheria
(*b*) Infective hepatitis
(*c*) Measles
(*d*) None of the above

96. Which one of the following combinations is of DPT vaccine?
(*a*) Toxoid, live and killed
(*b*) Toxoid, killed and toxoid
(*c*) Live, killed and toxoid
(*d*) Killed, killed and toxoid

97. One of the following is used in DPT vaccine:
(*a*) Magnesium sulphate
(*b*) Aluminium phosphate
(*c*) Aluminium sulphate
(*d*) Magnesium hydroxide

98. Bull neck in diphtheria is due to:
(*a*) Retropharyngeal abscess
(*b*) Laryngeal oedema
(*c*) Cellulitis
(*d*) Lymphadenopathy

99. The most common age group for diphtheria is:
(*a*) 1–2 years (*b*) 2–5 years
(*c*) 2–7 years (*d*) 2–9 years

100. The infectivity of a patient with diphtheria is:
(*a*) Till cough subsides
(*b*) Till patient is febrile
(*c*) Life-long
(*d*) For 15 days after infection

101. Which of the following diseases has incubation period less than one week?
(*a*) Tuberculosis (*b*) Leprosy
(*c*) Influenza (*d*) Food poisoning

102. All are features of influenza epidemic *except*:
(*a*) Large number of subclinical cases
(*b*) Long Incubation period
(*c*) Absence of cross immunity
(*d*) Sudden outburst

103. Which of the following vaccine is contraindicated in pregnancy?
(*a*) Rubella (*b*) OPV
(*c*) BCG (*d*) Hepatitis

104. True about mumps is all except:
(*a*) Incubation period 2–3 weeks
(*b*) Aseptic meningitis may be present
(*c*) Even after B/L orchitis's sterility is unusual
(*d*) Hyperamylasia falls in pancreatis

105. Following statements is *not true* regarding mumps:
(*a*) caused by paramyxovirus
(*b*) Incubation period is less than one week
(*c*) About 31–40% of infections are clinically in apparent
(*d*) Orchitis occurs in about one in 4 males 25%

106. Incubation period for mumps is:
(*a*) 18 days (*b*) 14 days
(*c*) 10 days (*d*) 5 days

107. Which of the following diseases gives life-long immunity after an attack?
(*a*) Typhoid (*b*) Mumps
(*c*) Tetanus (*d*) Diphtheria

108. Which of the following vaccine was introduced most lately?
(*a*) Mumps (*b*) Pertusis
(*c*) Measles (*d*) Rubella

109. What is *not* usually a feature of rubella:
(*a*) Low grade fever
(*b*) Arthralgia
(*c*) Posterior auricular lymphade-nopathy
(*d*) The rash begins on the trunk

110. Vaccine contraindicated during pregnancy is:
(*a*) Rubella (*b*) OPV
(*c*) Tetanus (*d*) Influenza

111. Keratomalacia is associated with:
(*a*) Measles (*b*) Mumps
(*c*) Rubella (*d*) Diarrhoea
(*e*) Chickenpox

112. *True* about measles vaccines are:
(*a*) Given subcutaneous
(*b*) Highly efficacy
(*c*) Given below 1 year of age
(*d*) Diluent does not require for storage

113. All of the following are *true* for measles vaccine *except*:
(*a*) Fever can occur 6–10 days after vaccination
(*b*) Immunity develops 11–12 days after vaccination
(*c*) There is spread of virus from vaccine to contacts
(*d*) Single dose of vaccine gives 95% protection

114. Measles vaccine given to a contact of measles case exerts protective effect within:
(*a*) 1 day (*b*) 3 day
(*c*) 7 days (*d*) 10 days

115. Measles vaccine should be used within the following time after reconstitution:
(*a*) 1 hour (*b*) 2 hours
(*c*) 3 hours (*d*) 1/2 hour

116. In all carriers cause transmission *except*:
(*a*) Cholera (*b*) Typhoid
(*c*) Measles (*d*) Poliomyelitis

117. Carriers are *not* an important source of transmission in:
(*a*) Typhoid (*b*) Poliomyelitis
(*c*) Diphtheria (*d*) Measles

118. Carriers are *not* seen in:
(*a*) Cholera (*b*) Diphtheria
(*c*) Typhoid (*d*) Measles

119. Carriers are associated with transmission of disease in all except:
(*a*) Typhoid (*b*) Cholera
(*c*) Measles (*d*) Diphtheria

120. Following are complication of chickenpox except:
(*a*) Rey's syndrome (*b*) Meningitis
(*c*) Pneumonia (*d*) Enteritis

121. All stages of rash are seen in:
(*a*) Chickenpox (*b*) Smallpox
(*c*) Measles (*d*) Typhoid

122. *True* about chickenpox rash:
(*a*) Centrifugal (*b*) Pleomorphic
(*c*) Umbilicated (*d*) Deep seated

123. Chickenpox is characterised by all *except*:
(*a*) Live virus can be isolated from crust
(*b*) Rapid transformation of stage
(*c*) Rash is centripetal in distribution
(*d*) Lesions appear in brain usually

124. Which is *not* a complication of chickenpox?
(*a*) Pancreatitis
(*b*) Pneumonia
(*c*) Encephalitis
(*d*) Thrombocytopenia

125. Communication period of chickenpox is:
(*a*) Till last scab falls off
(*b*) 4–5 days after rash
(*c*) In the incubation period
(*d*) Only upto fill fever lasts

ANSWERS

1	2	3	4	5	6	7	8	9	10
(d)	(a)	(d)	(a)	(c)	(c)	(d)	(c)	(a)	(c)
11	**12**	**13**	**14**	**15**	**16**	**17**	**18**	**19**	**20**
(b)	(d)	(b)	(a)	(a)	(a)	(d)	(c)	(c)	(b)
21	**22**	**23**	**24**	**25**	**26**	**27**	**28**	**29**	**30**
(b)	(c)	(d)	(c)	(d)	(d)	(c)	(a)	(d)	(c)
31	**32**	**33**	**34**	**35**	**36**	**37**	**38**	**39**	**40**
(d)	(a)	(d)	(b)	(d)	(b)	(c)	(c)	(a)	(b)
41	**42**	**43**	**44**	**45**	**46**	**47**	**48**	**49**	**50**
(d)	(c)	(b)	(c)	(d)	(a)	(a)	(a)	(d)	(c)
51	**52**	**53**	**54**	**55**	**56**	**57**	**58**	**59**	**60**
(c)	(a)	(d)	(d)	(d)	(c)	(d)	(c)	(a)	(d)
61	**62**	**63**	**64**	**65**	**66**	**67**	**68**	**69**	**70**
(c)	(b)	(a)	(d)	(c)	(c)	(b)	(b)	(a)	(b)
71	**72**	**73**	**74**	**75**	**76**	**77**	**78**	**79**	**80**
(d)	(c)	(c)	(a)	(a)	(a)	(a)	(a)	(b)	(d)
81	**82**	**83**	**84**	**85**	**86**	**87**	**88**	**89**	**90**
(c)	(d)	(c)	(d)	(d)	(d)	(d)	(a)	(a)	(b)
91	**92**	**93**	**94**	**95**	**96**	**97**	**98**	**99**	**100**
(c)	(a)	(b)	(a)	(a)	(d)	(b)	(d)	(b)	(d)
101	**102**	**103**	**104**	**105**	**106**	**107**	**108**	**109**	**110**
(d)	(b)	(a)	(d)	(b)	(a)	(b)	(d)	(d)	(a)
111	**112**	**113**	**114**	**115**	**116**	**117**	**118**	**119**	**120**
(c)	(d)	(c)	(c)	(a)	(c)	(d)	(d)	(c)	(d)
121	**122**	**123**	**124**	**125**					
(a)	(b)	(a)	(a)	(b)					

7

Parasitology & Entomology

Parasitology

The science that deals with the study of parasites is known as *parasitology*.

1. **Protozoa:** First animal unicellular organism with nucleus and cytoplasm. They causes diseases.
   1. Intestines—*Entamoeba histolytica*, *Giardia lamblia*.
   2. Mouth, vagina urethra - *Trichomonas Naginalo's*.
   3. Blood: malaria *Trypanosoma, Leishmania*.

   E. histolytica is a natural parasite with world wide distribution. It exists into two forms, vegetative or trophozoites, these forms are formed in the body.

   Cysts: Resistant from infectious form. Cysts are resistant to gastric juice get excysted in intestine and trophozoities are liberated. These trophozoites (pathogenic phase) penetrate mucosa and submucosa carried by blood to liver and sometimes to lung and brain.

   Giardia: It has trophozoite and cystic stages. It localizes in upper part of small intestine and causes pain in abdomen and diarrhoea.

   Trichomonas: *Trichomonas* (Hominis) in intestine vaginalis in vagina and urethra. Trophozoite is infective and man is the only host.

   Malaria Parasite: There are four types of malaria parasites: *Plasmodium vivax, P. falciparum, P. malaria, P. ovale* is not found in India. *P. vivax* is very common (70%).

   Leishmania: It cannot be differentiated morphologically culturally or by animal inoculation. Life cycle is completed in two hosts. Leishmania stage which alone is seen in man and leptomonad which is seen in insects or culture media. Insect is sandfly. It causes the disease kala azar.

   - *L. donovani* causes visceral leishmaniasis (Kalaazar)
   - *L. tropica* causes oriental sore.
   - *L. toroziliensis* causes mucocutaneous leishmaniasis.

2. **Hookworm:** (*Ancylostoma duodenale*) It is a blood feeding parasite, attached to small intestinal wall with hook changes occur in larvae and 3rd stage larvae are infective. Treatment consists of supportive diet iron supplement, Bephenium hydroxynaphthoate (alcopor) and Mebendazole.
3. **Round Worm:** (*Ascaris lumbricoidese*) It is a commonest of all human helminths and transmitted easily if standard of personal hygiene is very low. After piercing small intestine, via venules and lymphatics it comes to right heart and thereafter to lungs. It comes to glottis and swallowed in oesophagus and passed forward to stomach and small intestine where it matures further into adult.
4. **Thread Worm:** *(Enterobius vermicularis)*: Also called as Ring worm or oxyuris. The mode of transfer from perianal area to mouth is through fingers underneath nail, food contaminated by fingers or undergarment. Eggs once swallowed hatch in small intestines, and then enter caecum and mature. Person complains of perianal

itching (sleep may be disturbed because of this). Prevention consists of avoiding auto infection but improving personal hygiene cutting nails short, biting of nails is forbidden. Drugs effective are piperazine citrate and riprinium embonate.

5. **Filarial Worm:** Adult female live in human tissue and continuously produce elongated active microfilariae. These are picked up by certain mosquitoes (*culex* and *mansonoid*) where it grows into the infective form. Next blood meal of suck mosquito would deliever these parasites to other human host. *Wuchereria boncrafti* is most widely distributed. Next comes *Brugia malayi*, presence of large number of microfilaries in blood is a periodic phenomenon and it depends upon the biting adopted by the specific mosquito.

6. **Hydatid disease:** caused by Echinococus granulosus. Adults live in the small intestine of dogs, eggs are passed in faeces of dog. They are swallowed by men because of fonding of dog or because of close relations with dog.

   Gradually embryos develop into cysts which attain more and more diameter. In man it becomes a dead end infectious. However in case of sheep if dog eats cyst containing raw flesh or if such dead animal the life cycle can continue in the dog.

General Measures of Control and Prevention of Parasite Infection

These measures may be anyone of control of source of infection, control of transmission, control over entry into a human host *etc.* Control measures can be applied to different levels of life cycle. Application of two or more measures at one time is more beneficial than single control measure.

1. Reducing the possibility of new infections in the community (Attack *on human host*): Drug treatment for parasite, which will kill ova, eggs, which transmitted through faeces or microfilaria circulating in blood will be reduced (possibility of mosquito infestation will be reduced).
2. Attack on the host other than human beings: Attack on mosquito distribution or removal of breeding place such as Larvicide, Adulticide, Protection against bites. Control over the Dogs (killing or therapy) and rats.
3. Environmental sanitation measures:
   - *(i)* Safe water supply and proper disposal of sewage and other waste.
   - *(ii)* Slaughter house and meat inspection for control of hydatid, beef tape worm.
4. Protection of human host: Improved personal hygiene protective clothing and shoes hook worm and strongyloid control.
5. Food hygiene and proper cooking: Fish tape worm beef and park tape worm.

Entomology

Medical entomology includes scientific research on the behaviour, ecology, and epidemiology of arthropod disease vectors, and involves a tremendous outreach to the public, including local and state officials and other stake holders in the interest of public safety.

Vector: An insect helping in transmitting disease agent from diseased person to healthy one is called a vector.

Modes of disease transmission

- *(i) Mechanical:* This type of transmission is mainly seen in houseflies physical contamination of mouth parts, body hairs. It occurs when it flies from faeces to food to be used by human being.
- *(ii)* Biological transmission.

Types of hosts infection

1. *Definitive host:* The host which harbours the sexually matured forms of a disease agent is called a definitive host *e.g.*, mosquito for malaria parasite.
2. *Intermediate host:* The host harbouring sexually immature forms of the disease agent is called an intermediate host *e.g.*, man in malaria.

Important diseases and their vectors

1. **Dengue fever** - Vectors: Aedes aegypti (main vector) Aedes albopictus (minor vector) threatens -50 million people are infected by dengue annually, 25,000 die. Threatens 2.5 billion people in more than 100 countries.
2. **Malaria** - Vectors: Anopheles mosquitoes - 500 million become severely ill with malaria every year and more than 1 million die.
3. **Leishmaniasis** - Vectors: species in the genus Lutzomyia in the New World and Phlebotomus in the Old World. Two million people infected.
4. **Bubonic plague** - Principle vector: Xenopsylla cheopis At least 100 flea species can transmit plague. Re-emerging major threat several thousand human cases per year.High pathogenicity and rapid spread.
5. **Sleeping sickness** - Vector: Tsetse fly, not all species. Sleeping sickness threatens millions of people in 36 countries of sub-Saharan Africa
6. **Typhus** - Vectors: mites, fleas and body lice 16 million cases a year, resulting in 600,000 deaths annually.
7. **Wuchereria bancrofti** - most common vectors: the mosquito species: Culex, Anopheles, Mansonia, and Aedes; affects over 120 million people.
8. **Yellow Fever** - Principle vectors: Aedes simpsoni, A. africanus, and A. aegypti in Africa, species in Haemagogus genus in South America, and species in Sabethes genus in France -200,000 estimated cases of yellow fever (with 30,000 deaths) per year.
9. **Japanese encephalitis** - Several mosquito vectors, the most important being Culex tritaeniorhynchus.
10. **Chagas disease** - Vector: assassin bugs of the subfamily Triatominae. The major vectors are species in the genera Triatoma, Rhodnius, and Panstrongylus.
11. **Chikungunya** - Vectors: Aedes mosquitoes

MOSQUITOES

Four important types of mosquito are: *Anopheles*, *culex*, *Aedes* and *Mansonoids*. There are four stages of development in each mosquito. All mosquitoes breed on surface of water and egg, larva, pupa and the adult are their stages of life cycle.

Diseases Transmitted by Mosquitoes

(i) *Anopheles* - Malaria

(ii) *Culex* - Filariasis, certain viral encephalitis

(iii) *Aedes* - Dengue, chikengunya fever, yellow fever

(iv) *Mansonoids* - Filariasis

Control of Mosquitoes:

(i) Environmental control:-

a. Control of breeding places

b. Anti larval measure: using insecticides like fenthion, abate *etc*.

(ii) Anti adult measures: DDT, gammaxane

a. Biological control

b. Genetic control

c. Health education to people

HOUSEFLIES

It does not bite but transmits the disease agent mechanically from dirt to food.

Disease Transmitted by Houseflies

It takes nourishment from human excreta, respiratory tracts secretion and discharge of wounds and sputum. It exhibits equal preference to food to be consumed by man. Therefore contaminated food consumption leads to various diarrhoea and dysentry disorders, typhoid, paratyphoid, cholera and gastroenteritis. It also helps transmitting such infection as conjunctivitis, trechoma, tuberculosis *etc*.

Control of Housefly

1. Environmental control
2. Using insecticides
3. Fly papers

RAT FLEAS

Following disease is caused by rat flea

(i) Bubonic plague
(ii) Endemic typhus

Control of fleas:

(i) Insecticides
(ii) Use of repellents
(iii) Control of rats

CYCLOPS

It has a body, a tail and two pairs of antannae (one short, other long) size about 1mm just visible to naked eye.

Medical importance

Intermediate host of guinea worm (*Dracontiasis*) infestation and fish tape worm, water containing cyclops when drunk causes infection.

Control of Cyclops

1. Environmental control: Removal of steps from step wells construction of sanitary wells.
2. Physical methods
3. Chemical methods
4. Biological methods
5. Health education

DDT (Dichlorodiphenyltrichloroethane)

It is a white powder. It is practically insoluble in water. It is a contact poison, absorbed through the surfaces of legs and body. It causes the paralysis of locomotion of legs and wings.

BHC (Benzene hexachloride)

It is a white crystalline substance with musty odour. In pure form the drug is called as lindane which is a fine white odourless powder. It acts in similar way as DDT but action is much faster and can also kill by vaporisation. It is spread in a pouch of 50 mg per sq foot. Residual insecticide action can last for 3-5 months.

Malathion

Malathion and diazinon are two least toxic compounds to men. It is a clear liquid with yellowish brown colour. It has a unpleasant smell, powder from it can be given in sugar bait for housefly control.

Pyrethrum

Extract from dried heads of the flowers of Crysanthesmum plant is known as pyrethrum. *Pyrethrim* I and II are active component of pyrethrum. The compound is very unstable. It needs frequent application for controlling the insects as it has no residual action. The most important advantage of this insecticide is the 'knock down' effect on the insect immediately after spray.

SOME IMPORTANT PARASITES

1. Entamoeba histolytica

Entamoeba histolytica is a pathogenic Protozoa which causes the amoebic dysentery in man. Mainly it is found in the large intestine of man spread to the brain, liver and lungs. The disease caused by it is known as amoebiasis. It is world wide in distribution but abundantly found in tropical regions. The adult and harmful stage of Entamoeba is called trophozoite. It feeds upon debris of tissue and R.B.C.

Structure: It is microscopic acellular animalcule. Its active trophic form measures 25-30 in diameter while the smaller less active form measures 8- to 12- in diameter. It is similar to the Amoeba in structure. Generally it possesses a single pseudopodium.

Life Cycle: The life cycle to *Entamoeba histolytica* is completed in a single host so it is known as monogenetic. Transmission from one host to another takes place during encysted form through contaminated vegetables, water and food or by flies and cockroaches etc. An acute infection causes dysentry but chronic cases may pass infectious cysts in the faeces.

Reproduction: It reproduces by binary fission and encystment.

(i) *Binary fission:* In binary fission nucleus undergoes mitosis and nuclear division is followed by cell-body. In this way two daughter cells are formed which grow rapidly in size. Fully matured form penetrates the mucous lining of the intestine causing ulcers and bleeding ulcers.

(ii) *Encystment:* During encystment these are liberated into the lumen of colon from the ulcers. These are less active and become small and ulcers. These are less active and become small and rounded. They secrete a thin resistant colourless and transparent cyst wall around themselves. It contains reserve food in the form of diffused glycogen granules and 2-4 bar like chromatoid bodies. Ingested R.B.C. disappear. The cyst is protective in nature. Now nucleus divides into two and further division result into four daughter nuclei. This is known as quadrinucleated stage.

Cystic Stage: The mature tetranucleate cysts come out with the faeces of the host. The stored glycogen is used as food in this stage. These cysts are destroyed in unfavourable conditions *e.g.*, high temperature. At low temperature, these cyst can survive upto one and half months. The freshly laid cysts are green and refractile and appear as shining spheres. These cyst may easily be identified during pathological test. (Immature cyst is binucleated.

Transmission: The cysts may enter the body of new hosts through the contaminated vegetables, water and food. After reaching the intestine of host the cyst is broken down due to action of digestive juices or enzymes. The metacystic stage (only one) comes out from the cyst which gives rise to eight young Entamoebae after nuclear and cytoplasmic division. At the time of hatching four nuclei are present.

These young Entamoebae develop to change into adult trophozoites which secrete proteinous enzyme capable to dissolve the mucous membrane of intestine and ulcers are formed. In this way new infection is set and parasite causes the amoebic dysentry. They may digest the R.B.C. and blood from capillaries which is mixed with mucous causing bleeding with faeces.

Treatment: In primary infection Yeast and Enterovioform tablets are recommended with Sulphogonodine. The other medicines such as compound of Arsenic and Iodine are Neoysept, Diodoquin, Furamide *etc.* In secondary infection some percentage Arsenic and Iodine increase in compounds. Chronic and acute cases are treated with Emetin tablets, injections, *etc.*

Prevention: One should follow the principle of hygiene. Water, vegetables and food should be protected from infection.

2. Fasciola hepatica

Fasciola hepatica, commonly known as liver fluke is an endoparasite of sheep which resides in the liver and bile duct. It is world wide distributed. It causes liver rot disease in sheep.

Structure: It is flattened leaf like having somewhat oval shape. The size varies from 4-6 cms, colour of the body is slightly pinkish with brown margins.

The anterior end of the body possesses a minute circular mouth surrounded by an oral or anterior sucker. Posterior or ventral sucker lies just after the oral sucker on the ventral surface. In between the two suckers lies a genital pore, At the extreme posterior, the aperture of Laurer's canal is also developed.

Life Cycle: The liver fluke is hermaphrodite i.e. male and female reproductive organs are present in the same individual. It completes its life cycle in two hosts. The primary host is sheep or cattle while secondary host is a snail. Thus the cycle is digenetic.

Copulation: Although it is hermaphrodite but cross fertilization takes place. The cirrus of one is inserted into the opening of Laurer's canal of other. The sperms pass into the laurer's canal and finally reach to the oviduct.

Fertilization: The fertilization takes place with the help of sperms and ova in the oviduct.

Eggs: Fertilized eggs are surrounded by yolk and shell in the ootype. The shape of the egg is like a capsule having lid or operculum. The eggs pass through uterus and reach in the intestine of the host.

Cleavage: The cleavage starts in the uterus. The first cleavage is complete but unequal producing small granular propagatory cell and a large somatic cell. The somatic cell gives rise to the ectoderm of larva after division. Remaining propagatory cell divides to give rise to two types of cell:

(i) *Group of somatic cells:* These are responsible for the formation of body structure of embryo.

(ii) *Group of germ cells:* They lie in the posterior part of the larval body and responsible for the formation of new larval stage after development.

Within two weeks a ciliated larva is formed which is known as miracidium. It comes out and swims in the water.

Miracidium larva: It is conical in shape having large number of cilia all over the body. Cilia help in swimming in the water. Towards the anterior end a small apical papilla is present. In the apical region multinucleated apical gland and unicellular penetrating glands are present which open outside through the papilla.

Infection to the secondary host (Lymnaea): The larva is very active and swims freely in the water. If it finds its secondary host, the water snail, Lymnaea or Planorbis within a day, it bores, the pulmonary sac with the help of the papilla and the secretion of penetrating glands, otherwise it dies. Here cilia are lost and it develops into a new larval stage, the sporocyst.

Sporocyst: It is a sac like structure covered by cuticle. The cilia and epidermal cells are lost. Eyes spot, brain glands etc. degenerate. The subepithilial cells, muscles, and mesenchyme are as such and germ balls and protonephridia are present.

The germ balls produce daughter sporocysts which again produce third type of larva the redia.

Redia: It is an elongated sac like larva which comes out by rupturing cyst and migrates to liver or digestive gland of the snail. A small mouth is present at the anterior end. There is an aperature in the side wall near the collar which is known as birth pore.

Cercaria: It is a heart shaped larva with tail which resembles with the adult fluke in appearance. Its body is covered by thin cuticle. The rudiments of most of the adult organs are present. There is a mouth surrounded by oral sucker. Ventral sucker or posterior sucker or acetabullum is present on the ventral side. Pharynx is suctorial and intestine is bifid. Paired excretory ducts with flame cells and genital rudiments are present. Cystogenous cells is the characteristic feature of it which are responsible for the formation of cyst.

Metacercaria: It is similar to cercaria but tail and cystogenous cells are absent, Cyst is present around it. Flame cells have increased in number and excretory bladder opens out side by an aperture.

Infection to new host: Further development of metacercaria can only take place if it is swallowed by the main host, the sheep within few weeks. With the help of water plants or vegetation the cercariae reach in the intestine of sheep. The cyst is dissolved by the action of digestive juices and young fluke emerges which bores the intestinal wall. After 2 or 3 weeks they infect the liver and may enter in the bile duct for development to change into the adult forms.

3. Ascaris

Habit and Habitat: *Ascaris lumbricoides* is a common parasite found in the large intestine of man. It is world wide in distribution. The number of worms may be 500 or more in a single host.

Life Cycle: The life cycle of *Ascaris* is monogenetic *i.e.*, complete in one host only.

Copulation and Fertilization: The copulation in *Ascaris* takes place inside the host. The sperms of male which are Amoeboid are passed into the vagina of female and finally fertilize the eggs in oviduct or upper part of uterus (proximal part of uterus). The fertilized egg is surrounded by chitinous egg shell and a layer of albumen.

Infection: Embryonated or infective eggs (with 2nd stage larva) transfer through contaminated food, drinks and raw vegetables and taken by the host. The duodenal secretions stimulate the larva which comes out of egg shell. It contains nerve ring and alimentary canal.

Primary Migration of Larva: It first enters the host-intestine by penetration and reaches the liver through portal system or lymph channels. After a few days it reaches into the postcaval vein and then to the heart. From the heart through pulmonary artery, it reaches into the lung. Here it settles down in capillaries of alveoli for some time and undergoes two moultings one after the other. It increases in size measuring 1 to 2.1 mm in length. After third moulting it again starts its migration.

Secondary Migration of Larva: Larva comes into the air passages and then into the pharynx from alveoli. Here it causes coughing by irritation of the pharyngeal wall. Either it is swallowed again into the intestine with coughing or spitted out. Inside the intestine it moults for the last time (4th moulting) and assumes the adult form after development.

Economic Importance

1. Larvae cause the inflammation in the lungs. Sometimes symptoms of pneumonia, fever, anaemia eosinophilia may also appear.
2. The mature forms may cause abdominal pain, diarrhoea, headache etc, In huge quantity they may block the intestine.
3. Presence of the parasite causes abdominal pain and intestinal ulcers.
4. The parasites often cause toxic effects such as vomitting, allergies, urticaria and may cause loss of sight.

Prevention: Infection may be checked by taking preventive measures:

1. Raw vegetables, leaves, fruits and roots should be thoroughly washed and properly cooked.
2. The use of contaminated water and food should be avoided.
3. Sanitation should be proper.
4. Extra nails should be cut off from the fingers.
5. Before taking meal hands should be cleaned properly.
6. Children should not play in the dirty places.

4. Wuchereria Bancrofti (filarial worm)

Habit and Habitat: *Wuchereria bancrofti* lives in the lymphatic vessels and lymph nodes of man. The life cycle is completed in two hosts so it is a digenetic nematode. It is found in the tropical and sub-tropical countries.

Life Cycle: It is a digenetic nematode having following host:

1. Primary host-man
2. Secondary host-mosquito (Culex)

1. *Life cycle in Primary host (Man) :* The adult worm (female) gives rise to microfilariae larvae. They are surrounded by a delicate sheath. Microfilariae appear in peripheral blood circulation during night while during day they disappear. They are active and can move with and against the blood stream. Each is a colourless cylindrical form with tapering head. The body contains granules which are arranged along the central axis.

   Further development of microfilariae takes place only in the intermediate host, when they are sucked by mosquito.
2. *Life cycle in Secondary host (Mosquito):* The microfilariae are collected in the anterior part of stomach from where after casting their sheath they migrate to the thoracic muscles. Inside the muscles these increase in length. They change into thick short forms and represent first stage larvae having rudimentary canal. The second stage larvae are formed within three to six days as larvae grow rapidly, moult once and

attain a size of 212m - 325m. Metamorphosis takes place after about 102 hours. The tail is lost and development of digestive system, body cavity and genital organs takes place to change into third stage larvae measuring 1200m to 2000m in length and 15m-20m in breadth. The larvae migrate into the mouth parts of the mosquito.

Infection in Man: When the infected mosquito which is the carrier of the disease bites a man, numerous microfilariae are injected into the blood or deposited on the skin near the wound. Now larvae reach the lymphatic channels and settle down at some point and finally change into adults after metamorphosis. Near about in one year the adult form become sexually mature to reproduce new larval forms.

The parasite causes filarial fever, mental depression, headache *etc*. In case of heavy infections larval forms or adult forms block the lymph channels or vessels. Thickening of the lymphatic vessels takes place by the proliferation of endothelial cells. The lymph which cannot get back into circulatory system accumulates in the organs and causes them to swell to fantastic proportions. Generally liver, spleen, scrutum, vulva, legs and groins become greatly enlarged. This is commonly known as elephantiasis or filariasis. The disease may be eliminated by giving the compound of Antimony and Arsenic *e.g.*, Mel W, Hetrazon Msb. To control the infection preventive measures should be followed *viz*. destruction of mosquito, protection against mosquito bites *etc*.

OBJECTIVE QUESTIONS

1. The active or trophic forms of *Entamoeba histolytica* feed upon:
(*a*) Blood
(*b*) Food in the intestine
(*c*) Mucosa and submucosa of colon
(*d*) Erythrocytes, mucosa and submucosa of colon

2. In malarial infection, lysolecithin that destroys the RBCs is secreted by:
(*a*) Spleen (*b*) WBCs
(*c*) Liver (*d*) Plasmodium

3. If Amoeba is kept in distilled water its contractile vacuole:
(*a*) Works slowly
(*b*) Works faster
(*c*) Remain as such
(*d*) Disappear

4. Sir Ronald Ross discovered that:
(*a*) Malaria is caused by foul air
(*b*) Malaria is transmitted by *Anopheles*
(*c*) Four species of *Plasmodium* cause malaria
(*d*) Malaria is caused by protozoan

5. Cyst formation in Amoeba:
(*a*) Occurs in adverse conditions
(*b*) Does not occur
(*c*) Follows sexual union
(*d*) Preceeds sexual union

6. For prevention against amoebiasis, we should:
(*a*) Eat more food
(*b*) Use mosquito net
(*c*) Drink boiled water
(*d*) All

7. Golgi cycle is found in:
(*a*) W.B.C. (*b*) R.B.C.
(*c*) Liver cells (*d*) Stomach

8. Which is the locomotary organ of class suctoria:
(*a*) Pseudopodia (*b*) Flagellum
(*c*) Cilia (*d*) Tentacles

9. Zygote of which one is motile?
(*a*) Hydra (*b*) Plasmodium
(*c*) Ascaris (*d*) Pheretima

10. Quartan malaria is caused by *Plasmodium*:
(*a*) Ovale (*b*) Falciparum
(*c*) Malariae (*d*) Vivax

11. One of the following is Polymorphic:
(*a*) *Taenia solium* (*b*) *Trypanosoma*
(*c*) *Paramecium* (*d*) *Entamoeba*

12. In which form would you find chromatoid bodies in *Entamoeba histolytica*?
(*a*) In minuta (*b*) In mature cyst
(*c*) In trophozoite (*d*) None

13. The duration of erythrocytic cycle in *Plasmodium vivax* is:
(*a*) 48 hours (*b*) 24 hours
(*c*) Irregular (*d*) 72 hours

14. The infection stage of malarial parasite for human is
(*a*) Sporozoite (*b*) Leishmania
(*c*) Trypanosoma (*d*) Plasmodium

15. Paramecium contains:
(*a*) Two micronuclei
(*b*) One or more micronuclei
(*c*) Two macronuclei
(*d*) One micro and more macronuclei

16. Plasmodium vivax belongs to the class:
(*a*) Telesporea (*b*) Sarcodina
(*c*) Mastigophora (*d*) Ciliata

17. Malaria is an "Insect borne disease", was established by:
(*a*) Laveran (*b*) Golgi
(*c*) Sir Ronald Ross (*d*) Grassi

18. Reduction division of gametocytes in Plasmodium takes place:
(*a*) In the blood of man
(*b*) In the stomach of mosquito
(*c*) In the haemocoel of mosquito
(*d*) None of the above

19. Which of the following is a matching pair of the vector and the disease?
(*a*) Anopheles-malaria
(*b*) House fly - Yellow fever
(*c*) Body louse - Typhoid
(*d*) Sand fly - Plauge

20. The mode of nutrition in the free living Amoeba proteus is:
(*a*) Holophytic (*b*) Saprozoic
(*c*) Holozoic (*d*) Parasitic

21. Toxic malarial pigment is known as:
(*a*) Haematin (*b*) Globulin
(*c*) Proteolysin (*d*) Haemozoin

22. Infection of one of the following may reach lung, liver and brain.
(*a*) *Trypanosoma gambiense*
(*b*) *Entamoeba histolytica*
(*c*) *Plasmodium vivax*
(*d*) All the above

23. The technical name of pin worm or seat worm is
(*a*) *Trichinella* (*b*) *Ancylostoma*
(*c*) *Enterobius* (*d*) *Wuchereria*

24. Elephantiasis in man is caused by
(*a*) *Dracunculus* (Guinea worm)
(*b*) *Ancylostoma* (Hook worm)
(*c*) *Enterobius* (Pin worm)
(*d*) *Microfilairae* (Filaria worm)

25. Chenopodium oil is successfully used for expulsion of
(*a*) Tape worm (*b*) Liver fluke
(*c*) Flat worms (*d*) Round worm

26. Which one of the following has no intermediate host?
(*a*) Tape worm (*b*) Liver fluke
(*c*) Round worm (*d*) Plasmodium

27. In *Ascaris*, the 2nd moulting of larva takes place in
(*a*) Pharynx (*b*) Oesophagus
(*c*) Alveoli (*d*) Intestine

28. In *Ascaris*, the last moulting of larva takes place in
(*a*) Liver of man (*b*) Lungs of man
(*c*) Heart of man (*d*) Intestine of man

29. In Ascaris only the anterior part of the testis is functionable. Such a gonad is known as
(*a*) Monorchic (*b*) Didelphic
(*c*) Telogonia (*d*) Metagoni

30. The amphids are cuticular elevations of the ventro-lateral lips of Ascaris. These are
(*a*) Chemoreceptors (*b*) Olfactoreceptors
(*c*) Tactoreceptors (*d*) Gastoreceptors

31. Rhabditiform larva occurs in the life history of
(*a*) Round worm (*b*) Liver fluke
(*c*) Earthworm (*d*) Tape worm

32. Nematodes are called as
(*a*) Round worms
(*b*) Flat worm
(*c*) Blind worms
(*d*) Tubiculous worms

33. Ascaris lumbricoides completes its migration in man from intestine in about
(*a*) 10-14 days (*b*) 50-60 days
(*c*) 30-34 weeks (*d*) 1-2 years

34. The female Ascaris can be distinguished from the male by
(*a*) Curved posterior part
(*b*) Straight posterior part
(*c*) Pineal setae
(*d*) Shorter in size

35. Inner layer of Shelled egg of Ascaris is
(*a*) Proteinous (*b*) Lipoid
(*c*) Both (*d*) None

36. Infection of *Ascaris* is more in
(*a*) man (*b*) woman
(*c*) oldman (*d*) children

37. Cleavage in Ascaris
(*a*) Spiral & determinate
(*b*) Holoblastic
(*c*) Meroblastic
(*d*) All

38. One of the following is viviparous
(*a*) Filaria (*b*) Ascaris
(*c*) Fasciola (*d*) Taenia

39. Sense organs of Ascaris are
(*a*) Epidermal cords
(*b*) Spicules
(*c*) Papillae and amphids
(*d*) Circumcentric ring

40. Infection of *Ascaris* usually occur by
(*a*) Mosquito bite
(*b*) Tse tse fly
(*c*) Imperfectly cooked pork
(*d*) Contaminated water and vegetables

41. In *Ascaris*, the mode of formation of ova is
(*a*) Telogonic (*b*) Budding
(*c*) Hypergonic (*d*) Diphylefic

42. Elephantiasis disease is transmitted by
(*a*) Sand fly (*b*) Fruit fly
(*c*) House fly (*d*) Mosquito

43. The infective stage in the life cycle of Ascaris is
(*a*) Fertilized egg (*b*) Cyst
(*c*) Secondary larva (*d*) Tertiany larva

44. Filarial larvae are found in:
(*a*) Spleen septa of man
(*b*) Liver capsule of man
(*c*) Wall of Intestine of man
(*d*) Blood of man

45. Intermediate host of wuchereria is
(*a*) Culex (*b*) Anopheles
(*c*) House fly (*d*) Tse Tse fly

46. Parasitic *Amoeba* with single pseudopodium
(*a*) *Amoeba proteus*
(*b*) *Amoeba pilasa*
(*c*) *Amoeba verrucosa*
(*d*) *Entamoeba*

47. Euglena reproduce
(*a*) Asexually
(*b*) Sexually
(*c*) Both asexually and sexually
(*d*) Conjugation

48. Schuffmner's dots are found in life cycle of *Plasmodium* in
(*a*) R.B.C. of man
(*b*) Liver cells of man
(*c*) Gamete formation in mosquito
(*d*) All of above

49. Schizogony in *Plasmodium* takes place in
(*a*) R.B.C. of man
(*b*) Lumen of stomach of mosquito
(*c*) Liver of Man
(*d*) Liver or R.B.C. of Man

50. Asexual reproduction is most common among protozoans because:
(*a*) Sexes not well differentiated in them.
(*b*) They can multiply fast

(*c*) It has nutritional importance
(*d*) Many of them live as parasites

51. The excretion in *Entamoeba histolytica* takes place by:
(*a*) Contractile vacuoles
(*b*) General surface
(*c*) Food vacuoles
(*d*) None

52. Zygote of which one is motile?
(*a*) *Hydra*
(*b*) *Plasmodium*
(*c*) *Ascaris*
(*d*) *Pheretima*

53. Reduction division of gametocytes in Plasmodium takes place:
(*a*) In the blood of man
(*b*) In the stomach of mosquito
(*c*) In the haemocoel of mosquito
(*d*) None of the above

54. In life cycle of malarial parasite, the sporozoites are stored in
(*a*) Liver of man
(*b*) Blood of man
(*c*) Stomach of female Anopheles
(*d*) Salivary glands of female Anopheles

55. Sol & Gel theory was advocated by:
(*a*) Dobell
(*b*) Hyman
(*c*) Dellinger
(*d*) Mast & Pantin

56. "Sleeping sickness" is due to the bite of:
(*a*) Sand fly
(*b*) Tse-Tse Fly
(*c*) Bed Bug
(*d*) White fly

57. During binary fission Amoeba divides by:
(*a*) Amitotis (*b*) Mitotis
(*c*) Meiosis (*d*) None

ANSWERS

1	2	3	4	5	6	7	8	9	10
(*d*)	(*a*)	(*a*)	(*b*)	(*a*)	(*d*)	(*d*)	(*b*)	(*c*)	(*c*)
11	**12**	**13**	**14**	**15**	**16**	**17**	**18**	**19**	**20**
(*b*)	(*b*)	(*a*)	(*a*)	(*b*)	(*a*)	(*a*)	(*b*)	(*a*)	(*c*)
21	**22**	**23**	**24**	**25**	**26**	**27**	**28**	**29**	**30**
(*d*)	(*b*)	(*c*)	(*d*)	(*d*)	(*c*)	(*c*)	(*d*)	(*c*)	(*a*)
31	**32**	**33**	**34**	**35**	**36**	**37**	**38**	**39**	**40**
(*a*)	(*a*)	(*a*)	(*b*)	(*b*)	(*d*)	(*a*)	(*a*)	(*c*)	(*d*)
41	**42**	**43**	**44**	**45**	**46**	**47**	**48**	**49**	**50**
(a)	(d)	(c)	(d)	(a)	(d)	(a)	(a)	(d)	(b)
51	**52**	**53**	**54**	**55**	**56**	**57**			
(*b*)	(*b*)	(*d*)	(*d*)	(*d*)	(*b*)	(*b*)			

Family Welfare

Maternal and Child Health

The term "maternal and child health" refers to the promotive, preventive, curative and rehabilative health care for mothers and children. It includes the sub-areas of maternal health, child health, family planning school health, handicapped children, adolescence, and health aspects of care of children in special settings such as day care.

The specific objectives of MCH are: (a) reducing of maternal, prenatal, infant and childhood mortality and morbidity; (b) promotion of reproductive health; and (c) promotion of the physical and psychologist development of the child and adolescent within the family. The ultimate objective of MCH services is life-long health.

Antenatal Care

Antenatal care is the care of the women during pregnancy. Ideally this care should being soon after conception and continue throughout pregnancy. In some countries notification of pregnancy is required to bring the mother in the preventive care cycle as early as possible.

Objectives:

The objectives of antenatal care are:

1. To promote protect and maintain the health of the mother during pregnancy.
2. To detect "high risk" cases and give them special attention.
3. To foresee complications and prevent them.
4. To remove anxiety and dread associated with delivery
5. To reduce maternal and infant mortality and morbidity.
6. To teach the mother elements of child care, nutrition, personal hygiene, and environmental sanitation.
7. To sensitise the mother to the need for family planning including advice to cases seeking medical termination of pregnancy.

Intranatal Care

Child birth is a normal physiological process, but complications may rise. Septicaemia may result from unskilled and septic manipulations, and tetanus neonatorum from the use of unsterilized instruments. The need for effective intranantal care is therefore indispensable, even if the delivery is going to be a normal one. The emphasis is on the cleanliness.

The aims of good intranatal care are:

i) thorough asepsis

ii) delivery with minimum injury to the infant and the mother.

iii) readiness to deal with complications such as prolonged labour, anterpartum haemorrhage, convulsions, malpresentations, prolapse of the cord *etc.*

iv) care of the body at delivery resuscitation, care of the cord, care of the eyes *etc.*

Postnatal Care

Care of the mother (and the newborn) after delivery is known as postnatal or post partal care. Broadly this care falls into two areas: care of the mother which is primarily the responsibility of the obstetrician and care of the newborn, which is combined responsibility of the obstetrician and paediatrician. This combined area of responsibility is also known as perinatology.

Care of the Mother "Under Five Clinic"

The objectives of postpartal care are:

1. To prevent complication of the postpartal period.
2. To provide care for the rapid restoration of the mother to optimum health.
3. To check adequency of breast feeding
4. To provide family planning services.
5. To provide basic health education to mother.

Care of Children

The section focuses on children in the age group 0-14 years. This is the most important age group in all societies, not because they constitute about 40 per cent of the total population but because there is a renewed awareness that the determinants of chronic disease in later life and health behaviour are laid down at this stage. The childhood period is also a vital period because of the so called socialization process, that is, transmission of attitudes customs and behaviour.

It is customary to divide the childhood into the following age-periods:

1. Infancy (up to 1 year of age)
   (a) Neonatal period (first 28 days of life)
   (b) Post neonatal period (28th day to 1 year)
2. Pre-school age (1-4 years)
3. School age (5-14 years)

Delivering the MCH Services

MCH (mother and child health) is not a new speciality. It is a method of delivering health care to special group in the population which is especially vulnerable to disease, disability or death. These groups (*i.e.*, chidren under the age 5 years and women in the reproductive age group (15-44 years) comprise about 31.6 per cent of the total population in India (75).

The MCH services encompass the curative, preventive and social aspects of obstetrics, paediatrics, family welfare, nutrition, child development and health education. The specific objectives of MCH are:

1. reduction of morbidity rates for mothers and children
2. promotion of reproductive health, and
3. promotion of the physical and psychological development of the child within the family.

Through concern with child development and the health education of parents and children, the ultimate objective of MCH services is life-long health.

Child Health Problems

- Low birth weight
- Malnutrition
- Behavioural Problems

Recent Trends in MCH Care

Maternal and child care was traditionally designed and provided in the form of vertical programmes with "standard" technical content based on models from a few developed countries. Applied in different socioeconomic situations, such vertical programmes have been unable to provide more than minimum coverage because of their cost, and unable to solve the priority problems of the majority of mothers and children.

These are as follows:—

1. *Integration of care:* Conventional MCH services tended to be fragmented into antenatal care, postnatal care, infant care, family planning etc.
2. *Risk approach:* A new and promising means of improving the coverage and efficiency of MCH care and family planning is the risk use of scarce resources. It is based on the early detection of mothers and children with high risk factors.
   It is also possible to assess the "degrees" of risk of each factor, by scoring according to their (a) magnitude *i.e.*, extent and severity; (b) treatability-responsiveness to treatment and control; (c) cost effect in terms of alleviating human suffering; and (d) community attitude - social concern.
3. *Manpower changes:* The special category of "maternal and child health worker" (*e.g.*, auxiliary - nurse - midwives, health visitors) at the peripheral level is gradually being phased out. A wide range of workers are now considered necessary for maternal and child health works. It includes:

(i) Professionals: Specialists
(ii) Field workers: Multipurpose workers, Health Guides, dais (traditional birth attendants), balsevikas, anganwadi, workers, extention workers, *etc.*
iii) Voluntary workers: Members of women's organizations

4. *Primary health care:* Primary health care is now recognized as a way of making essential health care available to all. It has all the elements necessary to make a positive impact on the health of mothers and children - *i.e.*, MCH care, family planning, control of infections, education about health problems and how to prevent them, and measures to ensure nutritious food- all closely related. Primary health care emphasizes family oriented care and support, and community self reliance in health matters.

MATERNAL AND CHILD HEALTH

1. **Maternal and Child Health:** MCH includes all matters pertaining to health (physical, mental, social), of women throughout reproductive cycle (15-45 years) and children of all ages from conception to adolescence. It also includes special health services needed by handicapped children.
2. **MCH Problems:** Advanced countries are having problems of mortality, congenital malformation, genetic and certain behavioural problems. In developing countries the problems are maternal mortality and morbidity, child mortality and morbidity, spacing of pregnancies, limitation of family size, preventation of communicable disease, improvement of nourishment to prevent malnutrition from prenatal period to the period of weaning.
   Infection of mother may cause low birth weight, abortion, puerperal sepsis. Baby may get infection with labour, delievery and weaning period. Diarrhoea respiratory infections, skin infection, tuberculosis and malaria are common ailments. Diphtheria, whooping cough tetanus, measles, polio can also occur.
3. **Antenatal care:** The basic aim is that every pregnancy should end with healthy baby and healthy mother.
   1. To promote, protect and maintain the health of the mother during pregnancy
   2. To detect complications and treat them
   3. To detect high risk cases and manage them.
4. **Prenatal advice:** Mother is most receptive at this time for advice.
   Prenatal advice for:
   1. *Diet*: Full average diet is indicated along with extra protein (20gml/day)
   2. Personal hygiene is necessary for following:
   3. Personal cleanliness daily bath, wearing of clean clothes.
5. **Child care:** Mothercraft education consists of nutrition education, childrearing, cooking, family planning education, family budgeting is taught. Fear of Pregnancy is Removed. Specific protection is given.
   1. *For anaemia*: Iron and folic acid tablets 60 mg + 500 mg from 2nd trimester. given routinely to every expectant mother.
   2. Nutritional supplements are given at MCH centres and at ICDS projects.
   3. *Tetanus*: 2 injections are given of tetanus toxoids.
   4. *Syphilis*: routine VDRL is done, if positive it is adequately treated.
   5. Rh status: If Rh negative mother and Rh positive baby.
6. **Care of New Born:** (Neonatal care)
   Immediate care:
   1. *Maintenance of respiration*: All secretion and contents from mouth and nose should be cleaned. The baby must breathe and cry. Keep the baby upside down for 1-2 minutes, use suction machine if necessary.

2. *Care of Umbical Cord*: Tie the cord when pulsation stop by two ligature and then cut it clean and dress use aseptic precautions.
3. *Care of Eyes*: Clean the eye with sterile swab and put 1%. terramycine or silvernitrate drops.
4. *Care of Skin*: Apply oil and give a bath, observe whether baby is breathless, not passing stools, persistent vomitting, convulsions report to the doctor.

7. Organisation of MCH Services:
Organisation in rural areas:
1. Primary health centre through 3 tier system of health care delivery (PHC, Subcentre and village level)
2. Private Practitioners
3. ICDS
4. Cottage hospitals
5. certain welfare centres.

8. MCH Services in Urban Areas:
Responsibility is with local bodies and provision of MCH service is at the discretion of local bodies:
Maternity hospitals are run by local bodies with full time doctor, Ayas, nurses, honorary doctors *etc*.
Some of these are run by state government, some by central government and some by voluntary agencies and local bodies.

9. Juvenile Delinquency: A delinquent child is defined as who has comitted an offence *e.g.*, theft, sexual assult, murder, burglary etc., Child means a boy less than 18 years and girls less than 16 years of age. Delinquent truly means any abnormal behaviour which results in antisocial practices. These are managed by improvement in family life, proper schooling, giving recreational facilities and child guidance cinics.

10. Laws Utilized for Welfare of Women and Children:
1. *Age of Marriage*: of a girl from 15 years raised to 18 years.
This will improve literacy, fertility will be low and the girl will be more mature.
2. *MTP Act 1971*: Helps in maintaing health of mother and also getting rid of an unwanted child.
3. *Hindu Adoption Act of 1956*: gives women a pleasure of becoming mother by law particularly for infertile women.
4. Factory Act provides a creche for 30 working women in industry for their children upto 5 years of age.
5. *Maternity Benefit Acts*: (According ESIS, government, semi government) 90 days paid leave for delivery and 42 days leave for MTP or abortion is given so as to restore health.
6. *Suppression of Immoral Traffic Act (1956)*: Help women and girls to get rehabilitated socially from becoming prostitutes by punishing brothel keepers.

11. Laws Related to Children:
1. Children Act (1960): Provides the care, maintenance welfare, training, education and rehabilitation of delinquent children. It covers the neglected, destitute, socially handicapped, uncontrollable, victimized and delinquent children.
2. Factory Act: Children should not carry heavy load, they should not be given night shift. If at all they are to be kept as employees, their fitness should be certified by certified surgeons.

12. Infant Mortality Rate: Defined as the number of infant deaths per 1000 live births in a year. This is considered as most sensitive index of health and level of living of the people.

13. Demography: The study of population is known as Demography. Demography has been defined as the statistical study of the characteristic of human population with reference to size, growth, distribution, migration, vital statistics and the effects of all these on social and economic conditions.

14. Factors reducing birth are:
1. High divorce rate
2. Ban on remarriages of widows and divorcees.

3. High standard of living
4. Prolonged breast feeding
5. Popularity of abortion
6. Acceptance of family planning habit.

15. Factors Affecting Mortality: Reducing death rate

1. Absence of natural checks–famine, epidemics
2. Mass control of diseases–small pox, plague, cholera, malaria *etc*.
3. Advance in Medical Sciences–drugs, insecticides *etc*.
4. Better health care—Primary health centres etc.
5. National Health Programme.

16. Scope of Family Welfare:

1. *Before marriage:* Sex education, parent—craft education, Premarital and genetic counselling (advice before marriage and on genetic matters)
2. *After marriage*: Supply of contraceptives, Sterilization.
3. *Fertile couples*: MTP, screening for disease of genital tract, Parent craft and genetic counselling.
4. *Infertile couples:* Investigation and treatment of sterility, Artificial Insemination, Adoption.

17. Family Planning Methods are:

1. *Abstinence:* Means intercourse is avoided. This can not be considered as a method of contraceptives, it is difficult to bring into practice.
2. *Coitus interruptus*: In this method male partner withdraws penis so that ejaculation occurs outside the vagina. It is suspected that some get mental disturbance due to this. Failure rate is 15-20 pregnancy per 1100 women year.
3. *Rhythm method*: (Safe period) for those who will not adopt any other method of family planning because of religious or other reasons, the rhythm method is advised.

18. Cervical Cap: Widely used in Europe, also in our country in the past. It is a small bell shaped device, of rubber or metal that fits directly around cervix. A small quantity of spermicide can be applied. The cap can be kept in the position till next menses. This is better for elongated cervix. Initial examination by doctor is necessary. It should be checked before use.

19. Intrauterine Contraceptive Device: (I.U.C.D): In this method control of conception is by introducing a foreign body into uterus.

Lippe's Loop: It is made up of polyetheylene. It is monotaxic. It consists of loop itself, the inserter, plunger, the guards and threads. It is double 'S' shaped. It contains small amount of barium sulphate for gray visualisation. The loop has attached threads made up of fine neylon which protrude into vagina.

Advantages of loop:

1. No hospitalization, no complex procedure for insertion. It takes only 2 minutes for insertion.
2. It does not affect coitus.
3. It can be removed when pregnancy is desired.
4. It can be kept in place for 2-3 days.

20. Copper T : Second generation I.U.C.D. This is a small T shaped radioopaque, polyethylene device. Around its vertical arm is encircled a fine copper wire of area 200 mm from lower end of vertical arm 2 long strings project.

Sterilization: It is not necessary as it is available in sterilized pack. Copper T is introduced into uterus with the help of inserter which consists of a hollow tube and solid plunger. The copper T is straightened in the inserter and is pushed by plunger in uterine cavity with due precaution of asepsis, the thread should be in the vagina as in case of loop.

Mechanism of action: Copper from Copper T releases minute of copper which has spermicidal action and along with polyethelene T the action of implantation of fertilized ovum does not occur.

Copper T is effective for 3 years, hence should be replaced after 3 years

21. Injectable Pills MPA: (Medroxy Progesterone acetate) is given intramuscularly every 3 months 150 mg or 6 months 300 mg. This is safe, effective and acceptable.

Advantages : Highly effective method for irregular patient and minimum motivation is required, it does not affect lactation. It is costly has low failure rate (less than 1/000 women year).

22. Tubectomy: is done by

(*a*) abdominal route, minilap (small incision)

(*b*) vaginal route

(*c*) laparoscopic route

Time of operation

1. after delivery or abortion
2. in between deliveries

23. Sterilization (Male Sterlity): This is an operation done on men and consists incutting and ligating the two ends of vas deferens that carry spermatozoa from testis. After operation fertilization of women's ova is not possible and pregnancy is prevented.

Advantages

1. It does not require hospitalization.
2. Does not interfere with sexual desire or intercourse.
3. It does not reduce the capacity for physical or mental work.

24. Birth Control Method: They are used when pregnancy is suspected or confirmed.

1. Menstrual regulation
2. Abortion (Termination of pregnancy)

25. Medical Termination of Pregnancy Act, 1971

Indication of MTP

1. *Medical:* In this continuation of pregnancy can prove dangerous to mother.
2. *Tygemic:* Risk of baby born will be with congenital malformations (abnormal development)
3. *Humanitarian:* Pregnancy due to rape.
4. *Failure of contraceptives:* Methods have not been mentioned in the act therefore any method can be considered. Written consent of guardian is necessary if abortion is to be performed in a woman less than 18 years and in lunatics.

OBJECTIVE QUESTIONS

1. Breast milk compared to cow's milk has:

(*a*) More calories
(*b*) More fat
(*c*) More lactose
(*d*) More proteins

2. Milk is deficient in:

(*a*) Ca (*b*) Vitamin A
(*c*) Vitamin D (*d*) Fe

3. One of the following is 'biologically complete food:

(*a*) Groundnut (*b*) Wheat
(*c*) Soya bean (*d*) Milk

4. Protein in human milk is:

(*a*) 1.3 gm (*b*) 2.3 gm
(*c*) 3.3 gm (*d*) 4.5 gm

5. Highest amount of protein is seen in:

(*a*) Soya beans
(*b*) Groundnut
(*c*) Bengal gram
(*d*) Mysore Dal

6. When an abandoned child is legally accepted by a couple, it is called as:

(*a*) Remand home placement and foster home placement
(*b*) Remand home placement and Borstal placement
(*c*) Adoption and foster home placement
(*d*) Adoption and remand home placement

7. A 14 year old boy having lost his father a year ago, is caught shoplifting. The boy will be sent to:

(*a*) An orphanage
(*b*) An anganwadi
(*c*) A prison
(*d*) A remand home

8. Presence of the following substance reveals the fact of postcontamination of water:
(*a*) Chlorides (*b*) Nitrates
(*c*) Sulphates (*d*) Nitrites

9. Mental retardation is defined if IQ is below:
(*a*) 90 (*b*) 80
(*c*) 70 (*d*) 60

10. The approximate number of mentally retarded persons in India is around:
(*a*) 4-8 millions (*b*) 1-15 millions
(*c*) 15-20 millions (*d*) 20-25 millions

11. Per capita space for students in a classroom should not be less than —— sq. feet:
(*a*) 5 (*b*) 10
(*c*) 20 (*d*) 50

12. Ideal desk recommended for a school child is:
(*a*) Minus desk (*b*) Plus desk
(*c*) Zero desk (*d*) Any of the above

13. In school health services the most important functionary should be:
(*a*) School teacher (*b*) Health worker
(*c*) Medical officer (*d*) Health assistant

14. Which country had introduced school health services for the first time?
(*a*) France
(*b*) Russia
(*c*) United States of America
(*d*) India

15. The School Health Programmes came into vogue in:
(*a*) 1946 (*b*) 1948
(*c*) 1950 (*d*) 1960

16. IMR upto:
(*a*) Less than 1 year
(*b*) Equal to 1 year
(*c*) up to 1 year
(*d*) More than 1 year

17. Commonest cause of neonatal mortality in India is:
(*a*) Diarrhoeal diseases
(*b*) Birth injuries
(*c*) Low birth weight
(*d*) Congenital anomalies

18. Postnatal (early) death rate mainly depends upon:
(*a*) Environmental factors
(*b*) Antenatal care
(*c*) Events during birth
(*d*) Events during early neonatal period

19. Which state has the lowest infant mortality rate:
(*a*) Kerala (*b*) Tamil Nadu
(*c*) West Bengal (*d*) Madhya Pradesh

20. Infantile death is taken only below:
(*a*) 7 days (*b*) 1 months
(*c*) 1 year (*d*) 2 years

21. Neonatal mortality in proportion of IMR is:
(*a*) 65-75% (*b*) 50-60%
(*c*) 35-45% (*d*) 25-35%

22. The numerator used to define neonatal death rate is:
(*a*) All infants below one year of age
(*b*) Infants between 1 to 12 months
(*c*) Infant below 1 week of age
(*d*) Infants below 28 days of age

23. Stillbirth rate includes babies dead after
(*a*) 20 weeks (*b*) 24 weeks
(*c*) 28 weeks (*d*) 32 weeks

24. Denominator of preinatal mortality is:
(*a*) Live birth
(*b*) Stillbirth
(*c*) Live and stillbirth
(*d*) Live birth minus stillbirth

25. In the calculation of IMR which is the time period considered?
(*a*) 7 days (*b*) 28 days
(*c*) Before 1 year (*d*) 1-5 years

26. The commonest cause of maternal mortality in India is:
(*a*) Anaemia (*b*) Haemorrhage
(*c*) Abortion (*d*) Sepsis

27. Most rare cause of maternal mortality is:
(*a*) Abortion (*b*) Anaemia
(*c*) Toxaemia (*d*) Haemorrhage

28. Most common indirect cause of maternal mortality in India:
(*a*) Infection (*b*) Anaemia
(*c*) Heart disease (*d*) Accidents

29. All are common causes of maternal mortality in India except:
(*a*) Anaemia (*b*) Haemorrhage
(*c*) Toxaemia (*d*) Diabetes

30. In India, all are direct causes of maternal mortality except:
(*a*) Cardiac disease (*b*) Eclampsia
(*c*) Haemorrhage (*d*) Abortion

31. Denominator of maternal mortality rate is:
(*a*) Total number of female deaths
(*b*) Total number of live births
(*c*) 1000 live births
(*d*) 1000 female deaths

32. In a population of 10,000 with birth rate 36 per 1,000 and 5 maternal deaths, the MMR is:
(*a*) 14.5 (*b*) 13.8
(*c*) 20 (*d*) 5

33. All of the following are leading obstetrical causes of maternal mortality in India except:
(*a*) Severe anaemia
(*b*) Toxaemia of pregnancy
(*c*) Vascular accidents
(*d*) Abortions

34. Targeted infant mortality rate for 2000 AD:
(*a*) 50 (*b*) 60
(*c*) 70 (*d*) 80

35. All of the following are causes of postneonatal death in India except:
(*a*) Tetanus
(*b*) Respiratory infection
(*c*) Diarrhoea
(*d*) Malnutrition

36. English disease is a term used for:
(*a*) Chaga's disease
(*b*) Rheumatoid arthritis
(*c*) Chronic bronchitis
(*d*) Bronchiectasis

37. MCH care is assessed by:
(*a*) Death rate
(*b*) Birth rate
(*c*) Maternal-mortality rate
(*d*) Anemia in mother

38. Which is not true about growth chart used in India:
(*a*) There are 3 curves
(*b*) Top most curve corresponds to 50th percentile of Harvard
(*c*) Second curve corresponds to 80% of that standard
(*d*) Children with normal weight fall above the line

39. Growth is monitored by:
(*a*) Height
(*b*) Weight
(*c*) Growth chart
(*d*) Anthrabiometric measurement
(*e*) Mid-arm circumference

40. Road to health card has 2 reference points, which are:
(*a*) 30th percentile for boys and 3rd percentile for girls
(*b*) 50th percentile for boys and 3rd percentile for girls
(*c*) 50th percentile for boys and 5th percentile for girls
(*d*) 80th percentile for boys and 10th percentile for girls

41. The average birth weight in India is:
(*a*) 2.5 kg (*b*) 2.8 kg
(*c*) 3.00 kg (*d*) 3.2 kg

42. "Road to health card" line is
(*a*) 3rd percentile (*b*) 50th percentile
(*c*) 80th percentile (*d*) 97 percentile

43. Which is true about road to health card?
(*a*) 4 lines are present
(*b*) Top line rep. 50% of percentile
(*c*) Child between 1st and 2nd line is normal
(*d*) Lowest line corres to 70% of std.

44. Following is different between human and cow milk:
(*a*) Proteins and fat
(*b*) Proteins and sugar
(*c*) Proteins and lactose
(*d*) Minerals

45. A healthy mother with a healthy child should start artificial feeding by:
(*a*) 3 months (*b*) 5-6 months
(*c*) 1 year (*d*) 1-5 years

46. Perinatal mortality rate in India is:
(*a*) Late fetal death (stillbirth) + death under 1 week

(*b*) Late fetal death (stillbirth) + death under 2 weeks
(*c*) Late fetal and early neonatal death weighing over 1000 gm at birth
(*d*) Late fetal and early neonatal death weighing over 1500 gm at birth

47. Small-for-date babies are prevented by:
(*a*) Spacing of baby
(*b*) Antenatal care
(*c*) Nutritional supplement
(*d*) Immunisation

48. Low birth weight means a weight of less than:
(*a*) 2.8 kg (*b*) 2.7 kg
(*c*) 2.5 kg (*d*) 2.3 kg

49. By 2000 AD India has to reduce the birth of infants weighing below 2.5 kg to:
(*a*) 10% (*b*) 20%
(*c*) 30% (*d*) 40%

50. National goals of *Health for all by* 2000 AD:
(*a*) Infant mortality rate 60
(*b*) Crude death rate 9
(*c*) Crude birth rate 21
(*d*) Life expectancy at birth 70 years

ANSWERS

1	**2**	**3**	**4**	**5**	**6**	**7**	**8**	**9**	**10**
(*c*)	(*d*)	(*d*)	(*a*)	(*a*)	(*c*)	(*d*)	(*b*)	(*c*)	(*c*)
11	**12**	**13**	**14**	**15**	**16**	**17**	**18**	**19**	**20**
(*b*)	(*a*)	(*a*)	(*d*)	(*d*)	(*a*)	(*c*)	(*a*)	(*a*)	(*c*)
21	**22**	**23**	**24**	**25**	**26**	**27**	**28**	**29**	**30**
(*b*)	(*d*)	(*c*)	(*a*)	(*c*)	(*b*)	(*a*)	(*d*)	(*d*)	(*a*)
31	**32**	**33**	**34**	**35**	**36**	**37**	**38**	**39**	**40**
(*b*)	(*b*)	(*c*)	(*b*)	(*a*)	(*c*)	(*c*)	(*a*)	(*c*)	(*b*)
41	**42**	**43**	**44**	**45**	**46**	**47**	**48**	**49**	**50**
(*b*)	(*b*)	(*a*)	(*c*)	(*b*)	(*a*)	(*a*)	(*c*)	(*a*)	(*d*)

Health Education

Health Education is a process that informs, motivates and helps people to adopt and maintain healthy practices and lifestyles, advocates environmental changes as needed to facilitate this goal and conducts professional training and research to the same end".

Objectives of Health Education

Under the above definition, the three main objectives of health education are :

(a) *Informing people:* For thousands of years, disease and death have been accepted as normal phenomenon. Therefore, it become necessary to educate the peoples about the necessity of health.

(b) *Motivating people:* The second objective is more important than the first. Simply telling peope about health is not enough. They must be motivated to change their habits and ways of living, since many present day problems of community health require alteration of human behaviour or changes in the health practices which are deterimental to health.

(c) *Guiding into action:* Under the above definition, health education can and should be conducted by a variety of health, education and communication personnel, in a variety of settings, starting with the physician. People need help to adopt and maintain healthy practices and life-styles, which may be totally new to them. Governments have a major responsibility to provide the necessary infrastructure of health services.

Content of Health Education

Health education is as wide as community health. In practice, the content of health education may be divided into 8 main divisions:

1. *Human Biology:* Much of the teaching pertaining to human biology is done in schools.
2. *Nutrition:* The aim of health education in nutrition is to guide people to choose optimum and balanced diets which contain nutrients necessary for energy, growth, and repair — but not to teach the familiar jargon of calories and the biochemistry of nutrients. Education is given on the nutritive value of foods. High price of foods is not always poof of its high nutitional contents.
3. *Hygiene:* This has two aspects-personal and environmental. The aim of personal hygiene is to promote standards of personal cleanliness within the setting of the conditions where people live. *Personal Hygiene* includes bathing, clothing, washing hands and toilet; care of feet, nails and teeth; spitting, coughing, sneezing, personal appearance and inculcation of clean habits in the young. Training in personal hygiene should begin at a very early age and must be carried through school age. *Environmental Hygiene* has two aspects-domestic and community. Domestic hygiene comprises that of the home, use of soap, need for fresh air, light and ventilation; hygienic storage of foods; hygienic disposal of wastes, need to avoid pests, rats, mice and insects.

4. *Family Health Care:* Family health is traditionally centred round mother and child health care. However, the focus has expanded to embrace concern for the family as a unit. Currently family health care programmes embrace human growth.
5. *Control of Communicable and Non-Communicable Diseases:* There is a wide range of specific communicable and non-communicable diseases needing health education activity, to mention a few-malaria, sexually transmitted diseases, trachoma, leprosy, tuberculosis, malnutrition, cardio-vascular diseases, drug addiction, alcoholism, accidents etc.
6. *Mental Health:* Mental health problems occur everywhere. They become more prominent when major killer diseases are brought under control. There is a tendency to an increase in the prevalence of mental diseases.
7. *Prevention of Accidents:* Accidents are a feature of the complexity of modern life in the developed countries, they are taking an increasing toll of life and limb.
8. *Use of Health Services:* One of the declared aims of health education is to inform the public about the health services that are available in the community, and how to use them. They should not be misused or abused.

Table : Health Education and Propaganda

Education	*Propaganda or Publicity*
1. Knowledge and skills actively acquired	— Knowledge instilled in the minds of people
2. Makes people think for themselves	— Prevents or discourages thinking by ready made slogans
3. Disciplines primitive desires	— Arouses and stimulates primitive desires
4. Develops reflective behaviour. Train people to use judgements before acting	— Develops reflective behaviour; aims at impulsive actions
5. Appeals to reason	— Appeals to emotion
6. Develops individuality, personality and self-expression	— Develops a standard pattern of attitudes and behaviours according to the mould used
7. Knowledge acquired through self-reliant activity	— Knowledge is spoonfed and passively received
8. The process is behaviour centred aims at developing favourable attitudes and habits and skills	— The process is information centred-no change of attitude or behaviour designed.

Principles of Health Education

Before we come to the practice of health education, we must know the principles involved. Health education brings together the art and science of medicine, and the principles and practice of general education. The link is to be found in the school and behavioural sciences—sociology, psychology. It is possible to abstract certain principles of learning and use them in health education.

1. *Interest:* It is a psychological principle that people are unlikely to listen to those things which are not to their interest. It is salutary to remind ourselves that health teaching should relate to the interests of the people. The public is not interested in health slogans such as “Take care of your health” or “be healthy”. A health education programme of this kind would be as useless as asking people to “be healthy”, as a nutrition programme asking people to “eat good food”.
2. *Participation:* It is a keyword in health education. Participation is based on the psychological principle of active learning; it is better than passive learning. Group

discussion, panel discussion workshop all provide opportunities for active learning. Personal involvement is more likely to lead to personal acceptance.

3. *Known to Unknown*: In health education work, we proceed from the known to the unknown *i.e.*, start where the people are and with what they understand and then proceed to new knowledge. We use the existing knowledge of the people as pegs on which to hang new knowledge. In this way systematic knowledge is built up. New Knowledge will bring about a new, enlarged understanding which can give rise to an insight into the problem.
4. *Comprehension:* In health education we must know the level of understanding, education and literacy of people to whom the teaching is directed. One barrier to communication is using words which cannot be understood. A doctor asked the diabetic to cut down starchy foods. A doctor prescribed medicine in the familiar jargon "one teaspoonful three times a day"; the patient, a village woman, has never seen a teaspoon, and could not follow the doctor's directions. In health education, we should always communicate in the language people understand, and never use words which are strange and new to the people.
5. *Reinforcement:* Few people can learn all that is new in a single contact. Repetition at intervals is extremely useful. It assists comprehension and understanding. Every health compaign needs reinforcement; we may call it a "booster dose".

Barriers of Communication

These can be:

1. Physiological – difficulties in hearing, expression
2. Psychological – emotional disturbances, neurosis
3. Environmental – noise, invisibility congestion
4. Cultural – levels of knowledge and understanding, customs, beliefs, religion, attitudes

The barriers should be identified and removed for achieving effective communication.

Administration and Organisation

Governments have a responsibility for assisting and guiding the health education of the general public. For this purpose, the Central Health Education Bureau was established in Ministry of Health in 1956 at Delhi with the assistance of the Technical Co-operation Mission of the United States. The Central Health Education Bureau consists of training, media research, and evaluation divisions in addition to an administrative section. The functions of the Bureau are:

(1) to interpret the services of the central Ministry of Health so as to win the support for the maximum use of its various services;

(2) to procure and publish educational material for distribution throughout the country;

(3) to help Central Health Services, and voluntary organisations and State Health Ministries requesting technical assistance;

(4) to promote and coordinate health education work in the country, particularly by initiating and conducting specialized research, studies, and the effective use of education by health workers throughout the country.

HEALTH CARE OF THE COMMUNITY

Since health is influenced by a number of factors such as adequate food, housing, basic sanitation, healthy lifestyles, protection against environmental hazards and communicable diseases, the frontiers of health extend beyond the narrow limits of medical care. It is thus clear that "health care" implies more than "medical care". The term "medical care" is not synonymous "health care". It refers chiefly to those personal services that are provided directly by physicians or rendered as the result of physicians's instructions. It ranges from domiciliary care to resident hospital care. Medical care is a subset of health care system.

Health care is a public right, and it is the responsiblity of governments to provide this care to all people in equal measure. These principles have been recognized by nearly all governments of the world and enshrined in their respective constitutions. In India, health care is completely a governmental function.

Levels of Health Care

It is customary to describe health care services at 3 levels, *viz*., primary, secondary and tertiary care levels. These levels represents different types of care involving varying degrees of complexity.

1. *Primary care level:* It is the first level of contact of individuals, the family and community with the national health system, where "primary health care". ("essential" health care) is provided. As a level of care, it is close to the people, where most of their health problems can be dealt with and resolved. It is at this level that health care will be most effective within the context to the areas's needs and limitations. In the Indian context, primary health care is provided by the complex of primary health centres and their subcentres through the agency of multipurpose health workers, village health guides and trained dais.
2. *Secondary care level*: The next higher level of care is the secondary (intermediate) health care level. At this level more complex problems are dealt with. In India, this kind of care is generally provided in district hospitals and community health centres which also serve as the first referral level.
3. *Tertiary Care Level:* The tertiary level is a more specialized required specific facilities and attention of highly specialized health workers. This care is provided by the regional or central level institutions, *e.g.*, Medical College, Hospitals, All India Institutes, Regional Hospitals, Specialized Hospitals and other Apex Institutions.

Elements of Primary Health Care

Although specific services provided will vary in different countries and communities, the Alma-Ata Declartion has outlined 8 essential components of primary health care.

1. education concerning prevailing health problems and the methods of preventing and controlling them;
2. promotion of food supply and proper nutrition;
3. an adequate supply of safe water and basic sanitation;
4. maternal and child health care, including family planning;
5. immunization against major infections diseases;
6. prevention and control of locally endemic diseases;
7. appropriate treatment of common diseases and injuries; and
8. provision of essential drugs.

Principles of Primary Health Care:

1. *Equitable distribution:* The first key principle in the primary health care strategy is equity or equitable distribution of health services, *i.e.*, health services must be shared equally by all people irrespective of their ability to pay, and all (rich or poor, urban or rural) must have access to health services. At present, health services are mainly concentrated in the major towns and cities resulting in inequality of care to the people in rural areas. The worst hit are the needy and vulnerable groups of the population in rural areas and urban slums.
2. *Community Participation:* Not with standing the overall responsibility of the Central and State Governments, the involvement of individuals, families, and communities in promotion of their own health and welfare, is an essential ingredient of primary health care.
3. *Intersectoral coordination:* There is an increasing realization of the fact that the components of primary health care cannot be provided by the health sector alone. The declaration of Alma-Ata states that "primary health care involves in addition to the

health sector, all related sectors and aspects of national community development, food, industry, education, housing, public works, communication and others sectors".

4. *Appropriate technology:* Appropriate technology has been defined as "technology that is scientifically sound, adaptable to local needs, and acceptable to those who apply it and those for whom it is used, and that can be maintained by the people themselves in keeping with the principle of self reliance with the resources the community and country can afford.

Health Status and Health Problems

An assesment of the health status and health problems is the first requisite for any planned effort to develop health care services. This is also known as Community Diagnosis. The data required for analysing the health situation and for defining the health problems comprise the following:

1. Morbidity and Mortality statistics.
2. Demographic conditions of the population.
3. Environmental conditions which have a bearing on health.
4. Socio-economic factors which have a direct effect on health.
5. Cultural background, attitudes, beliefs, and practices which affect health.
6. Medical and health services available.
7. Other services available.

An analysis of the health situation in the light of the above data will bring out the health problems and health needs of the community. These problems are then ranked according to priority or urgency for allocation of resources.

Health Problems

The Health problems of India may be conveniently grouped under the following heads:

1. Communicable disease problems
2. Nutritional problems
3. Environmental sanitation problems
4. Medical care problems
5. Population problems

PRIMARY HEALTH CARE IN INDIA

In 1977, the Government of India launched a Rural Health Scheme, based on the principle of "Placing people's health in people's hands" It is a three tier system of health care delivery in rural areas based on the recommendation of the Shrivastava Committee in 1975. Close on the heels of these recommendation an International conference at Alma-Ata in 1978, set the goal of an acceptable level of health care approach. As a signatory to the Alma-Ata Declacation, the Government of India is committed to achieving the goal of Health for All through primary health care approach which seeks to provide universal comprehensive health care at a cost which is affordable.

Keeping in view, the WHO goal of "Health for All" evolved a National Health Policy based on primary health care approach. It was approved by Parliament in 1983. The National Health Policy has laid down a plan of action for reorienting and shaping the existing rural health infra-structure with specific goals to be achieved by 1985, 1990 and 1995 within the framework of the sixth (1980-85) and seventh (1985-90) Five Year Plans and the new 20 point programme. Steps are already under way to implement the National Health Policy objectives towards achieving Health for All by the year 2000. These are described below:

1. Village Level

One of the basic tenets of primary health care is universal coverage and equitable distribution of health resources. That is, health care must penetrate into the farthest reaches of rural areas, and that everyone should have access to it. To implement this policy at the village level, the following schemes are in operation:

(a) Village Health Guides Scheme
(b) Training of Local Dais
(c) ICDS Scheme

(a) Village Health Guides: A Village Health Guides is a person with an aptitude for social service and is not a full time government functionary. The Village Health

Guides Scheme was intoduced on 2nd October 1977 with the idea of securing people's participation in the care of their own health. The scheme was launched in all states except Kerela, Karnataka, Tamil Nadu, Arunachal Pradesh and Jammu and Kashmir which had alternative systems (*e.g.*, Mini-health centres in Tamil Nadu) of providing health services at the village level.

The guidelines for their selection are:

(*a*) they should be permanent residents of the local community, preferable women;

(*b*) they should be able to read and write, having minimum formal education at least up to the VI standard;

(*c*) they should be acceptable to all sections of the community and;

(*d*) they should be able to spare at least 2 to 3 hours every day for community health work.

(b) *Local Dais:* Most deliveries in rural areas are still handled by untrained dais who are often the only people immediately available to women during the preinatal period. An extensive programme has been under taken, under the Rural Health Scheme, to train all categories of local dais (traditional birth attendants) in the country to improve their knowledge in the elementary concepts of maternal and child health and sterilization, besides obstetric skills. The training is for 30 working days.

(c) *Anganwadi Worker:* Angan literally means a courtyard. Under the ICDS (Integrated Child Development Services) scheme, there is an anganwadi worker for a population of 1000. There are about 100 such workwes in each ICDS project. As of date over 5320 ICDS blocks are functioning in the country. The anganwadi worker is selected from the community she is expected to serve. She undergoes training in various aspects of health, nutrition, and child development for 4 months. She is a part-time worker and is paid an honorarium of Rs 200–250 per month for the services rendered, which include health check-up, immunization, supplementary nutrition, health education, non-formal pre-school education and referral services.

2. Sub-Centre Level

The sup-centre is the peripheral outpost of the existing health delivery system in rural areas. They are being established on the basis of one sub-centre for every 5000 population in general and one for every 3000 population in hilly, tribal and backward areas. As on 30th June 1996, 132730 sub-centres were established in the country; the total requirement is estimated to be 1.38 Lakh.

3. Primary Health Centre Level

The concept of primary health centre is not new to India. The Bhore committee in 1946 gave the concept of a primary health centre as a basic health unit, to provide, as close to the people as possible, an integrated curative and preventive health care to the rural population with emphasis on preventive and promotive aspects of health care.

The Declaration of Alma-Ata Conference in 1978 setting the goal of Health for All by 2000 AD has ushered in a new philosophy of equity, and a new approach, the primary health care approach. The National Health Plan (1983) proposed reorganization of primary health centres on the basis of one PHC for every 30,000 rural population in the plains, and one PHC for every 20,000 population in hilly, tribal and backward areas for more effective coverage.

Functions of the PHC

The functions of the primary health center in India cover all the 8 "essential" elements of primary health care as outlined in the Atma-Ata declaration. They are:

1. Medical care
2. MCH including family planning
3. Safe water supply and basic sanitation
4. Prevention and control of locally endemic diseases
5. Collection and reporting of vital statistics

6. Education about health
7. National Health Programmes
8. Referral services

4. Community Health Centres

As on 30th June 2002, 5299 community health centres were establisted by upgrading the primary health centres, Each community health centre covering a population of 80,000 to 1.20 lakh (one in each community development block) with 30 beds and specialists in surgery, medicine, obstetrics and gynaecology, and paediatrics with x-ray and laboratory facilities. For strengthening preventive and promotive aspects of health care, a new non-medical post called **community health officer** has been created at each community health centre. The community health officer is selected from amongst the supervisory category of staff at the PHC and district level with minimum of 7 years experience in rural health programmes. Some states have not accepted this scheme and have opted for a second medical officer.

Voluntary Health Agencies

The voluntary health agencies occupy an important place in community health programmes. "A voluntary health agency may be defined as an organisation that is administered by an autonomous board which holds meetings, collects funds for its support chiefly from private sources and expends money, whether with or without paid workers, in conducting a programme directed primarily to furthering the public health by providing health services or health education, or by advancing research or legislation for health, or by a combination of these activities". The one country where voluntary health agencies have developed and flourished to an enormous extent is the United States.

Functions

The types of service rendered by voluntary health agencies have been classified as:

(a) *Supplementing the Work of Government Agencies:* It is well known that government agencies cannot provide complete service because they operate under financial and statutory restrictions. The voluntary health agencies can help strengthen the work of government agencies by lending personal, or by contributing funds for special equipment, supplies or services.

(b) *Pioneering:* The voluntary health agencies are in a position to explore ways and means of doing new things. Research is one formof pioneering. When the efforts succeed and bear fruit, the government agencies can step in and take over the project for the benefit of the larger numbers.The family planning programme in India is an example of pioneering by the volutary agencies which first spearheaded the movement, in the face of much opposition. When the importance of family planning was realised, the government accepted family planning as a national policy.

(c) *Education:* There is unlimited scope for health education in India. The government agencies cannot cope with the problem, unless it is supplemented by voluntary effort on the part of the people.

(d) *Demonstration:* By putting up demonstrations and experimental projects, the voluntary health agencies have advanced the cause of public health. The demonstrations of bore hole latrines by the Rockefeller Foundation to solve the problem of hookworm in India is a case in point. The bore-hole latrine and its modifications have since become an essential part of the environmental sanitation programme in India.

(e) *Guiding the Work of Government Agencies:* By setting a good example the voluntary health agencies can always guide and criticise the work of government agencies.

(f) *Advancing Health Legislation:* The voluntary agencies can also mobilise public opinion and advance legislation on health matters for the benefit of the whole community.

VOLUNTATY HEALTH AGENCIES IN INDIA

1. Indian Red Cross Society

The Indian Red Cross Society was established in 1920. It has a network of over 400 branches all over India. It has been executing programmes for the promotion of health, prevention of disease and mitigation of suffering among the people. Its activities are:

(a) *Relief Work:* When disaster strikes any part of the country in the shape of earthquakes, floods, drought, epidemics, *etc*, the Red Cross Society immediately mobilises all its resources and goes to the rescue of the affected people.

(b) *Milk and Medical Supplies:* A number of hospitals, dispensaries, maternity and child welfare centres, schools and orphanges receive assistance from the society every year. The assistance given consists mainly of milk powder, medicines, vitamins and other supplies.

(c) *Armed Forces:* The care of the sick and the wounded among the members of the forces is one of the primary obligations of the Red cross. The society runs a well-equipped hospital, "the Red cross Home" in Bangalore-the only one of its kind in India and the Far East-for permanently disabled ex-serviceman.

(d) *Maternal and Child Welfare Services:* There are a large number of maternity and child welfare centres all over India, either directly administered by or are affiliated to the Red cross. There is a bureau of maternity and child welfare, which provides technical advice and financial aid to schemes for establishing model maternity and child welfare centres.

(e) *Family Planning:* Several states in India are running family planning clinics under the auspices of the Indian Red Cross.

(f) *Blood Bank and First Aid:* Some of the state branches have started blood banks. The St. John Ambulance Association in India which is part of the Red Cross has trained several lakh men and women in first aid, home nursing and allied subjects.

2. Hind Kusht Nivaran Sangh

The Hind Kusht Nivaran Sangh was founded in 1950 with its headquarters in New Delhi. Its precursor was the Indian Council of the British Empire Leprosy Relief Association (B.E.L.R.A.) which was dissolved in 1950. The programme of work of the sangh includes rendering of financial assistance to various leprosy homes and clinics, health education through publications and posters, training of medical workers and physiotherapists, conducting All-India Leprasy workers Conferences and publication of 'Leprosy in India', a quarterly journal. The sangh has branches all over India and works in close cooperation with the Government and other voluntary agencies.

3. Indian Council for Child Welfare

Indian council for child welfare was established in 1952. It is affiliated with the International Union for Child Welfare. Since its formation, the I.C.C.W. has built up a network of state councils and district councils all over the country. The services of I.C.C.W. are devoted to secure for India's children those opportunities and facilities, by law and other means which are necessary to enable them to develop physically, mentally, morally, spiritually and socially in a healthy and normal manner and in conditions of freedom and dignity.

4. Tuberculosis Association of India

The Tuberculosis Association of India was formed in 1939. It has branches in all the states in India. The activities of this Association comprise organising a T.B. seal compaign every year to raise funds, training of doctors, health visitors and social workers in antituberculosis work, promotion of health edvcation and promotion of consultations and conferences. The following institutions are under the management of the Association: The New Delhi Tuberculosis Centre, the Lady Linlithgow Sanatorium at Kasauli, The King Edward VII sanatorium at Dharampur and the Tuberculosis Hospital at Mehrauli.

5. Bharat Sevak Samaj

The Bharat Sevak Samaj which is a non-political and non-official organisation was formed in 1952. One of the prime objectives of the Bharat Sevak Samaj (B.S.S) is to help people to achieve health by their own actions and efforts. The B.S.S. has branches in all the states and in nearly all the districts. Improvement of sanitation in villages is one of the important activities of the B.S.S.

6. Central Social Welfare Board

The Central Social Welfare Board is an autonomous organisation under the general administrative control of the ministry of Education. It was set up by the Government of India in August 1953. The functions of the Board are:

(1) Surveying the needs and requirements of voluntary welfare organisations in the country

(2) promoting and setting up of social welfare organisations on a voluntary basis

(3) rendering of financial aid to deserving existing organisations and institutions. The Board inintiated, in 1968, "Family and child Welfare services" in rural areas for the welfare of women and children.The activities of these projects comprise teaching of craft, social education, literacy classes, maternity aid for women, distribution of milk, balwadis, and organisation of play centres for children. Then Board has also started a scheme of Industrial Cooperatives to help the lower-middle class women in Urban areas supplement their family income by doing paid work.

7. The Kasturba Memorial Fund

Created in commemoration of Kasturba Gandhi, after her death in 1944, the Fund was raised with the main object of improving the lot of women, especially in the villages, through gram-sevikas. The trust has nearly a crore of rupees and is actively engaged in various welfare projects in the country.

8. Family Planning Association of India

The Family Planning Association was formed in 1949 with its headquarters at Mumbai. It has done pioneering work in propagating family planning in India. The Association has branches all over the Country. These branches are running family planning clinics with grants-in-aid from the government. The association has trained serveral hundred doctors, health visitors and social workers. One of the activities of the Headquarters is to answer enquiries on family planning by correspondance or by personal interviews.

9. All India Women's Conference

It is the only women's voluntary welfare organisation in the country. Estabilished in 1926, it has now branches all over the country. Most of the branches are running M.C.H. cilinics, Medical centres, and adult education centres, milk centres and family planning clinics.

10. The All-India Relief Society

The All-India Relief society was established in 1946 with a view to coordinate different institutions working for the blind. It organises eye relief camps and other measures for the relief of the blind.

11. Professional Bodies

The Indian Medical Association, All India Licentiates Association, All India Dental Association, The Trained Nurses Association of India are all voluntary agencies of men and women who are qualified in their respective specialities and possess registerable qualifications. These professional bodies conduct annual conferences, publish journals, arrange scientific sessions and exhibitions, foster research, set up standards of professional education and organise refief camps during periods of natural calamities.

12. International agencies

The Rockefeller Foundation, Ford Foundation and CARE (Cooperative for American Relief Everywhere) are examples of voluntary international health agencies.

Vital Statistics and Elementary Statistics

1. Vital Statistics means data collected from vital events and compilation of data. Vital events are birth, death, marriage, divorce and adoption.
2. **Health Statistics:** Data derived from sickness events in a community or items of services provided *i.e.,* it includes—
   (a) *State of health*—Morbidity, Mortality.
   (b) *Factor affecting health*: Nutrition, housing, social, economic and environmental factors.
   (c) *Services:* Preventive, curative, rehabilitory.
3. **Sources of Vital Statistics:**
   1. Census
   2. Registration of birth, death and marriage
   3. National sample survey.

   The Census: The census is defined as the total process of collecting, compiling and publishing demographic, economic and social data pertaining to a specified time to all persons in a country.
4. **Uses of Vital Statistics:**
   1. For planning various activities related to health.
   2. For evaluation of planned activity.
   3. To know geographical distribution and health trends.
   4. For comparison of various indicators from one country with another.
   5. Research in community health problems.
5. **Classifications of Death:** Death should be classified according to the International Classification of Diseases (ICD). This classification is revised by the WHO approximately every 10 years. The latest revision being the Ninth Revision which has come into force on 1st January 1979. The new revision is intended to be much more useful than the previous ones. It includes recommendation concerning maternal and prenatal morbidity and mortality and a proposed fcrm of certificate of cause of prenatal death.

OBJECTIVE QUESTIONS

1. Health education is:
   (a) Health promotion
   (b) Health distortion
   (c) Thorough public health
   (d) Not prevalent
2. In the process of health education of community the most important step is:
   (a) Contact to doctors
   (b) Community discussion
   (c) Announces to community by loudspeaker
   (d) Knowing to local needs
3. Following are used in planning of health education *except*:
   (a) cover felt needs
   (b) using simple words
   (c) catchy slogans
   (d) Ensuring participation
4. WHO constitution was made in:
   (a) 1947 (b) 1950
   (c) 1952 (d) 1956
5. In health education programme a group of 10 people are speaking on a topic of common interest called as:
   (a) Workshop
   (b) Panel discussion
   (c) Group discussion
   (d) Symposium
6. *Not* a feature of mass media education:
   (a) Deals with local problem of communication
   (b) Easily understandable
   (c) wide approachable
   (d) Rapid

7. The Bhore Committee was set up in:
(*a*) 1943 (*b*) 1946
(*c*) 1947 (*d*) 1952

8. PHC was introduced as a result of ——— report:
(*a*) Bhore Committee
(*b*) Kartar Singh
(*c*) Mudaliar
(*d*) Planning Commission

9. All are *true* about Mudaliar committee *except*:
(*a*) To improve the quality of health care
(*b*) Strengthening of district hospital
(*c*) Consolidation of advances made in the first two five-year plan
(*d*) Each primary centre covers a population of 80,000

10. Which one of the following was not recommended by the Mudaliar services
(*a*) Strengthening the district hospital with specialist services
(*b*) Each primary health centre to serve 8000 population
(*c*) Constitution of all India Health services
(*d*) Integration of medical and health services

11. Match *List-I (Health Planning Committees)* with *List-II (Main Recommendations/ Important Results)* and select the correct answer using the codes given below the lists:

List-I
A. Shrivastava Committee
B. Chadah Committee
C. Kartar Singh Committee
D. Jungal Wallah Committee

List-II
1. Malaria workers to look after FP work also.
2. Integration of services from the highest to the lowest level.
3. Led to creation of health guides.
4. Led to creation of multipurpose worker.

Codes:

	A	B	C	D
(*a*)	3	4	1	2
(*b*)	3	1	4	2
(*c*)	2	1	4	3
(*d*)	2	4	1	3

12. Recommendation of Shrivastava committee was:
(*a*) Abolition of private practive
(*b*) Creation of multipurpose health workers
(*c*) Creation of PHO
(*d*) All of the above

13. Panchayat Raj means:
(*a*) Local health care centre
(*b*) Community health care centre
(*c*) Primary health care
(*d*) Local self rule government

14. The community development programme is meant:
(*a*) To bring about a special and economic change in village life through the effort of the villagers themselves
(*b*) To arrange welfare programmes for women and children
(*c*) To improve agriculture product through better manure and seeds
(*d*) To plan development pro-gramme in a village high population of 60 and 80 thousand

15. Drinking water is best made free of cyclops by:
(*a*) Filtration
(*b*) Boiling
(*c*) Chlorination
(*d*) None of the above

16. Diethyl toluamide is an effective:
(*a*) Larvicidal
(*b*) Agent against pupal of anopheles
(*c*) Repellent
(*d*) Space spray
(*e*) None of the above

17. Match *List-I (Vectors)* with *List-II (Diseases transmitted)* and select the correct answer using the code given below the lists:

List-I

A. *Culex* mosquito
B. Sand fly
C. *Aedes* mosquito
D. Head louse

List-II

1. Relapsing fever
2. Yellow fever
3. Japanese encephalitis
4. Kala-azar

Codes:

	A	B	C	D
(*a*)	3	1	2	4
(*b*)	4	1	3	2
(*c*)	2	4	3	1
(*d*)	4	3	2	1

18. Which of the following disease is found in India?
(*a*) Westnile fever
(*b*) Murray valley encephalitis
(*c*) Yellow fever
(*d*) Colorado tick fever

19. *Aedes* is vector for all except:
(*a*) Dengue
(*b*) Yellow fever
(*c*) Encephalitis
(*d*) Hemorrhagic fever

20. Which is *not* transmitted by culex?
(*a*) Dengue (*b*) Filaria
(*c*) Viral arthritis (*d*) Westnile fever

21. Diseases spread by mosquito are:
(*a*) Malaria
(*b*) Toxoplasmosis
(*c*) Histoplasma
(*d*) Sleeping sickness

22. *Culex* mosquito can transmit:
(*a*) Malaria (*b*) Kala-azar
(*c*) Dengue fever (*d*) None of the above

23. "Nuisance mosquito" is:
(*a*) *Anopheles* (*b*) *Culex*
(*c*) *Ades* (*d*) Tse-tse fly

24. The maximum permissible level of occupational exposure to radiation is —— — per year:
(*a*) 5 rem (*b*) 2 rem
(*c*) 10 rem (*d*) 50 rem

25. Rat flea transmits all the following *except*:
(*a*) Plague
(*b*) Salmonellosis
(*c*) *H. Dimunita*
(*d*) Murine fever

26. Which of the following is *not* an arthropod-borne infection in India?
(*a*) Japanese B encephalitis
(*b*) KDF
(*c*) Dengue
(*d*) Tanapox virus

27. The vector of Kyasanus Forest diseases is:
(*a*) *Anopheles* mosquito
(*b*) *Culex* mosquito
(*c*) Flea
(*d*) Tick

28. Trench fever is transmitted by:
(*a*) Flea
(*b*) Louse
(*c*) Tick mosquito
(*d*) None of the above

29. Hard tick transmits:
(*a*) Oroyo fever
(*b*) Oriental sore
(*c*) Leishmanials
(*d*) Tick typhus

30. For proper functioning, an oxidation pond requires:
(*a*) Algae, sunlight and ferns
(*b*) Algae, scavenging bacteria and sunlight
(*c*) Algae, saprophytic bacteria and sunlight
(*d*) Algae, human pathogenic bacteria and sunlight

31. *True* about septic tank is:
(*a*) Disinfectants should be used periodically
(*b*) Anaerobic digestion takes place inside and aerobic digestion takes place out side
(*c*) Minimum capacity of the tank is 100 gallons
(*d*) A retention period of 24 hours is insufficient

32. An inexpensive and efficient method of sewage disposal for a small community is:
(*a*) River outfall
(*b*) Oxidation pond
(*c*) Trickling filter
(*d*) Activated sludge

33. Trickling filter is used in:
(*a*) Primary treatment of sewage
(*b*) Secondary treatment of sewage
(*c*) Sewage effluent treatment
(*d*) Sewage farming treatment

34. Biological oxygen demand denotes contamination with:
(*a*) Bacteria (coliforms)
(*b*) Organic matter
(*c*) Nitrates
(*d*) Algae

35. Oxygen demand calculated in water is for evaluating its:
(*a*) Biological Value (BOD)
(*b*) Organic nature
(*c*) Stand by time
(*d*) *E. coli* ratio

36. Strength of sewage is expressed in terms of:
(*a*) Biological oxygen demand
(*b*) Chemical oxygen demand
(*c*) Suspended solids
(*d*) *E. coli* count

37. Anaerobic digestion of sludge is seen in:
(*a*) Aquaprivy
(*b*) Effluent
(*c*) Septic tank
(*d*) All of the above

38. Septic tank decomposition takes place by:
(*a*) Anaerobic (*b*) Aerobic
(*c*) Both (*d*) None

39. Which of the following is not a sanitary latrine?
(*a*) Aquaprivy
(*b*) Bore hole
(*c*) RCA type
(*d*) Service latrine

40. Accepted depth of water in water-seal latrine should not be more than ——— cm.
(*a*) 2.5 (*b*) 4.0
(*c*) 5.0 (*d*) 2.5

41. Which is the latrine of choice for camps?
(*a*) Aquaprivy
(*b*) Trench hole
(*c*) Pit latrine
(*d*) Chemical

42. Pit latrine has depth of ——— feet:
(*a*) 2-4 (*b*) 4-6
(*c*) 6-10 (*d*) 10-12

43. Sanitation barrier is:
(*a*) Segregation of faeces
(*b*) Control of flies
(*c*) Excreta disposal
(*d*) Proper water supply

44. Soakage pit is used for hygenic disposal of:
(*a*) Garbage (*b*) Rubbish
(*c*) Sewage (*d*) Sludge

45. The disposal of night soil and refuge is by:
(*a*) Chemical sterilization
(*b*) Burning
(*c*) Composting
(*d*) Any of the above

46. Controlled tipping is a method of disposal of:
(*a*) Sewage
(*b*) Human excreta
(*c*) Sludge
(*d*) Rufuse

47. Red Cross was founded by:
(*a*) Hippocrates
(*b*) Henry Durant
(*c*) Galen
(*d*) Madam curie

48. Kata thermometer is used to measure:
(*a*) Maximum temperature
(*b*) Minimum temperature
(*c*) Radiant heat
(*d*) Cooling power of air

49. A rupture of ear drum may actually occur at a decibel level above:
(*a*) 40 (*b*) 80
(*c*) 120 (*d*) 160

ANSWERS

1	2	3	4	5	6	7	8	9	10
(*a*)	(*d*)	(*c*)	(*a*)	(*c*)	(*a*)	(*a*)	(*b*)	(*d*)	(*b*)
11	**12**	**13**	**14**	**15**	**16**	**17**	**18**	**19**	**20**
(*a*)	(*b*)	(*d*)	(*a*)	(*a*)	(*c*)	(*d*)	(*a*)	(*c*)	(*a*)
21	**22**	**23**	**24**	**25**	**26**	**27**	**28**	**29**	**30**
(*a*)	(*d*)	(*b*)	(*a*)	(*b*)	(*d*)	(*d*)	(*b*)	(*d*)	(*c*)
31	**32**	**33**	**34**	**35**	**36**	**37**	**38**	**39**	**40**
(*b*)	(*b*)	(*b*)	(*b*)	(*b*)	(*a*)	(*c*)	(*a*)	(*a*)	(*d*)
41	**42**	**43**	**44**	**45**	**46**	**47**	**48**	**49**	
(*d*)	(*d*)	(*a*)	(*c*)	(*c*)	(*d*)	(*b*)	(*d*)	(*d*)	

10

Health Administration & Programmes

HEALTH PROGRAMMES

1. National Health Programme

Bhore committee's report in 1946 revealed important National problem of health. After independance the Government of India started health services in the country for people. This was very difficult work considering India is a big country. People are ignorant, mainly rural population. The work has to be done slowly due to limited resources.

Disease also spreads fast from one state to another by trade and commerce by pilgrimage. Considering certain problems requiring help from both centre as well as state, Central Government has role of planning, guiding, funding and co-ordinating National Health programmes. This is very necessary for having uniform action of control all over the country state Government has to implement these programmes.

These programmes are not static. New programmes are added like National cancer control programmes, National AIDS control programme and old ones like National Small pox Eradication Programme was deleted after its purpose was served. The trained manpower of this programme is utilized for new programme of E.P.I. *the programmes are*:

1. Control of communicable diseases Malaria, diarrhoea, tuberculosis, leprosy, filariasis, trachoma, AIDS
2. Environmental: sanitation water supply, excreta disposal, refuse disposal, minimum needs programme.
3. Nutrition: Goitre, supplementary feeding, nutrition education, Anaemia, Xeropthalmia
4. Population control (Family planning)
5. Rural health
6. Non-communicable diseases (cancer, diabetes), Blindness
7. Comprehensive (minimum need programme, Twenty point programme)

(a) National programmes for communicable diseases

1. Expanded programme on Immunisation converted to universal Immunisation Programme
2. National Malaria Eradication Programme
3. National filaria control programme
4. National Tuberculosis control programme
5. National leprosy Eradication Programme
6. Diarrhoeal Diseases control programme
7. STD control programme
8. Guinea worm eradication Programme
9. National AIDS control programme

(b) Environmental Sanitation

National water supply and Sanitation Programme

(c) Comprehensive Development

1. Minimum needs Programme
2. 20 points programme

(d) National Family Welfare Programme

(e) National Programme on Nutrition

1. Applied nutritional Anemia Prophylaxis Programme
2. Mid day meal programme
3. Special nutrition programme
4. ICDS
5. National Goitre control programme, renamed as Iodine Deficiency Disorders Programme

(f) **Non-communicable diseases**

(i) National cancer control programme
(ii) National diabetes control programme

2. National Malaria Control Programme

In the 1950 malaria was the India's biggest Health Problems. In order to fight this disease nation wide Malaria control programme was launched in 1953. Results of this programme were spactacular. Cases of malaria were decreases from 7.5 crores in 1952 to 2 million in 1958. Encouraged by these results and there was fear of insect vectors might develop resistance. The programme was upgraded to National Malaria Eradication Programme is implemented in 1958. India commitment to the goal of Health for All by 2000 AD.

In the control programme, strategy was insecticidal spray (D.D.T.) to kill anophele mosquitoes and thereby breaking chain of transmission of disease. Antimalarial drugs were given at low or no cost and larval control measures were introduced.

National Malaria Eradication Programme was to be carried out in 4 phases:-

(i) Preparatory phase
(ii) Attack phase
(iii) Consolidation phase
(iv) Maintenance phase

3. National Tuberculosis Control Programme, National Tuberculosis Programme (NTP), District Tuberculosis Programme (DTP)

National Tuberculosis programme started in 1962 with long term objective to reduce tuberculosis in the community to the level when it is not a public health problem.

The national Tuberculosis Institute Banglore serves as apex institute for this programme. Tuberculosis research centre at Chennai carries out various clinical trials to find out most suitable regimen of antitubercular drugs. National Tuberculosis institute also helps to solve problem at district tuberculosis centres. There are 17 tuberculosis training and demostration centres are functioning in the country to undertake training of medical and paramedical personnel.

4. National Leprosy Eradication Programme (NLCP), 1955

The National leprosy control programme was launched in 1955 as a programme with assistance from central government with following activities:

1. Early detection of cases
2. Domiciliary treatment with DDS

With strong political will the programme was redesignated as National Leprosy Eradication Programme. The activities of this programme are:

1. Early detection of cases by population survey. School survey, contact examination and voluntary referral
2. Short term multidrug therapy.
3. Health education
4. Rehabilitation activities
5. National Leprosy Control Plan changed to National Leprosy Eradication Programme on 1983.

The programme is implemented through establishment till 1988

1. Leprosy control units and modified leprosy control units	708
2. SET centres	7400
3. Urban leprosy centres	942
4. Reconstructive surgery units	75
5. Leprosy training centre	42
6. Leprosy Rehabilitation Promotion units	12

All 76 highly endemic districts are brought under MDR during 1980-90. Another 1225 MDR have opend upto 2005 (Dec).

5. MDR (Multi Drug Therapy)

In absence of specific protection of leprosy by a vaccine the policy of leprosy control was based on chemotherapy. Initially with dapsone but due to use of single drug, resistance of organism of leprosy was noted.

Hence new strategy with multiple drug is adopted.

Objectives of MDR are:

(a) Break chain of transmission by making patient free from bacteria

(b) To cure the patient

(c) To prevent drug resistance

Advantages of MDR are:

(a) Duration of treatment reduced

(b) Better patient's co-operation

(c) Cost effective

(d) Decreased work load to health worker.

6. STD Control Programme

The programme is operated on a regional basis with regional STD teaching cum Training centres establishment at Delhi, Chennai, Hyderabad, Calcutta and Nagpur. At these centres reference laboratories and Regional Survey cum mobile STDs centres are established. They are actively engaged in training and orientation programmes of the medical and para medical personnel, conducting short orientation courses for laboratory technicians. They also carryout inter laboratory evaluation of VDRL and research related to epidemiological profile and laboratory diagnosis particularly in the backward and tribal areas of the country.

7. AIDS Control Programme

The Government of India in 1985 constituted a task force to look into this problem. An AIDS cell was established in the DGHS, New Delhi to coordinate all activities pertaining to AIDS in the country.

National Policy is as:

1. Establishment of surveillance centre to cover the whole country.
2. Identification of high risk groups and their screening *i.e.*, pregnant women, prostitutes, blood donors, homosexual and drug addict.
3. Specific guidelines for management of detected cases and their follow up.
4. Formulating guidelines for blood banks, blood donors dialysis units.
5. IEC activities by mass media research.

8. National Cancer Control

At present 150 general hospitals offer facilities for cancer treatment by surgery, radiotherapy and chemotherapy. Teletheraphy cobalt unit for treatment of cancer is available in 54 medical colleges and 45 other medical institutions. At centre, there is cancer control Board headed by Minister of family welfare. 15 states and union territories have set up state cancer control board. There are 10 regional cancer centres.

Activities of Regional Cancer Centres:

1. Surveys
2. Diagnosis, Treatment and follow up
3. Training of personnel both medical and para-medical
4. Mass examination, health education and industrial hygiene
5. Research fundamental applied.

National Cancer Control Project:

Started by government of India and works for:

1. Control of tobacco related cancers using primary prevention
2. Early diagnosis and treatment of cervical and oral cancer.
3. Research evaluation and provision of more therapeutic facilities.

9. National Goitre Control Programme:

Also known as Iodine Deficiency Disorder control programme. The Government of India launched National Goitre Control Programme in 1952 which had following activities:

1. Survey of areas where goitre is detected
2. Production and supply of iodized salt to the endemic areas to control goitre.
3. Re-survey after 5 years to know impact of the programme.

Main strategy was iodization of salt and distribution of the salt to area of endemic goitre region. It is estimated that presently 40-50 million have goitre. 2.2 million severely mentally retarded, 6.6 million suffer from mild neurological deficit. All states and 4 out of 7 union territories showing endemic goitre.

10. Integrated Child Development Services

The ICDS programme is a (Maternal and Child health) Programme. It is more than a nutrition programme and aims at total development of the child. Only the nutritional component of ICDS is described initially. It consists of growth monitoring supplementary nutrition and nutrition education. The supplementary nutrition is given for 300 days a year on the spot feeding as far as possible. All beneficiaries receive daily ration of 300 kilocalories and 8 to 10 g protein. Severely malnourished children and pregnant women receive daily supplementary nutrition providing 600 kcal and 18-20 g protein.

The cost of supplementary nutrition is as follows:

Supplementary Nutrition	Cost
Moderately malnourished children (6 months to 72 months)	75 paise per child per day
Severely malnourished children (6 months to 72 months)	125 paise per child per day
Pregnant and nursing mother	105 paise per beneficiary per day

11. National Immunization Schedule (Revised)

Beneficiaries	*Age*	*Vaccine*	*No. of doses*	*Route of administration*
Infants	6 weeks to	DPT	3	Intra muscular
	9 months	Polio	3	Oral
		BCG	1	Intra dermal
	9 to 12 months	Measles		Subcutaneous
Children	16 to 24 months	DPT	1	Intra-muscular
		Polio	1	oral
	5 to 6 years	DT	1	Intra muscular
		Typhoid	2	Subcutaneous
	10 years	Tetanus toxoid	1	Intramuscular
		Typhoid		Sub cutaneous
	16 years	Tetanus toxoid	1	Sub cutaneous
		Typhoid	1	
Pregnant women	16-36 weeks	Tetanus toxoid	1	Intra-muscular

OBJECTIVE QUESTIONS

1. Problem village is all except:
   (*a*) Where no water source in a distance of 1.6 km from community
   (*b*) Water is more than depth of 15m
   (*c*) There is excess on Na^+, K^+, F^- salts
   (*d*) Risks of guinea worm infection

2. Cancer control programme was launched in:
   (*a*) 1976 (*b*) 1986
   (*c*) 1970 (*d*) 1992

3. The national Diabetes control Programme in India includes all the following activities,

except:

(*a*) Primary prevention of diabetes through genetic testing and genetic counselling

(*b*) Identification of high-risk subjects at an early stage, with appropriate health education

(*c*) Early diagnosis and manage-ment of cases

(*d*) Prevention, arrest or slowing of metabolic and cardio-vascular complications of the disease

4. In community Needs Assessments approach as part of the Reproductive and Child Health Programme, the target for various health activities are set at the level of:

(*a*) Community
(*b*) Sub-centre
(*c*) Primary health centre
(*d*) District

5. The "safe motherhood schemes" (CSSM) major thrust area is:

(*a*) Promotion of reproductive health
(*b*) Elimination of maternal morbidity
(*c*) Fertility regulation
(*d*) To provide essential prenatal, natal and postnatal services

6. In the reproductive and child health (RCH) programme the main addition over and above the child survival and safe motherhood programme is:

(*a*) Care of reproductive tract infection
(*b*) Essential newborn care
(*c*) First referral unit
(*d*) At-risk

7. Under reproductive and Child Health Programme, following two indicators are used:

(*a*) Life expectancy at age 1 and MMR
(*b*) Crude birth rate and IMR
(*c*) Crude death rate and IMR
(*d*) CDR and CBR

8. In the expanded programme of immunisation it is proposed to achieve target of ——— immunisation of children by 1990.

(*a*) 80% (*b*) 90%
(*c*) 95% (*d*) 100%

9. Target for EPI to be achieved by 1990 was:

(*a*) 60% coverage
(*b*) 80% coverage
(*c*) 90% coverage
(*d*) 100% coverage

10. In the National Goiter Control Programme, iodine is supplied:

(*a*) In drinking water
(*b*) In salt as iodine
(*c*) In salt as iodate
(*d*) As IM injectioin of iodised oil

11. The goal set for AD 2005 by the National programme for the control of blindness in India is to reduce blindness to:

(*a*) 0.3 per cent of total population
(*b*) 0.6 per cent of total population
(*c*) 1.2 per cent of total population
(*d*) 2.4 per cent of total population

12. Under the National Programme for Prevention of Blindness, Vitamin A is to be given to:

(*a*) All children between the ages of 1 to 5 years at 6 monthly intervals
(*b*) Children with history of night blindness
(*c*) Children with severe protein energy malnutrition
(*d*) Children with Bitot spots

13. Under the national TB programme, for a PHC to be called a PHI-R, requisite is:

(*a*) Microscopy
(*b*) Microscopy plus radiology
(*c*) Radiology
(*d*) Specialities of doctors

14. Consider the following statements:
The Revised National Tuberculosis Control Programme has a strategy base that reflects in:

1. Accountability of system
2. Increasing case detection
3. Ensuring DOTS based drugs for every patient

Which of these statements is/are correct?
(*a*) 1 and 2 (*b*) 2 and 3
(*c*) 3 only (*d*) 1, 2 and 3

15. Main aim of tuberculosis treatment is
(*a*) Radiological cure
(*b*) Contact tracing
(*c*) Bacteriological cure
(*d*) To prevent complication

16. Goal of national tuberculosis control programme (NTCP) is:
(*a*) To eradicate TB
(*b*) To decrease the transmission of TB
(*c*) To treat all sputum +ve patients
(*d*) To decrease the incidence of TB to such a low level that it is no longer a major public health problem
(*e*) BCG vaccination of all infants

17. False about DOTS is:
(*a*) Continuation phase drugs are given in a multiblister pack
(*b*) Medication is to be taken in presence of a health worker
(*c*) Biweekly dosage and DOT at time
(*d*) Improves compliance

18. District TB control programme is mainly concerned with:
(*a*) Finding out new cases
(*b*) Finding out resistant cases
(*c*) Detecting cases and treatment
(*d*) All of the above

19. The screening method of choice in prevalance of leprosy is 1 in 1000 is
(*a*) Contact survey (*b*) Group survey
(*c*) Mass survey (*d*) Any of the above

20. Under the National Leprosy Eradication Programme mass surveys are undertaken when the prevalence of leprosy is
(*a*) 1/1000 (*b*) 3/1000
(*c*) 5/1000 (*d*) 10/1000

21. India has entered which phase of demographic cycle:
(*a*) High stationary
(*b*) Low stationary
(*c*) Early expanding
(*d*) Late expanding

22. High prevalance zone for leprosy has cases per 1,000 population as:
(*a*) 1-2 (*b*) 2-5
(*c*) 5-10 (*d*) 10-20

23. Which of the following is/are used as operational indicator in antileprosy activity?
(*a*) Incidence
(*b*) Incidence and prevalence
(*c*) Relapse rate and case detection ratio
(*d*) Incidence and case detection ratio

24. The multidrug regimen under the national leprosy eradication programme (NLEP) for the treatment of all multi-bacillary leprosy would include:
(*a*) Clofazimine thiacetazone and dapsone
(*b*) Clofazimine rifampicin and dapsone
(*c*) Ethionamide, rifampicin and dapsone
(*d*) Propionamide, rifampicin and dapsone

25. In leprosy control programme, indicator of efficacy of early diagnosis case is:
(*a*) Disability rate among newly used
(*b*) Lepromin +ve% among used
(*c*) Ratio of, multi/pauci bacillary cases
(*d*) All of the above

26. The screening method of choice in prevalence of leprosy is 1 in 1000 is:
(*a*) Contact survey
(*b*) Group survey
(*c*) Mass survey
(*d*) Any of the above

27. Longest incubation period, among the following is of:
(*a*) Malaria (*b*) Hepatitis
(*c*) Leprosy (*d*) Filaria

28. In the national leprosy eradication programme (NLEP), mass surgery are done if the prevalance is:
(*a*) 1/1000 (*b*) 2/2,000
(*c*) 6/1000 (*d*) 10/1,000

29. Which of the following is not monitored in malaria surveillance now:
(*a*) ABER
(*b*) Infant parasite rate

(c) Annual parasite incidence
(d) Slide positivity rate

30. National programmes are now organised for the following in India except:
(a) Filariasis
(b) Leprosy
(c) Smallpox
(d) Trachoma

31. The objective of minimum needs programme does not include:
(a) One PHC for 30,000 population
(b) Link-mid-day meal programme to sanitation
(c) Integration of health, water and sanitation
(d) Urban area given priority

32. Under NMEP the minimum annual blood examination rate should be:
(a) 10% (b) 12%
(c) 14% (d) 18%

33. Modified programme for National Malaria Eradication Programme is based on:
(a) API
(b) ABER
(c) Infant parasite rate
(d) Spleen rate

34. In NMEP, the recommendation for area API-2 are A/E:
(a) Presumptive treatment
(b) DDT spraying fortwiced in a year
(c) Epidemiological investigation of all cases
(d) Follow-up every case for one year and monthly blood & mears

35. Which is not true of malaria eradication programme (MEP):
(a) started in 1953
(b) modified plan started in 1970
(c) incidence was 2 million cases in 1958
(d) incidence decreased to 50,000 in 1961

36. The expected reduction in API by 2000 AD in India is:
(a) 1/10 (b) 1/100
(c) 1/1000 (d) 0.5/1000

37. Under NMEP, the function of fever depot treatment is:
(a) Diagnosis of cases + spraying
(b) collection of slides + treatment of fever
(c) Treatment fever cases only
(d) Treatment + slide collection + spraying

38. Under NMEP, the minimum annual blood examination rate should be:
(a) 10% (b) 12%
(c) 14% (d) 18%

39. All of the following statements about National Malaria Control Programme are true except:
(a) Number of slides examined should amount to atleast 10% of the population under surveillance in a year
(b) Annual parasite incidence based on active and passive surveillance and cases confir-med by blood examination
(c) Annual blood examination rate is calculated from the number of slides examined per 100 cases of fever
(d) The slide positivity rate provides information on the trend of malaria transmission

40. Under NMEP, for areas with API more than 2 the vector is refractory to DDT, the new recommendation is:
(a) HCH-1 round/year
(b) HCH-2 rounds/year
(c) HCH-3 rounds/year
(d) Malathione-2 rounds/year

41. Under the National Malaria Eradication programme, radical treatment for P.vivax malaria is given for:
(a) 1 days (b) 5 days
(c) 7 days (d) 14 days

42. Under NMEP for areas with API more than 2 and vector refractory to DDT, the recommendations is:
(a) Malathion-3 rounds/year
(b) HCH-1 round/year
(c) HCH-2 rounds/year
(d) HCH-3 rounds/year

ANSWERS

1	2	3	4	5	6	7	8	9	10
(c)	(a)	(a)	(d)	(d)	(a)	(a)	(d)	(d)	(b)
11	**12**	**13**	**14**	**15**	**16**	**17**	**18**	**19**	**20**
(a)	(a)	(b)	(b)	(c)	(d)	(d)	(c)	(b)	(d)
21	**22**	**23**	**24**	**25**	**26**	**27**	**28**	**29**	**30**
(d)	(d)	(d)	(b)	(a)	(b)	(c)	(d)	(b)	(c)
31	**32**	**33**	**34**	**35**	**36**	**37**	**38**	**39**	**40**
(d)	(a)	(a)	(c)	(b)	(c)	(b)	(a)	(c)	(c)
41	**42**								
(b)	(d)								

10

Health Environment

1. Disposal of the Dead Human

(a) In Africa dead bodies are carried into the forest to be eaten by beasts of pray.

(b) Some tribes at Guinea throw the corpses into sea.

(c) Parsees in India place the dead body in a round tower called Tower of silence to be eaten by vultures and other birds.

(d) The bodies of high religious persons are sometime preserved by process involving use of salt and butter (Tibet). St. Xaviers body has been preserved in India.

(e) In the past Egyptians were using process of mummification for preservation.

Some of the methods mentioned above do not seem hygienic but are practised on religious grounds. Otherwise two broad methods of disposal of dead in the world are

1. Burning or cremation
2. Burial

Burning or Cremation: This is the most satisfactory method of disposal of the dead:-

1. Traditional burning is done with woods, cakes of cow dung *etc*.
2. Electric furnace - bodies are burnt rapidly and completely, this method is also less costly.

2. Requirement for a Burning Ground

(a) Cremetery should be 500 ft away from a residence.

(b) A land of 100m × 100m is sufficient.

(c) Fencing up to seven feet is desirable.

(d) Proper access is necessary.

(e) The area should not get water logged during rainy season.

(f) Sufficient light and water supply is necessary.

(g) There should be sufficient number of pyres and there should be shed for cremation during the rainy season.

3. Burial Ground

Object is speedy resolution and complete oxidation.

(a) Soil should be sandy, porous and either naturally or artificially drained to a depth of 8 ft. Clay soil is bad because it cannot be drained properly and allows product of put refaction to escape through cracks that are produced in dry weather.

(b) Trees should be planted so that toxic gases given out from decaying body will be absorbed.

(c) The body is removed in a coffin, but the body should be placed in easily destructible coffin for better decomposition. Muslims do use coffins.

(d) The burial should be properly marked and a paved passage should exist between the grave (space for burial 7 × 4' and space between 4)

(e) The body should be buried at a depth 3 to 5 feet.

(f) The area should be properly lighted.

4. Disposal of the Dead Animal Bodies

Disposal of the body of dead animal should be in such a way that it does not create nuisance or pollution is also very important. Small animal bodies like rats *etc.* can be removed along with other item of solid waste garbage. The dead bodies of animals like dogs are better removed by burial in a shallow pit and covered with earth or garbage. This is done in the usual dumping ground where the garbage is normally dumped.

The disposal of bigger animals like cows, buffaloes and calves has to be done more carefully. The skin of these animals are valuable and they are skinned. In some of metropolitan towns *e.g.,* Bombay, a special contract is being given for removal of the bodies of these animals with a condition that skinning is done in a distant secluded place and then the remains are disposed of in a way that nuisance is not created. Special care is necessary in cities where there are airports since the dead bodies of these animals attract birds *etc.* which are a danger to aircraft.

5. Engineering Methods of Disease Control

Public health engineering is very important aspect in preventing and controlling diseases and in maintaining public health. For some diseases, (occupational diseases) prevention is the proper method, if control and control by treatment is of little use. For example if water pollution is not prevented there may be epidemic of cholera, infectious hepatitis *etc*, and treating individuals does not prevent the spread of the diseases. There are many diseases—communicable, occupational and even nutritional which can be prevented and controlled by engineering methods for example:

1. Purifications of water (filtration, chlorination)
2. Proper distribution of pipes and lines
3. Provision of latrines or water carriage system for excreta disposal.
4. Proper disposal of garbage
5. Removal of step wells (for prevention of guinea worm disease)

Food borne: Cholera, enteric fever, dysenteries, polio, infectious hepatitis, food poisoing, intestinal worm which can be controlled by:

(a) Purification of water

(b) Proper refuse disposal

(c) Rat control (Rat proofing of houses and godowns *etc.* for prevention of contamination of food by rat)

Arthropod borne: Malaria, Filariasis, plague, scrub, typhus, leishmaniasis which can be controlled by:

(a) Filling up of places where water collection occur (pits, ditches, wells not in use *etc.*)

(b) while constructing roads, bridges, railroads *etc.* natural flow of water should not be obstructed.

(c) waste water disposal

(d) Mosquito proofing of houses

(e) Providing tight fitting covers for septic tanks wire mesh for ventilation, pipes of septic tanks.

(f) Cutting down of vegetation (for control of soft ticks).

(g) Filling in cracks or fissuers in walls of building (for control of sand flies).

Airborne: Measles, rubella, chickenpox, mumps, influenza, diphtheria, whooping cough, tuberculosis, cerebro spinal fever which can be controlled by:

(a). Provision of proper shelter with adequate light and ventilation

(b) Improvement of clearance of slums

(c) Dust control

6. Occupational

1. Diseases due to physical agents (heat, cold, pressure, electricity, noise and radiation)
2. Diseases due to chemical agents (organic and inorganic dust, metals poisonous chemicals *etc.*)

3. Accidents and injuries which can be controlled by:
   (a) Maintaining environmental sanitation disposal of refuse.
   (b) Proper maintenance of machines and taking safety measures to prevent accidents.

Nutritional: Dental caries and fluorosis which can be controlled by:

(a) Addition of fluorides to drinking water for dental caries

(b) Removal of excess of fluorides: For fluorosis.

(c) Soil transmitted: Ancylostomiasis (Hook worm) which can be controlled by provision of sanitary latrines in rural areas).

Air and Ventilation

	Inspired air	*Expried air*	*Change*
Oxygen	20.9%	16.5%	O_2 is less by 4.4%
carbon dioxide	.04%	4.44%	CO_2 is more by 4.4%
Nitrogen	79%	79%	No change
Water vapour	As in air	saturated	increased
Tempera-ture	As in air	Body temperature	increased
Organic matters	As in air	Increased	Increased
Other gases	In traces	Remains the same	No change

7. Air is Made Impure by:

1. *Breathing of man and animals:* The O_2 becomes less and CO_2, temperature, humidity and organic impurities are increased.
2. *Combustion (i.e., burning):* By combustion, O_2 becomes less and CO_2, CO, soot SO_2 *etc.* are given out. Temperature also rises:
   (a) Burning: For burning of 500 grams of coal 350 cc ft of oxygen or air is required. It gives out 1% unburnt carbon particles as soot CO_2, CO, CS_2, H_2S, SO_2, NH_3 and water vapour are also given out.
   (b) Coal gas is produced by destructive distillation of coal *i.e.,* by heating coal without oxygen. The gas has 46% H_2S, 37% marsh gas, 7% CO and a few other gases.
3. *Decomposition of organic matters:* During decomposition CO_2, NH_3, H_2S *etc.* are given out. These gases cause loss of health, lowers the vitality and susceptibility of disease increases.

8. Air is Purified in Nature by:

1. Action of the wind, it dilutes the impurities
2. Rain washes out impurities in air *i.e.,* dust, soot gases.
3. Sunlight due to its heat kills the insects and germs and ultra violet rays in sunlight is protoplasmic poison to the germs.
4. Breathing of plant during sunlight takes up CO_2 from the air, breaks up CO_2 to C and O_2 is given out in air and hence air contains more oxygen and less CO_2.
5. Oxygen and ozone in air oxidise and kill the germs.

9. Comfortable Room:

1. Temperature should be about 75°F
2. Humidity to be about 65% to 70%
3. D.K. to be 5 to 6
4. W.K. to be 15 to 18
5. CO_2 should not be more than 0.6% to 0.7%
6. Movement of air in the room should be 10 times per hour.
7. No dust in air.

10. Indicators of Pollution:

1. *SO_2:-* Major contaminant in many urban and industrial areas produced by burning of coal and fuel oil usually measured in air pollution surveys.

2. *Soiling index or smoke index*: Air is filtered through a papertape and density is measured by photo-electric meter.

3. *Suspended particles*: For domestic heating and industry and expressed as µg/m^3 (Microframs/abc meters) CO, NO_2 and lead are also measured.

11. Health Effects:

1. *Effects on man*: Immediate ones are increased morbidity and mortality, irritation to eyes, asthma 12000 died in Bhopal in 1984).

2. *Delayed effects*: Chronic bronchitis, asthma, primary lung cancer.

   Poor visibility leads to accidents unpleasant odour leads to nausea vomiting.

3. *Effects on plants and animals*: Plants are very sensitive to SO_2 Fluorine compound, smog, *etc*. spotting and burning of leaves, destruction of crops retarded growth of plants cattle suffer from cachexia by eating leaves and plants.

4. Social and economic aspects:
   - *(a)* Acidity of rain and fog causes corrosion of buildings hydrogen sulfide causes discolouration of lead point.
   - *(b)* Fluorine causes etching of glass. Tar and soot adhere on which they impinge, ozone causes damage to rubber goods.

12. Instruments used to measure atmospheric pressure are called "barometers". Barograph is an instrument which continuously records atmospheric pressure.

13. Effects of Atmospheric Pressure on Health

At high altitude oxygen pressure is less and air becomes thinner. Above 25000 feet breathing equipment is necessary. The physiological effects at high atitudes are:-

- *(a)* Increased rate of respiration (which is normally 18 per minute).
- *(b)* Concentration of haemoglobin in blood increases so that more oxygen can be carried.
- *(c)* Amount of blood pumped at every beat of heart is increases for improving circulation.

14. Barometer

In its simplest form consists of a tube about 80 cm long. It is filled with mercury and inverted in a pot containing mercury. It will be seen that the mercury level falls and come to 76 cm heigh at sea level. If we go up the pressure will fall by 1 cm for every 120 metres of ascent

15. Eupatheometer

It is a type of comfort indicator. There are 2 thermometer, one with black bulb and other with silvery bulb. Like kata the bulbs are heated and time taken for the thermometer to fall from upper mark to lower mark is noted. For example if the fall is 30 sec and 21 seconds and the scale at the black corresponding to 30 and 21 are 35 and 20 then the equivalent comfort = 35 + 20 = 55F.

16. Heat Stroke or Sunstroke

In this condition body temperature rises to 110°F the skin is dry. There is delirium fits and person may become unconscious. If the body temperature is not brought down immediately, death occurs.

Treatment: The patient's body should be cooled by ice water bath. The rectal temperature is brought down to 103°F and then kept constant between 102°F and 101°F. Bed rest should be taken for many days.

17. Prevention of Heat Stress

This is done by:

1. *Taking plenty of water*: For those who do heavy work in the sun 1 litre/hour is required.
2. People should work less where air temperature and humidity are high. There

should be period of rest between heavy work.

3. Clothes should be light in weight and colour and should be loose.
4. Goggles, hats *etc.* should be worn
5. Proper ventilation or air conditioning should be provided in places where people are subjected to heat stress like industries *etc*.

18. Cold Stress

This is seen where air temperature goes down as in places near north and south poles, in Europe and America during winter or at high altitudes like Himalayas. The main effects are due to failure of proper blood circulation. There is numbness of skin, weakness of muscles, drowsiness and unconsciousness. Gangrene may occur in finger toes *etc.* Treatment consists of warming the affected parts in water at 44°C for 20 minutes. Hot drinks should be taken frequently.

19. Hygrometers

Hygrometers are instruments to find out the moisture present in the air. It can be found out by direct method *i.e.,* Daniells Hygrometer. Regnault's Hygrometer, Dini's Hygrometer. It can be found out by indirect method *i.e.,* by Dry and Wet Bulb Hygrometer and by sling psychrometer.

20. Noise

Noise is an important health problem due to occupational and inoccupational sources. 'Noise' in broad term means any sound which is loud, unpleasant. It is also said that this is the wrong sound in the wrong place, at wrong time. Noise is defined as the discardent sound which results from nonperiodic vibration of air. Characteristic of noise are pitch (frequency of cycles) Intensity (loud- ness) and quality.

— Noise is measured in unit of decible
— 0 Decibel sound can just be heard
— 120 Decibel sound can be felt as a wave.

Sources of Noise

Sources	*Decibels*	*Sensation*
1. Boiler markershop	120	Extremely loud
2. Pneumatic drill	110	Very loud
3. Siren	100	Fairly loud
4. Radio	70	Loud
5. Public library	40	Quiet
6. Silence	0	Inaudible

21. Effects of Noise:

On animal: Temporary rise in breathing heart rate, rise of blood pressure, degeneration of hair cells etc.

On man:- The auditory effects:

1. Short exposure to high intensity causes rupture of ear drums.
2. Prolonged hearing loss occurs and patient's hearing can be preserved if source of noise is removed.

22. Legal Measures

1. Permissible level of noise 90 db for 8 hours shift.
2. Noise induced deafness is a notifiable disease to factory Inspector.
3. Noise induced deafness is a compensable disease and compensation can be obtained from management.

Acceptable noise levels (DBA)

Residential	bed room	-	25
	living room	-	40
Commercial	office	-	35-45
	restaurants	-	40-60
Industrial	workshop	-	40-60
	laboratory	-	40-50
Educational	classroom	-	30-40
	library	-	35-45
Hospitals	wards	-	20-35

LIGHTING

23. Characteristics of Proper Light

1. *Sufficient*: varies with intended use 5 foot candles in staircase to 100 foot candles in industries.

2. *Distribution*: uniform with same intensity
3. *Absence of glare*: Excessive contrast is avoided because it causes acute discomfort.
4. *Steadiness*: No flicker but constancy is required
5. Absence of sharp shadows natural light or artificial light with frequency nearer day light. Proper surroundings with adequate reflection from surfaces.

24. Measurement of Light

Day light factor: defined as ratio of illumination at a given point exposed simultaneously to the whole hemisphere of sky excluding direct sunlight.

$$\text{D.F.} = \frac{\text{Instantaneous illumination indoors}}{\text{Simultaneous occuring illumination outdoors}} \times 100$$

25. Biological Effects of Light

Bilirubin excretion is increased. Affects body temperature, physical activity, melanix synthesis and activation of vitamin D.

26. Radiation Hazards

Radio-activity is the decomposition of an atom accompanied by emision of radiant energy such as alpha, beta, gamma or x-rays.

Radiation is the giving off of electro-magnetic waves on particulate rays.

Mechanism of action of radiation: These act on cytoplasm and cause denaturation of protein, affect nucleus and cell division is affected resulting daughter cells are badly damaged.

27. Effects of Radiation on Man:

Factors producing effects are:

1. Type of radiation 2. dose of radiation 3. Time of radiation 4. Exposure of whole body or part 5. distance from source of radiation 6. Protective clothing if any

Acute: large dose of short duration

Chronic: Small dose over long period

Acute radiation syndrome: 400 - 500 rads 50% death and 100% will manifest sickness, nausea vomiting, hairloss, diarrhoea with blood, ulcers in mouth, fever and death 3000 Rad's-100% will die in one week.

28. Specific Protection from Radiation

1. Using minimum effective dose
2. Avoidance of indiscriminate use
3. Use of lead aprons, goggles
4. Use of filters and image intensifier
5. Decreasing time of exposures
6. Using shield and keeping distance
7. Enclosing procedure totally.

29. International Agencies Helping Protection Against Radiation Exposure

1. World Health Organisation (W.H.O.)
2. IAEA (The International Atomic Energy Association)
3. ICRP (The International Commi-ssion on Radiological Protection)

OBJECTIVE QUESTION

1. The following are found resistant to DDT except:
(*a*) Phlebotomus
(*b*) Culex fatigans
(*c*) Anopheles stephensi
(*d*) Musca domestic

2. The essential ingredient in the space sprays for vector control is:
(*a*) Malathion
(*b*) Phenothion
(*c*) Pyrethrum
(*d*) BHC

3. Paris green is larvicidal for:
(*a*) Anopheles
(*b*) Culex
(*c*) Aedes
(*d*) None of the above

4. Least toxic organophosphorus compound is:
(*a*) Paris green (*b*) Malathion
(*c*) Parathion (*d*) DDT

5. Effect of pyrethrum on mosquitoes is described as
(*a*) Residual (*b*) Repellent
(*c*) Known down (*d*) Contact

6. Abate is:
(*a*) Cyanide cpd
(*b*) Organophosphorus cpd
(*c*) Organochlorine cpd
(*d*) None of the above

7. Which one of the following insecticides is commonly used for ultra low-volume fogging?
(*a*) Abate (*b*) DDT
(*c*) Paris green (*d*) Malathion

8. Residual effect of malathion is for:
(*a*) 3 months (*b*) 6 months
(*c*) 9 months (*d*) 12 months

9. All are organophosphorus compounds except:
(*a*) Malathion (*b*) Propoxur
(*c*) Abdate (*d*) Fenethion

10. Which is an insecticide of vegetable origin?
(*a*) Abate (*b*) BHC
(*c*) Propoxur (*d*) Pyrethrum

11. The following are organo-phosphorus insecticides except:
(*a*) Fenthion (*b*) Parathion
(*c*) Chlorpyriphos (*d*) Pyrethrum

12. Which of the following is an organochlorine compound:
(*a*) Gardone (*b*) Dicapthon
(*c*) Kepone (*d*) Propoxur

13. To facilitate cross ventilation in educational institutions the recommended combined space for doors and windows as a percentage of floor space is:
(*a*) 10% (*b*) 15%
(*c*) 25% (*d*) 35%

14. Air pollution may cause:
(*a*) Dermatitis
(*b*) Carcinoma bronchus
(*c*) Bronchiectasis
(*d*) Pneumonia

15. Quality standards proposed by the Indian Central Pollution Control Board are based on limits of concentrations of:
(*a*) suspended particulate matter and sulphur dioxide
(*b*) suspended particulate matter, sulphur dioxide and oxides of nitrogen
(*c*) suspended particulate matter, sulphur dioxide of nitrogen and oxidents
(*d*) suspended particulate matter, sulphur dioxide, oxides of nitrogen and carbon monoxide

16. The following are indicators of the general level of air pollution except:
(*a*) Sulphur dioxide concentration
(*b*) Soiling index
(*c*) Formaldehyde concentration
(*d*) Total suspended particles

17. The best indicator(s) for monitoring of air pollution is/are:
(*a*) Sulphur dioxide and suspenden particles
(*b*) Sulphur dioxide
(*c*) Oxides of nitrogen and polyaromatic hydrocarbons
(*d*) Carbon monoxide

18. Indicators of air pollution are all except:
(*a*) Soiling index
(*b*) Concentration of SO_2
(*c*) Concentration of formal-dehyde
(*d*) Soot, dust and suspended particles

19. Not a primary air pollutant:
(*a*) Smoke and dust (*b*) So_2
(*c*) No_2 (*d*) Ozone

20. Corrected effective temperature is labelled as comfortable if it is (in degree F):
(*a*) Between 70 and 76
(*b*) Between 77 and 80
(*c*) Between 81 and 82
(*d*) Above 83

21. Temporary and permanent hardness of water is removed by:
(*a*) Boiling
(*b*) Addition of lime
(*c*) Permutit method
(*d*) All

22. Permanent hardness of water is not due to:
(*a*) Calcium bicarbonate
(*b*) Calcium sulphate
(*c*) Magnesium sulphate
(*d*) Nitrates

23. A water sample is said to be moderately hard when hardness-producing ion is about:
(*a*) 50 ppm
(*b*) 50-150 ppm
(*c*) 150-300 ppm
(*d*) 300 ppm

24. Sodium permutit is used for:
(*a*) Disinfection of water
(*b*) Sterilisation of water
(*c*) Removal of hardness of water
(*d*) Testing residual chlorine

25. UNDP is an international agency which works for:
(*a*) Developement of children
(*b*) Development of human and natural resources in a country
(*c*) Economic development of the country
(*d*) Research and technological development of the country

26. Old pollution of water is indicated by:
(*a*) Nitrates
(*b*) Nitrites
(*c*) Free and saline NH_3
(*d*) Chlorides

27. Primary health care as a principle of WHO was founded at:
(*a*) Geneva
(*b*) New York
(*c*) Alma Ata
(*d*) Austria

28. Nitrate level in water would not be more than - mg/l:
(*a*) 0.5 (*b*) 1.0
(*c*) 2.0 (*d*) 4.0

29. The organism which is NOT an indicator of faecal pollution is
(*a*) Staphylococcus
(*b*) Streptococcus
(*c*) E.coli
(*d*) Clostridium perfringens

30. The following organism because of its easy culture methods is widely used as bacteriological indicator of water pollution:
(*a*) Faecal streptococci
(*b*) Escherichia coli
(*c*) Clostridium perfringens
(*d*) Salmonella typhi

31. WHO standard for safe drinking water is:
(*a*) Less than 3 coliforms/100 ml
(*b*) 10 coliforms/100 ml
(*c*) Less than 20 coliforms/100 ml
(*d*) Less than 100 coliforms/100 ml

32. Which statement is not true about chlorination of well:
(*a*) Chlorine demand has to be estimated
(*b*) Volume of water has to be determined
(*c*) Bleaching powder solution has to be added immediately
(*d*) A contact period of 1 hour is allowed

33. In chlorination all are true except:
(*a*) Chlorine is a stable compound
(*b*) Available chlorine is 33%
(*c*) Rapid and brief action
(*d*) Minimum recommended concentration of free chlorine is 0.5% mg/1 hour

34. Difference in breast milk of a mother delivering preterm baby and mother delivering term baby has less quantity of:
(*a*) Lactose (*b*) Calcium
(*c*) Calories (*d*) Proteins

35. In orthotoludine tests all are correct except:
(*a*) Free chlorine is estimated
(*b*) 0.1 ml of reagent is used for 1 ml of water
(*c*) Yellow colour
(*d*) Read in 10 seconds

36. The residual chlorine content of drinking water should be:
(*a*) 0.5 ppm (*b*) 0.6 ppm
(*c*) 0.8 ppm (*d*) 1.2 ppm

37. Which of the following diseases is not susceptible by chlorination:
(*a*) Bacillary dysentry
(*b*) Typhoid fever
(*c*) Cholera
(*d*) Giardiasis

38. Which of the following is an important disinfectant on account of effectively destroying gram-positive and gram-negative bacteria, viruses and even spores at low pH levels:
(*a*) Phenol
(*b*) Alcohol
(*c*) Chlorine
(*d*) Hexachlorophene

39. For disinfecting large bodies of water, the most efficient and cost-effective method of applying chlorine is:
(*a*) Bleaching powder
(*b*) Chloramine
(*c*) Chlorine gas
(*d*) Perchloron

40. Noise pollution presents clinically as all except:
(*a*) Increase urinary output
(*b*) Decrease sexual activity
(*c*) Deafness
(*d*) Insomnia

ANSWERS

1	**2**	**3**	**4**	**5**	**6**	**7**	**8**	**9**	**10**
(*a*)	(*c*)	(*a*)	(*b*)	(*d*)	(*b*)	(*b*)	(*a*)	(*b*)	(*d*)
11	**12**	**13**	**14**	**15**	**16**	**17**	**18**	**19**	**20**
(*d*)	(*c*)	(*a*)	(*b*)	(*c*)	(*c*)	(*a*)	(*c*)	(*c*)	(*b*)
21	**22**	**23**	**24**	**25**	**26**	**27**	**28**	**29**	**30**
(*c*)	(*a*)	(*b*)	(*c*)	(*b*)	(*a*)	(*c*)	(*b*)	(*b*)	(*b*)
31	**32**	**33**	**34**	**35**	**36**	**37**	**38**	**39**	**40**
(*a*)	(*c*)	(*a*)	(*d*)	(*a*)	(*a*)	(*d*)	(*a*)	(*a*)	(*d*)

PRACTICE TEST PAPERS

PAPER SET-I

1. The substance that is used as bloodless scalpel is
(*a*) quartz-crystal (*b*) radioisotope
(*c*) X-ray (*d*) laser

2. The disorder characterised by reduction in the number of helper T-cells develops in
(*a*) *Myasthenia gravis*
(*b*) Cancer
(*c*) AIDS
(*d*) Taysach's disease

3. Which of the following algae are used as a source of food by astronauts?
(*a*) *Chlorella*
(*b*) *Spirogyra*
(*c*) *Chara*
(*d*) *Batrachospermum*

4. All the listed are diseases caused by protozoa except one
(*a*) Delhi-boils (*b*) Gambia fever
(*c*) Malaria (*d*) Filariasis

5. The body of Hydra is
(*a*) medusoid (*b*) polypoid
(*c*) both (a) and (b) (*d*) none

6. All the following are larval forms, except one
(*a*) Planula (*b*) Amphiblastula
(*c*) Glochidium (*d*) Neurula

7. The organism that is completely domesticated and never found in the wild is
(*a*) Honey bee (*b*) Lac insect
(*c*) *Bombyx mori* (*d*) Eriworm

8. Animals which feed on blood are called
(*a*) carnivores (*b*) herbivores
(*c*) detrivores (*d*) sanguivores

9. Apart from mammals, one other group of animal maintain constant body temperature, they are
(*a*) amphibians (*b*) reptiles
(*c*) birds (*d*) fishes

10. The tip of our nose contains
(*a*) elastic cartilage (*b*) calcified cartilage
(*c*) fibrous cartilage (*d*) hyaline cartilage

11. The process of formation of blood cell is called
(*a*) organogenesis (*b*) oogenesis
(*c*) haemopoiesis (*d*) spermiogenesis

12. Which of the following is the bone cell?
(*a*) Kupffer cell (*b*) Chondroblast
(*c*) Osteoblast (*d*) Osteoclast

13. No energy is required for the absorption of
(*a*) fat (*b*) proteins
(*c*) carbohydrates (*d*) all the three

14. The only vitamin secreted in human urine is
(*a*) B-complex (*b*) C
(*c*) D (*d*) K

15. In man, what can be vestigial among the following
(*a*) long hairs growing on pinna
(*b*) nails of fingers
(*c*) canine teeth
(*d*) nictitating membrane

16. One of the following is *not* a biofertilizer what is it?
(*a*) *Anabaena* (*b*) *Rhizobium*
(*c*) *Azospirillum* (*d*) *Spirogyra*

17. The fat content of milk is rich in
(*a*) cow (*b*) goat
(*c*) buffalo (*d*) sheep

18. The products resulting from atmospheric reaction of hydrocarbons and nitrogen oxides in the presence of sunlight are
(*a*) Gaseous pollutants
(*b*) Particulate pollutants
(*c*) Secondary pollutants
(*d*) Primary pollutants

19. Secondary pollutant is
(*a*) CO_2 (*b*) O_2
(*c*) CH_4 (*d*) O_3

20. Acid rain is caused by
(*a*) SO_2 and NO_2 (*b*) SO_3 and SO_2
(*c*) NO and NO_2 (*d*) SO_2 and H_2O

21. Which of the following is a carcinogenic?
(*a*) Gaseous pollutant
(*b*) Particulate pollutant
(*c*) Secondary pollutant
(*d*) All of the above

22. Tobacco contains seven polycyclic hydrocarbons and a radioactive substance is
(*a*) I-131 (*b*) Co-132
(*c*) U-235 (*d*) Po-210

23. The most important method of conservation of pollutant is
(*a*) oxidation in air
(*b*) chemical neutralisation of acid and bases
(*c*) both of these
(*d*) None of these

24. Humus helps in the
(*a*) making the soil granular
(*b*) plant growth
(*c*) it increases the water holding capacity of clay soil and sand soil
(*d*) All of the above

25. Mangrove vegetation living in saline marsh belong to
(*a*) Heliophytes (*b*) Epiphytes
(*c*) Halophytes (*d*) Sciophytes

26. The ozone layer present in the
(*a*) Trophosphere (*b*) Stratosphere
(*c*) Ozonosphere (*d*) Ionosphere

27. "Green House gases" are
(*a*) CO_2 only
(*b*) Chloroflurocarbons and CH_4
(*c*) Oxides of Nitrogen
(*d*) All of the above

28. The % of fresh water present in the world is
(*a*) 97% (*b*) 50%
(*c*) 100% (*d*) 3%

29. The reservoir of the gaseous cycles and the sedimentary cycle is/are
(*a*) Atmosphere only
(*b*) Lithosphere only
(*c*) Hydrosphere only
(*d*) Atmosphere & Lithosphere

30. Green house effect is caused by
(*a*) low CO_2 content
(*b*) high CO_2 content
(*c*) intermittent CO_2 content
(*d*) not by CO_2

31. Forest community is an example of
(*a*) Habitat (*b*) Niche
(*c*) Lians (*d*) Biosphere

32. Earthworms help farmers by
(*a*) making soil porus and increasing its fertility
(*b*) reducing alkalinity and acidity of soil
(*c*) causing soil erosion
(*d*) destroying bacteria present in the soil

33. A. Though hermophrodite, *Pheretima* practises cross fertilization.
B. This is because mating occurs in summer season.
(*a*) A is true, B is false
(*b*) A is false, B is true
(*c*) Both are true, but B is correct explanation of A
(*d*) Both are true, but B is not correct explanation of A.

34. The substance due to which the skin of *Pheritima* appears brown is
(*a*) Melanin (*b*) Haemoglobin
(*c*) Haemocyanin (*d*) Porphyrin

35. Insects are able to fly because
(*a*) of their chitinous wings
(*b*) of their ability to work
(*c*) sexes are seperate
(*d*) all of the above

36. Arthropods have
(*a*) bilaterally symmetrical with jointed exoskleton
(*b*) a segmented body with simple or compound eyes
(*c*) body consists of trunk, thorax and abdomen
(*d*) all of the above

37. Pheromons are secreted by
(*a*) Insects (*b*) Cephalopods
(*c*) Scyphozoas (*d*) Gastropods

38. Compound eyes have small units of its own lens are called
(*a*) ommatidium (*b*) synangium
(*c*) archegonium (*d*) conidium

39. In Arthropods
(*a*) fertilization is external in crustaceans but in others fertilisation is internal
(*b*) oviparous condition is seen
(*c*) viviparous condition is seen
(*d*) all of the above

40. The process of transformation of a larva into an adult is called
(*a*) Moulting (*b*) Ecdysis
(*c*) Metamorphosis (*d*) Syngamy

41. In arthropods, youngones that resemble adults, but do not have wings and reproductive organs are
(*a*) Nymph (*b*) ommatidia
(*c*) zygospore (*d*) egg

42. Arthropods have to shed their chitinous covering for growth by
(*a*) Moulting (*b*) Ecdysis
(*c*) Metamorphosis (*d*) both (a) and (b)

43. "Fossils arthropods" over 600 million years old are
(*a*) Arachnidans (*b*) Cephalopodans
(*c*) Trilobites (*d*) Trophocorans

44. Set of animals directly useful to human is
(*a*) Dragon fly, locust and silkmoth
(*b*) silkmoth, honey bee and grain beetle
(*c*) Honey bee, silkmoth and lac insect
(*d*) lac insect, silkmoth and locust

45. "Cantheridine" is got from
(*a*) cochinal insect (*b*) spanish fly
(*c*) red ant (*d*) boll weevil

46. Life history of cockroach belongs to
(*a*) Ametabola (*b*) Hemimetabola
(*c*) Paurometabola (*d*) Holometabola

47. Maggot is
(*a*) larva of culex
(*b*) pupa of housefly
(*c*) larva of housefly
(*d*) larva of dragon fly

48. Largest praying insect is
(*a*) Dragon fly (*b*) Spanish fly
(*c*) Praying mantis (*d*) Silver fish

49. Mouth part of cockroach is
(*a*) cutting type
(*b*) happing type
(*c*) siphonning type
(*d*) bitting and chewing type

50. Male cockroach differs from female cockroach because of the presence of
(*a*) Long antennae (*b*) Anal zera
(*c*) Amphids (*d*) Anal styles

51. An insect without mandibles is
(*a*) *Musca* (*b*) *Aphis*
(*c*) *Blatta* (*d*) *Anopheles*

52. The body cavity of cockroach is
(*a*) Coelom (*b*) Pseudocoel
(*c*) Haemocoel (*d*) Coelenteron

53. Conglobate gland occurs in male reproductive organs of
(*a*) frog (*b*) prawn
(*c*) earthworm (*d*) cockroach

54. *Anopheles* eggs float in water due to presence of
(*a*) zygotic nucleus (*b*) yolk
(*c*) air floats (*d*) air bubbles

55. Which one of the following stages is necessary in the life cycle of an animal in which complete metamorphosis occurs?
(*a*) Adult (*b*) Egg
(*c*) Larva (*d*) All of the above

56. In housefly, the mouth parts are specialised for
(*a*) sponging liquid food
(*b*) blood sucking
(*c*) chewing
(*d*) sucking flower juice

57. In hot summer and cold winter, the no. of malaria cases as well as anopheles declines. Reappearance of malaria in humid condition is due to
(*a*) surviving malarial parasites in humid carriers
(*b*) surviving sporozoites in surviving mosquitoes
(*c*) monkeys
(*d*) mosquito larva in permanent waters

58. Kala-azar and oriental sore are spread by
(*a*) housefly (*b*) bed bug
(*c*) sand fly (*d*) fruit fly

59. Bed bug spreads
(*a*) Yellow fever (*b*) Typhoid
(*c*) Trench fever (*d*) Typhus

60. Yellow fever is transmitted by
(*a*) *Culex* (*b*) *Ades strini*
(*c*) *Aedes* (*d*) *Anopheles*

61. Adult *Culex* and *Anophels* can be distinguished with the help of
(*a*) Mouth parts (*b*) Antennal wings
(*c*) sitting posture (*d*) feeding habit

62. Common feature of earthworm and cockroach is
(*a*) excretion by nephridia
(*b*) moulting of cuticle
(*c*) ventral nerve cord
(*d*) hermophroditism

63. Blood does not transport O_2 in
(*a*) earthworm
(*b*) mosquito
(*c*) cockroach
(*d*) mammalian foetus

64. Main excretory product in cockroach and other insect is
(*a*) urea (*b*) NH_3
(*c*) guanine (*d*) uric acid

65. Male mosquito cannot pierce our skin, because it has no
(*a*) mandibles (*b*) antennal
(*c*) proboscis (*d*) manillae

66. Vision in cockroach is
(*a*) mosaic (*b*) housefly type
(*c*) triploid (*d*) cat type

67. How many times between hatching and its complete development, the young cockroach undergoes ecdysis-
(*a*) not more than 7
(*b*) not more than 8
(*c*) not more than 9
(*d*) not more than 10

68. The Government of India passed the "Wildlife Protection Act" in the year
(*a*) 1972 (*b*) 1986
(*c*) 1982 (*d*) 1947

69. The expanded form of M.A.B. is
(*a*) Man and Biology
(*b*) Man and Botany
(*c*) Man and its Biography
(*d*) Man and Biosphere

70. Sunder Lal Bahugana is related to
(*a*) Green Revolution
(*b*) White Revolution
(*c*) India's Independence
(*d*) Chipko Movement

71. The expanded form of I.U.C. N is
(*a*) International Union of Conservation of Natural Resources
(*b*) International Union of Comondos of Navy
(*c*) Interstate Union of commissioner of N.C.C.
(*d*) International union of conservation of Nature and Natural resources

72. The component of a living cell affected by the pollutant SO_2 is
(*a*) Nucleus
(*b*) All cell membrane system
(*c*) Cell wall
(*d*) D.N.A

73. Which of the following will not cause any atmospheric pollution?
(*a*) H_2 (*b*) CO_2
(*c*) CO (*d*) SO_2

74. Photochemical smog is related to the pollution of
(*a*) Soil (*b*) Water
(*c*) Noise (*d*) Air

75. Which of the following enhances B.O.D. of water?
(*a*) Algae
(*b*) Sand
(*c*) Moss
(*d*) Sugar mill effluants

76. The most serious threat to the wild life comes from
(*a*) organic evolution
(*b*) biological control
(*c*) creation of new species
(*d*) habitat destruction

77. Most severe environmental hazard to mankind is due to
(*a*) Air pollution
(*b*) Noise pollution
(*c*) Water pollution
(*d*) Radioactive pollution

78. The ultraviolet radiation from the sun cause reaction that produce
(*a*) Co (*b*) SO_2
(*c*) F_2 (*d*) O_3 (Ozone)

79. The major cause of pollution is
(*a*) Man
(*b*) Plants
(*c*) Animals
(*d*) Man & Animals

80. The smallest bone of the body found in
(*a*) ears (*b*) eyes
(*c*) nose (*d*) fingers

ANSWERS

1	2	3	4	5	6	7	8	9	10
(*d*)	(*c*)	(*a*)	(*d*)	(*b*)	(*d*)	(*c*)	(*d*)	(*c*)	(*a*)
11	**12**	**13**	**14**	**15**	**16**	**17**	**18**	**19**	**20**
(*c*)	(*c*)	(*a*)	(*b*)	(*d*)	(*d*)	(*c*)	(*b*)	(*d*)	(*a*)
21	**22**	**23**	**24**	**25**	**26**	**27**	**28**	**29**	**30**
(*d*)	(*a*)	(*c*)	(*c*)	(*c*)	(*b*)	(*b*)	(*d*)	(*d*)	(*b*)
31	**32**	**33**	**34**	**35**	**36**	**37**	**38**	**39**	**40**
(*b*)	(*a*)	(*c*)	(*c*)	(*a*)	(*d*)	(*a*)	(*a*)	(*d*)	(*c*)
41	**42**	**43**	**44**	**45**	**46**	**47**	**48**	**49**	**50**
(*a*)	(*b*)	(*a*)	(*c*)	(*a*)	(*b*)	(*c*)	(*c*)	(*c*)	(*d*)
51	**52**	**53**	**54**	**55**	**56**	**57**	**58**	**59**	**60**
(*a*)	(*b*)	(*d*)	(*b*)	(*d*)	(*a*)	(*b*)	(*c*)	(*c*)	(*a*)
61	**62**	**63**	**64**	**65**	**66**	**67**	**68**	**69**	**70**
(*a*)	(*a*)	(*a*)	(*b*)	(*a*)	(*a*)	(*a*)	(*a*)	(*d*)	(*d*)
71	**72**	**73**	**74**	**75**	**76**	**77**	**78**	**79**	**80**
(*d*)	(*d*)	(*a*)	(*b*)	(*d*)	(*d*)	(*d*)	(*d*)	(*d*)	(*a*)

PAPER SET-II

1. Which of the following insecticides is the most persistent in soil?
(*a*) Malathion (*b*) Aldrin
(*c*) F-BHC (*d*) Parathion

2. D.D.T. is a:
(*a*) Biodegradable pollutant
(*b*) Green house gas
(*c*) Non biodegradable pollutant
(*d*) All of the above

3. Spraying of D.D.T. on crop produces pollution of:
(*a*) Air only
(*b*) Air and soil only
(*c*) Air and water only
(*d*) Air, soil and water

4. CO is harmful to human being because:
(*a*) it decreases CO_2 concentration
(*b*) it is carcinogenic
(*c*) it depletes O_3 layer
(*d*) it competes O_2 to combine with haomoglobin

5. P.A.N. is:
(*a*) Photochemical smog
(*b*) Peroxyacetyl nitrate
(*c*) Pan and noise
(*d*) None of these

6. The P.A.N. blocks:
(*a*) glycolysis (*b*) ATP synthesis
(*c*) CO_2 fixation (*d*) Hill reaction

7. "The Environmental Protection Act" promuglated in India in the year:
(*a*) 1974 (*b*) 1988
(*c*) 1981 (*d*) 1986

8. Bhopal gas disaster occured in the year:
(*a*) 1988 (*b*) 1986
(*c*) 1984 (*d*) 1982

9. The automobile emmission can be reduced by adding the following in the petrol:
(*a*) Ca-salts (*b*) Co-salt
(*c*) Si-salt (*d*) Ba-salt

10. The "Blue baby syndrome" is caused due to pollution by:
(*a*) Chlorides (*b*) Cyanides
(*c*) Fluorides (*d*) Nitrates

11. The most harmful pesticide is:
(*a*) P.A.N. (*b*) 2, 4 8-D
(*c*) D.D.T. (*d*) 2, 4-D

12. Lead is considered as:
(*a*) Air pollutant (*b*) Water pollutant
(*c*) Soil pollutant (*d*) All of the above

13. Bhopal gas disaster is due to
(*a*) Lead
(*b*) Cyanides
(*c*) Mercury
(*d*) Methyl isocyanides

14. The effect of radioactive pollutants depend upon:
(*a*) half-life & energy releasing capacity
(*b*) rate of diffusion
(*c*) rate of deposition of the radioactive element
(*d*) all of the above

15. The part of body which is firstly most affected by noise pollution:
(*a*) Pinna (*b*) Ear drum
(*c*) Both of these (*d*) None of these

16. The range of normal human hearing is:
(*a*) 15 hz to 15,000 hz
(*b*) 15 db to 800 db
(*c*) Both of these
(*d*) None of these

17. When excess of sweage is dumped into the river the B.O.D. is:
(*a*) Slightly decreased (*b*) Unchanged
(*c*) Decreases (*d*) Increases

18. "Minimata" disease is caused due to water pollution by:
(*a*) Pb (*b*) R-CHO
(*c*) R-OH (*d*) Hg

19. Mulching helps in:
(*a*) Moisture conservation
(*b*) Weed control
(*c*) Improvement of soil
(*d*) Increasing soil fertility

20. The part of earth in which life exists:
(*a*) lithosphere (*b*) biomes
(*c*) hydrosphere (*d*) atmosphere

21. Plants growing in loose non-saline soil are:
(*a*) Lithophytes (*b*) Halophytes
(*c*) Mesophytes (*d*) Xerophytes

22. One of the following crops is the most effective in controlling soil erosion:
(*a*) Green gram (*b*) Maize
(*c*) Capsicum (*d*) Pigeon pea

23. Taj Mahal is threatened due to the presence of which gas in the air?
(*a*) Chlorine (*b*) O_2
(*c*) NO_2 (*d*) SO_2

24. The amount of oxygen taken up by the micro-organism present in water is:
(*a*) M.A.B. (*b*) I.C.O.H
(*c*) P.A.N (*d*) B.O.D

25. The expanded form of B.O.D. is:
(*a*) Biological oxygen demand
(*b*) Biophysical oxygen demand
(*c*) Ban on destroying forest
(*d*) Biochemical oxygen demand

26. The term pesticides includes:
(*a*) Herbicides (*b*) Insecticides
(*c*) Fungicides (*d*) All of these

27. Eutrophication is observed in the:
(*a*) lakes and rivers (*b*) sea and ponds
(*c*) ponds and rivers (*d*) lakes and tanks

28. The main causes of soil erosion in India are:
(*a*) Deforestation (*b*) Over grazing
(*c*) Both of these (*d*) Desertification

29. The term synecology refers to the study of:
(*a*) Environment
(*b*) Individual organism
(*c*) Plant community
(*d*) All of these

30. A number of different inter related populations belonging to different species in a common environment called:
(*a*) Biotic community
(*b*) Pond community
(*c*) Ecology
(*d*) Eco-system

31. The different species of organism occuring in a pond is:
(*a*) Biotic community
(*b*) Pond community
(*c*) Plant community
(*d*) All of these

32. Interspecific relation is:
(*a*) Scavenging (*b*) Symbiosis
(*c*) Predation (*d*) parasitism

33. Chemical compound secreated by animals, meant for community and coordination of organs in an individual are:
(*a*) Pheromones (*b*) Ecocysone
(*c*) Scent glands (*d*) None of these

34. The sub ordinate to a species as a unit of cooperative aggregation of individual is:
(*a*) Consumer (*b*) Population
(*c*) Pollution (*d*) Genus

35. For describing a population which is most important:
(*a*) given space
(*b*) time
(*c*) number of individuals
(*d*) all of these

36. Population density is:
(where D = Population density, N = Total number of population added in a particular year, S = total sum of population.)
(*a*) $D = \frac{S}{N}$ (*b*) $D = \frac{N}{S}$
(*c*) $S = \frac{N}{D}$ (*d*) $N = \frac{D}{S}$

37. Which is not a determinant of population size?
(*a*) Malacity (*b*) Immigration
(*c*) Mortality (*d*) Migration

38. A population tends to increase and decrease respectively by:
(*a*) Motility, Immigration and Mortality, Emigration
(*b*) Motility, Mortality and Emigration, Immigration
(*c*) Emigration, Motility and Immigration, Mortality
(*d*) Migration, Motility and Immigration, Emigration

39. The study of trends in human population growth and the prediction of future development is called

(*a*) Topography (*b*) Grentology
(*c*) Demography (*d*) Socalism

40. The toxin produced by the bacteria of tuberculosis is

(*a*) Vibrin (*b*) Aflotoxin
(*c*) Cytotix (*d*) Tuberculion

41. An important features of human population is/are:

(*a*) that its growth is more stable in the developed countries
(*b*) that its growth is more stable in the developing countries
(*c*) that its growth is more stable in both countries
(*d*) depending upon the president of that country

42. Insect societies are the product of:

(*a*) Chemical evolution
(*b*) Organic evolution
(*c*) Pae dogenesis
(*d*) Biological evolution

43. Several members of a species may cover a defined area in search of food and mates called:

(*a*) Homo range (*b*) Range of territory
(*c*) Zone of overlap (*d*) Territory

44. Polymorphism helps in:

(*a*) Adaption of the species
(*b*) Survival of the species
(*c*) Both of above
(*d*) Survival and reproduction of species

45. The main factor which maintains the distinctness of different species is

(*a*) Reproductive isolation
(*b*) Differential reproduction
(*c*) Binary fission
(*d*) Sterility

46. Family life or family formation is the Characteristics of:

(*a*) Men only (*b*) All animals
(*c*) All birds (*d*) Few animals

47. The territorial boundaries of animals are marked by:

(*a*) Reproduction (*b*) Digestion
(*c*) Evolution (*d*) Urination

48. Indirect transmission of diseases by contaminated toys, garments, crockery, soaps *etc.* known as:

(*a*) Vectors (*b*) Formite borne
(*c*) Air borne (*d*) Vechical borne

49. Indirect transmission of disease by ice, water, food, blood *etc.* known as:

(*a*) Vectors (*b*) Fomite borne
(*c*) Air borne (*d*) Fomile borne

50. Which of the following disease is 100% fatal if not controlled?

(*a*) Rabbies (*b*) Hydrophobia
(*c*) Influenza (*d*) (a) & (b) both

51. Virulence of a pathogen depends on:

(*a*) Toxigenicity
(*b*) Invasiveness
(*c*) Both of above
(*d*) Toxicity and Replicative action

52. The term "Vaccination" was proposed by:

(*a*) Louis Pasteur
(*b*) Robert Koch
(*c*) Anton Leewenhock
(*d*) Edward Jenner

53. Histamine is released by:

(*a*) Phagocytes (*b*) Monocytes
(*c*) Adipocytes (*d*) Lymphocytes

54. Compounds that are released by WBC's in order to set the body thermostat at a higher temperature is:

(*a*) carcinogens (*b*) pathogens
(*c*) cyrpogens (*d*) pyrogens

55. Antibodies are:

(*a*) proteinaceous in nature
(*b*) polysaccharides
(*c*) lipoprotein
(*d*) all of the above

56. The major cells of immune system are:

(*a*) Antibodies
(*b*) Lympocytes
(*c*) Erythrocytes
(*d*) Antigens

57. T- and B- cells of immune system develops in foetus and adults in:
(*a*) brain and liver
(*b*) liver and thymus
(*c*) liver and brain
(*d*) liver and bone marrow

58. The number of antibodies produced by B-cells (approximately) are:
(*a*) 20 lakh/day
(*b*) 20 thousands/day
(*c*) 200 billions/day
(*d*) 20 trillions/day

59. The function of T-cells is:
(*a*) production of antibodies
(*b*) cellular immunity
(*c*) both of above
(*d*) none of above

60. The life span of T-cells is:
(*a*) 2-3 years
(*b*) 3-4 years
(*c*) 4-5 years
(*d*) up to the death of an individual

61. The function of helper T-cells is/are:
(*a*) Stimulation of antibody production by B-cells
(*b*) Toxigenicity and invasireness
(*c*) Supress the total immune system
(*d*) All of the above

62. The memory cells are produced by:
(*a*) B-cells (*b*) T-cells
(*c*) Active cells (*d*) None of these

63. The memory cells are stored in:
(*a*) Liver and Lymphnodes
(*b*) Only in liver
(*c*) Only in lymphnodes
(*d*) Spleen and lymphnodes

64. Passive immunity was discovered by:
(*a*) Edward Jenner (*b*) Emil vex Behring
(*c*) Louis Pasteur (*d*) Robert koch

65. Proteins that are released by cells in response to a viral infection which they help combat is:
(*a*) Immunoglobins (*b*) Interferons
(*c*) Pyrogens (*d*) None of the above

66. Sometimes people are born without T-and B-cells and this disorder is known as
(*a*) AIDS (*b*) ARC
(*c*) Hepatitis (*d*) SCID

67. The SCID is:
(*a*) Severe chronic immuno-deficiency
(*b*) Special chronic immuno-deficiency
(*c*) Severe chronic immuno-deficiency
(*d*) None of the above

68. The AIDS is:
(*a*) Acquired Immune Deficiency syndrome
(*b*) Apply Immuno Deficiency syndrome
(*c*) Average Indian development sangh
(*d*) None of the above

69. Which of the following disorder is characterised by a reduction in the number of helper T-cells that activate other lymphocytes:
(*a*) AIDS
(*b*) SCID
(*c*) ARC
(*d*) None of the above

70. AIDS related complex is
(*a*) SCID (*b*) ARC
(*c*) Lymphocytes (*d*) SCOID

71. AIDS caused by the virus
(*a*) HCLV III (*b*) HIV III
(*c*) RDX (*d*) ZLN

72. HIV is:
(*a*) Higher Immunized Vaccine
(*b*) Human Immunodeficiency virus
(*c*) Highest Immunisation Value
(*d*) None of the above

73. The mild form of AIDS is/are
(*a*) ARC (*b*) SCID
(*c*) HIV (*d*) All of these

74. Antigenic determinant bind to which portion of the antibody molecule:
(*a*) heavy chains (*b*) light chains
(*c*) both of these (*d*) none of these

75. The cell that actually produce the antibodies are:
(*a*) Helper T-cells (*b*) Cytogenic T-cells
(*c*) Killer T-cells (*d*) Plasma cells

76. A person without thymus (gland) would not be able to
(*a*) produce antibodies
(*b*) cytogenic T-cells
(*c*) regulate body temperature
(*d*) all of these

77. When an antigen and antibody reaction occur in the tissue instead of in the blood it is called
(*a*) Droplet infection
(*b*) Anaphylactic shock
(*c*) Congenital disease
(*d*) SQUID

78. Match the following

A. leprosy	1. *Mycobacterium leprae*
B. filaria	2. *Wuchereria bancrofti*
C.. syphilis	3. *Troponema pallidium*
D. Gonorrhoea	4. *Neisseria gonorrhoeace*

Codes:

	A	B	C	D
(*a*)	1	2	3	4
(*b*)	4	3	2	1
(*c*)	2	3	4	1
(*d*)	1	2	4	3

79. B.C.G. is a vaccine for
(*a*) Tuberculosis (*b*) Cholera
(*c*) Hepatitis (*d*) All of these

ANSWERS

1	2	3	4	5	6	7	8	9	10
(*d*)	(*a*)	(*d*)	(*d*)	(*b*)	(*d*)	(*a*)	(*a*)	(*b*)	(*c*)
11	**12**	**13**	**14**	**15**	**16**	**17**	**18**	**19**	**20**
(*a*)	(*a*)	(*d*)	(*d*)	(*b*)	(*c*)	(*d*)	(*a*)	(*b*)	(*b*)
21	**22**	**23**	**24**	**25**	**26**	**27**	**28**	**29**	**30**
(*c*)	(*a*)	(*d*)	(*d*)	(*d*)	(*d*)	(*d*)	(*c*)	(*c*)	(*a*)
31	**32**	**33**	**34**	**35**	**36**	**37**	**38**	**39**	**40**
(*b*)	(*b*)	(*a*)	(*b*)	(*d*)	(*a*)	(*a*)	(*c*)	(*c*)	(*d*)
41	**42**	**43**	**44**	**45**	**46**	**47**	**48**	**49**	**50**
(*a*)	(*d*)	(*c*)	(*c*)	(*a*)	(*a*)	(*a*)	(*d*)	(*b*)	(*d*)
51	**52**	**53**	**54**	**55**	**56**	**57**	**58**	**59**	**60**
(*c*)	(*d*)	(*a*)	(*b*)	(*a*)	(*b*)	(*b*)	(*b*)	(*c*)	(*a*)
61	**62**	**63**	**64**	**65**	**66**	**67**	**68**	**69**	**70**
(*a*)	(*a*)	(*a*)	(*b*)	(*b*)	(*d*)	(*a*)	(*b*)	(*a*)	(*b*)
71	**72**	**73**	**74**	**75**	**76**	**77**	**78**	**79**	
(*b*)	(*b*)	(*a*)	(*c*)	(*c*)	(*d*)	(*b*)	(*a*)	(*a*)	

PAPER SET-III

1. The favourite site of the bacteria of T.B. is:
(*a*) Brain (*b*) Lungs
(*c*) Liver (*d*) Stomach

2. The vaccine D.P.T. is applied to cure
(*a*) Diphtheria, whooping cough and Tetanus
(*b*) Diabetes, Pertusis and Tetanus
(*c*) Diphtheria, Pertusis and T.B.
(*d*) Diabetes, whooping cough and Tuberculosis

3. Which is mainly a water borne disease?
(*a*) Tuberculosis (*b*) Pertusis
(*c*) Diphtheria (*d*) Cholera

4. Sexually transmitted diseases (S.T.D.) is/are:
(*a*) Leprosy (*b*) Syphilis
(*c*) T.B. (*d*) Tetanus

5. Which one may leads to female sterility?
(*a*) Syphilis (*b*) Genorrchoea
(*c*) Leprosy (*d*) All of the above

6. The main symptoms of tetanus are:
(*a*) Lock jaw
(*b*) Painfill muscular spasms
(*c*) Both of these
(*d*) Swelling of lymphnodes

7. Painful swelling of parotid glands is the characteristic of disease:
(*a*) Measles (*b*) Mumps
(*c*) Chicken pox (*d*) All of these

8. Red spots on the body during measles is known as:
(*a*) puteda (*b*) nebula
(*c*) sparts (*d*) oil zone

9. There is no vaccine for the:
(*a*) Measles (*b*) Small pox
(*c*) Mumps (*d*) Chicken pox

10. "Ironlung" used in:
(*a*) T.B (*b*) Poliomyelitis
(*c*) Trachoma (*d*) All of the above

11. "Oral rehydration" theraphy is used in:
(*a*) Tuberculosis (*b*) Diphtheria
(*c*) Chlorosis (*d*) Cholera

12. Vector of Filariasis is:
(*a*) *Ades* (*b*) *Culex*
(*c*) *Anaphelles* (*d*) *Maggot*

13. Chronic hyperglycemia leads to:
(*a*) Mumps (*b*) Filaria
(*c*) Arthrits (*d*) Diabetes

14. If uric acid is not excreted from the body the disease developed is
(*a*) Artheritis (*b*) Gout
(*c*) Diabetes (*d*) None of these

15. Cancer is mainly due to:
(*a*) cell proliferation (*b*) cell maturation
(*c*) both of these (*d*) none of these

16. The spreading of cancerous cells to different parts of body by blood and lymph is known as:
(*a*) Metastasis
(*b*) Homostasis
(*c*) Benign tumors
(*d*) Malignant tumors

17. Cancer causing agents and genes respectively known as:
(*a*) carcinogenes and pyrogens
(*b*) oncogenes and interferons
(*c*) pyrogens and carcinogenes
(*d*) carcinogens and oncogenes

18. Breast cancer, lung cancer, cancer of stomach and pancreas are the types of
(*a*) Carcinomas (Ectodermal)
(*b*) Sarcomas (in tissue from mesoderm)
(*c*) Leukaemias (in blood)
(*d*) (b) and (c) both

19. Bone tumours, muscle tumours and the cancer of lymph nodes are the types of
(*a*) Lukaemias (*b*) Sarcomas
(*c*) Carcinomas (*d*) None of these

20. Excessive production of leucocytes causes:
(*a*) carcinomas
(*b*) sarcomas
(*c*) leukaemias
(*d*) benign tumours

21. In India the major form of cancer in man and woman respectively are
(a) Breast cancer and Mouth cancer
(b) Stomach cancer and Breast cancer
(c) Throat cancer and Vaginal cancer
(d) Mouth, throat cancer and uterine cervical cancer

22. A common weed that the source of the anticancer drugs (*e.g.*, vincristion, viattastin) is
(a) Vinca rosea
(b) Pepper nigrum
(c) Digitalis sp
(d) No drug ever produced for cancer

23. Which disease causes blindness in India?
(a) Trachoma (b) Retainsis
(c) Poliomyelis (d) None of these

24. Aflatoxin causes the cancer of
(a) skin (b) lungs
(c) vagina (d) liver

25. Individuals with alkinism (disorder) can't syntheses
(a) Melanin (b) Insulin
(c) W.B.C. (d) R.B.C

26. Dominantly inherited diseases are
(a) Dwarfism
(b) Polydactyly
(c) Huntington's disease
(d) All of the above

27. Trisomy arises due to
(a) mutation of chromosomes
(b) variation of x-chromosomes
(c) non-disjunction during egg cell formation
(d) all of the above

28. Autosomal abnormality due to 21st trisomy is known as
(a) Tunner's syndrome
(b) Taysach's disease
(c) Down's syndrome
(d) Klinefelter's disease

29. The XYY sex chromosome abnormality in male is known as
(a) Down's syndrome
(b) Klinefelter's syndrome
(c) Turner's syndrome
(d) None of these

30. The absence of one X in female (XO) is known as
(a) Down's syndrome
(b) Taysachs disease
(c) Klienfelter's syndrome
(d) Turner's syndrome

31. XO-individual formed by
(a) Y-carrying sperm fertilising on O-ovum
(b) X-carrying sperm fertilising an O-ovum
(c) Due to Turner's syndrome
(d) All of these

32. A recessive disease, phenylketo-nuria mainly occurs due to
(a) Enzymes (b) Proteins
(c) Aminoacids (d) Vitamins

33. The type of mental illness in which a patient recognised 'mad' is
(a) Neurosis (b) Phycosis
(c) Epilepsy (d) Addition

34. E.C.T. is
(a) shock treatment
(b) anaphylactic shock
(c) electrocardiotest
(d) None of these

35. The physical and mental dependence on drugs is
(a) Epilepsy (b) Addiction
(c) Depression (d) Emphysema

36. The effect of nicotine on pregnant woman is
(a) She will die
(b) Retardation of the growth of the foetus
(c) Both of these
(d) None of these

37. Tobacco obtained from
(a) *Nicotiana tobacum* and *N. rustica*
(b) *N. tobaccum* alone
(c) *N. rustica* alone
(d) None of these

38. If a persons drinks alcohol his vision becomes blurred and steady often the field of vision is reduced. It is
(a) Tunnel vision (b) Complex vision
(c) Compound vision (d) Affect vision

39. The organ which is more affected by taking alcohol is
(*a*) lungs (*b*) liver
(*c*) stomach (*d*) heart

40. Liver cells replaced by fibrous tissue due to excess intake of alcohol is:
(*a*) Fatty liver syndrome leads to cirrhosis
(*b*) Twener's syndrome leads to phycosis
(*c*) Klinefeller's syndrome leads to Neurosis
(*d*) Down's syndrome leads to sterilism

41. Psychotropic drugs includes
(*a*) Sedatives and Tranquillisers
(*b*) Hallucinogens and stimulants
(*c*) Opiate narcotics and Mood alternating drugs
(*d*) All of the above

42. Drugs that either causes deep sleep after taking or without inducing sleep is
(*a*) Sedatives and Transquellisers
(*b*) Valliam and Barbiturates
(*c*) Both of these
(*d*) None of these

43. Drugs that suppress brain function and relieves intense pain is
(*a*) Sedatives (*b*) Trantuillisers
(*c*) Vallium (*d*) Opiale narcotics

44. The most dangerous drug of the group opiate narcotics is
(*a*) Morphine
(*b*) Heroin
(*c*) Codoine
(*d*) Pethidine and Methadone

45. Caffeine (tea, coffee) are the examples of
(*a*) Sedatives (*b*) Stimulants
(*c*) Tranquillisers (*d*) All of these

46. Drugs that causes chronic phycosis and users claim that they can 'see sounds' and 'hear colour' is
(*a*) Sedatives and Tranquillisers
(*b*) Opiate marcotics
(*c*) Stimulant
(*d*) Hallucinogens

47. The L.S.D., charas, Bhang, Ganja, Haskish, Psilocytin, are the example of
(*a*) Sedatives (*b*) Hallucinnogens
(*c*) Stimulants (*d*) None of these

48. Charas, Bhang, and Ganja extracted from
(*a*) *Nicotiana tobacum*
(*b*) *Cannabis sativa*
(*c*) *Risum stilum*
(*d*) *Vinca rosea*

49. The Universal Immunisation programme of India launched in the year
(*a*) 1975 (*b*) 1985
(*c*) 1990 (*d*) 1992

50. E.C.G. is mainly for detecting the disorder of
(*a*) Heart (*b*) Brain
(*c*) Liver (*d*) Stomach

51. Electronencephalograph (EEG) was first used by
(*a*) Hans Berger (*b*) Einthoven
(*c*) Calvin (*d*) E. Iggort

52. To cure epilipsy and brain diseases, the instrument used
(*a*) ECG (*b*) EEG
(*c*) EPS (*d*) CT-Scan

53. Super Conducting Quantum Interference devices (SQUID) and Managetoence Phalography (MET) are the types of
(*a*) ECG
(*b*) EPS
(*c*) EEG
(*d*) None of the above

54. Diagonastic instrument for estimating the levels of biochemical substances in the blood, like cholestrol, glucose, urea and electrolytes is
(*a*) Endoscope (*b*) E.C.G.
(*c*) EPS (*d*) Autoanalyser

55. The study of x-rays for the detection and treatment of diseases is known as
(*a*) Opthalmology (*b*) X-logy
(*c*) Hematology (*d*) Radiology

56. CT-Scan is
(*a*) Computerised Tomographic Scanning
(*b*) Common Test of Stomach Scan
(*c*) Computerised Topographic Scanning
(*d*) (a) and (c) both

57. One of the earliest animals to be domesticated is
(*a*) Cat (*b*) Cow
(*c*) Dog (*d*) Rat

58. The temperature at which the cow's embryo kept is
(*a*) 0°C
(*b*) –196°C
(*c*) 25°C (Standard room temp)
(*d*) –203°C

59. The poor man's cow is
(*a*) Goat (*b*) Cow
(*c*) Sheep (*d*) Pigs

60. 'Pashmina' is got from
(*a*) Kashmiri goat (*b*) sheep
(*c*) yalk (*d*) all of the above

61. 'Meatmaking machines' of man is
(*a*) sheep (*b*) cow
(*c*) goat (*d*) pig

62. The study of breeding and management of bee for the production of honey is
(*a*) Apiculture (*b*) Sericulture
(*c*) Anemoculture (*d*) none of these

63. Edible fishes are
(*a*) Rohu (*b*) Katla
(*c*) Magure (*d*) All of the above

64. Salmon (fish) is used in the manufacture of
(*a*) Oils (*b*) Ingredients
(*c*) Vit. A (*d*) Soaps

65. Bordeaux mixture is a
(*a*) Herbicide (*b*) Fungicide
(*c*) Weedicide (*d*) Nematicide

66. Bordeaux is a mixture of
(*a*) $CuSO_4 + Ca(OH)_2 + H_2O$
(*b*) $CuSO_4 + NaOH + H_2O$
(*c*) $H_2SO_4 + Fe(OH)_3 + H_2O$
(*d*) $H_2O + NH_4OH + NaCl$

67. 'Downy mildew' caused by
(*a*) *Plasmodium falciparum*
(*b*) *Plasmopora viticola*
(*c*) *Bahrnia vitis*
(*d*) None of the above

68. The oldest and famous synthetic pesticide is/are
(*a*) DDT (*b*) BHC
(*c*) 2, 4-D (*d*) All of the above

69. Chemical used in the mosquito repellants (*e.g.*, Baygon) is
(*a*) Carbofuran (*b*) Aldicarb
(*c*) Temik (*d*) Propoxur

70. Which one have strong effect on Nervous system?
(*a*) Organochlomines
(*b*) Pyrethoids
(*c*) Carbamates
(*d*) Organophosphates

71. Which one affect fifty tissues of a animal?
(*a*) Carbomates
(*b*) Pyrethrids
(*c*) Organochloines
(*d*) Organophosphates

72. Bordeaux mixture was discovered by
(*a*) Millar Det
(*b*) R. Koch
(*c*) C-Bayer
(*d*) Pasteur

73. 'Pyrethrin is extracted from the plant
(*a*) *Chrysanthemum zinerarifolium*
(*b*) *Cleaslpinia indica*
(*c*) *Ceaselpinia suppur*
(*d*) *Pinus sp.*

74. Khaira disease of Rice is due to
(*a*) less amount of Mg in the soil
(*b*) less amount of M_2 in the soil
(*c*) more amount of NO_2^- in the soil
(*d*) more amount of Cl^- in the soil

75. I.P.M is
(*a*) Integrated Pest Management
(*b*) Indian Pest Management
(*c*) Italian Pacific March
(*d*) None of the above

76. "Bhopal Gas Tragedy" is due to
(*a*) Ethyl isocyanide
(*b*) Methyl isocyanide
(*c*) Methanol
(*d*) Ethanol

77. A mixture of cattle dung and crop residues are called
(*a*) Farmyard manure
(*b*) Composite manure
(*c*) Green manure
(*d*) None of the above

78. A mixture of rotted vegetables and animal refuse is
(*a*) Farmyard manure
(*b*) Composite manure
(*c*) Green manure
(*d*) None of the above

79. The main source of biofertilisers are
(*a*) Bacteria, Virus, Fungi
(*b*) Bacteria, Cyanobacteria, Fungi
(*c*) Bacteria, Fungi, Algae
(*d*) Fungi, Virus, and Bacteria

80. An excellent biofertilisers for rice is
(*a*) *Azolla anabeana* (*b*) *Azolla pinnata*
(*c*) RZD-120 (*d*) All of the above

81. Edaphic factors pertain to:
(*a*) Soil (*b*) Altitude of a site
(*c*) Water content (*d*) Temperature

ANSWERS

1	**2**	**3**	**4**	**5**	**6**	**7**	**8**	**9**	**10**
(*b*)	(*b*)	(*d*)	(*b*)	(*b*)	(*a*)	(*b*)	(*b*)	(*c*)	(*d*)
11	**12**	**13**	**14**	**15**	**16**	**17**	**18**	**19**	**20**
(*c*)	(*a*)	(*a*)	(*b*)	(*d*)	(*a*)	(*d*)	(*c*)	(*c*)	(*d*)
21	**22**	**23**	**24**	**25**	**26**	**27**	**28**	**29**	**30**
(*c*)	(*a*)	(*c*)	(*b*)	(*b*)	(*a*)	(*d*)	(*c*)	(*a*)	(*d*)
31	**32**	**33**	**34**	**35**	**36**	**37**	**38**	**39**	**40**
(*c*)	(*a*)	(*c*)	(*b*)	(*b*)	(*a*)	(*a*)	(*b*)	(*a*)	(*b*)
41	**42**	**43**	**44**	**45**	**46**	**47**	**48**	**49**	**50**
(*b*)	(*c*)	(*a*)	(*b*)	(*a*)	(*b*)	(*a*)	(*a*)	(*a*)	(*c*)
51	**52**	**53**	**54**	**55**	**56**	**57**	**58**	**59**	**60**
(*c*)	(*a*)	(*a*)	(*d*)	(*d*)	(*c*)	(*b*)	(*a*)	(*d*)	(*c*)
61	**62**	**63**	**64**	**65**	**66**	**67**	**68**	**69**	**70**
(*a*)	(*d*)	(*c*)	(*c*)	(*a*)	(*b*)	(*d*)	(*d*)	(*b*)	(*d*)
71	**72**	**73**	**74**	**75**	**76**	**77**	**78**	**79**	**80**
(*c*)	(*b*)	(*c*)	(*a*)	(*b*)	(*b*)	(*c*)	(*b*)	(*d*)	(*a*)
81									
(*a*)									

PAPER SET-IV

1. An example of biodegradable pollutant is
   (a) pesticide
   (b) carcases
   (c) smog
   (d) aluminium cans
2. The paper industry in India depends mainly on
   (a) bamboo
   (b) bagasse
   (c) conifers
   (d) both (a) and (b)
3. Which of the following condi-tions results from an excess of growth harmone?
   (a) Diabetes insipidus
   (b) Acromegaly
   (d) Hyperthyroidism
   (d) High B.P.
4. The epithelium of the urinary bladder
   (a) is protective in nature
   (b) has an absorptive function
   (c) prevents dehydration
   (d) is adapted to great changes in surface area
5. The lowest concentration of nitrogenous waste may be found in the blood passing through
   (a) renal artery
   (b) renal vein
   (c) pulmonary artery
   (d) pulmonary vein
6. The first larva that escapes out of the egg of *Fasciola* is
   (a) *cercaria* (b) *mirocidium*
   (c) *radia* (d) *metacercaria*
7. Which of the following is a micronutrient?
   (a) Mg (b) K
   (c) Ca (d) Zn
8. Litmus a natural dye is obtained from
   (a) algae (b) fungi
   (c) lichens (d) bryophytes
9. Terramycin is obtained from
   (a) streptomyces lavendulae
   (b) streptomyces rimosus
   (c) streptomyces griseus
   (d) none of the above
10. Enzymes enhance the rate of a chemical reaction by
    (a) changing the equilibrium point of the reaction
    (b) lowering the activation energy of the reaction
    (c) combining with the product as soon as it is formed
    (d) forming a rectant product complex
11. Match the following :-

A. Pure silk	1. *Samia cynthia*
B. Tasar	2. *Anthareae assamensia*
C. Muga	3. *Bombyx mori*
D. Tri	4. *Anthareae paplio*

Codes:	A	B	C	D
(a)	3	4	2	1
(b)	1	2	3	4
(c)	4	3	2	1
(d)	3	4	1	2

12. Fungi growing on dung are
    (a) epizoic
    (b) epixylous
    (c) epirhizous
    (d) coprophilic
13. Match the following

A. Annelida	1. Ammocoetes
B. Cyclostomata	2. Trochophore
C. Echinodermata	3. Tornaria
D. Hemichordata	4. Auricularia

Codes:	A	B	C	D
(a)	2	4	1	3
(b)	1	2	3	4
(c)	3	1	2	4
(d)	4	1	3	2

14. Branch of science concerned with improvement of mankind by applying laws of heredity.

(a) Euthenics (b) Eugenics
(c) Ethology (d) Genetics

15. An ecosystem is a complex interacting system of

(a) individuals
(b) populations
(c) communities with physical environment
(d) communities and their soil condition

16. The first human fossil was of

(a) Java man
(b) Ramapithecus
(c) Austra lopithecus
(d) Dryopithecus

17. The psychic area responsible for intelligence, memory and such other mental faculties is an association area of

(a) parietal lobe (b) occipital lobe
(c) frontal lobe (d) hypothalamus

18. Shagreen obtained from sharks is

(a) the oil extracted from liver
(b) the edible muscle
(c) the skin used for polishing
(d) the heterocercal tail used as momento

19. The human eye cannot see objects smaller than

(a) 10 microns (b) 100 microns
(c) 1,000 microns (d) 10,000 microns

20. Which one of the following stain is used for vital staining of components of living cells

(a) Wright's stain
(b) Malochite green
(c) Acetocarmine
(d) Safranin

21. The use and disuse principle of evolution was proposed by

(a) Hugo de Vries (b) Lamarck
(c) Weismann (d) Darwin

22. Synecology is the study of

(a) individual organism
(b) environment
(c) a community of living object
(d) none of the above

23. Unstriated muscle are

(a) voluntary and occur in heart wall
(b) involuntary an occur in intestinal wall
(c) involuntary and occur in heart wall
(d) voluntary and occur in intestinal wall

24. A person decide to live exclusively on a diet of mild egg and bread. He would suffer from

(a) marasmus
(b) night blindness
(c) scurvey
(d) rickets

25. Bile emulsifies fats because of the presence of

(a) Bile pigments
(b) Bile salts
(c) Esterases
(d) Cholesterol

26. Which of the following is a copper containing pigment

(a) Haemoglobin
(b) Haemoerythrin
(c) Haemocyanin
(d) Chlorocruorin

27. Which of the following promotes persistence of larval character?

(a) Insulin
(b) Thyroxin
(c) Ecdysone
(d) Juvenile harmone

28. Green Revolution was usherd in by hybrid varieties of

(a) wheat
(b) rice
(c) maize
(d) all of the above

29. In an electrocardiogram the P was denotes

(a) atrial activity
(b) proper functioning of heart
(c) ventricular contraction
(d) genetic engineering

30. Chalones are
(*a*) insect prisons
(*b*) auto anti bodies
(*c*) mitotic inhibitors
(*d*) growth promoting substances

31. Population explosion of small organism in a lake causes a viral aspect named
(*a*) bloom
(*b*) climax
(*c*) dominance
(*d*) ecological succession

32. Plastic though very useful are considered hazardous because they are
(*a*) insoluble in water
(*b*) too hard
(*c*) poisonous
(*d*) non biodegradable

33. Bhopal gas tragedy occurred because of inhalation of air containing too much of
(*a*) carbox dioxide (*b*) carbox monoxide
(*c*) methyl isocyanate (*d*) hydrogen sulphide

34. Divers disease is the same as
(*a*) Emphysema
(*b*) Decompression sickness
(*c*) Asphyxia
(*d*) Dyspnoea

35. BOD stands for
(*a*) Basic Oxygen Demand
(*b*) Biochemical Oxygen Deficit
(*c*) Basic Oxygen Deficit
(*d*) Biological Oxygen Demand

36. Conservation of forest can best be done by
(*a*) controlled grazing and falling of trees
(*b*) afforestation measures
(*c*) prevention of people from collecting forest produce
(*d*) all of the above

37. The first EEG was taken by
(*a*) Honst Berger (*b*) Einthoven
(*c*) Chardeck (*d*) Dr. Sethi

38. The hardest material in our body is
(*a*) enamel (*b*) dentine
(*c*) bone (*d*) tendon

39. The largest whale aquarium in Asia is situated at
(*a*) Lucknow, UP (*b*) Dehradun, UP
(*c*) Japan (*d*) Tarapur, Mumbai

40. Which of the following organs cannot be investigated by ultrasound?
(*a*) Bladder (*b*) Foetus
(*c*) Brain (*d*) Kidney

41. The computer is an important part in processing data in
(*a*) Electrocardio gram
(*b*) NMR imaging
(*c*) CT scan
(*d*) both (b) and (c)

42. The first medical application of x-rays was made by
(*a*) Roentgen (*b*) Becquerel
(*c*) Marie curie (*d*) Pierre curie

43. Which one of the following statement is *false*?
(*a*) Blood constitutes 8% of total body weight
(*b*) Blood has a pH of 6.5 to 7.0
(*c*) The male human body normally contains 5-6 litres of blood
(*d*) Blood has more plasma than cells

44. DNA finger printing cannot be done using
(*a*) RBC (*b*) WBC
(*c*) Sperm (*d*) Cheek cells

45. Ketone body formation occurs mainly when there is excess metabolism of
(*a*) carbohydrates
(*b*) proteins
(*c*) lipids
(*d*) a - ketoglutaric acid

46. Van Mahotsava launched in 1950
(*a*) is a measure against deforestation
(*b*) refers to afforestation prog-rammes
(*c*) refers to social forestry
(*d*) to prevent soil erosion

47. Water pollution is best controlled by
(*a*) treating effluents to remove injurious chemicals

(b) rearing more fishes
(c) cultivating useful water plants
(d) draining the polluted water into sea

48. Inheritance of skin colour in man is due to
(a) polygenes
(b) multiple alleles
(c) pleiotropism
(d) co-dominance

49. One of the following parasites does not require two hosts to complete its life cycle
(a) Liver fluke (b) Tapeworm
(c) Round worm (d) Guinea worm

50. Mountaineers should live on high carbohydrates diet because carbohydrate
(a) are high energy compounds
(b) are easily digestible
(c) can be changed to amino acid
(d) need less respiratory oxygen

51. A couple preparing for marriage have their blood typed along with the other required blood bests. Both are AB. They ask you what the types of blood group their children cannot have. Your answer would be
(a) A (b) AB
(c) B (d) O

52. Persons with Klinefelter's syndrome are
(a) sterile males (b) intersex
(c) superfemales (d) normal males

53. Baldness in human helps to explain
(a) sex linked genes
(b) sex influenced genes
(c) sex limited genes
(d) autosomal inheritance

54. Insulin decreases blood glucose level by
(a) promoting uptake of glucose by liver
(b) glycogenesis in liver
(c) uptake and utilization of glucose by muscle cells
(d) all of the above

55. The bacteriophage during infec-tion injects
(a) Capsid only
(b) Capsomeres
(c) DNA only
(d) DNA and tail fibres

56. One of the following is not caused due to noise pollution
(a) Temporary or permanent impairment of hearing
(b) Neurological disorders
(c) Muscular Spasm
(d) Headaches

57. Conditional reflexes were discovered by
(a) Hopkins (b) Pavlov
(c) Jenner (d) Haldane

58. Chewing gum is prepared using the
(a) latex of *Achras zapota*
(b) resin of *Pinus exelsa*
(c) gum of *Moringa oleifera*
(d) gum of *Acacia arabica*

59. Salvia, Lavendula, Mentha and Pogostemon are all sources of
(a) industrial lubricants
(b) cooking oils
(c) aromatic oils
(d) beverages

60. From which of the following is opium obtained
(a) Dried leaves
(b) Roots
(c) Latex from unripe capsules
(d) seeds

61. Tendon connects
(a) skin with muscles
(b) bone with muscles
(c) cartilage with muscles
(d) bone with bone

62. Insects have blood which
(a) resembles human blood in colour
(b) circulates through arteries and veins
(c) circulates through an open system
(d) has haemoglobin in the cells

63. Which of the following is responsible for increasing the heart beat
(a) Acetylcholine (b) Adrenaline
(c) Melatonix (d) F.S.H.

64. Diabetes insipidus is caused due to the deficiency of
(*a*) insulin (*b*) glucagons
(*c*) aldosterone (*d*) vasopressin

65. A decrease in the level of oestrogen and progesterone causes
(*a*) growth and dilation of myometrium
(*b*) formation of placenta
(*c*) constriction of uterine blood vessels leading to sloughing of uterine epithelium
(*d*) release of an ovum from ovaries

66. Equilibrium in atmosphere is maintained by
(*a*) producers
(*b*) producers and consumers
(*c*) decomposers
(*d*) producer, consumer, decomposer

67. Insectivoraes plants grow in the soil which is deficient in
(*a*) phosphorus (*b*) nitrogen
(*c*) sulphur (*d*) water

68. An ecosystem must have a continuous external sources of
(*a*) food (*b*) mineral
(*c*) energy (*d*) all of the above

69. The plant *Rauwoffia serpentina* can be used to control
(*a*) diabetes
(*b*) sleeping sickness
(*c*) blood pressure
(*d*) meningitis

70. Which is Gram negative?
(*a*) *Esherichia coli*
(*b*) *Staphylococcus aureus*
(*c*) *Streptococcus durans*
(*d*) All pathogenic bacteria

71. Blue revolution refers to
(*a*) manifold increase in the production of edible oils
(*b*) richer fish harvest from seas
(*c*) exploration of sea bed wealth
(*d*) better utilization of atmosp-heric gases for industrial purposes

72. Sugarcane juice is rich in
(*a*) sucrose (*b*) fructose
(*c*) glucose (*d*) all of these.

73. The respiration of the fat toliolein can be shown as follow $C_{57}H_{104}O_6 + 80O_2 \rightarrow 57CO_2 + 52H_2O$ which of the following represent the respiratory quotient (R.Q.) for this fat?
(*a*) $\frac{80\ O_2}{57\ CO_2} = 1.4$ (*b*) $\frac{80\ O_2}{52\ H_2O} = 1.5$
(*c*) $\frac{57\ CO_2}{80\ O_2} = 0.71$ (*d*) $\frac{52\ H_2O}{80\ O_2} = 0.65$

74. The causal organism of the disease scorpie in goats and sheeps and kuru in humans is a
(*a*) PPLO (*b*) Prion
(*c*) Viroid (*d*) Virion

75. The tallest tree in the world is
(*a*) *Pinus* (*b*) *Sequoia*
(*c*) *Ginkgo* (*d*) *Ficus*

76. The possible phenotypes for ABO blood groups are
(*a*) 4 (*b*) 6
(*c*) 8 (*d*) 16

77. The life span of human sperms in female genital tract is
(*a*) 24-48 hrs (*b*) less than 24 hrs
(*c*) 4-5 days (*d*) 1-2 days

78. An individual with both male and female tissues, a sex mosaic is known as
(*a*) Hemizygous
(*b*) Gynandromorph
(*c*) Hermophrodite
(*d*) Hypomorph

79. In the life cycle of silk moth the economically important stage is
(*a*) egg (*b*) caterpillar
(*c*) pupa (*d*) adult

80. Which one of the following is both a local anaesthetic as well as stimulant:
(*a*) Cocaine (*b*) Alcohal
(*c*) Heroine (*d*) Quinine

ANSWERS

1	2	3	4	5	6	7	8	9	10
(b)	(d)	(b)	(d)	(b)	(a)	(d)	(c)	(c)	(b)
11	**12**	**13**	**14**	**15**	**16**	**17**	**18**	**19**	**20**
(a)	(d)	(a)	(b)	(c)	(c)	(c)	(c)	(b)	(b)
21	**22**	**23**	**24**	**25**	**26**	**27**	**28**	**29**	**30**
(b)	(c)	(b)	(c)	(b)	(c)	(d)	(a)	(a)	(c)
31	**32**	**33**	**34**	**35**	**36**	**37**	**38**	**39**	**40**
(a)	(d)	(c)	(b)	(d)	(d)	(a)	(a)	(d)	(c)
41	**42**	**43**	**44**	**45**	**46**	**47**	**48**	**49**	**50**
(d)	(a)	(b)	(a)	(b)	(b)	(a)	(a)	(a)	(d)
51	**52**	**53**	**54**	**55**	**56**	**57**	**58**	**59**	**60**
(d)	(a)	(a)	(d)	(c)	(c)	(b)	(a)	(c)	(c)
61	**62**	**63**	**64**	**65**	**66**	**67**	**68**	**69**	**70**
(b)	(c)	(b)	(d)	(c)	(d)	(b)	(c)	(c)	(a)
71	**72**	**73**	**74**	**75**	**76**	**77**	**78**	**79**	**80**
(b)	(a)	(c)	(b)	(b)	(a)	(a)	(b)	(c)	(a)

PAPER SET-V

1. The main food of tadpole is
   (a) worms
   (b) small fishes
   (c) insects
   (d) aquatic algae and other vegetable matter
2. The present ineffectiveness of DDT in mosquito control is because of
   (a) conversion of DDT to DDE on exposure to atmosphere
   (b) stoppage of use of DDT as it was finding its way into the food articles of man
   (c) proliferation of breeds of mosquito, which can convert DDT to DDE
   (d) all of the above
3. Green house effect is a condition in which
   (a) the ozone layer surrounding the earth is broken down
   (b) there is an increase in the carbon dioxide content of the atmosphere
   (c) there is an increase in the temperature of the atmosphere due to the absorption of infra-red radiation by the increased CO_2 in the atmosphere
   (d) increased cosmic ray bombardment with the surface of the earth
4. The reason why most antibiotics have no effect on viruses is
   (a) they kill all bacteria which act as host of virus
   (b) viruses are too small in size for the antibiotics to act
   (c) viruses have no metabolism of their own
   (d) all of the above
5. Which one of the following statement about the effects of deforestation is not correct
   (a) If leads to soil erosion
   (b) It alters the local weather pattern
   (c) It speeds up nutrient recycling
   (d) It destroy the natural habitat of wild animal
6. The method recommended for discouraging human population growth in the shortest period is
   (a) educating people
   (b) adopting preventive and contraceptive measures
   (c) encouraging emigration
   (d) increasing the standard of living
7. The salts used by the diatoms and sponges in a pond ecosystem is
   (a) nitrates (b) phosphorus
   (c) sulphur (d) silicates
8. The commonest anaesthetic in use today is
   (a) halothane (b) chloroform
   (c) ether (d) alcohal
9. The immediate cause of induction of ovulation in the human female in the large plasma surge of
   (a) LH (b) FSH
   (b) Estradiol (d) Progesterone
10. A pathogenic protozoan that does not need a vector for completing its life cycle is
    (a) *Plasmodium vivax*
    (b) *Trypanosoma gambiense*
    (c) *Leishmania donovani*
    (d) *Entamoeba histolytica*
11. If you measure the concentration of carbondioxide above a forest when would you expect it to be maximum
    (a) Early morning
    (b) Mid morning
    (c) Afternoon
    (d) After sunset
12. Fruit juices are rich in
    (a) vitamin A (b) calcium
    (c) potassium (d) sodium
13. Absence of trees and presence of dwarf plants are the characteristic of
    (a) tropical rain forest
    (b) tundra
    (c) coniferous forest
    (d) deciduoces forest

14. Bone formation and growth is aided by
(*a*) vitamin D (*b*) vitamin B
(*c*) vitamin K (*d*) vitamin E

15. During urine formation. The part of nephron concerned with secreting urea and reabsorption of water is
(*a*) Glomerulus (*b*) Water
(*c*) Urinary bladder (*d*) Henle's loop

16. Diseases causitive organism

A. Dysentary	1. *Entamoeba histolytica*
B. Liver rot of sheep	2. *Wuchereria bancrofti*
C. Filariasis	3. vitamin A deficiency
D. Yerophthdrria	4. *Ascaris lumbricoides*
	5. *Fasciola hepatica*

Codes:	A	B	C	D
(*a*)	1	5	2	3
(*b*)	1	2	3	4
(*c*)	4	3	1	2
(*d*)	5	3	1	2

17. Drugs which produce confusion in visual perception and brain disturbance are called
(*a*) tranquillisers
(*b*) psychedelic or hallucinogenic
(*c*) narcotics
(*d*) ultrasonography

18. Which one of the following is widely applied in the investigation and management of infertility in woman
(*a*) X-rays (*b*) CT scan
(*c*) PET (*d*) Ultrasonography

19. What will happen if some fresh water protozoans are transferred to seawater ?
(*a*) The contractile vacuoles will work faster
(*b*) The contractile vacuoles will grow larger
(*c*) There will be no change in the contractile vacuoles
(*d*) The contractile vacuoles will disappear

20. Which of the following is not involved in blood coagulation
(*a*) fibrin (*b*) thrombocytes
(*c*) plasma (*d*) factor X

21. Diaslema is
(*a*) a toothless space in the jaws of rabbits
(*b*) a type of tooth in rabbit
(*c*) milk teeth in young ones
(*d*) a part of the pelvic girdle

22. Which one of the following is a renewable resource?
(*a*) Fossil fuels (*b*) Minerals
(*c*) Petroleum (*d*) soil

23. In people addicted to alcohol the liver get damaged because it
(*a*) has to metabolise the alcohol
(*b*) stores excess of glycogen
(*c*) is over stimulated to secret bile
(*d*) accumulates excess of fats

24. Ozone layer is present in
(*a*) Atmosphere (*b*) Stratosphere
(*c*) Ionosphere (*d*) Biosphere

25. A large population of denitrifying bacteria in the field is detrimental to the vegetation because
(*a*) they promote ammonification
(*b*) they convert nitrates to nitrites
(*c*) they generate molecular nitrogen
(*d*) all of the above

26. The step in cheese making that formerly used calf rennet but is now replaced by microbial enzymes is
(*a*) curding of milk
(*b*) coagulation of solids in the souring milk
(*c*) moisture removal from curd
(*d*) ripening of cheese

27. In a food chain the largest population is that of
(*a*) primary consumer
(*b*) secondary consumer
(*c*) decomposers
(*d*) producers

28. If a person picks a hot empty metal tin he will drop it immediately while an equally hot expensive dish with food in it will be put down quickly but gently. This latter

response is due to
(a) conditional reflex (b) spinal reflex
(c) visceral reflex (d) both (a) and (b)

29. The organism which appear first after volcanic eruption are
(a) Welwitschia (b) Ephedra
(c) Stangeria (d) Ginkgo biloba

30. The term *antibiotic* was coined by
(a) Selman Waksman
(b) Babes
(c) Paul Vaillemin
(d) Fleming

31. The mineral essential for formation of thyroxine is
(a) calcium (b) phosphorus
(b) sodium (d) Iodine

32. HCl secreted by the stomach is neutralised by
(a) Gastric juice (b) Pancreatic juice
(c) Bile (d) Intestinal secretion

33. A severe landslide may lay bare a hillside. In time however such a bare cliff face may become clothed by a verdant green cover. This process is known as
(a) ecological colonisation
(b) afforestation
(c) primary succession
(d) none of the above

34. The intermediate host of *Fasciola hepatica* is
(a) Helix (b) Bulinus
(c) Pila (d) Pinctada

35. Which of the following is present in approximately similar concentration in both plasma and urine?
(a) K^+ (b) NO^+
(c) PO_4^{3-} (d) SO_4^{2-}

36. National Orchidarium of India is situated at
(a) Shimla (b) Kolkata
(c) Bangalore (d) Yercaud

37. Match the following

A. Tape worm	1. obligates parasites frequently inefficient in that they kill their host
B. Mosquitoes	2. Transmitted by primary host eating secondry host
C. Malarial parasites	3. have free living larvae and parasitic adults
D. Wasps	4. May have free living adults and parasitic larvae

Codes:

	A	B	C	D
(a)	3	2	4	1
(b)	1	2	3	4
(c)	4	3	1	2
(d)	2	3	1	4

38. From the data given below, point out the country which will have the least population growth rate?

	Country	*Birth rate / 1000*	*Death rate*
(a)	M	15	5
(b)	N	25	10
(c)	O	35	18
(d)	P	48	41

39. Which one of the early theories to explain inheritance is similar to the present day concept of heredity?
(a) Aristotle's theory
(b) Preformation theory
(c) Encasement theory
(d) Theory of epigenesis

40. Which of the following is absent in the mouth parts of house fly?
(a) Maxillary palps (b) Hypopharynx
(c) Labellum (d) Mandibles

41. Bladder worm stage of Taenia is
(a) Onchosphere (b) *Cysticercus*
(c) *Strobila* (d) *Rostellum*

42. The revolving power of human eye is
(a) 10 microns (b) 100 microns
(c) 1000 microns (d) 50 microns

43. The endangered species of India are listed in
(a) all records of botanical survey of India
(b) all records of zoological survey of India
(c) the Red Data Book
(d) none of the above

44. The compound microscope invented by
(a) Zernike (b) Knoll and Ruska
(c) Robert Hooke (d) Janssens

45. Which of the following is the most characteristic feature of a neritic environment?
(*a*) low atmospheric humidity
(*b*) extremes of temperature
(*c*) low precipitation
(*d*) high rate of vapourisation

46. Insulin, allow molecular polysaccharide is found in the roots of
(*a*) wheat (*b*) mango
(*c*) dahlia (*d*) sugarcane

47. Chicken pox is caused by
(*a*) Adeno virus (*b*) SV-40 virus
(*c*) Varicella virus (*d*) Bacteriophase T_2

48. Match the following

A. Vital capacity	1. volume of air taken in by the lungs of mammal breathing normally at rest during one respiratory cycle
B. Expiratory reserve volume	2. volume of air remaining in the lungs after maximum expiration
C. Residual volume	3. volume of air that it is possible to expel from the lungs after normal expiration
D. Tidal volume	4. volume of air that it is possible to expel after forced inspiration

Codes:	A	B	C	D
(*a*)	3	2	1	4
(*b*)	1	2	3	4
(*c*)	4	3	2	1
(*d*)	2	3	1	4

49. The class of protozoans characterised by parasitic form is
(*a*) *Sacromastigophora*
(*b*) *Rhizopoda*
(*c*) *Sporozoa*
(*d*) *Ciliata*

50. Deficiency of Somatotropic harmone in children leads to
(*a*) Gigantism (*b*) Acromegaly
(*c*) Dwarfism (*d*) Cretinism

51. When man inhales air containing normal concentration of oxygen as well as carbon monoxide, he suffers from suffocation because
(*a*) carbon monoxide reacts with oxygen forming a compound which is toxic to the tissues
(*b*) haemoglobin combines with carbon monoxide instead of oxygen and the product cannot dissociate
(*c*) carbon monoxide affects the diaphragm and intercostal muscles
(*d*) carbon monoxide affects the nerves of the lungs

52. Which one of the following is called 'Pond silk?
(*a*) *Chlorella* (*b*) *Chlamydomonas*
(*c*) *Spirogyra* (*d*) *Nostoc*

53. The epithet meat making machines is used with reference to
(*a*) Cattle (*b*) Pigs
(*c*) Deer (*d*) All of the above

54. Bordeaux mixture was first tested upon
(*a*) downy mildew of grapes
(*b*) late blight of potato
(*c*) white rust of crucifers
(*d*) tikka disease of ground nut

55. Male mosquito is unable to pierce the skin of man because
(*a*) reduced mandibles
(*b*) mandibles absent
(*c*) antennae short
(*d*) none of these

56. PLO are the bacteria like organism which differ from the latter in
(*a*) lacking cell wall and mesosomes
(*b*) being larger than bacteria
(*c*) having ribosomes in their cytoplasm
(*d*) exhibiting binary fission

57. Which one of the following is both a local anaesthetic as well as stimulant?
(*a*) Cocaine (*b*) Alcohol
(*c*) Herion (*d*) Quinine

58. Aspirin is a
(*a*) mixture of acetylsalicyclic acid, cocaine and atropine
(*b*) single chemical substance the acetylsalicyclic acid
(*c*) plant product
(*d*) compound isolated from peanuts

59. The larva of *Ascaris* is formed
(*a*) Parechymula (*b*) Planula
(*c*) Rhabditiform (*d*) Bag larva

60. The largest gland in the human body is
(*a*) Salivary gland
(*b*) Gastric gland
(*c*) Intestinal gland
(*d*) Liver

61. The vaccine produced by genetic engineering recently are against the disease
(*a*) AIDS (*b*) Herpes
(*c*) Jaundice (*d*) Polio

62. The most abundant inorganic salts in the body are those of
(*a*) calcium (*b*) iodine
(*c*) iron (*d*) sodium

63. Trophic level are formed by
(*a*) only plants
(*b*) only animals
(*c*) organism linked in food chain
(*d*) none of the above

64. Olteomalacia in adults and rickets in children are caused by the deficiency of
(*a*) vitamin A (*b*) vitamin B_7
(*c*) vitamin D (*d*) vitamin C

65. A normal man respires in a minute
(*a*) 25-30 times (*b*) 10-15 times
(*c*) 14-18 times (*d*) 20-25 times

66. If a woman is pregnant and suffering from some suspected disease the method of diagnosis that is comparatively safe is
(*a*) CT scan
(*b*) X ray radio graphey
(*c*) Sonography
(*d*) PET scan

67. Mother during pregnancy are given this vaccine
(*a*) BCG
(*b*) Typhoid vaccine
(*c*) Tetanus toxoid
(*d*) All of the above

68. The Vitamin K is
(*a*) Tocopherol (*b*) Calciferol
(*c*) Phglloquinone (*d*) Retinol

69. Which one of the following is a biofertilizer?
(*a*) Urea (*b*) *Azospirillum*
(*c*) Superphosphate (*d*) Compost

70. The intermediate host of liver fluke is
(*a*) Pig
(*b*) Cyclops
(*c*) Snail
(*d*) Any aquatic invertebrate

71. The smallest organelle in a cell is
(*a*) lysosome (*b*) spherosome
(*c*) peroxisome (*d*) ribosome

72. Silent valley of Kerela is worth preserving because it
(*a*) is the only evergreen forest in India
(*b*) contains costly timber trees
(*c*) is a good picnic spot
(*d*) contains rare species of animals and plants

73. Bath sponge is obtained from
(*a*) *Euplectella* (*b*) *Euspongia*
(*c*) *Leucosolenia* (*d*) *Spongilla*

74. The main function of the large intestine is
(*a*) storage of waste products
(*b*) digestion of cellulose
(*c*) absorption of water
(*d*) absorption of amino acids

75. Vaccination against tetanizing toxin of tetanus is given to develop
(*a*) innate immunity
(*b*) active immunity
(*c*) passive immunity
(*d*) auto immunity

76. Humulin, the first human insulin is manufactured using
(*a*) transgenic animals
(*b*) transgenic plants
(*c*) recombinent *E. coli* clones
(*d*) *Rhizopus stolonifer*

77. The biogenetic law explains "*ontogeny repeats phylogeny*" It was proposed by
(*a*) Jean Baptiste Lamarck
(*b*) Ernst Heinurich Haeckel
(*c*) A.F.L Weismann
(*d*) T.H. Morgan

78. The important mineral constituent of the haemoglobin is
(a) potassium (b) sodium
(c) magnesium (d) iron

79. Name a genetical disease wherein the blood does not clot
(a) Haematuria (b) Haemophilia
(c) Haemolysis (d) Haemorrhage

ANSWERS

1	2	3	4	5	6	7	8	9	10
(d)	(c)	(c)	(c)	(c)	(b)	(d)	(a)	(a)	(d)
11	**12**	**13**	**14**	**15**	**16**	**17**	**18**	**19**	**20**
(d)	(c)	(b)	(a)	(d)	(a)	(b)	(d)	(d)	(c)
21	**22**	**23**	**24**	**25**	**26**	**27**	**28**	**29**	**30**
(a)	(d)	(d)	(b)	(c)	(b)	(c)	(d)	(a)	(a)
31	**32**	**33**	**34**	**35**	**36**	**37**	**38**	**39**	**40**
(d)	(b)	(c)	(b)	(b)	(d)	(a)	(d)	(d)	(d)
41	**42**	**43**	**44**	**45**	**46**	**47**	**48**	**49**	**50**
(b)	(b)	(c)	(d)	(b)	(c)	(a)	(a)	(c)	(c)
51	**52**	**53**	**54**	**55**	**56**	**57**	**58**	**59**	**60**
(b)	(c)	(b)	(a)	(a)	(a)	(a)	(b)	(c)	(d)
61	**62**	**63**	**64**	**65**	**66**	**67**	**68**	**69**	**70**
(b)	(a)	(c)	(c)	(c)	(c)	(c)	(c)	(b)	(c)
71	**72**	**73**	**74**	**75**	**76**	**77**	**78**	**79**	
(d)	(a)	(b)	(d)	(b)	(c)	(b)	(d)	(b)	

PAPER SET-VI

1. The functional unit of the kidney is
(*a*) neuron
(*b*) nephron
(*c*) malpighian body
(*d*) convoluted tubules

2. The hardest material in the human body is the
(*a*) bone
(*b*) cartilage
(*c*) enamel of the tooth
(*d*) dentine of the tooth

3. The triple vaccination given to the children is preventive against
(*a*) tuberculosis, whooping cough, diphtheria
(*b*) whooping cough, tetanus, diphtheria
(*c*) common cold, polio, tetanus
(*d*) peneumonia, tetanus, polio

4. The largest flower found is:
(*a*) Giant water lily
(*b*) *Dahlia*
(*c*) *Rafflesia*
(*d*) Sunflower

5. A virus that cause dystrophy of the muscles is
(*a*) AIDS virus (*b*) Rubella virus
(*c*) Mumps virus (*d*) Polio virus

6. Earth worm cannot live in dry soil because
(*a*) it cannot perform locomotion
(*b*) it needs water for reproduction and life history
(*c*) it require soil moisture for respiration
(*d*) it has to consume plenty of water

7. The main source of infection of rabies from an infected dog is through its
(*a*) faeces (*b*) urine
(*c*) skin (*d*) saliva

8. Vaccination was introduced by
(*a*) Alexander Flemming
(*b*) Edward Jenner
(*c*) Landsteiner
(*d*) William Harvey

9. The nutrition in plasmodium is
(*a*) holozoic (*b*) holophytic
(*c*) saprozoic (*d*) parasitic

10. The brain is covered by membrane called
(*a*) pleura (*b*) pericardium
(*c*) meninges (*d*) peritoneum

11. Generally animal virus contains
(*a*) RNA (*b*) DNA
(*b*) Plastids (*d*) Mitochondria

12. The environmental factor that reduces the rate of transpiration is
(*a*) high humidity
(*b*) high temperature
(*c*) high light intensity
(*d*) high wind velocity

13. Vitamins are
(*a*) energy producer
(*b*) body builders
(*c*) regulators
(*d*) heat producer

14. Infection is transmitted when the primary host consumes the secondary host in the case of
(*a*) *Fasciola hepatica*
(*b*) *Taenia solium*
(*c*) *Trypanosoma gambiense*
(*d*) *Wuchereria bancrofti*

15. In the nephron, the urine gets concentrated in the
(*a*) Glomerulus
(*b*) Bowman's capsule
(*c*) Proximal convoluted tube
(*d*) Henle's loop and distal convoluted tube

16. The blood smear of the person revealed the differential count of WBC to be as follow
Neutrophils : 65%
Eosinophils : 6%
Basophils : 1%
Lymphocytes : 25%
Monocytes : 5%
The person is likely to be suffering from
(*a*) leukemia
(*b*) bacterial infection
(*c*) allergic reaction
(*d*) harmful effect of certain drug

17. The insectivorous plants make use of the insect for their ____ requirement.
(*a*) food (*b*) nitrogen
(*c*) water (*d*) mineral

18. Potamine poisoining means
(a) poison by chemicals
(b) poison by gas
(c) food poisoing due to bacteria
(d) none of the above

19. Bile contains
(a) protein digesting enzymes
(b) carbohydrate digesting enzymes
(c) fat splitting enzymes
(d) no enzyme

20. Pasteurisation of milk means
(a) removal of fat
(b) addition of vitamin A and D
(c) heating to 110°C for 30 minutes followed by quick cooling
(d) heating to 60°C for 30 minutes followed by quick cooling

21. Which type of soil is best suited for the cultivation of cotton in India?
(a) Loamy soil (b) Black soil
(c) Sandy soil (d) Clayey soil

22. Dialysis is performed on patient suffering from
(a) heart trouble (b) lung trouble
(c) ulcer (d) kidney failure

23. Cataract is caused by the
(a) accumulation of dust in the eye
(b) lens getting opaque
(c) nerves supplying the eyes getting weak
(d) conjunctiva becoming thickened

24. An anti-viral substance, known to prevent the synthesis of new virus in the cell is known as
(a) transferon (b) antibody
(c) interferon (d) inferon

25. A gas which could become a pollutant in failure is
(a) SO_2 (b) CO_2
(c) CO (d) NO_2

26. During the second conception, if the RH- mother has RH + foetus it will
(a) have no effect
(b) enable the embryo to grow fast
(c) cause erythroblastosis foetalis when RBC of foetus get destroyed and at times leading
(d) change the RH^+ of foetus to RH^-

27. Salivary amylase is inactivated in the stomach by
(a) pepsin
(b) rising level of HCl
(c) rennin
(d) gastric lipase

28. In recent years, Scientists have developed yeast strains capable of producing the human insulin called humulin. This has been possible because of advance in
(a) hybridoma technique
(b) recombinant DNA technology
(c) method of cloning
(d) tissue culture

29. Kwashirorkar, an African word to signify "rejected ones" affecting children to under developed and developing countries with symptoms of stunted growth, loss of appetite, amaemia portruding bellies, match stick legs, resulting in great mortality, is due to the deficiency of
(a) vitamins (b) fats
(c) proteins (d) carbohydrates

30. Reflex actions are
(a) conscious actions
(b) automatic instantaneous actions controlled by the spinal cord
(c) slow reaction to external stimuli
(d) controlled by autonomous nervous system

31. Greek word *Hygeia* means
(a) Goddess of Health
(b) Goddess of Love
(c) Goddess of Study
(d) None of the above

32. The smallest flower is that of the
(a) onion
(b) mustard
(c) fig
(d) *Wolfia microscopica*

33. Antibacterial drug produced from an alga is
(a) chlorellin (b) clavicin
(c) Asperagillin (d) penicillin

34. *Artemisia maritima* yields a drug called san toxin. It is used as an
(a) antidote to snake poison
(b) antacid
(c) antiseptic
(d) antithelminthic

35. Major pollutant emitted by automobiles is
(a) SO_2 (b) CO_2
(c) NO (d) CO

36. The ecological pyramid that can never be inverted is
(*a*) pyramid of biomass
(*b*) pyramid of energy
(*c*) pyramid of number
(*d*) any one of the above

37. Forest Research Institute is situated at
(*a*) Dehradun (*b*) Shimla
(*c*) Mumbai (*d*) Kolkata

38. An ecological study undertaken in rain forest of North Eastern India is
(*a*) biological (*b*) autoecological
(*c*) synecological (*d*) statistical

39. Stratified epithelium is characterstic of
(*a*) mammalian skin (*b*) oesophagus
(*c*) urinary bladder (*d*) both (a) and (c)

40. Phagocytosis is a phenomenon associated with
(*a*) neutrophils and monocytes
(*b*) eosinophils and basophils
(*c*) neutrophils and lymophocytes
(*d*) monocytes and lymphcytes

41. In which of the following cases, the parasite requires only one host to complete its life cycle?
(*a*) *Ascaris lumbricoides*
(*b*) *Dracunculus medinensis*
(*c*) *Fasciola hepatica*
(*d*) *Trypanosoma gambiense*

42. The one thing that is common between earthworm and cockroach is
(*a*) haemocoel
(*b*) respiratory pigment heamo-globin
(*c*) nephridia
(*d*) double ventral nerve cord

43. The joint that is present between the head of Femur and Acetabulum cavity is
(*a*) hinge joint
(*b*) pivot joint
(*c*) ball and socket joint
(*d*) gliding joint

44. The vitamin involved in the process of blood coagulation is
(*a*) vitamin K (*b*) vitamin B_6
(*c*) vitamin C (*d*) vitamin D

45. The term "Fatigue" is most appropriately used with reference to
(*a*) brain
(*b*) neuromuscular junction
(*c*) nerve
(*d*) cyton

46. Match the following

A.	Planula	1.	liver fluke
B.	Trochophore	2.	obelia
C.	Miracidium	3.	Mereis
D.	Bipinnaria	4.	mosquito
		5.	star fish

Codes:	A	B	C	D
(*a*)	1	2	3	5
(*b*)	2	3	4	5
(*c*)	1	2	3	4
(*d*)	5	4	3	2

47.

A.	Biopesticide	1.	Azolla Anabaena Symbiont
B.	Bioherbicide	2.	Phytophthora palmivora
C.	Biofertilizer	3.	Azadirachta indica
D.	Mycoherbicide	4.	Cochineal insect
		5.	Arthrobotrys

Codes:	A	B	C	D
(*a*)	3	4	2	1
(*b*)	2	3	4	1
(*c*)	1	2	3	4
(*d*)	2	1	3	4

48. Match the following

A.	SO_2	1.	Biomagnification
B.	DDT	2.	lichen desert
C.	Chlorofluoro carbon	3.	knock knee
D.	Mercury	4.	Ozone hole
		5.	Minamata disease

Codes:	A	B	C	D
(*a*)	2	1	4	5
(*b*)	1	2	3	4
(*c*)	5	4	3	2
(*d*)	4	3	2	1

49. DDT has been banned in many developed countries because of its
(*a*) high toxicity to mammals
(*b*) high degree of persistence in the environment
(*c*) low toxicity to insect
(*d*) high solubility in water

50. The one important advantage of conventional radiography is
(*a*) ready availability

(b) low hazard
(c) intermediate cost
(d) general physician's familiarity with interpretation, indication and reliability

51. When a person is injured severly his brain release compounds which tend to decrease his pain these compounds are called
(a) entephalins (b) amphetamines
(c) histamines (d) antihistamines

52. The advantage of an NMR imaging over a CT scan is that
(a) it is comparatively free from hazardous radiation
(b) it can obtain images in any plane
(c) it has greater sensitivity for brain lesions
(d) all of the above

53. Fear of water is a symptom of
(a) Dysentery (b) Diarrhoea
(c) Cholera (d) Rabies

54. Gerontology is the science that studies
(a) Foetuses
(b) Death
(c) Physiological disorders
(d) Old age

55. Yellow bone marrow
(a) is yellowish due to the reduced blood supply
(b) is haemopoietically dormant
(c) cannot form blood cells
(d) is haemopoetically very active

56. *Salk* vaccine is used to combat
(a) AIDS (b) Rabies
(c) Polio (d) Herpes virus

57. A housefly has
(a) 2 pairs of legs and 1 pair of wings
(b) 3 pairs of legs and 1 pair of wings
(c) 3 pairs of legs and 2 pairs of wings
(d) 2 pairs of legs and 2 pairs of wings

58. The ophthalmologist removes from a dead eye donor his
(a) iris (b) cornea
(c) lens (d) eyeball

59. Jute is formed of
(a) leaf fibres (b) cornea
(c) bast fibres (d) xylem fibres

60. The ultimate source of energy for the entire biosphere is
(a) soil (b) sun
(c) the ocean (d) atmosphere

61. In the human brain, the seat of intelligence is
(a) cerebrum
(b) cerebellum
(c) medulla oblongata
(d) pons

62. Haemoglobin is found dissolved in the plasma of
(a) cockroach (b) frog
(c) earthworm (d) snail

63. The kung tribe living in the kalahari desert of South Africa depend for their food needs on the seeds of
(a) *Cerus grandiflorus*
(b) *Ananas comosus*
(c) *Bauhinia esculenta*
(d) *Welwitschia mirabilis*

64. Choose the correct pair
(a) Protista – all unicellular, eukaryotic organisms
(b) Fungi – only saprophytes
(c) Monera – single envelope system
(d) animal – only parasites

65. Hydroponics is
(a) the art of cutting shrub bery to artistic shapes
(b) the art of growing miniature-sized plants
(c) growing plants in a soilless medium
(d) growing plants in magnetized water

66. In man, normal blood glucose level per 100ml of blood is
(a) 50-80 mg (b) 80-120 mg
(c) 100-150 mg (d) 120-180 mg

67. Average life span of RBC in human is
(a) 90 days (b) 120 days
(c) 45 days (d) 150 days

68. Ecological horizon is a term applied to
(a) the different layers in soil profile
(b) the distant areas where sky and earth seem to meet
(c) the different type of vegetation in a tropical forest
(d) any one of the above

69. Bombay duck is a
(a) marine edible fish found at the coast of Maharashtra

(b) fresh water edible fish endemic to the ponds and lakes of Maharashtra
(c) culinary preparation in Maharashtrian homes
(d) snail found in the backwaters of Mahim coast

70. The dental formula 2,1,2,3 / 2,1,2,3 is of
(a) man (b) frog
(c) rabbit (d) horse

71. *Trypanosoma*, an endoparasite in man is found in
(a) blood (b) lungs
(c) liver (d) alimentary canal

72. Malignant tertian malaria is caused by
(a) *Plasmodium vivax*
(b) *Plasmodium falciparum*
(c) *Plasmodium malariae*
(d) *Plasmodium ovale*

73. Bladderworm stage of *Taenia* is
(a) Onchosphere (b) Cysticercus
(c) Strobila (d) Rasteltum

74. What is the secretion, in which a part of the cell is lost along with it known as?
(a) Wodorine (b) Holocine
(c) Aorine (d) Merocrine

75. The wings of pollen grain of *Pinus* are formed by
(a) Exine (b) Mesosporium
(c) Intine (d) Exo-intine

76. Edaphic factors pertain to
(a) water content in the environment
(b) soil
(c) altitude of a site
(d) temperature variations

77. Darwin's theory of natural selection fails to give a satisfactory explanation for
(a) overproduction
(b) struggle for existence
(c) variation
(d) survival of the fittest

78. The egg of lizard belongs to
(a) Microlecithal type
(b) Macrolecithal type
(c) Alecithal type
(d) Mesolecithal type

79. Assuming that there is no linkage and crossing over the segregation of Medelian factors during meiosis occurs at
(a) Diplotene (b) Metaphase-I
(c) Anaphase-I (d) Anaphase II

80. The stage in the life history of Plasmodium which can found both in the primary and secondary host is
(a) Merozoite (b) Trophozoite
(c) Ookinete (d) Gametocyte

ANSWERS

1	2	3	4	5	6	7	8	9	10
(b)	(c)	(b)	(c)	(d)	(c)	(d)	(b)	(d)	(c)
11	**12**	**13**	**14**	**15**	**16**	**17**	**18**	**19**	**20**
(b)	(c)	(d)	(b)	(c)	(b)	(c)	(d)	(b)	(d)
21	**22**	**23**	**24**	**25**	**26**	**27**	**28**	**29**	**30**
(b)	(d)	(b)	(c)	(b)	(c)	(b)	(b)	(c)	(b)
31	**32**	**33**	**34**	**35**	**36**	**37**	**38**	**39**	**40**
(a)	(d)	(a)	(d)	(d)	(b)	(a)	(c)	(d)	(a)
41	**42**	**43**	**44**	**45**	**46**	**47**	**48**	**49**	**50**
(a)	(d)	(c)	(a)	(b)	(a)	(a)	(a)	(b)	(d)
51	**52**	**53**	**54**	**55**	**56**	**57**	**58**	**59**	**60**
(a)	(d)	(d)	(d)	(b)	(c)	(b)	(b)	(c)	(b)
61	**62**	**63**	**64**	**65**	**66**	**67**	**68**	**69**	**70**
(a)	(c)	(c)	(a)	(c)	(b)	(b)	(c)	(a)	(a)
71	**72**	**73**	**74**	**75**	**76**	**77**	**78**	**79**	**80**
(a)	(b)	(b)	(d)	(d)	(b)	(c)	(b)	(c)	(d)

PAPER SET-VII

1. The system that is absent in *Taenia solium*
(*a*) nervous (*b*) reproductive
(*c*) excretory (*d*) digestive

2. Which one of the following has *no* intermediate host?
(*a*) Tapeworm (*b*) Liverfluke
(*c*) Roundworm (*d*) *Plasmodium*

3. The mouth part of female *Anopheles* mosquito are of
(*a*) Biting & Chewing type
(*b*) Piercing type
(*c*) Sponging type
(*d*) None of these

4. One of the following animal groups is exclusively marine
(*a*) coelentrates (*b*) sponges
(*c*) Echinoderms (*d*) Molluscs

5. Abscisic acid (ABA) causes
(*a*) faster leaf fall
(*b*) dormancy
(*c*) retardation of growth
(*d*) all of these

6. The most abundant inorganic salt in our body is
(*a*) Ca (*b*) I_2
(*c*) Fe (*d*) Na

7. Which one of the following disease kill more people?
(*a*) Malaria
(*b*) Plague
(*c*) AIDS
(*d*) Water-borne diseases

8. Bhopal gas disaster occured in
(*a*) 1986 (*b*) 1988
(*c*) 1982 (*d*) 1984

9. Browning of paper in old books is caused by
(*a*) collection of dust
(*b*) excessive use
(*c*) oxidation of cellulose
(*d*) presence of silver fish

10. The role of molybdenum is
(*a*) carbon assimilation
(*b*) chromosome contraction
(*c*) flowering induction
(*d*) nitrogen fixation

11. *Revenala madagascarensis* is commonly called
(*a*) fish tail palm
(*b*) talipot palm
(*c*) traveller's palm
(*d*) palmyra palm

12. Stethoscope was invented by
(*a*) Laennec (*b*) Edward Jenner
(*c*) Robert Koch (*d*) Einthoven

13. Lichens are the best indicator of ______ pollution of a place.
(*a*) air (*b*) water
(*c*) soil (*d*) noise

14. Oncology is the study of
(*a*) dead cells (*b*) living cells
(*c*) cancer cells (*d*) dividing cells

15. The ability to distinguish between two close points as two seperate points in the fields of a microscope is known as
(*a*) focal point
(*b*) resolving power
(*c*) diffraction
(*d*) critical point

16. ______ is a bacterial disease
(*a*) Rabies (*b*) Small pox
(*c*) Measles (*d*) Tuberculosis

17. Auxanometer is an instrument to measure
(*a*) Transpiration
(*b*) Growth
(*c*) Respiration
(*d*) Photosynthesis

18. Tracer technique makes use of
(*a*) micronutrients
(*b*) radioisotopes
(*c*) vitamins
(*d*) enzymes

19. The average age of Indian women is
(*a*) 50 years (*b*) 55 years
(*c*) 65 years (*d*) 70 years

20. Ciliated epithelium is found in
(a) oviduct
(b) primary bronchioles
(c) buccal cavity of frog
(d) all of the above

21. Rods and cones of the retina are referred to as
(a) phonoreceptors
(b) chemoreceptors
(c) photoreceptors
(d) mechanoreceptors

22. "Rigor Mortis" occurs
(a) when muscle is stretched beyond its capacity
(b) when muscle is devoid of supply of oxygen
(c) in muscles of dead animals
(d) when muscles are fatigued

23. Minamata disease of Japan is caused by
(a) carbon monoxide poisoning
(b) insecticide poisoning
(c) mercury poisoning
(d) radioactive fall out

24. Rabies vaccine was initially developed by
(a) Louis Pasteur *(b)* Robert Gallo
(c) Robert Koch *(d)* William Harvey

25. The immunological functions of the body is controlled by
(a) albumins
(b) alpha globulins
(c) beta globulins
(d) gamma globulins

26. The number of bones in the human skull is
(a) 14 *(b)* 22
(c) 30 *(d)* 8

27. The scientist known for using X-rays to cause mutation is
(a) T.H morgan
(b) H.J. Muller
(c) Friedrich Miescher
(d) D.E. moore

28. Cancer cell are more easily damaged by radiation than normal cells because they are
(a) starved of nutrients
(b) non dividing
(c) undergoing rapid division
(d) abnormal

29. An alkaloid used in the treatment of cold, asthma and hayfever is obtained from
(a) Atropha belladona
(b) Ephedra vulgaria
(c) Pinus roxburghii
(d) None of the above

30. During rainy days, wooden doors swells by the process of
(a) osmosis *(b)* exosmosis
(c) imbibition *(d)* all of the above

31. The formation of gametocytes of *Plasmodium* takes place in
(a) the stomach of female Anopheles mosquito
(b) the salivary gland of female Anopheles mosquito
(c) the blood of man
(d) the liver of man

32. Which of the following vitamin is generally excreted in urine by human?
(a) Vitamin A *(b)* Vitamin C
(c) Vitamin K *(d)* Vitamin B_6

33. Which of the following is the chief function of bile juice?
(a) Digest fats by enzymes
(b) Emulsify fats for digestion
(c) Pegalate digestion of protein
(d) Emulsify protein for digestion

34. What is the total number of bones in the body of man?
(a) 305 *(b)* 206
(c) 606 *(d)* 636

35. B.O.D is a measure of polluting organic matter present in a sample of
(a) water
(b) air
(c) soil
(d) bottom mud from a pond

36. Which one of the following forest is known to be a "forest that never burns"?
(a) Coniferoces forest
(b) Tropical rain forest
(c) Deciduous forest
(d) Tundra forest

37. Which of the following is normally not an atmospheric pollutant?
(*a*) CO (*b*) Hydrocarbon
(*c*) SO_2 (*d*) CO_2

38. Deltoid ridge is found in the
(*a*) humerus
(*b*) femur
(*c*) radio-ulna
(*d*) junction between the tibia and fibula

39. The mineral elements which plays an important role in Nitrogen Metobolism is
(*a*) In (*b*) Mo
(*c*) Cu (*d*) S

40. The energy currency of the cell is
(*a*) GTP (*b*) CAMP
(*c*) AMP (*d*) ATP

41. A dialyser is useful when _____ fails to function
(*a*) heart (*b*) liver
(*c*) kidney (*d*) brain

42. Sunandini is a better breed milk cow, developed in
(*a*) Kerala
(*b*) Haryana
(*c*) Andhra Pradesh
(*d*) Bihar

43. Match the following :

A. Parasitism	1. Intraspecific relationship
B. Harmful insect	2. Termites
C. Social life	3. Aphid
D. Mating competition	4. Interspecific relationship
	5. Elephant

Codes:	A	B	C	D
(*a*)	2	3	4	1
(*b*)	2	3	4	5
(*c*)	1	2	3	5
(*d*)	2	4	3	1

44. A person in a tightly closed room with an open hearth dies due to
(*a*) heat
(*b*) carbon monoxide poisoing
(*c*) carbon dioxide accumulation
(*d*) nitrogen excess in blood

45. The larva of tapeworm is known as
(*a*) cercaria (*b*) redia
(*c*) cysticercus (*d*) miracidium

46. Penicillin as an antibiotic was found out by
(*a*) Louis Pasteur (*b*) Flemming
(*c*) Iwanowski (*d*) Jenner

47. Enzymes having the same properties and different molecular structure are termed as
(*a*) isoenzymes
(*b*) coenzymes
(*c*) apoenzymes
(*d*) holoenzymes

48. The deficiency of thyroid during the childhood results in the retardation of physical, mental and sexual development. This condition is referred to as:-
(*a*) dwarfism
(*b*) cretinism
(*c*) myxodema
(*d*) addison's disease

49. Viruses that parasitize bacterial cells called bacteriophages were discovered in 1917 by
(*a*) Iwanowski (*b*) Stanley
(*c*) D' herelle (*d*) Loeway

50. The spread of *Entamoeba histolytica* is by
(*a*) bite of sand fly
(*b*) bite of Anopheles mosquito
(*c*) direct contact with the infected individual
(*d*) consuming contaminated food and water

51. Lock jaw is caused by
(*a*) virus
(*b*) *Clostridium tetani*
(*c*) *Eyco bacterium*
(*d*) *Vibrio cholerae*

52. Carbohydrates are
(*a*) body builders
(*b*) regulators
(*c*) energy producer
(*c*) none of the above

53. Saliva of man contains an enzyme called
(*a*) erepsin (*b*) ptyalin
(*c*) amylase (*d*) maltase

54. Elephantiasis is caused by
(a) *Ascaris lumbricoides*
(b) *Wuchereria bancrofti*
(c) *Taenia solium*
(d) *Ancylostoma duodenale*

55. The largest mammal that ever lived or is living is
(a) Giraffe (b) Elephant
(c) Blue whale (d) Hippopotamus

56. Decreases in the number of leucocytes is termed as
(a) leukaemia (b) leukopenia
(c) polyerythremia (d) haemolysis

57. Noise pollution results when the sound increases beyond ______ decibel and is continuous
(a) 80 (b) 120
(c) 45 (d) 200

58. Peristalsis is brought about by contraction of
(a) abdominal muscles
(b) diaphragm
(c) smooth muscles of gut
(d) gravitational force

59. Sweat secretion is
(a) a continuous process
(b) under nervous control
(c) process of exretion
(d) all of the above

60. The apparatus used for ascertaining the proper working of the heart is
(a) sphygmomanometer
(b) electrocardiograph
(c) electroencephalograph
(c) haematemesis

61. Virus was discovered by
(a) Stanely
(b) Louis Pasteur
(c) Dmitri Iwanowski
(d) Jenner

62. The largest number of species of animals belong to the phylum
(a) Chordata (b) Arthropoda
(c) Mollusca (d) Coelenterata

63. The ends of bones are connected together by the
(a) tendons (b) ligaments
(c) muscles (d) cartilage

64. Colour blindness is caused by
(a) vitamin A deficiency
(b) opacity of lens
(c) weak optic nerve
(d) gene mutation

65. "Sleeping Sickness" of Africa is caused by
(a) Plasmodium vivax
(b) Leishmania
(c) Trypanosoma gambiense
(d) Entamoeba histolytica

66. Universal donor belongs to the blood group
(a) A (b) AB
(c) B (d) O

67. A pulse rate of 140 per minute is a characterstic of
(a) an elephant (b) an old man
(c) an adult (d) a new born baby

68. Meat pickled with salt remains unspoilt by bacteria for a long time because
(a) the salt dehydrates the meat
(b) the salt forms a protective coating
(c) the salt prevents respiration to bacteria
(d) the bacteria lose their water by plasmolysis and hence get dried and ineffective.

69. The harmone which prepares the uterus for the implantation of the fertilized ovum is
(a) oxytocin (b) prolaction
(c) progesterone (d) thyrotropin

70. Food poisioning is caused by
(a) *P. vivax*
(b) *Salmonella spp.*
(c) *Leismania spp.*
(d) None of these

71. Vitamin D deficiency leads to ricket in children and asteomalacia in adults because it is essential for the metabolism of
(a) sulphates of sodium and potassium
(b) calcium and phospharus
(c) iron
(d) iodine

72. Introducing weakend or dead pathogens into an animal result in.
(*a*) passive immunity
(*b*) active immunity
(*c*) no immunological reactions
(*d*) the pathogens being attacked by neutrophils

73. Bacteriphages are
(*a*) Bactericidal viruses
(*b*) Bactericidal drugs
(*c*) Insecticidal bacteria
(*d*) Bacteria of intestine

74. The animal can synthesise in their body
(*a*) All types of vitamins
(*b*) vitamin A only
(*c*) vitamin D only
(*d*) vitamin B and C

75. Bowman's capsule and the glomerulus of the kidney tubule are together known as
(*a*) Henele's loop
(*b*) Malpighian capsule
(*c*) Nephron
(*d*) Coiled tube

76. The tuberculosis in man is caused by
(*a*) *Bacillus anthracis*
(*b*) *Vibrio cholerale*
(*c*) *Corynebacterium diphtherial*
(*d*) *Mycobacterium*

77. Iodine deficiency results in the deficiency of
(*a*) parathormone (*b*) thyroxin
(*c*) oxytocin (*d*) insulin

78. An organism fully in tune with its environment is said to have found its
(*a*) ecosystem
(*b*) ecological niche
(*c*) biome
(*d*) biosphere

79. Some fungi live on dead plants and animals and they are termed
(*a*) autotrophs
(*b*) parasites
(*c*) saprobes
(*d*) commensals

80. Saprophytes are usually found growing in
(*a*) compost (*b*) detritus
(*c*) humus (*d*) all of the above

ANSWERS

1	**2**	**3**	**4**	**5**	**6**	**7**	**8**	**9**	**10**
(*d*)	(*c*)	(*b*)	(*c*)	(*d*)	(*a*)	(*d*)	(*d*)	(*c*)	(*d*)
11	**12**	**13**	**14**	**15**	**16**	**17**	**18**	**19**	**20**
(*c*)	(*a*)	(*a*)	(*c*)	(*b*)	(*d*)	(*b*)	(*b*)	(*c*)	(*d*)
21	**22**	**23**	**24**	**25**	**26**	**27**	**28**	**29**	**30**
(*c*)	(*c*)	(*c*)	(*a*)	(*a*)	(*b*)	(*b*)	(*c*)	(*b*)	(*c*)
31	**32**	**33**	**34**	**35**	**36**	**37**	**38**	**39**	**40**
(*c*)	(*b*)	(*b*)	(*b*)	(*a*)	(*b*)	(*d*)	(*a*)	(*b*)	(*d*)
41	**42**	**43**	**44**	**45**	**46**	**47**	**48**	**49**	**50**
(*c*)	(*a*)	(*a*)	(*b*)	(*c*)	(*b*)	(*a*)	(*b*)	(*b*)	(*d*)
51	**52**	**53**	**54**	**55**	**56**	**57**	**58**	**59**	**60**
(*b*)	(*c*)	(*b*)	(*b*)	(*c*)	(*b*)	(*a*)	(*c*)	(*d*)	(*b*)
61	**62**	**63**	**64**	**65**	**66**	**67**	**68**	**69**	**70**
(*c*)	(*b*)	(*b*)	(*d*)	(*c*)	(*d*)	(*d*)	(*d*)	(*c*)	(*b*)
71	**72**	**73**	**74**	**75**	**76**	**77**	**78**	**79**	**80**
(*b*)	(*b*)	(*a*)	(*c*)	(*b*)	(*d*)	(*b*)	(*b*)	(*c*)	(*d*)

PAPER SET-VIII

1. Anti Xerophthalmic vitamin is
   (*a*) vitamin A (*b*) vitamin B_1
   (*c*) vitamin D (*d*) vitamin K

2. Purple bacteria resort to ——— nutrition.
   (*a*) saprophytic
   (*b*) chemotrophic
   (*c*) chemoautotrophic
   (*d*) parasitic

3. The human blood was first classified into blood groups by
   (*a*) Willpam Harvery
   (*b*) Landsteiner
   (*c*) Maleighi
   (*d*) Howell

4. Scurvy is due to the absence of
   (*a*) vitamin B_1 (*b*) vitamin B_6
   (*c*) vitamin C (*d*) vitamin K

5. The longest bone in the human body is
   (*a*) tibia (*b*) femur
   (*c*) humerus (*d*) rib

6. Food poisioning called potamine poisoning caused at times by consuming affected tinned food symptomised by fits, double vision, paralysis starting from the face spreading downwards, difficulty in swallowing *etc.* is due to
   (*a*) Virus
   (*b*) *Clostridium botulinum*
   (*c*) *Streptococci*
   (*d*) *Staphylococcus*

7. Merely for the purpose of monetary gains, a harmone injection is given in the udder of dry cows to give milk and the harmone is
   (*a*) thyroxine
   (*b*) paratharmone
   (*c*) oxytocin
   (*d*) insulin

8. Plague bacilli are transmitted from root to
   (*a*) air
   (*b*) water
   (*c*) flea
   (*d*) contaminated food

9. Hookworm infection is common among
   (*a*) factory workers
   (*b*) masons
   (*c*) hospital workers
   (*d*) agricultural workers

10. A man of blood group O marries a woman of blood group A. The wife's father is of blood group O. What is the probability that their children will belong to blood group O?
    (*a*) 25% (*b*) 50%
    (*c*) 75% (*d*) 100%

11. LSD(lysergic acid diethylamide) a dangerous habit forming drug converting the addicts into hopeless incurable cases is a
    (*a*) transquiliser
    (*b*) stimulant
    (*c*) depressant
    (*d*) hallusinogenic drug

12. Ergotamine, an alkaloid derived from a parasitic fungus, claviceps, popularity called ergot
    (*a*) is a depressant
    (*b*) is a vitamin
    (*c*) stimulates smooth muscles of uterus hastening labour
    (*d*) causes cardiac arrest

13. For myopia (short sightedness) the kind of lens to be used is
    (*a*) convex lens
    (*b*) plano convex
    (*c*) concave
    (*d*) cylindrical lens

14. As per present knowledge the pH factor is present in
    (*a*) all mammals
    (*b*) man only
    (*c*) all vertebrates
    (*d*) man and rhesus monkeys only

15. Small pox is caused by
(*a*) bacteria (*b*) virus
(*c*) fungus (*d*) algae

16. Nitrogen is an important constituent of
(*a*) carbohydrates
(*b*) fat
(*c*) protein
(*d*) all mineral salt

17. The part of the brain that control the regulation of temperature in the human body is
(*a*) cerebrum
(*b*) cerebellum
(*c*) hypothalamus
(*d*) medulla

18. The type of anaemia in which RBCs fail to measure is
(*a*) haemdytic anaemia
(*b*) pericius anaemia
(*c*) aplastic anaemia
(*d*) haemorrhagic anaemia

19. Carbon dioxide is mostly transported in the blood in the form of
(*a*) carboxy haemoglobin
(*b*) carbino haemoglobin
(*c*) carbonic acid
(*d*) bicarbonate of sodium and potassium

20. The blood of an accident victim when mixed with aggulutinxin A resulted in clumping of RBC. The blood group of the victim may be
(*a*) A (*b*) B
(*c*) O (*d*) AB or B

21. The enzyme erepsin acts on
(*a*) carbohydrates (*b*) fats
(*c*) proteins (*d*) mineral salts

22. The phase of contraction of heart is termed as
(*a*) heartbeat (*b*) systole
(*c*) diastole (*d*) heart sound

23. In insects, the larva does not change into an adult unless this hormone is secreted
(*a*) prothoracicotropin
(*b*) ecdysone
(*c*) juvenile hormone
(*d*) diapause hormone

24. RBCs are destroyed in the
(*a*) bone marrow (*b*) yolk sac
(*c*) liver (*d*) kidney

25. Food poisoning by taking spoilt fish, meat, egg, powder *etc.* resulting in vomiting, severe abdominal pain, occasionally in death is due to the bacteria
(*a*) *Rhizobium*
(*b*) *Vibrio cholerae*
(*c*) *Salmonella*
(*d*) *Mycobacterium*

26. Sulphur bacteria is
(*a*) autotropic
(*b*) chemoautotrophic
(*c*) saprophytic
(*d*) parasitic

27. A non-infectious unnatural and unusual reaction of a person to any substance or condition for which he is hypersensitive is termed as
(*a*) infection (*b*) immunity
(*c*) allergy (*d*) toxin

28. Fluorine is needed for the
(*a*) synthesis of thyroxine
(*b*) enamel of the teeth
(*c*) hardening of the bones
(*d*) nerve impulse transmission

29. Villi are microscopical hair like structures helpful in absorption and they are present in the
(*a*) stomach (*b*) duodenum
(*c*) ileum (*d*) colon

30. The system that is simple and primitive in the star fish is
(*a*) reproductive system
(*b*) digestive system
(*c*) nervous system
(*d*) water vescular system

31. The biggest chemical factory in the human body is the
(*a*) intestine (*b*) liver
(*c*) brain (*d*) pancreas

32. In *Plasmodium,* the zygote exhibits wriggling movement and this stage is termed
(*a*) spore
(*b*) sporozoite
(*c*) ookinete
(*d*) ex-flagellation

33. A person suffers laceration on his arm. On careful observation the doctor could conclude that a vein was cut which one of the following points helped the doctor to confirm his observation.
(*a*) Amount of blood loss was less
(*b*) Blood flow was not in spurts
(*c*) Colour of blood was not red
(*d*) Cut was very deep

34. Maggots are the larva of
(*a*) butterfly
(*b*) housefly
(*c*) cockroach
(*d*) dragonfly

35. Bakeries use yeast in bread making because it
(*a*) increase the taste
(*b*) make the bread soft and spongy
(*c*) keeps the bread fresh for a few days
(*d*) add vitamin B

36. *Escherichia coli*, used in genetical experiment inhibits our
(*a*) stomach (*b*) liver
(*c*) intestine (*d*) lungs

37. The process of destroying disease producing microorganism and their spores is termed as
(*a*) pasteurisation
(*b*) antibiotic
(*c*) sterilization
(*d*) sanitation

38. The action of the bile on fats is a process of
(*a*) hydrolysis (*b*) oxidation
(*c*) reduction (*d*) saponification

39. Inability to see after dusk due to deficiency of vitamin A is termed
(*a*) colour blindness (*b*) nyctalopia
(*c*) myopia (*d*) glaucoma

40. Most communicable disease are caused by bacteria and viruses which is expressed as germ theory of disease and the credit to establishing this theory goes to
(*a*) Edward Jenner
(*b*) Hippocrates
(*c*) Louis Pasteur and Robert Koch
(*d*) Landsteiner

41. Which of the following parasite has no intermediate host during its life history?
(*a*) *Liver fluke*
(*b*) *Plasmodium*
(*c*) *Taenia*
(*d*) *Ascaris*

42. In the ECG, the *P wave* is altered. It indicates that
(*a*) the atrial functioning is abnormal
(*b*) ventricles are functioning normally
(*c*) rate of conduction of impulse is very fast
(*d*) the person has suffered a heart attack

43. Citrus fruits and Indian gooseberry contain rich amount of
(*a*) vitamin B
(*b*) vitamin C
(*c*) vitamin E
(*d*) vitamin K

44. The water soluble vitamins are
(*a*) vitamins A,B and C
(*b*) vitamin B and C
(*c*) vitamin C and A
(*d*) none of the above

45. The reserve volume of air in man is
(*a*) 8000 ml (*b*) 3000 ml
(*c*) 1000 ml (*d*) 500 ml

46. The B.O.D. of fresh water pond is high when its water is
(*a*) clear
(*b*) polluted
(*c*) not exposed to sun
(*d*) full of aquatic life

47. *Entamoeba histolytica* differ from *Amoeba proteus* in that it does not have

(a) pseudopodia
(b) contractile vacuole
(c) food vacuole
(d) nucleus

48. Gram positive bacteria have
(a) thick and homogeneous cell wall
(b) as much as 70% peptido-glycon in their cell wall
(c) less than 10% lipids in cell wall
(d) none of the above

49. The sugar present in honey is
(a) glucose (b) maltose
(c) lactose (d) fructose

50. When there are no antigens in RBC and both A and B antibodies are present in the plasma such a person belongs to the blood group
(a) A (b) B
(c) AB (d) O

51. The blindspot of the eye is
(a) dead spot
(b) spot outside receptive surface
(c) spot covered by nerves on the retina
(d) non receptor to light

52. The reservoir host of *Trypanosoma gambiense* is
(a) sheep (b) horse
(c) buffalo (d) antelope

53. A mammal's thermostat is the
(a) medulla
(b) hypothalamus
(c) cerebral peduncles
(d) pons

54. Asthma is respiratory disease caused due to
(a) infection of trachea
(b) infection of lungs
(c) bleeding into pleural cavity
(d) sparms in bronchial muscles

55. Which one of the following is *not* a beneficial organism?
(a) *Penicillium*
(b) *Agaricus*
(c) *Diatoms*
(d) *Bacillus anthracis*

56. Whisky is an alcohol distillate obtained by fermenting
(a) juice of sugarcane
(b) juice of fruits
(c) mash of cereals
(d) molasses

57. Individual suffer hallucinations mental depression and changed personalities when they take the drug
(a) barbiturates
(b) lysergic acid diethylamide (LSD)
(c) morphine
(d) all of the above

58. Yeast is a good source of vitamin
(a) A (b) B
(c) D (d) E

59. Who applied the cell theory of plants?
(a) Schwann (b) C.P. Swanson
(c) Schleiden (d) R. Virchow

60. A technique for diluting the distribution of radioactive isotopes previously incorporated into cell is called
(a) cell fractionation
(b) autoradiography
(c) phase-4 contrast microscopy
(d) tissue culture

61. Which of the following microscopes has the highest resolving power?
(a) Phase contrast microscope
(b) Fluorescent microscope
(c) Polarizing microscope
(d) Electron microscope

62. If an organism, heterozygous for two pairs of genes represented by AaBb undergoes meiosis then the possible genotypic combination of the gametes will be
(a) AB, ab
(b) Aa, Bb
(c) AB, ab, Aa, aB
(d) data insufficient

63. A man who carries a sex linked gene on his Y chromosome will transmit this gene to

(a) all his daughters
(b) all his sons
(c) half of his sons
(d) half of his daughters

64. If a boy's father has haemophilia and his mother has one gene for haemophilia. What is the chance that the boy will inherit the disease?
(a) 0% (b) 50%
(c) 75% (d) 100%

65. All the living organism on the earth constitute
(a) biome (b) biosphere
(c) community (d) population

66. Plants and animals living in a given area form
(a) population (b) biome
(c) community (d) ecosystern

67. Bladder worm is the larva of
(a) *Ascaris* (b) *Taenia*
(c) *Nereis* (d) *Fasciola*

68. Which of the following animals has a true coelom?
(a) *Ascaris* (b) *Fasciola*
(c) *Obelia* (d) *Pheretima*

69. How many pair of hearts does an earthworm (*Pheretima posthuma*) possess?
(a) 3 (b) 4
(c) 5 (d) 6

70. Which of the following is fat soluble vitamin?
(a) Niacin
(b) Biotin
(c) Ascorbic acid
(d) Calciferol

71. Which of the following is a biologically incompetent marriage?
(a) Man RH–ve and woman RH+ve
(b) Man RH+ve and woman RH+ve
(c) Man RH+ve and woman RH–ve
(d) Man RH–ve and woman RH–ve

72. Glucose is completely absorbed in
(a) loop of Henle
(b) proximal convoluted tubule
(c) distal convoluted tubule
(d) collecting tubule

73. Ammonia is converted into urea through a cycle of chemical reaction. This is called
(a) Bio-oxidation
(b) Ornithine cycle
(c) Arginine cycle
(d) Cori's cycle

74. The joint which enables you to turn your head from side to side is called
(a) hinge joint
(b) pivot joint
(c) uniqaial joint
(d) soddle joint

75. Which one of the following is not an addictive?
(a) Nicotine (b) Caffeine
(c) Alcohol (d) Aspirin

76. If ______ is not the major component of an individual diet he or she can develop pellagra
(a) leafy egetable (b) milk
(c) eggs (d) corn

77. Table sugar is
(a) Glucose (b) Lactose
(c) Sucrose (d) Fructose

78. Chloroflurocarbon pose a danger to the natural concentration of
(a) carbon dioxide
(b) oxygen
(c) nitrogen
(d) ozone

79. A bullock is different from a bull in that it is
(a) sterilized by castration
(b) naturally incapable of sperm production
(c) naturally stronger
(d) more aggressive

80. Impatiens balsamina serves as an indicator plant in respect of
(a) aluminium (b) zinc
(c) gold (d) copper

ANSWERS

1	2	3	4	5	6	7	8	9	10
(a)	(c)	(b)	(c)	(b)	(b)	(c)	(c)	(d)	(b)
11	**12**	**13**	**14**	**15**	**16**	**17**	**18**	**19**	**20**
(d)	(c)	(c)	(d)	(b)	(c)	(c)	(b)	(d)	(d)
21	**22**	**23**	**24**	**25**	**26**	**27**	**28**	**29**	**30**
(c)	(b)	(b)	(c)	(c)	(b)	(c)	(b)	(c)	(c)
31	**32**	**33**	**34**	**35**	**36**	**37**	**38**	**39**	**40**
(b)	(c)	(b)	(b)	(b)	(c)	(c)	(d)	(b)	(c)
41	**42**	**43**	**44**	**45**	**46**	**47**	**48**	**49**	**50**
(d)	(a)	(b)	(b)	(b)	(b)	(b)	(c)	(d)	(d)
51	**52**	**53**	**54**	**55**	**56**	**57**	**58**	**59**	**60**
(c)	(d)	(b)	(d)	(d)	(c)	(d)	(b)	(c)	(b)
61	**62**	**63**	**64**	**65**	**66**	**67**	**68**	**69**	**70**
(d)	(c)	(b)	(b)	(b)	(c)	(b)	(d)	(b)	(c)
71	**72**	**73**	**74**	**75**	**76**	**77**	**78**	**79**	**80**
(c)	(b)	(b)	(b)	(d)	(d)	(c)	(d)	(a)	(b)

Test of English Language

Chapter 1

COMMON ERRORS

(A) ONE WORD SUBSTITUTES

1. You are a man of *words.* (word)
2. I did all my *works.* (work)
3. I have placed *order* for a book. (orders)
4. I am out of *sort.* (sorts)
5. He applied himself to *study.* (studies)
6. There is no *place* on this berth. (room)
7. I am resting in the *shadow* of a tree. (shade)
8. He *walked* on his cycle. (rode)
9. I have no *rupees.* (money)
10. The house is beyond *repairs.* (repair)
11. His *four fathers* were great men. (forefathers)
12. He is given free *boarding* and lodging. (board)
13. There is a *bevy* of boys. (bevy of girls)
14. This house is made of *bricks.* (brick)
15. There is a *crowd* of grapes. (bunch)
16. He has not paid the *foods* charges. (food)
17. I enjoy *freeship.* (free-studentship)
18. He has applied for *lecturership.* (lectureship)
19. A *towny man* gets a lot of comforts. (A townsman)
20. He is true to his *words.* (word)
21. I am a man of *part.* (parts)
22. I have sent *a request* for casual leave. (an application)
23. He is out of *door.* (doors)
24. He is out of *spirit.* (spirits)
25. They are *sworn* enemies. (avowed)
26. I *richly* deserve this honour. (highly, greatly)
27. He *highly* deserves this punishment. (richly)
28. He is very *coward.* (is a coward or is very cowardly)
29. It is *totally* clear to me. (perfectly, thoroughly)
30. It is *totally right.* (all right/perfectly right)
31. The pot is *vacant.* (empty)
32. I admire her *womanish* virtues. (womanly)
33. It is a historical event. (historic)
34. My tooth is *giving pain* (aching)
35. I *took* my admission. (I was admitted or I got myself admitted)
36. I *took* my birth in 1920. (I was born)
37. It is *utterly* right. (wholly, perfectly)
38. I have done *good* at the examination. (well)
39. The thief stood *in front of* the judge. (before)
40. My salary is Rs. 400/- *per month.* (per mensem)
41. My salary is Rs. 4800/- *per year.* (per annum)
42. Please credit this amount to my *name.* (account)
43. *Good bye,* Ram, I am glad to see you. (Good evening)
44. *Good night,* sir, you are welcome. (Good evening)
45. The *weather* of this place suits me. (climate)
46. He is *devoted* to gambling. (addicted)
47. You are *addicted* to literature. (devoted)
48. There is *lack of* poverty here. (absence of)
49. This great poem is very *artful.* (artistic)
50. I gave him a cheque *of* Rs. 500/- (for)
51. I like your *childish* nature. (child-like)
52. She is *somewhat* tall for her age. (too, rather)
53. The great saint is *notorious* in the spiritual field. (famous)
54. You are a *luxuriant* man. (luxurious)
55. Please *shut* the tap. (close)
56. Bread is made *of* flour. (from)
57. Shakespeare was an *imaginary* poet. (imaginative)
58. As he is *sick,* he is absent. (ill)
59. What's the cause *for* delay? (of)
60. There is no cause *of* complain. (for)
61. *Whom* are you speaking to? (Who)
62. The teacher *told* that the earth is round. (said)
63. *See* this word in the dictionary. (look up)
64. Have you *seen* all the examination papers? (examined)

65. The doctor *saw* my pulse. (felt)
66. He *saw* my certificates. (looked into)
67. He *stopped* at my house for a week. (stayed)
68. He *tells* me a fool. (calls)
69. I *told* him good morning. (wished)
70. Will you *forego* your holiday? (forgo)
71. Please excuse *me* coming late. (my)
72. I can't question his *bonafide.* (bona fides)
73. This scheme has been *approved of* by VC. (approved by the VC)
74. I didn't *approve* this marriage proposal. (approve of)
75. You *enjoy* bad health. (You have)
76. Columbus *invented* America. (discovered)
77. I *hope* that I shall fail. (I am afraid)
78. The smoke is *raising* from huts. (rising)
79. He was *hung* for murder. (hanged)
80. She refused to look at me, *much more* speak to me. (much less)
81. He went with me *so far as* Mumbai. (as far as)
82. I cannot stay here *any more.* (any longer)
83. I went there *especially* to see him. (specially)
84. His words are as sweet as *sugar.* (honey)
85. He invited me but I *denied.* (declined)
86. He *denied* to help me. (refused)
87. She *gave* a speech. (made)
88. A lot of men suspect the existence of God. (doubt)
89. I don't like *that he should go out.* (I don't like him to go out)
90. The ship was *drowned* in the sea. (The ship sank)
91. Fish *float* in the river. (swim)
92. A piece of wood is *swimming.* (floating)
93. The picture was *hanged.* (hung)
94. I cannot *rise* it. (raise)
95. I will do it *some way* or another. (some way or other/one way or another)
96. Please *await* me here. (wait for)
97. He jumped *at* a conclusion. (to)
98. Neither of them saw *each other.* (saw the other)
99. The two cars followed *each other.* (One car followed the other)
100. His name is *full-known.* (well-known)
101. *Except for* your help I would have been ruined. (Without or But for)
102. He *shook my hand.* (shook hands with me or shook me by the hand)
103. It is an apple of *contention.* (discord)
104. *What to speak* of helping, he did not even see me. (Not to speak)
105. She is as busy as an *ant.* (as a bee)
106. It is a *forgone* conclusion. (foregone)
107. Do not *speak* a lie. (tell)
108. He is as firm as a *hill.* (rock)
109. He *talks* English well. (speaks)
110. It is as heavy as *stone.* (lead)
111. The matter *shook* in the balance. (trembled)
112. He is as gentle as a *cow.* (lamb, dove)
113. He is as greedy as a *cat.* (wolf)
114. He is as faithful as a *horse* (dog)
115. He *turned every* stone. (He left no stone unturned)
116. My friend *visualises* that the Five-Year Plan is good. (feels)
117. It is as white as *milk.* (snow)
118. I have *given* examination this year. (appeared at, taken)
119. He *broke the news* of my grand success. (communicated)
120. I could not help *to laugh.* (laughing)

(B) SUPERFLUOUS WORDS

1. He died at the age of *serventy years.* (seventy)
2. He picked *up* a quarrel. (picked a quarrel)
3. I am awaiting *for* your reply. (awaiting your reply)
4. The fact is *true.* (It is a fact)
5. He is my *own* father. (He is my father)
6. I met a *child of* five years *old.* (a five-year old child)
7. The clock has struck *six hours.* (six)
8. It is *almost quite* right. (quite right or almost right)
9. He is a man of *good* position. (man of position)
10. It is *rather* unique. (It is unique)
11. I walked on *my feet.* (on foot)
12. I *think myself.* (I think)

13. He will *return back* in a week. (return or come back)
14. He is out of *good* temper. (out of temper)
15. She is in a *bad* temper. (in a temper)
16. My watch is in *proper* order. (is in order)
17. Unless you *do not* work hard, you will not pass. (Unless you work)
18. Wait here until I *do not* return. (until I return)
19. Her face resembles *to* her mother. (resembles her mother's)
20. I recommended *for* him to the Principal. (recommended him)
21. I am contesting *for* a seat. (contesting a seat)
22. I am investigating *into* the case. (investigating the case)
23. Let us discuss *about* the problem. (discuss the problem)
24. I doubt as *to* whether he is honest. (doubt whether)
25. The poet describes *about* nature. (describes nature)
26. She made a *fine* figure. (made a figure)
27. There is no *other* alternative. (no alternative)
28. You are my only *one* friend. (only friend)
29. I think/consider him *to be* a good student. (him a good student)
30. I consider it *as* a good thing. (consider it a good thing)
31. He was proved *to be* wrong. (proved wrong)
32. I ordered *for* his dismissal. (ordered his dismissal)
33. He is my *cousin brother*. (cousin)
34. This is just the *right thing*. (just the thing)
35. I forbade him *not* to smoke. (him to smoke)

(C) WORDS OMITTED

1. Do not *take to* your heart. (take this to)
2. I *find hard* to do it. (find it hard)
3. I *know him* a good man. (know him to be)
4. His services were *dispensed.* (despensed with)
5. I have *disposed* the business. (disposed of)
6. She does not *listen* my advice. (listen to)
7. He does not know *to read and write*. (how to read and write)
8. It is *regarded* sacred. (regarded as)
9. I took him *a thief*. (for a thief)
10. I have a pen to *write*. (to write with)
11. I *consider wrong* to use unfair means. (consider it wrong)
12. *Suffice* to say. (Suffice it to say)
13. *Yours* of the 10th instant is to hand. (Your letter of the 10th)
14. Please come to *mine*. (my house, place, residence)
15. She *avenged* on her enemy. (avenged herself)
16. When he *grows* he will enter a college. (grows up)
17. She is *five feet*. (five feet tall)
18. He *met* an accident. (met with)
19. Go there and *enjoy*. (enjoy yourself)
20. I *pray* God. (pray to God)
21. I *replied* him. (replied to him)
22. I *wrote* him to come. (wrote to him)
23. *Open* page 15. (Open at)
24. He resides in a *boarding*. (boarding house)
25. You have a house to *live*. (to live in)
26. You are *for possible* mishap. (for a possible)
27. Why do not you *come with* me? (come along)
28. The tree *grew tall* to be retained. (grew too tall)
29. Shekhar Kapoor directed *Elizabeth*. (the movie Elizabeth)
30. You can *count me* for support. (count on me)

(D) WORDS NOT PROPERLY RELATED

1. The storm burst just when the king reached the shore with great violence.
(The storm burst with great violence just when the king reached the shore).
2. I told him that he would fail as plainly as possible.
(I told him as plainly as was possible that he would fail).

3. Lost a cane by a gentleman with a carved head. (Lost by a gentleman a cane with a carved head).
4. He gave a stool to the servant that had four legs. (He gave the servant a stool that had four legs).
5. The death occurred yesterday afternoon at his residence of Mr Brown. (The death of Mr Brown occurred at his residence yesterday afternoon).
6. A motor car may be driven across the bridge which weighs less than two tons. (A motor car, which weighs less than two tonnes, may be driven across the bridge.)
7. My *family members.* (The members of my family)
8. Many *worth seeing* places. (Many places worth seeing)
9. *All round* the year. (All the year round)
10. I saw a dead horse while walking across the field. (While walking across the field, I saw a dead horse).
11. He shot himself dead after bidding his wife good-bye with a gun. (After bidding his wife good-bye, he shot himself dead with a gun).
12. He was murdered, sleeping in cold blood while he was. (He was murderd in cold blood while he was sleeping).
13. A large number of seats have been occupied by scholars that have no backs. (A large number of seats which have no backs, have been occupied by scholars).
14. Standing on the roof a helicopter flew over me. (While I was standing)
15. Playing in the field a ghost was seen. (While we were playing)
16. Walking in the morning a snake bit him. (While he was walking)
17. While plucking flowers a wasp stung him. (While he was plucking...)
18. Waiting for a taxi a lizard fell on his head. (As he was waiting for a taxi...)
19. Wanted a house by a government officer that has at least four bed rooms. (Wanted by a government officer a house that has at least four bed rooms.)
20. Wanted a piano by a gentleman with carved legs. (Wanted by a gentleman, a piano with carved legs).
21. He boarded the plane after coming out of the taxi that was waiting at the runway. (After coming out of the taxi, he boarded the plane that was waiting at the runway)
22. The chairman spoke at length about the company but the members of the board sipped tea. (The chairman spoke at length about the company while the members of the board sipped tea.)
23. Wanted a girl to be handled my wife who would wash utensils and clean the kitchen. (Wanted a girl to wash utensils and clean the kitchen, to be handled only by my wife)
24. Fearing attack, he pushed the sword by me. (Fear an attack by me, he pushed the sword.)
25. As the truck lost control, he hit the car. (When he lost control, the truck hit the car)

EXERCISE

1. (A) Cholera is/(B) raging in the/(C) town for/ (D) over a month./(E) No Error.
2. (A) He cannot pull / (B) on / (C) with / (D) his wife. / (E) No Error.
3. (A) The speech he / (B) gave at the function / (C) was very / (D) impressive. / (E) No Error.
4. (A) I and he / (B) was admitted in / (C) this / (D) college. / (E) No Error.
5. (A) Inspite of / (B) the instructions to / (C) the contrary,/ (D) he came down at once. / (E) No Error.
6. (A) Hardly / (B) had I / (C) reached the / (D) station than the train left. / (E) No Error.
7. (A) Not seldom / (B) he / (C) comes late to / (D) school. / (E) No Error.
8. (A) Not only has he / (B) passed the / (C) examination, but also, he / (D) has distinguished. / (E) No Error.

9. (A) From / (B) all the / (C) hill stations, which I know, Gulmarg is / (D) the most delightful. / (E) No Error.

10. (A) He takes ordinarily / (B) his / (C) dinner at / (D) 8.30 P.M. everyday. / (E) No Error.

11. (A) The members of / (B) his / (C) family are / (D) coming in this train./ (E) No Error.

12. (A) I fail to / (B) understand what / (C) have you / (D) been doing all these days. / (E) No Error.

13. (A) I have / (B) warned the / (C) class for / (D) making a noise. / (E) No Error.

14. (A) The / (B) reason of his being / (C) angry / (D) is because he is hungry. / (E) No Error.

15. (A) He is / (B) twenty / (C) years old, / (D) Isn't it. / (E) No Error.

16. (A) He / (B) has lost / (C) match from / (D) his rival. / (E) No Error.

17. (A) Not un-often / (B) I have / (C) asked / (D) him to speak the truth. / (E) No Error.

18. (A) He did not / (B) like me / (C) coming in / (D) that careless fashion. / (E) No Error.

19. (A) This year, the / (B) monsoon failed and this caused / (C) a terrible famine throughout / (D) the province. / (E) No Error.

20. (A) He advised / (B) everybody to / (C) look after their / (D) own interest. / (E) No Error.

21. (A) People do not / (B) save money like / (C) they / (D) used to. / (D) No Error.

22. (A) Neither of / (B) them were / (C) prepared for / (D) the emergency. / (E) No Error.

23. (A) I want you to pick up / (B) the box of / (C) eggs and carefully / (D) carry it. / (E) No Error.

24. (A) He has / (B) been / (C) more / (D) successful than me. / (E) No Error.

25. (A) If I were / (B) he, / (C) I should / (E) go. / (E) No Error.

26. (A) Who / (B) are / (C) you / (E) referring to? / (E) No Error.

27. (A) She is / (B) the / (C) tallest / (D) of the two girls./ (E) No Error.

28. (A) People should make it / (B) a rule never to / (C) interfere with / (D) the affairs of others. / (E) No Error.

29. (A) Nobody in / (B) their / (C) senses would / (D) have done that. / (E) No Error.

30. (A) He was / (B) one of the / (C) wisest man / (D) who have ever lived. / (E) No Error.

31. (A) I would / (B) not say that / (C) if / (D) I were him. / (E) No Error.

32. (A) As a / (B) dramatist, Shaw is / (C) superior / (D) than Galsworthy. / (E) No Error.

33. (A) Kalidas is / (B) greater than / (C) any / (D) Indian dramatist. / (E) No Error.

34. (A) Boys study because / (B) they / (C) may earn their / (D) livelihood. / (e) No Error.

35. (A) Supposing if / (B) you are / (C) arrested, what will / (D) you do? / (E) No Error.

36. (A) Though he / (B) was / (C) busy, but / (D) he talked to me. / (E) No Error.

37. (A) The / (B) sceneries of Himalayas are / (C) second to / (D) none. / (E) No Error.

38. (A) I do / (B) not / (C) know that when / (D) he will come./ (E) No Error.

39. (A) Many / (B) a / (C) sleepless / (D) nights I spend. / (E) No Error.

40. (A) He / (B) was / (C) hung / (D) for murder. / (E) No Error.

41. (A) He / (B) was / (C) settled in / (D) United States. / (E) No Error.

42. (A) Do not / (B) find / (C) fault in / (D) his work. / (D) No Error.

43. (A) He has / (B) been reading very / (C) hard since / (D) last fourteen days. / (E) No Error.

44. (A) Less / (B) books are / (C) needed in / (D) the library now. / (E) No Error.

45. (A) He has / (B) been / (C) accused / (D) for theft. / (E) No Error.

46. (A) I request / (B) your favour of granting / (C) me / (D) permission to apply elsewhere. / (D) No Error.

47. (A) His failure is / (B) to be / (C) attributed to / (D) nothing else than pride. / (E) No Error.

48. (A) I / (B) ask him that why / (C) he / (D) had injured me. / (E) No Error.

49. (A) The trophy has / (B) been / (C) competed / (d) by ten teams. / (E) No Error.

50. (A) His both hands / (B) have / (C) been / (D) injured. / (E) No Error.

51. (A) We do / (B) not have any / (C) more place / (D) in this compartment. / (E) No Error.

52. (A) Such a / (B) boy, who / (C) does not study, is not / (D) liked by his teachers. / (E) No Error.

53. (A) My sister is / (B) two years / (C) older than / (D) me./ (E) No Error.

54. (A) Unless he / (B) will work / (C) hard, he / (D) will not succeed. / (E) No Error.

55. (A) When two / (B) years old, / (C) my / (D) uncle married./ (E) No Error.

56. (A) The / (B) train is / (C) running in / (E) time. / (E) No Error.

57. (A) They / (B) are / (C) fast / (D) enemies. / (E) No Error.

58. (A) Good Night, / (B) Sir, Have / (C) a cup of / (E) tea. / (E) No Error.

EXPLANATORY ANSWERS

1. A : Replace *is* by *has been.*

2. B : Replace it by *well.*

3. A : It should be *which he gave.*

4. B : The verb should be plural as *were.*

5. D : Replace *came down* by *returned.*

6. D : Replace *than* by *when* because *hardly* is followed by *when.*

7. A : Delete *not* because *seldom* has negative sense.

8. D : It should be *distinguished himself.*

9. A : replace *From* by *Of.*

10. A : Put *ordinarily* in the beginning of the sentence.

11. D : It should be *by.*

12. C : An interrogative clause cannot follow a principal clause. So it should be *you have.*

13. C : Replace *for* by *against.*

14. D : Replace *because* by *that.*

15. D : The tag question should be *Isn't he?*

16. C : Replace *from* by *to.*

17. A : It should be *unoften*—double negatives should not be used.

18. B : A gerund is preceded by a possessive pronoun. So it should be *my.*

19. C : Replace *throughout* by *in.*

20. C : Replace *their* by *his* because it must agree with *everybody.*

21. B : Replace *like* by *as* because it is a comparison.

22. B : The verb should be singular, *i.e., was.*

23. C : Put *carefully* after *it.*

24. D : It should be 'I' because the complete sentence is than *I have been.*

25. C : Replace *should* by *would.*

26. A : Replace *Who* by *Whom.*

27. C : While comparing two, comparative degree should be used.

28. B : It should be *not to.*

29. B : Replace *their* by *his.*

30. C : It should be *men* because *one of the* means out of *many.*

31. D : Replace *him* by *he.*

32. D : *Superior* is followed by *to* and not *than.*

33. C : It should be *any other.*

34. A : Replace *because* by *so that.*

35. A : Delete *if* because *supposing* and if do not go together.

36. C : Replace *but* by *yet.*

37. B : It should *scenery of the Himalayas is.*

38. C : Delete *that* because it cannot be used with *when.*

39. D : *Many* a followed by a singular noun so it should be *night.*

40. C : It should be *hanged* because *hung* means suspended.

41. D : Artice *the* should be used with United States.

42. C : Replace *in* by *with.*

43. C : For period of time *for* should be used.

44. A : For countable things *Fewer* should be used.

45. D : Replace *for* by *of.*

46. B : The phrase should be *you to grant.*

47. D : *else* is followed by *but.*

48. B : Delete *that* because it cannot go with *why.*

49. D : It should be *competed for by.*

50. A : The phrase should be *Both of his hands.*

51. C : Use *room* for *place* because for sitting place – *room* should be used.

52. B : *Such* is followed by *as.*

53. C : It should be *elder to* because for brothers and sisters *'older'* should not be used.

54. B : Replace by *works* because we cannot use double *'will'* in one sentence.

55. A : The sentence means that the uncle was two years old. So it should be *When I was two years.*

56. C : "running to time" means *not late.*

57. C : For enemies the word *bitter* should be used.

58. A : We say *Good evening* when we meet a person.

Chapter 2

BASIC VOCABULARY

A-SYNONYMS

Synonyms are the words of the same grammatical class that have a similar but not an identical meaning. Some of them have been appended below:

1. Amusement—is that which occupies the vacant mind.

Diversion—is that which turns the thoughts aside into a new direction.

Recreation—is that which refreshes the mind after work.

1. Abandon, Desert, Forsake
2. Abbreviate, Abridge, Summarise, Sum Up, Shorten
3. Abdicate, Resign, Relinquish
4. Abhor, Detest, Hate
5. Abnormal, Unusal, Unnatural
6. Accomplish, Effect, Execute, Achieve
7. Accurate, Exact, Precise
8. Accuse, Charge, Blame, Condemn, Denounce
9. Adversity, Calamity, Misery, Tribulation
10. Alleviate, Mitigate, Relieve
11. Amaze, Astonish
12. Amusement, Entertainment, Diversion, Recreation
13. Anger, Vexation, Annoyance, Wrath, Resentment
14. Anger, Wrath, Indignation, Displeasure, Resentment
15. Announce, Proclaim, Declare
16. Answer, Reply
17. Apparently, Ostensibly, Clearly, Straight forwardly
18. Ask, Request, Beg, Beseech, Supplicate, Entreat, Implore, Solicit, Urge
19. Assent, Acquiesce
20. Astute, Shrewds, Perspicacious, Canny, Wily, Crafty
21. Attachment, Affection, Tenderness, Fondness, Love, Living
22. Autocrat, Despot, Tyrant, Monarch
23. Avaricious, Miserly, Stingy, Penurious
24. Aversion, Antipathy, Dislike, Hatred, Repugnance
25. Awkward, Clumsy
26. Barren, Unproductive, Sterile
27. Base, Low, Mean, Ignoble
28. Bear, Suffer, Endure
29. Beautiful, Handsome, Pretty, Lovely, Fine, Exquisite
30. Benevolent, Beneficent, Munificent, Liberal, Bountiful
31. Bias, Prepossession, Prejudice
32. Bold, Daring, Audacious
33. Bravery, Courage, Gallantry, Fortitude
34. Brief, Concise, Terse, Pity
35. Build, Erect, Construct

2. Character—is the sum of man's qualities.

Reputation—is what people think of the qualities of a man.

3. Command—a loftier term; an order by a superior in the armed forces.

Injunction—comes from some superior authority often as to general conduct.

Order—an order from some arranging or directing authority in respect of particular acts.

4. Confess—we confess to some one that we are wrong.

Admit—we admit to ourselves that we are mistaken.

5. Continuous—an action uninterrupted as long as it lasts.

Continual-that which is constantly renewed and recurring, though interrupted.

Perpetual-that which is continuous and lasting.
Eternal-lasting through all the past and also, into the future.

36. Calamity, Disaster, Catastrophe
37. Callous, Cruel, Hard
38. Calm, Tranquil, Quiet
39. Careless, Negligent, Unintentional, Inadvertent
40. Charming, Lovable, Amiable
41. Cheat, Imposter, Thug
42. Civil, Courteous, Affable, Polite
43. Civil, Polite, Courteous, Polished, Well-bred
44. Class, Category, Type
45. Coarse, Crude, Vulgar
46. Cold, Frigid, Indifferent, Passionless
47. Colossal, Gigantic, Huge, Anormous
48. Completely, Entirely, Scarcely, Hardly
49. Comprehend, Understand, Apprehend
50. Comprise, Include, Consist of
51. Compulsion, Restraint, Constraint
52. Confess, Acknowledge, Own, Avow, Admit
53. Confuse, Confound, Derange
54. Conscious, Aware
55. Consolation, Comfort, Solace
56. Contemplation, Meditation, Negotiation
57. Contentment, Satisfaction
58. Contrary, Opposite, Reverse
59. Cordial, Warm, Friendly, Hearty
60. Couple, Pair, Duo
61. Courteous, Polite, Civil, Affable
62. Criterion, Standard, Test, Rule
63. Cruel, Barbarous, Inhuman, Savage
64. Cruel, Savage, Brutal
65. Customary, Fashionable, Conventional

6. **Crime**—violation of a law of the Country
   Vice—violation of a moral law
   Sin—violation of a religious law
7. **Delightful**—applies the pleasures of the mind and to those of the senses except taste.
   Delicious—applies only to the pleasures of the senses.
8. **Discover**—we discover something that existed before but was unknown.
   Invent—we invent new combinations.
9. **Dismay**—a state of gloomy apprehension.
   Daunt—a man is daunted by a suden obstacle.
   Appal—a man is appalled by a sense of overwhilming

66. Dangerous, Perilous, Hazardous
67. Decay, Decline, Wither, Fade
68. Deceipt, Beguile, Fraud
69. Decorate, Adorn, Embelish, Ornament
70. Deference, Respect, Reverence, Veneration
71. Delude, Mislead
72. Demeanour, Behaviour
73. Depot, Autocrat, Tyrant
74. Despise, Condemn, Scorn, Disdain, Hate
75. Dexterity, Address, Skill, Cleverness
76. Distinguish, Discriminate, Differentiate, Discern
77. Divine, Godlike, Heavenly
78. Dreadful, Terrifying, Appaling

10. **Efficacious**—remedy.
    Efficient—physician.
    Effective—medicine effective in its working.
    Effectual—patient effectually cured.

79. Earnest, Serious, Solemn
80. Effect, Consequence, Result
81. Enemy, Antagonist, Adversary, Opponent
82. Envy, Jealousy, Vani
83. Error, Mistake, Blunder
84. Error, Mistake, Blunder, Fault
85. Eternal, Everlasting, Perpetual, Immortal
86. Expense, Cost

11. **Enormous**—is used of size or extent that is awkward or unpleasing.
    Vast—refers to space.
    Huge—refers to bulk; a stronger word than 'big.'
    Big—refers to bulk.
12. **Famous**—for one's achievements
    Illustrious—due to one's high rank
    Notable—for some special act
    Renowned—for one's achievements
    Noted—in either a good or a bad sense
    Notorious—is always used in a bad sense

87. Faith, Belief, Credulity
88. False, Imaginary, Spurious
89. Famous, Celebrated, Illustrious, Renowned
90. Fascinate, Enchant, Charm
91. Figure, Emblem, Symbol, Type
92. Force, Compel, Coerce, Oblige, Constrain
93. Fortitude, Courage, Valour, Bravery, Interpidity, Gallantry, Heroism

94. Frailty, Foible, Failing
95. Frank, Candid, Ingenuous
96. Fraud, Knavery
97. Funny, Jocose, Ludicrous, Ridiculous, Absurd

13. Give—a general term.
Confer—implies superior authority in the giver.
Grant—an answer to a petition.

14. Grave—because of important considerations; serious; opposed to levity.
Sober—calm and moderate in actions, behaviour and mannerisms; opposed to flightiness.
Solemn—because of something peculiar and rare; often with the idea of religious awe.

15. General—relating to a genus or whole class, opposed to special.
Universal—includes every particular part.

16. Glad—sense of pleasure.
Delighted—expresses a stronger sense of pleasure, than glad.
Gratified—implies that we satisfy the desires or inclinations of other person.
Merry—we show our actions or bearing when we are merry.

17. Habit—internal principle.
Custom—external action, a habit of devotion leads to the custom of praying.

18. Idle—opposed to busy, dislikes doing work.
Lazy—opposed to alert, dislikes taking trouble.
Negligent—opposed to diligent; dislikes taking trouble.

19. Import—is the actual significance of words as they are in a sentence.
Sense—'sense' is the possible significance that the words bear in a sentence.
Meaning—'meaning' is the significance intended by the writer.

20. Leave—a general term; we leave persons or things with the intention of returning.
Quit—we quit things, jobs, countries, homes and never return.
Forsake—we forsake or desert persons.
Desert—to leave due to fault in the person who does so.
Relinquish—to leave things with regret.
Renounce—to leave in a formal way in public.
Abandon—we abandon things hopelessly.

21. Liberty—implies previous constraint.
Freedom—absence of constraint at the present movement.

22. Liberal—allowing freedom of movements, actions and thoughts; an absence of servile niggardliness.
Generous—nobleness of feeling, placing others before oneself.
Charitable—points to the spirit of love or kindness in which, an action is done.

23. Lie—intentional of truth; more offensive than falsehood.
Falsehood—less offensive than lie.
Untruth—more softened than falsehood.
Deception—Deliberately created falsehood that appears to be sight and moral.
Fiction—merely something invented or imagined.

24. Nearly—is applied to questions of quantity, time and space.
Almost—is applied to the degree of severity or the limit.

25. Observe—is a general or a continuous act; we observe a person's demeanour.
Remark—is a special or single act; we remark peculiarities.
Notice—is to observe in a cursory way.

26. Part—a segment of a house, building, contract, business, family, society; used in general parlance.
Portion—is a part set aside for a special purpose.

27. Passive—means doing nothing.
Patient—refers to the mental condition.

28. Permit—to give a decided acquiescence.
Allow—to abstain from refusal.
Suffer—not to oppose a thing, though our feelings may be against it.

29. Pity—often implies an approach to contempt.
Compassion—has more tenderness than pity.
Sympathy—implies more of fellow-feeling; having an empathetic attitude towards someone in distress.

30. Praise—a person for what he does (for his actions); it also refers to the of feelings and the sentiments.

Admire—a person for what he is (for his natural qualities); it refers to the feelings rather than the expressions of feelings.

Extol—praise or admire vehemently.

Commend—a person for what he does.

Eulogise—praise or admire in a set discourse of poetry or prose.

31. Pride—implies to claim to respect or attention too highly viewing equals as inferiors and superiors as equals.

Vanity—an excessive desire for recognition, approbation and applause for qualities we possess or do not possess.

Haughtiness—develops from pride, applies to manners and development only.

Arrogance—is in a person without any deference; considering himself infallible.

Self-conceit—a very high opinion of oneself.

32. Religious—scrupulous in one's conduct towards God.

Pious—implies a reverence for what is good and desire to do good.

Godly—means endeavouring to be like God.

Devout—devoted to the worship and service of God.

Righteous—means upright and honest in one's dealings.

33. Safety—a well-grounded security.

Security—An absence of all fears or anxieties.

34. Secret—not known; not shared with people at large; normally used for thoughts, concepts or information.

Hidden—beyond vision or knowledge; normally used for objects and tangible items.

Concealed—hidden, withdrawn or removed from observation; refusing to reveal or divulge.

Covert—not openly expressed; concealed; secretive.

98. Gentle, Tender, Kind, Soft
99. Genuine, Authentic
100. Genuine, Authentic
101. Gift, Present, Donation
102. Gloomy, Dark, Sombre
103. Graceful, Elegant, Thankful
104. Guard, Keep, Preserve
105. Hamper, Hinder, Impede
106. Help, Aid, Assistance
107. Hidden, Secret, Covert, Tacit
108. Idle, Lazy, Indolent, Slothful
109. Illusion, Delusion
110. Imaginary, Fancied, Utopian
111. Impalacable, Unrelenting, Inexorable
112. Impracticable, Impossible, Utopian
113. Increase, Enlarge, Augment, Perpetuate
114. Inevitable, Unavoidable
115. Insolent, Impudent, Impertinent, Shameless
116. Intensify, Heighten, Aggravate
117. Irresolute, Undecided, Wavering, Vacillating
118. Joy, Felicity, Happiness, Bliss
119. Joyful, Glad, Pleased, Delighted, Exhilarated
120. Judicious, Discreet, Prudent
121. Laborious, Assiduous, Industrious, Hard working
122. Lawless, Unlawful, Illegal
123. Lenient, Mild, Forbearing
124. Lethargy, Sluggishness
125. Linger, Later, Stay, Prolong
126. Lively, Bright, Brisk
127. Mad, Insane, Imbecile
128. Magnificent, Grand, Splendid
129. Misfortune, Adversity, Misery, Crisis
130. Misfortune, Calamity, Disaster
131. Modest, Diffident, Bashful, Shy, Demure, Reserved
132. Obscene, Indecent, Filthy, Vulgar
133. Obtuse, Dull, Stupid
134. Obvious, Clear, Evident
135. Occurrence, Event, Circumstance
136. Only, Solely, Alone, Merely, Simply
137. Opportunity, Occasion, Juncture
138. Pain, Grief, Sorrow, Agony, Anguish
139. Pardon, Forgive
140. Pardon, Forgive, Excuse, Exculpate
141. Patience, Fortitude, Resignation
142. Perpendicular, Vertical, Erect, Towering, Standing
143. Person, Individual Creature, Being
144. Power, Strength, Force, Authority
145. Premature, Nascent, Novice, Beginner
146. Privacy, Retirement, Solitude, Loneliness, Desolation
147. Prohibit, Forbid
148. Prompt, Incite, Instigate, Provoke
149. Queer, Odd, Quaint, Singular

150. Recover, Regain, Retrieve
151. Regret, Lament, Deplore
152. Remember, Recollect
153. Reproof, Reprimand, Censure, Remonstrate, Reproach
154. Reserved, Reticent, Indolent, Withdrawn
155. Residue, Remainder, Remnant
156. Respect, Esteem, Prestige, Reverance
157. Respite, Reprieve, Solace, Comfort
158. Return, Restore, Surrender
159. Revenge, Vengeance
160. Rigid, Stiff, Unyielding
161. Rise, Ascend, Mount, Soar
162. Rival, Competitor
163. Rude, Impertinent, Insolent, Impudent
164. Savage, Barbarian, Cruel
165. Scarce, Rare
166. See, Look, Behold, Discern, Perceive
167. Separate, Part, Divide, Bifurcate
168. Severe, Harsh, Rigorous, Stern, Austere, Strict
169. Shame, Disgrace, Dishonour
170. Sincere, Frank, Candid
171. Size, Bulk, Volume
172. Slander, Calumny, Detraction, Defamation
173. Sly, Cunning, Crafty, Deceitful
174. Sorrow, Distress, Affliction
175. Store, Collect, Accumulate
176. Sublime, Elevated, Exalted
177. Suffering, Pain, Agony, Anguish
178. Sufficient, Adequate, Enough
179. Suitable, Apposite, Appropriate, Befitting
180. Superfluous, Needless, Unnecessary
181. Supernatural, Unnatural, Non-natural, Preternatural
182. Synonymous, Equivalent, Identical
183. Teach, Instruct, Inform, Educate
184. Tell, Say, Relate, Recount, Describe
185. Timidity, Shyness, Basefulness, Diffidence
186. True, Authentic
187. Truism, Platitude, Commonplace, Cabal
188. Truth, Veracity, Fact
189. Useful, Advantageous, Expedient
190. Vacant, Empty, Void, Hiatus, Space
191. Vain, Useless, Fruitless, Ineffectual
192. Variance, Variety, Variation
193. Vulgarism, Vulgarity, Obscenity, Lewdness
194. Wisdom, Learning, Acquaintance, Knowledge
195. Wit, Humour
196. Wretched, Miserable, Unfortunate
197. Zeal, Passion
198. Zenith, Top, Summit, Peak

35. **Sensuous**—addressing the senses, less objectionable form of sensual.
Sensitive—quick to respond impressions, decisions, actions.
Sensible—capable of responding to impressions.
Sentiment—having the faculty of feeling.
Sentimental—having an excess of sentiments.
Sensual—generally means voluptuous; lewd.

36. **Silly**—deficiency of intellect; implies contempt.
Foolish—an abuse of intellect; implies blame.
Dull—slown in understanding.
Stupid—expresses a cloudy perception of everything.
Weak—some moral deficiency.
Simple—normal; no crafty attitudes or appe-rances; plain; sans any decorations or hype.
Absurd—applies to an action; implies something laughable.

37. **Shun**—a person or vices; to give up.
Avoid—a person or a thing or an action.
Elude—to avoid or escape by speed, trick or cleverness; to remain out of one's reach.

38. **Stop**—to arrest motion.
Stay—to remain where the motion is arrested.

39. **Strict**—is used for one who likes to keep close to rules and regulations.
Severe—one who keeps so close to them as to punish the slightest infringement.

40. **Sublime**—strongest and highest of the following words means the loftiest style of excellence.
Magnificent—applied to anything on a large and grand scale.
Splendid—is less stronger in its significance than magnificent; applies to abstract qualities; something brilliant.
Grand—used for something in a great or lofty style.
Superb—nearly the same as magnificent; the most impressive or splendid or exalted kind.

41. **Sympathy**—felt for our equals when they are

in distress.

Compassion—for inferiors with an effort to relieve them.

Pity—does not imply any sense of connection with the object pitied.

Fellow-feeling—refers to the joyful as well as to sad circumstances.

42. Teach—teaching is a branch of knowledge.

Instruct—instruction applies to theory; to brief about an operation or an act.

Inform—a matter of fact made known.

Educate—includes the harmoniosis; drawing out of all the faculties of the person being educated.

43. Temporal—relative to time; opposed to eternity.

Temporary—lasting only for a time.

44. Timid—applies to a person's state of mind or to his disposition.

Timorous—applies only to a person's disposition.

Cowardly—is used alike of character or conduct.

Dastardly—is used alike of character or conduct; it implies to meanness.

45. Transient—for short duration; temporary and varying in degree.

Transitory—having the nature of transient, transitory life.

Fleeting—is actually passing away, fleeting hours.

46. Trifling—a matter of small or little importance; no contempt.

Trivial—small matter often exaggerated; implies contempt.

47. Understand—to follow things without little or no difficulty.

Comprehend—refers to things that are difficult to follow.

48. Utility—of an invention or a discovery.

Usefulness—of the article discovered or invented.

49. Weightly—reasons; arguments.

Heavy—cares; discourses.

50. Wisdom—means ready and accurate perception of analogies.

Prudence—a lower kind of 'wisdom.'

51. Wonder—at what is extraordinary loftly, great or stricking.

Surprise—at what is unexpected.

Strange—refers to something that is uncommon or odd.

B. ANTONYMS

Pairs of words having opposite or contrary meanings are called *antonyms*.

1. Abbreviate-expand
2. Ability-disability, incompetence
3. Absurd-sane, rational
4. Abundance-want
5. Accept-reject, refuse
6. Accord-discord, disagreement
7. Accumulate-scatter, fritter
8. Accustomed-unusual
9. Acquisition-loss
10. Acquit-dislike
11. Active-inert
12. Admit-reject
13. Adopt-reject
14. Advance-retreat
15. Adversity-prosperity
16. Affectation-naturalness
17. Affinity-aversion
18. Alert-careless, absent-minded
19. Amiability-petulance
20. Ample-scanty, meagre
21. Analysis-synthesis
22. Ancient-modern
23. Antipathy-sympathy
24. Appreciate-depreciate
25. Approach-repel
26. Arrival-departure
27. Arrogant-Humble
28. Artificial-natural
29. Ascent-descent
30. Assemble-disperse
31. Assist-harass
32. Assured-doubtful

33. Attack-repel
34. Attract-repel
35. Authentic-spurious
36. Awkward-graceful, dexterous
37. Barbarous-civilised
38. Barren-fertile
39. Base-noble, virtuous
40. Beautiful-ugly
41. Beautify-disfigure
42. Belief-disbelief
43. Beneficial-injurious
44. Benevolent-cruel, callous
45. Bliss-misery
46. Blustering-gentle, quite
47. Boisterous-quiet, calm
48. Bold-timid, cowardly
49. Borrow-lend
50. Bravery-cowardice
51. Brutal-humane, kindly
52. Brutality-humanity
53. Butter-fingured-tenacious
54. Callous-soft, tender
55. Care-neglect
56. Cautious-reckless
57. Celebrated-obscure
58. Censure-praise
59. Certain-uncertain
60. Chaste-impure, unchaste
61. Cheap-dear
62. Cheerful-gloomy, depressed
63. Cheerfulness-dejection
64. Choose-reject
65. Coarse-fine
66. Collect-disperse
67. Combatant-non-combatant
68. Comic-tragic, serious
69. Compare-contrast
70. Compassionate-merciless
71. Competent-incompetent
72. Complex-simple
73. Complicate-simplify
74. Compress-expand
75. Conceal reveal
76. Conceited-modest, unassuming
77. Concord-discord
78. Condemn-praise
79. Condense-lengthen, expand
80. Confess-deny
81. Confidence-diffidence, distrust, doubt
82. Consolidate-weaken
83. Conspicuous-inconspicuous
84. Continue-discontinue
85. Contract-expand
86. Converge-diverge
87. Cordial-cold, frigid
88. Costly-cheap
89. Courageous-timorous
90. Create-destroy
91. Credit-discredit, debit
92. Crude-refined
93. Cruel-kind, gentle
94. Danger-safety
95. Darkness-light
96. Decrease-uncrease
97. Deep-shallow
98. Defame-praise, laud
99. Deficit-surplus
100. Definite-indefinite, vague
101. Delay-haste
102. Deligent-lazy
103. Delight-displeasure, sorrow
104. Demote-promote
105. Dense-sparse
106. Descend-ascend
107. Despair-hope
108. Destruction-construction
109. Diffident-confident
110. Diminish-increase
111. Discourage-encourage
112. Distant-near
113. Distress-comfort
114. Dwarf-giant
115. Early-late
116. Earthly-heavenly, celestial
117. Economy-extravagance
118. Elegance-ugliness
119. Elenate-depress
120. Eligible-ineligible
121. Emancipate-enslave
122. Energetic-weak
123. Enmity-friendship
124. Enormous-small

125. Enrich-impoverish
126. Enthusiasm-indifference
127. Entrance-exit
128. Equality-inequality
129. Equitable-unjust
130. Evade-face
131. Exceptional-ordinary
132. Exonerate-implicate
133. Expedient-unexpedient
134. Expeditious-dialatory
135. Experience-inexperience
136. Explicit-implicit
137. Exquisite-detestable
138. Exterior-interior
139. External-internal
140. Extraordinary-ordinary
141. Extravagant-Economical
142. Exult-lament
143. Fabulous-actual, real
144. Fact-fiction
145. Failure-success
146. Fair-foul
147. False-true
148. Familiar-strange
149. Famous-obscure, unknown, notorious
150. Fanciful-practical, pragmatic
151. Fatigue-refresh
152. Ferocious-mild, gentle
153. Fickle-constant, confident
154. Fictitious-true, genuine
155. Fidgety-placid, self-possessed
156. Fine-coarse, rough
157. Flexible-stiff, rigid
158. Folly-wisdom
159. Foreign-native
160. Freedom-slavery
161. Fresh-stale
162. Futility-utility
163. Gaiety-mourning, melancholy
164. Gain-loss, profit
165. General-particular
166. Generous-mean, avaricious
167. Generosity-stinginess
168. Genuine-false, spurious
169. Gloomy-gay, vivacious
170. Good-bad, wicked
171. Growth-decline, retardation
172. Guilty-innocent
173. Happiness-sorrow, sadness
174. Hard-soft, polite
175. Haughty-humble, suave
176. Healthy-diseased
177. Heavy-light
178. Help-hinder, obstruct
179. Homogeneous-heterogenous
180. Honest-dishonest
181. Honour-dishonour, shame
182. Hope-despair
183. Hospitable-inhospitable
184. Humane-cruel
185. Humble-proud
186. Humility-arrogance
187. Hypocrisy-sincerity
188. Illuminate-darken
189. Imbecile-sane
190. Immaculate-soiled, spotted
191. Impede-expedite
192. Impolite-rude
193. Import-export
194. Include-exclude
195. Increase-decrease
196. Indolent-active, energetic
197. Induce-dissuade
198. Industrious-lazy
199. Inferior-superior
200. Inhale-exhale
201. Initial-final
202. Insert-extract
203. Insufficiently-plentitude
204. Intelligible-unintelligible
205. Interest-boredom
206. Interested-disinterested
207. Interesting-uninteresting
208. Invariable-fluctuating
209. Joint-separate
210. Joyful-sad, depressed
211. Joy-sadness, sorrow
212. Junior-senior
213. Justice-injustice
214. Keen-indifferent
215. Knowledge-ignorance
216. Lack-plenty

217. Lanquid-energetic, vigorous
218. Legal-illegal
219. Legible-Illegible
220. Lentence-severity
221. Lessen-extend, enlarge
222. Liberty-slavery
223. Liquid-solid
224. Logical-irrational
225. Long-short
226. Loose-tight
227. Loyal-treacherous, disloyal
228. Luscious-unpalatable, insipid
229. Mad-sane
230. Magnify-reduce
231. Major-minor
232. Malice-goodwill
233. Material-spiritual
234. Meagre-plentiful
235. Meek-ungovernable
236. Miraculous-common place, ordinary
237. Miserly-generous
238. Moderation-fanaticism
239. Moral-immoral
240. Morbid-healthy
241. Motion-rest
242. Native-foreign
243. Natural-artificial
244. Neat-untidy
245. Noble-base, ignoble
246. Normal-abnormal
247. Notorious-reputable
248. Obligation-claim
249. Obscure-clarify
250. Obstinate-yielding
251. Offensive-pleasing, defensive
252. Ominous-auspicious
253. Optimism-pessimism
254. Optional-compulsory
255. Ordinary-uncommon, rare
256. Outward-inward
257. Parsimony-prodigality
258. Part (noun)-whole
259. Part (verb)-join
260. Partial-fair, impartial
261. Particular-general
262. Passion-coolness
263. Pathetic-joyous, happy, exuberant
264. Peace-war, confrontable, tussle, battle
265. Permanent-temporary, momentary, fleeting
266. Permit-prohibit
267. Persist-relinquish
268. Persuade-dissuade
269. Petulance-amiability
270. Physical-mental, psychological
271. Please-displease
272. Pleasure-pain
273. Plenteous-unsufficient
274. Plentiful-scarce
275. Plenty-scarcity
276. Poor-rich, wealthy
277. Pompous-modest
278. Practicable-Impracticable
279. Praise-condemn, defame
280. Precious-cheap, worthless
281. Preliminary-final
282. Premium-discount
283. Pride-humility
284. Profit-loss
285. Progressive-retrogade
286. Prospect-retrospect
287. Prosperity-adversity
288. Prudent-imprudent, reckless
289. Pursue-avoid
290. Quarrelsome-peaceful, friendly
291. Quick-slow, tardy
292. Raise-lower
293. Rapid-slow, tardy
294. Rare-common, ordinary
295. Rash-steady, cautious
296. Real-false
297. Rear-front
298. Recklessness-prudence, wisdom
299. Recover-relapse
300. Rectify-falsify
301. Refinement-coarseness
302. Rejoice-lament, grieve
303. Relevant-irrelevant
304. Relieve-aggravate
305. Religious-secular, irreligious
306. Relish-dislike, shun
307. Remote-near
308. Repress-encourage

309. Repulsive-attractive
310. Resolute-vacillating
311. Resolve-hesitate
312. Restless-calm
313. Restone-appropriate
314. Reveal-hide
315. Rigid-flexible
316. Romantic-prosaic, classical
317. Rough-smooth
318. Ruthless-humane, polite, kind
319. Sacred-profane, unholy
320. Safety-danger, peril
321. Sane-insane, irrational
322. Satisfaction-dissatifaction
323. Savage-civilised
324. Scanty-plentiful
325. Secret-open, public
326. Security-peril, risk
327. Security-peril, risk
328. Sedulousness-indolence
329. Sensible-insensible, senseless
330. Sensitive-insensitive
331. Separate-joint
332. Serious-trifling, light
333. Service-disservice
334. Severe-mild
335. Shallow-deep
336. Sharp-blunt
337. Shy-bold, impudent
338. Simple-intricate, complex
339. Sin-virtue
340. Slow-prompt
341. Smart-dull, slow
342. Smile-frown
343. Sober-excited
344. Soft-hard, stubborn
345. Solidity-liquefy
346. Special-ordinary
347. Speedy-slow
348. Stationary-moving
349. Steadfast-wavering, fickle
350. Straight-crooked
351. Sublime-ridiculous
352. Summit-base
353. Surplus-deficit
354. Sweet-bitter, sour
355. Swift-slow
356. Synonym-antonym
357. Tainted-pure
358. Tame-wild
359. Tedious-lively
360. Temperate-intemperate
361. Tender-hard, strong
362. Thin-fat, stout
363. Thrifty-extravagant
364. Thrive-decline
365. Tolerance-intolerance, bigotry
366. Tractable-refractory
367. Tranquil-agitated
368. Transient-lasting, durable, stable
369. Transparent-opaque
370. Triumph-fail
371. Truth-falsehood
372. Uniform-variable
373. Union-disunion, discord, split
374. Vague-definite
375. Vain-modest, effective
376. Variety-uniformity
377. Venturesome-timid
378. Vigilant-careless, heedless
379. Vindictive-forgiving
380. Violent-gentle
381. Violent-gentle
382. Visible-invisible
383. Vital-immaterial
384. Vivacious-languid
385. Voluntary-compulsory
386. Voluntary-compulsory
387. Volunteer-desert
388. Vulgar-refined
389. Warmth-coolness
390. Wave-wax
391. Wearisome-refreshing
392. Winsome-unprepossessing
393. Woeful-cheerful
394. Worry-comfort
395. Worthless-priceless
396. Yield-resist
397. Youth-age
398. Zeal-indifference
399. Zenith-nadir
400. Zest-dislike

Chapter 3

Idioms and Phrases in Common Usage

1. **To bear in mind:** (to remember) While reading a book we should *bear in mind* the special conditions under which, its author has lived.
2. **To make the best of a bad bargain:** (to bear hardships as best as one can) It is true that your employer is a hard taskmaster but you must *make the best of a bad bargain.*
3. **Into the bargain:** (in addition) He married a rich widow's daughter and got her property *into the bargain.*
4. **Blue blood:** (noble birth) King Edward could not marry Miss Simpson because she had no *blue blood* in her veins.
5. **Bad blood:** (enmity or angry feeling) The recent quarrel has created *bad blood* between the two friends.
6. **To the backbone:** (thoroughly) He is a patriot *to the backbone.*
7. **To have an axe to grind:** (to have a selfish motive) He flatters his boss for he has *an exe to grind.*
8. **An apple of discord:** (bone of contention or cause of dispute) Kashmir is the *apple of discord* between India and Pakistan.
9. **All and sundry:** (everyone without distinction) *All and sundry* cannot be invited to this function because it is a special occasion.
10. **To give oneself airs:** (to be vain and haughty) All people dislike a man who *gives himself airs.*
11. **To be all agog:** (eager and excited) Upon returning home after five years, he found his family *all agog.*
12. **To come of age:** (to become major) He will manage all his affairs when he *comes of age.*
13. **To be above board:** (fair and open) He is honest and so, all his dealings are *above board.*
14. **A black sheep:** (a disloyal person) The robber said that there was *a black sheep* in the gang who had betrayed by giving its secrets to the police.
15. **Bag and baggage:** (with all one's belongings) When he was transferred, he left Agra with his *bag and baggage.*
16. **A bird of passage:** (a temporary resident) My friend cannot settle in this city because he is *a bird of passage.*
17. **Birds of the same feather:** (persons of the same character) One thief likes to accompany another for the *birds of the same feather* flock together.
18. **To kill two birds with one stone:** (to accomplish two purposes at once) He *killed two birds with one stone* for he visited Kanpur and enjoyed the cricket match as well.
19. **To bid fair:** (to give a promise of) This intelligent student *bid fair* to top the list this year in the university examinations.
20. **To be on the horns of a dilemma:** (to face a perplexing choice between two unpleasant things) My poor friend *is on the horns of a dilemma* for if he goes abroad, he will break his wife's heart and if does not, he will mar his future.
21. **Between the devil and the deep sea:** (between two equally great evils when there is no escape either way) He is *between the devil and*

the deep sea for he must either resign or face an enquiry of the charges against him of embezzlement.

22. **Between scylla and charybdis:** (between two dangers in which, if a man avoids the one, he falls into the other) If he escapes *the scylla* of sensuality, he will run into the *charybdis* of drinking.
23. **To get the better of:** (to overcome) The fight seemed equal for a while but he *got the better of* his enemy in the end.
24. **To hit below the belt:** (to take unfair advantage) While referring to his rival's private life he *hit below the belt* beg the quest and thus played foul to him.
25. **To talk big:** (to boast) My friend always *talks big.*
26. **To have a bee in one's bonnet:** (to be eccentric) The old man seems *to have a bee in his bonnet* for he changes his desire so many times.
27. **To beat about the bush:** (to talk irrelevantly) A good speaker does not *beat about the bush* when he speaks in a public meeting.
28. **To take up the cudgels:** (to hold a brief)- A good man does not *take up the cudgels* on behalf of a wrong-doer nor does he hold a brief for a criminal.
29. **As the crow flies:** (in a straight line) The plane, which took Pt. Nehru to Delhi, flew *as the crow flies.*
30. **To shed crocodile tears:** (hypocritical or false grief) She hated the old miser and so she *shed crocodile tears* at his death.
31. **A cock and bull story:** (a false story or explanation) When he is late, he explains his irregularities with *a cock and bull story.*
32. **To cut one's coat according to one's cloth:** (to live within one's means)- With a small salary, I cannot visit the cinema every week for I have *to cut my coat according to my cloth.*
33. **To put the cart before the horse:** (to be preposterous or foolish by putting before what should be put behind)- If you teach them the geography of the world before the geography of India, you will *put the cart before the horse.*
34. **To take the bull by its horns:** (to attack a danger boldly) Next morning he took courage to face his powerful enemy in the office and *took the bull by the horns.*
35. **To nip in the bud:** (to suppress or end at an early stage) This kind of indiscipline among students should be *nipped in the bud.*
36. **To make a clean breast of:** (to make complete confession) The thief *made a clean breast of* his guilt when the policeman beat him.
37. **To be born with a silver spoon in one's mouth:** (to be born rich) Pt. Nehru was born with *a silver spoon in his mouth.*
38. **Bread and butter:** (means of livelihood) It is a question of *bread and butter,* so he should not quarrel with his boss.
39. **In the good books of:** (to enjoy the favour of) He is *in the good books of* his principal and so, he hopes to get the appointment.
40. **Blue-stocking:** (a literary women) India has produced many *a blue-stocking* like Sarojini Naidu.
41. **Blood is thicker than water:** (one cannot ignore family ties) *Blood is thicker than water* and so, he has appointed his brother as the incharge of this office.
42. **To beat black and blue:** (to thrash mercilessly) The police caught the thief and *beat him black and blue.*
43. **To throw down the gaunlet of glove:** (challenge) This wrestler has *thrown the gaunlet* to all the champions present in the arena.
44. **In full swing:** (something at its peak in activity) When I reached there, the fair was *in full swing.*
45. **To take time by the forelock:** (to make usage of the opportunity) Napolean *took time by the forelock* and began every job fifteen minutes earlier than its schedule.
46. **To follow suit:** (to do what the predecessor has done) When the chief guest began to take tea, we *followed suit.*

47. **By fits and starts:** (irregularly)- She is not an achiever because she works *by fits and starts.*
48. **A feather in one's cap:** (a thing of pride and distinction) That he has become a member of the executive council is another *feather in his cap.*
49. **A far cry:** (a long distance in time or space) It is *a far cry* from this city Newyork.
50. **To take exception to:** (to object to) This remark from you is a reflection on me, and so, I *take exception to it.*
51. **A white elephant:** (something costly to maintain) This foreign engineer in our iron and steel factory draws a fat salary and so, it is difficult for us to keep such *a white elephant* for a long time.
52. **To eat one's words:** (to whitdraw one's words) Being rash to pass a disgraceful remark, he had *to eat his words.*
53. **To set by the ears:** (to cause a quarrel) It is the old man's will, which has *set* all the family *by the ears.*
54. **Throw dust in one's eyes:** (to deceive) A man cannot *throw dust in my eyes* when I know the facts.
55. **Double-dealing** (deceiving) Being an honest man, he is incapable of *double-dealing.*
56. **To go to the wall:** (to fare badly) The new hands will *go to the wall* due to this retrenchment in our factory.
57. **A dog in the manger policy:** (preventing others from what is useless to oneself) In spite of this surity to loose in the forthcoming elections he follows *a dog in the manger policy* and does not give a chance to me.
58. **To carry favour with:** (to flatter for favour) This clever and worldly wise man does not fail *to carry favour with* any officer in the town.
59. **To eat the humble pie:** (to be humiliated) He wrote an apology and thus *ate the humble pie* for being rude to his uncle.
60. **To ride the high horse:** (to think big or to put on airs) Being the brother of a minister, he *rides the high horse.*
61. **To out-herod Herod:** (to make more noise and bluster than Herod or to exceed Herod in oppression) He *out-heroded Herod* in his verbal attack on his rival or, Hitler *out-heroded Herod* in his dealings with the Jews.
62. **Helter-skelter:** (in confusion or disorder) When they saw a headmaster they ran away *helter-skelter.*
63. **To take to one's heels:** (to run away) When the thief saw a policeman coming towards him he *took to his heels.*
64. **Over head and ears:** (overwhelmingly)- He is *over head and ears in debt.*
65. **To make hay while the sun shines:** (to take full advantage of an opportunity) This is a golden opportunity for you and so, you should *make hay while the sun shines.*
66. **To bury the hatchet:** (to stop quarrelling) He has *buried the hatchet* and has befriended his rival.
67. **To harp on the same string:** (to be always talking about the same thing) He bores me by *harping on the same string* continually.
68. **To die in harness:** (to die while doing one's duty or work) He is an industrious and hard-working man and hopes *to die in harness* only.
69. **Handwriting on the wall:** (the warning of the forthcoming disaster) That the Congress has lost many seats in the recent general elections, is *the handwriting on the wall,* which it cannot ignore easily.
70. **Hand in glove with:** (to be intimate and friendly) He is *hand in glove with* his neighbour these days.
71. **To split hairs:** (to advance hair-splitting arguments) I request you to state the main issue at once and not to waste my time in *splitting hairs.*
72. **To bring same grist to the mill:** (to be a source of some income) Every member of this family earns something and so, even the children *bring same grist to the mill.*
73. **To gird up the one's lions:** (to get ready far hard work) Let all of us *gird up our lions* to improve the lot of the poor people in the country.

74. To lead by the nose: (to make one do what someone else likes) Every person can *lead him by the nose* for he is a very simple man.

75. To hit the nail on the head: (to give the exact answer or solution) Without beating about the bush, you should *hit at the nail on the head.*

76. To move heaven and earth: (to do everything possible) He has *moved heaven and earth* for his reinstatement.

77. To mince matters: (to be soft-tongued) Without *mincing matters,* I told him that his son was weak in English.

78. To make a mountain of a mole-hill: (to magnify a trivial matter) This is a trivial matter and so, you should not *make a mountain of a mole-hill.*

79. To cry over spilt milk: (to regret in vain) When you are robbed of your money, you should not *cry over spilt milk.*

80. To be at loggerheads: (to quarrel) They are *at loggerheads* over the division of work in the library.

81. The loaves and fishes: (the material advantages) He is more than sixty years old but he sticks to his office for *the loaves and fishes.*

82. To leave in the lurch: (to leave in difficulty) My friends *left me in the lurch* when they cycled ahead without telling me the way to my house.

83. To laugh in one's sleeves: (to laugh secretly) This simple man does not know that his companions are *laughing in their sleeves* and are thus making a butt of him.

84. To strike while the iron is hot: (to act while an opportunity lasts) The present education minister is favourable to our teachers community and so, we should approach him for an increase in our dearness allowance. Indeed, we should *strike while the iron is hot.*

85. To have many irons in the fire: (to be busy with many things at the same time) He has *many irons in the fire* and so, he cannot call any moment of time his own.

86. Inns and outs: (all the details) I can give my judgement only when I know all the *inns and outs* of this matter.

87. To break the ice: (to begin conversation after silence) After a long silence, he *broke the ice* and began to persuade his angry friend to accompany him.

88. The rank and file: (common people) The revolt against the present ministry has not spread in the *rank and file* because it is still confined to the upper classes.

89. To call in question: (to dispute) It is not wise *to call* the authority of a *boss in question.*

90. To feel one's pulse: (to know one's feelings) Shastriji had *felt the pulse* of every citizen in India and he knew that the nation is behind him over the Kashmir issue.

91. Pros and cons: (points for and against) A man can judge this case only after he has examined its *pros and cons* carefully.

92. At a premium: (valued highly) Dishonesty is *at a premium* in this line of trade.

93. Pell mell: (in a confused or disorderly manner) When the class room caught fire, the student left it *pell mell.*

94. To cast pearls before swine: (waste advice or something valuable before those who cannot appreciate its value) By delivering a thrilling speech before the illiterate and ignorant people, he *cast pearls before swine.*

95. Pandora's box: (a source of many evils) Autocracy has proved to be a *Pandora's box.*

96. To palm off: (to pass off an inferior article as superior) He cannot buy woollen cloth from this shop-keeper because once, he has *palmed off* an ordinary rug for a genuine Dhariwal product.

97. To hold out an olive branch: (to try for peace) India has always *held out the olive branch* in her disputes with the neighbouring countries.

98. A fly in the ointment: (a defect marring the excellence) The poor relative seems to be *a fly in the ointment* in the company of rich people.

99. Out of sorts: (not feeling well) He is feeling *out of sorts* and so, he has taken leave today.

100. To pour oil on troubled waters: (to soothe or pacify) They do not stop quarrelling with each other even when I have made my best efforts *to pour oil on troubled waters.*

101. At odds: (in conflict) They are *at odds* because they seldom meet each other.

102. Null and void: (of no legal validity) This bond will be *null and void* after five years.

103. To smell a rat: (to know that something is wrong) When I saw the window open from a distance, I *smell a rat.*

104. At six and sevens: (in disorder) He was surprised to find everything in his drawing room *at sixes and sevens.*

105. To give the cold shoulder: (to treat in a cold manner) When I approached him for a favour, he *gave me the cold shoulder.*

106. To talk shop: (to talk one's own profession) He is a cloth-deeler but he seldom *talks shop* while going with me to the Ganges.

107. At sea: (to be perplexed) All the doors being closed, I am perfectly *at sea* to understand how the thief entered the room and took away my cash and clothes.

108. Scot-free: (unpunished) Three boys were punished but the real mischief-monger went *scot-free.*

109. A good samaritan: (a really kind and charitable person) He proved the poor begger's *good samaritan* by arranging for his medical treatment.

110. The salt of the earth: (the people, who preserve the society by the good influence of their character) Those men and women who live for their countrymen, are *the salt of the earth.*

111. To cross the Rubicon: (to take a fateful step) When he resigned, he *crossed the Rubicon* because he will no longer be reinstated.

112. A red letter day: (a happy and memorable day) Being the Republic day, the twenty-sixth January is *a red letter day* in the history of India.

113. Red tape: (long and tedious process through which, a file moves before a final order is passed) The scheme of cooperative societies is likely to be held up for a week due to *red tape.*

114. Red handed: (in the act) The thief was caught *red-handed* by the watchmen who found him inside the room.

115. To read between the lines: (to understand the hidden meaning) This is all right but *reading between the lines,* I find that it will not help us in the execution of our plan.

116. To rise from the ranks: (to rise to an eminent position from a very humble position) Napoleon *rose from the ranks* as he started as an ordinary soldier.

117. A wild goose chase: (a foolish and useless quest) If you visit the Himalayas to see the snow-man only, it will be a *wild goose chase* only.

118. To hold water: (to be put to test) The argument which you have given, will not *hold water.*

119. Of the first water: (of the finest quality or of diamond) Every word let out by his tongue is *of the first water.*

120. To throw cold water: (to discourage) This is a very good scheme but the old man is likely to *throw cold water* on it.

121. With a vengeance: (anything in the extreme) This lawlessness is a manifestation of the fact that newly-won freedom is freedom *with a vengeance.*

122. To blow one's own trumpt: (to boast or praise oneself) Nowadays, a man has *to blow his own trumpet* if he wants to achieve success in any walk of life.

123. To play truant: (to be absent without leave) He has *played truant* more than once and so, he is not in the good books of his teacher.

124. Touch and go: (a situation in which, a little thing may turn the balance) The fate of the present ministry hangs in the balance, so, it is but *a touch and go* affair.

125. With the tongue in the cheek: (insincerily or ironically) This man is a bad character; so, while praising honesty and truth, he talks *with the tongue in the cheek.*

126. On tenterhooks: (in agonised suspense) I request you to tell me about your decision and not to keep me *on tenterhooks.*

127. **A storm in a tea-cup:** (a noisy quarrel or insignificant disturbance over a trivial matter) There was *a storm in a tea-cup* when they failed to decide whether the amount of subscription should be raised or not.

128. **On the spur of the moment:** (on impulse or without deliberation) This witty man answers all questions *on the spur of the moment.*

129. **At stake:** (in danger) His reputation is at *stake* and so, he should fulfil his promise.

130. **To sow wild oats:** (to lead a wild reckless life in youth) He repents now in his old age for having *sown wild oats* in his youth.

131. **To end up in smoke:** (to fail badly, to come to nothing) He lacks practical wisdom and therefore, this scheme will *end up in smoke.*

132. **To set at nought:** (to defy) His boss has dismissed him for having *set* his authority *at nought.*

133. **Turn to account:** (make useful) He has *turned to account* every useful thing he got from me.

134. **With one accord:** (unanimously) All the students declared to go on a picnic *with one accord.*

135. **To play the game:** (to act honestly, to observe rules) A God-fearing man *plays the game* and does not deceive his friends.

136. **By hook or by crook:** (by fair means or by foul) He has made up his mind to become rich *by hook or by crook.*

137. **A maiden speech:** (the first speech in public) He has never spoken in public in the past but he has done very well in this *maiden speech.*

138. **A dark horse:** (little known of unexpected winner) By winning the race, it has proved to be *a dark horse* as it was not expected to do it at this age.

139. **A wet blanket:** (a person who checks conversation, damps enthusiasm) The entry of this strict teacher proved to be *a wet blanket* to the fun enjoyed by the students.

140. **Within an ace of:** (the smallest possible amount, hair's breath) It was *within an ace of* what he desired.

141. **Gone to his account:** (dead) I am sorry that this gentle creature has *gone to his account.*

142. **To give a wide berth:** (to keep at a distance or to avoid) We should *give a wide berth* to all bad people.

143. **A French leave:** (absence without leave) The teacher had to explain to the principal why he went on *a French leave.*

144. **Yeoman's service:** (hard and faithful work) As a supply minister, he has given the *yeoman's service* to the public and deserves all possible tribute for it.

145. **Out of the wood:** (out of a difficult situation) The shortage of food-grains still continue and so, we are not yet *out of the wood.*

146. **To keep the wolf from the door:** (to escape starvation) The poor workers cannot continue this strike for a long time for they have to *keep the wolf from the door.*

147. **At one's wit's end:** (not to know what to do) I am *at my wit's end* for I am unable to decide what to do with this mischievous boy.

148. **A turn-coat:** (a time server) He flatters the present chief minister as he did in the case of his predecessor becasuse he is *a turn-coat* and does not really belong to any party.

149. **A Utopian scheme:** (a scheme or plan too ideal to be realised) I don't think that this Land Gift Movement is to prove *a Utopian scheme* only.

150. **To feather one's nest:** (to secure money or comfort) Everyone of these selfish time-servers and turn-coats *feather their own nest* when they talk of giving service to other people.

151. **To pay lip service:** (not to be sincere in praise) I know that you are not really favouring me and so, I would request you not to *pay lip service* to me.

152. **Cat's paw:** (a person used as a tool by another) I cannot to be a *cat's paw* in his hand.

153. **To go against the grain:** (not tasteful or according to inclination) These days, many students opt for English even when it has *gone against their grain.*

154. **To burn one's boats:** (to leave no means to retreat or to take a final decision) While speaking on the Quit India Resolution, he said

that they had *burnt their boats* and so, there was no going back.

155. The heel of Achilles: (weak or vulnerable point) Every great man has *the heel of Achilles* in his personality if he is a human being.

156. The gift of the gab: (the power of speech) These days, a man cannot become a leader if he has not been favoured by nature with *the gift of the gab.*

157. At the eleventh hour: (at the last minute) He has approached me *at the eleventh hour* and so, I could not do much for him.

158. Kith and kin: (a near relative) He is his *kith and kin,* and so, he is bound to favour him.

159. In the wake: (after something) Flood brings cholera *in its wake* and so, all possible medical arrangements should be in advance.

160. Palmy days: (prosperous times) He is now a beggar but he still dreams of his *palmy days.*

161. At the outset: (in the very beginning) He has missed the catch *at the outset* but now, he is playing well.

162. To make amends for: (to compensate for damage, injury or insult) He has apologised *to make amends for* the insolent behaviour in the class.

163. To make short work of: (to dispose of speedily or end suddenly) The locusts have *made short work of* the rabi crop this year.

164. To hang fire: (to remain suspended or to be slow in going off) If this thing *hangs fire* now, it will never be completed (or the bomb is hanging fire and so, it is not to go off soon).

165. To go by the board: (to come to nothing) All his schemes to start a co-operative society in this village have *gone by the board.*

166. To chew the cud: (to meditate on some idea) He promised to give his judgement only after *chewing the cud* on the scheme.

167. To count the chickens before they are hatched: (to anticipate gains) You have started this business only yesterday, and you have begun *to count the chickens before they are hatched.*

168. To bear the burnt of: (to endure the main force, strain or shock of) It was the *pipal* tree that had to *bear the burnt of* the lightning on Monday but the neighbouring trees escaped narrowly.

169. To beggar description: (beyond description) The beauty of the Taj, which is a great wonder of the world is *beggars description.*

170. To call a spade a spade: (to be plain and blunt in speech) If you want me to speak of this matter, I will *call* a *spade a spade* and will not mince matters.

171. To make the flesh creep: (to scare with terror) This murder will *make any man's flesh creep.*

172. To have a finger in every pie: (to meddle in every affair) He is so ambitious that he *has a finger in every pie.*

173. Wool gathering: (absent-minded) He was *wool gathering* when the teacher introduced this difficult lesson.

174. Will-o-the-wisp: (anything that deludes) Man's life is a struggle in which, happiness is like the *will-o-the-wisp*, it deludes him for ever.

175. To flog a dead horse: (to revive a dead issue) If you raise questions regarding the integration of Kashmir with India, you will only *flog a dead horse.*

176. By leaps and bounds: (quickly) The population of India is increasing *by leaps and bounds.*

177. With open arms: (warmly, affectionately) My friend welcomed me *with open arms* when I visited his place last year.

178. To give the devil his due: (to admit the merits of a bad person also) He is wicked but intelligent man; so, you should *give the devil his due* by admitting this intellectual superiority.

179. The sword of Democles: (an ever present and imminent danger)The fear of examination hangs for ever over the students like a *sword of Democles.*

180. A sop to cerberus: (something to pacify a troublesome enemy) The mill owner offered him a good job as *sop to cerberus* because he created trouble among the workers.

181. A bolt from the blue: (sudden and sad

occurrence) The news of his uncle's death came to him as a *bolt from the blue.*

182. A sleeping partner: (one who invests money and shares in the profit but not in the management of a business) Ram is only *sleeping partner* of this firm and so, he seldom looks into these matters.

183. Hall mark: (stamp or mark of genuine excellence) Simplicity is always the *hall mark* of a saintly man like Gandhiji.

184. To wash dirty linen in public: (to discuss personal and private matters before strangers) When he was defeated, he began *to wash dirty linen in public* against his rival.

185. To take to task: (to require explanation) I will *take him task* for idling away five hours.

186. To stem the tide of: (to check) If you want to make India a great nation, you should first *stem the tide of* hunger and poverty.

187. To set the Thames on fire: (to try to do an impossible thing)- If you aim at reaching the Sun, you will try to set *the Thames on fire.*

188. To sail in the same boat with: (to be equally exposed to danger) I was satisfied to know that I had my neighbour *sailing with me in the same boat.*

189. In accordance with a: (in obedience to) *In accordance with* this order I have to stay here for a week.

190. Up to the mark: (up to the standard) He is working hard but he is still not *up to the mark* in this subject.

191. To wind up: (stop) Inspite of these heavy losses, he is not *to wind up* his business.

192. To tide over: (overcome) He has *tided over* all the difficulties on the way to his success.

193. To drive home: (make clear) I followed this point only when my friend *drove it home.*

194. A narrow escape: (a lucky or close escape) He had a *narrow escape* from death in the accident.

195. To draw upon: (take help from) He will *draw upon* all his resources to get out of the present crisis.

196. Out of place: (strange) A crow, in the company of swans looks quite *out of place.*

197. To bring to book: (to be tried in the count) If you commit this crime, you will *be brought to book* by the police.

198. In cold blood: (cruelly) The robbers committed the murder of a helpless traveller *in cold blood.*

199. The see eye to eye: (agree) I do not *see eye to eye* with my friend in the matter of co-education.

200. With a grain of salt: (with reservations) *With a grain of salt,* you have to believe his statemant.

201. To lose ground: (defeat, decrease) It is because of this case of forgery that my friend has begun to *lose ground* in his popularity.

202. Hard up: (scarcity) He has sustained a heavy loss in business recently and so, he is *hard up* for money.

203. To make both ends meet: (to live within one's income) It is with sad to note that he is now able *to make both ends meet.*

204. Point blank: (direct) He refused to accompany me and I did not like this *point-blank* refusal.

205. To rise to the occasion: (to prove worthy) When Bhama Shah saw Rana Pratap and his family facing many hardships in the forests of the Aravalli hills, he *rose to the occasion* and helped master with men and money.

206. With a view to: (for the purpose of) I have come to Kanpur *with a view to* meeting my friend Sant Kumar.

207. To back out: (left) He has *backed out* even when himself undertook this project for its completion.

208. The lion's share: (the biggest share) Those people, who shirk money should not demand *the lion's share* in the people incomes.

Chapter 4

USAGE OF PREPOSITIONS

Prepositions are generally placed in front of those words, which they control. They could also come after the words they govern, notably in questions and in relative and interrogative clauses.

Examples:

What can I cut the apple *with*?

This is the house he was telling me *about*?

Many verbs get strongly associated with certain prepositions in one of the following ways:

(A) With verb and prepositions keeping their basic meanings.

Examples:

Take the book *in* your hand and open it *at* page 49.

He is sitting *on* an armchair and looking *out of* the gate.

He spoke *about* his holidays.

(B) As a compound having an idiomatic meaning.

Examples:

She did not *take* to me at first. (Like)

She *took after* her father. (resembled)

Babita *set about* preparing dinner. (began to prepare)

The boat *made for* the bank. (went towards)

Prepositions indicate various relationships between words or phrases, the most usual being those of time, space (position, direction etc.), manner, agent and mental or emotional attitudes.

Examples:

The book is *on* the desk. (space, position or place)

The boy ran *toward* the house. (direction)

The man arrived *at* ten O'clock. (time)

He travels *by* train. (manner)

The book was written *by* him. (agent)

He spoke *about* his holidays. (mental associa-tion)

We can conceive of various space-relationships with the notions either of Rest or of Motion.

Rest

(i)	Rest near with contact	→ **At** →	Babita was *at* home.
(ii)	Rest near with-out contact	→ **By** →	I stood *by* him.
	Rest near with-out contact	→ **with** →	I sat *with* her.
(iii)	Rest on the surface	→ **On** →	The house is *on* the hill.
(iv)	Rest in the interior	→ **In** →	He rides *in* a carriage.

Motion

(i)	Motion to-wards, result-ing in contact	→ **To** →	Babita gone *to* school.
(ii)	Motion to-wards, before	→ **For** →	She sailed *for* Japan it results in contact.
(iii)	Motion away from the upper surface	→ {**Of** / **Off**} →	The balloon passed within 10 metres *of* the ground, the jum-ped *off* the chair
(iv)	Motion away from exterior	→ **From** →	He has come *from* the school.
(v)	Motion along the interior	→ **Through** →	He went *through* the garden.
(vi)	Motion to a higher point	→ **Up** →	He ran *up* the ladder.

Prepositions of Place or Position

A list of some prepositions that indicate relation-ships of place or position has been appended below:

1. At Babita is *at* the store.

2.	**To**	Babita went *to* school.
	From	Babita came *from* school.
3.	**In**	She is sitting *in* an arm chair.
	On	She is sitting *on* the sofa.
4.	**By**	The matches are over there *by* the Cigarettes.
	Beside	The book is *beside* the desk.
	Near	Babita is sitting *near* the window.
	Against	Do not lean *against* the wall.
5.	**Over**	The kite is *over* our head.
	Under	The book is *under* the desk.
	Beneath	The closet is *beneath* the stairs.
	Underneath	Put a pad *underneath* the neg.
	On top of	He is working *on top of* the house.
6.	**Behind**	The boy is *behind* the desk.
	In back of	He is standing *in back of* Babita.
	In front of	Her school is *in front of* my house.
7.	**Up**	I saw her walking *up* the street.
	Down	I met her two miles *down* the road.
8.	**Across**	She walked *across* the park.
	Around	I took a walk *around* the 'K' block.
	Through	I went *through* the park.
9.	**Between**	She is sitting *between* Gopal and Govind.
	Among	Her letter is somewhere *among* these papers.
10.	**Inside**	Keep this box *inside* the house.
	Outside	Do not leave the chair *outside* the house.
11.	**After**	Stop for a while *after* each question.
	Before	While giving dates, place the month *before* the day.
12.	**Above**	This town is *above* sea level.
	Below	This city is *below* sea level.
13.	**At the top of**	His name is *at the top of* the list.
	At the bottom of	My name is *at the bottom* of the list.
	At the Head of	He is *at the head of* his class.

Prepositions of Direction

The following is a list of some prepositions that indicate relationship of direction.

Into	I walked *into* the room.
Out of	They ran *out of* the burning house.
Toward	He walked *toward* the tent.
By way of	You can go to Mumbai *by way of* Pune.

Prepositions of Time

A list of some prepositions that indicate relationships of time has been appended below:

1.	**At**	The match will start *at* 2 O'clock.
	By	He reached there *by* 2 O'clock.
2.	**In**	He will come *in* an hour.
	On	Her birthday is *on* November 19.
3.	**For**	I stayed *for* three days.
	During	I go there *during* the summer holidays.
	Since	I have been living here *since* 1940.
4.	**After**	Meet me *after* 10 O'clock.
	Before	Come to me *before* 6 O'clock.
5.	**Until**	Stay here *until* Monday.
	Till	Wait here *till* 5 O'clock.
6.	**At the beginning of**	Meet me *at the beginning of the* week.
	At the end of	Go to him *at the end of the* month.
	In the middle of	I will meet him *in the middle of* the week.
7.	**Around**	I will come to you at *around* 7 O'clock.
	About	It is now *about* 5 O'clock.

Prepositions of Manner

A list of some prepositions that indicate relationships of manner has been appended below:

1.	**By**	You can go *by* bus.
2.	**On**	He went *on* foot.
3.	**In**	We came here *in* a car.
4.	**With**	She greeted me *with* a smile.
5.	**Like**	He walks *like* an old man.

Some other Types of Prepositions

1. Agent (Or Instrument) — With or By
   Open the door *with* this key.
   The door is opened *by* him.
2. Accompaniment — With
   He went *with* her to the market.
3. Purpose — For
   This book is meant *for* you only.
4. Association — Of
   I got the news *of* her success.
5. Measure — Of and By
   I want three slices *of* bread.
   Cloth is not sold *by the yard*.
6. Similarity — Like
   You look *like* your brother.
7. In the capacity of — As
   He will serve *as* chairman.

Some Prepositions and Their Usage

1. ABOUT

About *(on-by-out, on that which is by the outside)*: It means close proximity to the outside. It is used figuratively in the following senses:

(a) Close to, on the verge of:

(*i*) It is *about* three O'clock.
(*ii*) He is *about* to be married.
(*iii*) This happened *about* a year ago.
(*iv*) He is much *about* the same as he was last year. (very nearly).

(b) Engaged in (of occupations):

(*i*) What are you *about*? (What are you doing?)
(*ii*) I send him *about* (to engage in) his business.

(c) On all sides of, concerning:

(*i*) I want to consult *about* a matter.
(*ii*) Tell us *about* him.

(d) Adverbial Usage:

(*i*) He went two miles *about.* (He made a circuit of two miles).
(*ii*) He turned *about.* (round)
(*iii*) He decided to bring it *about.* (to cause to happen)
(*iv*) They cast *about* for an opportunity. (tried to find)
(*v*) I am too ill to get *about.* (to leave the house)
(*vi*) They were hanging *about.* (loitering near).

2. ABOVE

Above *(on-by-up; on that which is on the upper side)*: It means close proximity to the upper surface. It is used in the sense of higher in status in terms of position or order. It is used figuratively in the sense of the following:

(*a*) Out of the range of, beyond
His conduct is *above* suspicion.

(*b*) More than (of quantity or degree)
(*i*) Not *above* fifty boys were present.
(*ii*) I value this *above* everything.

(*c*) Superior to
She is *above* such meanness.

3. ACROSS

Across *(on cross, cross-wise)*: It indicates intersection and hence, it is used to indicate.

(*a*) Motion from one side of thing to the other:
A road runs *acorss* the farm.

(*b*) Position on the otherside of a thing:
Her cottage is just *across* the street.

(*c*) Position on both sides of a thing:
(*i*) He threw the load *across* his shoulders.
(*ii*) I came *across* her.

4. AFTER

After *(after, more off)*: It points out distance measured from the back part of a thing. It is used in the sense of the following:

(*a*) Behind (with the notion of sequence of time):
Day *after* day passed by.

(*b*) In accordance with, in imitation of:
(*i*) He is a man *after* my own heart.
(*ii*) This boy takes *after* his father.

(*c*) In quest of, in regard to:
(*i*) They are seekers *after* God.
(*ii*) What are you *after*? (What are you doing?)

(*d*) As a result of, and so, inspite of:
I succeeded *after* all.

5. AGAINST

Against *(on going, in the way)*: It indicates opposition. It is used figuratively in the sense of :

(*a*) Opposed to, in opposition to:
This is *against* the law.

(*b*) In provision for, with reference to some necessity or danger:

It is good to save something *against* a rainy day. (hard times)

6. ALONG

Along *(over against in length, length-wise):* It points out motion or position by the side of a thing or in the direction of its length.

Flowers were blooming *all along* the valley.

7. AMONG, AMONGST

Among *(in the crowd or company of)*: It indicates motion to or position in the midst of. It is used in the sense of-

(a) **In the number of:**
He is the strongest *among* the boys of this school.

(b) **By the joint action of:**
Settle this matter *among* yourselves.

(c) **For distribution to:**
Share this money *among* you.

8. AROUND, ROUND

Around *(on round, in a round or circle)*: It indicates proximity on all sides. Round is its shortened form.

(a) **On every side of:**
Treses grew *around* her house.

(b) **Circuitously about:**
He is travelling *round* the world.

(c) **Adverbial Use:**
(*i*) Go *round* (make a circuit).
(*ii*) Come *round* (revive)
(*iii*) All *round* (in every direction).
(*iv*) *Round* about (indirect)

9. BEFORE

Before *(By fore)*: It marks motion or position in front of.

(*a*) He appeared *before* the judge.
(*b*) They ran away *before* him.

10. BEHIND

Behind *(By hind)*: It marks motion or position at the back of.

(*a*) The sun is *behind* a cloud.
(*b*) The train is *behind* time.

11. BELOW

Below *(By low)*: It indicates motion to or position at a lower point.

(*a*) The article is *below* the mark.
(*b*) He struck me *below* the knee.

12. BENEATH

Beneath *(By the nither part)*: It indicates motion to or position at a lower point.

(*a*) She dived *beneath* the water.
(*b*) She is buried *beneath* this stone.

13. BESIDE, BESIDES

Beside *(By side)* : It indicates motion or position by the side of. It is used in the sense of:

(a) **Aside from, outside of :**
This is *beside* the mark.

(b) **In addition to** *(also in the from besides) :*
Besides three children at home, she has two at school.

14. BETWEEN

Between *(By twain)*: It means in the middle of two.

(*a*) He reads *between* the lines.
(*b*) I will some *between* twelve and one O'clock.

15. BEYOND

Beyond *(By yonder)* : It means on the further side of and so outside the limits of.

(*a*) The matter is *beyond* dispute.
(*b*) His behaviour is *beyond* all praise.

16. OUT OF

Out of : It is a compound preposition. It indicates:

(a) **Motion from the interior and so origin, derivation:**
He turned him *out of* the house.

(b) **Rest on the outside, and so, exclusion, defect, loss:**
(*i*) He is *out of* prison.
(*ii*) He is a fish *out of* water.
(*iii*) *Out of* sight, *out of* mind.
(*iv*) I am *out of* pocket by that bargain.

(c) **Adverbial Usage:**
(*i*) He was *out.* (Not at home).
(*ii*) Find *out* the truth. (discover).
(*iii*) The book will soon be *out.* (published).
(*iv*) Fire is *out.* (extinguished).
(*v*) The day was *out.* (ended).
(*vi*) Congress I is *out* in Punjab. (not in Government office).
(*vii*) He laughed *out.* (without restraint)

(*viii*) You are *out* in that matter. (in error).
(*ix*) Write *out* the lesson. (copy in full).
(*x*) Look out the baby. (Take care).

17. TOWARD, TOWARDS

Toward, Towards *(tending to)* : It means in the direction of. It is used in the sense of—

(a) Approaching to, and so near to:
He wrote it *towards* the end of the book.

(b) With a view to, for the aid of:
I did everything *towards* that object.

(c) With reference to, regarding:
Do everything *towards* God and *toward* man.

18. WITHOUT

Without *(on the outside of)* : It is used to express exclusion or deficiency with reference to attendant circumstances only.

(*a*) He was left *without* money in the world.
(*b*) He tried his best *without* success.

19. WITHIN

Within *(in the interior of, and so inside the limits of):*

(*a*) He kept within doors.
(*b*) I will come within an hour.

20. WITH

With : At first 'With' had the meaning of from—with hold, withdraw, to put with, to differ with, to break with.

Then it took the meaning of against—withstand, to be angry with, to *bigh* with.

Lastly it gained its modern sense of association–I will go with you; I am with you.

It is used in relation to—

(a) Attendant Circumstances:
I will go there *with* pleasure.

(b) The point of reference of an action or a feeling:
He is popular *with* the boys.

(c) Instrumentality:
He did it *with* his own hands.

21. UP

Up : *'Up'* indicates *motion to* and sometimes *rest at* a higher point.

(*a*) He is gone upstairs
(*b*) It is a very *up hill* task.

'Up' has its adverbial use also.

(*a*) He always gets *up* early.
(*b*) Let us be *up* and doing.
(*c*) Prices are looking *up.* (have a tendency to rise).
(*d*) He offered *up* (put) a prayer.
(*e*) To keep *up.* (maintain)
(*f*) Brought *up.* (educated)
(*g*) Threw *up.* (abandoned) or gave up.
(*h*) Bear *up.* (be firm)
(*i*) Came *up.* (arrived)
(*i*) Caught *up.* (overtook)
(*j*) Hard *up.* (in difficulty)
(*k*) Made *up.* (compensated)

22. UNDER

Under: It marks position or motion beneath. It has the meaning of—

(a) In subordination to, subject to:
(*i*) Be patient *under* misfortune.
(*ii*) The case is *under* trial.
(*iii*) It is a post *under* Government.

(b) Falling short of, less than:
I will not give it you *under* four rupees.

(c) Covered, represented, designated by:
He deceived me *under* the mask.

(d) Adverbial use:
(*i*) He brought the fever *under.* (subdued)
(*ii*) He was obliged to knock under. (to yield)

23. FOR, DURING, SINCE

For : In expressions of time, *for* refers to a period of time, frequently stated in terms of the number of hours, days, weeks, and so forth, and in such expressions as *for a long (short) time, for several (a few) minutes, for a little while,* and so forth.

(*a*) We waited *for* fifteen minutes.
(*b*) We waited *for* two hours.
(*c*) We waited *for* several hours.
(*d*) We waited *for* a long time.

During: During also refers to a period to time, frequently stated as a block of time—*during the summer, during the year, during the semester, during my vacation* etc.

(*a*) It rained a great deal *during* the winter.
(*b*) It rained a great deal *during* the year.
(*c*) It rained a great deal *during* the spring semester.
(*d*) It rained a great deal *during* April.

(*e*) It rained a great deal *during* 1955.

In many cases *FOR* refers to something more or less continuous, *during,* to something intermittent. *For* is followed by the indefinite article—*during,* by the definite article.

(*a*) It rained for a day or so. (It rained almost continuously for a day or so).

(*b*) It rained during the day. (It rained sometime during the day or perhaps off and on during the day).

Since: 'Since' refers to a period of time that extends from a point of time in the past to the present or to another point of time in the past. The tense of the verb is usually the present perfect continuous or past continuous.

(*a*) It has been raining *since* five O'clock.

(*b*) I have been here *since* May 10th.

(*c*) I have been here *since* June 1952.

(*d*) I had been teaching there *since* November 1965.

24. ON TIME, IN TIME

On Time: It means *'On schedule.'*

I was there *on time.* (I was there at the appointed time)

In Time: It usually means before an appointed time (often with time left over to do something).

I reached the office in time.

25. FROM, TO *OR* FROM, UNTIL

These expressions have approximately the same meanings and are usually interchangeable in expressions of time.

(*a*) He works *from* 8 A.M. *to* 5 P.M.

(*b*) He works *from* 8 A.M. *until* 5 P.M.

26. AT

At: It indicates external proximity with the notion of contact actual or intended. It is used to denote—

(*a*) **Proximity in relation to a point in space, in the phrases:**

(*i*) She is sick *at* heart.

(*ii*) I keep him *at* arm's length.

(*iii*) She is quite *at* home on this topic.

(*b*) **Proximity in relation to a point in time:**

(*i*) He came *at* day break.

(*ii*) He went *at* 5 O'clock.

(**Note:** *on, in* and *by* used in relation to space of time—*on* monday, *in* the morning (but *on* the morning of Tuesday, the 14th' etc. *by* day not at day. At length-after a long time, finally).

(*c*) **Proximity in relation to value or degree:**

(*i*) The cow is valued *at* Rs. 100.

(*ii*) I wil sell this thing *at* cost price.

(*iii*) She set my advice *at* nought. (valued it at nothing, despise it).

(*d*) **Proximity in relation to the notions of consequence or dependence:**

(*i*) She calmed me *at* (by means of) a word.

(*ii*) He came *at* my call.

(*iii*) I am a tenant *at* will (of my landlord).

(*e*) **Proximity in relation to the notions of occupation, situation, condition:**

(*i*) The storm was *at* its height.

(*ii*) My mind is *at* ease.

(*iii*) He has to play *at* cricket.

(*iv*) He is *at* work.

(*f*) **Adverbial use:** *At* is used in adverbial phrases—often with the notion of *degree* or *reckoning* understood.

(*i*) He is a fool *at* best.

(*ii*) I am not *at* all tired.

(*g*) In an address *at* is used with the house number+the name of the street.

He lives at 66/222 Bhusa Toli.

(*h*) In referring to location *at* ordinarily indicates a specified location.

She will meet me at the library.

(*i*) *At* is sometimes used in referring to the arrival of a train and so forth.

The train will arrive *at* Kanpur *at* 8.10 A.M.

27. BY

By: It indicates proximity often without contact either in connection with rest or motion. It is used to denote—

(*a*) **Proximity is relation to time:**

(*i*) I shall come *by* 12 O'clock. (not later than 12 O'clock).

(*b*) **Agency:**

(*i*) I can read *by moonlight.*

(*ii*) He has two children *by* his first wife.

(*iii*) He wants to travel *by* rail.

(*c*) **Manner:**

(*i*) I caught him *by* the leg.

(ii) He paid the money by instalments.

(d) Measure, standard, amount:

(i) It is 10 O'clock *by* (not in) my watch.

(ii) He is teacher *by* profession.

(iii) He sells *by* whole sale.

(iv) He is taller *by* four inches.

(e) Adjuration, appeal:

(i) I swear *by* Heaven.

(ii) I beseech you *by* the mercies of God. (Bible).

(f) Adverbial use: *By* is used as an adverb—

(i) They passed *by* on the other side.

(ii) He laid *by* a rupee every week. (saved).

(iii) Go *by* (avoid)

(iv) *By* and *by* (near and near, very near, very soon).

(v) *By* the *by* [near the near (time)]

28. FOR

For *(Fore):* In Old English it meant *before, in front of.* Now it is used in relation to the three main notions of (A) substitution, (B) causality, (C) opposition.

(A) Substitution—with the meanings of—

(a) In the place of, instead of:

(i) I passed him *for* a rich man. (He was regarded as rich).

(ii) That was meant *for* a joke.

(iii) I took you *for* a gentleman. (regarded)

(b) In exchange for:

(i) An eye *for* an eye and a tooth *for* a tooth.

(ii) He sells mangoes *at* six for a rupee.

(c) In correspondence to:

These two books are page *for* page and line *for* line alike.

(B) Causality-with the meanings of—

(a) On behalf of, in favour of, in the interest of:

(i) Our P. M. is *for* peace.

(ii) He should think *for* himself.

(b) For the sake of, on account of:

(i) She did it *for* love of me.

(ii) I am sorry *for* you.

(c) In regard of, in point of:

(i) As *for* me, I do not object.

(ii) He is small *for* his age.

(d) For the purpose of:

(i) This is not fit *for* food.

(ii) He gasped *for* breath.

(e) In the direction of:

(i) He started *for* Kanpur.

(f) To the extent of:

(i) I failed *for* 10,000 rupees.

(ii) He was silent *for* a time.

29. INTO

Into: Motion inward is usually indicated by *Into.* It marks—

(a) Motion or direction inward:

(i) Please enter *into* the room.

(ii) I will take you *into* my confidence.

(iii) She has driven me *into* a corner.

(b) Change of condition:

(i) He has grown *into* a youngman.

(ii) I reasoned him *into* submission. (induced him to submit by reasoning with him).

30. OF, OFF

Of, Off: They are different forms of the same word. They indicate motion away from or rest at a distance from something. They have the meanings of—

(a) From, with the notion, of separation:

(i) She acquitted you *of* blame.

(ii) He got *off* his horse.

(iii) He is *off* duty.

(b) Proceeding from, with the notion of source or starting point:

(i) He comes *of* good family.

(ii) Evil must come *of* evil.

(c) Resulting from, with the notion of cause:

(i) He died *of* cancer.

(ii) I am sick *of* waiting.

(d) Appertaining to, with the notions of:

(i) Possession-

Bread is the staff of life.

(ii) Material, and so distinguishing characteristic—

1. It is a bar of iron.

2. Service is not a bed *of* roses.

(iii) Apposition—

1. The month of May.

2. A jewel of a servant. (most valuable servant).

(iv) Partition—

I am not *of* your religion.

(v) Point of reference, object—

1. He is hard of heart.

2. He is lame of both legs.

(e) **Adverbial uses:** 'off' is used as an adverb in-

Give *off* (emit), Take *off* (depart), Be *off* (go away),Cast *off* (discard), Set *off* (started), Came *off* (took place), Warned *off*, (advised), Well *off* (rich, prosperous), *off* and on (at intervals).

31. ON, UPON

On : It is from the same root as in and originally meant at or near with the added notion of superposition.

Hence *on, upon* (up-on) are used to indicate contact.

With the upper surface in relation to—

(a) **Place:**

(i) Kanpur stands *on* the Ganga.

(ii) Refreshment is *on* the table.

(iii) He gave me blow *upon* blow.

(b) **Time:**

(i) Come on Sunday.

(c) **Attendant circumstances:**

(i) I have hit *upon* a plan.

(ii) I am not *on* speaking terms with him.

(iii) Her house is *on* fire.

(iv) I call upon you to be firm [request].

(d) **On acquires the notion of:**

Reliance, dependence, aim—Sheep feed on grass. It is used in the sense of—

(i) *Because of*—

I congratulated her *on* her success.

(ii) *Just after, and so in consequence of*—

On hearing this, he ran away.

(iii) *In direction of, with a view to, against*—

1. The guns opened fire *on* the fort.

2. He went *on* a pilgrimage.

(iv) *In accordance with, Independence upon*—

I will act *on* your suggestion-*on* your advice.

(v) *On condition of*—

He lends money *on* good security.

(e) **Adverbial use :** *On* is used as an adverb—

Go *on*, live *on*, laid *on*, later *on*, carried *on*, fall *on*, get *on*, hold *on*.

(f) ***On* occurs in numerous adverbial phrases:**

On the wing [in flight], *on* the alert [ready], *on* all hands [in all directions], *on* no account [for no reason whatever], *on* a par [equal], *on* hand [in present possession], *on* occasion [at need], *on* the want [in a state of decline].

32. OVER

Over: It indicates (*A*) Position above—I wept *over* his grave.

(*B*) Motion above—He travelled over the mountains.

(*C*) Position beyond—My home is over the sea.

Hence it is used with the sense of—

(a) **Above (in place time or other relations):**

(i) I am *over* head and ears in debt.

(ii) She was absent *over* two hours.

(iii) He ruled *over* a vast empire.

(b) **About the surface of, across:**

(i) Think *over* my proposal.

(ii) He ferried them *over* the river.

(c) **On the other side of, beyond:**

(i) He lives *over* the way. (on the other side of the street)

(ii) He stayed *over* the next day.

(d) **Adverbial Use:**

(i) My ancestors came *over* here three hundred years ago.

(ii) He gave over the attempt. (abandoned).

(iii) He called over the names (read aloud).

(iv) It is all *over* with him (ruined or dead).

33. TO

To : It indicates motion towards a point in space or time, with the notion of reaching it. It is used to mark—

(a) **The direction of an action or a feeling towards on object or state—**

(i) He is a friend *to* the poor.

(ii) I am pray *to* anxiety.

(b) **Reference to some standard:**

She tried *to* convince me.

(d) **Adaptation, consonance:**

It is not *to* my advantage.

(e) **Comparison:**

As three is *to* six, so is four *to* eight.

(f) **Purpose:**

I went *to* see her.

(g) **Degree, limit:**

I was frightened *to* death. [Excessively]

(j) **Result:**

The shirt was torn *to* pieces.

(k) **Adverbial use:**

To and fro, go *to,* fall *to,* bring *to,* etc.

Usage of Prepositions

1. The following words take the preposition FOR after them.

Nouns: Affection, ambition, anxiety, apology, appetite, aptitude, blame, candidate, capacity, compassion, compensation, contempt, craving, desire, esteem, fitness, fondness, guarantee, leisure, liking, match, motive, need, opportunity, partiality, passion, pity, pretext, prediction, relish, remorse, reputation, ability, basis, care, cause, demand, disgust, distaste, excuse, facility, fondness, grief, hatred, love, punishment, qualification, receipt, regard, regret, remedy, request, respect, search, shame, sorrow, sympathy, taste, prediction; zest, amends, application, atonement, authority, bargain, cloak, competition, consideration, eagerness, emulation, fine, forbearance, freedom, gratitude, greediness, hope, inclination, intercession, lust, margin, longing, martyr, necessity, nerve, penance, penetration, predilection, preference, preparation, provocation, reason, readiness, receptacle, recompense, repentance, request, respect, responsibility, reverence, surety, satisfaction, specific, stickler, use, warrant, yearning, zeal, zeet.

Adverbs: Anxiously, effectively, fortunately, sufficiently,

Adjectives and Participles: Anxious, celebrated, conspicuous, customary, designed, zealous, destined, eager, eligible, eminent, fit, grateful, notorious, prepared, proper, qualified, ready, sorry, sufficient, suited, useful, solicitous, suitable.

Chapter 5

ONE WORD SUBSTITUTION

1. Persons, who lived during the same time period —*Contemporaries*
2. Members who are all of one mind—*Unanimous*
3. A thing, which cannot be seen —*Invisible*
4. A voice, which cannot be heard —*Inaudible*
5. A person, who cannot be elected or selected —*Inelligible*
6. Writing which cannot be read —*Illegible*
7. Words, which cannot be understood —*Unintelligible*
8. A match in which, neither party wins —*Drawn*
9. An animal that lives on flesh —*Carnivorous*
10. A plan, which cannot be put into practice —*Impracticable*
11. A person who lacks courage —*Coward*
12. A thing or person liked by all —*Populdr*
13. A person who can neither read nor write —*Illiterate*
14. One who abandons his faith —*Apostate*
15. One who is opposed to war and violence —*Pacifist*
16. One who takes a dark view of life —*Pessimist*
17. One who takes a bright view of life—*Optimist*
18. Person skilled in many languages —*Linguist*
19. Writer of pamphlets —*Pamphleteer*
20. Writer of comedies —*Comedian*
21. Writer of tragedies —*Tragedian*
22. Writer of sonnets —*Sonneteer*
23. Writer of drama —*Dramatist*
24. One who enters a country, not his own, for settling there —*Immigrant*
25. One who leaves one's country for settling abroad —*Emigrant*
26. One who is disposed to weeping—*Lachrimose*
27. One who falsely pretends skill in medicine —*Quack Or Charlatan*
28. One who is disposed to quarrel with all —*Bellicose Or Quarrelsome*
29. One who has regard for others —*Altruist*
30. One who is between boyhood and manhood —*Adolescent*
31. One who keeps away from pleasure —*Abstinent*
32. A remedy for all diseases —*Panacea*
33. One travelling on foot —*Pedestrian*
34. To cut off the head —*Behead*
35. To tell before-hand —*Predict*
36. Words no longer in usage —*Obsolete*
37. The murder of one's father —*Patricide*
38. The murder of one's brother —*Fratricide*
39. At the same time —*Simultaneously*
40. Speaking without preparation —*Extempore*
41. Without payment or recompense —*Gratis*
42. One who knows everything —*Omniscient*
43. The life of a person written by himself —*Autobiography*
44. A post with a salary but no work —*Sinecure*
45. A post with no salary —*Honrary*
46. One who lives on vegetables —*Vegetarian*
47. A thing fit to be eaten —*Edible*
48. A child born after its father's death Or A book published after its author's death–*Posthumous*
49. One who represents the government of his country abroad —*Ambassador*
50. One living at the same time or age as another —*Contemporary*
51. One who acts mechanically without free will of one's own —*Automated*
52. An athelete who has defeated all his rivals —*Champion*
53. One resolved not to marry —*Celebate*
54. One who holds fast to irrational view—*Bigot*
55. One (person or nation) engaged in regular warfare —*Belligerent*

56. One who is born out of wedlock —*Bastard*

57. One who believes everything easily —*Credulous*

58. One who is engaged in illegitimate traffic of controlled goods or commodities in short supply —*Black Marketeer*

59. One who makes excessive profits in trade —*Profiteer*

60. One who indulges in boastful talk—*Braggart*

61. Lover of one's own country or nation —*Patriot Or Nationalist*

62. One who likes to inflict pain upon oneself —*Masochist*

63. One who is desirous of doing evil to others —*Malevolent*

64. One who is desirous of doing good to others —*Benevolent*

65. Lover of mankind —*Philanthropist*

66. Hater of marriage —*Misogamist*

67. Hater of women —*Misogynist*

68. Hater of mankind —*Misanthrope*

69. One who is not fully developed —*Immature*

70. One who talks during sleep —*Somnaloquist*

71. One who walks during sleep—*Somnambulist*

72. A child under seven years of age —*Infant*

73. One who abstains from drinking—*Teetoteller*

74. One who believes that pleasure is the chief objective in life —*Hedonist*

75. One who is opposed to old traditions —*Heterodox*

76. One who respects traditions —*Orthodox*

77. One who believes that all things in the universe are manifestations of one God —*Pantheist*

78. One who does not believe in gods —*Atheist*

79. One who believes in many gods —*Polytheist*

80. One who believes in one God —*Monotheist*

81. A breaker of idols and conventions —*Iconoclast*

82. One who deserts his faith or principles —*Renegade*

83. A poem of fourteen lines —*Sonnet*

84. A figure having eight sides —*Octagon*

85. A figure having seven sides —*Heptagon*

86. A figure having six sides —*Hexagon*

87. A figure having five sides —*Pentagon*

88. A figure having four sides —*Quadrilateral*

89. A figure having three sides —*Triangle*

90. Celebration after 100 years —*Centenary*

91. Yearly celebration —*Anniversary*

92. Place where prostitutes live —*Brothel*

93. Fight between two persons with or without arms —*Duel*

94. Place where public records are kept—*Archive*

95. Chest in which, a corpse is buried —*Coffin*

96. Trap for catching birds and animals —*Snare*

97. Buiding set apart for lodging horses—*Stable*

98. A group of rhymed lines —*Stanza*

99. Systematic collection and analysis of facts and data —*Statistics*

100. Export and import duties —*Tariffs*

101. Duty levied on goods entering a town —*Octroi*

102. A collection of choicest poems —*Anthology*

103. Equipment for warfare —*Armament*

104. Substance, which can kill germs—*Germicide*

105. Substance, which can kill insects —*Insecticide*

106. Four-footed animal —*Quadruped*

107. Two-footed animal —*Biped*

108. Vessel to spit in —*Spitoon*

109. Material through which, light cannot pass at all —*Opaque*

110. Material through which, light can pass only partially —*Transparent*

111. One who always thinks that he is ill —*Valetudinarian*

112. One who always thinks of himself —*Egoist*

113. One who abstains from animal foods —*Vegetarian*

114. One who alters his principles to changing circumstances —*Opportunist*

115. One who is given to the indulgence of animal appetites —*Sensualist*

116. One who is a lover of books —*Bibloiphilist*

117. One who is addicted to one's own pet nations —*Faddist*

118. One who denies all existing doctrines —*Nihilist*

119. Use of a delicate word or expression in place of an offensive one —*Euphemism*

120. A morbid impulse to steal —*Kleptomania*

121. A mania for versifying —*Metromania*
122. An inordinate craving for music—*Melomania*
123. Insanity characterised by excessive self-exultation —*Megalomania*
124. A rage for collecting rare books —*Bibliomania*
125. Uncontrollable desire for alcohol —*Dipsomania*
126. Delusion that one is God —*Theomania*
127. Want of or lack of blood —*Anaemia*
128. Morbid dread of water —*Hydrophobia*
129. Dread or hatred of books —*Bibliophobia*
130. Unreasonable dread of being poisoned —*Toxiphobia*
131. Roundabout way of expressing one's ideas —*Circumlocution*
132. Tendency to appoint one's own relatives for high posts —*Nepotism*
133. Habit of giving special privileges to one's friends and relatives —*Favouritism*
134. Language commonly understood by many people —*Lingua Franca*
135. Art of growing gardens —*Horticulture*
136. A society which has no government —*Anarchy*
137. Government by a dictator —*Dictatorship*
138. Government by two independent authorities —*Dyarchy*
139. Government by the wealthy —*Plutocracy*
140. Government by the few —*Oligarchy*
141. Government by the mob —*Mobocracy*
142. Government by the people —*Democracy*
143. Government by a king —*Monarchy*
144. Death caused by electricity —*Electrocution*
145. A free fight in which, many persons take part —*Riot*
146. Large-scale killings —*Massacre*
147. Murder of one's ownself —*Suicide*
148. Murder of mother —*Matricide*
149. Murder of an infant —*Infanticide*
150. Murder of a king —*Regicide*
151. Murder of human being —*Homicide*
152. Theft of literary ideas and material —*Plagiarism*
153. A poem of three lines —*Triplet*
154. A poem of two lines —*Couplet*
155. One who starves the body for the good of the soul —*Ascetic*
156. One who is not sure of the existence of God —*Agnostic*
157. Government by the officials —*Bureaucracy*
158. Motivated to get some money through criminal acts —*Mercenary*
159. Speaking many languages —*Multi-lingual*
160. Speaking two languages —*Bi-lingual*
161. Not in consonance with reason —*Irrational*
162. In consonance with reason —*Rational*
163. That the loss of which, cannot be made good —*Irremediable*
164. Easily set on fire —*Inflammable*
165. Sure to happen —*Inevitable*
166. Not clearly expressed, only implied—*Implicit*
167. Clearly expressed —*Explicit*
168. Living both on land and in water —*Amphibious*
169. Living in water —*Aquatic*
170. Just about to happen —*Imminent*
171. That, which cannot be excused—*Inexcusable*
172. That, which cannot be explained —*Inexplicable*
173. That, which cannot be expressed —*Inexpressible or Ineffable or Unutterable*
174. That, which cannot die —*Immortal*
175. That, which cannot perish —*Imperishable*
176. That, which cannot be exhausted —*Inexhaustible*
177. That, which cannot be conquered —*Invincible*
178. Only in title —*Titular*
179. Only in name —*Nominal*
180. Occurring in five years —*Quinquennial*
181. To talk in childish prattle —*Lisp*
182. To speak in a way, which may be interpreted in two contradictory ways —*Equivocate*
183. To outrage the sanctity of a religious place —*Desecrate*
184. To accuse a pesson of treason or any serious crime before a competent tribunal —*Impeach*
185. To despatch things to a foreign land—*Export*
186. To bring things from a foreign land —*Import*
187. The passage of the soul after death into another body —*Transmigration*

188. Morbid fear of men (in women) —*Androphobia*
189. An impracticable ideal —*Utopia*
190. Remarks, which do not really apply to the subject under discussion —*Irrelevant*
191. Words inscribed on the tomb of a person —*Epitaph*
192. Speech made to oneself when one is alone —*Soliloquy*
193. One who is new in any business or profession —*Novice*
194. One who possesses several talents or gifts —*Versatile*
195. One who eats too much —*Glutton*
196. One who changes one's principles or party —*Turncoat*
197. One who lives upon others —*Parasite*
198. A man of unusual habits —*Eccentric*
199. One who is all-powerful —*Omnipotent*
200. One who is present everywhere—*Omnipresent*
201. A letter, poem etc. whose anthor is unknown —*Anonymous*
202. With one voice' a decision-opinion on which, all are agreed —*Unanimous*
203. The action of looking back on past time —*Retrospection*
204. The action of looking within or into one's own mind —*Introspection*
205. Vigilant and cautious observation of events or circumstances —*Circumspection*
206. One who can make himself at home in all countries —*Cosmopolitan*
207. One who is always inclines to find faults —*Censorious*
208. People working together in the same office or department —*Colleagues*
209. A person having little or no sympathy —*Callous*
210. Marrying more than one husband at a time —*Polyandry*
211. Marrying more than one wife or more than one husband at a time —*Polygamy*
212. Marrying one husband or one wife at a time —*Monogamy*
213. A woman with dark complexion and brown hair —*Brunette*
214. A woman of fair complexion and light hair —*Blonde*
215. To talk impiously about sacred things or texts —*Blasphemy*
216. A statement open to more than one interpretation —*Ambiguous*
217. One who does something not professionally but for pleasure —*Amateur*
218. To turn friends into enemies —*Alienate*
219. A man who has too much enthusiasm for his own religion and hates other religion —*Fanatic*
220. A state of complete chastity on the part of a woman —*Virginity*
221. A place where clothes are kept —*Wardrobe*
222. A person who has long experience of any occupation —*Veteran*
223. A style or text full of words —*Verbose*

Chapter 6

COMPREHENSION

By comprehension we mean 'grasping a piece of writing *intelligently*', which is slightly different from 'understanding' of any piece of writing. As we know, according to the law of nature, individuals differ in their levels of intelligence. So, the readers of any passage would also differ in their capacity and aptitude in grasping the exact message contained therein. That is why, there are persons who would read any piece of writing once only and could get fully apprised while others could read it to get something out of it, Hence, comprehension is related to the grasping the idea contained in any passage.

Essentional Pre-requisites of Comprehension: While attempting comprehension you will read a passage to satisfy yourself. See carefully:

(a) what is actually conveyed by the narrator;
(b) in what connection he has conveyed all that; and
(c) what is his contention/objective or what he wants to say by it.

Treatment of comprehension passage: First thing to be done on your part is to read the whole passage thoroughly and attempt to grasp fully, the meanings and the context of the same. No matter whether you read it twice or thrice for the purpose. After reading it to your satisfaction, attempt the questions. Every question is followed by *multiple choice* answers. You have to choose the right answer out of them. While attempting to mark your choice, you may, if you so feel, read the passage once again for the purpose. It will help you in clearing your doubt about the right choice.

While choosing your answer, note the following:

(A) Actually you are not writing an answer yourself but choosing the *best* or the *correct* answer out of the lot presented for the purpose.

(B) While making the choice of the correct answer beware of the distractors. Plainly speaking, distractors are meant to distract you from the correct answers. The language used therein sometimes is mixed with the language of the actual text of the passage just to mislead you. *Fresh reading of passage dealing with the question would help you much in this regard.*

(C) Note it finally that the more you will read the more you will understand the actual sense sought to be conveyed by the narrator. Therefore, read and compare every suggested answer with the original passage and in this way, clear yourself of the distractors to mark the correct answer. *Do not act in a hurried manner.*

By now, it should be very clear to the readers what is meant by comprehension and how a passage for comprehension is dealt with properly. All this can be summed up to help them evolve a method to accord comprehension treatment to the passage.

(i) You should read the passage as a whole once, twice or thrice *to grasp* the sense of the narrator *completely* in the first instance.

(ii) The *phrases, idioms* and *technical terms,* if any, should be very carefully read again and again and should be *understood in the context of the meanings of one another.* Their exact sense should be noted in mind.

(iii) The *speed of reading* for comprehension is *faster* in the beginning and then *slowed down* in successive rounds. It would enable you to *understand* the *passage intelligently* and exactly.

(iv) Use the method of re-reading the passage to solve your difficulty for choosing your answer.

PASSAGE-1

Mrs. Loisel now learned what it was like to be really poor. She made up her mind to face it and played her part bravely. This terrible debt had to be paid and she would pay it. The maid was dismissed; the flat was given up and they moved into a *garret.*

She did all the rough household work; washed up after meals and ruined her finger nails scrubbing dirty dishes and pans. She did all the washing and hung it out on the line to dry. Every morning, she carried the rubbish down to the street and brought the water, pausing for breath at the top of each *flight of stairs.* Dressed like a working woman, she went with her basket on her arm to the *greengrocer,* the *grocer* and the *butcher,* bargaining, arguing and fighting for every penny.

Her husband spent his evenings, working at some shopkeepers' account, and at night, he would often copy papers at a few pennies a page.

Thus life went on for ten years.

At the end of that time, they had paid off everything to the last penny, including the interest on the loan.

Mrs. Loisel now looked like an old woman. She had become a typical poor man's wife, rough and coarse. Her hair was neglected, her dress was untidy, her hands were red. But now and then, when her husband was at the office, she would sit by the window and her thoughts would go back to that far away evening, the evening of her beauty and her success. What would have been the end of it if she had not lost the necklace? Who could say? How strange and varied are the chances of life. How small a thing can save or ruin you.

One Sunday, she went for a walk in the Champa Elysees* and she caught sight of a lady with a child. She recognized Mrs. Forestier, who looked as young, as pretty and as attractive as ever. Mrs. Loisel felt a wave of sadness pass over her. Should she speak to her? Why not? Now that the debt was paid, why should she not tell her the whole story? She went up to her.

"Good morning, Jeanne."

Her friend did not recognize her and said, "I'm afraid I don't know you; you must have made a mistake."

"No, I am Mathilde Loisel."

Her friend uttered a cry.

'Oh' my poor dear Mathilde! How you have changed!"

"Yes, I have been through a very hard time since I saw you last."

* A park in Paris

"What do you mean?"

"You remember the diamond necklace you lent me to wear?"

"Yes, Well?'

"Well, I lost it."

"I don't understand. You brought it back to me."

"What I brought you back was another one, exactly like it and for the ten years, we have been busy paying for it. You must understand that it was not an easy matter for people like us, who hadn't a penny. However, it's all over now. I can't tell you what a relief it is!"

Mrs. Forestier stopped dead.

"You mean that you bought a diamond necklace to replace mine?"

"Yes. And you never noticed it? They were certainly very much alike."

She smiled with pride and satisfaction. But Mrs. Forestier seized both her hands in great distress.

"Oh, my poor, dear Mathilde! Why? Mine was only imitation. At the most it was worth five hundred francs!"

Questions

1. Mrs. Loisel was not a well off lady but still, she took to pay back the huge amount of necklace
   A. in a half-hearted way
   B. in a reluctant manner
   C. quite unwillingly
   D. in a determined way
   E. under compulsion of law

2. Entire money was paid up by her without excuse but
   A. it took ten years for Loisel to clear off the dues in instalments
   B. it took ten years for them to save that much amount to pay back
   C. it took lesser period in paying back the money
   D. they had not paid back in full the amount of necklace even during a period of ten years
   E. they were running short of a little amount to pay back the amount in full at the end of ten years

3. Mrs. Loisel struggled very hard to pay back the amount and it
   A. had made her weak and ill

B. had no effect on her health
C. had made her demoralised and ill humoured
D. had bereft her of her memory
E. had affected her looks

4. When Mrs. Loisel met Mrs. Forestier she
A. told her that she had lost the necklace but promised to return another exactly like it
B. admitted that she had replaced Mrs. Forestier's diamond necklace with a necklace of imitation diamonds
C. told her that the necklace she had returned was not the same that she had borrowed
D. accused Mrs. Forestier of being a cause of ten years sufferings
E. begged her pardon to avoid talk about the necklace that has caused her so much worry

5. Mrs. Forestier told Mrs. Loisel to the effect that
A. the necklace that was returned was made of imitation diamonds
B. the necklace borrowed by Mrs. Loisel was not of real diamonds
C. the necklace returned valued just 500 francs
D. the necklace that she had returned valued less than 500 francs
E. the necklace she had lent was of real diamonds

PASSAGE-2

Imagine a ship built to sail amongst the ice at the North Pole. The ship has a hull two feet thick. This hull is shaped so that when the ice closes in on the ship she* is pushed up—like a piece of soap in your hand and drifts in the top layer of the ice. A ship like this was built for the great Norwegian explorer Fridjof Nansen.

One day, while he was walking by the sea, Nansen found a piece of Russian wood. Obviously the wood had drifted south across the Arctic Circle from Siberia. Nansen thought that if a piece of wood could make the journey so could he. If he had a ship which rested on the ice he would be able to drift across the Arctic Sea. And so the 'Fram' (which means 'forward') was built.

In June, 1893, Nansen left Oslo with a crew of 13 men and 30 dogs for the sledges. Many people thought his plans were mad and said that he was going to meet his death. By September, the 'Fram' had reached Cape Chelyuskin, the most northerly point of Siberia. Here, the ice became 30 ft thick and began to close in on the 'Fram.' But just as Nansen had said, the ship rose up, came to rest on the ice, and began to drift. For an year she drifted northwards, then slowly westwards. Nansen then decided to rush to the North Pole with his companion Hjelmar Johansen. At that time, no explorer had ever reached the Pole.

They set off with 28 dogs, 3 sledges, 2 small boats, a tent, sleeping bags and food. By April 1895 they were within 200 miles of the Pole.

This was nearer to the Pole than any other explorer had ever been. But conditions were terrible. The temperature dropped to 40 degrees below freezing point. The dogs became exhausted. Their clothes froze on their bodies. In the end they had to turn back. The two men and their dogs travelled for four months through ice and snow. Frozen, exhausted and with sinking spirits, they struggled on through mile after mile of snow.

Once Nansen was nearly killed by animals. On another occasion, they tied their small boats to an iceberg and climbed up to make observations. The boats broke loose and began to drift. Nansen knew that they would not be able to go on without the boats. Still wearing his heavy clothes, he dived into the freezing water and swam after the boats. Then, after he had got them back, Nansen's boat was nearly destroyed by an animal.

At last, they reached Franz Josef Land, which is still inside the Arctic Circle. They decided to spend the winter there because it would have been dangerous to travel in a Polar winter. They built a hut of stone and covered it with animal skins and then, settled down for a long cold wait. They spent the winter hunting, talking and writing. In this way, they stopped themselves from going mad with loneliness.

In May, when spring came, they set out again on their march Southwards. A month later, they

* She-the feminine pronoun is used for ships and boats in English.

walked into a party of British explorers. The British had been in the Arctic for two years and were waiting for their ship to take them home. The ship arrived and took Nansen and Johansen back to Norway.

But what had happened to the 'Fram'? There was no word. Her movements were as much a mystery as those of Nansen and Johansen had been. Astonishingly, a week after Nansen's return, the 'Fram' drifted back to Norway—exactly three years after she had left. Nansen was given a hero's welcome and so were the men of the 'Fram.'

Questions

1. For going on journey across the Arctic, Nansen got an idea of a particular ship, especially designed for the purpose because
   - A. he must travel by a newly designed ship to go on exploration mission
   - B. he must have a ship that would sail around the frozen Arctic
   - C. he must have a ship that would plough through the ice
   - D. he must have a ship that would slide the top layer of the ice
   - E. he must have a ship that would rest on the ice and drift
2. How did Nansen plan to go on exploration mission across the Arctic?
   - A. He planned to go to Russia across the Arctic sea
   - B. He planned to sail towards the North Pole
   - C. He planned to sail north-west toward the Pole
   - D. He planned to proceed Northward on the ice
   - E. He planned to go across the Arctic from north to south
3. What happened when Nansen and Johansen tried to reach the North Pole proceeding West ward?
   - A. they lost the way and were misled
   - B. they reached the pole but could not stay there
   - C. they reached the Pole and passed the winter there
   - D. they approached closer to the pole but were forced to keep away by weather extremities
4. What happened to Nansen and Johansen while they were on return journey?
   - A. They met unknown explorers who played host to them
   - B. They met British explorers who offered them lift to Norway
   - C. They met the British explorers who took them home in their ship
   - D. They met the British explorers and took them home in their ship—the 'Fram'
   - E. They got a ship that had just landed a party of explorers and reached home
5. What happened to 'Fram' after it was abandoned by Nansen and Johansen?
   - A. The ship was destroyed by the snow storm
   - B. Returned to Norway after a very long time
   - C. Returned to Norway shortly after Nansen
   - D. Nothing was heard of it
   - E. The ship was remodelled by some other explorers and taken away by them

PASSAGE-3

The French expedition led by Maurice Herzog climbed Annapurna, the 26,493 ft mountain in the Himalayan mountains of Nepal in 1950. This was the first mountain of over 26,000 feet to be climbed, nearly 1,000 ft higher than Tilman's Nanda Devi. At the time of Herzog's climb, some twenty-two previous expeditions had attempted to reach a summit of 26,000 feet. All had failed.

At first, things went according to plan. By May 28th, the mountaineers had established four camps on Annapurna, a base camp at about 16,750 feet and higher camps at 19,350 ft, 21,650 feet and 23,500 feet. Then, two things went wrong. Two of Herzog's companions, whom he had sent high to establish a fifth camp near the summit, were overcome by high altitude sickness and frostbite, an injury to the body caused by intense cold. They failed to set up the camp. With another companion, Louis Lachenal, Herzog took over from them and on June 2nd, made a camp of sorts—a tent on an ice shelf—at 24,600 feet. The monsoon was almost on them and a weather forecast that they had heard on the radio just before coming up was bad. They spent a miserable night in their tent and it snowed heavily.

With dawn the weather got a little better and

they decided to go for the summit, still nearly 2000 feet above them. Neither was using oxygen, both were beginning to suffer from frostbite. After eight hours' climbing they got to the top. Then the weather showed signs of breaking and they had to go down as quickly as they could. On the way down, Herzog took off his gloves for a moment to get something out of his climbing bag—he does not recall what—and he dropped the gloves. They rolled over a cliff.

The loss was disastrous. To be gloveless at 26,000 ft with bad weather coming on might easily mean the loss of his hands from frostbite. There was nothing to be done but to go on down.

They reached their tent of the night before to find that two more of the party, Lionel Terray and Goston Rebuffat, had come to their aid. Terray and Rebuffat undoubtedly saved their lives, for both Herzog and Lachenal were severely frostbitten and Herzog's hands were in a terrible condition.

In the morning the four of them set off on the descent to the next camp but in snow and thick mist, they lost their way. They walked this way and that for the whole day. At nightfall, they were still lost not knowing where they were continuing the descent. Next morning, Lachenal could barely walk. Herzog could not stand unless Terray and Rebuffat supported him. Herzog decided that he was simply getting in the way and told them to leave him and try to save their own lives. The others refused to leave him. In this condition, they were lucky to be found by a search party from the camp.

The behaviour of Herzog and his companions in disaster is beyond criticism as it is beyond praise. As a leader of the expedition, Herzog was unquestionably right to tell the others to abandon him in order to have a better chance themselves but they were equally right to disobey. At the same time, had they left him to die on the mountain, they could not have been criticised; three lives for one is a proper exchange. Herzog's condition was hindering the others, fatally, for all he or they knew. Yet the determination of Herzog's companions to die with him rather than leave him somehow stands out above all arguments about what would have been sensible.

Questions

1. The writer commenting on expedition to Annapurna has remarked to the effect that

A. before Tilman none had climbed the height of 26,000 ft

B. Herzog was the first mountaineer to reach the height of 26,000 ft

C. there had been no expedition till then to climb to that height

D. there had been twenty-two expeditions to climb Annapurna but all had failed

E. Tilman had climbed to a height of 26,000 ft before Herzog

2. What had been the fate of the French expedition under review?

A. It took an ill-start and ended in damn failure

B. It took a good and successful start but ended in sorrow

C. It took an odd start but later got to the right course as per plan

D. It was very disheartening in the beginning

E. It had taken a good start in the beginning but failed later

3. What happened to Lachenal and Herzog when they set out for final assault to Annapurna?

A. They were overcome by mountain sickness and frostbite and gave up the idea of proceeding on

B. They reached Annapurna all right but descended immediately

C. They had returned leaving uncanned 2,000 feet height below Annapurna

D. They had reached the summit but due to aggressive weather returned without camping or rest

E. They were parted on way and descended back to their camp in confusion

4. What happened when Lachenal and Herzog were returning from Annapurna to the lower camp?

A. Both had broken their shins

B. Herzog had lost his gloves

C. Rebuffat and Terray met to help them

D. Both were affected by frostbite

E. Herzog told his companion to go back and abandon him

5. What did Herzog decide while on way to descent to the fourth camp?

A. Herzog decided—for other—to leave as

Rebuffat was getting in the way

B. Herzog decided to leave Lachenal because he could only walk with difficulty

C. Herzog ordered others to leave him and save their own lives

D. Herzog asked others to leave him in anticipation of getting a better chance of recovering later in due course

E. Herzog asked others to leave so that they could arrange better treatment for him

PASSAGE-4

The Great Wall of China is said to be the one structure built by man on earth, which would be visible to observers on the moon. It covers a distance of 1,500 miles as the crow flies. From the Liaotung Peninsula Westward to the last fortress in Central Asia, it crosses the Northern provinces of China. But its actual course, twisting and turning, sweeping across deep valleys, covers over 2,000 miles.

In the Eastern section, its height varies from 15 to 30 feet and its width from about 25 feet at the bottom to 15 feet at the top where there is a pathway wide enough for six horsemen to ride side by side, protected by parapets. When the wall was first built, it had about 25,000 towers, each 40 feet square and 40 feet high projecting from it every few hundred yards with holes from which, the defenders could shoot at attackers. Thousands of these towers are still standing. There are also many watch-towers on the enemy side, outside the wall on hilltops or passes. These and the towers of the wall were used for signalling with smoke or flags by day and with fire by night. The approach of invaders could be reported at once and reinforcements could be sent to any part of the frontier.

The great Emperor Shih Huang Ti joined three earlier frontier walls to form a Great Wall, which was to act as a boundary between China and the north and keep out the feared nomads of the Mongolian steppes. The wall was designed to strengthen the nation's defences; it was not then, as it later became in Ming times, a substitute for a strong army and State.

Construction was started in about 221 B.C. and the structure was practically complete when Shih Huang Ti died in 210 B.C. The man who did most in carrying out the Emperor's plans was general Meng Tien, who, in 221 B.C., led an expedition against the Tartars with an army of 3,00,000, and drove them back from the Yellow River into the steppes and set his men to work on building the Wall. They were later joined by the thousands of convicts. Year in, year out, in icy winds and snowstorms in winter and in duststorms in summer, the work went on and so many men died that the wall was sometimes called the longest cemetery in the world. The core of the Wall is earth and stone, faced with brick and set in a stone foundation. In hilly places, the design was altered; two parallel ditches were dug out of the rock, 25 feet apart and great blocks of stone were laid in the trenches to a height of several feet. Along each side of these stones, baked bricks—about two feet long—were laid at right angles to the face of the Wall, joined together with a white mortar so hard that no nail could be driven into it. The space between the two brick walls was filled with earth, which was beaten down hard. North of Peking, the Wall follows mountain summits of such an altitude and steepness that even goats can hardly climb them. Further West, the Wall often follows the easiest route and here again, its design changes and it is built of yellow earth faced with a thin layer of brick or stone.

Emperor Wu Ti (140-86 B.C.) resumed work on the Wall and extended it to its greatest length and built fortresses in Central Asia itself. The emperors of the Ming Dynasty (A.D. 1386-1644) carried out more work on the Wall repairing its whole length and establishing new walls West of the Yellow River. The Wall, which now exists, dates from the Ming Dynasty but many of its foundations are nearly 2,000 years old; the long line of gray bricks goes back into China's past, dividing two ways of life, separating the nomad from the peaceful farmer.

Questions

1. What do you know about the length of the Great Wall of China?

   A. The Great Wall of 1,500 miles long crossing even length of twisting valleys, etc.

   B. The Great Wall is 2,000 miles long leaving the twisting valleys

   C. The Great Wall is 2,000 miles long overall,

including twisting walls

D. The Great Wall is 1,500 miles long through the twisting valleys

E. The Great Wall was originally 3,000 miles long but now, it is just 1,500 miles

2. What was the idea behind raising the Great Wall?

A. To facilitate weather conditions of that part of China

B. To engage the convicts in hard labour

C. To check the invaders from the North without necessitating massive army

D. To watch the movement of enemy and keep them off the invasion attempts

E. It was built for patrolling purposes throughout the region

3. What was the Wisdom of Emperor Shih Huang Ti in constructing Great Wall?

A. He considered the wall as more powerful means of defence than a massive army

B. He had already used three separate walls to protect the frontiers

C. He was the first ruler to use walls as reliable means of defence

D. He joined three old walls to make the Great Wall for protection from the North

E. The Wall was a multi-purpose project to engage the convicts, to protect the country and facilitate the military movement

4. What do you come to know about the design and construction of the Great Wall?

A. The entire Wall is constructed in a uniformed way

B. The entire Wall is constructed with the same material

C. The same method of construction is used for the entire Wall

D. Different methods of construction are used in different parts of the country

E. There is difference in the outward design of the structure in different regions

5. Who carried over the most part of the work on Great Wall?

A. Shih Huang Ti

B. General Meng Ten

C. Emperor Wu Ti

D. The Ming Emperors

E. The Generals of the Chinese Army of the post Ming era

PASSAGE-5

Countries in the higher stages of development accumulate capital far more easily than those in the less advanced stages. This is one reason why lending between advanced and less advanced countries—at low or zero rates of interest and for long terms of repayment-should be considered normal and natural.

But even loans at low or zero rates or outright grants of capital have their dangers. Even where a country has reached a stage, where it can use capital in quantity, borrowing from abroad can be a substitute for earnings from abroad. The poor country must take advantage of the tendency for the more advanced nations to become what Keynes* called "high-cost, high-living" countries. Friends of many developing countries must view with some concern the rather poor performance of their exports. At a roughly similar stage in her industrialisation, Japan had no alternative but to force her products on to the markets of the world. This did not make the Japanese universally popular but it did provide the earnings for investments, which ensured her further growth. It is doubtful if such aid, however generous, can be a substitute for such earnings and for the independence and self-confidence they bring.

The borrowing of technology is also a complex matter. One advantage of being second in line is that the country so placed can take advantage of what has been worked out, often with considerable mental labour and cost, by those who have gone before. But one must know why the thing was worked out. High-yielding maize hybrids, improved fertilizer usage, are both advances of general application. They are as appropriate and important for the less as for the more developed country. But much of the technology of the more advanced countries was developed because of their shortage of labour, the mechanical cotton picker and the modern heavy farm tractor are inventions of this sort. Their usage on farms in the United States reflects the fact that labour for hire is scarce. This technology should not be

* Keynes-the famous British Economist

taken over in the earlier stages of development in countries with unemployment problems.

So much for the borrowing of capital and technology. I come now to the borrowing of organisation, a term I use broadly to include government and its services and educational, welfare and economic organisation. The argument goes-because a particular organisation or service exists in a more advanced country, it must make an important contribution to development and should be re-created in countries that are in the less advanced stages. It will aid in their development too.

This line of reasoning is a rich source of error. Often and I think usually, the organisation and services of the more advanced countries are not the cause of its development but its result. They either reflect the needs of more advanced development or they are made possible by the level of development and income that country has reached. Unwise borrowing of such organisations will not help development but hinder it. The government of India is a complex thing, which reflects the great variety of tasks undertaken by India in her stage of development. An equally complex organisation would be a great misfortune for one of the newer African States, for the time being, with a far simpler range of tasks.

If luxuries like specialised educational institutions, prefabricated housing and a wide range of public services are adopted before their time, they will draw resources from the tasks that are vital for development.

A hundred years ago, the development of the trans-Mississippi plains in the United States called, above all else, for a land policy, which would get the land settled and ploughed and a transportation system, which would get the products to market. To this end, the government surveyed the land, gave 160 acres to anyone who had proved this good intensions by farming it for a few months and subsidised the building of a railway. These essentials having been provided, development proceeded at amazing speed. It was our unquestioned good fortune that community education experts, home economists and public safety advisers had not been invented. Had these existed, attention would have been drawn from the central task of getting the farms settled and the railway built.

Today, in the United States, these more elaborate services can be easily afforded. And in the present stage of our development, they may be needed. Transferred to Africa or even to India, they may be redundant or damaging as they would have been in the United States in its comparable stage of economic development.

Questions

1. What is meant by 'capital' in the passage?

A. The money earned by traders and industrialists as profit

B. The money that is paid by a borrower in excess to the money borrowed

C. The money advanced by a lender for developmental purposes that would bring interest

D. The amount of money and material that can be put to earn more money

E. The money that is saved in course of time—shorter or longer

2. What is the advantage of advanced and economically developed countries regarding supply of capital over under-developed countries?

A. Developed countries make huge profits from under-developed countries

B. Under-developed countries or less developed countries have rare chances of accumulation of capital internally

C. Developed countries can easily attract capital from less developed countries

D. They are able to accumulate money at a higher rate than any of the under-developed countries

E. They want to keep their money engaged

3. In what way, are the exports helpful to the under-developed countries?

A. It would incline developed countries to provide them big loans

B. They can import latest stuff and material to improve their standard of living

C. The earnings from export would raise their capacities to enhance the rate of growth

D. They will be able to repay the loans at an early date

E. They can easily modernise their industry

4. What advantage is available to under-developed countries in respect of exports that the developed countries lack?
   A. They may improve their position quickly and instead of borrowing may earn from foreign countries
   B. The exports from under-developed countries are encouraging by the advanced countries and appreciated
   C. The cost of production of the same commodity in under-developed countries is lower than in the developed countries
   D. Developed countries grow a tendency of lavish spending without caring for enhancing their earnings
   E. Export promotion in under-developed countries grows the industries rapidly
5. What is particular with Japan in quoting as an instance in context of exports?
   A. Japan had flooded the under-developed countries with very cheap commodities
   B. Japan had exported on competitive rates in foreign countries
   C. Japan is exporting not less than the developing countries had been when they were in the same stage of industrial development
   D. Japan had taken to export intensely while she was still an under-developed country like others are
   E. Japan is exporting to pay off foreign debts

PASSAGE-6

To avoid the various foolish opinions to which, mankind is prone, no superhuman brain is required. A few simple rules will keep you, not only from all errors, but also from silly errors.

If the matter is one that can be settled by observation, make the observation yourself. Aristotle could have avoided the mistake of thinking that women have fewer teeth than men, by the simple device of asking Mrs. Aristotle to keep her mouth open while he counted. Thinking that you know when, in fact, you do not, is a bad mistake to which, we are all prone. I believe myself that hedgehogs eat black beetles because I have been told that they do; but if I was writing a book on the habits of hedgehogs, I should not commit myself until I had seen one enjoying this diet. Aristotle, however, was less cautious. Ancient and mediaeval writers knew all about unicorns and salamanders; not one of them thought it necessary to avoid dogmatic statements about them because he had never seen one of them.

Many matters, however, are less easily brought to the test of experience. If, like most of the mankind, you have strong convictions on many such matters, there are ways in which, you can learn about your own bias. If an opinion contrary to your own makes you angry, that is a sign that you are subconsciously aware of having no good reason for thinking as you do. If someone says that two and two are five or that Iceland is on the equator, you feel pity rather than anger, unless you know so little of arithmetic or geography that his opinion shakes your own contrary conviction. The most savage controversies are those about the kind of opinion as to which, there is no good evidence, either way. Persecution is used in theology, not in arithmetic, because in arithmetic there is knowledge, but in theology there is only opinion. So, whenever you find yourself getting angry about a difference of opinion, be on the alert; you will probably find, on examination, that your belief is going beyond what the evidence warrants.

A good way of ridding yourself of certain types of dogmatism is to become aware of opinions held in social circles different from your own. When I was young, I lived much outside my own country—in France, Germany, Italy and the United States. I found this very profitable in reducing the intensity of my insular prejudices. If you cannot travel, talk to people with whom you disagree and read a newspaper belonging to a party that is not yours. If the people and the newspaper seem mad, stupid and wicked, remind yourself that you seem so to them. In this opinion, both parties may be right but they cannot both be wrong. This thought should generate a certain caution.

Questions

1. What is the writer's comment on Aristotle in the passage?
   A. Aristotle averted the mistake of thinking that women have lesser teeth than men
   B. Aristotle might have thought about women

as having lesser teeth in their mouths than men

C. Aristotle could have avoided the mistake of thinking that women have lesser teeth than men

D. Aristotle thought women have lesser teeth in their mouths than men

E. Aristotle could not avoid the mistake of thinking that women have lesser teeth than men

2. Writer explains his view by saying that if he is going to write a book on hedgehogs

A. he would state that they are black beetles as he had heard and believed about it

B. he would like to check statement by means of his own observation about hedgehogs

C. he would not stick to the view that hedgehogs are black beetles

D. he won't commit the opinion that hedgehogs are black beetles

E. he would verify the statement that they are black beetles before making it

3. What does the writer mean by latest of experience mentioned in the passage?

A. Verify the facts through a highly qualified and well informed person

B. Ascertain the facts from a person who has specialised knowledge of the subject

C. Verify the facts by making personal observations

D. Experimenting by testing that the matter causes reaction in you

E. To verify the matter in the light of common belief

4. What is the comment of the writer about the unicorn and salamanders mentioned in the stories of ancient and mediaeval eras?

A. The two were neither observed nor did they exist

B. They were observed by the writers

C. The two existed but were not observed or seen by those writers

D. The two were in existence in the past only

E. The two may exist but are not observed by the modern writers so far

5. How has the writer defined a dogmatic statement in the context of passage?

A. The one that is undoubting

B. The one that is beyond questioning

C. The one that is taken for granted

D. The one that is probable

E. The one that is highly convincing

ANSWERS

Passage 1

1	2	3	4	5
D	B	D	D	C

Passage 2

1	2	3	4	5
D	D	C	E	D

Passage 3

1	2	3	4	5
D	D	C	B	5. D

Passage 4

1	2	3	4	5
D	A	E	C	B

Passage 5

1	2	3	4	5
E	E	D	C	C

Passage 6

1	2	3	4	5
B	D	D	B	C

Passage 7

1	2	3	4	5
C	D	D	D	B

Passage 8

1	2	3	4	5
D	D	C	C	D

Passage 9

1	2	3	4	5
C	E	C	A	A

Chapter 7

WORDS COMMONLY MIS-SPELT

Note : *The common and more important words have been italicised.*

A

accredited
accrue
accumulate
accurate
accused
accuse
accussation
accustomed
achieve
acknowledge
acquaintance
acquiesce
acquire
acquisition
acquit
actually
actuality
additional
address
addressee
adequate
adequacy
adhere
adherent
adjourn
admirable
administrator
admission
adopt
adulterate
advantageous
adventure
adventurous
adversary
advise
advisable
advertisement
aerial
aerie (or aery)
aeronaut
aesthetic
affectionate
affiliate
affirmation
affix
afflict
affluence
affray
against
agape
agency
aggravate
aggression
aggrieved
agitator
agony
agree
agreeable
agreement
agriculture
aide-de-camp
alcohol
alert
alien
alienate
allegory
alliance
alliteration
allot
allowance
allude
allusion
almighty
aloud
almost
aloof
amass
amateur
ambiguity
ambitious
amenity
ambiguous
amiable
analysis
anarchy
ancestor
anchor
ancient
anecdote
angelic
anger
angry
anguish
annihilate
announce
annual
annually
anonymous
antidote
antiquity
antiseptic
anoint
antique
antithesis
anxious
anxiety
apology
apologise
apostle
apparatus
apparent
appearance
appellation
appetite
appreciate
apprentice
approach
approve
appropriate
approval
approximate
aptitude
aquatic
architecture
ascertain
ascetic
assemblage
assent
assignation
attendance
audience
autobiography
awe

B

bailiff
balcony
balloon
balm
banana
bankruptcy
banquet
barbarous

barrier
bazaar
beauteous
beautify
beguile
behaviour
believe
benediction
beneficent
beneficial
bequeath
besiege
bestow
bewitch
bias
bicycle
binocular
biography
bivouac
bizarre
blasphemy
bough
bounteous
bouquet
breath
brunette
buffet
bungalow
buoyant
bureaucracy
business
butcher

C

cadence
cadre
cafe
calender
calibre
callous
calumny
candour
canoe
canonise
canvas
canvass
cap-a-pie
caprice
career
carriage
carcass
caricature
casualty
catalogue
celebrate
celestial
cemetry
censure
centenary
ceremonial
champion
character
Christmas
chronicle
circumstantial
coalesce
coalition
coerce
coffee
coincide
collaborate
collapse
commemorate
communication
comparable
competition
complement
comparison
comprehension
condolence
conference
conscious
consecutive
contemporary
contemptible
correspondence
countenance
creature
cubicle
curiosity
cylinder

D

daffodil
daunt
dearth
deceased
deceit
deceive
decency
decision
declaration
deference
deficiency
defiance
defy
deity
deliberate
delineate
delirious
deliverance
demoniac
demurrage
dependant
dependence
depression
derision
descend
descent
despot
develop
devour
diagnosis
diarrhoea
dictionary
difference
diffident
digression
dilemma
discern
discipline
disciplinarian
disguise
dissolution
donor
doughty
drudgery
dubious
dwelling
dynasty

E

earnest
eccentricity
ecstasy
effeminate
efficacious
effrontery
eighty
elapse
elegance
elegiac
elementary
eligible
emancipation
embarrassed
embroidery
empyrean
enamel
enamour
endeavour
endow
endure
enfranchise
enthusiasm
entreaty
envisage
ennoble
equilibrium
ethereal
evaporate
exaltation
exasperate
excellence
exception
exhilarate
explanation
explosion
extinguish
extravagance

F

fashion
fascinate
feature
feign
felicitous
february
feudal
fibre
fiend
fierce
fiery
figure
flourish
foible
forebode
forecast
forgo
foreign
foretell
foreword
forfeit
forty
fourteen
fraud
freight
freer
fruition
fulness
furlong
furniture

G

galloping
gaudy
gauging
genius
genealogy
gorgeous
glutton
gnaw
good-bye
grieve
guarantee
guardian
guild
guise
gymnasium

H

half-caste
hammock
handiwork
handkerchief
harangue
harass
hasten
heinous
heroes
heroine
heterogenous
hideous
holiday
horde
humorous
humorist
hurricane
hypocrite
hyprocrisy
hygiene
hysterical

I

ideal
idiom
idiosyncrasy
idolatry
ignominy
illiteracy
illusion
immanent
immeasurable
imminent
impassable
impartial
impenetrable
impiety
impostor
impoverish
inaccessible
inadequate
inalienable
inappropriate
incandescent
inclement
inconsolable
inconvenient
incredulous
indefatigable
indigenous
indiscretion
indispensable
indomitable
infallible
infinitesimal
inflammation
influential
ingenious
ingenuity
ingenuous
ingratiate
ingredient
inoculation
inquisitor
insurrection
irresistible
itch
itinerant

J

jealous
jeopardise
jessamine
jovial
judgement
jungle

K

kaleidoscope
knack
kennel
knot
knowledge
knuckle

L

laboratory
laborious
labyrinth
language
leapard
ligitimate
library
lieutinant
liquefy
litigant
liveable
livelihood
lovable
luxurious

M

magnificent
magnify
maintenance
majority
manageable
manifesto
manoeuvre
mantelshelf
marketed
marshalled
martial
marvelled
marvellous
masquerade
mattress
mayoralty
meagre
measuring
medicinal
mediocre
memorandum
mercenary
meteor
mileage
milennium
millionaire

miniature
minstrel
mischievous
mischhief
misjudgement
modelled
modified
modifying
moisten
moneyed
monitor
monologue
mortal
murkiness
murky
muscular
myriad

N

navigable
negotiate
night
nestling
niche
niece
ninth
notable
noticeable
notified
notifying
novice
noxious
nuisance
nutrition
nymph

O

oasis
obedience
obeisance
obituary
oblique
obliterate
obnoxious
obscure
obsequious
observance
offence
offensive
olympic
omelet (omelette)
omen
omniscient
onomatopoeia
opium
oppress
opulent
ordinary
original
ounce
outcast
ovation
overawe
overhaul
overwhelming
owner

P

pacify
pageant
paladin
palatial
palsy
paltry
pamphlet
panacea
panegyric
pantheism
paralysis
parchment
paroxysm
particoloured
partition
passionate
pastoral
pastry
pasture
patient
patronage
pecuniary
pedestal
peevish
penance
penitent
penitence
penury
perceptible
perennial
permanence
permissible
persecute
perspire
persuasion
perturbation
perversion
phantom
philosophy
phthisis
picturesque
peer
pigeon
pillage
pique
piquant
pitiful
plausible
plebian
pledge
pneumonia
precis
precocious
predicament
predilection
preference
premium
presumptuous
pretentious
prior
procrastinate
profession
prohibit
proprietor
provisional
psalm
pseudonym
pungent
pursuit
pyre

Q

quack
quaint
quarrel
quarrelled
quarrelsome
quarterly
quell
querulous
question
quiescent
quixotic
quorum

R

raciness
radiance
reillery
raspberry
ravenous
realm
recede
receivable
receive
receipt
receptacle
recompense
reconcilable
reconciliatory
recurrence
reducible
reference
regrettable
regiment
relief
relieve
religious
remedy
reminiscence
remitted
removable
remuneration
repelling
repetition
replaceable

repository
reprehensible
reprieve
reproducible
reprovable
repudiator
reputable
requittal
resolvable
resplendent
resurrection
resumption
retraceable
retractable
retrievable
retrieve
revel
revival
rhetoric
rheumatism
rhyme
rhythm
ribald
ridiculous
righteous
rigorous
ruling
rumour

S

sabbath
sacrament
sacrifice
sacrificial
sacrilege
sacrilegious
sagacious
sagacity
saleable
salutary
satchel
safeless
saucer
sauciness
saviour
scabbard
scenery
schedule
scheme
scholar
schooner
science
scintillate
scurrilous
scythe
secede
secrecy
sedentary
sensibility
sepulchre
shield
shoeing
shriek
siege
sieve
silkiness
similarly
simultaneous
sinecure
silful
slyly
smoulder
solecism
solemnize
soliloquy
soliloquize
sombre
somersault
sootiness
sorcery
souvenir
spasm
specify
spectre
sphere
splendour
spontaneous
sprightly
squalid
squalor
squeak
squire
stalwart
staunch
stratagem
stupefy
subservience
subterranean
subtle
succour
succumb
sufficient
suffrage
sumptuous
supercillious
superfluous
superintendent
supersede
superstition
supervisor
suppressor
supremacy
surfeit
surliness
survivor
susceptible
suspense
suspicious
suspensor
sycophant
syllable
sylvan
symbol
symmetrical
symphony
symptom
synonymous

T

tacit
taciturnity
tactician
tameable
tambourine
tawdry
teasel
technique
tedious
temerity
temperament
temperance
tempestuous
temporary
tenable
tenacious
tenement
tenor
tenuity
termagant
tertiary
testimonial
therapeutics
thistle
thorough
threatening
threshold
tithe
torpor
tortuous
tournament
traceable
traitorous
tranquillity
transcend
transference
transferred
transgressor
treasurer
tremendous
tremulous
turbulence
twelfth
twentieth
tying
tyrant

U

ulterior
ultra vires
umbrella
umpire
unalloyed
unanimous

unassuming
unconscionable
undultatory
unfledged
ungrudging
unintelligible
unison
unsavoury

vacancy
vaccinate
vacillate
vacuum
valedictory
valiant
valley
valuable
vaseline
vegetable
vehement
veiled

unspeakable
unthinkable
unwieldy
upbraid
usurp
utilitarian
utterance
uxorious

V

veneer
vengeance
venison
venomous
ventilator
venturesome
venturous
veracious
veracity
verandah
verify
vestige

vicinity
vicissitude
victual
vigour
vigorous

wagon
waif
waltz
wary
warily
wasteful
weasel
weird
whirl

yacht
yeoman

zodiac

vitiate
vivacity
vivify
votary

W

wholesome
wield
wilful
wilfulness
withhold
witticism
wreak
wrought

Y

yield

Z

zoology

Chapter 8

SOME PURPLE PATCHES

NUMBERED PARAGRAPH

In the following passage, some of the words have been left out. First read the passage over and try to understand what it is about. Then fill in the blanks with the help of the alternatives given. Mark your correct Answer.

PASSAGE-1

Many parents greet their children's teenage years with needless dread. While teens (1) assault us with heavy-metal music (2) outlandhish clothes and spend all (3) time with friends, such behaviour (4) adds up to full-scale revolt. Teenage (5), according to psychologist Laurence Steinberg has been (6) exaggerated. Sociologist Sanford Dornbusch agrees. "The (7) that teenagers inevitably rebel is a (8) that has the potential for great family (9)" says Dornbusch. He believes that notion can (10) communication during this critical time for parents to influence youngsters.

1. A. should B. may C. must D. can

2. A. put B. show C. dress D. flaunt

3. A. our B. their C. his D. her

4. A. infrequently B. sporadically C. scarcely D. always

5. A. revolution B. mania C. subversion D. rebellion

6. A. greatly B. hardly C. never D. always

7. A. surmise B. idea C. complaint D. accusation

8. A. story B. reality C. fact D. myth

9. A. ruin B. harm C. defeat D. downfall

10. A. damage B. destroy C. injure D. suffocate

PASSAGE-2

Nations which have (11) upon programmes of economic development often run into unsuspected barriers which threaten, and often (12) the (13) needed growth of the economy. Industrialisation (14), productivity fails to respond and the nations' goals of a rising standard of living for its people are (15). The cities are (16) up and urban unemployment steadily grows. Very probably there is an equal measure of (17) in the countryside. The poorest quarter of the population in developing lands (18) being left almost entirely behind in the vast (19) of the modern technological society. The "marginal men", the (20) strugglers for survival on the (21) of farm and city, may (22) more than two billion. Can we (23) any human order surviving with so (24) a mass of (25) piling up at its base?

11. A. decided B. progressed C. insisted D. embarked E. initiated

12. A. activate B. deteriorate C. halt D. cut E. enlighten

13. A. positively B. hopefully C. alarmingly D. deceptively E. desperately

14. A. falters B. deviates C. fluctuates D. lowers E. dissolves

15. A. postponed B. frustrated C. suspended D. criticised E. fulfilled

16. A. piling B. filing C. growing D. developing E. enlarging

17. A. worklessness B. shortage C. imbalance D. employment E. diversity

18. A. believes B. condemns C. suffers D. risks E. endeavours

19. A. struggle B. surface
C. result D. abundance
E. transformation

20. A. brave B. aged
C. wretched D. ultimate
E. honest

21. A. fringes B. ground
C. surface D. background
E. environment

22. A. account B. project
C. extend D. mount
E. number

23. A. hope B. suspect
C. question D. imagine
E. argue

24. A. little B. far
C. gross D. long
E. many

25. A. population B. misery
C. generation D. degradation
E. humility

PASSAGE-3

Women have (**26**) made (**27**) in the corporate workplace but certainly not as much as they had (**28**) We have new laws, rules and (**29**) relating to women in the workplace, but what we have not changed much is male (**30**) Women have fallen short in their goals because we (**31**) the potency of the male need to (**32**) their power. We can abide (**33**) by the laws and rules, we create in order to (**34**) women an equal opportunity in the corporate workplace and still not (**35**) the problems that afflicted and eventually capsized the women's raft.

26. A. seldom B. not
C. optimistically D. undoubtedly
E. perhaps

27. A. attempts B. progress
C. decisions D. efforts
E. automation

28. A. prescribed B. informed
C. encompassed D. predisposed
E. expected

29. A. problems B. revolutions
C. policies D. cases
E. activities

30. A. behaviour B. population
C. achievements D. patterns
E. hatred

31. A. risk B. minimise
C. respect D. retaliate
E. underestimate

32. A. know B. maintain
C. evolve D. absolve
E. diminish

33. A. them B. partially
C. occasionally D. scrupulously
E. excessively

34. A. deprive B. donate
C. assure D. deny
E. share

35. A. emphasise B. explore
C. judge D. mentioned
E. overcome

PASSAGE-4

Children are loved by all human beings. But (**36**) this world of human (**37**) ther is no (**38**) nuisance than a boy (**39**) the age of fourteen. He is neither ornamental (**40**) useful. It is impossible to (**41**) affection on him as on a (**42**) boy and he always getting (**43**) the way. If he talks with a childish lisp he is called a baby, and if he answers in a grown-up way he is called impertinent. In fact, any talk from him is resented. Then he is (**44**) the unattractive, growing age. He grows out (**45**) his clothes, with indecent haste. His voice begins to break and loses its childish charm.

36. A. in B. for
C. of D. on

37. A. life B. world
C. affairs D. beings

38. A. bad B. worse
C. worst D. better

39. A. of B. in
C. on D. at

40. A. nor B. or
C. and D. so

41. A. showering B. repose
C. show D. shower

42. A. big B. little
C. tiny D. small

43. A. on B. in
C. through D. off

44. A. at B. of
C. on D. with

45. A. beyond B. from
C. of D. through

PASSAGE-5

New industries supported by foreign interests (46) offer (47) salaries to their employees at all levels of responsibility than (48) locally-owned industries. They need (49) people and are (50) to pay high wages to (51) them. Local industries often (52) the high salaries offered by foreign-supported industries, arguing that this will (53) raise all wages to an excessive level. Workers in local industries, seeing the sharp (54) in job-pay will agitate for an improvement in their salaries. This eventually will drain the resources and (55) their profitability.

46. A. hardly B. reluctantly
C. seldom D. never
E. usually

47. A. disproportionate B. better
C. proportionate D. comparable
E. unreasonable

48. A. did B. could
C. do D. their
E. does

49. A. local B. several
C. more D. talented
E. less

50. A. willing B. bound
C. forced D. reluctant
E. authorised

51. A. entertain B. retain
C. enrich D. hire
E. bribe

52. A. uphold B. imitate
C. protest D. pay
E. accept

53. A. hardly B. considerably
C. not D. unreasonably
E. artificially

54. A. difference B. cut
C. hike D. decrease
E. injustice

55. A. augment B. fulfil
C. enhance D. lower
E. check

PASSAGE-6

The people of Orissa, where 70 per cent of the cultivable (56) is rain-fed had no choice but to migrate because of the (57) drought. Migration is an annual (58) in the drought-prone districts of this State. Madhya Pradesh (59) a favourite (60) besides Andhra Pradesh, Delhi and even Punjab. A survey (61) that every year more than 50,000 people migrate from one district alone. But this year more than 20,000 have already migrated (62) from one block of this district.

56. A. grain B. crop
C. water D. area
E. length

57. A. fear B. weak
C. best D. simple
E. severe

58. A. claim B. affair
C. festival D. right
E. demand

59. A. be B. were
C. is D. may
E. are

60. A. opportunity B. agency
C. destination D. force
E. course

61. A. shows B. collects
C. provided D. obtains
E. conducted

62. A. into B. above
C. beyond D. from
E. although

PASSAGE-7

To the curious and the (63) the sea still presents the challenge of the unknown, for ignorance is still the (64) characteristic of man's relations to the sea. But now, more than ever, necessity (65) us onward in our exploration of the sea. We now have submarines capable of (66) submergence for many months (67) missiles capable of (68) many times greater than that (69) by World War II. For (70) reasons, therefore, we need (71) to learn more about the (72) of ocean bottom, about deep ocean currents, temperature, density and so on.

63. A. outgoing B. courageous C. formidable D. watchful E. intelligent

64. A. outstanding B. remarkable C. valuable D. critical E. distinguishing

65. A. projects B. excites C. goads D. propels E. makes

66. A. provocative B. turbulant C. deadly D. durable E. steady

67. A. guiding B. subjecting C. providing D. holding E. directing

68. A. expansion B. destruction C. projection D. domination E. aggression

69. A. forced B. witnessed C. experienced D. conceived E. wrought

70. A. traditional B. academic C. deliberate D. strategic E. historical

71. A. ugrently B. drastically C. judiciously D. cautiously E. wilfully

72. A. tenacity B. distribution C. topography D. resources E. velocity

PASSAGE-8

Energy is the most important (73) for economic development (74) a country and (75) in the quality of life of its people. Recent developments in the (76) of science and technology have revolutionised the industrial (77) of the country due to which the energy (78) has increased mainifold. But these developments also (79) a huge quantity of undesirable but (80) wastes which are regularly thrown into rivers, ponds, etc. Waste products from thermal power plants (81) fly ash is one of such wastes which has drawn the (82) of scientists and academicians.

73. A. matter B. factor C. output D. attribute E. ingredient

74. A. on B. about C. of D. for E. in

75. A. dilution B. deterioration C. development D. improvement E. decline

76. A. field B. range C. respect D. scope E. place

77. A. input B. sickness C. consumption D. backwardness E. growth

78. A. requirement B. scenario C. strength D. accumulation E. level

79. A. utilise B. generate C. regulate D. maintain E. retain

80. A. marginal B. sustainable C. needful D. unavoidable E. useful

81. A. often B. occasionally C. rarely D. instantly E. mainly

82. A. research B. thought C. attention D. morale E. minds

ANSWERS

1	2	3	4	5	6	7	8	9	10
B	D	B	D	D	A	B	B	A	D
11	12	13	14	15	16	17	18	19	20
D	D	E	A	B	C	A	C	A	A
21	22	23	24	25	26	27	28	29	30
A	E	A	C	A	D	B	E	C	A
31	32	33	34	35	36	37	38	39	40
C	B	E	C	E	A	D	B	A	A
41	42	43	44	45	46	47	48	49	50
D	B	B	A	C	E	B	C	D	A
51	52	53	54	55	56	57	58	59	60
B	C	D	A	D	D	E	B	C	C
61	62	63	64	65	66	67	68	69	70
A	D	D	B	C	E	D	B	B	D
71	72	73	74	75	76	77	78	79	80
A	C	B	C	D	A	E	A	B	D
81	82								
E	C								

REARRANGEMENT OF SENTENCES

TYPE-ONE

Each of the following passages contains five sentences marked a, b, c, d and e. Rearrange the five sentences in proper sequence in order to form a meaningful paragraph. Answer the questions named below each of the passages.

PASSAGE-1

a. Both of them are human beings.
b. They have the same desires, passions, emotions and sentiments.
c. Both of them are made of five elements.
d. Both men and women are created by the same God.
e. They are made of the same flesh and blood.

Questions

1. Which of the following will be the FIRST sentence?

A. a B. b
C. c D. d
E. e

2. Which of the following will be the SECOND sentence?

A. a B. b
C. c D. d
E. e

3. Which of the following will be the THIRD sentence?

A. a B. b
C. c D. d
E. e

4. Which of the following will be the FOURTH sentence?

A. a B. b
C. c D. d
E. e

5. Which of the following will be the FIFTH sentence?

A. a B. b
C. c D. d
E. e

PASSAGE-2

a. All of them are very dedicated to the institute.
b. It was started with only four faculty members.
c. It is one of the reasons for its recognition in such a short period.
d. Now it has a team of fifty highly qualified persons.
e. This institute is only four years old.

Questions

6. Which of the following should be the FIRST sentence?

A. a B. b
C. c D. d
E. e

7. Which of the following should be the SECOND sentence?

A. a B. b
C. c D. d
E. e

8. Which of the following should be the THIRD sentence?

A. a B. b
C. c D. d
E. e

9. Which of the following should be the FOURTH sentence?

A. a B. b
C. c D. d
E. e

10. Which of the following should be the FIFTH sentence?

A. a B. b
C. c D. d
E. e

PASSAGE-3

a. She came back wet and with a cold.
b. It was raining in Torents.
c. Ram had been sick for some days.
d. Many things were needed in the house.
e. Despite it, Ram's wife went out to market.

Questions

11. Which sentence should come FIRST in the passage?

A. a B. b
C. c D. d
E. e

12. Which sentence should come SECOND in the passage?

A. a B. b
C. c D. d
E. e

13. Which sentence should come THIRD in the passage?

A. a B. b
C. c D. d
E. e

14. Which sentence should come FOURTH in the passage?

A. a B. b
C. c D. d
E. e

15. Which sentence should come FIFTH in the passage?

A. a B. b
C. c D. d
E. e

PASSAGE-4

a. The patient became helpless.
b. The patient went to the doctor.
c. He wanted to give him some present.
d. The docotr totally refused to do so.
e. He requested him to accept it.

Questions

16. Which of the following should be the FIRST sentence?

A. a B. b
C. c D. d
E. e

17. Which of the following should be the SECOND sentence?

A. a B. b
C. c D. d
E. e

18. Which of the following should be the THIRD sentence?

A. a
B. b
C. c
D. d
E. e

19. Which of the following should be the FOURTH sentence?

A. a
B. b
C. c
D. d
E. e

20. Which of the following should be the FIFTH sentence?

A. a
B. b
C. c
D. d
E. e

PASSAGE-5

a. Children sat listening to him for almost an hour.
b. At the stories were full of crime and mystery.
c. Ramesh conceded to their request.
d. That hour was fascinating for them.
e. Children requested Ramesh to tell them stories.

Questions

21. Which of the following will be the FIRST sentence?

A. a
B. b
C. c
D. d
E. e

22. Which of the following will be the SECOND sentence?

A. a
B. b
C. c
D. d
E. e

23. Which of the following will be the THIRD sentence?

A. a
B. b
C. c
D. d
E. e

24. Which of the following will be the FOURTH sentence?

A. a
B. b
C. c
D. d
E. e

25. Which of the following will be the FIFTH sentence?

A. a
B. b
C. c
D. d
E. e

ANSWERS

Passage-1

The proper sequence of the sentences is:

Both men and women are created by the same God. They are made of the same flesh and blood. Both of them are made of five elements. They have the same desires, passions, emotions and sentiments. Both of them are human beings.

1. D   2. E   3. C   4. B   5. A

Passage-2

The proper sequence of the sentences is:

This institute is only four years old. It was started with only four faculty members. Now it has a team of fifty highly qualified persons. All of them are very dedicated to the institute. It is one of the reasons for its recognition in such a short period.

6. E   7. B   8. D   9. A   10. C

Passage-3

The proper sequence of the sentenees is:

Ram had been sick for some days. Many things were needed in the house. It was raining in Torrents. Despite it, Ram's wife went out to rharket. She came back wet and with a cold.

11. C   12. D   13. B   14. E   15. A

Passage-4

The proper sequence of the sentences is:

The patient went to the doctor. He wanted to give him some present. He requested him to accept it. The doctor totally refused to do so. The patient became helpless.

16. B   17. C   18. E   19. D   20. A

Passage-5

The proper sequence of the sentenees is:

Children requested Ramesh to tell them stories. Ramesh conceded to their request. Children sat listening to him for almost an hour. All the stories were full of crime and mysterv That hour was fascinating for them.

21. E   22. C   23. A   24. B   25. D

TYPE-TWO

In questions below, each passage consists of six sentences. The first and the sixth sentences are given in the beginning. The middle four sentences in each have been removed and jumbled up. These are labelled P, Q, R and S. Find out the proper order for the four sentences.

1. S_1 : Since the sixties there has been an increasing interest in human neurophysiology, which deals with the neural bases of mental activity and behaviour.

S_6 : So far the journal has published a mixture of articles including reports and investigations.

P : It has format which is very similar to that of *Brain and Language*, a sister journal.

Q : Since then, a number of journals devoted entirely to this area of research have appeared.

R : Before the 1960's when this field was the concern of a small number of investigators, research articles were scattered in various neurological journals.

S : *Brain and Cognition* is one such journal.

The proper sequence should be:

A. R Q S P B. Q R S P
C. Q S P R D. R S P Q

2. S_1 : She said on the phone that she would report for duty next day.

S_6 : Eventually we reported to the police.

P : We waited for a few days, then we decided to go to her place.

Q : But she did not.

R : We found it locked.

S : Even after that we waited for her for quite a few days.

The proper sequence should be:

A. P R S Q B. Q P S R
C. Q P R S D. S Q P R

3. S_1: A force of attraction exists between everybody in the universe.

S_6 : The greater the mass, the greater is the earth's force of attraction on it—we call this force of attraction gravity.

P : Normally it is very small but when one of the bodies is a planet, like the earth, the force is considerable.

Q : It has been investigated by many scientists including Galileo and Newton.

R : Everything on or near the surface of the earth is attracted by the mass of the earth.

S : This gravitational force depends on the mass of the bodies involved.

The proper sequence should be:

A. P R Q S B. P R S Q
C. Q S R P D. Q S P R

4. S_1 : Metals are today being replaced by polymers in many applications.

S_6 : Many Indian Institutes of Science and Technology run special programmes on polymer science.

P : Above all, they are cheaper and easier to process, making them a viable alternative to metals.

Q : Polymers are essentially long chains of hydrocarbon molecules.

R : Today polymers as strong as metals have been developed.

S : These have replaced the traditional chromium-plated metallic bumpers in cars.

The proper sequence should be:

A. Q R S P B. R S Q P
C. R Q S P D. Q R P S

5. S_1 : Biological evolution has not fitted man to any specific environment.

S_6 : That brilliant sequence of cultural peaks can most appropriately be termed the ascent of Man.

P : It is by no means a biological evolution, but it is a cultural one.

Q : His imagination, his reason, his emotional subtlety and toughness, make it possible for him not to accept the environment but to change it.

R : And that series of inventions by which man from age to age has reshaped his environment is a different kind of evolution.

S : Among the multitude of animals which scamper, fly, burrow and swim around us, he is the only one who is not locked into his environment.

The proper sequence should be:

A. Q P R S B. S R Q P
C. Q R S P D. S Q R P

6. S_1: Growing up means not only getting larger, but also using our senses and our brains to become more aware of the things around us.

S_6: In other words, we must develop and use our ability to reason, because the destruction or the preservation of the places in which we live depends on us.

P : Not only does he have a memory but he is able to think and reason.

Q : In this, man differs from all other animals.

R : Before we spray our roadside plants or turn sewage into our rivers, we should pause to think what the results of our actions are likely to be.

S : That is to say, he is able to plan what he is going to do in the light of his experience before the does it.

The proper sequence should be:

A. Q R S P B. S P Q R
C. S P R Q D. Q P S R

7. S_1: It is regrettable that there is widespread corruption in the country at all levels.

S_6: This is indeed a tragedy of great magnitude.

P : So there is hardly anything that the government can do about it now.

Q : And there are graft and other malpractices too.

R : The impression that corruption is a universal phenomenon persists and the people do not cooperate in checking this evil.

S : Recently several offenders were brought to book, but they were not given deterrent punishment.

The proper sequence should be:

A. Q S R P B. S Q R P
C. R S Q P D. P Q S R

8. S_1 : Smoke oozed up between the planks.

S_6: Most people bore the shock bravely.

P : Passengers wee told to be ready to quit the ship.

Q : The rising gale fanned the smouldering fire.

R : Everyone now knew there was a fire on board.

S : Flame broke out here and there.

The proper sequence should be:

A. S R Q P B. Q P S R
C. R S P Q D. Q S R P

9. S_1 : It was dark moonless night.

S_6: They all seemed to him to be poor and ordinary—mere childish words.

P : He turned over the pages, reading passages here and there.

Q : He heard them on the floor.

R : The poet took down his books of poems from his shelves.

S : Some of them contained his earliest writings which he had almost forgotten.

The proper sequence should be:

A. R P Q S B. R Q S P
C. R S P Q D. R P S Q

10. S_1 : A noise started above their heads.

S_6: Nearly two hundred lives were lost on the fateful day.

P : But people did not take it seriously.

Q : That was to show everyone that there was something wrong.

R : It was a dangerous thing to do.

S : For, within minutes the ship began to sink.

The proper sequence should be:

A. P Q R S B. P R Q S
C. Q P R S D. Q P S R

11. S_1 : The cooperative system of doing business is a good way of encouraging ordinary workers to work hard.

S_6: The main object is to maintain the interest of every member of the society and to ensure that the members participate actively in the projects of the society.

P : If the society is to be well run, it is necessary to prevent insincere officials being elected to the committee which is solely responsible for the running of the business.

Q : They get this from experienced and professional workers who are not only familiar with the cooperative system, but also with efficient methods of doing business.

R : To a large extent, many cooperative societies need advice and guidance.

S : The capital necessary to start a business venture is obtained by the workers' contributions.

The proper sequence should be:

A. S Q P R B. P Q S R

C. S R Q P D. P S R Q

12. S_1 : American private lives may seem shallow.

S_6 : This would not happen in China, he said.

P : Students would walk away with books they had not paid for.

Q : A Chinese journalist commented on a curious institution: the library.

R : Their public morality, however, impressed visitors.

S : But in general they returned them.

The proper sequence should be:

A. P S Q R B. Q P S R

C. R Q P S D. R P S Q

13. S_1 : The *Bhagavadgita* recognises the nature of man and the needs of man.

S_6 : A man who does not harmonise them, is not truly human.

P : All these three aspects constitute the nature of man.

Q : It shows how the human being is a rational one, an ethical one and a spiritual one.

R : More than all, it must be a spiritual experience.

S : Nothing can give him fulfilment unless it satisfies his reason, his ethical conscience.

The proper sequence should be:

A. P S R Q B. R S P Q

C. Q P S R D. P S Q R

14. S_1 : I usually sleep quite well in the train, but this time I slept only a little.

S_6 : It was shut all night, as usual.

P : Most people wanted it shut and I wanted it open.

Q : As usual, I got angry about the window.

R : The quarrel left me completely upset.

S : There were too many people and too much luggage all around.

The proper sequence should be:

A. R S Q P B. S Q P R

C. S Q R P D. R S P Q

15. S_1 : For decades, American society has been called a melting pot.

S_6 : In recent years, such differences—accentuated by the arrival of immigrants from Asia and other parts of the world in the United States—have become something to celebrate and to nurture.

P : Differences remained—in appearance, mannerisms, customs, speech, religion and more.

Q : The term has long been a cliche, and a half-truth.

R : But homogenisation was never achieved.

S : Yes, immigrants from diverse cultures and traditions did cast off vestiges of their native lands and become almost imperceptibly woven into the American fabric.

The proper sequence should be:

A. Q R S P B. S Q R P

C. S Q P R D. Q S R P

16. S_1 : While talking to a group, one should feel self-confident and courageous.

S_6 : Any man can develop his capacity if he has the desire to do so.

P : Nor is it a gift bestowed by Providence on only a few.

Q : One should also learn how to think calmly and clearly.

R : It is like the ability to play golf.

S : It is not as difficult as most men imagine.

The proper sequence should be:

A. S Q P R B. Q S P R

C. Q R S P D. R S Q P

17. S_1 : In 1934, William Golding published a small volume of poems.

S_6 : *But Lord of the Flies* which came out in 1954 was welcomed as "a most absorbing and instructive tale".

P : During the World War II (1939-45) he joined the Royal Navy and was present at the sinking of the *Bismarck*.

Q : He returned to teaching in 1945 and gave it up in 1962, and is now a full-time writer.

R : In 1939, he married and started teaching at Bishop Wordsworth's School in Salisbury

S : At first his novels were not accepted.

The proper sequence should be:

A. R P Q S B. R P S Q

C. S R P Q D. S Q P R

18. S_1 : Our ancestors thought that anything which moved itself was alive.

S_6 : Therefore some scientists think that life is just a very complicated mechanism.

P : The philosopher Descartes thought that both men and animals were machines.

Q : But a machine such as a motorcar or a steamship moves itself, and as soon as machines which moved themselves had been made, people asked, "Is man a machine?"

R : And before the days of machinery that was a good definition.

S : He also thought that the human machine was partly controlled by the soul action on a certain part of the brain, while animals had no souls

The proper sequence should be:

A. P R S Q B. R P Q S

C. P S Q R D. R Q P S

19. S_1 : But how does a new word get into the dictionary?

S_6 : He sorts them according to their grammatical function, and carefully writes a definition.

P : When a new dictionary is being edited, a lexicographer collects all the alphabetically arranged citation slips for a particular word.

Q : The dictionary makers notice it and make a note of it on a citation slip.

R : The moment a new word is coined, it usually enters the spoken language.

S : The word then passes from the realm of hearing to the realm of writing.

The proper sequence should be:

A. P Q R S B. P R S Q

C. R Q P S D. R S Q P

20. S_1 : There is a touching story of Professor Hardy visiting Ramanujan as he lay desperately ill in hospital at Putney.

S_6 : It is the lowest number that can be expressed in two different ways as the sum of two cubes."

P : 'No, Hardy, that is not a dull number in the very least.

Q : Hardy, who was a very shy man, could not find the words for his distress.

R : It was 1729.

S : The best he could do, as he got to the bedside was: "I say, Ramanujan, I thought the number of the taxi I came down in was a very dull number".

The proper sequence should be:

A. P R S Q B. Q S R P

C. Q S P R D. S Q R P

21. S_1 : The heart is the pump of life.

S_6 : All this was made possible by the invention of the heart-lung machine.

P : They have even succeeded in heart transplants.

Q : Nowadays surgeons are able to stop a patient's heart and carry out complicated operations.

R : A few years ago it was impossible to operate on a patient whose heart was not working properly.

S : If the heart stops we die in about five minutes.

The proper sequence should be:

A. S R Q P B. S P R Q

C. S Q P R D. S R P Q

22. S_1 : On vacation in Tangier, Morocco, my friend and I sat down at a street cafe!

S_6 : Finally a man walked over to me and whispered, "Hey buddy ..... this guy's your waiter and he wants your order."

P : At one point, he bent over with a big smile, showing me a single gold tooth and a dingy fez.

Q : Soon I felt the presence of someone standing alongside me.

R : But this one wouldn't budge.

S : We had been cautioned about beggars and were told to ignore them.

The proper sequence should be:

A. S Q R P B. S Q P R

C. Q S R P D. Q S P R

23. S_1 : There is only one monkey we can thoroughly recommend as an indoor pet.

S_6 : Finally, let me say that no other monkey has a better temper or more winning ways.

P : They quickly die from colds and coughs after the first winter fogs.

Q : It is the beautiful and intelligent Capuchin monkey.

R : The lively little Capuchins, however, may be left for years in an English house without the least danger to their health.

S : The Marmosets, it is true, are more beautiful than the Capuchins and just as pleasing, but they are too delicate for the English climate.

The proper sequence should be:

A. P Q R S B. Q R P S

C. Q S P R D. R P S Q

24. Hungry, with a population of about ten million, lies between Czechoslovakia to the north and Yugoslavia to the south.

S_6 : The new industries derive mainly from agricultural production.

P : Here a great deal of grain is grown.

Q : In recent years, however, progress has been made also in the field of industrialisation.

R : Most of this country consists of an extremely fertile plain, through which the river Danube flows.

S : In addition to grain, the plain produces potatoes, sugar, wine and livestock.

The proper sequence should be:

A. Q R S P B. R P S Q

C. P R S Q D. R Q S P

25. S_1 : Throughout history man has used energy from the sun.

S_6: This energy comes from inside atoms.

P_6 : Today, when we burn wood or use electric current we are drawing on energy.

Q : However, we now have a new supply of energy.

R : All our ordinary life depends on the sun.

S : This has come from the sun.

The proper sequence should be:

A. S Q P R B. R Q P S

C. Q S R P D. P S R Q

26. S_1 : In India marriages are usually arranged by parents.

S_6 : She felt she was a modern girl and not a subject for bargaining

P : Sometimes girls and boys do not like the idea of arranged marriages.

Q : Most young people accept this state of affairs.

R : Shanta was like that.

S : They assume their parents can make good choices.

The proper sequence should be:

A. S P R Q B. P S R Q

C. Q S P R D. R Q P S

27. S_1 : I had halted on the road.

S_6 : I decided to watch him for a while and then go home.

P : As soon as I saw the elephant I knew I should not shoot him.

Q : It is a serious matter to shoot a working elephant.

R : I knew that his 'must' was already passing off.

S : The elephant was standing eighty yards from the road.

The proper sequence should be:

A. S P Q R B. P Q S R

C. R Q P S D. S R P Q

28. S_1 : A man can be physically confined within stone walls.

S_6 : No tyranny can intimidate a lover of liberty.

P : But his mind and spirit will still be free.

Q : Thus his freedom of action may be restricted.

R : His hopes and aspirations still remain with him.

S : Hence, he will be free spiritually if not physically.

The proper sequence should be:
A. P Q R S B. S R Q P
C. Q P R S D. Q P S R

29. S_1 : The dictionary is the best friend for your task.
S_6 : Soon you will realize that this is an exciting task
P : That may not be possible always.
Q : It is wise to look it up immediately.
R : Then it must be firmly written on the memory and traced at the first opportunity.
S : Never allow a strange word to pass unchallenged.
The proper sequence should be:
A. P Q R S B. S P Q R
C. Q R P S D. S Q P R

30. S_1 : Far away in a little street there is a poor house.
S_6 : His mother has nothing to give but water, so he is crying
P : Her face is thin and worn and her hands are coarse, pricked by a needle, for she is a seam-stress.
Q : One of the windows is open and through it I can see a poor woman.
R : He has a fever and a asking for oranges.
S : In a bed in a corner of the room her little boy is lying ill.
The proper sequence should be:
A. S R Q P B. P Q S R
C. Q P S R D. R S P Q

31. S_1 : Calcutta unlike other cities, kept its trams.
S_6 : The foundation stone was laid in 1972.
P : As a result, there is horrendous congestion.
Q : It was going to be the first in South Asia.
R : They run down the centre of the road.
S : To ease in the city decided to build an underground railway line.
The proper sequence should be:
A. P R S Q B. P S Q R
C. S Q R P D. R P S Q

32. S_1 : We now know that oceans are very deep.
S_6 : This reaches from India to the Antarctic.
P : For example, the Indian Ocean has a range called the Indian Ridge.
Q : Much of it is fairly flat.
R : However, there are great mountain ranges as well.
S : On average the bottom is two and a half to three and a half miles down.
The proper sequence should be:
A. S Q P R B. P Q S R
C. R S Q P D. Q P R S

33. S_1 : As he passed beneath her he heard the swish of her wings.
S_6 : The next moment he felt his wings spread outwards.
P : He was not falling head long now.
Q : Then monstrous terror seized him
R : But it only lasted a minute.
S : He could hear nothing.
The proper sequence should be:
A. P S Q R B. Q S P R
C. Q S R P D. P R Q S

34. S_1 : When a satellite is launched, the rocket begins by going slowly upwards through the air.
S_6 : Consequently, the rocket still does not become too hot.
P : However, the higher it goes, the less air it meets.
Q : As the rocket goes higher, it travels faster.
R : For the atmosphere becomes thinner.
S : As a result there is less friction.
The proper sequence should be:
A. Q P R S B. Q S P R
C. P Q R S D. P Q S R

35. S_1 : Sunbirds are among the smallest of Indian birds.
S_6 : Our common sunbirds are the purple sunbird, the glossy black species and purplerumped sunbird, the yellow and maroon species
P : Though they are functionally similar to the hummingbirds of the New World, they are totally unrelated.
Q : They do eat small insects too.
R : They are also some of the most brilliantly-coloured birds.
S : Sunbirds feed on nectar mostly and help in pollination.
The proper sequence should be:
A. S Q P R B. R P S Q
C. Q P R S D. P S R Q

ANSWERS

1	2	3	4	5	6	7	8	9	10
A	C	D	A	C	D	A	A	D	C
11	12	13	14	15	16	17	18	19	20
A	B	B	B	B	B	A	C	A	B
21	22	23	24	25	26	27	28	29	30
A	C	B	B	D	C	B	A	D	C
31	32	33	34	35					
D	A	C	A	A					

SENTENCE IMPROVEMENT

In questions given below, a part of the sentence is italicised. Below are given alternatives to the italicised part which may improve the sentence. Choose the correct alternative. In case no improvement is needed, option 'D' is the answer.

1. If you *cross the line* you will be disqualified.
A. cross upon the line
B. cross on the line
C. cross out the line
D. No improvement

2. My friend was in hospital for a week *after* an accident.
A. through
B. following
C. for
D. No improvement

3. I want *you to clearly understand* that excuses won't do.
A. you clearly to understand
B. you to understand clearly
C. to clearly understand you
D. No improvement

4. I *have lived* in Delhi since I was four.
A. am living
B. lived
C. had lived
D. No improvement

5. To get one's name in the Rowland Ward's book of hunting records was the *hot* ambition of every serious hunter.
A. extreme
B. burning
C. high
D. No improvement

6. In fact, if it hadn't been for his *invaluable advice* on so many occasions I wouldn't have achieved anything in life.
A. remarkable advice
B. valuable advices
C. priceless suggestions
D. No improvement

7. The greatest thing in style is to have *a use* of metaphor.
A. knowledge
B. command
C. need
D. No improvement

8. John *had told* me that he hasn't done it yet.
A. told
B. tells
C. was telling
D. No improvement

9. The record for the biggest tiger hunt has not been *met* since 1911 when Lord Hardinge, then Viceroy of India, shot a tiger that measured eleven feet six and three-fourth inches.
A. improved
B. broken
C. bettered
D. No improvement

10. Whatever to our other problems, we have no *shortcoming* to cheap labour in India.
A. default
B. deficit
C. scarcity
D. No improvement

11. Mr. Smith arrived *at* India in June last year.
A. to
B. by
C. in
D. No improvement

12. If he *would have tried* he would have succeeded.
A. is tried
B. was tried
C. had tried
D. No improvement

13. I will not go to school, if *it shall rain tomorrow.*
A. it would rain tomorrow
B. it will rain tomorrow
C. it rains tomorrow
D. No improvement

14. Why the dinosaurs died out *is not known.*
A. it is not known
B. the reason is not known
C. that is not known
D. No improvement

15. He could not *look* anything in the dark room.
A. look at
B. see
C. see through
D. No improvement

16. He *was fined* for careless driving.
A. got fined
B. fined
C. was to be fined
D. No improvement

17. We look forward to *hear* from you.
A. hearing
B. have heard
C. listen
D. No improvement

18. When the examinations were over *Anil and me* went to our native town.
A. me and Anil
B. Anil and I
C. I and Anil
D. No improvement

19. Will you kindly *open* the knot?
A. unite
B. break
C. loose
D. No improvement

20. Realising is the significance of technical education for a developing country, the government *laid aside* a large sum on it during the last plan-period.
A. laid up
B. set aside
C. laid out
D. No improvement

21. Other countries *have eradicated* this disease ten years ago.
A. eradicated
B. had eradicated
C. did eradicated
D. No improvement

22. We were *not* the wiser for all his effort to explain the case to us.
A. none
B. neither
C. nevertheless
D. No improvement

23. If I stood alone in defence of truth, and the whole world *is banded* against me and against truth, I would fight them all.
A. will be banded
B. were banded
C. banded
D. No improvement

24. During his long discourse, he did not *touch* that point.
A. touch upon
B. touch on
C. touch of
D. No improvement

25. He *has not and can never be* in the good books of his employer because he lakes honesty.
A. has not and cannot be
B. has not and can never been
C. has not been and can never be
D. No improvement.

ANSWERS

1	2	3	4	5	6	7	8	9	10
D	B	D	D	C	D	A	B	B	C
11	12	13	14	15	16	17	18	19	20
C	C	C	D	B	D	A	B	A	B
21	22	23	24	25					
A	A	B	B	C					

COMPLETION OF SENTENCES

There is a blank space in each of the following sentences. Fill in the blank by choosing the correct word or group of words from the alternatives— A, B, C and D.

1. I shall go .... for higher studies.
A. alien B. foreign
C. abroad D. emigrated

2. She gave me .... to drink.
A. some water B. little water
C. any water D. few water

3. You should not avoid .... him.
A. for meeting B. in meeting
C. to meet D. meeing

4. Are you .... your lessons?
A. busy for preparing
B. busy preparing
C. busy to prepare
D. busy of preparing

5. If you .... hard, you would have succeeded.
A. worked
B. had worked
C. were working
D. would have worked

6. It is long since I .... her.
A. met B. had met
C. have met D. will have met

7. She did nothing but ....
A. complaining B. complain
C. complained D. None of these

8. He is more intelligent .... in the class.
A. than all the boys
B. than any other
C. than any other boys
D. to all the boys

9. Can you write faster .... ?
A. to I B. to me
C. than me D. than I

10. She insisted .... the work.
A. on my doing
B. in my doing
C. in me doing
D. on me doing

11. A series of lectures .... arranged.
A. are B. were
C. have been D. has been

12. I admitted that I was ....
A. on the wrong
B. on wrong
C. in wrong
D. in the wrong

13. Do you speak Bengali? Yes. I learnt .... in Calcutta.
A. how speak it
B. it to speak
C. speak it
D. how to speak it

14. Why was he so late? I do not know ....
A. what the reason was
B. what the reason can be
C. can what the reason be
D. what could the reason be

15. I am not prepared to .... him in this matter.
A. go off B. go with
C. go for D. go up

ANSWERS

1	2	3	4	5	6	7	8	9	10
C	A	D	B	B	A	B	C	D	A
11	12	13	14	15					
D	D	D	A	B					

MATHEMATICS

QUANTITATIVE APTITUDE

1

NUMBERS

A **number** tells us that how many units are there in a given quantity. A number denotes one or more units of same kind of thing. For example **Two** books, **Three** tables, **Ten** pens, **Fifteen** penciles etc.

TYPES OF NUMBERS

1. **Whole Numbers** : The numbers 0, 1, 2, 3, 4, 5.....etc. are called whole numbers. 54 is a whole number while $3\frac{1}{4}$ is not a whole number.
2. **Even Numbers :** The numbers which are divisible by 2 are called even numbers. For example 2, 4, 8, 24, 38 etc.
3. **Odd Numbers :** The numbers which are not divisible by 2 are called odd numbers. For example 1, 3, 5, 7, 9, 11, 13, 15 etc.
4. **Prime Numbers :** The numbers which are only divisible by 1 or the number itself are called prime numbers. For example 2, 3, 5, 11, 17 etc.
5. **Composite Numbers :** The numbers which are not prime, are called composite numbers. Prime numbers and composite numbers together make a set of natural numbers.
6. **Consecutive Numbers :** The numbers are called consecutive numbers when one number is successor of the other. For example 3, 4, 5, 6, 7 and 8 are consecutive while 3, 4, 5, 6, 7 and 9 are not consecutive numbers. 4, 6, 8, 10 are even consecutive numbers while 7, 9, 11, 13 are odd consecutive numbers.
7. **Rational Numbers :** A number which can be expressed in the form A/B, where A and B are integers and B is different from zero, is called rational number. For example 8, $\frac{9}{8}, \frac{25}{27}$, 0 etc. are rational numbers.
8. **Irrational Numbers :** A number which cannot be expressed in the form A/B is called irrational number. Where A and B are integers and B is different from zero. For example $\sqrt{11}, \sqrt{13}, \sqrt{15}, 6+\sqrt{7}$ are irrational numbers.
9. **Face value of a number :** Face value of a digit in a number is the digit itself. For example in 75, Face value of 7 is 7 and Face value of 5 is 5.
10. **Place value of a number :** Place value of a digit in a number is according to its place. For example in 75, place value of 7 is 70 because 7 is in ten's place and place value of 5 is 5.

Important Note :

(*i*)	The number 1 is neither composite nor prime.
(*ii*)	2 is only a number which is even and prime.

Remember the following while solving problems :

1.	(*a*)	0 is neither positive nor negative integer.
	(*b*)	'+1' is the smallest integer in positive integers and '– 1' is the largest integer in negative integers.
2.	(*c*)	In a whole square number, 0, 1, 4, 5, 6 and 9 may be at its units's place.
	(*d*)	In a cubic number 0 to 9 any digit may be at its unit's place.

3. (e) Sum of numbers from 1 to n

$$= \frac{n(n+1)}{2}$$

(f) Sum of odd numbers from 1 to n

$$= \left(\frac{\text{Last odd number } + 1}{2}\right)^2$$

(g) Sum of even numbers from 1 to n

$$= \frac{\text{Last even number}}{2} \times \left(\frac{\text{Last even number}}{2} + 1\right)$$

Example 1. *What is the sum of numbers 1 to 40?*

Solution. $\because$ Sum of the numbers from 1 to n

$$= \frac{n(n+1)}{2}$$

$\therefore$ Sum of the numbers from 1 to 40,

$$= \frac{40(40+1)}{2} = 20 \times 41 = 820.$$

Example 2. *In three numbers, first number is double the second and thrice the third. If the sum of three numbers is 33 then what will be these numbers?*

Solution. Let first number = x

$\therefore$ second number $= \frac{x}{2}$

and third number $= \frac{x}{3}$

According to problem,

Sum of three numbers = 33

$$\therefore \quad x + \frac{x}{2} + \frac{x}{3} = 33 \Rightarrow \frac{11x}{6} = 33 \Rightarrow x = 18$$

Therefore numbers will be 18,

$$\left(\frac{18}{2} = 9\right) \text{ and } \left(\frac{18}{3} = 6\right).$$

Example 3. *If the difference between two numbers is 3 and difference between their squares is 39, then what will be the larger number ?*

Solution. Let the larger number and smaller number be x and y respectively.

According to problem,

$$x - y = 3 \quad \text{... (i)}$$

$$x^2 - y^2 = 39 \quad \text{... (ii)}$$

From (i) and (ii)

$$x^2 - y^2 = 39 \Rightarrow (x+y)(x-y) = 39$$

$$\Rightarrow (x+y) \times 3 = 39 \Rightarrow x + y = \frac{39}{3} = 13 \quad \text{...(iii)}$$

From (i) and (iii), $2x = 3 + 13 = 16$

$$\Rightarrow x = \frac{16}{2} = 8$$

$\therefore$ Larger number = 8.

Example 4. *When a number is divided by 7, the remainder is 4 and when the number is divided by 6, the remainder is 3. What will be the number ?*

Solution. $\because$ Number = Divisor × Quotient + Remainder

In First position,

Number = 7 × Quotient + 4 ... (i)

In Second position,

Number = 6 × Quotient + 3 ... (ii)

It is clear from the two equations that Quotient is 5 in first position and quotient is 6 in second position.

$\therefore$ Number = 7 × 5 + 4 = 39.

Example 5. *When a number is divided by 144, the remainder is 90. If the number is divided by 9, then what is the remainder ?*

Solution. $\because$ 144 is divisible by 9 and 90 is divisible by 9.

$\therefore$ When the number is divided by 9, it will be divisible completely by 9 and remainder will be 0.

Example 6. *What will be the sum of odd numbers from 10 to 60 ?*

Solution. $\because$ Sum of odd numbers from 1 to n

$$= \left(\frac{\text{Last number } + 1}{2}\right)^2$$

$\therefore$ Sum of odd numbers from 1 to 60

$$= \left(\frac{59+1}{2}\right)^2 = \left(\frac{60}{2}\right)^2 = (30)^2 = 900$$

and Sum of odd numbers from 1 to 10

$$=\left(\frac{9+1}{2}\right)^2=\left(\frac{10}{2}\right)^2=(5)^2=25$$

∴ Sum of odd numbers from 10 to 60
= 900 – 25 = 875.

Example 7. *What will be the sum of even numbers from 18 to 54 ?*

Solution. ∵ Sum of even numbers from 1 to *n*

$$=\frac{\text{Last number}}{2}\left(\frac{\text{Last number}}{2}+1\right)$$

∴ Sum of even numbers from 1 to 54

$$=\frac{54}{2}\left(\frac{54}{2}+1\right)=27(27+1)$$

= 27 × 28 = 756

and sum of even numbers from 1 to 17

$$=\frac{16}{2}\left(\frac{16}{2}+1\right)=8\times 9=72$$

∴ Sum of even numbers from 18 to 54
= 756 – 76 = 684.

EXERCISE

In the following questions four answer choices are given in which one is correct. Choose the correct answer.

1. Product of two prime numbers will be :
A. Even number B. Odd number
C. Composite number D. Whole number

2. A number which is both even and prime is :
A. 1 B. 3
C. 5 D. 2

3. A number having 2, 3 and 7 as a prime factor is :
A. 52 B. 42
C. 32 D. 72

4. If a number A is less than a number B, then what will be the number which is greater than A and smaller than B ?
A. $\frac{A+B}{2}$ B. $\frac{A-B}{2}$
C. $\frac{B-A}{2}$ D. $\frac{A\times B}{2}$

5. In the following which is the greatest number ?
A. $(4)^2$ B. $[(2+2)^2]^2$
C. $(2\times 2\times 2)^2$ D. $(2+2+2)^2$

6. If x and y are odd numbers, then which of the following will be even number ?
A. $x\div y$ B. $x\times y$
C. $x+y$ D. $x-y$

7. In a question of Division, Divisor is 9, quotient is 114 and Remainder is 5, then what will be the dividend ?
A. 931 B. 1031
C. 1131 D. 1233

8. Largest number of four digits is :
A. 9989 B. 9888
C. 9999 D. 9000

9. Smallest number of four digits is :
A. 1001 B. 1111
C. 1011 D. 1000

10. What is the difference in place value and face value of 3 in 5309 ?
A. 257 B. 297
C. 327 D. 307

11. What is the difference in place values of 7 in 6707 ?
A. 693 B. 783
C. 893 D. 393

12. If 17 is added to 8 times of a number, the result is 209. What is the number ?
A. 23 B. 27
C. 24 D. 29

13. If 8 is added in square root of a number, the result is 34. What is the number ?
A. 566 B. 872
C. 766 D. 676

14. The difference of squares of two consecutive numbers is 31. What are the numbers ?
A. 14 and 17 B. 15 and 16
C. 16 and 15 D. 13 and 14

15. The difference of squares of two consecutive numbers is 21. What are the numbers ?
A. 10 and 11
B. 11 and 10
C. 12 and 9
D. 8 and 13

16. If sum of two numbers x and y is equal to double of x then value of y will be ?
A. A $= x$
B. $> x$
C. C $< x$
D. Negative number

17. What will be the difference in smallest number of 4 digits and largest number of 2 digits ?
A. 801
B. 901
C. 1
D. 91

18. The sum of two numbers is 10 and their product is 20. What will be the sum of their reciprocals ?
A. 1
B. 2
C. $\frac{1}{2}$
D. $\frac{1}{10}$

19. A positive integer x is multiplied by 4. If the product is equal to cube of x, then what will be the value of x ?
A. 2
B. 8
C. 4
D. 3

20. The product of three consecutive natural numbers will be divisible by :
A. 3
B. 6
C. 9
D. 15

21. What will be the smallest number which is a multiple of 7 and gives remainder 3 when divided by 4 or 12 or 16 ?
A. 195
B. 168
C. 140
D. 147

22. If $\frac{2}{3}$ of fifth-part of a number is equal to 6, then number is :
A. 45
B. 48
C. 64
D. 52

23. The sum of digits of a two digit number is 8 and their product is 12. What will be the difference of two digits ?
A. 6
B. 4
C. 8
D. 12

24. If 19 is subtracted from a two digit number then resulting number is two-third of the original number. What is the sum of two digits of the number ?
A. 12
B. 15
C. 17
D. 14

25. If 5 times of a number is divided by 10, the quotient is 4. What is the number ?
A. 10
B. 12
C. 16
D. 8

26. What will be added to 11148 so that the sum is divisible by 7 ?
A. 7
B. 3
C. 9
D. 5

27. What will be the sum of odd numbers between 25 and 75 ?
A. 1500
B. 1300
C. 1600
D. 1800

28. If a number is squared then which of the following digits will not be in unit's place ?
A. 1
B. 4
C. 5
D. 2

29. The digit in unit's place in the product of $52 \times 84 \times 96 \times 108$ will be :
A. 4
B. 6
C. 2
D. 8

30. Find the numbers which are divisible by 9 in between 200 and 400.
A. 19
B. 22
C. 21
D. 26

31. What will be the smallest number of 7 digits using 0, 1, 2, 3, 4, 5 and 6 ?
A. 1204536
B. 1023456
C. 1042356
D. 1032456

32. The sum of two digits of a number is 15. If 9 is added to the number, the digits are interchanged. What is the number ?
A. 69
B. 87
C. 96
D. 78

33. Naunihal was asked to multiply a number by $\frac{7}{5}$ but by mistake he multiplied the number by $\frac{5}{7}$. If his answer was 144 less than correct answer, the number was
A. 210
B. 310
C. 284
D. 264

EXPLANATORY ANSWERS

1. B : ∵ Product of two prime numbers is an odd number. For example product of two prime numbers 7 and 11 = 7 × 11 = 77 which is an odd number. Therefore answer choice is (B).

2. D : ∵ 2 is a number which is even and prime also. Therefore answer choice is (D).

3. B : ∵ ∴ Prime factors of the numbers are 2, 3 and 7.

∴ Number = 2 × 3 × 7 = 42.

4. A : According to problem, A < B

$\Rightarrow$ A + A < B + A

$\Rightarrow$ 2 A < B + A

$\Rightarrow$ $A < \frac{A+B}{2} < B$

Therefor, it is clear that $\frac{A+B}{2}$ is greater than A and smaller than B.

∴ Answer choice is (A).

5. A : ∴ $(4)^2 = 16$, $[(2+2)^2]^2 = (4^2)^2 = 256$,

$(2 \times 2 \times 2)^2 = 8^2 = 64$

$(2+2+2)^2 = (6)^2 = 36$

∴ Answer choice is (B).

6. C : The sum of two odd numbers is always an even number. Therefore answer choice is (C).

7. B : ∵ Dividend = Divisor × Quotient + Remainder

∴ Dividend = 9 × 114 + 5 = 1026 + 5 = 1031.

8. C : ∵ Largest number of 4 digits = 9999

Therefore answer choice is (C).

9. D : ∵ Smallest number of 4 digits = 1000

Therefor answer choice is (D).

10. B : ∵ Place value of 3 in 5309 = 3 × 100 = 300

Face value of 3 in 5309 = 3

Difference = 300 – 3 = 297.

11. A : Place value of 7 in the unit's place of 6707 = 7 × 1 = 7.

Place value of 7 in the hundred's place of 6707

= 7 × 100 = 700

Difference = 700 – 7 = 693.

12. C : Let the number be x

According to problem,

$x \times 8 + 17 = 209$

$8x = 209 - 17 = 192$

$x = \frac{192}{8} = 24$

∴ Number = 24.

13. D : Let the number be x

According to problem,

Square root of number = $\sqrt{x}$

∴ $\sqrt{x} + 8 = 34$

$\Rightarrow \sqrt{x} = 34 - 8 = 26$

$\Rightarrow x = 26 \times 26 = 676$

∴ Number = 676.

14. B : Let two consecutive numbers be x, $(x + 1)$

According to problem,

$(x+1)^2 - (x)^2 = 31$

$\Rightarrow x^2 + 2x + 1 - x^2 = 31$

$\Rightarrow 2x + 1 = 31$

$\Rightarrow 2x = 31 - 1 = 30$

$\Rightarrow x = \frac{30}{2} = 15$

∴ Numbers are 15 and 16.

15. A : Let two consecutive numbers are x, $(x + 1)$

According to problem,

$(x+1)^2 - (x)^2 = 21$

$\Rightarrow x^2 + 2x + 1 - x^2 = 21 \Rightarrow 2x + 1 = 21$

$\Rightarrow 2x = 21 - 1 = 20$

$\Rightarrow x = \frac{20}{2} = 10$

∴ Number are 10 and 11.

16. A : According to problem,

$x + y = 2x \Rightarrow y = x$

∴ Value of y = value of x

∴ Answer choice is (A).

17. B : ∵ Least number of 4 digits = 1000

Largest number of 2 digits = 99

Difference = 1000 – 99 = 901.

18. C : Let the two numbers be x and y

According to problem,

$x + y = 10$ ...(*i*)

and $xy = 20$ ....(*ii*)

Form (*i*) and (*ii*)

$$\frac{x+y}{xy} = \frac{10}{20} \Rightarrow \frac{1}{y} + \frac{1}{x} = \frac{1}{2}$$

∴ Sum of reciprocals of the numbers $= \frac{1}{2}$

∴ Answer choic is (C).

19. A : According to problem,

$x \times 4 =$ cube of x

∴ $4x = x^3 \Rightarrow x^2 = 4$

$\Rightarrow x = +2, -2$

Because x is positive integer.

∴ $x = +2$

∴ Answer choice is (A).

20. B : Product of three consecutive numbers is always divisible by 6. Therefore answer choice is (B).

21. D : ∵ L.C.M. of 4, 12 and 16 = 48

∴ Number = 48 + 3 = 51, but 51 is not a multiple of 7.

So we have to consider 48 × 2 + 3, 48 × 3 + 3 ... etc.

Now 48 × 3 + 3 = 144 + 3 = 147 which is a multiple of 7

∴ Answer choice is (D).

22. A : Let the number be x

Fifth part of the number $= \frac{x}{5}$

According to problem,

$$\frac{x}{5} \times \frac{2}{3} = 6 \Rightarrow \frac{x}{5} = 9 \Rightarrow x = 45$$

∴ Number = 45.

23. B : Let in the two digit number unit's and ten's digits be x and y respectively.

Number $= 10y + x$

Sum of the digits $= y + x = 8$ ...(*i*)

Product of digits $= yx = 12$ ...(*ii*)

From (*i*) and (*ii*)

$(y - x)^2 = (y + x)^2 - 4yx = (8)^2 - 4 \times 12$

$= 64 - 48 = 16$ ...(*iii*)

∴ $y - x = 4$

From (*i*) and (*iii*)

$2y = 12 \Rightarrow y = 6$

and $6 + x = 8 \Rightarrow x = 2$

∴ Difference of digits

$= 6 - 2 = 4$

24. A : Let the two digits number $= 10x + y$

According to problem,

$$(10x + y) - 19 = (10x + y) \times \frac{2}{3}$$

$$(10x + y) - (10x + y) \times \frac{2}{3} = 19$$

∴ $(10x + y) \times \frac{1}{3} = 19$

∴ $10x + y = 19 \times 3 = 57$

∴ Number = 57 and sum of the digits $= 5 + 7 = 12$

25. D : Let the number be x

5 times of the number $= 5x$

∴ $\frac{5x}{10} = 4 \Rightarrow 5x = 40$

$\Rightarrow x = \frac{40}{5} = 8$

∴ Number = 8.

26. B : ∵

```
7)11148(1592
  7
  41
  35
   64
   63
    18
    14
     4
```

11148 = 7 × 1592 + 4. Therefore it is clear that if 3 is added to 11148 then 11151 is divisible by 7.

27. B : ∵ Sum of odd numbers from 1 to n

$$= \left(\frac{\text{Last odd number} + 1}{2}\right)^2$$

∴ Sum of odd numbers from 1 to 75

$$= \left(\frac{75+1}{2}\right)^2 = (38)^2 = 1444$$

Sum of odd numbers from 1 to 24

$$=\left(\frac{23+1}{2}\right)^2=(12)^2=144$$

$\therefore$ Sum of odd numbers from 25 to 75 $= 1444 - 144 = 1300$.

28. D : When a number is squared then the digit at unit's place can be 0, 1, 4, 5, 6 and 9. Therefore 2 cannot be in unit's place of a squared number.

$\therefore$ Answer choice is (D).

29. A : Product of unit's digits in $52 \times 84 \times 96 \times 108$
$= 2 \times 4 \times 6 \times 8 = 384$

$\therefore$ Unit's digit in $384 = 4$

$\therefore$ Unit's digits in the product of $52 \times 84 \times 96 \times 108 = 4$.

30. B. : $\because$ Numbers divisible by 9 in between 1 to

$$400 = \frac{400}{9} = 44$$

Numbers divisibly by 9 in between 1 to 200

$$= \frac{200}{9} = 22$$

$\therefore$ Numbers divisible by 9 in between 200 to 400 $= 44 - 22 = 22$.

31. B : 7 digit's least number using 0, 1, 2, 3, 4, 5 and 6 = 1023456.

32. D : Let the number $= (10x + y)$

According to problem,

$$x + y = 15 \qquad ...(i)$$

and $(10x + y) + 9 = 10y + x$

$\Rightarrow \quad 9y - 9x = 9$

$\Rightarrow \quad y - x = 1 \qquad ...(ii)$

From (*i*) and (*ii*)

$2y = 16 \Rightarrow \quad y = 8$

$x + 8 = 15 \Rightarrow \quad x = 7$

$\therefore$ Number $= 10 \times 7 + 8 = 70 + 8 = 78$

33. A : Let the number $= x$

Correct answer $= \frac{7}{5}$ of $x = \frac{7x}{5}$

Wrong answer $= \frac{5}{7}$ of $x = \frac{5x}{7}$

According to problem,

Correct answer = Wrong answer + 144

$$\therefore \quad \frac{7x}{5} = \frac{5x}{7} + 144$$

$$\therefore \quad \frac{7x}{5} - \frac{5x}{7} = 144$$

$$\Rightarrow \quad \frac{24x}{35} = 144$$

$$\Rightarrow \quad x = \frac{144 \times 35}{24} = 210$$

$\therefore$ Number = 210.

2

FRACTIONS

Fraction : Fraction is a number which denotes the equal parts of a thing or a number.

For example : One-fourth part $= \frac{1}{4}$

Half part $= \frac{1}{2}$

Types of Fractions :

1. Proper Fraction : When numerator is less than the denominator, the fraction is called proper fraction.

For example : $\frac{2}{5}, \frac{1}{6}, \frac{3}{7}$....... etc. are proper fractions.

2. Improper Fraction : When numerator is greater than the denominator, the fraction is called improper fraction.

For example : $\frac{3}{2}, \frac{5}{2}, \frac{7}{5}$....... etc. are improper fractions.

So, improper fraction is always greater than proper fraction.

3. Mixed Fraction : In mixed fraction there is a whole number along with proper fraction.

For example : $2\frac{1}{4}$ is a mixed fraction in which 2 is a whole number and $\frac{1}{4}$ is proper fraction. It can be written as :

$$2\frac{1}{4} = 2 + \frac{1}{4}$$

To Convert Mixed Fraction into Improper Fraction

For example : $2\frac{1}{4}$ is a mixed fraction. Multiply 2 by 4 and to the product add 1. Now numerator $= 2 \times 4 + 1 = 9$ and denominator = 4.

Therefore $2\frac{1}{4}$ can be written as $\frac{9}{4}$ which is a improper fraction.

Like Fraction : The fractions whose denominators are equal, are called like fractions.

For example : $\frac{1}{8}, \frac{3}{8}, \frac{5}{8}, \frac{7}{8}$.

Unlike Fraction : The fractions whose denominators are unequal, are called unlike fractions.

For example : $\frac{1}{2}, \frac{2}{3}, \frac{3}{5}, \frac{3}{7}$

To Convert Unlike Fractions Into Like Fractions

For example : We have to convert $\frac{3}{4}, \frac{4}{5}$ and $\frac{2}{7}$ into like fractions. First of all we have to find the L.C.M. of their denominators. ∵ L.C.M of 4, 5 and 7 = 140. By dividing 140 by 4, 5 and 7 we get 35, 28 and 20. To convert these fractions into like fractions we have to multiply and divide these fractions respectively by 35, 28 and 20.

$$\frac{3}{4} = \frac{3}{4} \times \frac{35}{35} = \frac{105}{140}$$

$$\frac{4}{5}=\frac{4}{5}\times\frac{28}{28}=\frac{112}{140}$$

$$\frac{2}{7}=\frac{2}{7}\times\frac{20}{20}=\frac{40}{140}$$

Addition of Fractions : Let us add $\frac{2}{3}+\frac{3}{5}+\frac{1}{2}$.

First of all we find the L.C.M. of 3, 5 and 2 (denominators of fractions).

L.C.M. of 3, 5 and 2 = 30

Dividing 30 by 3, 5 and 2 we get 10, 6 and 15.

Now we have to multiply and divide the first, second and third fractions by 10, 6 and 15 respectively.

$$\frac{2}{3}=\frac{2}{3}\times\frac{10}{10}=\frac{20}{30},\ \frac{3}{5}=\frac{3}{5}\times\frac{6}{6}=\frac{18}{30}$$

and $\frac{1}{2}=\frac{1}{2}\times\frac{15}{15}=\frac{15}{30}$

$$\therefore\ \frac{2}{3}+\frac{3}{5}+\frac{1}{2}=\frac{20}{30}+\frac{18}{30}+\frac{15}{30}$$

$$=\frac{20+18+15}{30}=\frac{53}{30}=1\frac{23}{30}.$$

Subtraction of Fractions : Let us subtract $\frac{11}{12}-\frac{5}{9}$. First of all we have to find L.C.M. of denominators of given fractions.

$\therefore$ L.C.M. of 12 and 9 = 36.

$\because$ By dividing 36 by 12 and 9 we get 3 and 4 respectively.

$\therefore$ We have to multiply and divide first and second fraction by 3 and 4 respectively.

$$\therefore\ \frac{11}{12}=\frac{11}{12}\times\frac{3}{3}=\frac{33}{36}\text{ and }\frac{5}{9}=\frac{5}{9}\times\frac{4}{4}=\frac{20}{36}$$

$$\therefore\left(\frac{11}{12}-\frac{5}{9}\right)=\left(\frac{33}{36}-\frac{20}{36}\right)=\frac{33-20}{36}=\frac{13}{36}.$$

Multiplication of Fractions : Remember the following :

(*i*) Multiply the fractions by changing them into proper fractions.

(*ii*) If a fraction is multiplied by a whole number, then its numerator is multiplied by whole number and denominator remains the same.

(*iii*) Product of two fractions

$$=\frac{\text{Product of numerators of two fractions}}{\text{Product of denominators of two fractions}}$$

For example : $1\frac{4}{5}\times\frac{15}{18}$

$$1\frac{4}{5}=1+\frac{4}{5}=\frac{5+4}{5}=\frac{9}{5}$$

$$\therefore\ 1\frac{4}{5}\times\frac{15}{18}=\frac{9}{5}\times\frac{15}{18}=\frac{3}{2}$$

Division of Fractions : When we divide a fraction by another fraction then first of all we change (÷) sign into (×) sign and invert the fraction after (÷) sign. For example, if it is $\div\frac{2}{5}$ then it becomes $\times\frac{5}{2}$. Now multiply the fractions.

For example : $\frac{3}{4}\div2\frac{1}{2}$

$$\frac{3}{4}\div2\frac{1}{2}=\frac{3}{4}\div\frac{5}{2}=\frac{3}{4}\times\frac{2}{5}=\frac{3}{10}.$$

Important Note : (*i*) When solving the problems involving Addition (+), Substraction (−), Multiplication (×), and Division (÷) simultaneously we use "BODMAS" Rule. Explanation of 'BODMAS' word is

B → Bracket	[{(−)}]
O → of	OF
D → Division	÷
M → Multiplication	×
A → Addition	+
S → Substraction	−

First of all we solve bar, then common braket ( ), then curdly bracket { }, then square bracker [ ], then 'of', then 'division', then 'multiplication', then addition and in the last 'subtraction'.

(*ii*) In Questions 'of' indicates 'multiplicaton'.

Example 1. *Evaluate* $7\frac{5}{9}+\frac{85}{9}$.

Solution $7\frac{5}{9}=7+\frac{5}{9}$

$$7\frac{5}{9}+\frac{85}{9}=7+\left(\frac{5}{9}+\frac{85}{9}\right)=7+\left(\frac{90}{9}\right)$$

$$=7+10=17.$$

Example 2. *What is the value of*

$$\left(\frac{2}{7}+\frac{3}{7}+\frac{4}{7}+\frac{5}{7}\right)?$$

Solution. $\frac{2}{7}+\frac{3}{7}+\frac{4}{7}+\frac{5}{7}$

$$=\frac{2+3+4+5}{7}=\frac{14}{7}=2$$

Example 3. $3\frac{1}{3}+5\frac{3}{8}+2\frac{1}{4}=?$

Solution. $\because\quad 3\frac{1}{3}=3+\frac{1}{3},$

$$5\frac{3}{8}=5+\frac{3}{8},\ 2\frac{1}{4}=2+\frac{1}{4}$$

$$\therefore\quad 3\frac{1}{3}+5\frac{3}{8}+2\frac{1}{4}=3+\frac{1}{3}+5+\frac{3}{8}+2+\frac{1}{4}$$

$$=10+\frac{1}{3}+\frac{3}{8}+\frac{1}{4}$$

$$=10+\left(\frac{8+9+6}{24}\right)$$

$$=10+\frac{23}{24}=10\frac{23}{24}.$$

Example 4. *Find the value of* $3\frac{1}{2}+2\frac{1}{3}-3\frac{1}{4}$.

Solution. $3\frac{1}{2}+2\frac{1}{3}-3\frac{1}{4}$

$$=\left(3+2-3+\frac{1}{2}+\frac{1}{3}-\frac{1}{4}\right)$$

$$=2+\left(\frac{6+4-3}{12}\right)=2+\frac{7}{12}=2\frac{7}{12}.$$

Example 5. *Find the value of* $\frac{1}{3}\times\frac{9}{11}\div2\frac{1}{2}$.

Solution. $\because\ \frac{1}{3}\times\frac{9}{11}\div2\frac{1}{2}=\frac{1}{3}\times\frac{9}{11}\div\frac{5}{2}$

$$=\frac{1}{3}\times\frac{9}{11}\times\frac{2}{5}\quad\textbf{(BODMAS rule)}$$

$$=\frac{6}{55}.$$

Example 6. *Find the value of* : $\left(5\frac{1}{4}\div7\right)$.

Solution. $5\frac{1}{4}\div7\ \Rightarrow\ \frac{21}{4}$

$$\Rightarrow\ \frac{21}{4}\times\frac{1}{7}=\frac{3}{4}$$

Example 7. *What is the value of*

$$\left(17\div\frac{51}{3}\times\frac{51}{17}\right)?$$

Solution. $17\div\frac{51}{3}\times\frac{51}{17}=17\times\frac{3}{51}\times\frac{51}{17}=3.$

Example 8. *What is the value of (36800 ÷ 230 + 230)?*

Solution. $36800\div230+230$

$$=\frac{36800}{230}+230\qquad\textbf{[BODMAS Rule]}$$

$$=160+230=390.$$

Example 9. *Find the value of* :

$$870\times5\frac{2}{3}+4\frac{4}{5}\div1\frac{3}{5}.$$

Solution. $870\times5\frac{2}{3}+4\frac{4}{5}\div1\frac{3}{5}$

$$=870\times\frac{17}{3}+\frac{24}{5}\div\frac{8}{5}$$

$$=870\times\frac{17}{3}+\left(\frac{24}{5}\times\frac{5}{8}\right)$$

[Using BODMAS Rule]

$$=(290\times17)+3=4930+3=4933.$$

Example 10. *If 36 – ? = 3 × 4 – 2 × 5, then what is the value of (?).*

Solution. $36-?=3\times4-2\times5$

$\Rightarrow\quad 36-?=12-10\quad$ **[BODMAS Rule]**

$\Rightarrow\quad 36-?=2$

$\Rightarrow\quad ?=36-2=34$

Therefore $\quad ?=34$

Example 11. $72 \div (3)^2 \div (2)^2 = ?$

Solution. $72 \div (3)^2 \div (2)^2 = ?$

$\Rightarrow \quad \frac{72}{(3)^2} \div (2)^2 = ?$

$\Rightarrow \quad \frac{72}{9} \div (2)^2 = ?$

$\Rightarrow \quad 8 \div (2)^2 = ?$

$\Rightarrow \quad \frac{8}{(2)^2} = ?$

$\Rightarrow \quad \frac{8}{4} = 2 = ?$

Points to Remember : **If there is equal sign in questions of fractions, then fraction should be solved from left to right.**

EXERCISE

Each of the following question is provided with four multiple choice answers. Choose the correct answer in place of sign (?).

1. $535 + 1229 = ?$
A. 1874 B. 1764
C. 1774 D. 1664

2. $0.0095 \div 0.05 = ?$
A. .019 B. 1.9
C. 0.19 D. .29

3. $\frac{7}{4} - \frac{4}{7} = \frac{5}{28} + ?$
A. 2 B. $\frac{1}{7}$
C. $\frac{2}{9}$ D. 1

4. $5\frac{1}{5} \times 10\frac{1}{10} = ?$
A. 52.52 B. 42.45
C. 53.52 D. 65.30

5. $22 \times 5 = 22$ of ?%
A. 4500 B. 5000
C. 500 D. 750

6. 200 of $\frac{1}{25} \div 8 = ?$
A. 1 B. 3
C. 8 D. 5

7. $\frac{5}{3} + \frac{7}{6} + \frac{8}{3} + \frac{1}{2} = ?$
A. $\frac{4}{9}$ B. 6
C. 4 D. 2

8. $1\frac{1}{5} + 2\frac{2}{5} + 3\frac{10}{25} = ?$
A. 6 B. 7
C. 5 D. 4

9. $\frac{40 \times 0.4 \times 0.04}{4 + 4 \div 4} = ?$
A. .128 B. .148
C. .15 D. .248

10. $0.11 + 0.19 \times 0.5 = ?$
A. 0.105 B. 0.205
C. 0.305 D. 0.215

11. $\sqrt{\frac{25}{15625}} = \sqrt{\frac{?}{30625}}$
A. 36 B. 49
C. 64 D. 81

12. $50 \div 5 \div 5 = ?$
A. 2 B. 10
C. $\frac{1}{5}$ D. 4

13. $(242 - 17)^2 - (7 \times 5)^2 = ?$
A. 49400 B. 94400
C. 48400 D. 45000

14. 64 of ?% = 20 + 20 of 20%.
A. 47.5 B. 38.6
C. 37.5 D. 37.2

15. $\frac{187}{17} \times \frac{196}{14} \times \frac{1}{11} = ?$
A. 18 B. 14
C. 17 D. 13

16. $\dfrac{(21-3)+128+120}{98.5-94.7}=?$

A. 50 B. 65
C. 70 D. 69

17. ? × 12 = 336 of 75%

A. 21 B. 22
C. 28 D. 25

18. 5 of 10% + 10 of 5% = ? of 15%

A. $7\frac{1}{3}$ B. $6\frac{2}{3}$
C. $8\frac{2}{3}$ D. $9\frac{1}{6}$

19. 4 × 32 of 75% ÷ 3 = ?

A. 32 B. 45
C. 44 D. 43

20. $4\frac{2}{3}-1\frac{5}{9}+4\frac{8}{6}=?$

A. $8\frac{1}{3}$ B. $8\frac{4}{9}$
C. $7\frac{4}{9}$ D. $6\frac{2}{3}$

21. $\dfrac{40\times 15+25}{26+4\div 4-2}=?$

A. 25 B. 30
C. 31 D. 42

22. $\sqrt{?}-3=19$

A. 844 B. 375
C. 484 D. 400

23. $5\frac{2}{3}\div\left(2-\frac{1}{2}\right)=?$

A. $\frac{26}{17}$ B. $\frac{34}{9}$
C. $\frac{38}{3}$ D. $\frac{37}{6}$

24. $\dfrac{16\times 2}{0.6+1.0}=?$

A. 20 B. 22
C. 16 D. 18

25. $2\frac{1}{3}+?+1\frac{1}{6}=5\frac{1}{4}$

A. $2\frac{4}{5}$ B. $1\frac{4}{7}$
C. $1\frac{3}{4}$ D. $1\frac{5}{6}$

26. $12\sqrt{2}+48\div 8=?$

A. $6(2\sqrt{2}+1)$ B. $12\sqrt{2}+5$
C. $2\sqrt{2}+6$ D. $5(2\sqrt{2}+1)$

27. $5\frac{3}{4}+7\frac{4}{5}+3\frac{5}{6}=?$

A. $18\frac{17}{60}$ B. $17\frac{23}{60}$
C. $17\frac{22}{41}$ D. $23\frac{1}{60}$

28. 100 × 0.2 + 0.01 × 1000 + 110 =?

A. 144 B. 140
C. 141 D. 159

29. $\frac{6}{11}+\frac{7}{8}\div\frac{77}{40}=?$

A. 1 B. 4
C. 7 D. 6

30. $\frac{1}{2}+\frac{1}{4}+?=\frac{25}{28}$

A. $\frac{1}{6}$ B. $\frac{1}{7}$
C. $\frac{1}{8}$ D. $\frac{1}{4}$

31. $18 \text{ of } \frac{3}{81}+\frac{1}{3}=?$

A. 2 B. 5
C. 1 D. 4

32. $\dfrac{\frac{1}{2}-\frac{1}{4}}{\frac{1}{8}+\frac{3}{4}}=?$

A. $\frac{3}{7}$ B. $\frac{4}{7}$
C. $\frac{1}{7}$ D. $\frac{2}{7}$

33. $3.5 \div 1.75 + 6.4 = ?$

A. 7.4 B. 8.4

C. 8.1 D. 9.3

34. $\frac{201.6 \div 14}{144 \div 2} = ?$

A. .2 B. .5

C. .7 D. .6

35. $4 \div [5 + 1 - (4 - 3)] = ?$

A. – 2 B. 2

C. – 1 D. 3

36. $1.5 + 4\,(2 - .5) + .1 - .4 = ?$

A. 7.2 B. 6.8

C. 7.9 D. 9.0

37. $374 - 85 \div 17 = ?$

A. 639 B. 963

C. 369 D. 350

38. $(374 - 85) \div 17 = ?$

A. 13 B. 15

C. 18 D. 17

39. $3\frac{1}{2}\left(\frac{2}{5} \div \frac{1}{5}\right) = ?$

A. 7 B. 8

C. 9 D. 12

40. $4 \times 9 \div \sqrt{144} = ?$

A. 3 B. 4

C. 8 D. 15

41. $\frac{7}{3} \div \frac{35}{18} \div \frac{54}{20} = ?$

A. $\frac{4}{7}$ B. $\frac{4}{9}$

C. $\frac{3}{7}$ D. $\frac{7}{9}$

42. $(36 + 12 - 4) \div 4 = ?$

A. 14 B. 18

C. 11 D. 20

43. $2\frac{1}{3} \times 4\frac{1}{5} \div \frac{7}{15} = ?$

A. 21 B. 23

C. 29 D. 31

44. $\frac{3}{4} + \frac{1}{3} - \frac{1}{4} + \frac{1}{3} = ?$

A. $2\frac{1}{3}$ B. $1\frac{1}{6}$

C. $1\frac{2}{3}$ D. $3\frac{5}{6}$

45. $1\frac{1}{3} \times 2\frac{3}{4} \times 3\frac{4}{5} \times 1\frac{5}{11} = ?$

A. $20\frac{15}{17}$ B. $20\frac{4}{3}$

C. $16\frac{4}{9}$ D. $18\frac{3}{10}$

46. $\left(2\frac{3}{7} + \frac{4}{7}\right)^2 \div 3 + 2 = ?$

A. 5 B. 6

C. 8 D. 17

47. $\left(1\frac{3}{5} - \frac{2}{3} \div \frac{12}{13} + \frac{7}{5} \times \frac{1}{3}\right) = ?$

A. $2\frac{31}{70}$ B. $1\frac{33}{70}$

C. $2\frac{31}{90}$ D. $1\frac{31}{90}$

48. $(999^2 - 998^2) \div 10 \times 100 + 3 = ?$

A. 29974 B. 19973

C. 18973 D. 15997

49. $\left(\frac{2}{3} + \frac{1}{2}\right) \div \left(\frac{2}{3} - \frac{1}{2}\right) \div 7 = ?$

A. 4 B. 1

C. $\frac{1}{3}$ D. 2

50. $1 + [1 \div \{5 \div 4 - 1 \div (13 \div 3 - 1 \div 3)\}] = ?$

A. 8 B. $\frac{1}{8}$

C. 2 D. 10

51. $(20 \div 5) \div 2 + (16 \div 8) \times 2 + (10 \div 5) \times (3 \div 2) = ?$

A. 11 B. 9

C. 10 D. 25

EXPLANATORY ANSWERS

1. B : 535 + 1229 = 1764

2. C : $\because$ $0.0095 \div 0.005 \Rightarrow \frac{0.0095}{0.05} = \frac{.95}{5} = .19$

3. D : $\because \frac{7}{4} - \frac{4}{7} = \frac{5}{28} + ? \Rightarrow \frac{7 \times 7 - 4 \times 4}{4 \times 7}$

$= \frac{5}{28} + ?$

$\Rightarrow \frac{49 - 16}{28} = \frac{5}{28} + ? \Rightarrow \frac{33}{28} = \frac{5}{28} + ?$

$\Rightarrow 1\frac{5}{28} = \frac{5}{28} + ? \qquad \Rightarrow 1\frac{5}{28} = \frac{5}{28} + ?$

$\Rightarrow ? = 1$

4. A : $\because 5\frac{1}{5} \times 10\frac{1}{10} = ?$

$\Rightarrow \frac{26}{5} \times \frac{101}{10} = ? \Rightarrow 52.52 = ?$

5. C : $\because$ 22 × 5 = 22 of ? % $\Rightarrow 110 = 22 \times \frac{?}{100}$

$\Rightarrow \frac{110 \times 100}{22} = ? \quad \Rightarrow 500 = ?$

6. A : $\because$ 200 of $\frac{1}{25} \div 8 = ? \quad \Rightarrow 8 \div 8 = ?$

$\Rightarrow \frac{8}{8} = ? \quad \Rightarrow 1 = ?$

7. B : $\because \frac{5}{3} + \frac{7}{6} + \frac{8}{3} + \frac{1}{2} = ?$

$\Rightarrow \frac{5 \times 2 + 7 \times 1 + 8 \times 2 + 1 \times 3}{6}$

$\Rightarrow \frac{10 + 7 + 16 + 3}{6} = ?$

$\Rightarrow \frac{36}{6} = ? \quad \Rightarrow 6 = ?$

8. B : $\because 1\frac{1}{5} + 2\frac{2}{5} + 3\frac{10}{25} = ?$

$\Rightarrow 1 + \frac{1}{5} + 2 + 2 + 2\frac{2}{5} + 3 + \frac{10}{25} = ?$

$\Rightarrow (1 + 2 + 3) + \frac{1}{5} + \frac{2}{5} + \frac{10}{25} = ?$

$\Rightarrow 6 + 1 = ? \Rightarrow 7 = ?$

9. A : $\because \frac{40 \times 0.4 \times 0.04}{4 + 4 \div 4} = ?$

$\Rightarrow \frac{.64}{4 + \frac{4}{4}} = ? \qquad \Rightarrow \frac{.64}{4 + 1} = ?$

$\Rightarrow \frac{.64}{5} = ? \qquad \Rightarrow .128 = ?$

10. B : $\because$ 0.11 + 0.19 × 0.5 = ? $\Rightarrow$ 0.11 + 0.095 = ?

$\Rightarrow$ 0.205 = ?

11. B : $\sqrt{\frac{25}{15625}} = \sqrt{\frac{?}{30625}} \Rightarrow \frac{25}{15625} = \frac{?}{30625}$

$\Rightarrow ? = \frac{25 \times 30625}{15625} = 49$

12. A : $\because 50 \div 5 \div 5 = ?$

$\Rightarrow \frac{50}{5} \div 5 = ? \Rightarrow 10 \div 5 = ?$

$\Rightarrow \frac{10}{5} = ? \quad \Rightarrow 2 = ?$

13. A : $\because (242 - 17)^2 - (7 \times 5)^2 = ?$

$\Rightarrow (225)^2 - (35)^2 = ?$

$\Rightarrow (225 + 35)(225 - 35) = ?$

$\Rightarrow 260 \times 190 = ? \quad \Rightarrow 49400 = ?$

14. C : $\because$ 64 of ?% = 20 + 20 of 20%

$\Rightarrow 64 \times \frac{?}{100} = 20 + 4$

$\Rightarrow 64 \times \frac{?}{100} = 24$

$\Rightarrow ? = \frac{24 \times 100}{64} = 37.5$

15. B : $\because \frac{187}{17} \times \frac{196}{14} \times \frac{1}{11} = ? \Rightarrow \frac{187}{187} \times \frac{196}{14} = ?$

$\Rightarrow 14 = ?$

16. C : $\because \frac{(21 - 3) + 128 + 120}{98.5 - 94.7} = ?$

$\Rightarrow \frac{18+248}{3.8} = ? = \frac{2.66}{3.8} = ? \Rightarrow 70 = ?$

17. A : $\because ? \times 12 + 336$ of $75\% \Rightarrow ? \times 12 = 252$

$\Rightarrow ? - \frac{252}{12} - 2$

18. B : $\because 5$ of $10\% + 10$ of $5\% = ?$ of 15%

$\Rightarrow .5 + .5 = .15 \times ?$

$\Rightarrow ? = \frac{1.0}{.15} = \frac{100}{15} = 6\frac{2}{3}$

19. A : $\because 4 \times 32$ of $75\% \div 3 = ? \Rightarrow 4 \times 24 \div 3 = ?$

$\Rightarrow 4 \times \frac{24}{3} = ?$

$\Rightarrow 4 \times 8 = ?$

$\Rightarrow 32 = ?$

20. B : $\because 4\frac{2}{3} - 1\frac{5}{9} + 4\frac{8}{6} = ?$

$\Rightarrow 4 + \frac{2}{3} - 1 - \frac{5}{9} + 4 + \frac{8}{6} = ?$

$\Rightarrow (4-1+4) + \left(\frac{2}{3} - \frac{5}{9} + \frac{8}{6}\right) = ?$

$\Rightarrow 7 + \frac{12-10+24}{18} = ?$

$\Rightarrow 7 + \frac{26}{18} = ? \Rightarrow 7 + 1\frac{4}{9} = ?$

$\Rightarrow 8\frac{4}{9} = ?$

21. A : $\because \frac{40 \times 15 + 25}{26 + 4 \div 4 - 2} = ?$

$\Rightarrow \frac{600+25}{26+\frac{4}{4}-2} = ?$

$\Rightarrow \frac{625}{26+1-2} = ? \quad \frac{625}{26+1-2} = ?$

$\Rightarrow 25 = ?$

22. C : $\because \sqrt{?} - 3 = 19$

$\Rightarrow \sqrt{?} = 19 + 3 = 22$

$\Rightarrow ? = 22 \times 22 = 484.$

23. B : $\because 5\frac{2}{3} \div \left(2 - \frac{1}{2}\right) = ? \Rightarrow \frac{17}{3} \div \frac{3}{2} = ?$

$\Rightarrow \frac{17}{3} \times \frac{2}{3} = ? \Rightarrow \frac{34}{9} = ?$

24. A : $\because \frac{16 \times 2}{0.6 + 1.0} = ? \Rightarrow \frac{32}{1.6} = ? \Rightarrow 20 = ?$

25. C : $\because 2\frac{1}{3} + ? + 1\frac{1}{6} = 5\frac{1}{4}$

$\Rightarrow \frac{7}{3} + ? + \frac{7}{6} = \frac{21}{4}$

$\Rightarrow ? = \frac{21}{4} - \left(\frac{7}{3} + \frac{7}{6}\right) = \frac{21}{4} - \frac{7}{2} = \frac{7}{4} = 1\frac{3}{4}$

26. A : $\because 12\sqrt{2} + 48 \div 8 = ?$

$\Rightarrow 12\sqrt{2} + \frac{48}{8} = ? \Rightarrow 12\sqrt{2} + 6 = ?$

$\Rightarrow 6\left(2\sqrt{2} + 1\right) = ?$

27. B : $\because 5\frac{3}{4} + 7\frac{4}{5} + 3\frac{5}{6} = ?$

$\Rightarrow (5+7+3) + \left(\frac{3}{4} + \frac{4}{5} + \frac{5}{6}\right) = ?$

$\Rightarrow 15 + \frac{143}{60} = ?$

$\Rightarrow 15 + 2\frac{23}{60} = ?$

$\Rightarrow 17\frac{23}{60} = ?$

28. B : $\because 100 \times 0.2 + 0.01 \times 1000 + 110 = ?$

$\Rightarrow 20 + 10 + 110 = ? \Rightarrow 140 = ?$

29. A : $\because \frac{6}{11} + \frac{7}{8} \div \frac{77}{40} = ? \Rightarrow \frac{6}{11} + \frac{7}{8} \times \frac{40}{77} = ?$

$\Rightarrow \frac{6}{11} + \frac{5}{11} = ? \Rightarrow \frac{11}{11} = ? \Rightarrow 1 = ?$

30. B : $\because \frac{1}{2} + \frac{1}{4} + ? = \frac{25}{28} \Rightarrow \frac{3}{4} + ? = \frac{25}{28}$

$\Rightarrow ? = \frac{25}{28} - \frac{3}{4}$

$\Rightarrow ? = \frac{25-21}{28} = \frac{4}{28} = \frac{1}{7}$

31. C : $\because 18$ of $\frac{3}{81} + \frac{1}{3} = ? \Rightarrow \frac{2}{3} + \frac{1}{3} = ?$

$\Rightarrow \frac{3}{3} = ? \Rightarrow 1 = ?$

32. D : $\because \dfrac{\frac{1}{2}-\frac{1}{4}}{\frac{1}{8}+\frac{3}{4}} = ? \Rightarrow \dfrac{\frac{1}{4}}{\frac{7}{8}} = ? \Rightarrow \frac{8}{4\times 7} = ?$

$\Rightarrow \frac{2}{7} = ?$

33. B : $\because 3.5 \div 1.75 + 6.4 = ? \Rightarrow \frac{3.5}{1.75} + 6.4 = ?$

$\Rightarrow 2 + 6.4 = ? \Rightarrow 8.4 = ?$

34. A : $\because \frac{201.6 \div 14}{144 \div 2} = ? \Rightarrow \dfrac{\frac{201.6}{14}}{\frac{144}{2}} = ?$

$\Rightarrow \frac{14.4}{7.2} = ? \Rightarrow 2 = ?$

35. C : $\because 4 - [5 + 1 - (4 - 3)] = ?$

$\Rightarrow 4 - [5 + 1 - 1] = ? \Rightarrow 4 - 5 = ?$

$\Rightarrow -1 = ?$

36. A : $\because 1.5 + 4(2 - .5) + .1 - .4 = ?$

$\Rightarrow 1.5 + 4 \times 1.5 + .1 - .4 = ?$

$\Rightarrow 1.5 + 6 + .1 - .4 = ? \Rightarrow 7.2 = ?$

37. C : $\because 374 - 85 \div 17 = ?$

$\Rightarrow 374 - \frac{85}{17} = ? \Rightarrow 374 - 5 = ? \Rightarrow 369 = ?$

38. D : $\because (374 - 85) \div 17 = ? \Rightarrow 289 \div 17 = ?$

$\Rightarrow \frac{289}{17} = ? \Rightarrow 17 = ?$

39. A : $\because 3\frac{1}{2}\left(\frac{2}{5} \div \frac{1}{5}\right) = ? \Rightarrow \frac{7}{2}\left(\frac{2}{5} \times \frac{5}{1}\right) = ?$

$\Rightarrow \frac{7}{2} \times 2 = ? \Rightarrow 7 = ?$

40. A : $\because 4 \times 9 \div \sqrt{144} = ? \Rightarrow 4 \times 9 \div 12 = ?$

$\Rightarrow 4 \times \frac{9}{12} = ? \Rightarrow \frac{4 \times 9}{12} = ? \Rightarrow 3 = ?$

41. B: $\because \frac{7}{3} \div \frac{35}{18} \div \frac{54}{20} = ? \Rightarrow \frac{7}{3} \times \frac{18}{35} \div \frac{54}{20} = ?$

$\Rightarrow \frac{7}{3} \times \frac{18}{35} \times \frac{20}{54} = ? \Rightarrow \frac{4}{9} = ?$

42. C : $\because (36 + 12 - 4) \div 4 = ? \Rightarrow 44 \div 4 = ?$

$\Rightarrow \frac{44}{4} = ? \Rightarrow 11 = ?$

43. A : $\because 2\frac{1}{3} \times 4\frac{1}{5} \div \frac{7}{15} = ? \Rightarrow \frac{7}{3} \times \frac{21}{5} \div \frac{7}{15} = ?$

$\Rightarrow \frac{7}{3} \times \frac{21}{5} \times \frac{15}{7} = ? \Rightarrow 21 = ?$

44. B : $\because \frac{3}{4} + \frac{1}{3} - \frac{1}{4} + \frac{1}{3} = ?$

$\Rightarrow \left(\frac{3}{4} - \frac{1}{4}\right) + \left(\frac{1}{3} + \frac{1}{3}\right) = ?$

$\Rightarrow \frac{1}{2} + \frac{2}{3} = \frac{7}{6} = ? \Rightarrow 1\frac{1}{6} = ?$

45. B : $\because 1\frac{1}{3} \times 2\frac{3}{4} \times 3\frac{4}{5} \times 1\frac{5}{11} = ?$

$\Rightarrow \frac{4}{3} \times \frac{11}{4} \times \frac{19}{5} \times \frac{16}{11} = ? \Rightarrow \frac{304}{15} = ?$

$\Rightarrow 20\frac{4}{15} = ?$

46. A : $\because \left(2\frac{3}{7} + \frac{4}{7}\right)^2 \div 3 + 2 = ?$

$\Rightarrow (2 + 1)^2 \div 3 + 2 = ? \Rightarrow 3^2 \div 3 + 2 = ?$

$\Rightarrow \frac{3^2}{3} + 2 = ? \Rightarrow 3 + 2 = ? \Rightarrow 5 = ?$

47. D : $1\frac{3}{5} - \frac{2}{3} \div \frac{12}{13} + \frac{7}{5} \times \frac{1}{3} = ?$

$\Rightarrow \frac{8}{5} - \frac{2}{3} \times \frac{13}{12} + \frac{7}{5} \times \frac{1}{3} = ?$

$\Rightarrow \frac{8}{5} - \frac{13}{18} + \frac{17}{15} = ? \Rightarrow \frac{144 - 65 + 42}{90} = ?$

$\Rightarrow \frac{121}{90} = ? \Rightarrow 1\frac{31}{90} = ?$

48. B : $\because (999^2 - 998^2) \div 10 \times 100 + 3 = ?$

$\Rightarrow [(999 + 998)(999 - 998)] \div 10 \times 100 + 3 = ?$

$\Rightarrow 1997 \div 10 \times 100 + 3 = ?$

$\Rightarrow \frac{1997}{10} \times 100 + 3 = ?$

$\Rightarrow 19970 + 3 = ? \Rightarrow 19973 = ?$

49. B : $\because \left(\frac{2}{3}+\frac{1}{2}\right) \div \left(\frac{2}{3}-\frac{1}{2}\right) \div 7 = ?$

$\Rightarrow \frac{7}{6} \div \frac{1}{6} \div 7 = ?$

$\Rightarrow \frac{7}{6} \times 6 \div 7 = ? \Rightarrow \frac{7}{6} \times 6 \times \frac{1}{7} = ?$

$\Rightarrow 1 = ?$

50. C : $\because 1 + [1 \div \{5 \div 4 - 1 \div (13 \div 3 - 1 \div 3)\}] = ?$

$\Rightarrow 1 + \left[1 \div \left\{5 \div 4 - 1 \div \left(\frac{13}{3} - \frac{1}{3}\right)\right\}\right] = ?$

$\Rightarrow 1 + [1 \div \{5 \div 4 - 1 \div 4\}] = ?$

$\Rightarrow 1 + \left[1 \div \left\{\frac{5}{4} - \frac{1}{4}\right\}\right] = ?$

$\Rightarrow 1 + [1 \div 1] = ? \Rightarrow 1 + 1 = ? \Rightarrow 2 = ?$

51. B : $\because (20 \div 5) \div 2 + (16 \div 8) \times 2 + (10 \div 5) \times (3 \div 2) = ?$

$\Rightarrow 4 \div 2 + 2 \times 2 + 2 \times \frac{3}{2} = ?$

$\Rightarrow 2 + 2 \times 2 + 2 \times \frac{3}{2} = ?$

$\Rightarrow 2 + 4 + 3 = ?$

$\Rightarrow 9 = ?$

3

SQUARE ROOT AND CUBE ROOT

Square Root : When a number is multiplied by itself, then square root of the product is that number. It is expressed by the sign ($\sqrt{\ }$).

Cube Root : When a number is multiplied three times by the number itself, then cube root of the product is that number. It is expressed by the sign ($\sqrt[3]{\ }$).

Important Note :

> The square root of a fraction is obtained by dividing the square root of numerator by square root of denominator.

Example 1. *What is the square root of 36 ?*

Solution. Square root of

$36 = \sqrt{36} = \sqrt{6\times6} = 6.$

Example 2. *Find the square root of 1444.*

Solution.

```
      3  8
 3 | 14 44
   |  9
68 |  5 44
   |  5 44
   |    ×
```

∴ Square root of 1444

$= \sqrt{1444} = \sqrt{38\times38} = 38.$

Example 3. *Find the square root of 172.3969.*

Solution.

```
        13 .13
   3 | 1 72. 39 69
     | 1
  23 |   72
     |   69
 261 |    339
     |    261
2623 |     7869
     |     7869
     |        ×
```

∴ Square root of 172.3969 = $\sqrt{172.3969}$

$= \sqrt{13.13\times13.13} = 13.13.$

Example 4. *Find cube root of 729.*

Solution. Cube root of 729

$= \sqrt[3]{729}$

$= \sqrt[3]{9\times9\times9} = 9.$

Example 5. *Find the value of* $\sqrt[3]{.000008}$.

Solution. $\sqrt[3]{.000008}$

$= \sqrt[3]{8\times10^{-6}}$

$= \sqrt[3]{2\times2\times2\times10^{-2}\times10^{-2}\times10^{-2}}$

$= 2\times10^{-2}$

$= .02.$

Example 6. *Find cube root of* $3\frac{3}{8}$.

Solution. $\because\ 3\frac{3}{8} = \frac{27}{8}$

$\therefore$ Cube root of $\frac{27}{8} = \sqrt[3]{\frac{27}{8}}$

$= \sqrt[3]{\frac{3\times3\times3}{2\times2\times2}} = \frac{3}{2}.$

Example 7. *Find cube root of 1.728.*

Solution. $\because$ 1.728

$= 2\times2\times2\times2\times2\times2\times3\times3\times3\times10^{-3}$

∴ Cube root of 1.728,

$= \sqrt[3]{\overline{2\times2\times2}\times\overline{2\times2\times2}\times\overline{3\times3\times3}\times10^{-3}}$

$= 2\times2\times3\times10^{-1}$

$= 12\times10^{-1} = 1.2.$

Example 8. *Find the least square number which is divisible by 8, 12 and 16.*

Solution. Least number divisible by 8, 12 and 16 will be equal to L.C.M. of 8, 12 and 16.

L.C.M. of 8, 12 and 16 = 48

But 48 is not a square number.

$48 = \overline{2 \times 2} \times \overline{2 \times 2} \times 3$

So, it is clear that we have to multiply 48 by 3 to get a square number.

∴ Least square number

$= 48 \times 3 = 144.$

Example 9. *What least number should be added to 21018 so that the sum is complete square ?*

Solution.

$$\begin{array}{r|l} & 145 \\ \hline 1 & 2\ 10\ 18 \\ & 1 \\ \hline 24 & 110 \\ & 96 \\ \hline 284 & 1418 \\ & 1425 \\ \hline & -7 \end{array}$$

It is clear that if 7 is added to the number then the sum is a perfect square.

EXERCISE

In the following questions four answer choices are given in which one is correct. Choose the correct answer.

1. What is the square root of $5\frac{19}{25}$?
   A. $3\frac{2}{5}$ B. $2\frac{3}{5}$
   C. $2\frac{2}{5}$ D. $2\frac{1}{5}$
2. What is the value of $\sqrt{0.049}$?
   A. .07 B. .09
   C. .06 D. .08
3. What is the value of $\sqrt{128+\sqrt{260-\sqrt{16}}}$?
   A. 18 B. 16
   C. 14 D. 12
4. What is the cube root of 1331 ?
   A. 21 B. 31
   C. 11 D. 41
5. What is the cube root of $2\frac{10}{27}$?
   A. $1\frac{2}{3}$ B. $1\frac{1}{3}$
   C. $1\frac{1}{9}$ D. $1\frac{5}{3}$
6. What is the value of $\sqrt{.9}$?
   A. .94 B. .97
   C. .93 D. .95
7. If $\sqrt{49} \times \frac{1}{5} = 7 \times \sqrt{x}$, then what is the value of x?
   A. $\frac{2}{5}$ B. $\frac{1}{25}$
   C. $\frac{3}{25}$ D. $\frac{4}{5}$
8. If $\frac{?}{\sqrt{0.81}} = 150 + \sqrt{.09}$, then what is the value of (?)
   A. 137.27 B. 131.9
   C. 135.27 D. 127.3
9. If $\frac{10^2+12^2}{\sqrt{1400}} = \sqrt{x}$, then what is the value of x?
   A. 148.84
   B. 184.48
   C. 144.84
   D. 164.84
10. If $\sqrt{625-225} = \sqrt{?} + 10$ then what is the value of (?) sign ?
    A. 125 B. 150
    C. 100 D. 200
11. If $\sqrt{5} = 2.2361$ and $\sqrt{3} = 1.732$ the, what is the value of $\frac{1}{\sqrt{3}+\sqrt{5}}$?
    A. 0.152 B. 0.215
    C. 0.252 D. 0.172
12. If $\sqrt{169} = 13$ the, what is the value of $\sqrt{0.000169} + \sqrt{0.0169}$?
    A. 0.143 B. 0.139
    C. 0.133 D. 0.153

13. What is the value of $3\times\sqrt{15}\times\sqrt{5}-4\times\sqrt{27}$?

A. $3\sqrt{9}$ B. $3\sqrt{7}$
C. $3\sqrt{3}$ D. $3\sqrt{5}$

14. What is the value of

$\sqrt{\sqrt[3]{0.000729}+\sqrt{.0961}}$?

A. .63 B. .73
C. .83 D. .93

15. If $\frac{18}{\sqrt{36}}\times\frac{24}{\sqrt{9}}\times\frac{120}{\sqrt{?}}=720$, then what is the value of (?) sign ?

A. 8 B. 7
C. 16 D. 9

16. If $\frac{\sqrt{144}}{12^2}+\frac{24^2}{\sqrt{576}}+\frac{\sqrt{5184}}{36^2}=x$, then what is the value of the x ?

A. $20\frac{5}{36}$ B. $24\frac{7}{36}$
C. $22\frac{7}{36}$ D. $24\frac{5}{36}$

17. What is the value of

$\left(2+\sqrt{2}\right)+\frac{1}{\left(2+\sqrt{2}\right)}+\frac{1}{\left(\sqrt{2}-2\right)}$?

A. 4 B. 8
C. 2 D. 6

18. What is the least square number of 4 digits ?

A. 1012 B. 1024
C. 1032 D. 1016

19. What is the least number which is subtracted from 1026 so that the remainder is a perfect square ?

A. 2 B. 4
C. 6 D. 8

20. What is the least number which when mutiplied by 216 × 10^2 then product is a perfect square ?

A. 5 B. 4
C. 3 D. 6

21. A gardener grows 5625 trees in the garden. If he grows trees in such a way that number of trees in a row is equal to the number of rows. What is the number of rows ?

A. 65 B. 75
C. 95 D. 85

22. Each student of a class deposited so many rupees in subscription for Picnic, as many as the students were in the class. If 3 teachers deposited together Rs. 450 then total subscription was Rs. 1350. What was the number of students in the class ?

A. 35 B. 40
C. 30 D. 45

EXPLANATORY ANSWERS

1. C : ∵ $5\frac{19}{25}=\frac{144}{25}$

∴ Square root of $\frac{144}{25}=\sqrt{\frac{144}{25}}=\frac{\sqrt{12\times12}}{\sqrt{5\times5}}$

$=\frac{12}{5}=2\frac{2}{5}$

∴ Square root of $5\frac{19}{25}=2\frac{2}{5}$.

2. A : ∵ .0049 = .07 × .07

∴ $\sqrt{.0049}=\sqrt{.07\times.07}=.07$

Therefore value of $\sqrt{.0049}=.07$.

3. D : ∵ $\sqrt{16}=\sqrt{4\times4}=4$ and

$\sqrt{260-\sqrt{16}}=\sqrt{260-4}=\sqrt{256}$

∵ $\sqrt{256}=\sqrt{16\times16}=16$

∴ $\sqrt{128+\sqrt{260-\sqrt{16}}}=\sqrt{128+\sqrt{260-4}}$

$=\sqrt{128+\sqrt{256}}$

$=\sqrt{128+16}=\sqrt{144}=\sqrt{12\times12}=12$.

4. C : Cube root of 1331

$=\sqrt[3]{1331}=\sqrt[3]{11\times11\times11}=11$.

5. B : ∵ $2\frac{10}{27}=\frac{64}{27}$

$\therefore$ Cube root of

$$2\frac{10}{27} = \sqrt[3]{\frac{64}{27}} = \sqrt[3]{\frac{4\times4\times4}{3\times3\times3}} = \frac{4}{3} = 1\frac{1}{3}.$$

6. D : $\because$ $.09 = .9000$

$$\begin{array}{r|l} & .94 \\ 9 & .90\ 00 \\ & 81 \\ \hline 184 & \ \ 900 \\ & \ \ 736 \\ \hline & \ \ 164 \end{array}$$

So, it is clear that $\sqrt{.9} = .95$ approx.

7. B : $\because$ $\sqrt{49} = 7$ $\quad\therefore$ $\sqrt{49} \times \frac{1}{5} = 7 \times \sqrt{x}$

$$\Rightarrow 7\times\frac{1}{5} = 7\times\sqrt{x}$$

$$\Rightarrow \frac{1}{5} = \sqrt{x} \Rightarrow x = \left(\frac{1}{5}\right)^2 = \frac{1}{25}$$

8. C: $\because$ $\sqrt{0.81} = .9$ and $\sqrt{.09} = .3$

$$\therefore \frac{?}{\sqrt{0.81}} = 150 + \sqrt{.09}$$

$$\Rightarrow \frac{?}{.9} = 150 + .3 = 150.3$$

$$\Rightarrow ? = 150.3 \times .9 = 135.27.$$

9. A : $\because$ $10^2 + 12^2 = 100 + 144 = 244$

and $\sqrt{400} = 20$

$$\therefore \frac{10^2 + 12^2}{\sqrt{400}} = \sqrt{x} \Rightarrow \frac{244}{20} = \sqrt{x}$$

$$\Rightarrow 12.2 = \sqrt{x} \qquad \Rightarrow x = 148.84.$$

10.C : $\because$ $\sqrt{625-225} = \sqrt{400} = 20$

$$\therefore \sqrt{625-225} = \sqrt{?} + 10$$

$$\Rightarrow 20 = \sqrt{?} + 10 \quad \Rightarrow \quad \sqrt{?} = 10$$

$$\Rightarrow ? = 100.$$

11.C : $\because$ $\frac{1}{\sqrt{3}+\sqrt{5}} = \frac{1}{\sqrt{3}+\sqrt{5}} \times \frac{\sqrt{5}-\sqrt{3}}{\sqrt{5}-\sqrt{3}}$

$$= \frac{\sqrt{5}-\sqrt{3}}{(\sqrt{5})^2 - (\sqrt{3})^2}$$

$$= \frac{\sqrt{5}-\sqrt{3}}{5-3} = \frac{\sqrt{5}-\sqrt{3}}{2} = \frac{2.2361-1.7321}{2}$$

$= 0.252.$

12. A : $\because$ $\sqrt{0.000169} = 0.013$ and $\sqrt{0.0169} = 0.13$

$$\therefore \sqrt{0.000169} + \sqrt{0.0169} = 0.013 + 0.13 = 0.143.$$

13.C : $3\times\sqrt{15}\times\sqrt{5} = 3\times\sqrt{5\times3}\times\sqrt{5}$

$$= 3\times\sqrt{5}\times\sqrt{3}\times\sqrt{5} = 15\sqrt{3}$$

and $4\times\sqrt{27} = 4\times\sqrt{9\times3} = 4\times\sqrt{9}\times\sqrt{3} = 12\sqrt{3}$

$$\therefore \quad 3\times\sqrt{15}\times\sqrt{5} - 4\times\sqrt{27} = 15\sqrt{3} - 12\sqrt{3} = 3\sqrt{3}.$$

14. A : $\because$ $\sqrt[3]{0.000729} = \sqrt[3]{.09\times.09\times.09} = .09$ and

$\sqrt{.0961} = \sqrt{.31\times.31} = .3$

$$\therefore \sqrt{\sqrt[3]{.000729} + \sqrt{.0961}} = \sqrt{.09 + .31} = \sqrt{.4}$$

$$\begin{array}{r|l} & .63 \\ 6 & .40\ 00 \\ & 36 \\ \hline 123 & \ \ 400 \\ & \ \ 369 \\ \hline & \ \ \ \ 31 \end{array}$$

$.4 = .4000$

$\therefore$ $\sqrt{.4} = .63$ approx.

$$\therefore \sqrt{\sqrt[3]{.000729} + \sqrt{.0961}} = .63.$$

15. C : $\because$ $\frac{18}{\sqrt{36}} \times \frac{24}{\sqrt{9}} \times \frac{120}{\sqrt{?}} = 720$

$$\Rightarrow \frac{18}{6} \times \frac{24}{3} \times \frac{120}{\sqrt{?}} = 720$$

$$\sqrt{?} = \frac{18\times24\times120}{6\times3\times720} = 4$$

$$\Rightarrow ? = 4^2 = 16.$$

16. D : $\because$ $\frac{\sqrt{144}}{12^2} + \frac{24^2}{\sqrt{576}} + \frac{\sqrt{5184}}{36^2} = x$

$$\Rightarrow \frac{12}{12^2}+\frac{24^2}{24}+\frac{72}{36^2}=x$$

$$\Rightarrow \frac{1}{12}+24+\frac{1}{18}=x$$

$$\Rightarrow x=24\frac{5}{36}$$

17.C : $\because \frac{1}{2+\sqrt{2}}=\frac{2-\sqrt{2}}{4-2}=\frac{2-\sqrt{2}}{2}$

and $\frac{1}{\sqrt{2}-2}=\frac{\sqrt{2}+2}{2-4}=\frac{\sqrt{2}+2}{-2}$

$\therefore \quad 2+\sqrt{2}+\frac{1}{2+\sqrt{2}}+\frac{1}{\sqrt{2}-2}$

$=2+\sqrt{2}+\frac{2-\sqrt{2}}{2}-\frac{\sqrt{2}+2}{2}$

$=2+\sqrt{2}-\sqrt{2}=2.$

18. B : $\because$ Least number of four digits = 1000

But this is not a square number

$1000=(31)^2+39$

So, we have to find $(32)^2$

$32^2=1024$

$\therefore$ Least number of four digits which is a perfect square = 1024.

19. A : $\because$

```
        32
   3 | 10 26
     |  9
  62 |  1 26
     |  1 24
     |     2
```

So, it is clear that we have to subtract 2 from 1026 to get a remainder 1024 which is a perfect square of 32.

20. D : $\because 216\times10^2=6\times6\times6\times10\times10$

So, it is clear that we have to multiply the above number by 6 to make it a perfect square.

21. B : $\because$ Number of rows in the garden will be square root of 5625.

```
         75
    7 | 56 25
      | 49
  145 |  7 25
      |  7 25
      |     ×
```

Square root of 5625 $=\sqrt{5625}=75$

$\therefore$ Number of rows = 75.

22. C : Total subscription of teachers and students

= Rs. 1350

Subscription of students

= Rs. (1350 – 450) = Rs. 900

Number of students = $\sqrt{900}$

```
       30
   3 | 9 00
     | 9
   6 |   00
```

$\therefore$ Number of students = 30.

4

HCF AND LCM

Highest Common Factor : The highest common factor (H.C.F.) of two or more numbers is the largest or the highest among common factors.

Lowest Common Multiple : The lowest common multiple (L.C.M.) of two or more numbers is the smallest number which is a multiple of each of the given numbers.

Remember the following while solving the problems :

(*i*) H.C.F. of fractions

$$= \frac{\text{H.C.F of numerators}}{\text{L.C.M. of denominators}}$$

(*ii*) L.C.M. of fractions

$$= \frac{\text{L.C.M. of numerators}}{\text{H.C.F. of denominators}}$$

(*iii*) Product of two numbers = H.C.F. × L.C.M.

Example 1. *Find the H.C.F. of 18, 24 and 60.*

Solution. ∵ $18 = 2 \times 3 \times 3$

$24 = 2 \times 2 \times 2 \times 3$

$60 = 2 \times 2 \times 3 \times 5$

∴ From the prime factors of the above numbers it is clear that 2×3 is common in prime factors of three numbers.

∴ Required H.C.F. = 6

Example 2. *Find the L.C.M. of 40, 30, 25 and 20.*

Solution. ∵ $40 = 2 \times 2 \times 2 \times 5$

$30 = 2 \times 3 \times 5$

$25 = 5 \times 5$

$20 = 2 \times 2 \times 5$

From the prime factors of the above four numbers we note that 2 occurs as a prime factor maximum three times, 3 one time and 5 two times.

∴ Required L.C.M. = $2 \times 2 \times 2 \times 3 \times 5 \times 5$

= 600.

Example 3. *Find H.C.F. of $\frac{4}{9}$, $\frac{10}{21}$ and $\frac{20}{63}$.*

Solution. ∵ H.C.F. of fractions

$$= \frac{\text{H.C.F. of numerators}}{\text{L.C.M. of denominators}}$$

∴ H.C.F. of 4, 10 and 20 = 2

L.C.M. of 9, 21 and 63 = 63

∴ H.C.F of $\frac{4}{9}$, $\frac{10}{21}$ and $\frac{20}{63} = \frac{2}{63}$.

Example 4. *Find that how many times the H.C.F. of 48 and 64 is contained in L.C.M. ?*

Solution. $48 = 2 \times 2 \times 2 \times 2 \times 3$

$64 = 2 \times 2 \times 2 \times 2 \times 2 \times 2$

Common factors = $2 \times 2 \times 2 \times 2 = 16$

∴ Required H.C.F. = 16

To find L.C.M of 48 and 64

$48 = 2 \times 2 \times 2 \times 2 \times 3$

$64 = 2 \times 2 \times 2 \times 2 \times 2 \times 2$

Prime factors occurring maximum times

$= 2 \times 2 \times 2 \times 2 \times 2 \times 2 \times 3 = 192$

∴ Required L.C.M. = 192 = 16 × 12.

It is clear that H.C.F. of 48 and 64 is contained 12 times in the L.C.M. of 48 and 64.

Example 5. *L.C.M. and H.C.F. of two numbers is 60 and 4 respectively. If one number is 20, then find the other number.*

Solution. First number × second number

= H.C.F. × L.C.M.

20 × second number = 4 × 60

$$\text{Second number} = \frac{40 \times 60}{20} = 12.$$

Example 6. *Product of two numbers is 7200. If their H.C.F. is 20 then what will be the L.C.M. ?*

Solution. L.C.M. × H.C.F. = Product of two numbers

$$\text{L.C.M.} \times 20 = 7200$$

$$\therefore \quad \text{L.C.M.} = \frac{7200}{20} = 360.$$

Example 7. *What will be the largest number which divides 221, 491 and 116 leaving same remainder in each case ?*

Solution. First we have to find the difference between first number and second number, second number and third number and then find the H.C.F. of the difference to get the required largest number.

∴ Difference of first and second number
= 491 – 221 = 270

Difference of second and third number
= 491 – 116 = 375

270 = 2 × 3× 3× 3 × 5

375 = 3 × 5 × 5×5

H.C.F. = 3 × 5 = 15

∴ Required largest number = 15.

Example 8. *Determine the lowest number which when divided by 5, 6, 8, 9 or 12 leaves remainder 1 in each case and exactly divisible by 13.*

Solution . First we have to find L.C.M. of 5, 6, 8, 9 or 12

5 = 5 × 1

6 = 2 × 3

8 = 2 × 2 × 2

9 = 3 × 3

12 = 2 × 3 × 3

Required L.C.M. = 2 × 2 × 2 × 3 × 3 × 5 = 360

Required number = 360 + 1 = 361

But this is not exactly divisible by 13.Therefore we have to consider 360 × 2 + 1, 360 × 3 + 1, 360 × 4 + 1 etc.

∴ Required lowest number
= 360 × 10 + 1 = 3601 which is exactly divisibly by 13.

EXERCISE

In the following questions four possible answer choice are given. In which one is correct. Choose the correct answer.

1. What will be H.C.F. of 12, 24 and 36 ?
A. 16 B. 18
C. 12 D. 36

2. What is L.C.M. of 70, 20 and 14 ?
A. 120 B. 140
C. 280 D. 70

3. What will be H.C.F. of 72, 108 and 56 ?
A. 4 B. 8
C. 12 D. 112

4. What will be L.C.M. of 6, 9, 12 and 18 ?
A. 18 B. 36
C. 6 D. 54

5. How many times H.C.F. of 24, 48 and 72 is contained in their L.C.M. ?
A. 2 times B. 4 times
C. 5 times D. 6 times

6. The ratio of two numbers is 11 : 15. If their H.C.F. is 13 then what will be the numbers respectively ?
A. 143, 195 B. 195, 143
C. 110, 150 D. 121, 165

7. What is the lowest number which is exactly divisible by 3, 4, 6 and 8 ?
A. 36 B. 24
C. 12 D. 48

8. What is the lowest perfect square number which is exactly divisbly by 56, 21 and 36 ?
A. 7050 B. 8056
C. 7040 D. 8100

9. Find the largest common divisor of 102 and 1170.
A. 10 B. 7
C. 6 D. 8

10. Find the lowest number between 50 and 100 which is exactly divisible by 3, 6 and 15.
A. 150 B. 75
C. 120 D. 60

11. What will be L.C.M. of $\frac{25}{14}$, $\frac{15}{8}$ and $\frac{40}{27}$?
A. 600 B. 500

C. 400 D. 440

12. What will be H.C.F. of $\frac{5}{6}$, $\frac{9}{10}$ and $\frac{12}{11}$?

A. $\frac{1}{380}$ B. $\frac{1}{330}$

C. $\frac{7}{330}$ D. $\frac{1}{440}$

13. What will be largest number which divides 27, 33 and 39 leaving remainder 2, 3, and 4 respectively ?

A. 4 B. 5

C. 3 D. 7

14. The product of two numbers is 380. What will be their L.C.M. if their H.C.F. is 1 ?

A. 130 B. 180

C. 230 D. 380

15. Find the lowest of 5 digits which is exactly divisbly by 12, 15 and 18.

A. 10080 B. 10800

C. 11820 D. 12080

16. What is the lowest number which is divisible by 24, 28 and 35 leaving 5 as remainder in each case ?

A. 775 B. 920

C. 845 D. 855

EXPLANTORY ANSWERS

1. C : ∵ $12 = \underline{2 \times 2 \times 3}$

$24 = 2 \times \underline{2 \times 2 \times 3}$

$36 = \underline{2 \times 2 \times 3} \times 3$

∴ Required H.C.F. $= 2 \times 2 \times 3 = 12$.

2. B : $70 = 2 \times 5 \times 7$

$20 = 2 \times 2 \times 5$

$14 = 2 \times 7$

∴ Required L.C.M. $= 2 \times 2 \times 5 \times 7 = 140$.

3. B : ∵ $72 = 2 \times 2 \times 2 \times 3 \times 3$

$108 = 2 \times 2 \times 3 \times 3 \times 3$

$56 = 2 \times 2 \times 2 \times 7$

∴ Required H.C.F. $= 2 \times 2 = 4$.

4. B : ∵ $6 = 2 \times 3$

$9 = 3 \times 3$

$12 = 2 \times 2 \times 3$

$18 = 2 \times 3 \times 3$

∴ Required L.C.M. $= 2 \times 2 \times 3 \times 3 = 36$.

5. D : $24 = 2 \times 2 \times 2 \times 3$

$48 = 2 \times 2 \times 2 \times 2 \times 3$

$72 = 2 \times 2 \times 2 \times 3 \times 3$

∴ Required H.C.F. $= 2 \times 2 \times 2 \times 3 = 24$

Required L.C.M. $= 2 \times 2 \times 2 \times 2 \times 3 \times 3$

$= 144 = 24 \times 6$

It is clear that H.C.F. of 24, 48 and 72 is contained 6 times in their L.C.M.

6. A: Let the numbers be $11x$ and $15x$ respectively.

H.C.F. of two numbers = 13 (Given)

It is clear that value of x is 13 because 11×13 and 15×13 have H.C.F. = 13.

∴ Numbers are $11 \times 13 = 143$ and $15 \times 13 = 195$.

7. B : It is clear from the problem that we have to find L.C.M. of 3, 4, 6 and 8.

$3 = 1 \times 3$

$4 = 2 \times 2$

$6 = 2 \times 3$

$8 = 2 \times 2 \times 2$

∴ Required L.C.M. $= 2 \times 2 \times 2 \times 3 = 24$

∴ Required lowest number divisibly by 3, 4, 6 and 8 = 24.

8. A. First of all we have to find L.C.M. of 56, 21 and 36.

$56 = 2 \times 2 \times 2 \times 7$

$21 = 3 \times 7$

$36 = 2 \times 2 \times 3 \times 3$

∴ Required L.C.M. $= 2 \times 2 \times 2 \times 3 \times 3 \times 7$

Because it is not a perfect square. To make it a perfect square we have to multiply it by 2×7.

∴ Lowest perfect square number

$= 2 \times 2 \times 2 \times 3 \times 3 \times 7 \times 2 \times 7 = 7056$.

9.C : $102 = 2 \times 3 \times 17$

$1170 = 2 \times 3 \times 3 \times 5 \times 13$

It is clear that highest common factor $= 2 \times 3 = 6$

∴ Largest common divisor = 6.

10. D : ∵ $3 = 3 \times 1$

$6 = 2 \times 3$

$15 = 3 \times 5$

$\therefore$ L.C.M. $= 2 \times 3 \times 5 = 30$

But 30 is not a number between 50 and 100.

$\therefore$ Required number divisible by 3, 6 and 15 and in between 50 and 100 $= 2 \times 30 = 60$.

11. A : L.C.M. of fractions

$$= \frac{\text{L.C.M. of numerators}}{\text{H.C.F. of denominators}}$$

$$\text{L.C.M. of } \frac{25}{14}, \frac{15}{8} \text{ and } \frac{40}{27}$$

$$= \frac{\text{L.C.M. of 25, 15 and 40}}{\text{H.C.F. of 14, 8 and 27}}$$

$\because$ $25 = 5 \times 5$, $15 = 3 \times 5$, $40 = 2 \times 2 \times 2 \times 5$

$\therefore$ Required L.C.M $= 2 \times 2 \times 2 \times 3 \times 5 \times 5$
$= 600$

$\because$ $14 = 2 \times 7$, $8 = 2 \times 2 \times 2$, $27 = 3 \times 3 \times 3$

$\therefore$ Required H.C.F. = 1

$$\therefore \text{L.C.M. of } \frac{25}{14}, \frac{15}{8} \text{ and } \frac{40}{27}$$

$$= \frac{600}{1} = 600.$$

12.B : L.C.M. of fractions,

$$= \frac{\text{H.C.F. of numerators}}{\text{L.C.M. of denominators}}$$

$$\therefore \text{H.C.F of } \frac{5}{6}, \frac{9}{10} \text{ and } \frac{12}{11}$$

$$= \frac{\text{H.C.F. of 5, 9 and 12}}{\text{L.C.M. of 6, 10 and 11}}$$

$\because$ $5 = 1 \times 5$, $9 = 3 \times 3$, $12 = 2 \times 2 \times 3$

$\therefore$ Required H.C.F. = 1

$\because$ $6 = 2 \times 3$, $10 = 2 \times 5$, $11 = 1 \times 11$

$\therefore$ Required L.C.M. $= 2 \times 3 \times 5 \times 11 = 330$

$$\therefore \text{H.C.F of } \frac{5}{6}, \frac{9}{10} \text{ and } \frac{12}{11} = \frac{1}{330}.$$

13. B : In such problems, the remainder is subtracted from the numbers and then we find their H.C.F.

$27 - 2 = 25$, $33 - 3 = 30$ and $39 - 4 = 35$

Now we have to find H.C.F. of 25, 30 and 35.

$\because$ $25 = 5 \times 5$, $30 = 2 \times 3 \times 5$, $35 = 5 \times 7$

$\therefore$ Required H.C.F. = 5

$\therefore$ Required largest number = 5.

14. D : $\because$ Product of two numbers = L.C.M. × H.C.F.

380 = L.C.M. × 1

$$\Rightarrow \text{L.C.M.} = \frac{380}{1} = 380.$$

15. A : $12 = 2 \times 2 \times 3$, $15 = 3 \times 5$ and $18 = 2 \times 3 \times 3$

$\therefore$ Required L.C.M. $= 2 \times 2 \times 3 \times 3 \times 5 = 180$

Lowest number of 5 digits = 10000
$= 180 \times 55 + 100$

It is clear that lowest number of 5 digits exactly divisible by 12, 15 and 18 $= 180 \times 56 = 10080$.

16. C : $\because$ $24 = 2 \times 2 \times 2 \times 3$

$28 = 2 \times 2 \times 7$

$35 = 5 \times 7$

$\therefore$ Required L.C.M. $= 2 \times 2 \times 2 \times 3 \times 5 \times 7$
$= 840$

It is clear that lowest number which is divided by 24, 28 and 35 and leaves remainder 5 in each case $= 840 + 5 = 845$.

5

PERCENTAGE

A fraction with its denominator as 100 is called a **percent**. The numerator of the fraction is called rate percent. The symbol % is used for 'percent'.

While solving the problems involving fraction we have to remember the following :

(*i*) 4% means $\frac{4}{100}$ which is a simple fraction and $\frac{4}{100}$ means .04 which is a decimal fraction. Therefore value of 4% in simple fraction and decimal fraction is $\frac{4}{100}$ and .04 respectively.

(*ii*) In the problems involving fraction we should consider whole thing as 100%.

(*iii*) To convert a simple fraction and decimal fraction into percent fraction we multiply the fraction by 100.

(*iv*) There is no unit of percent.

Important Note : In problems 'of' means multiplication.

Example 1. *Convert 12% into simple fraction.*

Solution. 12% means $\frac{12}{100}$

$\therefore \quad 12\% = \frac{12}{100} = \frac{3}{25}$.

Example 2. *How* $\frac{9}{20}$ *will be written in percent fraction ?*

Solution. $\frac{9}{20}$ is a simple fraction.

To convert simple fraction into percent fraction we multiply it by 100.

$\therefore \quad \frac{9}{20} = \frac{9}{20} \times 100\% = 45\%$.

Example 3. *What is 20% of Rs. 300 ?*

Solution. 20% of Rs. 300 $= 300 \times \frac{20}{100}$ = Rs. 60.

Example 4. *If 10% of 20% of x = 5, then what is the value of x ?*

Solution. $\because$ 10% of 20% of $x = 5$

$\therefore \quad \frac{10}{100} \times \frac{20}{100} \times x = 5$

$\therefore \quad x = \frac{5 \times 100 \times 100}{10 \times 20} = 250$

$\therefore$ Value of $x = 250$.

Example 5. *The population of a village is 800. If there are 40% men, 35% women and remaining are children, then find the number of children in that village.*

Solution. Number of children

$= 100\% - (40\% + 35\%)$

$= 100\% - 75\% = 25\%$

$\therefore$ Number of children = 25% of 800

$= 800 \times \frac{25}{100} = 200$.

Example 6. *If 8% of A is equal to 14% of B, then how many % of B is equal to 20% of A ?*

Solution. $\because$ 8% of A = 14% of B

(8 × 2.5)% of A = (14 × 2.5)% of B

$\therefore$ 20% of A = 35% of B.

Example 7. *Gulson's monthly income is Rs. 1800. If he spends 15% on food, 15% on clothes, 10% on house rent and 50% on domestic goods then what is his saving ?*

Solution. Monthly saving

$= 100\% - (15\% + 15\% + 10\% + 50\%)$

$= 100\% - 90\% = 10\%$

$\therefore$ Gulson's monthly saving = 10% of Rs. 1800

$= 1800 \times \frac{10}{100}$ = Rs. 180.

Example 8. *40% persons read newspaper x and 50% persons read newspaper y. 10% persons read both newspapers. How many persons do not read any of the newspaper ?*

Solution. Suppose number of persons = 100

No. of persons who read newspaper x

$= 40\%$ of $100 = 40$

No. of persons who read newspaper y

$= 50\%$ of $100 = 50$

No. of persons who read both newspaper

$= 10\%$ of $100 = 10$

No. of persons who do not read any of the number of the newspaper

$= 100 - (40 + 50 - 10) = 20$

$\therefore$ Number precent = 20%.

Example 9. *10% of soldiers were killed in war, 10% of the remaining were died by disease and 10% of the remaining were disabled for war. If there are 729000 healthy soldiers in the military then what was the number of soldiers in the beginning ?*

Solution. Let number of soldiers in the beginning =100

No. of soldiers killed in war = 10% of 100 = 10

Remaining soldiers = 100 – 10 = 90

No. of solidiers died by disease = 10% of 90

= 9

Reamaining soldiers = 90 – 9 = 81

No. of soldiers disabled for war = 10% of 81

= 8.1

Remaining soldiers = 81 – 8.1 = 72.9

If number of healthy soldiers are 72.9 then number of soldiers in the beginning = 100

If number of healthy soldiers are 729000 then numbers of solidiers in the beginning

$$\frac{100 \times 729000}{72.9} = 1000000.$$

Example 10. *In an examination 75% students passed in English and 65% pased in mathematics. 15% failed in both subjects. If 495 students passed the examination in both subjects then find the total number of students.*

Solution. No. of students failed in English

= 100% – 75% = 25%

No. of students failed in Maths = 100% – 65%

= 35%

No. of students failed in both subjects = 15%

Total No. of students who failed

= (25 + 35 – 15) = 45%

Total no. of students who passed = 100% – 45%

= 55%

55% of total students = 495

$$\therefore \quad \text{Total students} = \frac{495 \times 100}{55} = 900.$$

Example 11. *In an examination A secured 10% less marks than B, B secured 25% more marks than C. C secured 20% less marks than D. If A secured 360 marks out of 500 then find the marks secured by D.*

Solution. Marks secured by A

$$= \frac{360}{500} \times 500 = 72\%$$

In first case : A secured 10% less marks than B

$\therefore$ Marks secured by B

$$= 72\% \times \frac{100\%}{100\% - 10\%}$$

$$= 72\% \times \frac{100\%}{90\%} = 80\%$$

In second case : B secured 25% more marks than C

$\therefore$ Marks secured by C

$$= 80\% \times \frac{100\%}{100\% + 25\%}$$

$$= 80\% \times \frac{100}{125} = 64\%$$

In third case : C secured 20% less more than D

$\therefore$ Marks secured by D

$$= 64\% \times \frac{100\%}{100\% - 20\%}$$

$$= 64\% \times \frac{100}{80} = 80\%$$

$\therefore$ D secured 80% marks.

EXERCISE

In the following questions four possible answer choices are given in which one is correct. Choose the correct answer.

1. Convert $\frac{3}{20}$ in percent fraction

A. 10% B. 6%
C. 15% D. 18%

2. Convert 35% in decimal fraction :

A. .035 B. .35
C. 3.5 D. 35

3. How much percent of one metre is 5 cm ?

A. 4% B. 10%
C. 5% D. 20%

4. By which number we should divide a number to get 20% of the number ?

A. 5 B. 4
C. 8 D. 2

5. If 55% of 80 + 30% of 90 + ? = 198, then what is the value of (?) sign ?

A. 120 B. 127
C. 117 D. 130

6. If $6\frac{2}{5} + 80\%$ of 35 $+ 26\frac{1}{3} = \oplus$ then what is the value of $\oplus$?

A. $60\frac{11}{15}$ B. $59\frac{4}{15}$
C. $70\frac{1}{15}$ D. $49\frac{11}{15}$

7. If 70% of ? = 455, then what is the value of (?) sign ?

A. 380 B. 650
C. 660 D. 655

8. The population of a city was 50000. It increased to 52000. What is the percentage increase in the population ?

A. 18% B. 27%
C. 25% D. 4%

9. If price of wheat increase by 60% then by which percent a family should decrease its consumption so that expenditure will not increase ?

A. 47.5% B. 31.5%
C. 37.5% D. 20.5%

10. There are 1800 students in school. If 20% are muslim, 15% sikh, 10% Christian and remaining are Hindu, then how many are Hindu students ?

A. 880 B. 990
C. 1024 D. 1120

11. Marks secured by Kamal Kant in English are equal to 40% of total marks secured by him in Hindi and Mathematics. If he secured 20 marks more in Hindi instead of Mathematics, then how many marks he secured in English ?

A. 780
B. Information is incomplete
C. 860
D. 540

12. Lavkush's salary is 30% more than Sanju's salary. If Sanju's salary is Rs. 600 then what is Lavkush's salary ?

A. Rs. 780 B. Rs. 670
C. Rs. 860 D. Rs. 920

13. Population of Shikarpur in 1961 was 44000. In 1971 it increased to 55000. What is the percentage increase in population ?

A. 22% B. 15%
C. 25% D. 20%

14. If price of an article decreases by 10% then 1 kg more article can be purchased in Rs. 25. What is the decreased price of the article ?

A. Rs. 2.50 /kg B. Rs. 1.75/kg
C. Rs. 2.25/kg D. Rs. 3.30/kg

15. If 5% of a number is 15 then what is the value of 30% of number ?

A. 80 B. 90
C. 87 D. 93

16. If one side of the rectangle is increased by 50% and other side is decreased by 50% then new area is how much percent less than original area?

A. 20% B. 50%
C. 25% D. 40%

17. If length and breadth of a rectangular field is increased by 20% and 10% respectively then how much percent the area increases ?
A. 32% B. 27%
C. 30% D. 10%

18. If the price of a machine increases by 20%, the sale decreases by 40%. What is the effect on cash collected ?
A. 16% less B. 28% less
C. 20% less D. 25% less

19. A worker earns Rs. 120 in 50 hours. If labour increases by $12\frac{1}{2}$% per hour then what is increased labour per hour ?
A. Rs. 2.70 B. Rs. 2.50
C. Rs. 1.85 D. Rs. 2.10

20. In a company there are 75% skilled workers and remaining are unskilled. 80% of skilled workers and 20% of unskilled workers are permanent. If number of temporary workers is 126, then what is the number of total workers ?
A. 480 B. 510
C. 360 D. 377

21. In an examination 51% students failed in English and 45% failed in Mathematics. If 21% failed in both subjects and 169 passed the examination, then how many students appeared in the examination ?
A. 760 B. 625
C. 625 D. 400

EXPLANATORY ANSWERS

1.C : $\because$ Percentage fraction of $\frac{3}{20}$

$= \frac{3}{20} \times 100\% = 15\%.$

2. B : Decimal fraction of 35% $= \frac{35}{100} = .35.$

3.C : Let x% of 1 metre = 5 cm

$\therefore \quad 100 \text{ cm} \times \frac{x}{100} = 5 \text{ cm}$

$\therefore \quad x = \frac{5 \times 100}{100} = 5$

Therefore, 5% of 1 metre = 5 cm.

4. A : Let 20% of the number be obtained by dividing it by x.

$\therefore \quad \frac{\text{Number}}{x} = 20\% \text{ of the number}$

$= \text{Number} \times \frac{20}{100}$

$\therefore \quad x = \frac{100 \times \text{Number}}{20 \times \text{Number}} = 5$

Therefore, by dividing the number by 5, we get 20% of the number.

5.B : 55% of 80 $= 80 \times \frac{50}{100} = 44$

30% of 90 $= 90 \times \frac{30}{100} = 27$

$\because$ 55% of 80 + 30% of 90 + ? = 198

$\Rightarrow \quad 44 + 27 + ? = 198$

$\Rightarrow \quad ? = 198 - 44 - 27 = 127$

$\Rightarrow \quad ? = 127$

6. A : $\because 6\frac{2}{5} = 6 + \frac{2}{5}$, 80% of 35 $= 35 \times \frac{80}{100} = 28$

and $26\frac{1}{3} = 26 + \frac{1}{3}$

$\because 6\frac{2}{5} + 80\% \text{ of } 35 + 26\frac{1}{3} = \oplus$

$\Rightarrow \quad 6 + \frac{2}{5} + 28 + 26 + \frac{1}{3} = \oplus$

$\Rightarrow \quad 60 + \frac{2}{5} + \frac{1}{3} = \oplus$

$\Rightarrow \quad 60 + \frac{11}{15} = \oplus$

$\oplus = 60\frac{11}{15}$

7.B : $\because$ 70% of ? = 455

$\therefore \quad ? \times \frac{70}{100} = 455$

$\therefore\ ? = \frac{455\times100}{70} = 650.$

8.D : $\because$ Population of a city in the beginning = 50,000

Population of a city in the end = 52,000

Increase in population = 52000 – 50000 = 2000

$\%\text{Increase} = \frac{2000}{50000}\times100 = 4\%.$

9.C : According to problem,

Let first price of 100 kg wheat = Rs. 100

Increase = 60%

$\therefore$ Increased price of 100 kg wheat = Rs. 160

Quantity of wheat purchased in Rs. 100

$= \frac{100}{160}\times100 = 62.5$ kg

$\therefore$ Decrease in consumption of wheat

= 100 – 62.5 = 37.5

$\therefore$ Percent decrease in consumption = 37.5%.

10. B : Percemtage of Hindu studens

= 100% – (20% + 15% + 10%)

=100% – 45% = 55%

$\therefore$ Number of Hindu students = 55% of 1800

$= \frac{1800\times55}{100} = 990$

11. B : Information is incomplete.

12 A : Lavkush's salary = Sanju's salary + 30% of Sanju's salary

= Rs. 600 + 30% of Rs. 600

$= \text{Rs. } 600 + \text{Rs. } \frac{30\times600}{100}$

= Rs. 600 + Rs. 180 = Rs. 780.

13. C : Shikarpur's population in 1961 = 44000

Shikarpur's population in 1971 = 55000

Increase = 55000 – 44000 = 11000

$\%\text{increase} = \frac{11000}{44000}\times100 = 25\%.$

14. A : According to problem,

Decrease in rate = 10%

$\therefore$ 10% decrease in Rs. 25

$= \text{Rs. } \frac{10\times25}{100} = \text{Rs. } 2.50$

$\therefore$ Decreased price of 1 kg article = Rs. 2.50.

15. B : Accroding to problem,

5% of the number = 15

$\therefore \text{Number}\times\frac{5}{100} = 15$

$\therefore \text{Number} = \frac{100\times15}{5} = 300$

$\therefore 30\% \text{ of the number} = \frac{30}{100}\times300 = 90.$

16. C : Let length and breadth of the rectangle be x and y respectively.

$\therefore$ Area of the rectangle = xy square units

In first case : Length is increased by 50%

$\therefore$ New length of the rectangle x + 50% of x

= $1.5x$

In second case : Breadth is decreased by 50%

$\therefore$ New breadth of the rectangle = y – 50 % of y

= $.5y$

$\therefore$ New area of the rectangle = $1.5x \times .5y$

= $.75xy$ square units

$\therefore$ Decrease in area = $xy - .75xy = .25xy$

$\%\text{ Decrease in area} = \frac{.25xy}{xy}\times100 = 25\%.$

17. A : Let length and breadth of rectangle field be x and y respectively.

Area of rectangular field = xy square unit

New length of rectangular field

= x + 20% of x = $1.2x$

New breath of rectangular field

= y + 10% of y = $1.1y$

New area of reactangular field $1.2x \times 1.1y$

= $1.32xy$ square unit

Increase in area = $1.32xy - xy = .32xy$

$\%\text{ increase in area} = \frac{.32xy}{xy}\times100 = 32\%.$

18. B : Let sale price of a machine be Rs. 100 and number of machines sold = 100

$\therefore$ Total sale = Rs. 100 × 100 = Rs. 10000

Increase in sale price = 20%

$\therefore$ New sale price of machine = Rs. 120

Decrease in sale = 40%

$\therefore$ Number of machines sold = 100 – 40 = 60

$\therefore$ Total new sale = 120 × 60 = Rs. 7200

Decrease in sale = Rs. (10000 – 7200)

= Rs. 2800

% Decrease in sale = $\frac{2800}{10000} \times 100 = 28\%$.

19. A : Total earing of 50 hours = Rs. 120

$\therefore$ Earing of 1 hour = $\frac{120}{50}$ = Rs. $\frac{12}{5}$

% Increase in earning = $12\frac{1}{2}\%$

$\therefore$ New earning of 1 hour

= Rs. $\frac{12}{5} + 12\frac{1}{2}\%$ of Rs. $\frac{12}{5}$

$= \frac{12}{5} + \frac{12}{5} \times \frac{25}{2 \times 100}$ = Rs. (2.40 + .30)

= Rs. 2.70.

20. C : Let No. of workers in the company = 100

$\therefore$ No. of skilled workers = 75% of 100 = 75

No. of unskilled workers = 25

Permanent workers out of skilled workers

= 80% of 75 = $\frac{80 \times 75}{100} = 60$

Permanent workers out of unskilled workers

= 20% of 25 = $\frac{20 \times 25}{100} = 5$

Total number of permanent workers

= 60 + 5 = 65

$\therefore$ Total number of temporary workers

= 100 – 65 = 35

If there are 35 temprory workers then total workers = 100

If there are 126 temporary workers then total

workers = $\frac{100 \times 126}{35} = 360$.

21. C : Let No. of students appeared in examination = 100

Failed in English = 51

Failed in Mathematics = 45

Failed in both subjects = 21

$\therefore$ Failed in only English + Failed in only Maths + Failed in both subjects

= (51 – 21) + (45 – 21) – 21

= 30 + 24 + 21 = 75

$\therefore$ Passed in both subjects = 100 – 75 = 25

If 25 passed then total students = 100

If 169 passed then total students

$= \frac{100 \times 169}{25} = 676$.

6

SIMPLE INTEREST

The money that you borrow is known as **Principal**, and the money that you pay for using somebody else's money is known as **interest**. The sum of principal and interest is known as the **amount.**

Points to Remember :

1. Amount = Principal + Interest
2. Simple Interest = $\frac{\text{Priciple} \times \text{Time} \times \text{Rate}}{100}$

Note : If amount of years is subtracted from the amount of P years then the remaining amount is the simple interest of (P – Q) years. (While P > Q)

Example 1. *What is the simple interest of Rs. 800 in 2 years at the rate of 5% per annum?*

Solution. Here, Principal = Rs. 800, Time = 2 years, Rate = 5% p.a.

$$\text{S.I.} = \frac{\text{P} \times \text{R} \times \text{T}}{100} = \frac{800 \times 5 \times 2}{100} = \text{Rs. } 80.$$

Example 2. *What is the simple interest of Rs. 5600 in 5 years at the rate of 6% per annum?*

Solution. Here, Principal = Rs. 5600, Rate = 6% per annum, Time = 5 years.

$$\text{S.I.} = \frac{\text{P} \times \text{R} \times \text{T}}{100} = \frac{5600 \times 5 \times 6}{100} = \text{Rs. } 1680.$$

Example 3. *At what rate percent per annum will Rs. 1000 amounts to Rs. 1120 in 3 years?*

Solution. Here, Principal = Rs. 1000, Amount = Rs. 1120

$\therefore$ Interest of 3 years = 1120 – 1000 = Rs. 120

$$\text{Rate} = \frac{\text{S.I.} \times 100}{\text{P} \times \text{T}} = \frac{120 \times 100}{1000 \times 3} = 4\%.$$

Example 4. *If the simple interest of a sum in 4 years at the rate of 4% per annum is Rs. 176 then find the sum.*

Solution. Let the sum = Rs. x, Time = 4 years

Rate = 4% per annum.

Interest = Rs. 176

$$\text{Principal} = \frac{\text{Simple interest} \times 100}{\text{Time} \times \text{Rate}}$$

$$= \frac{176 \times 100}{4 \times 4} = \text{Rs. } 1100.$$

Example 5. *Simple interest on a certain sum is Rs. 144. If rate percent is equat to the number of years then find the rate percent.*

Solution. Let the sum = Rs. 100, Rate = x %, Time = x years

$$\therefore \quad \text{Simple Interest} = \frac{\text{P} \times \text{R} \times \text{T}}{100}$$

$$144 = \frac{100 \times x \times x}{100} = x^2$$

$$\Rightarrow \quad x = \sqrt{144} = 12$$

$$\therefore \quad \text{Rate percent} = 12\%.$$

Example 6. *If the simple interest of Rs. 1500 in 2 years is Rs. 135 and in 3 years is Rs. 202.50, then find the rate of interest.*

Solution. Difference in interests of 3 years and 2 years = Rs. (202.50 – 135) = Rs. 67.50

$$\text{Rate} = \frac{\text{Simple Interest} \times 100}{\text{Principal} \times \text{Time}}$$

$$= \frac{67.50 \times 100}{1500 \times 1} = 4\frac{1}{2}\%.$$

Example 7. *Rs. 800 amounts to Rs. 928 in 4 years at certain rate. If interest rate is increased by 3% then what will be the amount?*

Solution. *In the first case* : Interest in 4 years = Rs. (928 – 800) = Rs. 128

$\therefore$ Rate $= \frac{\text{S.I.} \times 100}{\text{P} \times \text{T}} = \frac{128 \times 100}{800 \times 4} = 4\%$.

In second case : New rate = (4 + 3)% = 7%

$$\text{Simple Interest} = \frac{\text{P} \times \text{R} \times \text{T}}{100}$$

$$= \frac{800 \times 7 \times 4}{100} = \text{Rs. } 224$$

$\therefore$ Amount = Rs. (800 + 224) = Rs. 1024.

Example 8. *In what time will a sum of money triple itself at 4% per annum simple interest?*

Solution. Let sum of money = Rs. x

Amount = Rs. $3x$, Rate = 4%

Simple Interest = Rs. $(3x - x)$ = Rs. $2x$

$$\text{Time} = \frac{\text{S.I.} \times 100}{\text{P} \times \text{R}} = \frac{2x \times 100}{x \times 4} = 50 \text{ years}$$

$\therefore$ Sum will become triple in 50 years.

Example 9. *If a sum of money invested at simple interest amounts to Rs. 5184 in 2 years and Rs. 5832 in 3 years then find the sum and rate of interest.*

Solution. Simple interest of 1 year

= Amount in 3 years – Amount in 2 years

= Rs. (5832 – 5184) = Rs. 648

$\therefore$ Simple interest of 2 years = 2 × 648 = Rs. 1296

$\therefore$ Sum of money

= Amount in 2 years – Interest of 2 years

= Rs (5184 – 1296) = Rs. 3888

$$\text{Rate of interest} = \frac{\text{S.I.} \times 100}{\text{P} \times \text{T}}$$

$$= \frac{648 \times 100}{3888 \times 1} = \frac{50}{3} = 16\frac{2}{3}\%.$$

Example 10. *A man invests Rs. 500 for 4 years and Rs. 600 for 3 years and earns simple interest of Rs. 190. Find the rate of interest.*

Solution. Let rate of interest = x %

Ist case : Principal = Rs. 500, Time = 4 years, Rate = x%.

$$\text{S.I.} = \frac{500 \times 4 \times 3x}{100} = \text{Rs. } 20x$$

IInd case : Principal = Rs 600,

Time = 3 years, Rate = x %

$$\text{S.I.} = \frac{600 \times x}{100} = \text{Rs. } 18x$$

Total simple interest = Rs. $20x$ + Rs. $18x$

= Rs. $38x$

Rs. $38x$ = Rs. 190

$$\therefore \quad x = \frac{190}{38} = 5$$

$\therefore$ Rate of interest = 5%.

Example 11. *A man borrows Rs 8000 for 5 years at the rate $2\frac{1}{2}$% per annum. For what time another man will borrow a sum of Rs 100 at $2\frac{1}{2}$% so that interest may be same?*

Solution. Interest in first case

$$= \frac{8000 \times 2\frac{1}{4} \times 5}{100} = \frac{8000 \times 9 \times 5}{4 \times 100} = \text{Rs. } 900$$

Interest will be same for another man.

$\therefore$ Interest = Rs. 900, Principal = Rs. 10000,

Rate = $2\frac{1}{2}$%, $\Rightarrow$ Time $= \frac{\text{Interest} \times 100}{\text{Principal} \times \text{Rate}}$

$$= \frac{900 \times 100}{10000 \times \frac{5}{2}} = \frac{900 \times 100 \times 2}{10000 \times 5} = \frac{18}{5} = 3\frac{3}{5} \text{ years.}$$

EXERCISE

In the following questions four answer choices are given in which one is correct. Choose the correct answer.

1. What will be simple interest of Rs. 750 in $4\frac{1}{3}$ years at 6% per annum?

A. Rs. 180 B. Rs. 215

C. Rs. 195 D. Rs. 210

2. In what time Rs. 700 amounts to Rs. 805 at 5% per annum?

A. 3 years B. $2\frac{1}{2}$ years

C. $3\frac{1}{2}$ years D. 4 years

3. What sum amounts to Rs. 560 in 8 years at 5% per annum?
A. Rs. 360 B. Rs. 400
C. Rs. 420 D. Rs. 380

4. The simple interest on Rs. 1600 is Rs. 32 less than the simple interest on Rs. 2000 at the same rate 4%. Find the time period.
A. $1\frac{1}{2}$ years B. 1 yeares
C. 2 years D. 3 years

5. Deepak lent out sum money on simple interest. After 30 years he received three times his money. What is the rate of interest?
A. $6\frac{2}{3}\%$ B. $16\frac{2}{3}\%$
C. $8\frac{1}{3}\%$ D. $3\frac{1}{3}\%$

6. A sum of money lent out at simple interest amounts to Rs. 2800 in 2 years and to Rs. 3250 in 5 years. What is the sum of money?
A. Rs 2500 B. Rs 2400
C. Rs 2800 D. Rs 3000

7. Pramod lents out some money at $6\frac{1}{4}\%$ · per annum. In what time his interest will be equal to his sum?
A. 15 years B. 18 years
C. 16 years D. 17 years

8. If a sum of money in 4 years amounts to 11/10 times then what will be the rate of interest?
A. $3\frac{1}{2}\%$ B. $2\frac{1}{2}\%$
C. $4\frac{1}{2}\%$ D. $3\frac{1}{4}\%$

9. Equal amount of money lent out to Sonu and Monu for 2 years at 5% and 6% respectively. If interest paid by Monu was Rs. 20 more than Sonu, then what is the amount of money lent out to each?
A. Rs. 1000 B. Rs. 1020
B. Rs. 1050 D. Rs. 1120

10. Mohit borrowed Rs. 15000 for 3 years. If interest paid by him was Rs. 2700, then what was the rate of interest?
A. 8% B. 4%
C. 6% D. 3%

11. A sum of money amounts to Rs. 2750 in 2 years at 5% per annum. At what rate the same money amounts to Rs. 3000 in 2 years?
A. 12% B. 10%
C. 15% D. 20%

12. A sum of money doubles itself at simple interest in 16 years. What is the rate of interest?
A. $6\frac{2}{3}\%$ B. $5\frac{1}{4}\%$
C. $6\frac{1}{4}\%$ D. $3\frac{1}{4}\%$

13. A sum of money amounts to 4 times in 24 years at simple interest. What is the rate of interest?
A. $10\frac{1}{2}\%$ B. $12\frac{1}{2}\%$
C. $8\frac{1}{3}\%$ D. $12\frac{1}{3}\%$

14. The interest of one rupee in one month is 1 paise. What is the rate of interest?
A. 11% B. 10%
C. 8% D. 12%

15. The simple interest of Rs. 400 is Rs. 64. Find the number of years if rate of interest is one-fourth of number of years.
A. 8 B. 7
B. 4 D. 3

16. Rs. 500 amounts to Rs. 580 in 4 years. If the rate of interest is increased by 4% then what will be new amount?
A. Rs. 870 B. Rs. 675
C. Rs. 660 D. Rs. 790

17. If interest on Rs. 18860 is Rs. 740, then what will be the amount?
A. Rs. 18600 B. Rs. 19600
C. Rs. 19900 D. Rs. 18800

18. A money-lender borrowed Rs. 2400 for 2 years. If he paid 5% interest on $\frac{1}{3}$ part and 4% interest on remaining part then how much interest was

paid by him?

A. Rs. 217 B. Rs. 320

C. Rs. 370 D. Rs. 208

19. What will be the sum of money which earns monthly interest Rs 600 at 6% per annum?

A. Rs. 110000 B. Rs. 120000

C. Rs. 150000 D. Rs. 145000

20. What will be the amount of Rs. 150 in 4 months at the rate of 5 paise per rupee per month?

A. Rs. 180 B. Rs. 163

C. Rs. 153 D. Rs. 190

21. A bicycle can be purchased in Rs. 800. A customer can purchase it in 12 monthly instalments of Rs. 80. What is the rate of interest?

A. 18% B. 22%

C. 20% D. 15%

22. In what time the simple interest of Rs. 1600 at 5% will be equal to simple interest of Rs. 1000 for 6 years at 4% per annum?

A. $2\frac{1}{2}$ years B. 3 years

C. 4 years D. 6 years

EXPLANATORY ANSWERS

1. C : Here, Principal = Rs. 750,

Time $= 4\frac{1}{3} = \frac{13}{3}$ years, Rate = 6%

$$\text{Simple Interest} = \frac{\text{Principal} \times \text{Time} \times \text{Rate}}{100}$$

$$= \frac{750 \times \frac{13}{3} \times 6}{100}$$

$$= \frac{750 \times 13 \times 6}{3 \times 100} = \text{Rs. } 195$$

2. A : Here, Principal = Rs. 700, Amount = Rs. 805, Rate = 5%

Simple Interest = Amount – Principal

= 805 – 700 = Rs. 105

$$\text{Time} = \frac{\text{S.I.} \times 100}{\text{P} \times \text{R}} = \frac{105 \times 100}{700 \times 5} = 3 \text{ years}$$

3. A : Let Principal = Rs. x, Amount = Rs. 560

Time = 8 years, Rate = 5%

Simple Interest = Amount – Principal

= Rs. $(560 - x)$

$$\because \text{Simple Interest} = \frac{\text{Principal} \times \text{Time} \times \text{Rate}}{100}$$

$$\therefore \quad 560 - x = \frac{x \times 8 \times 5}{100} = \frac{2x}{5}$$

$$\Rightarrow \quad 2800 - 5x = 2x$$

$$\Rightarrow \quad 7x = 2800$$

$$\Rightarrow \quad x = \frac{28000}{7} = 400$$

$\therefore$ Principal = Rs. 400.

4. C : Let the time period for both sums = T years

In first case : P = Rs. 1600, Time = T years, R = 4%

$$\text{S.I.} = \frac{1600 \times T \times 4}{100} = \text{Rs. } 64T$$

In second case : P = Rs. 2000, R = 4%, Time = T years

$$\text{S.I.} = \frac{2000 \times T \times 4}{100} = \text{Rs. } 80T$$

According to problem,

$$64\,T = 80T - 32$$

$$80T - 64T = 32$$

$$16T = 32$$

$$\therefore \quad T = \frac{32}{16} = 2$$

$\therefore$ Time period = 2 years.

5. A : Let Principal = Rs. x

Then amount = Rs. $3x$, Time = 30 years

Simple Interest = Rs. $(3x - x)$ = Rs. $2x$

$$\text{Rate} = \frac{\text{Simple interest} \times 100}{\text{Principal} \times \text{Time}} = \frac{2x \times 100}{x \times 30}$$

$$= \frac{20}{3} = 6\frac{2}{3}\%$$

$\therefore$ Interest rate $= 6\frac{2}{3}\%$.

6. A : Amount in 2 years = Rs. 2800

Amount in 5 years = Rs. 3250

$\therefore$ Interest of 3 years = Rs. (3250 – 2800)
= Rs. 450

$\therefore$ Interest of 2 years = $\frac{450\times2}{3}$ = Rs. 300

$\therefore$ Sum of money = Amount of 2 years – interest of 2 years
= 2800 – 300 = Rs. 2500.

7. C : Let after T years interest be equal to the principal.

$\therefore$ Simple Interest $= \frac{P\times R\times T}{100}$; $R = \frac{25}{4}\%$

$$P = \frac{P\times\frac{25}{4}\times T}{100}$$

$$\Rightarrow \quad T = \frac{100\times4}{25} = 16.$$

$\therefore$ Required Time period = 16 years.

8. B : Let principal = Rs. x

Amount = Rs. $\frac{11}{10}x$, Time = 4 years

Simple Interest = Amount – Principal

$$= \text{Rs.}\left(\frac{11}{10}x - x\right) = \text{Rs. } \frac{x}{10}$$

$$\text{Simple Interest} = \frac{\text{Principal}\times\text{Time}\times\text{Rate}}{100}$$

$$\frac{x}{10} = \frac{x\times4\times\text{Rate}}{100}$$

$$\therefore \text{Rate} = \frac{100}{4\times10} = \frac{5}{2} = 2\frac{1}{2}\%$$

$\therefore$ Required rate $= 2\frac{1}{2}\%$.

9. A : Let sum of money lent out to Sonu and Monu = Rs. x

For Sonu : P = Rs. x, T = 2 years, R = 5%

$$\text{S.I.} = \frac{x\times2\times5}{100} = \text{Rs. } \frac{x}{10}$$

For Monu : P = Rs. x, T = 2 years, R = 6%

$$\text{S.I.} = \frac{x\times2\times6}{100} = \text{Rs. } \frac{6x}{50}$$

According to problem, Monu's interest is Rs. 20 more than Sonu's interest.

$$\therefore \frac{6x}{50} = \frac{x}{10} + 20$$

$$\Rightarrow \frac{6x}{50} - \frac{x}{10} = 20$$

$$\Rightarrow \frac{x}{50} = 20$$

$$\Rightarrow x = 20\times50 = 1000$$

$\therefore$ Sum of money lent out to each = Rs. 1000.

10 C : Here, Principal = Rs. 15000, Time = 3 years, S.I. = Rs. 2700

$$\therefore \text{Rate} = \frac{\text{S.I.}\times100}{P\times T} = \frac{2700\times100}{15000\times3} = 6\%.$$

11. B : Let the sum of money = Rs. x

In first case : Principal = Rs. x, Time = 2 years
Rate = 5%, Amount = Rs. 2750
Simple Interest = (Amount – Principal)

$$= \frac{P\times R\times T}{100}$$

$$\therefore \quad 2750 - x = \frac{x\times5\times2}{100} = \frac{x}{10}$$

$$\Rightarrow 27500 - 10x = x$$

$$\Rightarrow 11x = 27500$$

$$\Rightarrow x = \frac{27500}{11} = 2500$$

$\therefore$ Sum of money = Rs. 2500

In second case : Principal = Rs. 2500,
Amount = Rs. 3000
Time = 2 years
Simple Interest = (Amount – Principal)

$$= \frac{P\times R\times T}{100}$$

$$\therefore (3000-2500) = \frac{2500\times2\times\text{Rate}}{100}$$

$$\therefore \quad \text{Rate} = \frac{500\times100}{2500\times2} = 10\%.$$

12. C : Let the sum of money = Rs. x

$\therefore$ Amount = Rs. $2x$, Time = 16 years
Simple Interest = (Amount – Principal)

$$= \frac{P\times R\times T}{100}$$

$$2x - x = \frac{x\times16\times\text{Rate}}{100}$$

$\Rightarrow\ x = \dfrac{x \times 16 \times \text{Rate}}{100}$

$\Rightarrow$ Rate $= \dfrac{x \times 100}{x \times 16}$

$\Rightarrow$ Rate $= \dfrac{100}{16} = \dfrac{25}{4} = 6\dfrac{1}{4}\%$

$\therefore$ Required rate $= 6\dfrac{1}{4}\%$.

13. B : Let sum of money = Rs. x

$\therefore$ Amount = Rs. $4x$, Time = 24 years

Simple Interest = (Amount – Principal)

$= \dfrac{P \times R \times T}{100}$

$4x - x = \dfrac{x \times 24 \times \text{Rate}}{100}$

$3x = \dfrac{x \times 24 \times \text{Rate}}{100}$

$\therefore$ Rate $= \dfrac{3x \times 100}{x \times 24} = \dfrac{25}{2} = 12\dfrac{1}{2}\%$

$\therefore$ Required rate $= 12\dfrac{1}{2}\%$.

14. D : Here, Principal = 1 Re = 100 Paise,

Simple Interest = 1 Paise

Time = 1 month $= \dfrac{1}{12}$ year

Rate $= \dfrac{\text{S.I} \times 100}{P \times T} = \dfrac{1 \times 100}{100 \times \dfrac{1}{12}} = 12\%$

$\therefore$ Required rate = 12%.

15. A : Let Rate = $x\%$, Time = $4x$ years

Principal = Rs. 400, Interest = Rs. 64

Simple Interest $= \dfrac{P \times T \times R}{100}$

$\therefore\ 64 = \dfrac{400 \times 4x \times x}{100} = 16x^2$

$\Rightarrow x^2 = 4 \Rightarrow x = 2$

$\therefore$ Required time $= 4x = 4 \times 2 = 8$ years.

16. C : *In first case :* Simple Interest of 4 years

= 580 – 500 = Rs. 80.

Rate $= \dfrac{\text{S.I.} \times 100}{P \times T} = \dfrac{80 \times 100}{500 \times 4} = 4\%$

In the second case : New rate (4 + 4)% = 8%

Simple Interest $= \dfrac{P \times T \times R}{100} = \dfrac{500 \times 4 \times 8}{100}$

= Rs. 160

$\therefore$ New amount = 500 + 160 = Rs. 660.

17. B : Amount = Principal + Simple Interest

= 18860 + 740 = Rs. 19600.

18. D : Sum of money = Rs. 2400

$\dfrac{1}{3}$ part $= \dfrac{2400}{3}$ = Rs. 800

Remaining part = Rs. (2400 – 800) = Rs. 1600

In first case : P = Rs. 800, T = 2 years, R = 5%

S.I. $= \dfrac{800 \times 2 \times 5}{100}$ = Rs. 80.

In second case : P = Rs. 1600, T = 2 years, R = 4%

S.I. $= \dfrac{1600 \times 2 \times 4}{100}$ = Rs. 128

Total interest = Rs. (80 + 128) = Rs. 208.

19. B : Here, S.I. = Rs. 600,

Time = 1 month $= \dfrac{1}{12}$ year, R = 6%

Sum (Principal) $= \dfrac{\text{S.I} \times 100}{T \times R}$

$= \dfrac{600 \times 100}{\dfrac{1}{12} \times 6} = \dfrac{600 \times 100 \times 12}{6}$ = Rs. 120000.

20. A : Principal = Rs. 150, Time = 4 months,

Rate = 5 %

S.I. $= \dfrac{150 \times 4 \times 5}{100}$ = Rs. 30

Amount = Principal + Simple Interest

= Rs. (150 + 30) = Rs. 180.

21. C : Amount paid in 12 instalments of Rs. 80 per month = Rs. 80 × 12 = Rs. 960

Here, Princpal = Rs. 800, Amount = 960,

Time = 1 year

$\therefore$ Simple Interest = Amount – Principal

$$= \frac{P \times T \times R}{100}$$

$$\therefore\ 960 - 800 = \frac{800 \times Rate \times 1}{100}$$

$$\Rightarrow \frac{160}{8} = Rate$$

$$\Rightarrow \quad Rate = 20\%$$

22. B : *In first case :*

$$\text{Simple Interest} = \frac{P \times T \times R}{100} = \frac{1600 \times Time \times 5}{100}$$

In second case :

$$\text{Simple Interest} = \frac{1000 \times 6 \times 4}{100}$$

According to problem, the interest in both cases is equal.

$$\therefore \quad \frac{1600 \times Time \times 5}{100} = \frac{1000 \times 6 \times 4}{100}$$

$$\Rightarrow \text{Time} = 3 \text{ years}$$

$\therefore$ Required Time period = 3 years.

7

COMPOUND INTEREST

When interest is calculated on the amount (Principal plus interest) then it is called compound interest.

Important Formulae:

(*i*) Amount = Principal + Compound Interest

(*ii*) Compound Interest = Amount – Principal

Things to Remember:

(*i*) If interest is calculatated half yearly then rate is halved and time is doubled.

(*ii*) If interest is calculated quarterly then rate is divided by four and time is multiplied by four.

Important Note: For one year time simple interest and compound interest are equal when rate of interest per annum is given.

Example 1. *What will be the interest on Rs 15625 in 2 years when interest is compounded annually at the rate of 4%?*

Solution. Here, Principal = Rs. 15625, Time = 2 years, Rate = 4%

Compound Interest

$$= \text{Principal}\left[\left(1+\frac{R}{100}\right)^{\text{Time}} - 1\right]$$

$$= 15625\left[\left(1+\frac{4}{100}\right)^{2} - 1\right]$$

$$= 15625\left[\frac{26}{25}\times\frac{26}{25} - 1\right]$$

$$= 15625\left(\frac{676-625}{625}\right)$$

$$= \frac{15625\times 51}{625} = \text{Rs. } 1275.$$

Example 2. *If compound interest of a certain sum for 2 years at the rate of 5% P.A. is Rs 1230 then what will be the sum of money?*

Solution. Compound Interest

$$= \text{Principal}\left[\left(1+\frac{R}{100}\right)^{\text{Time}} - 1\right]$$

$$1230 = \text{Principal}\left[\left(1+\frac{5}{100}\right)^{2} - 1\right]$$

$$1230 = \text{Principal}\left[\frac{21}{20}\times\frac{21}{20} - 1\right]$$

$$1230 = \text{Principal} \times \frac{41}{400}$$

$$\therefore \text{ Principal} = \frac{1230\times 400}{41} = \text{Rs. } 12000$$

∴ Required sum of money = Rs. 12000.

Example 3. *Neeraj lent out Rs .400 for 2 years at compound interest. If he earned an interest Rs. 41 then what is the rate of interest?*

Solution. Here, Principal = Rs. 400,

Time = 2 years

Compound Interest = Rs. 41

$$\text{Compound Interest} = \text{Principal}\left[\left(1+\frac{R}{100}\right)^{\text{Time}} - 1\right]$$

$$41 = 400\left[\left(1+\frac{\text{Rate}}{100}\right)^{2} - 1\right]$$

$$41 = 400\left(1+\frac{\text{Rate}}{100}\right)^{2} - 400$$

$$\because\ 400\left(1+\frac{\text{Rate}}{100}\right)^{2} = 400 + 41 = 441$$

$$\therefore \left(1+\frac{\text{Rate}}{100}\right)^2 = \frac{441}{400} = \left(\frac{21}{20}\right)^2$$

$$\therefore \quad 1+\frac{\text{Rate}}{100} = \frac{21}{20}$$

$$\therefore \quad \frac{\text{Rate}}{100} = \frac{21}{20} - 1 = \frac{1}{20}$$

$$\therefore \quad \text{Rate} = \frac{1}{20} \times 100 = 5\%.$$

Example 4. *In how much time compund interest on Rs. 800 at the rate 10 % per annum will be Rs. 168?*

Solution. Here, Principal = Rs. 800, Rate = 10%
Compound Interest = Rs. 168
Compound Interest

$$= \text{Principal}\left[\left(1+\frac{\text{Rate}}{100}\right)^{\text{Time}} - 1\right]$$

$$\therefore \quad 168 = 800\left[\left(1+\frac{10}{100}\right)^{\text{Time}} - 1\right]$$

$$\therefore \quad 168 = 800\left(\frac{11}{10}\right)^{\text{Time}} - 800$$

$$\therefore \quad 800\left(\frac{11}{10}\right)^{\text{Time}} = 168 + 800 = 968$$

$$\therefore \quad \left(\frac{11}{10}\right)^{\text{Time}} = \frac{968}{800} = \frac{121}{100} = \left(\frac{11}{10}\right)^2$$

$$\Rightarrow \quad \text{Time} = 2 \text{ years.}$$

Example 5. *If a sum of money amounts to Rs. 2420 in 2 years and Rs. 2662 in 3 years when interest is compounded annually then what is rate of interest?*

Solution. Amount = Principal$\left(1+\frac{\text{Rate}}{100}\right)^{\text{Time}}$

In first case : $2420 = P\left(1+\frac{R}{100}\right)^2$

In second case : $2662 = P\left(1+\frac{R}{100}\right)^3$

$$\therefore \quad \frac{\left(1+\frac{R}{100}\right)^3}{\left(1+\frac{R}{100}\right)^2} = \frac{2662}{2420}$$

$$\Rightarrow \quad \left(1+\frac{R}{100}\right) = \frac{1331}{1210}$$

$$\Rightarrow \quad \frac{R}{100} = \frac{1331}{1210} - 1 = \frac{121}{1210} = \frac{1}{10}$$

$$\Rightarrow \quad \text{Rate} = 100 \times \frac{1}{10} = 10\%.$$

Example 6. *If the simple interest of a sum of money for 2 years at 10% per annum is Rs. 200 then what will be the compound interest of the same sum for the same time and same rate ?*

Solution. *In first case* :

$$\text{Principal} = \frac{\text{S.I.} \times 100}{\text{Time} \times \text{Rate}}$$

$$= \frac{200 \times 100}{2 \times 10} = \text{Rs. } 1000$$

$\therefore$ Sum = Rs. 1000

In second case :

$$\text{Compound Interest} = \text{Principal}\left[\left(1+\frac{R}{100}\right)^T - 1\right]$$

$$= 1000\left[\left(1+\frac{10}{100}\right)^2 - 1\right]$$

$$= 1000\left[\left(\frac{11}{10}\right)^2 - 1\right]$$

$$= 1000 \times \frac{21}{100} = \text{Rs. } 210.$$

Example 7. *On a certain sum the difference between compound and simple interest is Rs. 8. If rate is 4% and time period is 2 years then what is the sum?*

Solution. Simple Interest

$$= \frac{\text{Principal} \times \text{Rate} \times \text{Time}}{100}$$

$$= \frac{\text{Principal} \times 4 \times 2}{100} = \frac{2 \times \text{Principal}}{25}$$

$$\text{Compound interest} = \text{Principal}\left[\left(1+\frac{\text{Rate}}{100}\right)^{\text{Time}} - 1\right]$$

$$= \text{Principal}\left[\left(1+\frac{4}{100}\right)^{2} - 1\right]$$

$$= \text{Principal}\left[\frac{26}{25} \times \frac{26}{25} - 1\right] = \text{Principal} \times \frac{51}{625}$$

According to problem, Difference in interest = Rs. 8

$$\therefore \text{Principal} \times \frac{51}{625} - \text{Principal} \times \frac{2}{25} = 8$$

$$\therefore \text{Principal}\left(\frac{51-50}{625}\right) = 8$$

$\therefore$ Principal = 8 × 625 = Rs. 5000

$\therefore$ Sum of money = Rs. 5000.

Examplc 8. *A certain sum amonts to Rs. 800 in 4 years and amounts to Rs. 888 in 5 years when interest is compounded annually. What will be the amount in 6 years?*

Solution. $\because$ Amount of fourth year will be principal for fifth year.

$\therefore$ Amount of 5th year

$$= \text{Amount of 4th year}\left(1+\frac{R}{100}\right)^{1}$$

$$888 = 800\left(1+\frac{\text{Rate}}{100}\right) \Rightarrow \frac{888}{800} = 1+\frac{\text{Rate}}{100}$$

$$\Rightarrow \frac{\text{Rate}}{100} = \frac{888}{800} - 1 = \frac{88}{800}$$

$$\Rightarrow \text{Rate} = \frac{100 \times 88}{800} = 11\%$$

Amount of 6th year

$$= \text{Amount of 5th year}\left(1+\frac{\text{Rate}}{100}\right)^{\text{Time}}$$

$$= 888\left(1+\frac{11}{100}\right) = \frac{888 \times 11}{100} = \text{Rs. } 985.68$$

EXERCISE

In the following questions four answer choices are given in which one is correct. Choose the correct answer.

1. What will be the differenc in compound and simple interest for a sum of Rs. 1500 in 3 years at 4% per annum?

A. Rs 6.29 B. Rs 7.29
C. Rs 8.30 D. Rs 7.38

2. What will be the difference in compound and simple interst for a sum of Rs. 540 in 2 years at 10% per annum?

A. Rs 7.40 B. Rs 6.40
C. Rs 4.40 D. Rs 5.40

3. What is the sum which amounts to Rs. 12.10 in 2 years at 10% when interest is compounded annually?

A. Rs. 10 B. Rs. 9
C. Rs. 8 D. Rs. 11

4. Compound interest of Rs. 1024 in 3 years at certain rate is Rs. 204.25. What is rate percent?

A. $6\frac{1}{2}\%$ B. $6\frac{1}{4}\%$
C. $7\frac{1}{4}\%$ D. $5\frac{1}{4}\%$

5. What will be the amount of Rs. 4800 in 3 years at 5% when interest is compounded annually?

A. Rs. 5546.60 B. Rs. 5556.60
C. Rs. 4456.60 D. Rs. 5536.60

6. If a sum is lent out for 1 year at 12% p.a. compound interest then what is quarterly rate percent?

A. 3% B. 4%
C. 2% D. 5%

7. What will be the compound interest of Rs. 2550 in 1 year at 6% per annum when interest is compounded half yearly?
A. Rs. 145.28 B. Rs. 155.29
C. Rs. 255.29 D. Rs. 145.29

8. What sum will produce compound interest Rs. 496.50 in 3 years at 10% per annum?
A. Rs. 1200 B. Rs. 1500
C. Rs. 1300 D. Rs. 1600

9. A sum amounts to Rs. 110 in 1 year and Rs. 121 in 2 years when interst is compounded annually. What is the rate percent?
A. 9% B. 8%
C. 10% D. 11%

10. What will be the amount of Rs. 16000 in $1\frac{1}{2}$ years at 10% per annum when interest is compounded half yearly?
A. Rs. 19522 B. Rs. 19550
C. Rs. 16555 D. Rs. 18522

11. The persent population of a town is 12500. If it increases at the rate of 20% per annum then what will be the population after 3 years?
A. 21800 B. 22500
C. 21600 D. 23400

12. If simple interest of a certain sum for 2 years at 5% p.a. is Rs. 400 then what will be the compound interest of the same sum for same time and same rate?
A. Rs. 310 B. Rs. 520
C. Rs. 410 D. Rs. 430

13. If a sum of money doubles itself in 3 years at compound interest, then in how many years it will be four times?
A. 5 years B. 6 years
C. 3 years D. 4 years

14. If compound interest of a certain sum in 2 years at 8% p.a. is Rs. 83.20 then what will be simple interest for the same sum for the same time?
A. Rs. 80 B. Rs. 70
C. Rs. 90 D Rs. 85

15. If simple interest for a certain sum for 2 years at $7\frac{1}{2}$% p.a. is Rs. 345 then what will be the compound interest at the same rate and same time ?
A. Rs. 428.25 B. Rs. 357.93
C. Rs. 357.97 D. Rs. 457.93

16. If difference of simple and compound interest on Rs. 1200 for 2 years is Rs. 48 then what is the rate of interest ?
A. 25% B. 19%
C. 20% D. 15%

17. What is the difference of simple and compound interest for Rs. 800 in 2 years at 10% p.a. ?
A. Rs. 7 B. Rs. 5
C. Rs. 8 D. Rs. 9

18. What is the sum for which difference in simple and compound interest at 4% p.a. in 2 years is Rs. 2 ?
A. Rs. 1150 B. Rs. 1250
C. Rs. 1350 D. Rs. 1050

EXPLANATORY ANSWERS

1. B. : Here, Principal = Rs. 1500, Rate = 4%, Time = 3 years

$$\text{Simple Interest} = \frac{P \times T \times R}{100}$$

$$= \frac{1500 \times 3 \times 4}{100} = \text{Rs. } 180$$

Compound Interest

$$= \text{Principal}\left[\left(1+\frac{\text{Rate}}{100}\right)^{\text{Time}} - 1\right]$$

$$= 1500\left[\left(1+\frac{4}{100}\right)^3 - 1\right]$$

$$= 1500\left[\frac{26}{25} \times \frac{26}{25} \times \frac{26}{25} - 1\right]$$

$$= 1500\left[\frac{17576 - 15625}{15625}\right]$$

$$= \frac{1500 \times 1951}{15625} = \text{Rs. } 187.29$$

$\therefore$ Difference in interest

$= \text{Rs. } (187.29 - 180) = \text{Rs. } 7.29.$

2. D : Principal = Rs. 540, Rate = 10%, Time = 2 years

$$\text{Simple Interest} = \frac{P \times R \times T}{100} = \frac{540 \times 10 \times 2}{100} = \text{Rs. } 108$$

Compound Interest

$$= \text{Principal}\left[\left(1+\frac{\text{Rate}}{100}\right)^{\text{Time}} - 1\right]$$

$$= 540\left[\left(1+\frac{10}{100}\right)^2 - 1\right]$$

$$= 540\left(\frac{11}{10} \times \frac{11}{10} - 1\right) = \frac{540 \times 21}{100} = \text{Rs. } 113.40$$

Difference in interest = Rs. (113.40 – 108) = Rs. 5.40

3. A. : $\text{Amount} = \text{Principal}\left(1+\frac{\text{Rate}}{100}\right)^{\text{Time}}$

$$12.10 = \text{Principal}\left(1+\frac{10}{100}\right)^2$$

$$12.10 = \text{Principal}\left(\frac{11}{10}\right)^2$$

$$\text{Principal} = \frac{12.10 \times 100}{121} = \text{Rs. } 10$$

$\therefore$ Sum of money = Rs. 10.

4. B : Amount = Principal + Compound Interest

$$\text{Principal}\left(1+\frac{\text{Rate}}{100}\right)^{\text{Time}} = \text{Principal} + \text{Compound interest}$$

$$\therefore \quad 1024\left(1+\frac{\text{Rate}}{100}\right)^3 = 1024 + 204.25$$

$$= 128.25$$

$$\left(1+\frac{\text{Rate}}{100}\right)^3 = \frac{1228.25}{1024} = \frac{4913}{4096} = \left(\frac{17}{16}\right)^3$$

$$\therefore \left(1+\frac{\text{Rate}}{100}\right)^2 = \frac{17}{16}$$

$$\Rightarrow \frac{\text{Rate}}{100} = \frac{17}{16} - \frac{1}{16} \Rightarrow \text{Rate} = \frac{100}{16} = 6\frac{1}{4}\%.$$

5. B : $\text{Compound Interest} = 4800\left[\left(1+\frac{5}{100}\right)^3 - 1\right]$

$$= 4800\left[\left(\frac{21}{20}\right)^3 - 1\right] = 4800\left[\frac{21 \times 21 \times 21}{20 \times 20 \times 20} - 1\right]$$

$$= 4800\left[\frac{9261 - 8000}{8000}\right] = \frac{4800 \times 1261}{8000}$$

= Rs. 756.60

$\therefore$ Amount = Principal + Compound Interest = 4800 + 756.60 = Rs. 5556.60.

6. A : Rate of interest = 12 % p.a.

$$\therefore \text{ Quarterly rate} = \frac{12\%}{4} = 3\%.$$

7. B : Principal = Rs. 2550 , Rate = 6% p.a. = 3% half yearly

Time = 1 year = 2 half years

$$\text{Compound Interest} = 2550\left[\left(1+\frac{3}{100}\right)^2 - 1\right]$$

$$= 2550\left[\left(\frac{103}{100}\right)^2 - 1\right]$$

$$= 2550\left[\frac{10609 - 10000}{10000}\right] = \frac{2550 \times 609}{10000}$$

= Rs. 155.29.

8. B : Compound Interest

$$= \text{Principal}\left[\left(1+\frac{\text{Rate}}{100}\right)^{\text{Time}} - 1\right]$$

$$496.50 = \text{Principal}\left[\left(1+\frac{10}{1000}\right)^3 - 1\right] = \text{Rs. } 108$$

$$496.50 = \text{Principal}\left[\left(\frac{11}{10}\right)^3 - 1\right]$$

$$= \text{Principal} \times \frac{331}{1000}$$

$$\therefore \text{Principal} = \frac{496.50 \times 1000}{331} = \text{Rs. } 1500$$

$\therefore$ Required sum – Rs. 1500.

9. C : First year's amount will be principal for the second year.

$\therefore$ Amount of 2nd year

$$= \text{Amount of Ist year}\left(1+\frac{R}{100}\right)^{\text{Time}}$$

$$\therefore 121 = 110\left(1+\frac{R}{100}\right)^{1} \Rightarrow \frac{121}{110} = 1+\frac{R}{100}$$

$$\Rightarrow \frac{R}{100} = \frac{121}{110} - 1 = \frac{11}{110} = \frac{1}{10}$$

$$\Rightarrow R = \frac{100 \times 1}{10} = 10\%.$$

10. D : Here, Principal = Rs. 16000,

$$\text{Time} = 1\frac{1}{2} \text{ year} = 3 \text{ half years}$$

Rate = 10% p.a. = 5% half yearly

$$\therefore \text{Amount} = \text{Principal}\left(1+\frac{\text{Rate}}{100}\right)^{\text{Time}}$$

$$= 16000\left(1+\frac{5}{100}\right)^{3} = 16000\left(\frac{21}{20}\right)^{3}$$

$$= \frac{16000 \times 9261}{8000} = \text{Rs. } 18522.$$

11. C : Population of the town after 3 years

$$= \text{Present population}\left(1+\frac{\text{Rate}}{100}\right)^{\text{Time}}$$

$$= 12500\left(1+\frac{20}{100}\right)^{3} = 12500 \times \frac{6}{5} \times \frac{6}{5} \times \frac{6}{5}$$

$$= 21600.$$

12. C : *In first case* : Principal $= \frac{\text{S.I.} \times 100}{\text{Time} \times \text{Rate}}$

$$= \frac{400 \times 100}{2 \times 5} = \text{Rs. } 4000$$

In second case : Principal = Rs. 4000, Rate = 5%, Time = 2 years

Compound Interest

$$= \text{Principal}\left[\left(1+\frac{\text{Rate}}{100}\right)^{\text{Time}} - 1\right]$$

$$= 4000\left[\left(1+\frac{5}{100}\right)^{2} - 1\right]$$

$$= 4000\left[\left(\frac{21}{20}\right)^{2} - 1\right] = \frac{4000 \times 41}{400} = \text{Rs. } 410.$$

13. B : Let the sum = Rs. x

According to problem,

$$2x = x\left(1+\frac{\text{Rate}}{100}\right)^{3} \Rightarrow 2 = \left(1+\frac{\text{Rate}}{100}\right)^{3}$$

On squaring both sides

$$(2)^2 = \left(1+\frac{\text{Rate}}{100}\right)^{6} \Rightarrow 4 = \left(1+\frac{\text{Rate}}{100}\right)^{6}$$

Therefore, it is clear that sum will be 4 times in a period of 6 years.

14. A : Compound Interest

$$= \text{Principal}\left[\left(1+\frac{\text{Rate}}{100}\right)^{\text{Time}} - 1\right]$$

$$\therefore 83.20 = \text{Principal}\left[\left(1+\frac{8}{100}\right)^{2} - 1\right]$$

$$83.20 = \text{Principal}\left[\left(\frac{27}{25}\right)^{2} - 1\right]$$

$$= \text{Principal} \times \frac{104}{625}$$

$$\therefore \quad \text{Principal} = \frac{625 \times 83.20}{104} = \text{Rs. } 500$$

$$\therefore \text{Simple Interest} = \frac{P \times T \times R}{100} = \frac{500 \times 2 \times 8}{100}$$

$$= \text{Rs. } 80.$$

15. B : $\because$ Simple interest $= \frac{P \times T \times R}{100}$

$$345=\frac{P\times2\times7\frac{1}{2}}{100}$$

$\therefore$ Principal $=\frac{345\times100}{15}=$ Rs. 2300

Compound Interest

$$=\text{Principal}\left[\left(1+\frac{\text{Rate}}{100}\right)^{\text{Time}}-1\right]$$

$$=2300\left[\left(1+\frac{7\frac{1}{2}}{100}\right)^2-1\right]$$

$$=2300\left[\left(\frac{43}{40}\right)^2-1\right]$$

$$=2300\left[\frac{1849-1600}{1600}\right]$$

$$=\frac{2300\times249}{1600}=\text{Rs. }357.93.$$

16. C : Let the rate of interest $= x\%$

Principal = Rs. 1200, Time = 2 years

Simple Interest $=\frac{1200\times2\times x}{100}=$ Rs. $24x$

Compound Interest $=1200\left[\left(1+\frac{x}{100}\right)^2-1\right]$

$$=1200\left[\left(\frac{x}{100}\right)^2+\frac{2x}{100}\right]$$

According to problem,

$$1200\left[\frac{x^2}{10000}+\frac{2x}{100}\right]-24x=48$$

$$\Rightarrow \frac{12x^2}{100}+\frac{2400x}{100}-24x=48$$

$$\Rightarrow \frac{12x^2}{100}=48 \quad\Rightarrow\quad x^2=48$$

$\Rightarrow x=20$

$\therefore$ Rate of interest = 20%.

17. C : Principal = Rs. 800, Rate = 10%, Time = 2 years

$\therefore$ Simple Interest $=\frac{800\times10\times2}{100}=$ Rs. 160

Compound Interest $=800\left[\left(1+\frac{10}{100}\right)^2-1\right]$

$$=800\left[\left(\frac{11}{10}\right)^2-1\right]$$

$$=\frac{800\times21}{100}=\text{Rs. }168$$

Difference in interest = Rs. (168 – 160) = Rs. 8

18. B : Let sum of money = Rs. x

Rate = 4% , Time = 2 years

$\therefore$ Simple Interest $=\frac{x\times4\times2}{100}=$ Rs. $\frac{8x}{100}$

Compound Interest $=x\left[\left(1+\frac{4}{100}\right)^2-1\right]$

$$=x\left[\left(\frac{26}{25}\right)^2-1\right]=x\left[\frac{676-625}{625}\right]$$

$$=\text{Rs. }\frac{x\times51}{625}$$

According to problem,

$$\frac{x\times51}{625}-\frac{8x}{100}=2$$

$$\Rightarrow \frac{51x}{625}-\frac{2x}{25}=2$$

$$\Rightarrow \frac{51x-50x}{625}=2$$

$$\Rightarrow \frac{x}{625}=2$$

$\Rightarrow x = 625\times2 = 1250$

$\therefore$ Sum of the money = Rs. 1250

8

PROFIT AND LOSS

Cost Price : The amount paid to purchase an object is known as its cost price.

Selling Price : The amount at which an object is sold, is known as its selling price.

Points to Remember :

1. If selling price is more than cost price, then
   Profit = S.P. – C.P
   $$\text{Profit\%} = \frac{\text{Gain}\times 100}{\text{C.P.}}$$
2. If selling price is less than cost price, then
   Loss = C.P. – S.P.
   $$\text{Loss\%} = \frac{\text{Loss}\times 100}{\text{C.P.}}$$
3. In case of Gain%
   $$\text{S.P.} = \text{C.P.}\left(1+\frac{\text{Gain\%}}{100}\right)$$
4. In case of Loss%
   $$\text{S.P.} = \text{C.P.}\left(1-\frac{\text{Loss\%}}{100}\right)$$

> **Important Note** : Gain and loss are always calculated on the C.P.

Example 1. *If a watch is bought for Rs. 1200 and sold for Rs. 1500, then what is the gain percent?*

Solution. C.P. of the watch = Rs. 1200

S.P. of the watch = Rs. 1500

Gain = Rs. (1500 – 1200) = Rs. 300

$$\text{Gain\%} = \frac{\text{Gain}\times 100}{\text{C.P.}} = \frac{300\times 100}{1200} = 25\%.$$

Example 2. *By selling an article for Rs. 24, gain is 20%. What is the cost price of the article?*

Solution. $$\text{Cost Price} = \frac{\text{Selling Price}}{\left(1+\frac{\text{Gain\%}}{100}\right)}$$

$$= \frac{24}{\left(1+\frac{20}{100}\right)} = \frac{24}{120}\times 100 = \text{Rs. } 20$$

∴ Cost price of the article = Rs. 20.

Example 3. *By selling a radio for Rs. 450, loss is 10%. What is the cost price of the radio?*

Solution. $$\text{Cost Price} = \frac{\text{Selling Price}}{\left(1-\frac{\text{Loss\%}}{100}\right)}$$

$$= \frac{450}{\left(1-\frac{10}{100}\right)} = \frac{450}{90}\times 100 = \text{Rs. } 500$$

∴ Cost price of the radio = Rs. 500.

Example 4. *By selling a book for Rs. 144, gain is 20%. If it is sold for 30% gain, then what is the selling price of the book?*

Solution. *In First Case* : S.P. = Rs. 144, Gain% = 20%

$$\text{C.P.} = \frac{\text{S.P.}}{\left(1+\frac{\text{Gain\%}}{100}\right)} = \frac{144}{\left(1+\frac{20}{100}\right)}$$

$$= \frac{144\times 100}{120} = \text{Rs. } 120$$

∴ Cost price of the book = Rs. 120

In Second Case : C.P. = 120, Gain % = 30%

$$\text{S.P.} = \text{C.P.}\left(1+\frac{\text{Gain\%}}{100}\right)$$

$$= 120\left(1+\frac{30}{100}\right)$$

$$= \frac{120\times 130}{100} = \text{Rs. } 156$$

∴ Selling price of the book = Rs. 156.

Example 5. *By selling an article for Rs. 1230, loss is 18%. If the article is sold for Rs. 1600, then what is Gain% or Loss %?*

Solution. *In First Case :*

S.P. = Rs. 1230, Loss = 18%

$$\text{C.P.} = \frac{\text{S.P.}}{\left(1-\frac{\text{Loss\%}}{100}\right)} = \frac{1230}{\left(1-\frac{18}{100}\right)}$$

$$= \frac{1230 \times 100}{82} = \text{Rs. } 1500$$

In Second Case : C.P. = Rs. 1500, S.P. = Rs. 1600

Gain = Rs. (1600 – 1500) = Rs. 100

$$\text{Gain\%} = \frac{\text{Gain} \times 100}{\text{C.P.}} = \frac{100 \times 100}{1500}$$

$$= \frac{20}{3}\% = 6\frac{2}{3}\%.$$

Example 6. *A shopkeeper marks his goods 20% above cost price. He offers 10% discount to his customers. What is his gain percent?*

Solution. Let C.P. of the article = Rs. 100

Marked price of the article = Rs. 120

Discount = 10% of Rs. 120 = Rs. 12

S.P. = Rs. 120 – Rs. 12 = Rs. 108

Gain = S.P. – C.P. = Rs. (108 – 100) = Rs. 8

$$\text{Gain\%} = \frac{\text{Gain} \times 100}{\text{C.P.}} = \frac{8 \times 100}{100} = 8\%.$$

Example 7. *What price should a tradesman mark above the cost price to gain 5%, after allowing a discount of 20%?*

Solution. Let C.P. of the article = Rs. 100

and M.P. of the article = Rs. $(100 + x)$

S.P. of the article = Rs. 100 + 5% of Rs. 100

= Rs. 105

Discount on marked price = 20%

∴ S.P. = $(100 + x)$ – 20% of $(100 + x)$

$$105 = \frac{4}{5}(100 + x)$$

$$\Rightarrow \quad 100 + x = \frac{105 \times 5}{4} = \frac{525}{4}$$

$$\Rightarrow x = \frac{525}{4} - 100 = \frac{525 - 400}{4} = \frac{125}{4} = 32.25$$

∴ Marked price is 31.25% above the cost price.

Example 8. *A merchant sells two sewing machines each for Rs. 960. If he gains 20% on first machine and loses 20% on second machine, then what is his percent gain or loss in this transaction?*

Solution. For first sewing machine :

S.P. = Rs. 960, Gain% = 20%

$$\text{C.P.} = \frac{\text{S.P.}}{\left(1+\frac{\text{Gain\%}}{100}\right)} = \frac{960}{\left(1+\frac{20}{100}\right)}$$

$$= \frac{960 \times 100}{120} = \text{Rs. } 800$$

For second sewing machine

S.P. = Rs. 960, Loss% = 20%

$$\text{C.P.} = \frac{\text{S.P.}}{\left(1-\frac{\text{Loss\%}}{100}\right)} = \frac{960}{\left(1-\frac{20}{100}\right)}$$

$$= \frac{960 \times 100}{80} = \text{Rs. } 1200$$

Total C.P. of two machines = Rs. (800 + 1200)

= Rs. 2000

Total S.P. of two machines = Rs. (960 + 960)

= Rs. 1920

Loss = Rs. (2000 – 1920) = Rs. 80

$$\text{Loss\%} = \frac{\text{Loss} \times 100}{2000} = \frac{80 \times 100}{2000} = 4\%.$$

EXERCISE

In following questions four answer choices are given in which one is correct. Choose the correct answer.

1. Ram bought a cycle for Rs. 770 and sold it for Rs. 810. What is his gain?
   - A. Rs. 40
   - B. Rs. 30
   - C. Rs. 50
   - D. Rs. 55

2. A fruit seller sells 10 apples for a rupee and gains 60%. How many apples he bought for a rupee?
   - A. 14
   - B. 16
   - C. 15
   - D. 18

3. If C.P. of 5 mangoes is equal to S.P. of 4 mangoes, then what will be gain % ?

A. 20% B. $16\frac{2}{3}\%$

C. 25% D. 10%

4. Sheesh Ram sold a table for Rs. 540 and lost 10%. If he wants to gain 10%, then what is S.P. of the table?

A. Rs. 660 B. Rs. 680

C. Rs. 580 D. Rs. 550

5. A shopkeeper offers 10% discount on price list and still makes a profit of 25%. What is the cost price of an article whose list p;rice is Rs. 80?

A. Rs. 57.60 B. Rs. 60.40

C. Rs. 72.50 D. Rs. 75.60

6. A sofa set is sold for Rs. 632. The gain is equal to the loss when it is sold for Rs. 544. What is the cost price of the sofa-set?

A. Rs. 858 B. Rs. 588

C. Rs. 540 D. Rs. 637

7. A television is sold at 20% gain. If it is sold at 20% loss then selling price is less Rs. 120. What is the cost price of the television?

A. Rs. 600 B. Rs. 220

C. Rs. 300 D. Rs. 380

8. By selling an article for Rs. 31 a shopkeeper loses 7% . If he sells the article for Rs. 35, then what is gain% or loss%?

A. Loss 3% B. Gain 5%

C. Loss 5% D. Gain 3%

9. A bought a radio for Rs. 500 and sold it to B at 5% gain. After some time B sold it to C at 5% loss. What is cost price of the radio for C?

A. Rs. 498.75 B. Rs. 375.60

C. Rs. 370.25 D. Rs. 480.60

10. Ram bought 21 pens for Rs. 20 and he sold them at the rate of 20 for Rs. 21. What is his gain%?

A. 7.50% B. 10.25%

C. 10.50% D. 16.66%

11. If 11 pencils are bought for Rs. 10 and 10 pencils are sold for Rs. 11 then what is the gain%?

A. 18% B. 16%

C. 21% D. 10%

12. A man sells his radio for Rs. 770 and gains 1/7 of the selling price. What is his gain%?

A. $16\frac{2}{3}\%$ B. $6\frac{1}{3}\%$

C. $6\frac{2}{3}\%$ D. $33\frac{1}{3}\%$

13. A man sold a watch fo Rs. 432 on some loss. If he had sold the watch for Rs. 516 then he had gained equal to 1/3 of first loss. What is the cost price of the watch?

A. Rs. 420 B. Rs. 495

C. Rs. 550 D. Rs. 630

14. If an article is sold at a gain of 10% instead of a loss of 10% then difference in selling price is Rs. 55. What is the cost price of the article?

A. Rs. 275 B. Rs. 288

C. Rs. 310 D. Rs. 290

15. The cost price of an article is 60% of the marked price. If 20% discount is offered at marked price then what is the gain %?

A. $16\frac{2}{3}\%$ B. $6\frac{2}{3}\%$

C. $33\frac{1}{3}\%$ D. 40%

16. A shopkeeper sells an article at $12\frac{1}{2}\%$ loss. If he sells it for Rs. 92.50 more then he gains 6%. What is the cost price of the article?

A. Rs. 510 B. Rs. 500

C. Rs. 575 D. Rs. 600

17. A shopkeeper sells a bicycle at 10% gain. If he sells it for Rs. 10 more and if its cost price is 20% less than the first. Then he gains 40%. What is the cost price of the bicycle?

A. Rs. 500 B. Rs. 320

C. Rs. 380 D. Rs. 480

18. A merchant bought two cows for Rs 500. He sold one cow at 12% loss and the other at 8% gain. In this transaction he neither lost nor gained. What was the cost price of each cow?

A. Rs. 300 and Rs. 200

B. Rs. 200 and Rs. 300

C. Rs. 175 and Rs. 325

D. Rs. 240 and Rs. 260

19. A man bought some eggs at 4 for Rs. 3 and sold them at 5 for Rs. 4. In this transaction he gained Rs. 16. How many eggs did he purchase?

A. 410 B. 300

C. 320 D. 280

EXPLANATORY ANSWERS

1. A : Cost price of the cycle = Rs. 770

Selling price of the cycle = Rs. 810

Gain = S.P. – C.P. = Rs. (810 – 770) = Rs. 40.

2. B : S.P. = Re 1. Gain % = 60%

$$C.P. = \frac{S.P.}{\left(1+\frac{Gain\%}{100}\right)} = \frac{1}{\left(1+\frac{60}{100}\right)}$$

$$= \frac{1\times100}{160} = Re.\frac{5}{8}$$

Apples purchased in Re $\frac{5}{8}$ = 10

Apples purchased in Re 1 = $10\times\frac{8}{5} = 16$

So, he purchased 16 apples in one rupee.

3. C : Let C.P. of 5 mangoes = Rs. x

∴ S.P. of 4 mangoes = Rs. x

C.P. of 1 mango = Rs. $\frac{x}{5}$

S.P. of 1 mango = Rs. $\frac{x}{4}$

$$Gain\% = \frac{x}{4} - \frac{x}{5} = Rs.\ \frac{x}{20}$$

$$Gain\% = \frac{Gain\times100}{C.P.}$$

$$= \frac{x/20\times100}{\frac{x}{5}} = \frac{x\times100\times5}{20\times x} = 25\%.$$

4. A : *In First Case* : S.P. of the table = Rs. 540,

Loss% = 10%

$$C.P. = \frac{S.P.}{\left(1-\frac{Loss\%}{100}\right)} = \frac{540}{\left(1-\frac{10}{100}\right)}$$

$$= \frac{540}{90}\times100 = Rs.\ 600$$

In Second Case : C.P. = Rs. 600, Gain% = 10%

$$S.P. = C.P.\left(1+\frac{Gain\%}{100}\right)$$

$$= 600\left(1+\frac{10}{100}\right) = \frac{600\times110}{100} = Rs.\ 660$$

∴ S.P. of the table = Rs. 660.

5. A : Let C.P. of the article = Rs. x

According to problem, Gain = 25%

∴ S.P. of the article = Rs. x + 25% of Rs. x

$$= Rs.\ \frac{5x}{4}$$

List price of the article = Rs. 80

Discount = 10% of Rs. 80 = Rs. 8

∴ S.P. = Rs. 80 – Rs. 8 = Rs. 72

$$\therefore \frac{5x}{4} = 72 \Rightarrow 5x = 72\times4$$

$$\Rightarrow x = \frac{72\times4}{5} = Rs.\ 57.60$$

∴ Cost price of the article = Rs. 57.60.

6. B : Let cost price of the sofa-set = Rs. x

In First Case : C.P. = Rs. x, S.P. = Rs. 632

Gain = S.P. – C.P. = Rs. (632 – x)

In Second Case : C.P. = Rs. x, S.P = Rs. 544

Loss = C.P. – S.P. = Rs. (x – 544)

According to problem,

Gain in first case = Loss in second case

$$632 - x = x - 544$$

$$\Rightarrow 632 + 544 = 2x$$

$$\Rightarrow 1176 = 2x \Rightarrow x = \frac{1176}{2} = 588$$

∴ Cost price of sofa-set = Rs. 588.

7. C : Let C.P. of the television = Rs. x

In First Case : C.P. = Rs. x, Gain% = 20%

$$S.P. = x\times\frac{120}{100} = Rs.\ \frac{6x}{5}$$

In Second case : C.P. = Rs. x, Loss% = 20%

$$S.P. = x\times\frac{80}{100} = Rs.\ \frac{4x}{5}$$

According to problem,

$$\frac{6x}{5} - \frac{4x}{5} = Rs.\ 120$$

$$\Rightarrow \frac{6x-4x}{5} = 120$$

$\Rightarrow \quad 2x = 120\times5$

$\Rightarrow \quad x = \frac{120\times5}{2} = 300$

$\therefore$ C.P. of the television = Rs. 300.

8. B : *In First Case* :

S.P. of the article = Rs. 31, Loss = 7%

$$\text{C.P.} = \frac{\text{S.P.}}{\left(1-\frac{\text{Loss\%}}{100}\right)} = \frac{31}{\left(1-\frac{7}{100}\right)}$$

$$= \frac{31\times100}{93} = \text{Rs. } 33\frac{1}{3}$$

In Second Case : C.P. = Rs. $33\frac{1}{3}$,

S.P. = Rs. 35

$$\text{Gain} = \text{Rs.}\left(35-33\frac{1}{3}\right) = \text{Rs. } 1\frac{2}{3} = \text{Rs.}\frac{5}{3}$$

$$\text{Gain\%} = \frac{\text{Gain}\times100}{\text{C.P.}}$$

$$= \frac{\frac{5}{3}\times100}{\frac{100}{3}} = \frac{5\times100\times3}{3\times100} = 5\%.$$

9. A : *In First Case* : C.P. = Rs. 500, Gain% = 5%

$$\text{S.P. for A} = \frac{500\times105}{100} = \text{Rs. } 525$$

S.P. for A is equal to C.P. for B.

In Second Case : C.P. = Rs. 525, Loss = 5%

$$\therefore \text{ S.P. for B} = \frac{525\times95}{100} = \text{Rs. } 498.75$$

$\therefore$ C.P. for C = Rs. 498.75.

10. B : C.P. of 21 pens = Rs. 20

$$\text{C.P. of one pen} = \text{Rs. } \frac{20}{21}$$

S.P. of 20 pens = Rs. 21

$$\text{S.P. of 1 pen} = \text{Rs. } \frac{21}{20}$$

$$\text{Gain} = \text{S.P.}-\text{C.P.} = \frac{21}{20}-\frac{20}{21} = \text{Rs. } \frac{41}{420}$$

$$\text{Gain\%} = \frac{\text{Gain}\times100}{\text{C.P.}} = \frac{\frac{41}{420}\times100}{\frac{20}{21}}$$

$$\text{Gain\%} = \frac{41\times100\times21}{420\times20} = \frac{41}{4} = 10.25\%$$

11. C : C.P. of 11 pencils = Rs. 10

$$\text{C.P. of 1 pencil} = \text{Rs. } \frac{10}{11}$$

S.P. of 10 pencils = Rs. 11

$$\text{S.P. of 1 pencil} = \text{Rs. } \frac{11}{10}$$

$$\text{Gain} = \text{S.P.}-\text{C.P.} = \frac{11}{10}-\frac{10}{11} = \frac{21}{110}$$

$$\text{Gain\%} = \frac{\text{Gain}\times100}{\text{C.P.}} = \frac{\frac{21}{110}\times100}{\frac{10}{11}}$$

$$= \frac{21\times100\times11}{110\times10} = 21\%$$

12. A : S.P. of radio = Rs. 770

$$\text{Gain} = \frac{1}{7} \text{ of Rs. } 770 = \frac{770\times1}{7} = \text{Rs. } 110$$

C.P. of the radio = S.P. – Gain

= 770 – 110 = Rs. 660

$$\text{Gain\%} = \frac{\text{Gain}\times100}{\text{C.P.}} = \frac{110\times100}{660}$$

$$= \frac{50}{3} = 16\frac{2}{3}\%.$$

13. B. : *In First Case* : Let loss = Rs. x,

S.P. = Rs. 432

$\therefore$ C.P. of the watch = Rs. $(432+x)$

In Second Case :

S.P. of the watch = Rs. 516, Gain = $\frac{x}{3}$

$\therefore$ C.P. of the watch = Rs. $\left(516-\frac{x}{3}\right)$

According to problem,

$$432+x = 516-\frac{x}{3}$$

$\Rightarrow \quad x+\frac{x}{3}=516-432=84$

$\Rightarrow \quad \frac{4x}{3}=84 \Rightarrow x=\frac{84\times 3}{4}=63$

$\therefore$ C.P. of the watch = Rs. (432 + 63)
= Rs. 495.

14. A :Let C.P. of the article = Rs. x,

In First Case : Loss = 10%

$\therefore$ S.P. of the article $= x - 10\%$ of x

$= \text{Rs. } \frac{9x}{10}$

In Second Case : Gain = 10%

$\therefore$ S.P. of the article $= x + 10\%$ of x

$= \text{Rs. } \frac{11x}{10}$

According to problem,

$\frac{11x}{10}=\frac{9x}{10}+55 \Rightarrow \frac{11x}{10}-\frac{9x}{10}=55$

$\Rightarrow \frac{2x}{10}=55 \Rightarrow x=\frac{55\times 10}{2}=275$

$\therefore$ C.P. of the article = Rs. 275.

15. C :Let marked price of the article = Rs. 100

$\therefore$ C.P. of the article = 60% of Rs. 100
= Rs. 60

Discount = 20% at marked price

$\therefore$ S.P. = Rs. 100 – 20% of Rs. 100
= 100 – 20 = Rs. 80

Gain = S.P. – C. P. = Rs. 80 – Rs. 60
= Rs. 20

$\text{Gain\%}=\frac{\text{Gain}\times 100}{\text{C.P.}}=\frac{20\times 100}{60}=\frac{100}{3}$

$=33\frac{1}{3}\%.$

16. B :Let C.P. of the article = Rs. x

In First Case : C.P. = Rs. x,

$\text{Loss\%}=12\frac{1}{2}\%=\frac{25}{2}\%$

$\therefore \text{S.P.}=x\left[1-\frac{25/2}{100}\right]=x\times\frac{7}{8}=\text{Rs. }\frac{7x}{8}$

$\therefore$ *In Second Case* :

$\text{S.P.}=\text{Rs.}\left(\frac{7x}{8}+92.50\right)$, Gain% = 6%

$\therefore \quad \text{C.P.}=\frac{\text{S.P.}}{\left(1+\frac{\text{Gain\%}}{100}\right)}=\frac{\left(\frac{7x}{8}+92.50\right)}{\left(1+\frac{6}{100}\right)}$

$=\text{Rs.}\left(\frac{7x}{8}+92.50\right)\times\frac{100}{106}$

$x=\left(\frac{7x}{8}+92.50\right)\times\frac{100}{106}$

$\Rightarrow \quad 106x=\frac{175x}{2}+9250$

$\Rightarrow \quad 106x-\frac{175x}{2}=9250$

$\Rightarrow \quad \frac{37x}{2}=9250$

$\Rightarrow \quad x=\frac{9250\times 2}{37}=500$

$\therefore$ C.P. of the article = Rs. 500.

17. A :Let C.P. of the bicycle = Rs. x

In First Case :

S.P. of the bicycle = Rs. x + 10% of Rs. x

$= \text{Rs. } \frac{11x}{10}$

In Second Case :

$\text{S.P.} = \text{Rs.}\left(\frac{11x}{10}+10\right)$

C.P. = Rs. x – 20% of x = Rs. $\frac{4x}{5}$

Gain = 40%

$\text{S.P.}=\text{C.P.}\left(1+\frac{\text{Gain\%}}{100}\right)$

$\Rightarrow \frac{11x}{10}+10=\frac{4x}{5}\left(1+\frac{40}{100}\right)=\frac{4x}{5}\times\frac{7}{5}=\frac{28x}{25}$

$\Rightarrow \frac{28x}{25}-\frac{11x}{10}=10$

$\Rightarrow \frac{56x-55x}{50}=10 \Rightarrow \frac{x}{50}=10 \Rightarrow x=500$

$\therefore$ C.P. of bicycle = Rs. 500.

18. B : Let cost price of first cow = Rs. x

Then cost price of second cow = Rs.$(500 - x)$

For First Case : C.P. = Rs. x, Loss% = 12%

$$\therefore \quad \text{S.P.} = \frac{x \times 88}{100} = \text{Rs. } \frac{22x}{25}$$

For Second Case : C.P. = Rs. $(500 - x)$,

Gain% = 8%

$$\therefore \quad \text{S.P.} = (500 - x) \times \frac{108}{100} = \text{Rs. } (500 - x) \times \frac{27}{25}$$

$$\text{Total S.P.} = \frac{22x}{25} + (500 - x) \times \frac{27}{25}$$

$$= \frac{22x}{25} + 540 - \frac{27x}{25} = \left(540 - \frac{x}{5}\right)$$

Total C.P. = Rs. 500

According to problem, there is no loss, no gain.

$$\therefore \quad 540 - \frac{x}{5} = 500 \Rightarrow \frac{x}{5} = 40 \Rightarrow x = 200$$

$\therefore$ Cost price of first cow = Rs. 200

Cost price of second cow = Rs. (500 – 200)

= Rs. 300.

19. C : Let the eggs purchased by man = x

C.P. of 4 eggs = Rs. 3

C.P. of x eggs = Rs. $\frac{3x}{4}$

and S.P. of 5 eggs = Rs. 4

S.P. of x eggs = Rs. $\frac{4x}{5}$

According to problem, Gain = Rs. 16

S.P. – C.P. = Gain

$$\therefore \quad \frac{4x}{5} - \frac{3x}{4} = 16 \Rightarrow \frac{x}{20} = 16$$

$$\Rightarrow \quad x = 320$$

$\therefore$ The man purchased 320 eggs.

9

AVERAGE

To find the average of given quantities we divide the sum of given quantities by the number of quantities.

$$\text{Average} = \frac{\text{Sum of all quantities}}{\text{No. of quantities}}$$

Example 1. *Find the average of 40.8, 45.2, 39.8, 24.6 and 49.6.*

Solution : Sum of given quantities

$= 40.8 + 45.2 + 39.8 + 24.6 + 49.6 = 200.0$

No. of quantities = 5

$$\text{Average} = \frac{\text{Sum of quantities}}{\text{No. of quantities}} = \frac{200}{5} = 40.$$

Example 2. *The readintg of a freezer are 10°, – 14° and 16°. What will be the next reading if average is 2°?*

Solution. Let next reading of the freezer = $x°$

$$\text{Average} = \frac{\text{Sum of all quantities}}{\text{No. of quantities}}$$

$$2° = \frac{10° + (-14)° + 16° + x°}{4} = \frac{12° + x°}{4}$$

$\Rightarrow 8° = 12° + x° \Rightarrow x° = -12° + 8° = -4°$

$\therefore$ Next reading = – 4°.

Example 3. *If average of 5, 15, 20, 25 and x is 15 then what is the value of x?*

Solution. $\because$ $\text{Average} = \frac{\text{Sum of all quantities}}{\text{No. of quantities}}$

$$15 = \frac{5 + 15 + 20 + 25 + x}{5} = \frac{65 + x}{5}$$

$\Rightarrow$ $75 = 65 + x \Rightarrow x = 75 - 65 = 10$

$\therefore$ Value of x = 10.

Example 4. *Average weight of a class of 35 students is 47.5 kg. If the weight of the teacher is included then average weight increases by 500 gm. What is the weight of the teacher?*

Solution. $\because$ Average weight of 35 students = 47.5 kg

$\therefore$ Total weight of 35 students = 47.5 × 35 = 1662.5 kg

Average weight of (35 students + 1 teacher) = 47.5 × .5 = 48 kg

Total weight of (35 students + 1 teacher) = 48 × 36 = 1728 kg

Weight of the teacher = 1728 – 1662.5 = 65.5 kg.

Example 5. *Average of three numbers is 8. If average of first two numbers is 10 then what is the third number?*

Solution. $\because$ Average of three numbers = 8

Total of three numbers = 8 × 3 = 24

Average of first two numbers = 10

Total of first two numbers = 10 × 2 = 20

$\therefore$ Third number = Total of three numbers – Total of two numbers = 24 – 20 = 4.

Example 6. *Average weight of 5 men is 60 kg. If a new man enters then average weight increases by 1 kg. What is the weight of new man?*

Solution. Average weight of 5 men = 60 kg

Total weight of 5 men = 60 × 5 = 300 kg

Average weight of (5 men + 1 new man) = 60 + 1 = 61 kg

Total weight of (5 men + 1 new man) = 61 × 6 = 366 kg

$\therefore$ Weight of new man = 366 – 300 = 66 kg.

Example 7. *Average of 30 terms is 20 and average of other 20 terms is 30. What is average of all terms?*

Solution. $\because$ Average of 30 terms = 20

$\therefore$ Total of 30 terms = 30 × 20 = 600

and average of 20 terms = 30

$\therefore$ Total of 20 terms = 30 × 20 = 600

∴ Total of (30 + 20) terms = 600 + 600 = 1200

∴ Average of all terms $= \frac{1200}{50} = 24$.

Example 8. *Average of 10 numbers 4, 6, 8, 10, 12, 14, 16, 18, 20 and 22 is 13. If 5 is added to each number then what is the new average of all numbers?*

Solution. Average of 10 numbers = 13

∴ Total of 10 numbers = 13 × 10 = 130

If 5 is added to each number then total increment is 50

∴ Total of new 10 numbers = 130 + 50 = 180

∴ New average $= \frac{180}{10} = 18$.

Example 9. *Average height of 25 children is 140 cm. If 5 new children join the class then average height becomes 145 cm. What is the average height of 5 new children?*

Solution. ∵ Average height of 25 children = 140 cm

∴ Total of height 25 children = 140 × 25 = 3500 cm

∵ Average height of (25 + 5) children = 145 cm

∴ Total height of 30 children = 30 × 145 = 4350 cm

∴ Total height of 5 new children = 4350 – 3500 = 850 cm

∴ Average height of 5 new children $= \frac{850}{5} = 170$ cm.

EXERCISE

In the following questions four answer choices are given in which one is correct. Choose the correct answer.

1. What is the average of 20, 25, 22, and 23?
   A. $21\frac{1}{3}$ B. 25
   C. $22\frac{1}{2}$ D. $20\frac{1}{2}$
2. If average of three numbers is 13 then what is the sum of these numbers?
   A. 39 B. 37
   C. 32 D. 31
3. Average of 5 numbers is 9. If 2 is added to each number then what is new average?
   A. 11 B. 10
   C. 8 D. 15
4. What is the average of first five multiples of 7?
   A. 30 B. 21
   C. 29 D. 11
5. What is the average of first five prime numbers?
   A. 4.6 B. 5.9
   C. 5.6 D. 6.4
6. Average of 6 numbers is 12. If 2 is subtracted from each number, then what is the average of new numbers?
   A. 10 B. 8
   C. 9 D. 7
7. Average of three numbers is 20. If two numbers are 16 and 22, then what is the third number?
   A. 24 B. 18
   C. 20 D. 22
8. Average age of 40 boys of a class is 15 years. If the age of the teacher is included then their average age is 16. What is the age of the teacher?
   A. 61 years B. 73 years
   C. 56 years D. 84 years
9. In three numbers, the first number is double of the second and half of the third. If the average of three numbers is 56, then what is the largest number?
   A. 96 B. 108
   C. 92 D. 84
10. Average of students from class I to V is 29. if average of class I, II and III is 30, then what is the total strength of class IV and V ?
    A. 44 B. 55
    C. 30 D. 59
11. A shopkeeper earns Rs 504 in 12 days. In first 4 days his average income was Rs. 40.

What was his average income for the remaining days?

A. Rs. 43/day
B. Rs. 48/day
C. Rs. 52/day
D. Rs. 28/day

12. Average age of A, B and C is 36 years. If average age of B and C is 30 years and age of B is 22 years then what is the sum of the ages of A and C?

A. 68 years
B. 86 years
C. 58 years
D. 61 years

13. Average temperature of Monday, Tuesday, Wednesday and Thursday was 38°. Average temperature of Tuesday, Wednesday, Thursday and Friday was 40°. If temperature of Monday was 40° then what was the temperature of Friday?

A. 39°
B. 42°
C. 46°
D. 48°

14. If in a family of eight members, the income of father, mother and eldest son is Rs. 6000, Rs. 4000 and Rs. 2000 respectively, then what is the average income of one member of the family?

A. Rs. 1280
B. Rs. 1500
C. Rs. 1390
D. Rs. 1525

15. A motor cyclist covers a distance of 60 km at the speed of 20 km/hr. He returns from the same way at a speed of 40 Km/hr. What is his average speed for the whole journey?

A. $26\frac{2}{3}$ km/hr
B. $13\frac{7}{13}$ km/hr
C. $26\frac{1}{3}$ km/hr
D. $38\frac{1}{2}$ km/hr

16. Average price of 10 chairs and 6 tables is Rs. 30. If average price of tables is Rs. 50 then what is the average price of chairs?

A. Rs. 24
B. Rs. 18
C. Rs. 19.25
D. Rs. 16.80

17. Average score of 5 innings of a cricket's player is 20. If score of first 4 innings are 40, 30, 14 and 10 respectively then what is the score of fifth inning?

A. 6
D. 8
C. 4
D. 3

18. Average age of a family of 5 members is 20 years. If the age of youngest member is 8 years then what was the average age of other members of the family at the birth of the youngest member?

A. 11 years
B. 17 years
C. 15 years
D. 18 years

19. Average of 5 terms is 10. If average of first two terms is 7 and average of last two terms is 13, then what is the value of third term?

A. 8
B. 7
C. 10
D. 9

20. A man covers a distance of 6 km at the rate of 4 km/hr and he covers a distance of 4 km at the rate of 3 km/hr. what is his average speed?

A. $4\frac{1}{17}$ km/hr
B. $3\frac{9}{17}$ km/hr
C. $2\frac{9}{17}$ km/hr
D. $6\frac{1}{3}$ km/hr

EXPLANATORY ANSWERS

1. C : $\because$ Average $= \dfrac{\text{Sum of all quantities}}{\text{No. of quantities}}$

$$= \frac{20+25+22+23}{4} = \frac{90}{4} = 22\frac{1}{2}.$$

2. A : Average of three numbers = 13

$\therefore$ Total of three numbers = 13 × 3 = 39.

3. A : Average of three numbers = 9

$\therefore$ Sum of five numbers = 9 × 5 = 45

If 2 is added to each number, then increment in sum of five numbers is 2 × 5 = 10

$\therefore$ Sum of five new numbers = 45 + 10 = 55

$\therefore$ New average $= \frac{55}{5} = 11.$

4. B : First five multiples of 7 are 7, 14, 21, 28 and 35

$\therefore$ Average $= \frac{7+14+21+28+35}{5} = \frac{105}{5} = 21$

$\therefore$ Average of five multiples of 7 = 21.

5. C : First five prime numbers are 2, 3, 5, 7 and 11

$$\text{Average} = \frac{2+3+5+7+11}{5} = \frac{28}{5} = 5.6.$$

6. A : $\because$ Average of 6 numbers = 12

$\therefore$ Sum of 6 numbers = 12 × 6 = 72

If 2 is subtracted from each number, then

Sum of new 6 numbers = 72 – 2 × 6

= 72 – 12 = 60.

$$\text{Average of new numbers} = \frac{60}{6} = 10.$$

7. D : $\because$ Average of three numbers = 20

$\therefore$ Sum of three numbers = 20 × 3 = 60

Sum of two numbers = 16 + 22 = 38

$\therefore$ Third number = 60 – 38 = 22.

8. C : $\because$ Average age of 40 boys = 15 years

$\therefore$ Total age of 40 boys = 15 × 40 = 600 years

Average of (40 boys + 1 teacher) = 16 years

Total age of (40 boys + 1 teacher) = 16 × 41

= 656 years

$\therefore$ Age of the teacher = 656 – 600 = 56 years.

9. A : Let first number = $2x$,

Second number = x

Third number = $4x$

$$\text{Average} = \frac{\text{Sum of all quantities}}{\text{No. of quantities}}$$

$$56 = \frac{2x+x+4x}{3} = \frac{7x}{3}$$

$$\Rightarrow \quad 7x = 56 \times 3 \quad \Rightarrow x = \frac{56\times3}{7} = 24$$

$\therefore$ Largest number = 4 × 24 = 96.

10. B : Average No. of students in Class I to V = 29

Total No. of students in class I to V

= 29 × 5 = 145

Average No. of students in Class I to III = 30

Total No. of students in class I to III

= 30 × 3 = 90

Total No. of students in class IV to V

= 145 – 90 = 55.

11. A : Shopkeeper earns in 12 days = Rs. 504

Average income of first 4 days = Rs. 40

Total income of first 4 days

= Rs 40 × 4 = Rs. 160

Total income of remaining 8 days

= 504 – 160 = Rs. 344

Average income of remaining 8 days

$$= \frac{344}{8} = \text{Rs. } 43.$$

12. B : Average age of A, B and C = 36 years

Total age of A, B and C = 36 × 3

= 108 years

Average age of B and C = 30 years

Total age of B and C = 30 × 2 = 60 years

$\therefore$ Age of A = 108 – 60 = 48 years

Age of B = 22 years (Given)

$\therefore$ Age of C = 60 – 22 = 38 years

$\therefore$ Total age of A and C = 48 + 38 = 86 years.

13. D : $\because$ Average temperature of Monday, Tuesday, Wednesday and Thursday = 38°

$\therefore$ Total temperature of these 4 days

= 38° × 4 = 152°

$\because$ Average temperature of Tuesday, Wednesday, Thursday and Friday = 40°

$\therefore$ Total temperature of these 4 days

= 40° × 4 = 160°

Temperature of Monday = 40°

$\therefore$ Total temperature of Tuesday, Wednesday and Thursday = 152° – 40° = 112°

$\therefore$ Temperature of Friday = 160° – 112° = 48°.

14. B : Total income of eight members

= 6000 + 4000 + 2000 = Rs. 12000

Average income of one member

$$= \frac{12000}{8} = \text{Rs. } 1500.$$

15. A : $$\text{Time} = \frac{\text{Distance}}{\text{Speed}} = \frac{60}{20} = 3 \text{ hours}$$

In return journey,

$$\text{Time} = \frac{60}{40} = \frac{3}{2} \text{ hours}$$

$$\text{Total time} = 3 + \frac{3}{2} = \frac{9}{2} \text{ hours}$$

Total Distance = 60 + 60 = 120 km

$$\text{Average speed} = \frac{\text{Total Distance}}{\text{Total Time}}$$

$$= \frac{120}{\frac{9}{2}} = \frac{120\times2}{9} = \frac{240}{9} = 26\frac{2}{3} \text{ k/hr.}$$

16. B : Average price of (10 chairs + 6 tables)
= Rs. 30

Total price of (10 chairs + 6 tables)
= Rs. 30 × 16 = Rs. 480

Average price of 6 tables = Rs. 50 (Given)

Tota price of 6 tables
= Rs. 50 × 6 = Rs. 300

∴ Total price of 10 chairs
= Rs. (480 – 300)
= Rs. 180

∴ Average price of chairs = $\frac{180}{10}$ = Rs. 18.

17. A : Average score of 5 innings = 20

Total score of 5 innings = 50 × 5 = 100

Total score of first four innings
= 40 + 30 + 14 + 10 = 94

∴ Score of 5th inning = 100 – 94 = 6.

18. C: Average age of 5 members = 20 years

Total age of 5 members = 20 × 5 = 100 years

Age of the youngest member = 8 years

After the birth of youngest member, increment in age in 8 years = 8 × 5 = 40 years

Total of the age of 4 members at the time of birth of youngest member = 100 – 40 = 60 years

∴ Average age = $\frac{60}{4}$ = 15 years.

19. C : ∵ Average of 5 terms = 10

Total of 5 terms = 10 × 5 = 50

∵ Average of first two terms = 7

∴ Total of first two terms = 7 × 2 = 14

∵ Average of last two terms = 13

∴ Total of last two terms = 13 × 2 = 26

∴ Third term = Total of 5 terms – (Total of first two terms + total of last two terms)
= 50 – (14 + 26) = 50 – 40 = 10.

20. B : ∵ At the rate of 4 km/hr, time required for 6 km distance

$= \frac{6}{4} = \frac{3}{2}$ hours

∵ At the rate of 3 km/hr, time required for 4 km distance = $\frac{4}{3}$ hours

∴ Total time required = $\frac{3}{2} + \frac{4}{3} = \frac{17}{6}$ hours

Total distance covered = 6 + 4 = 10 km

Average speed = $\frac{10}{\frac{17}{6}} = \frac{10 \times 6}{17} = \frac{60}{17}$

$= 3\frac{9}{17}$ km / hr.

10

WORK, TIME AND WAGES

Points to Remember :

1. If a man completes a work in 20 days then he completes $\frac{1}{20}$ part of the work in one day.

2. If A's speed is double than B, then A will take half time to complete the work than B.

3. To complete a work if the number of persons are increased then time required to complete the work decreases in the same ratio.

4. In the problems of Time and Work we assume that a person is doing the work at uniform speed until an explanation is not given.

5. To find the labour we should remember that labour is equal to the ratio of work done by a worker.

Example 1. *Ram can complete a work in 6 days and Sham can complete it in 8 days. In how many days both can complete the work ?*

Solution. Ram's 1 day's work $= \frac{1}{6}$

Sham's 1 day's work $= \frac{1}{8}$

(Ram's + Sham's) 1 day's work $= \frac{1}{6} + \frac{1}{8} = \frac{7}{24}$

$\therefore$ Ram and Sham complete the work in

$\frac{24}{7}$ days $= 3\frac{1}{7}$ days

Example 2. *A and B together can complete a work in 6 days while A alone can complete it in 15 days. In how many days B alone can complete the work?*

Solution. (A + B)'s 1 day's work $= \frac{1}{6}$

A's 1 days work $= \frac{1}{15}$

$\therefore$ B's 1 day's work $= \frac{1}{6} - \frac{1}{15} = \frac{1}{10}$

$\therefore$ B will complete the work in 10 days.

Example 3. *3 men or 6 boys can complete a work in 8 days. In how many days 4 men and 4 boys will complete the same work?*

Solution. $\because$ 3 men = 6 boys

$\therefore$ 1 man = 2 boys

$\therefore$ 4 men + 4 boys = 8 boys + 4 boys

= 12 boys

$\because$ 6 boys can complete the work = 8 days

$\therefore$ 12 boys can complete the work in

$= \frac{8 \times 6}{12} = 4$ days

$\therefore$ 4 men and 4 boys can complete the work in 4 days.

Example 4. *Promod completed $\frac{3}{5}$ part of work in 9 days and he completed the remaining part of work with the help of Deepak in 4 days. In how many days can Deepak alone finish the whole work?*

Solution. $\because$ Pramod's 9 day's work $= \frac{3}{5}$

Pramod's 1 day's work $= \frac{3}{5} \times \frac{1}{9} = \frac{1}{15}$

Pradomd's 4 day's work $= \frac{1}{15} \times 4 = \frac{4}{15}$

Total work done by Pramod $= \frac{3}{5} + \frac{4}{15} = \frac{13}{15}$

$\therefore$ Remaining work $= 1 - \frac{13}{15} = \frac{2}{15}$

It is clear that Deepak completes $\frac{2}{15}$ work in 4 days.

$\therefore$ Deepak can complete the whole work in

$= \frac{4 \times 15}{2} = 30$ days

Example 5. *3 men or 5 boys can complete a work in 12 days. In how many days 6 men and 3 boys can complete double work?*

Solution. $\because$ 3 men = 5 days

$\therefore$ 6 men = 10 boys

$\therefore$ 6 men + 3 boys = 10 boys + 3 boys

= 13 boys

5 boys can do the work in = 12 days

1 boy can do the work in = 12 × 5 = 60 days

13 boys can do the work in = $\frac{60}{13}$

13 boys can do double work in

$$= \frac{60}{13} \times 2 = \frac{120}{13} = 9\frac{3}{13} \text{ days}$$

$\therefore$ 6 men and 3 boys can do double work in $9\frac{3}{13}$ days.

Example 6. *A can complete a work in a time double than B and triple than C. If three together can complete the work in 20 days then in how many days each can complete the work separately?*

Solution. $\because$ Suppose A can complete the work in x days

$\therefore$ B can complete the work in $\frac{x}{2}$ days

and C can complete the work in $\frac{x}{3}$ days

(A + B + C)'s 1 day's work

$$= \frac{1}{x} + \frac{1}{x/2} + \frac{1}{x/3}$$

$$= \frac{1}{x} + \frac{2}{x} + \frac{3}{x} = \frac{6}{x}$$

According to the problem,

$\therefore$ (A + B + C)'s 1 day's work = $\frac{1}{20}$

$\therefore$ A can complete the work in 120 days, B can complete it in 60 days and C can complete it in 40 days.

Example 7. *A and B can do a work in 12 days; B and C can do it in 15 days and C and A can do it in 20 days. In how many days three together can do the work?*

Solution. $\because$ (A + B)'s 1 day's work = $\frac{1}{12}$

(B + C)'s 1 day's work = $\frac{1}{15}$

(C + A)'s 1 day's work = $\frac{1}{20}$

$\therefore$ 2(A + B + C)'s 1 day's work

$$= \frac{1}{12} + \frac{1}{15} + \frac{1}{20}$$

$$= \frac{5+4+3}{60} = \frac{12}{60} = \frac{1}{5}$$

$\therefore$ (A + B + C)'s 1 day's work = $\frac{1}{5} \times \frac{1}{2} = \frac{1}{10}$

$\therefore$ A, B and C together can do the work in 10 days.

Example 8. *Two taps can fill a tank in 60 minutes and 75 minutes separately. There is a third tap which can empty the tank. If all the tree taps are opened at the same time then the tank fills in 50 minutes. In how much time the thired tap can empty the filled tank?*

Solution. The part of the tank filled in 1 minute by two taps

$$= \frac{1}{60} + \frac{1}{75} = \frac{9}{300} = \frac{3}{100}$$

The part of the tank filled in 1 minute by three tapes

$$= \frac{1}{50}$$

$\therefore$ Third tap empties the part of the tank in one minute

$$= \frac{3}{100} - \frac{1}{50} = \frac{1}{100}$$

$\therefore$ Third tap can empty the tank in 100 minutes.

EXERCISE

In the following questions four answer choices are given in which one is correct. Choose the correct answer.

1. Monika can do $\frac{1}{5}$ part of a work in one day. In how many days she can complete the work?
   A. 4 days B. 8 days
   C. 5 days D. 2 days

2. Kanchan can do a work in 20 days. If she worked for 6 days then what part of the work is left?
   A. $\frac{7}{9}$ B. $\frac{11}{9}$
   C. $\frac{7}{10}$ D. $\frac{1}{4}$

3. Meenu can read 8 pages of a novel in 30 minutes. If the novel contains 80 pages then what time she will take to read it completely?
   A. $4\frac{1}{2}$ hours B. $3\frac{1}{3}$ hours
   C. 4 hours D. 5 hours

4. 2 men or 5 women can do a work in 46 days. In how much time 4 men and 8 women can complete the work?
   A. $11\frac{7}{9}$ days B. $12\frac{7}{9}$ days
   C. $10\frac{7}{9}$ days D. $8\frac{1}{3}$ days

5. Kamlesh, Lazwati and Yashoda can do a work in 8, 12 and 24 days separately. In how many days three together can do the work?
   A. 4 days B. $4\frac{1}{2}$ days
   C. 3 days D. $5\frac{1}{2}$ days

6. A and B together can do a work in 28 days. They finished the work with the help of C in 21 days. In how many days C alone can do the work?
   A. 83 days B. 84 days
   C. 90 days D. 45 days

7. 4 boys and 6 women can do a work in 4 days while 2 boys and 4 women can do it in 7 days. In how many days 3 boys and 1 women can do the work?
   A. 8 days B. 10 days
   C. 12 days D. 13 days

8. Rajesh completed 3/5 part of a work in 9 days. He completed the reamaining work with the help of Suresh in 45 days. In how many days Suresh alone can do the work?
   A. 25 days B. 30 days
   C. 35 days D. 42 days

9. Sapna and Sandhya can do a work in 12 and 10 days respectively. If they work on alternative days and Sapna begins the work then in how many days the work will be completed?
   A. 8 days B. 11 days
   C. 14 days D. 5 days

10. A takes half time than B to do a work. C takes time equal to A and B together. If three together can do the work in 7 days then in how many days A alone can do the work?
    A. 21 days B. 10 days
    C. 8 days D. 34 days

11. A, B and C together contracted to do a work for Rs. 450. If ratio of their work is 9 : 5 : 4 respectively then find the share of A.
    A. Rs. 220 B. Rs. 225
    C. Rs. 325 D. Rs. 180

12. A can do a work in 16 days. If B's speed is double than A, then in how many days they together can do the work?
    A. $5\frac{1}{3}$ days B. $3\frac{1}{5}$ days
    C. $4\frac{1}{3}$ days D. $2\frac{1}{4}$ days

13. A, B and C can do a work in 20, 18 and 14 days respectively. B and C together did the work for

4 days and the remaining work was completed by A. Find the share of A in total wages of Rs. 2520.

A. Rs. 1380 B. Rs. 1440

C. Rs. 1210 D. Rs. 1240

14. Two taps can fill a tank in 15 and 12 minutes respectively. A third tap can empty it in 20 minutes. If all the taps are opened at the same time then in how much time the tank will be filled?

A. $8\frac{1}{2}$ minutes B. 10 minutes

C. $11\frac{1}{3}$ minutes D. 14 minutes

15. 4 men and 10 women were put on a work. They completed $\frac{1}{3}$ work in 4 days . After this 2 men and 2 women were increased. They completed 2/9 more work in 2 days . If the remaining work is to be completed in 3 days then how many more women must be increased?

A. 32 B. 8

C. 50 D. 55

EXPLANATORY ANSWERS

1. C : Monika does $\frac{1}{5}$ work in = 1 day

∴ Monika completes the work in 5 days.

2. C : ∵ Kanchan's 1 day's work = $\frac{1}{20}$

Kanchan's 6 days' work = $\frac{1}{20}\times 6 = \frac{3}{10}$

Remaining work = $1-\frac{3}{10}=\frac{7}{10}$.

3. D : Meenu reads 8 pages in 30 minutes

Meenu reads 1 page in $\frac{30}{8}$ minutes

Meenu reads 80 pages in

$\frac{30\times 80}{8}$ = 300 minutes = 5 hours.

4. B : ∵ 2 men = 5 women

∴ 4 men + 8 women = 10 women + 8 women

= 18 women

5 women can do the work in 46 days

1 woman can do the work in = 46 × 5 days

18 women can do the work in

$\frac{46\times 5}{18} = 12\frac{7}{9}$ days

4 men and 8 women can do the work in $12\frac{7}{9}$ days.

5. A : ∵ Kamlesh's 1 day's work = $\frac{1}{8}$

Lazwati's 1 day's work = $\frac{1}{12}$

Yashoda's 1 day's work = $\frac{1}{24}$

(Kamlesh + Lazwati + Yashoda)'s 1 day's work

$=\frac{1}{8}+\frac{1}{12}+\frac{1}{24}=\frac{3+2+1}{24}=\frac{6}{24}=\frac{1}{4}$

∴ They complete the work in 4 days.

6. B : ∵ (A + B)'s 1 day's work = $\frac{1}{28}$

(A + B + C)'s 1 day's work = $\frac{1}{21}$

∴ C's 1 day's work = $\frac{1}{21}-\frac{1}{28}$

$=\frac{4-3}{84}=\frac{1}{84}$

∴ C can do the work in 84 days.

7. A : *In First Case* :

(4 boys + 6 women) do the work in 4 days

∴ (2 boys + 3 women) do the work in

= 4 × 2 = 8 days

In Second Case :

(2 boys + 4 women) do the work in 7 days

1 day's work of (2 boys + 3 women) = $\frac{1}{8}$

1 day's work of (2 boys + 4 women) = $\frac{1}{7}$

$\therefore$ 1 day's work of 1 woman = $\frac{1}{7}-\frac{1}{8}=\frac{1}{56}$

$\therefore$ 1 day's work of 4 women = $4\times\frac{1}{56}=\frac{1}{14}$

$\therefore$ 1 day's work of 2 boys = $\frac{1}{7}-\frac{1}{14}=\frac{1}{14}$

$\therefore$ 1 day's work of 3 boys = $\frac{1}{14}\times\frac{3}{2}=\frac{3}{28}$

$\therefore$ 1 day's work of (3 boys + 1 woman)

$=\frac{3}{28}+\frac{1}{56}=\frac{1}{8}$

$\therefore$ 3 boys and 1 women can do the work in 8 days.

8. B : $\because$ Rajesh's 9 day's work = $\frac{3}{5}$

$\therefore$ Rajesh's 1 day's work = $\frac{3}{5}\times\frac{1}{9}=\frac{1}{15}$

$\therefore$ Rajesh's 4 day's work = $\frac{1}{15}\times 4=\frac{4}{15}$

$\therefore$ Total work done by Rajesh = $\frac{3}{5}+\frac{4}{15}$

$=\frac{9+4}{15}=\frac{13}{15}$

Remaining work = $1-\frac{13}{15}=\frac{2}{15}$

Suresh does $\frac{2}{15}$ work in = 4 days.

$\therefore$ Suresh does 1 work in = $\frac{4\times 15}{2}$ = 30 days

9. B : $\because$ Sapna's 1 day's work = $\frac{1}{12}$

Sandhya's 1 day's work = $\frac{1}{10}$

(Sapna + Sandhya)'s 1 day's work = $\frac{1}{12}+\frac{1}{10}$

$=\frac{5+6}{60}=\frac{11}{60}$

$\because$ They work on alternative days

$\therefore$ (Sapna + Sandhya)'s 5-5 day's work

$=\frac{11}{60}\times 5=\frac{11}{12}$

$\therefore$ Remaining work = $1-\frac{11}{12}=\frac{1}{12}$

Now Sapna's turn comes.

Sapna does $\frac{1}{12}$ work in 1 day

$\therefore$ Work will be completed in

= 5 + 5 + 1 = 11 days

10. A : Suppose A alone complete the work in x days

$\therefore$ B can complete the work in $2x$ days

$\therefore$ A's 1 day's work = $\frac{1}{x}$

B's 1 day's work = $\frac{1}{2x}$

C's day's work = $\frac{1}{x}+\frac{1}{2x}=\frac{3}{2x}$

$\therefore$ (A + B +C)'s 1 day's work = $\frac{1}{x}+\frac{1}{2x}+\frac{3}{2x}$

$=\frac{2+1+3}{2x}=\frac{6}{2x}=\frac{3}{x}$

According to problem,

(A + B + C)'s 1 day's work = $\frac{1}{7}$

$\therefore \quad \frac{3}{x}=\frac{1}{7} \Rightarrow x=3\times 7=21$

$\therefore$ A alone can do the work in 21 days.

11. B. : $\because$ Sum of the ratios = 9 + 5 + 4 = 18

$\therefore$ Share of A = $\frac{9}{18}\times 450$ = Rs. 225.

12. A : $\because$ A can do the work in = 16 days

$\therefore$ B can do the work in = 8 days.

$\therefore$ A's 1 day's work = $\frac{1}{16}$

B's 1 day's work = $\frac{1}{8}$

$(A + B)$'s 1 day's work $= \frac{1}{16} + \frac{1}{8} = \frac{3}{16}$

$(A + B)$ do $\frac{3}{16}$ work in = 1 day.

$\therefore$ $(A + B)$'s do one work in $= \frac{16}{3} = 5\frac{1}{3}$ days.

13. D : $\because$ $(B + C)$'s 1 day's work $= \frac{1}{18} + \frac{1}{14} = \frac{8}{63}$

$(B + C)$'s 4 day's work $= \frac{8}{63} \times 4 = \frac{32}{63}$

$(B + C)$'s do the work for 4 days and the remaining work is done by A alone.

$\therefore$ Remaining work $= 1 - \frac{32}{63} = \frac{31}{63}$

$\therefore$ Share of A $= \frac{31}{63} \times 2520 =$ Rs. 1240.

14. B : Part of the tank filled in 1 minute by taps (A + B + C)

$= \frac{1}{15} + \frac{1}{12} - \frac{1}{20} = \frac{4+5-3}{60} = \frac{6}{60} = \frac{1}{10}$

$\because$ $\frac{1}{10}$ part of the tank is filled in = 1 minute

$\therefore$ 1 part of the tank is filled in = 10 minutes

15. B : *In First Case* :

(4 men + 10 women)'s 4 day's work $= \frac{1}{3}$

$\therefore$ (4 men + 10 women)'s 1 day's work $= \frac{1}{12}$ ...(*i*)

In Second Case :

(6 men + 12 women)'s 2 day's work $= \frac{2}{9}$

$\therefore$ 16 men + 12 women's 1 day's work $= \frac{2}{9}$

From (*i*) and (*ii*)

(2 men + 5 women)'s 1 day's work $= \frac{1}{24}$

and (2 men + 4 women)'s 1 day's work

$= \frac{1}{9} \times \frac{1}{3} = \frac{1}{27}$

$\therefore$ 1 women's 1 day's work

$= \frac{1}{24} - \frac{1}{27} = \frac{1}{216}$

$\therefore$ 6 men's 1 day's work

$= \frac{1}{9} - \frac{1}{216} \times 12 = \frac{1}{9} - \frac{1}{18} = \frac{1}{18}$

Remaining work $= 1 - \left(\frac{1}{3} + \frac{2}{9}\right)$

$= 1 - \frac{5}{9} = \frac{4}{9}$

6 men's 3 day's work $= \frac{1}{18} \times 3 = \frac{1}{6}$

Now, remaining work

$= \frac{4}{9} - \frac{1}{6} = \frac{8-3}{18} = \frac{5}{18}$

$\because$ $\frac{1}{216}$ work is done in 1 day by 1 woman

$\therefore$ $\frac{5}{18}$ work is done in 3 days by

$= \frac{5}{18} \times \frac{216}{3} =$ 20 women

$\therefore$ Number of women increased = 20 – 12 = 8.

11

RATIO, PROPORTION AND PROPORTIONAL PARTS

Ratio : Ratio of two quantities is always expressed in the same units. We find the ratio by dividing one term by the other term. For example, the relation between 20 paise and 80 paise is the same as a relation between 1 cow and 4 cows. We express this relation as :

20 : 80 or 1 : 4

Proportion : When the two ratios are equal, they are called in proportion. If $\frac{a}{b} = \frac{c}{d}$, it means $\frac{a}{b}$ is in proportion to $\frac{c}{d}$ or $\frac{c}{d}$ is in proportion to $\frac{a}{b}$. It is expressed as following :

$$a : b :: c : d$$

In this relation the product of extreme terms is equal to the product of middle terms,

i.e., $a \times d = b \times c$.

Proportional Parts : To distribute a given quantity in required ratio is called proportional division and distributed parts are called proportional parts. For example : Divide a quantity X in the ratio A : B : C.

Sum of the ratios = A + B + C

$$\text{Part of A} = \frac{A}{A+B+C} \times X$$

$$\text{Part of B} = \frac{B}{A+B+C} \times X$$

$$\text{Part of C} = \frac{C}{A+B+C} \times X$$

Example 1. *If 0.75 : x :: 5 : 8, then what is the value of x ?*

Solution. 0.75 : x :: 5 : 8

Product of extreme terms = product of middle terms

$\therefore \quad 0.75 \times 8 = x \times 5$

$\Rightarrow \quad x = \frac{0.75 \times 8}{5} = 1.2$

$\therefore$ Value of x = 1.2.

Example 2. *What number should be subtracted from 23, 30, 57 and 78 so that remainders are in proportion ?*

Solution. Let the required number is x.

According to problem,

$(23 - x) : (30 - x) :: (57 - x) : (78 - x)$

$\therefore \quad (23 - x)(78 - x) = (30 - x)(57 - x)$

$\therefore \quad 23 \times 78 - 101x + x^2 = 30 \times 57 - 87x + x^2$

$\therefore \quad 23 \times 78 - 30 \times 57 = 101x - 87x$

$\therefore \quad 1794 - 1710 = 14x$

$\therefore \quad 84 = 14x$

$\Rightarrow \quad x = \frac{84}{14} = 6$

$\therefore$ Required number to be subtracted is 6.

Example 3. *Two numbers are in a ratio 5 : 8. If 2 is added to each number then their ratio becomes 2 : 3. What are the numbers ?*

Solution. Let the numbers be $5x$ and $8x$.

According to problem,

$(5x + 2) : (8x + 2) = 2 : 3$

$\therefore \quad (5x + 2) \times 3 = (8x + 2) \times 2$

$\therefore \quad 15x + 6 = 16x + 4 \Rightarrow x = 2$

$\therefore$ Numbers are $5 \times 2 = 10$ and $8 \times 2 = 16$.

Example 4. *Divide Rs. 1000 in A, B and C in the ratio 2 : 3 : 5.*

Solution. Sum of the ratio = 2 + 3 + 5 = 10

$\therefore$ A's part $= \frac{2}{10} \times 1000 =$ Rs. 200

$\text{B's part} = \frac{3}{10} \times 1000 = \text{Rs. } 300$

$\text{C's part} = \frac{5}{10} \times 1000 = \text{Rs. } 500$

Example 5. *If Rs. 9000 is divided among three workers in the ratio* $\frac{1}{3} : \frac{1}{4} : \frac{1}{6}$ *respectively, then what is the share of third worker ?*

Solution. Ratio in the wages of three workers

$$= \frac{1}{3} : \frac{1}{4} : \frac{1}{6} = 4 : 3 : 2$$

Sum of the ratios = 4 + 3 + 2 = 9

$$\text{Share of third worker} = \frac{2}{9} \times 9000 = \text{Rs. } 2000$$

Example 6. If $A : B = 5 : 7$ *and* $B : C = 9 : 11$, *then what is* $A : C$?

Solution. $A : B = 5 : 7 \Rightarrow \frac{A}{B} = \frac{5}{7}$

and $B : C = 11 \Rightarrow \frac{B}{C} = \frac{9}{11}$

$$\therefore \quad \frac{A}{B} \times \frac{B}{C} = \frac{5}{7} \times \frac{9}{11} \Rightarrow \frac{A}{C} = \frac{45}{77}$$

$$\Rightarrow A : C = 45 : 77$$

Example 7. *The sum of squares of three numbers is 116. If the ratio of numbers is 2 : 3 : 4, then what are the numbers respectively ?*

Solution. Let the numbers be $2x$, $3x$ and $4x$.

According to problem,

$$(2x)^2 + (3x)^2 + (4x)^2 = 116$$

$$\therefore \quad 4x^2 + 9x^2 + 16x^2 = 116$$

$$\therefore \quad 29x^2 = 116 \Rightarrow x^2 = \frac{116}{29} = 4$$

$$\Rightarrow \quad x = 2$$

∴ Numbers are 2 × 2 = 4, 3 × 2 = 6 and 4 × 2 = 8.

Example 8. *Two vessels of same capacity are filled with a mixture of milk and water. Milk is* $\frac{1}{2}$ *part and* $\frac{1}{3}$ *part respectively and remaining part of the vessels is filled with water. If the mixtures of these vessels is empetied in a third vessel, then what is the ratio of milk and water ?*

Solution. ∵ Both vessels are of same capacity.

∴ *In first vessel* : Milk = $\frac{1}{2}$, water = $\frac{1}{2}$

In second vessel : Milk = $\frac{1}{3}$, water = $\frac{1}{3}$

∴ *In third vessel* :

$$\text{Milk} = \frac{1}{2} + \frac{1}{3} = \frac{5}{6} \text{ part}$$

$$\text{Water} = \frac{1}{2} + \frac{2}{3} = \frac{7}{6} \text{ part}$$

$$\therefore \text{Ratio of Milk and Water} = \frac{5}{6} : \frac{7}{6} = 5 : 7.$$

Example 9. *In three vessels the ratio of water and milk is 6 : 7, 5 : 9 and 8 : 7 respectively. If the mixtures of three vessels are mixed then what is the ratio of water and milk ?*

Solution. *In First Vessel* : Water : Milk = 6 : 7

Sum of the ratio = 6 + 7 = 13

$$\therefore \quad \text{Water} = \frac{6}{13}, \text{ Milk} = \frac{7}{13}$$

In Second Vessel : Water : Milk = 5 : 9

Sum of the ratio = 5 + 9 = 14

$$\therefore \quad \text{Water} = \frac{5}{14}, \text{ Milk} = \frac{9}{14}$$

In Third Vessel : Water : Milk = 8 : 7

Sum of the ratio = 8 + 7 = 15

$$\therefore \quad \text{Water} = \frac{8}{15}, \text{ Milk} = \frac{7}{15}$$

When the mixtures of three vessels are mixed,

$$\text{Quantity of water} = \frac{6}{13} + \frac{5}{14} + \frac{8}{15} = \frac{3691}{2730}$$

$$\text{Quantity of milk} = \frac{7}{13} + \frac{9}{14} + \frac{7}{15} = \frac{4499}{2730}$$

$$\therefore \quad \text{Ratio} = \frac{3691}{2730} : \frac{4499}{2730} = 3691 : 4499.$$

EXERCISE

In the following questions four answer choices are given in which one is correct. Choose the correct answer.

1. What is the ratio of 20 paise and Rs. 3 ?
   A. 2 : 9 B. 1 : 14
   C. 1 : 15 D. 1 : 16
2. Which ratio is greater in 12 : 18 or 21 : 18 ?
   A. 12 : 18 B. 21 : 18
   C. Both are equal D. Nothing
3. What is fourth proportional of 7, 8 and 14 ?
   A. 16 B. 18
   C. 25 D. 36
4. What should be added to 8, 21, 13 and 31 so that the sum is in proportion ?
   A. 4 B. 8
   C. 5 D. 7
5. What is the value of x if $17 : 25 = x : 150$?
   A. 108 B. 102
   C. 96 D. 97
6. If $A = \frac{2}{5}B$ and $B = \frac{1}{3}C$ then what is A : B : C ?
   A. 5 : 2 : 15 B. 5 : 15 : 2
   C. 2 : 5 : 15 D. 15 : 2 : 5
7. What is the ratio between 50 cm and 4 m ?
   A. 1 : 8 B. 2 : 7
   C. 1 : 9 D. 3 : 8
8. If $\frac{A}{B} = \frac{1}{2}$, then what is the value of $\left(\frac{3}{4} + \frac{B-A}{B+A}\right)$?
   A. $\frac{15}{17}$ B. $\frac{13}{11}$
   C. $\frac{13}{12}$ D. $\frac{10}{13}$
9. The ratio of ages of Gulshan and Pankaj is 10 : 9. If Gulshan's age after 6 years be 26 years then what is the present age of Pankaj ?
   A. 18 years B. 10 years
   C. 17 years D. 20 years
10. If a man covers a distance in 7 hours and a tonga covers the same distance in $4\frac{1}{3}$ hours then what is the ratio of speed of man and tonga ?
    A. 7 : 15 B. 6 : 13
    C. 13 : 21 D. 13 : 20
11. One year ago the ratio of Tarun and Kamal Kant's ages was 4 : 5. If one year after the ratio of their ages is 5 : 6, then what is the present age of Tarun ?
    A. 7 years B. 9 years
    C. 11 years D. 6 years
12. A sum is distributed among A, B and C in the ratio 2 : 3 : 5 respectively. If C's share is 50% of the sum, then what is the share of B ?
    A. 550
    B. Question is incomplete
    C. 940
    D. cannot be calculated
13. There are coins of 25 paise and 10 paise in a bag in the ratio 6 : 17 respectively. If the total amount is Rs. 16 then what is the number of 10 paise's coin ?
    A. 88 B. 64
    C. 85 D. 72
14. In what ratio two types of tea costing Rs. 15 per kg and Rs. 20 per kg are mixed so that cost price of the mixture is Rs. 16.50 per kg ?
    A. 5 : 6 B. 7 : 3
    C. 6 : 7 D. 3 : 7
15. The ratio of sides of two squares is 3 : 4. What is the ratio of their perimeters ?
    A. 3 : 4 B. 2 : 5
    C. 4 : 5 D. 3 : 7
16. To make a table, the ratio of cost of wages, wood and paint is 7 : 5 : 3 respectively. If total cost of table is Rs. 780, then what is the cost of wages ?
    A. Rs. 380 B. Rs. 464
    C. Rs. 364 D. Rs. 330
17. If $\frac{x}{y} = \frac{3}{4}$ then what is the value of $(2x + 3y) : (3y - 2x)$?
    A. 3 : 1 B. 3 : 2

C. 1 : 2 D. 2 : 3

18. A sum is divided between A, B and C in the ratio 1 : 4 : 7. If difference in shares of A and B is Rs. 2400, then what is the share of C ?

A. Rs. 5800 B. Rs. 5600
C. Rs. 7750 D. Rs. 8750

19. The ratio of ages of Om Dutt, Ajay and Sanjay is 9 : 4 : 7. If the difference in ages of Ajay and Sanjay is 9 years, then what is the difference in the ages of Om Dutt and Ajay ?

A. 18 years B. 21 years
C. 15 years D. 11 years

EXPLANATORY ANSWERS

1. C : To find the ratio of 20 paise and Rs. 3, we convert Rupee into paise.
20 paise : Rs. 3 = 20 paise : 300 paise = 1 : 15.

2. B : $\because 12 : 18 = \frac{12}{18} = \frac{2}{3}$ or $\frac{4}{6}$

and $21 : 18 = \frac{21}{18} = \frac{7}{6}$

It is clear that $\frac{7}{6} > \frac{4}{6}$

$\therefore$ 21 : 18 is greater ratio.

3. A : Let fourth proportional = x

$\therefore 7 : 8 :: 14 : x \Rightarrow 7 \times x = 8 \times 14$

$\Rightarrow x = \frac{8 \times 14}{7} = 16$

$\therefore$ Fourth proportional = 16.

4. C : Let the required number to be added $= x$

According to problem,

$(8 + x) : (21 + x) :: (13 + x) : (31 + x)$

Product of extremes = Product of middle terms

$\therefore (8 + x)(31 + x) = (21 + x)(13 + x)$

$\therefore 248 + 39x + x^2 = 273 + 34x + x^2$

$\therefore 5x = 273 - 248 = 25$

$\therefore x = \frac{25}{5} = 5$

$\therefore$ Required number to be added is 5.

5. B : $\because 17 : 25 = x : 150 \Rightarrow 17 \times 150 = 25x$

$\Rightarrow x = \frac{17 \times 150}{25} = 102$

$\therefore$ Value of x is 102.

6. C : $\because A = \frac{2}{5}B \Rightarrow \frac{A}{B} = \frac{2}{5}$

$\Rightarrow A : B = 2 : 5$

$B = \frac{1}{3}C \Rightarrow \frac{B}{C} = \frac{1}{3}$

$\Rightarrow B : C = 1 : 3$

To equal the value of B in two ratios we multiply second ratio by 5.

A : B = 2 : 5

B : C = 1 : 3 or 5 : 15

Now A : B : C = 2 : 5 : 15.

7. A : 50 cm : 4 m $\Rightarrow$ 50 cm : 400 cm

$\Rightarrow$ 1 : 8.

8. C : $\because \frac{A}{B} = \frac{1}{2} \Rightarrow \frac{B-A}{B+A} = \frac{2-1}{2+1} = \frac{1}{3}$

$\therefore \left(\frac{3}{4} + \frac{B-A}{B+A}\right) = \frac{3}{4} + \frac{1}{3} = \frac{13}{12}.$

9. A : Let present ages of Gulshan and Pankaj be $10x$ and $9x$.

According to problem,

After 6 years Gulshan's age = 26 years

$\therefore 10x + 6 = 26 \Rightarrow 10x = 26 - 6 = 20$

$\Rightarrow x = \frac{20}{10} = 2$

$\therefore$ Pankaj's present age = 9 × 2 = 18 years.

10. C : Let distance = x km

Man's speed = $\frac{\text{Distance}}{\text{Time}} = \frac{x}{7}$ km / hr

Tonga's speed = $\frac{\text{Distance}}{\text{Time}} = \frac{x}{4\frac{1}{3}} = \frac{3x}{13}$ km / hr

Ratio of Man's and Tonga's speed

$\frac{x}{7} : \frac{3x}{13} = 13 : 21.$

11. B : Let present ages of Tarun and Kamalkant be x years and y years respectively.

In First Case : $\frac{x-1}{y-1} = \frac{4}{5}$ ...(*i*)

In Second Case : $\frac{x+1}{y+1} = \frac{5}{6}$ ...(*ii*)

From (*i*) and (*ii*),

$5x - 4y - 1 = 0$ ...(*iii*)

$6x - 5y + 1 = 0$ ...(*iv*)

Multiply (*iii*) by 5 and (*iv*) by 4, we get

$25x - 20y - 5 = 0$

$24x - 20y + 4 = 0$

$- \quad + \quad -$

$x \quad - 9 = 0$

$\therefore \quad x = 9$

$\therefore$ Tarun's present age is 9 years.

12. B : To find the share of B, sum of money must be given in the question. Therefore the question is incomplete.

13. B : Ratio of 25 paise coins and 10 paise coins

$= 6 : 17$

Ratio of amount of 25 paise coins and 10 paise coins

$= 6 \times 25 : 17 \times 10$

$= 150 : 170$

$= 15 : 17$

Sum of ratio $= 15 + 17 = 32$

Amount of 10 paise coins

$= \frac{17}{13} \times$ Rs. 16 = Rs. 8.50

$\therefore$ Number of 10 paise coins $= 8.50 \times 10 = 85$

14. B : $\because$ Cost of the mixture = Rs. 16.50 per kg

Tea costing Rs. 15 per kg is cheaper from the mixture = Rs. 1.50 per kg

Tea costing Rs. 20 per kg is dearer from the mixture =Rs. 3.50 per kg.

To equal the cost of cheaper and dearer tea we must multiply them by 3.50 and 1.50 respectively, *i.e.*, in the ratio of 7 : 3.

15. A : Let sides of the squares be $3x$ and $4x$ respectively.

$\therefore$ Perimeter of 1st square $= 4 \times 3x = 12x$

Permeter of 2nd square $= 4 \times 4x = 16x$

$\therefore$ Ratio of perimeters $= 12x : 16x = 3 : 4$.

16. C : Sum of the ratios $= 7 + 5 + 3 = 15$

$\therefore$ Cost of wages $= \frac{7}{15} \times$ Rs. 780 = Rs. 364.

17. A : $\because \frac{x}{y} = \frac{3}{4} \Rightarrow 4x = 3y$

$\therefore 2x + 3y = 2x + 4x = 6x$

and $3y - 2x = 4x - 2x = 2x$

$\therefore (2x + 3y) : (3y - 2x) = 6x : 2x = 3 : 1$.

18. B : $\because$ Difference in ratio of A and B $= 4 - 1 = 3$

$\therefore$ Share of C $= \frac{7}{3} \times$ Rs. 2400 = Rs. 5600.

19. C : $\because$ Difference in ratio of Ajay and Sanjay

$= 7 - 4 = 3$

Differnce in ratio of Om Dutt and Ajay

$= 9 - 4 = 5$

If difference in ratio is 3 then difference in ages

= 9 years

If difference in ratio is 5 then difference in ages

$= \frac{9}{3} \times 5 = 15$ years

$\therefore$ Difference in ages of Om Dutt and Ajay

= 15 years.

12

SPEED, TIME AND DISTANCE

Points to Remember :

1. Speed $= \dfrac{\text{Distance}}{\text{Time}}$
2. Distance = Speed × Time
3. Time $= \dfrac{\text{Distance}}{\text{Speed}}$

While solving the problem we should remember the following :

1. If two trains are moving in same direction, then
   Resulting speed = Difference of their speeds
2. If two trains are moving in opposite direction, then
   Resulting speed = Sum of their speeds
3. If a boat moves in direction of flow, then
   Resulting speed of the boat = speed of the boat in still water + speed of the flow
4. If a boat moves opposite to flow, then
   Resulting speed of the boat = Speed of the boat in still water – speed of the flow

5. 1 km/hr $= \dfrac{5}{18}$ m/s.

Example 1. *Ramesh covers a distance of* $4\frac{1}{2}$ *km in* $\frac{1}{2}$ *hr. What is his speed in m / s ?*

Solution. ∵ Speed $= \dfrac{\text{Distance}}{\text{Time}}$

$$= \frac{4\frac{1}{2}}{\frac{1}{2}} = 9 \text{ km / hr} = 9 \times \frac{5}{18} = 2.5 \text{ m / s}$$

Example 2. *A train covers a distance of 240 km in 8 hours. If its speed is increased by* $1\frac{1}{2}$ *times then what time it will take to cover a distance of 540 km ?*

Solution. *In First Case* :

$$\text{Speed} = \frac{\text{Distance}}{\text{Time}} = \frac{240}{8} = 30 \text{ km / hr}$$

In Second Case : Speed $= 30 \times 1\frac{1}{2} = 45$ km/hr and Distance = 540 km

$$\therefore \quad \text{Time} = \frac{\text{Distance}}{\text{Speed}} = \frac{540}{45} = 12 \text{ hours.}$$

Example 3. *A train covers a distance of 13 km in 12 minutes. If its speed is decreased by 5 km/hr then what time it will take to cover the same distance?*

Solution. *In First Case* :

$$\text{Speed} = \frac{13}{12/60} = 65 \text{ km / hr}$$

In Second Case : Speed = 65 – 5 = 60 km/hr
Distance = 13 km.

$$\text{Time} = \frac{\text{Distance}}{\text{Speed}} = \frac{13}{60} \text{ hour} = 13 \text{ minutes.}$$

Example 4. *In what time a 100 m long train moving with a speed of 30 km/hr crosses a man standing beside the railway line ?*

Soultion. Speed of the train = 30 km/hr

$$= 30 \times \frac{5}{18} = \frac{25}{3} \text{ m / s}$$

$$\text{Time} = \frac{\text{Distance}}{\text{Speed}} = \frac{100}{25/3} = 12 \text{ seconds.}$$

Example 5. *The lengths of a platform and a train are 130 m and 70 m respectively. If the speed of the train is 36 km/hr then how much time will it take to cross the platform ?*

Solution. ∵ The train crosses the platform.

∴ Total distance covered by the train

= 130 m + 70 m = 200 m.

Speed of the train = 36 km/hr

$= 36 \times \frac{5}{18} = 10$ m/s

∴ Required time $= \frac{200}{10} = 20$ seconds.

Example 6. *A train crosses a 300 m long platform in 20 seconds and crosses a pole in 10 seconds. What is the length of the train ?*

Solution. Let the length of the train = x metres.

In First Case : Distance covered by the train

= $(300 + x)$ metres

Time = 20 seconds.

∴ Speed of the train $= \frac{300+x}{20}$ m/s

In Second Case : Speed of the train $= \frac{x}{10}$ m/s

$\therefore \frac{300+x}{20} = \frac{x}{10}$

$\Rightarrow 3000 + 10x = 20x \quad \Rightarrow \quad 10x = 3000$

$\Rightarrow x = \frac{3000}{10} = 300$ m

∴ Length of the train = 300 m.

Example 7. *A boat covers a distance of 35 km in 5 hours in the direction of flow and it covers the same distance in 7 hours in opposite direction of flow. What is the speed of boat in still water ?*

Solution. In the direction of flow :

Speed of the boat $= \frac{35}{5} = 7$ km/hr

∴ Speed of the boat in still water + speed of flow = 7 km/hr

In opposite direction of flow :

Speed of the boat $= \frac{35}{7} = 5$ km / hr

∴ Speed of the boat in still water – speed of flow = 5 km/hr

∴ 2 × Speed of the boat in still water

= 7 + 5 = 12 km/hr

∴ Speed of the boat in still water

$= \frac{12}{2} = 6$ km / hr.

Example 8. *Two trains are running from two stations A and B at the speed of 22 km/hr and 38 km/hr towards each other at the same time. If the distance between two stations A and B is 1800 km then after how much time they will meet each other ?*

Solution. ∵ Two trains are running towards each other.

∴ Resulting speed = 22 + 38 = 60 km/hr

Time $= \frac{\text{Distance}}{\text{Speed}} = \frac{1800}{60} = 30$ hours

∴ Required time = 30 hours.

EXERCISE

In the following questions four answer choices are given in which one is correct. Choose the correct answer.

1. A train crosses a pole in 10 seconds. If the length of the train is 150 m, then what is the speed of the train ?
   A. 54 km/hr B. 60 km/hr
   C. 72 km/hr D. 45 km/hr
2. A train 160 m long crosses a platform of 160 m length in 16 seconds. What is the speed of the train ?
   A. 68 km/hr B. 70 km/hr
   C. 72 km/hr D. 62 km/hr
3. Two trains are running towards each other at the speed of 40 km/hr and 30 km/hr respectively on parallel lines. If the distance between two trains is 105 km, then after how much time they will meet each other ?
   A. $1\frac{1}{3}$ hr B. $1\frac{1}{2}$ hr
   C. 2 hr D. $1\frac{1}{4}$ hr

4. A train whose length is 120 m, crosses a bridge in 12 seconds at a speed of 60 km/hr. What is the length of the bridge ?
A. 75 m B. 80 m
C. 85 m D. 90 m

5. A boat in the direction of flow covers a distance of 60 km in 4 hours. If speed of the boat is double the speed of flow then how much distance it covers in 2 hours opposite the flow ?
A. 10 km B. 8 km
C. 11 km D. 15 km

6. Two men P and Q start a journey from same place at a speed of 3 km/hr and $3\frac{1}{2}$ km/hr respectively. If they move in same direction then what is the distance between them after 4 hours?
A 3 km B. $2\frac{1}{2}$ km
C. 2 km D. $3\frac{1}{2}$ km

7. A man covers a distance of 45 km in 9 hours. If his speed is increased 3 times then in how much time he covers a distance of 60 km ?
A. 4 hr B. 4 hr 10 minutes
C. $5\frac{1}{2}$ hr D. 5 hr 40 minutes

8. A 500 m long goods train crosses a platform in 36 seconds. If the length of the platform is 220 m then what is the speed of the goods train in km/hr ?
A. 60 B. 72
C. 80 D. 85

9. The length of a train and a platform is equal. The train at the speed of 90 km/hr crosses the platform in 1 minute. What is the length of platform ?
A. 750 m B. 690 m
C. 760 m D. 810 m

10. A man covered a certain distance of one side by cycle and other side by scooter in 2 hours 20 minutes. If he had covered the total distance by cycle then time consumed was 3 hours 30 minutes. In what time he can cover the total distance by scooter ?
A. 1 hr 15 minutes B. 1 hr 10 minutes
C. 1 hr 40 minutes D. 2 hr 5 minutes

11. A train 180 m long is running at a speed of 42 km/hr. In what time it crosses a man going at a speed of 6 km/hr in the same direction ?
A. 11 seconds B. 21 seconds
C. 23 seconds D. 18 seconds

12. A man travels a distance of 6 km at a speed of 4 km/hr and a distance of 4 km at a speed of 3 km/hr. What is his average speed in total journey ?
A. $3\frac{9}{17}$ km/hr B. $4\frac{9}{17}$ km/hr
C. $2\frac{1}{17}$ km/hr D. $3\frac{1}{17}$ km / hr

13. A man travels a distance at a speed of 8 km/hr and returns at a speed of 6 km/hr. If he takes $3\frac{1}{2}$ hr time in total journey, then how much distance he covered ?
A. 25 km B. 28 km
C. 24 km D. 30 km

14. The circumference of a motor wheel is $4\frac{2}{7}$ m. The wheel completes7 round in 4 seconds. What is the speed (km/hr) of the motor?
A. 22 B. 27
C. 30 D. 31

15. A certain distance is covered at a certain speed. If half the distance is covered in double time then what is the ratio of two speeds ?
A. 4 : 1 B. 4 : 3
C. 3 : 1 D. 1 : 4

16. The speed of a boat in still water is 8 km/hr. The boat takes equal time to cover a distance of 30 km in the direction of flow and 18 km against the flow. What is the speed of flow ?
A. $2\frac{1}{3}$ km/hr B. 2 km/hr
C. $2\frac{1}{4}$ km/hr D. $3\frac{1}{4}$ km/hr

17. A train starts from Delhi at 6.00 A.M. and reaches Meerut at 10 A.M. The other train starts from Meerut at 8 A.M. and reaches Delhi at 11 : 30 A.M. If the distance between Delhi and Meerut is 200 km, then at what time the two trains meet each other ?
A. 8 hours 56 mts B. 8 hours 46 mts
C. 7 hours 56 mts D. 8 hours 30 mts

EXPLANATORY ANSWERS

1. A : ∵ The train crosses the pole. So in given time it covers the distance equal to its length.

∴ Speed of the train

$= \frac{\text{Distance}}{\text{Time}} = \frac{150}{10} = 15 \text{ m/s}$

$= 15 \times \frac{18}{5} = 54 \text{ km/hr}$.

2. C : ∵ The train crosses the platform

∴ Distance covered by the train = Length of the train + Length of the plateform

= 160 + 160 = 320 m

Time = 16 seconds

∴ Speed of the train $= \frac{320}{16} = 20 \text{ m/s}$

$= 20 \times \frac{18}{5} = 72 \text{ km/hr}$.

3. B : ∵ Two trains are moving towards each other

∴ Resulting speed = 40 + 30 = 70 km/hr

Distance = 105 km

Time $= \frac{105}{70} = 1\frac{1}{2}$ hours

∴ Trains meet each other after $1\frac{1}{2}$ hours.

4. B : Let length of the bridge = x metres

Distance covered by train = Length of the train + Length of the bridge

= $(120 + x)$ metres

Time = 12 seconds

Speed $= \frac{120+x}{12}$ m/s $= \frac{120+x}{12} \times \frac{18}{5}$ km/hr

But speed of train = 60 km/hr (Given)

∴ $\frac{120+x}{12} \times \frac{18}{5} = 60$

⇒ $120 + x = \frac{12 \times 5 \times 60}{18} = 200$

⇒ $x = 200 - 120 = 80$

∴ Length of the bridge = 80 m.

5. A : In the direction of flow :

Speed of the boat $= \frac{60}{4} = 15 \text{ km/hr}$

∴ Speed of the boat in still water + speed of the flow = 15 km/hr

According to problem,

Speed of the boat in still water = 2 × speed of the flows

∴ 3 × speed of the flow = 15 km/hr

∴ Speed of the flow $= \frac{15}{3} = 5 \text{ km/hr}$

∴ Speed of the boat in still water = 15 – 5 = 10 km/hr.

Against the flow :

Distance covered by boat in 2 hours

= (speed of the boat in still water – speed of the flow) × 2

= (10 – 5) × 2 = 5 × 2 = 10 km.

6. C : ∵ Both men travel in same direction.

∴ Resulting speed $= 3\frac{1}{2} - 3 = \frac{1}{2}$ km/hr

∴ Distance between them after 4 hours

$= \frac{1}{2} \times 4 = 2$ km.

7. A : *In First Case* : Speed of the man

$= \frac{45}{9} = 5 \text{ km/hr}$.

In Second Case : Speed of the man

= 5 × 3 = 15 km/hr

Distance = 60 km

Time $= \frac{60}{15} = 4$ hours.

8. B : ∵ Goods train crosses the platform.

∴ Distance covered by train

= Length of the train + length of the platform

= 500 + 220 = 720 m

Time = 36 seconds

∴ Speed of the goods train

$= \frac{720}{36} = 20 \text{ m/s} = 20 \times \frac{18}{5} = 72 \text{ km/hr}$.

9. A : Let length of the train and platform be x m and x m respectively.

∴ Distance covered by train = $x + x = 2x$ m

Time = 1 minute = 60 seconds

$\therefore$ Speed of the train

$$= \frac{2x}{60} = \frac{x}{30} \text{ m/s} = \frac{x}{30} \times \frac{18}{5} \text{ km/hr}$$

But speed of the train = 90 km/hr (Given)

$$\therefore \quad \frac{3x}{25} = 90 \quad \Rightarrow \quad x = \frac{25 \times 9}{3} = 750$$

$\therefore$ Length of the platform = 750 m.

10. B : Let distance of one side = x km

Let speed of cycle and scooter be V_1, V_2 km/hr respectively.

$$\text{Time in first case} = \frac{x}{V_1} \text{ hr}$$

$$\text{Time in second case} = \frac{x}{V_2} \text{ hr}$$

$$\text{Total time} = 2 \text{ hour } 20 \text{ mts} = 2\frac{1}{3} \text{ hr}$$

$$\frac{x}{V_1} + \frac{x}{V_2} = 2\frac{1}{3} = \frac{7}{3} \qquad ...(i)$$

According to problem,

If he travels total distance by cycle, then

$$2 \times \frac{x}{V_1} = 3\frac{1}{2} = \frac{7}{2}$$

$$\therefore \quad \frac{x}{V_1} = \frac{7}{4}$$

By putting the value of $\frac{x}{V_1}$ in eqation (*i*)

$$\frac{7}{4} + \frac{x}{V_2} = \frac{7}{3}$$

$$\Rightarrow \quad \frac{x}{V_2} = \frac{7}{3} - \frac{7}{4} = \frac{7}{12}$$

If he travels total distance by scooter then

$$\text{Time} = 2 \times \frac{x}{V_2} = 2 \times \frac{7}{12} = \frac{7}{6} = 1 \text{ hour } 10 \text{ mts}.$$

11. D : $\because$ Train and man are travelling in same direction

$\therefore$ Resulting speed = 42 – 6 = 36 km/hr

$$= 36 \times \frac{5}{18} = 10 \text{ m/s}$$

Distance covered = 180 m

$$\therefore \quad \text{Time} = \frac{\text{Distance}}{\text{Speed}} = \frac{180}{10} = 18 \text{ seconds.}$$

12. A : Time required to cover a distance of 6 km at a speed of 4 km/hr $= \frac{6}{4} = \frac{3}{2}$ hr

Time required to cover a distance of 4 km at a speed of 3 km/hr

$$= \frac{4}{3} \text{ hr}$$

$$\text{Total time} = \frac{3}{2} + \frac{4}{3} = \frac{17}{6} \text{ hr}$$

Total Distance = 6 + 4 = 10 km

$\therefore$ Average speed

$$= \frac{10}{17/6} = \frac{10 \times 6}{17} = \frac{60}{17} = 3\frac{9}{17} \text{ km/hr}.$$

13. C : Let one side distance = x km

Time required to cover a distance of x km at a speed of 8 km/hr

$$= \frac{x}{8} \text{ hr}$$

Time required to cover a distance of x km at a speed of 6 km/hr

$$= \frac{x}{6} \text{ hr}$$

$$\text{Total time} = 3\frac{1}{2} \text{ hr (Given)}$$

$$\therefore \quad \frac{x}{8} + \frac{x}{6} = \frac{7}{2}$$

$$\Rightarrow \quad \frac{7x}{24} = \frac{7}{2} \quad \Rightarrow \quad x = 12$$

$\therefore$ Total disatnce = 2 × 12 = 24 km.

14. B : Circumference of the wheel $= 4\frac{2}{7} = \frac{30}{7}$ m

$\therefore$ Distance covered by the wheel in one round

$$= \frac{30}{7} \text{ m}$$

$\therefore$ Distance covered by the wheel in 7 rounds

$$= \frac{30 \times 7}{7} = 30 \text{ m}$$

According to problem, this distance is covered in 4 seconds.

$\therefore$ Speed $= \frac{\text{Distance}}{\text{Time}} = \frac{30}{4}$ m / s $= \frac{30}{4} \times \frac{18}{5}$

$= 27$ km / hr

$\therefore$ Speed of the motor is 27 km/hr.

15. A : Let distance $= x$ and speed $= V_1$

$\therefore$ time $(t) = \frac{x}{V_1}$ $\Rightarrow$ $V_1 = \frac{x}{t}$

According to problem,

Distance $= \frac{x}{2}$ and time $= 2t$

$\therefore$ Speed $(V_2) = \frac{x/2}{2t} = \frac{x}{4t}$

$\therefore$ $\frac{V_1}{V_2} = \frac{x/t}{x/4t} = \frac{4}{1}$

$\Rightarrow$ $V_1 : V_2 = 4 : 1$

16. B : Let speed of the flow $= x$ km/hr

In direction of flow

Speed of the boat

= (Speed in still water + speed of flow)

$= (8 + x)$ km/hr

Time required to cover a distance of 30 km

$= \left(\frac{30}{8+x}\right)$ hr

Against the flow :

Speed of the boat

= Speed of the boat in still water – speed of flow

$= (8 - x)$ km/hr

$\therefore$ Time required to cover a distance of 18 km

$= \left(\frac{18}{8-x}\right)$ hr

According to problem, time in both cases is equal.

$\therefore$ $\frac{30}{8+x} = \frac{18}{8-x}$

$\Rightarrow$ $48x = 96$ $\Rightarrow$ $x = 2$

$\therefore$ Speed of the flow = 2 km/hr.

17. A : $\because$ Time taken by first train from Delhi to Meerut

$= 10 - 6 = 4$ hours

$\therefore$ Speed of the first train $= \frac{200}{4} = 50$ km / hr

Time taken by second train from Meerut to Delhi

$= 11.30 - 8 = 3\frac{1}{2} = \frac{7}{2}$ hr

$\therefore$ Speed of the second train $= \frac{200}{7/2} = \frac{400}{7}$ km / hr

Because first trains starts 2 hours early than second train

$\therefore$ Distance covered by first train in 2 hours

$= 50 \times 2 = 100$ km

$\therefore$ Remaining distance $= 200 - 100 = 100$ km

Resulting speed $= 50 + \frac{400}{7} = \frac{750}{7}$ km / hr

$\therefore$ After 8 hours, time required to meet the train

$= \frac{\text{Distance}}{\text{Speed}} = \frac{100}{750/7}$ hr

$= \frac{700}{750}$ hr $= \frac{14}{15}$ hr $= 56$ minutes

Therefore the train will meet at 8.56.

13

DISCOUNT

Discount is the reduction or an allowance made from the amount of a bill in lieu of its immediate cash payment. The reduction made in consideration of making immediate payment is called discount or *true discount* (T.D.). The immediate cash payment is called *present worth* (P.W.) or present value.

Important Formulae

(i) Sum Due (S.D.) = P.W. + T.D.

(ii) P.W. = S.D. – T.D.

$$= \frac{100 \times \text{S.D.}}{100 + (\text{T} \times \text{R})} \text{ at Simple Interest}$$

$$= \frac{\text{S.D.}}{\left(1 + \frac{\text{R}}{100}\right)^n} \text{ at Compound Interest}$$

(iii) T.D. = S.D. – P.D.

(iv) T.D. on Sum Due = Interest on P.W.

(v) $\text{T.D.} = \frac{\text{S.D.} \times \text{R} \times \text{T}}{100 + (\text{R} \times \text{T})}$

(vi) $\text{T} = \frac{100 \times \text{T.D.}}{\text{P.W.} \times \text{R}}$

(vii) $\text{R} = \frac{100 \times \text{T.D}}{\text{P.W.} \times \text{T}}$

Example 1. Find the present worth and true discount on Rs. 6000 due 2 years at 10% per annum S.I.

Solution: $\text{P.W.} = \frac{100 \times 6000}{100 + (10 \times 2)} = \frac{100 \times 6000}{120}$

= Rs. 5000

Hence, T.D. = 6000 – 5000

= Rs. 1000

Example 2. Find the present worth of a bill of Rs. 6760 due 2 years hence at 4% C.I. Calculate T.D.

Solution: $\text{P.W.} = \frac{\text{A}}{\left(1 + \frac{\text{R}}{100}\right)^n} = \frac{6760}{\left(1 + \frac{4}{100}\right)^2}$

$= \frac{6760 \times 25 \times 25}{26 \times 26} = \text{Rs. } 6250$

T.D. = S.D. – P.W.

= Rs. 6760 – Rs. 6250 = Rs. 510

EXERCISE

1. Find the present worth of Rs. 264 due in 2 years hence at 5% per annum.

A. Rs. 200 B. Rs. 240
C. Rs. 250 D. Rs. 280

2. Find the true discount on a bill for Rs. 1270 due 7 months hence at 10% per annum.

A. Rs. 10 B. Rs. 35
C. Rs. 70 D. Rs. 170

3. What is the sum due 15 months hence whose present worth at 4% is Rs. 1000?

A. Rs. 1050 B. Rs. 1100
C. Rs. 1120 D. Rs. 1200

4. What is the rate of interest when the P.W. of Rs. 1245 due 15 months hence is Rs. 1200?

A. 3% B. $2\frac{1}{2}$%
C. 4% D. 5%

5. The sum due 219 days hence whose present worth at $5\frac{1}{2}$% of Rs. 400 is :

A. Rs. 300
B. Rs. 312
C. Rs. 390
D. Rs. 413.20

6. What is the rate of interest when the P.W. of Rs. 8175 due in 5 months Rs. 8000?

A. 4% B. 5%

C. $5\frac{1}{4}$% D. $5\frac{1}{2}$%

7. If the interest on Rs. 50 at $4\frac{1}{2}$% be equal to the discount of Rs. 59 for the same time and at the same rate when is the latter sum due?

A. 3 years B. 4 years

C. 5 years D. 2 years

8. What is the rate of interest when the present worth of Rs. 108.15 due in 146 days is Rs. 105?

A. 5% B. $6\frac{1}{2}$%

C. $7\frac{1}{2}$% D. 10%

9. The interest on a certain sum of money is Rs. 67.20 and the discount on the same sum of money for the same time and at the same rate is Rs. 60. What is the sum?

A. Rs. 560 B. Rs. 500

C. Rs. 460 D. Rs. 400

10. The true discount on a certain sum at a certain rate for 4 years is Rs. 100 on the same sum at the same rate and time, interest is Rs. 120. Find the sum.

A. Rs. 500 B. Rs. 400

C. Rs. 600 D. Rs. 400

EXPLANATORY ANSWERS

1. B: $\text{P.W.} = \text{Rs.}\frac{100\times 264}{100+5\times 2} = \text{Rs.}\frac{100\times 264}{110}$

$= \text{Rs. } 240$

2. C: $\text{T.D.} = \frac{1270\times 10\times 7}{\left(100+10\times\frac{7}{12}\right)12} = \frac{1270\times 10\times 7}{1270}$

$= \text{Rs. } 70$

3. A: $\text{T.D.} = 1000\times\frac{15}{12}\times\frac{4}{100} = \text{Rs. } 50$

Hence, S.D. = 1000 + 50 = Rs. 1050

4. A: T.D. = 1245 – 1200 = Rs. 45; hence,

$R = \frac{45\times 100\times 12}{1200\times 15} = 3\%$

5. D: $T = \frac{219}{365} = \frac{3}{5}$ year

$\text{T.D.} = 400\times\frac{11}{2\times 100}\times\frac{3}{5} = \text{Rs. } 13.20$

Hence, S.D. = 400 + 13.20 = Rs. 413.20

6. C: T.D. = Rs. 8175 – Rs. 8000 = Rs. 175

$R = \frac{175\times 100\times 12}{8000\times 5} = 5\frac{1}{4}\%$

7. B: Here, $\frac{50\times 9\times T}{100\times 2} = \frac{59\times 9\times T}{\left[100+\left(\frac{9}{2}.T\right)\right]2}$

$\Rightarrow 200 + 9T = 236$

$\Rightarrow 9T = 36 \qquad \therefore T = 4 \text{ years}$

8. C: $T = \frac{146}{365} = \frac{2}{5}$ year

B.D. = 108.15 – 105 = Rs. 3.15

$R = \frac{3.15\times 100\times 5}{105\times 2} = 7\frac{1}{2}\%$

9. A: $\because$ Interest on Sum – T.D. = Interest on T.D.

$\therefore$ Rs. 67.20 – Rs. 60 = Interest on Rs. 60

Now, $\text{Rs.}7\frac{1}{5}$ = Interest on Rs. 60

$\therefore \text{Rs.}67\frac{1}{5} = \text{Interest on } \frac{60}{7\frac{1}{5}}\times 67\frac{1}{5}$

Hence, the required sum $= \frac{60\times 5}{36}\times\frac{336}{5}$

= Rs. 560

10. C: Rs. 120 – Rs. 100 = Interest on Rs. 100

$\Rightarrow$ Rs. 20 = Interest on Rs. 100

Hence, Rs. 120 = Interest on $\frac{100}{20}\times 120$

= Rs. 600

Hence, sum = Rs. 600

14

PARTNERSHIP

When two or more than two persons agree to invest money to run a business jointly, this association or deal is called *partnership* and those who invest money are called *pertners.* The total investment is called the *capital.*

Kind of partners: There are two kinds of partners.

1. Working or active partner : When a partner devotes his time for the business in addition to invest his money, he is called a working partner. With mutual agreement, the active partners get some fixed percentage of profit as *working allowance.*

2. Sleeping or non-active partner : A partner who simply invests money, but does not attend to the business is called a sleeping partner.

Kind of partnership :

(i) **Simple partnership :** If the capitals of several partners are invested for the same period, it is called a simple partnership.

(ii) **Compound or complex partnership :** If the capitals of the partners are invested for different intervals of time, the partnership is called compound or complex.

Example 1: If A and B enter into a partnership, A contributes Rs. 7000 and B contributes Rs. 10000. If the profit at the end of the year amounts to Rs. 7310, what would be the share of B in the profit?

Solution: Ratio of their capitals

= 7000 : 10000 = 7 : 10

Hence, share of B = $\frac{10}{17} \times 7310$

= Rs. 4300

Example 2: A and B started a business with the investment of Rs. 4000 and Rs. 6000 respectively. In what ratio the profit earned at the end of the year will be distributed between them?

Solution: $\because$ Ratio of the capitals of A and B

= 4000 : 6000 = 2 : 3

$\therefore$ profit of A and B will be in the ratio of 2 : 3

EXERCISE

1. A and B started a business with the investment of Rs. 80000 and Rs. 60000 respectively. At the end of the year total profit in the business will be divided between them in the ratio of :
   A. 2 : 3 B. 3 : 4
   C. 2 : 1 D. 4 : 3

2. A and B started a business in partnership with the investment of Rs. 4000 and Rs. 6000 respectively. If at the end of the year total profit is Rs. 2250, what will each of them get?
   A. Rs. 900, Rs. 1350
   B. Rs. 800, Rs. 1450
   C. Rs. 1000, Rs. 1250
   D. Rs. 1200, Rs. 1050

3. Sonu, Monu and Mohit together start a business with the investment of Rs. 1800, Rs. 1500 and Rs. 1600 respectively. If at the end of the year, Monu gains a profit of Rs. 900 the total profit in the business is :
   A. Rs. 2880 B. Rs. 2940
   C. Rs. 3200 D. Rs. 3240

4. Omdutt started a business with a capital of Rs. 8000. After six months, Sanjay joined him with investment of some capital. If at the end of the year each of them gets equal amount as profit, how much did Sanjay invest in the business?
   A. Rs. 18000 B. Rs. 17500
   C. Rs. 16000 D. Rs. 16500

5. A, B and C buy a farm for Rs. 100000. A contributes Rs. 40000 in it. They sell it, and from the profit B gets Rs. 2750 and C gets Rs. 1750. What would be the profit of A?

A. Rs. 2780 B. Rs. 3000
C. Rs. 3280 D. Rs. 2785

6. A and B jointly invest Rs. 2100 and Rs. 3100 respectively in a firm. A is an active partner and hence he gets 25% of the profit separately. If their business yields them total Rs. 1040 as profit, what will be the gain of each of them?

A. Rs. 415, Rs. 625
B. Rs. 575, Rs. 465
C. Rs. 515, Rs. 525
D. Rs. 560, Rs. 480

7. Two partners invested Rs. 12500 and Rs. 8500 respectively in a business and decided that 60% of the profit incurred from the business will be equally divided between them while remaining profit will be assumed as interest on their capitals. If one of the partners gets Rs. 300 more profit than the other, what is the total profit in the business?

A. Rs. 3937.50 B. Rs. 4940.50
C. Rs. 3936.50 D. Rs. 4156

8. Neeraj and Birju are partners in a business. They divide between them the profit incurred in the business in such a proportion that $\frac{2}{5}$th portion of the profit gained by Neeraj is equal to $\frac{1}{3}$rd portion of the profit gained by Birju. If total profit in the business is Rs. 1210, find the profit earned by Birju.

A. Rs. 780 B. Rs. 660
C. Rs. 680 D. Rs. 590

9. A, B and C together took under lease a pasture ground for Rs. 888. If in this pasture ground A put his 20 sheep out to graze for 2½ months, B put his 30 sheep out to graze for 4 months and C put his 36 sheep out to graze for 3½ months, find the lease amount paid by each of them.

A. Rs. 205, Rs. 315, Rs. 378
B. Rs. 150, Rs. 360, Rs. 378
C. Rs. 170, Rs. 360, Rs. 358
D. Rs. 228, Rs. 360, Rs. 300

10. A, B and C started a business with the investment of Rs. 5000, Rs, 6000 and Rs. 4000 respectively. A is an active partner and therefore he gets 30% of the profit separately. Rest of the profit is divided in the ratio of their capitals. If at the end of year, A's profit is Rs. 200 more than the sum of the profits made by B and C, find the profit made by each of them.

A. Rs. 1620, Rs. 1242, Rs. 1178
B. Rs. 1720, Rs. 1252, Rs. 1228
C. Rs. 1510, Rs. 1187, Rs. 1133
D. Rs. 1600, Rs. 840, Rs. 560

EXPLANATORY ANSWERS

1. D: Ratio between their profits
$= 80000 : 60000 = 4 : 3$

2. A: Ratio of capitals of A and B
$= 4000 : 6000 = 2 : 3$

A's share in the profit $= \frac{2}{5} \times 2250 = $ Rs. 900

B's share in the profit $= \frac{3}{5} \times 2250$
= Rs. 1350

3. B: Ratio of their capitals $= 1800 : 1500 : 1600$
$= 18 : 15 : 16$

Sum of proportionals $= 18 + 15 + 16 = 49$
Monu's profit = Rs. 900

$\therefore$ Total profit in the business $= \frac{900}{15} \times 49$
= Rs. 2940

4. C: Investment by Omdutt for 1 month
= Rs. 8000×12 = Rs. 96000
Let Sanjay invested Rs. x for 6 months
$\therefore$ Capital of Sanjay for 1 month
= Rs. $x \times 6$ = Rs. $6x$
Now, $6x = 96000$ $\therefore$ x = Rs. 16000

5. B: Here, ratio of capitals of A and (B + C)

= 40000 : 60000 = 2 : 3

Profit of (B + C) = 2750 + 1750 = Rs. 4500

Hence, A's profit = $\frac{4500}{3} \times 2 =$ Rs. 3000

6. B: Separate profit for A = $\frac{1040 \times 25}{100} =$ Rs. 260

Remaining profit = Rs. (1040 – 260)

= Rs. 780

Ratio of capitals of A and B = 2100 : 3100

= 21 : 31

A's profit = $\frac{21}{52} \times 780$ = Rs. 315

B's profit = $\frac{31}{52} \times 780$ = Rs. 465

Total profit of A = Rs. (315 + 260)

= Rs. 575

Therefore A and B will make profit of Rs. 575 and Rs. 465 respectively.

7. A: Ratio of their capitals = 12500 : 8500

= 25 : 17

Hence, sum of their ratios = 25 + 17 = 42

and difference of ratios = 25 – 17 = 8

Now total profit taken as interest

$= \frac{300}{8} \times 42$ = Rs. 1575

Hence, total profit in the business

$= \frac{100}{40} \times 1575 =$ Rs. 3937.50

8. B: Let shares of Neeraj and Birju in profit are Rs. x and Rs. y respectively; then,

$\frac{2}{5}x = \frac{1}{3}y \qquad \therefore \quad x : y = 5 : 6$

Hence, share of Birju = $\frac{6}{11} \times 1210 =$ Rs. 660

9. B: Ratio of their shares = (20 × 5/2) : (30 × 4) : (36 × 7/2) = 25 : 60 : 63

Sum of proportionals = 25 + 60 + 63 = 148

Total lease amount = Rs. 888

∴ Amount paid by A = $\frac{25}{148} \times 888 =$ Rs. 150

Amount paid by B = $\frac{60}{148} \times 888$ = Rs. 360

Amount paid by C = $\frac{63}{148} \times 888$ = Rs. 378

10. D: Ratio of capitals of A, B and C

= 5000 : 6000 : 4000 = 5 : 6 : 4

Let total profit in the business = Rs. x; then

$\frac{30x}{100} + \frac{5}{15} \times \frac{70x}{100} - \frac{(6+4)}{15} \times \frac{70x}{100} = 200$

$\Rightarrow \frac{8x}{15} - \frac{7x}{15} = 200 \quad \therefore x =$ Rs. 3000

Hence, A's profit = $\frac{8 \times 3000}{15}$ = Rs. 1600

B's profit = $\frac{6}{15} \times \frac{7 \times 3000}{10}$ = Rs. 840;

C's profit = $\frac{4}{15} \times \frac{7 \times 3000}{10}$ = Rs. 560

15

MIXTURE AND ALLIGATION

Alligation deals with calculation of values or properties of a mixture. Alligation is the rule that enables us—

(1) to find the proportion in which the two or more ingredients at the given prices must be mixed to yield a mixture at the given price. This is termed as "Alligation Alternate".

(2) to calculate the average or mean value of a mixture when the prices of two or more ingredients which are to be mixed together and proportion in which they are to be mixed are given. This is termed as "Alligation Medial".

1. Rule of Alligation:

$$\frac{\text{A of Cheap mixture}}{\text{A of Dearer mixture}} = \frac{\text{CP of Dearer – Mean Price}}{\text{Mean Price – CP of Cheaper}}$$

Here cost price of unit quantity of the mixture is called the *Mean Price*.

The above rule may be represented schematically as under:

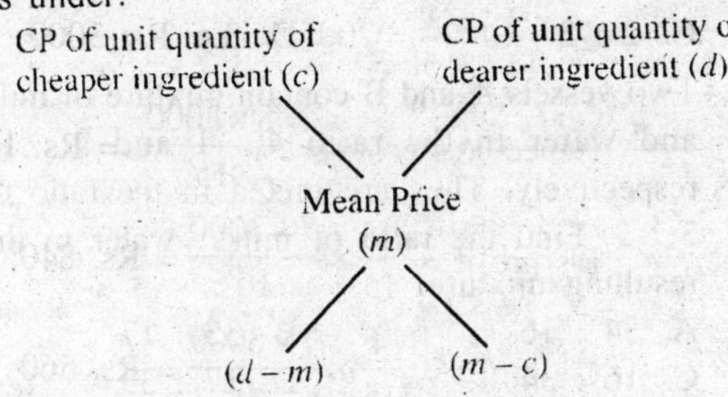

(Cheaper quantity) : (Dearer quantity) = $(d - m)$: $(m - c)$

This relationship is very helpful in solving problems on mixture involving percentage values, rates, prices, speeds etc.

2. m gm of sugar solution has x % sugar in it. To increase the sugar content in the solution to y %,

quantity of sugar need to be added $= \dfrac{m(y-x)}{100-y}$.

3. A vessel contains x litres of liquid A. y litres are withdrawn and replaced by liquid B. Next y litres of the mixture is withdrawn and again replaced by liquid B.

This operation is repeated n times.

$$\frac{\text{Quantity of liquid A left after } n\text{th operation}}{\text{Whole quantity of liquid A initially present}}$$

$$= \left(\frac{x-y}{x}\right)^n \text{ or } \left(1-\frac{y}{x}\right)^n$$

Example 2: Find the quantities of two types of wheat, one @ Rs. 6 per kg and the other @ Rs. 4 per kg. to get 20 kgs. of wheat mixture worth Rs. 4.5 per kg.

Solution:

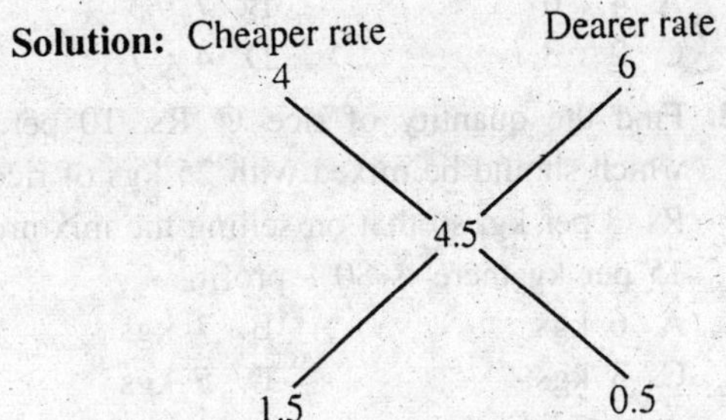

$$\frac{\text{Quantity of cheaper wheat}}{\text{Quantity of dearer wheat}} = \frac{1.5}{0.5} = \frac{3}{1}$$

Quantity of cheaper wheat

$$= \frac{3}{3+1} \times 20 = 15 \text{ kgs}$$

Quantity of dearer wheat

$= \frac{1}{3+1} \times 20 = 5$ kgs.

Example 1: In what proportion water be mixed with pure milk in order to make a profit of 20% by selling it at cost price?

Solution: Let cost price of pure milk be Re. 1 per litre.

The SP of mixture = Re. 1 per litre

Profit = 20%

So, CP of 1 litre of mixture

$= \text{Rs.}\left(1 \times \frac{100}{120}\right) = \text{Re. } \frac{5}{6}$

We assume that CP of 1 litre of water is zero.

Using the rule of alligation on 1 litre,

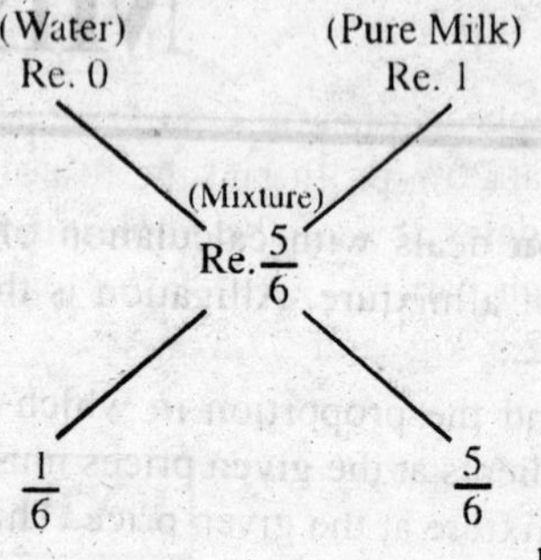

$$\frac{\text{Quantity of water}}{\text{Quantity of pure milk}} = \frac{\frac{1}{6}}{\frac{5}{6}} = \frac{1}{5}$$

or, Ratio of water to pure milk in the mixture = 1 : 5.

EXERCISE

1. In what proportion must tea at Rs. 62 per kg be mixed with tea at Rs. 72 per kg in order to obtain the mixture worth Rs. 65 per kg?

A. 4 : 6 B. 7 : 3
C. 2 : 3 D. 4 : 7

2. Find the quantity of rice @ Rs. 10 per kg. which should be mixed with 25 kgs of rice @ Rs. 8 per kg, so that on selling the mixture @ 15 per kg there is 80% profit.

A. 6 kgs B. 7 kgs
C. 3 kgs D. 5 kgs

3. A shopkeeper buys 26 kgs of milk @ Rs. 16 per kg. He also buys from another source an inferior quality of milk @ Rs. 10 per kg. How much quantity of the latter should he buy to mix it with the former so that he can sell the mixture @ Rs. 14 per kg without making any loss?

A. 13 kgs B. 12 kgs
C. 14 kgs D. 16 kgs

4. Two vessels A and B contain milk and water in the ratio 7 : 5 and 17 : 7 respectively. In what ratio mixtures from two vessels should be mixed to get a new mixture containing milk and water in the ratio 5 : 3?

A. 1 : 2 B. 2 : 1
C. 2 : 3 D. 3 : 2

5. Two vessels A and B contain mixture of milk and water in the ratio 4 : 1 and 9 : 11 respectively. They are mixed in the ratio of 3 : 2. Find the ratio of milk : water in the resulting mixture.

A. 34 : 16 B. 33 : 17
C. 16 : 34 D. 17 : 33

6. A person has two solutions of sugar with 30% and 50% concentration respectively. In what proportion should he mix two solutions to get 45% concentration in the resulting mixture?

A. 1 : 3 B. 3 : 1
C. 2 : 3 D. 3 : 2

7. 6 litres of milk and water mixture has 75% milk in it. How much milk should be added to the mixture to make it 90% pure?

A. 8 litres B. 9 litres
C. 10 litres D. 12 litres

8. In what ratio must water be added to spirit to gain 25% by selling it at cost price?

A. 1 : 4 B. 4 : 1

C. 3 : 4 D. 4 : 3

9. A shopkeeper has 50 kgs of rice. He sells a part of it at 20% profit and the rest at 40% profit. If he gains 25% on the whole, find the quantity of each part.

A. 12.5 kgs and 37.5 kgs

B. 37.5 kgs and 12.5 kgs

C. 23.5 kgs and 21.5 kgs

D. 21.5 kgs and 23.5 kgs

10. A shopkeeper has 100 kgs of tea. He sells a part of it at 20% profit and the rest at 5% loss. If his overall profit is 10%, find the quantity for each part.

A. 20 kgs B. 25 kgs

C. 30 kgs D. 40 kgs

EXPLANATORY ANSWERS

1. B:

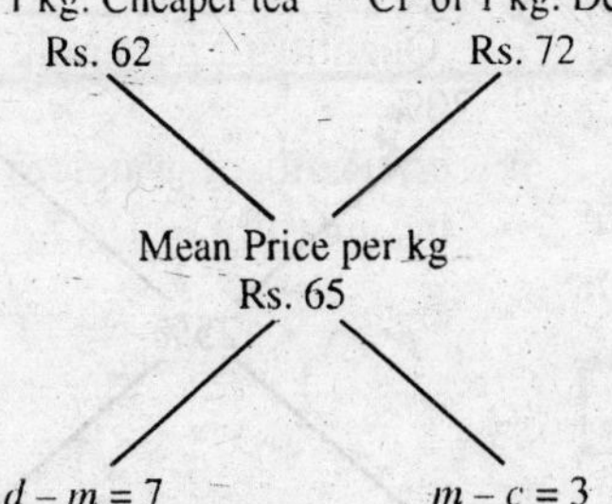

Using Alligation rule,

$$\frac{\text{Quantity of cheaper tea}}{\text{Quantity of dearer tea}} = \frac{d-m}{m-c} = \frac{7}{3}$$

Therefore, they must be mixed in the ratio of 7 : 3.

2. D: Cost price of the mixture $= 15 \times \frac{100}{180}$

$= \text{Rs. } \frac{25}{3}$ per kg

$$\frac{\text{Quantity of rice @ Rs. 8 per kg}}{\text{Quantity of rice @ Rs.10 per kg}} = \frac{5/3}{5/3} = \frac{5}{1}$$

Quantity of rice @ Rs. 10 per kg $= 25 \times \frac{1}{5}$

= 5 kgs.

3. A:

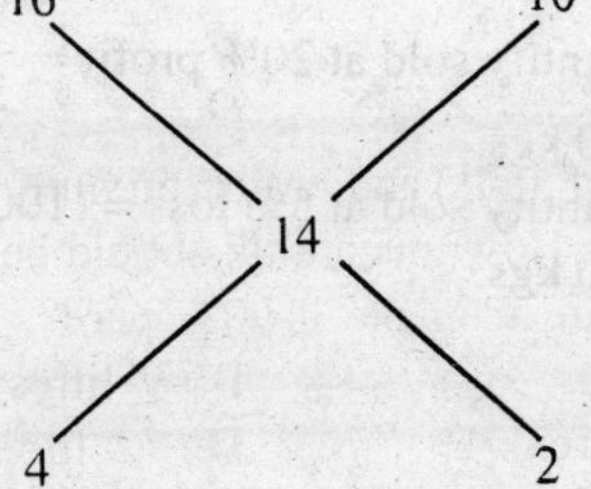

or 2 : 1

$$\frac{\text{Quantity of milk @ Rs.10 per kg}}{\text{Quantity of milk @ Rs. 16 per kg}} = \frac{1}{2}$$

So, quantity of milk @ Rs. 10 per kg. $= \frac{26}{2}$

= 13 kgs.

4. B: First of all we write the fraction of milk present in three mixtures.

In A : $\frac{7}{12}$

In B : $\frac{17}{24}$

In combination of A and B : $\frac{5}{8}$

We now apply alligation rule on these fractions.

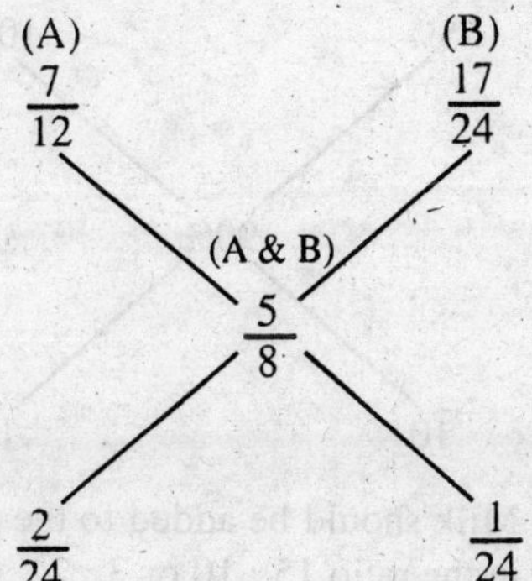

or, 2 : 1

So, Ratio of A : B = 2 : 1.

5. B: Fraction is *Milk* *Water*

A: $\frac{4}{5}$ $\frac{1}{5}$

B : $\frac{9}{20}$ $\frac{11}{20}$

$(3A + 2B) = A \text{ and } B : \left(\frac{12}{5}+\frac{9}{10}\right) \left(\frac{3}{5}+\frac{11}{10}\right)$

$\frac{33}{10}$ $\frac{17}{10}$

So, Ratio of milk : water in the resulting mixture = 33 : 17.

6. A: 

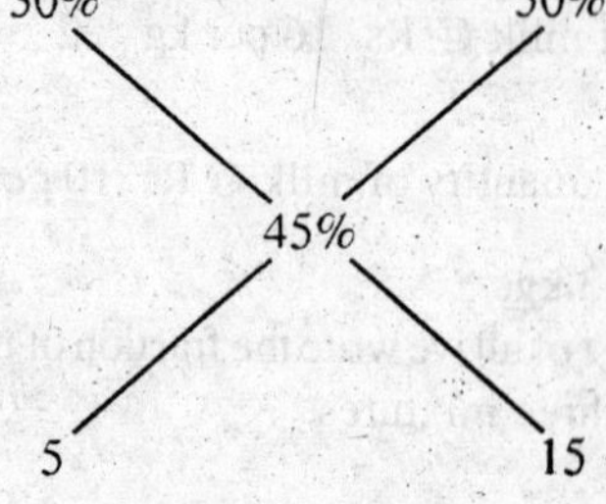

He should mix 30% and 50% in the ratio 5 : 15 or 1 : 3.

$\frac{30\% \text{ Solution}}{50\% \text{ Solution}} = \frac{1}{3}$

or 1 : 3

7. B: The given solution has 75% milk. Milk to be added has 100% milk.

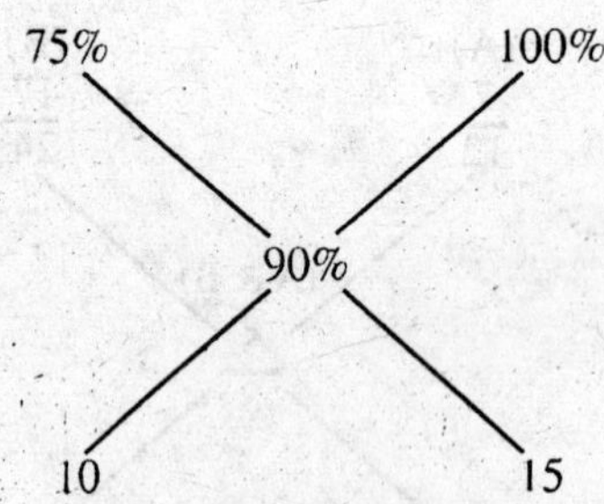

Milk should be added to the given mixture in the ratio 15 : 10 or 3 : 2.

$\therefore$ Quantity of milk to be added = $\frac{3}{2} \times 6$

= 9 litres.

8. A: Let cost price of spirit be Re. 1 per litre.
Then SP of mixture = Re. 1 per litre
Gain = 25%

So, CP of mixture = $1 \times \frac{100}{125}$ = Re. $\frac{4}{5}$

We assume that CP of water is zero.
Using alligation rule on cost price,
Water should be mixed to spirit in the ratio

$\frac{1}{5} : \frac{4}{5}$ or 1 : 4.

9. A:

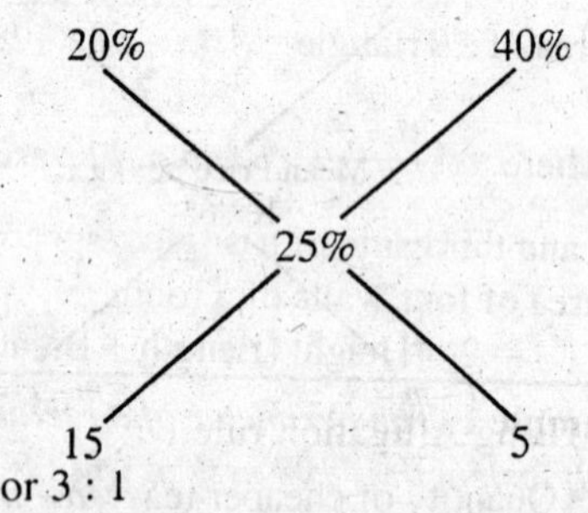

or 3 : 1

Quantity sold at 20% profit = $\frac{3}{3+1} \times 50$

= 37.5 kgs.

Quantity sold at 40% profit = (50 – 37.5)

= 12.5 kgs.

10. D:

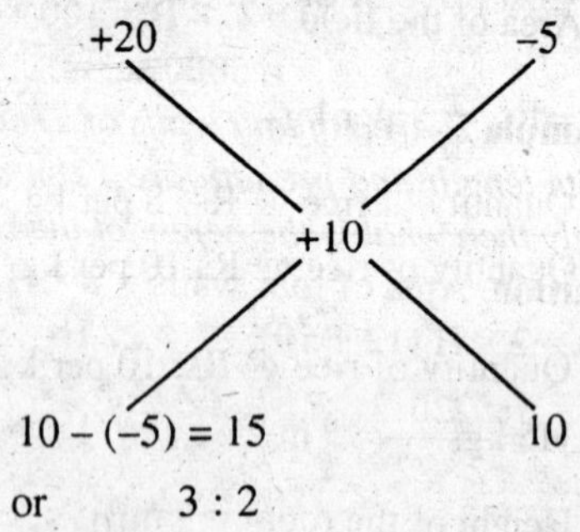

or 3 : 2

Quantity sold at 20% profit = $\frac{3}{3+2} \times 100$

= 60 kgs.

Quantity sold at 5% loss = (100 – 60)

= 40 kgs.

16

AREA

Important Formulae :

1. Area of a rectangle = Length × Breadth
2. Perimeter of a rectangle
   = 2(Length + Breadth)
3. Area of a square = $(\text{Side})^2$
4. Perimeter of square = 4 × Side
5. Area of a circle = $\pi \times (\text{Radius})^2$
6. Circumference of a circle = 2π × Radius
7. Area of a Triangle $=\sqrt{s(s-a)(s-b)(s-c)}$

   where $s=\dfrac{a+b+c}{2}$ and a, b, c are first, second and third side of triangle respectively.
8. Area of four walls of a room
   = 2 × Height (Length + Breadth)

Example 1. *The perimeter of a rectangle field is 300 m. If its length is 100 m then what is its area?*

Solution. Perimeter of the rectangular field
= 300 m

2(L + B) = 300

2(100 + B) = 300

(100 + B) = 150 ⇒ B = 50

∴ Area of the field = L × B = 100 × 50
= 5000 sq. m.

Example 2. *Area of four walls of a room is 220 sq. m. If its length and breadth are 12 m and 10 m respectively then what is the height of the room ?*

Solution. Area of four walls = 2 × H (L + B)

220 = 2 × H (12 + 10) = 2 × 22 H

$\therefore\ H=\dfrac{220}{2\times 22}=5$ m

∴ Height of the room = 5 m.

Example 3. *The breadth of a rectangular plot is one-third of its length. If perimeter of the plot is 240 m then what are its length and breadth ?*

Solution. Let length of plot = x m

$\therefore$ Breadth of plot $=\dfrac{x}{3}$ m

$\therefore$ Perimeter of plot $=2\left(x+\dfrac{x}{3}\right)=2\times\dfrac{4x}{3}$ m

But perimeter of plot = 240 m (Given)

$\therefore\ 2\times\dfrac{4x}{3}=240 \Rightarrow x=\dfrac{240\times 3}{2\times 4}=90$

$\therefore$ Length = 90 m, Breadth $=\dfrac{90}{3}=30$ m.

Example 4. *Length and breadth of a field are 250 m and 30 m respectively. A tank 30 m × 10 m × 6 m is dug in this field and the earth dug out is spread evenly over the remaining portion of the field. How much is the level of the field raised ?*

Solution. Area of the field
= 250 × 30 = 7500 sq. m.

Area of the tank = 30 × 10 = 300 sq. m.

∴ Area of the remaining field
= 7500 – 300 = 7200 sq. m.

Volume of the tank = 30 × 10 × 6 = 1800 cu. m.

Level of the earth raised

$=\dfrac{\text{Volume of the earth dug out}}{\text{Area}}$

$=\dfrac{1800}{7200}=\dfrac{1}{4}$ m = 25 cm.

Example 5. *The sides of a triangle are in a ratio of 3 : 4 : 5. If the perimeter of the triangle is 24 m then what is the area of triangle ?*

Solution. Let sides of the triangle be $3x$, $4x$ and $5x$ metres.

∴ Perimeter = $3x + 4x + 5x = 12x$

According to problem,

$12x=24\ x=\dfrac{24}{12}=2$

∴ Sides of the triangle are 3 × 2, 4 × 2, 5 × 2

i.e., 6 m, 8 m and 10 m

$\therefore\ s=\dfrac{a+b+c}{2}=\dfrac{6+8+10}{2}=\dfrac{24}{2}=12$

Area of triangle = $\sqrt{s(s-a)(s-b)(s-c)}$

$= \sqrt{12\times6\times4\times2} = \sqrt{24\times24} = 24$ sq. m.

Example 6. *There is a circular path around a circular field. If the difference between the circumference of field and path is 66 m then what is the width of the path ?*

$\left(\pi = \frac{22}{7}\right)$

Solution. Let radius of the field = r m

and outer radius = R m

$\therefore$ Width of the path = $(R-r)$ m

Outer perimeter = 2π R

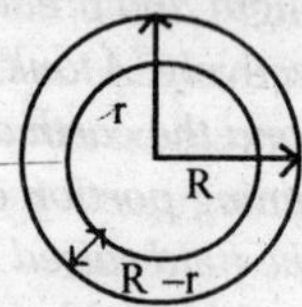

Inner perimeter = $2\pi r$

According to problem,

$2\pi R - 2\pi r = 66$

$\Rightarrow 2\pi(R-r) = 66$

$\Rightarrow R - r = \frac{66}{2\pi} = \frac{66}{2\times\frac{22}{7}} = \frac{66\times7}{2\times22} = \frac{21}{2} = 10.5$ m

$\therefore$ Width of the path = 10.5 m.

Example 7. *The length and breadth of a field are 150 m and 50 m respectively. It has two roads each 2 m wide running in the middle of it crossing each other at right angle. Find the cost to prepare the path at the rate of 35 paise per sq. m.*

Solution. Let the two paths be AB and CD

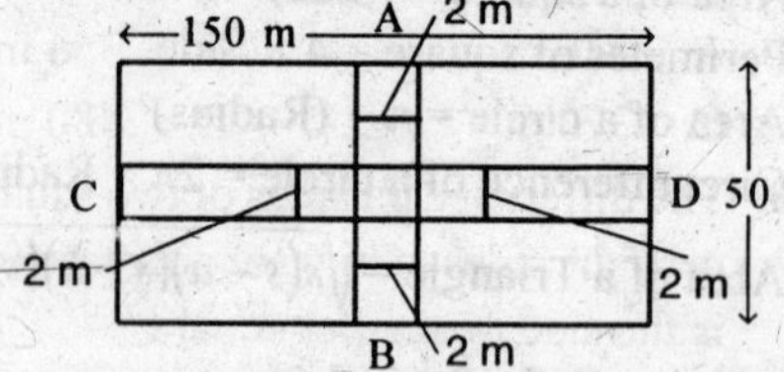

Area of the path AB = 50 × 2 = 100 sq. m

Area of the path CD = 150 × 2 = 300 sq. m.

Area of square PQRS = 2 × 2 = 4 sq. m

$\therefore$ Area of two paths = 100 + 300 – 4= 396 sq. m.

$\therefore$ Cost of preparing the path

$= 396 \times \frac{35}{100} =$ Rs. 138.60

EXERCISE

In the following questions four answer choices are given in which one is correct. Choose the correct answer.

1. If the side of a square field is 30 m then what is its area ?
A. 3600 sq. m B. 900 sq. m
C. 625 sq. m D. 810 sq. m

2. The circumference of a circle is 352 m. What is its radius ?
A. 56 m B. 48 m
C. 52 m D. 62 m

3. The ratio of circumference of two wheels is 2 : 1. If the circumference of bigger wheel is 396 cm then what is the radius of smaller wheel?
A. 31.5 cm B. 27.6 cm
C. 31.8 cm D. 25.5 cm

4. The circumference of two concentric circles are 176 m and 132 m. What is the difference between their radii ?
A. 8 m B. 9 m
C. 11 m D. 7 m

5. A rectangular field is 90 m × 50 m. Inside the field there is a path of width 5 m bordering the field. What is the area of the path ?
A. 1450 sq. m B. 1100 sq. m
C. 1000 sq. m D. 1300 sq. m

6. There is a path of width 3.5 m around a circular field. If radius of the field is 14 m then what is the area (sq. m) of the path ?
A. 346.5 B. 370.5
C. 446.5 D. 386.7

7. If the side of a square is decreased by 50% then how much percent its area decreases ?
A. 60% B. 75%
C. 50% D. 37.5%

8. If the length and breadth of a rectangle are 16 m and 12 m respectively then what is its diagonal?
A. 20 m B. 10 m
C. 18 m D. 14 m

9. The area of a field is 6150 sq. m. If its breadth is 50 m then what is its perimeter ?
A. 346 m B. 356 m
C. 370 m D. 480 m

10. The difference im areas of two squares is 700 sq. m. If the sides of bigger square is 40 m then what is the side of smaller square ?
A. 17 m B. 30 m
C. 16 m D. 12 m

11. The area of rectangular plot is 5400 sq. m. If the ratio of its sides is 3 : 2 then what is its perimeter ?
A. 288 m B. 289 m
C. 300 m D. 310 m

12. The length, breadth and height of a room are 5 m, 4 m and 2.5 m respectively. What is the area of its four walls ?
A. 45 sq. m B. 41 sq. m
C. 36 sq. m D. 25 sq. m

13. The height of a cone is 7 cm and diameter of its base is 14 cm. What is the volume of the cone ?
A. 411.6 cu m B. 359.3 cu m
C. 442.6 cu m D. 450.6 cu m

14. The inner diameter of a well is 8 m. If the well is 14 m deep then what is its volume ?
A. 459 cu m B. 981 cu m
C. 778 cu m D. 704 cu m

15. The height of a cone is 27 cm and radius of the base is 6 cm. If three such cones are melted and a big sphere is made then what is the radius of the sphere ?
A. 8 cm B. 12.5 cm
C. 11 cm D. 9 cm

16. A godown is 8 m × 6 m × 3 m . How many bags of wheat can be placed in this if one bag occupies a space 0.50 cu m?
A. 288 B. 270
C. 304 D. 316

17. A circular plot has a path around it. If the circumference of the circle is 88 m and width of the path is 2 m then what is the area of the path ? $\left(\pi = \frac{22}{7}\right)$
A. 288.6 sq. m B. 188.6 sq. m
C. 178.5 sq m D. 81.6 m

18. A room is 6 m × 4 m × 3 m . What is the cost of painting its walls at the rate of Rs. 1.25 per sq. m ?
A. Rs. 75 B. Rs. 65
C. Rs. 88 D. Rs. 94

19. If the length of a rectangular field is increased by 50% and breadth is decreased by 10% then what percent increase or decrease will be in its area ?
A. 20% increase B. 35% decrease
C. 35% increase D. 20% decrease

20. If two sides of a square paper are decreased by 30% and 40% respectively then how much percent the new area decreases ?
A. 58% B. 62%
C. 40% D. 70%

21. If the base of a right triangle is 8 cm and its diagonal is 10 cm then what is its area ?
A. 12 sq. cm B. 24 sq. cm
C. 16 sq. cm D. 25 sq. cm

22. There is a path around a circular grassy plot. If the radius of the plot is 20 m and area of the path is equal to the area of the plot then what is the cost of paving the path at the rate of Rs. 5.60 per sq. m ?
A. Rs. 8070 B. Rs. 7040
C. Rs. 7441 D. Rs. 8860

23. A rectangular grassy field is 24 m × 14 m. There is a path of width 1 m around it. How many square tiles of size 20 cm × 20 cm are required to cover the path ?
A. 1800 B. 1980
C. 2000 D. 2200

EXPLANATORY ANSWERS

1. B: $\because$ Side of square field = 30 m

$\therefore$ Area of the square field = $(30)^2 = 900$ sq. m.

2. A: $\because$ Circumference of circle $(2\pi R) = 352$ (where R is the radius)

$$\therefore 2 \times \frac{22}{7} \times R = 352 \Rightarrow R = \frac{352 \times 7}{2 \times 22} = 56$$

$\therefore$ Radius of the circle is 56 m.

3. A: Let radii of bigger and smaller wheel be R_1 and R_2 cm.

Circumference of bigger wheel = $2\pi R_1$ cm

Cicumference of smaller wheel = $2\pi R_2$ cm

According to problem,

$$\frac{2\pi R_1}{2\pi R_2} = \frac{2}{1}$$

$$\frac{396}{2\pi R_2} = \frac{2}{1}$$

$$\Rightarrow R_2 = \frac{396}{2 \times 2 \times \frac{22}{7}} \Rightarrow R_2 = \frac{396 \times 7}{2 \times 2 \times 22} = 31.5$$

$\therefore$ Radius of the smaller wheel is 31.5 cm.

4. D: Let the radii of two concentric circles be R_1 and R_2 m.

$\therefore$ Circumference of big circle $(2\pi R_1) = 176$ m and Circumference of small circle $(2\pi R_2) = 132$ m

$\therefore 2\pi R_1 - 2\pi R_2 = 176 - 132 \Rightarrow 2\pi (R_1 - R_2) = 44$

$$\Rightarrow R_1 - R_2 = \frac{44}{2 \times \frac{22}{7}} = 7$$

$\therefore$ Difference in radii of two circles = 7 m.

5. D: Area of rectangular field = 80×40 = 3200 sq. m.

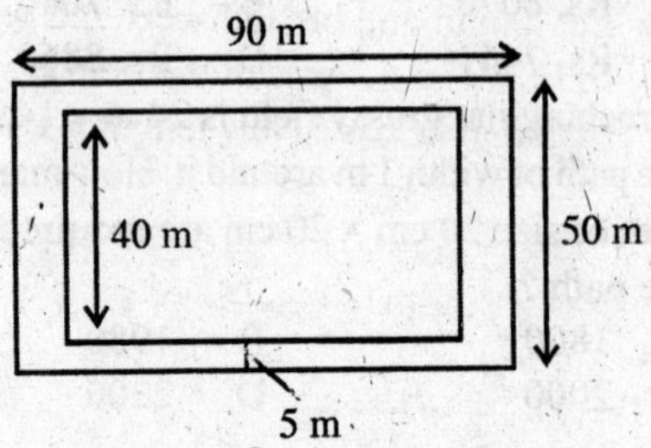

Area of outer rectangle = $90 \times 50 = 4500$ sq. m.

$\therefore$ Area of the path = $4500 - 3200 = 1300$ sq. m.

6. A: Radius of circular field = 14 m

$$= \pi r^2 = \frac{22}{7} \times 14 \times 14 = 616 \text{ sq. m}$$

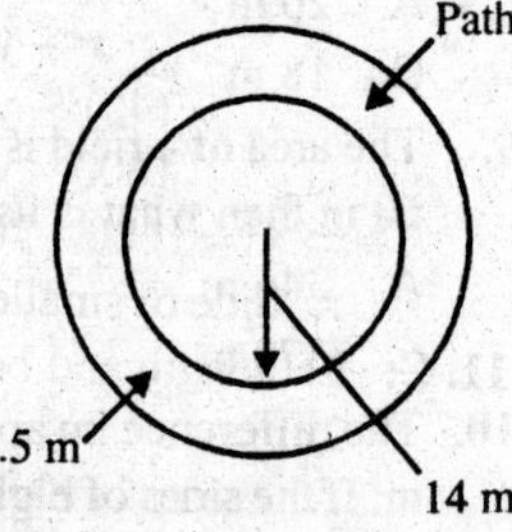

Radius of the circular field with path

(R) = 14 + 3.5

= 17.5 m

$\therefore$ Area of the circular field with path

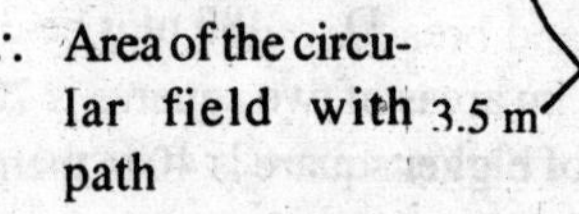

$$= \pi R^2 = \frac{22}{7} \times 17.5 \times 17.5 = 962.5 \text{ sq. m.}$$

$\therefore$ Area of the path = $962.5 - 616 = 346.5$ sq. m.

7. B: Let side of the square = x

$\therefore$ Area of the square = $(\text{side})^2 = x^2$

According to problem,

New side of the square = $x - 50\%$ of x

$$= x - \frac{x}{2} = \frac{x}{2}$$

$$\therefore \text{ New area of the square} = \left(\frac{x}{2}\right)^2 = \frac{x^2}{4}$$

$$\text{Decrease in area} = x^2 - \frac{x^2}{4} = \frac{3x^2}{4}$$

$$\% \text{ Decrease} = \frac{\frac{3x^2}{4} \times 100}{x^2} = 75\%$$

8. A: $\because$ Diagonal of the rectangle

$$= \sqrt{(\text{Length})^2 + (\text{Breadth})^2}$$

$$= \sqrt{(16)^2 + (12)^2} = \sqrt{256 + 144}$$

$$= \sqrt{400} = 20\text{m}.$$

9. A: Area of the rectangular field = Length × Breadth

$\therefore$ 6150 = Length × 50

$$\therefore \text{Length} = \frac{6150}{50} = 123 \text{ m}$$

$\therefore$ Perimeter $= 2(L + B) = 2(123 + 50)$
$= 2 \times 173 = 346$ m.

10. B: Let sides of bigger and smaller squares be x and y m.
$\therefore$ Area of bigger square $= x^2$
Area of smaller square $= y^2$
According to problem,
$x^2 - y^2 = 700$
$(40)^2 - y^2 = 700$
$1600 - y^2 = 700$
$\Rightarrow y^2 = 1600 - 700 = 900 \Rightarrow y = 30$
$\therefore$ Side of smaller square = 30 m.

11. C: Let length and breadth of the plot be $3x$ and $2x$ m.
$\therefore$ Area of the plot $= 3x \times 2x = 6x^2$ sq. m.
According to problem
$6x^2 = 5400 \Rightarrow x^2 = 900 \Rightarrow x = 30$
$\therefore$ Length $= 3 \times 30 = 90$ m, Breadth $= 2 \times 30 = 60$ m
$\therefore$ Perimeter $= 2(L + B) = 2(90 + 60)$
$= 2 \times 150 = 300$ m.

12. A: Area of four walls $= 2 \times H(L + B)$
$= 2 \times 2.5 (5 + 4) = 5 \times 9 = 45$ sq. m.

13. B: Volume of the cone $= \frac{1}{3}\pi r^2 h$
Radius $(r) = \frac{14}{2} = 7$ cm
Height $(h) = 7$ cm
$\therefore$ Volume of the cone
$= \frac{1}{3} \times \frac{22}{7} \times 7 \times 7 \times 7 = 350.3$ cu. cm.

14. D: Diameter of well = 8 m
$\therefore$ Radius of the well = 4 m
Depth of the well = 14 m
$\therefore$ Volume of the well $= \pi r^2 h$
$= \frac{22}{7} \times 4 \times 4 \times 14 = 704$ cu. cm.

15. D: Height of the cone $(h) = 27$ cm
Radius of the cone $(r) = 6$ cm
$\therefore$ Volume of the cone $= \frac{1}{3}\pi r^2 h$
$= \frac{1}{3}\pi \times 6 \times 6 \times 27$ cu cm.
Volume of 3 cones $= 3 \times \frac{1}{3}\pi \times 6 \times 6 \times 27$
$= \pi \times 6 \times 6 \times 27$ cu. cm.
According to problem,
Volume of sphere = Volume of 3 cones
$\frac{4}{3}\pi R^3 = \pi \times 6 \times 6 \times 27$ cu. cm
$\Rightarrow R^3 = \frac{\pi \times 6 \times 6 \times 27 \times 3}{4\pi} = 729$
$\Rightarrow R = 9$ cm
$\therefore$ Radius of the sphere = 9 cm.

16. A: Volume of Godown $= 8 \times 6 \times 3$ cu. m.
Volume of 1 bag = 0.50 cu. m.
No. of bags $= \frac{\text{Volume of Godown}}{\text{Volume of 1 bag}}$
$= \frac{8 \times 6 \times 3}{0.50} = 288$

17. B: Let radius of the circle = R m.
$\therefore$ Circumference of the circle $= 2\pi R$
$2\pi R = 88 \Rightarrow R = \frac{88}{2\pi}$
$= \frac{88}{2 \times \frac{22}{7}} = 14$
Area of the circle $= \pi R^2 = \pi \times 14 \times 14$
$= 196\pi$ sq. m.
Radius of the circle with path $= 14 + 2 = 16$ m
$\therefore$ Area of the circle with path $= \pi \times 16 \times 16$
$= 256\pi$ sq. m.
$\therefore$ Area of path $= 256\pi - 196\pi = 60\pi$ sq. m.
$= 60 \times \frac{22}{7} = 188.6$ sq. m.

18. A: Area of four walls $= 2H(L + B)$
$= 2 \times 3(6 + 4) = 6 \times 10 = 60$ sq. m.
Cost of painting the walls at the rate of Rs. 1.25 sq. m.
$= 60 \times 1.25 =$ Rs. 75.

19. C: Let length and breadth be x and y.
In First Case : Area of the field $= xy$ sq. units
In Second Case : New length $= x + 50\%$ of x
$= x + \frac{x}{2} = \frac{3x}{2}$
New breadth $= y - 10\%$ of y
$= y - \frac{y}{10} = \frac{9y}{10}$

New Area of the field,

$$= \frac{3x}{2} \times \frac{9y}{10} = \frac{27xy}{20} \text{ sq. units}$$

$$\text{Increase in area} = \frac{27xy}{20} - xy = \frac{7xy}{20} \text{ sq. units}$$

$$\% \text{ increase} = \frac{\frac{7xy}{20} \times 100}{xy} = 35\%$$

20. A: *In First Case:*

Area of square paper = x^2 sq. units

$$\text{One side} = x - 30\% \text{ of } x = \frac{7x}{10}$$

$$\text{Second side} = x - 40\% \text{ of } x = \frac{3x}{5}$$

$\therefore$ Area of rectangular paper

$$= \frac{7x}{10} \times \frac{3x}{5} = \frac{21x^2}{50} \text{ sq. units}$$

Decrease in area

$$= x^2 - \frac{21x^2}{50} = \frac{29x^2}{50} \text{ sq. units}$$

$$\% \text{ decrease} = \frac{\frac{29x^2}{50} \times 100}{x^2} = 58\%$$

21. B: $(\text{Diagonal})^2 = (\text{Base})^2 + (\text{Perpendicular})^2$

$10^2 = 8^2 + (\text{Perpendicular})^2$

$(\text{Perpendicular})^2 = 10^2 - 8^2 = 100 - 64 = 36$

$\therefore$ Perpendicular = 6

$\therefore$ Area of the right triangle

$$= \frac{1}{2} \times \text{Base} \times \text{Perpendicular}$$

$$= \frac{1}{2} \times 8 \times 6 = 24 \text{ sq. cm.}$$

22. B: Radius of the plot = 20 m

Area of the circular plot

$$= \pi r^2 = \frac{22}{7} \times (20)^2 \text{ sq. m}$$

According to problem

Area of the path = Area of the plot

$$= \frac{22}{7} (20)^2 \text{ sq. m.}$$

$$= \frac{22}{7} \times 400 \text{ sq. m}$$

Cost of paving the path

$$= \frac{22}{7} \times 400 \times 5.60 = \text{Rs. } 7040$$

20 m

Path

23. C: Area of grassy field = 24 × 14 = 336 sq. m.

Width of the path = 1 m

Length of the field with path = 24 + 2 = 26 m

Breadth of the field with path = 14 + 2 = 16 m

Area of the field with path = 26 × 16 = 416 sq. m.

Area of the path = 416 − 336 = 80 sq. m.

$$\text{Area of 1 square tile} = \frac{20}{100} \times \frac{20}{100} = 0.04 \text{ sq. m}$$

$$\text{No. of tiles} = \frac{80}{.04} = 2000.$$

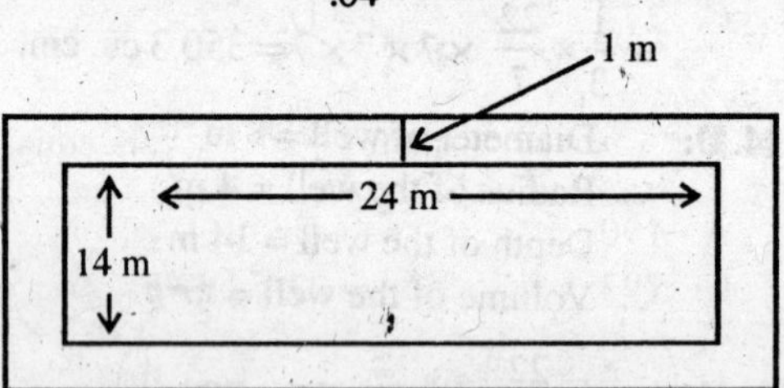

17

SIMPLE ALGEBRAIC OPERATIONS

The four fundamental operation of addition (+), subtraction (–), multiplication (×) and division (÷) when performed on algebraic quantities are called simple algebraic operations.

Algebraic formulae and their applications

Some Important Formulae

1. $(a + b)^2 = a^2 + 2ab + b^2$
2. $(a - b)^2 = a^2 - 2ab + b^2$
3. $a^2 - b^2 = (a + b)(a - b)$
4. $a^2 + b^2 = (a + b)^2 - 2ab$
5. $(a + b + c)^2$
   $= a^2 + b^2 + c^2 + 2ab + 2bc + 2ca$
6. $(a + b)^3 = a^3 + 3a^2b + 3ab^2 + b^3$
   $= a^3 + b^3 + 3ab(a + b)$
7. $(a - b)^3 = a^3 - 3a^2b + 3ab^2 - b^3$
   $= a^3 - b^3 - 3ab(a - b)$
8. $a^3 + b^3 = (a + b)(a^2 - ab + b^2)$ [for factorisation]
   $a^3 + b^3 = (a + b)^3 - 3ab(a + b)$ [for evaluation when $a+b$ and ab are given]
9. $a^3 - b^3 = (a - b)(a^2 + ab + b^2)$ [for factorisation]
   $a^3 - b^3 = (a - b)^3 + 3ab(a - b)$ [for evaluation]
10. If $a + b + c = 0$, then $a^3 + b^3 + c^3 = 3abc$

EXERCISE

1. If $\left(x+\frac{1}{x}\right)=5$, then $\left(x^2+\frac{1}{x^2}\right)$ is equal to:

A. 20 B. 24
C. 27 D. 23

2. If $\left(x+\frac{1}{x}\right)=4$, then $\left(x^4+\frac{1}{x^4}\right)$ is equal to:

A. 190 B. 180
C. 193 D. 194

3. If $\left(x^2+\frac{1}{x^2}\right)=66$, then $\left(x-\frac{1}{x}\right)$ is equal to:

A. 6 B. 12
C. 8 D. 9

4. If $a + b = 8$, $a - b = 4$, then $a^2 + b^2$ is equal to:

A. 20 B. 40
C. 10 D. 30

5. If $x^2 + 5x - 2k$, is exactly divisible by $(x - 1)$, then the value of k is:

A. 1 B. 2
C. 3 D. 4

6. If $x^2+\frac{1}{x^2}=7$, then the values of $x+\frac{1}{x}$ is :

A. 2 B. 3
C. 5 D. 6

7. If $x+\frac{1}{x}=4$, then the value of $x^3+\frac{1}{x^3}$ is :

A. 52 B. 64
C. 68 D. 76

8. If $x+y=8$ and $xy=7$ then the value of x^3+y^3 is :

A. 344 B. 342
C. 345 D. 340

9. If $(x-2)$, is a factor of $x^2+4x-2k$, then the value of k is:

A. 1 B. 3
C. 4 D. 6

10. If $x^{100}+2x^{99}+k$, is divisible by $(x+1)$, then the value of k is:

A. 1 B. 4
C. 3 D. 0

11. Value of k for which $(x-2)$ is a factor of (x^2-kx+2) is:

A. 2 B. 3
C. 4 D. 5

12. If $x-\frac{1}{x}=3$. The value of $x^2+\frac{1}{x^2}$ is :

A. 2 B. 12
C. 10 D. 11

13. If $x-\frac{1}{x}=2$, then $x^3-\frac{1}{x^3}$ is :

A. 14 B. 16
C. 15 D. 12

14. The value of k for which $x-1$ is a factor of $4x^3+3x^2-4x+k$, is :

A. 3 B. 1
C. −2 D. −3

15. If $x+2$ and $x-1$ are the factors of x^3+10x^2+mx+n, then the values of m and n are respectively :

A. 5 and −3 B. 17 and −8
C. 7 and −18 D. 23 and −19

16. Let $f(x)$ be a polynomial such that $f\left(-\frac{1}{2}\right)=0$, then a factor of $f(x)$ is :

A. $2x-1$ B. $2x+1$
C. $x-1$ D. $x+1$

17. One factor of x^4+x^2-20 is x^2+5. The other factor is :

A. x^2-4 B. $x-4$
C. x^2-5 D. $x+2$

18. If $a+b+c=0$ then $a^3+b^3+c^3$ is

A. $2abc$ B. $3abc$
C. abc D. $4abc$

34. The factors of x^8+x^4+1 are :

A. $(x^4+1-x^2),(x^2+1+x),(x^2+1-x)$

B. $(x^4+1-x^2),(x^2-1+x),(x^2+1+x)$

C. $(x^4-1+x^2),(x^2-1+x),(x^2+1+x)$

D. $(x^4-1+x^2),(x^2+1-x),(x^2+1+x)$

35. The expression $10xy^4-10x^4y$ can be expressed in factors as :

A. $10xy(x-y)(x^2+xy+y^2)$

B. $10xy(y-x)(x^2-xy+y^2)$

C. $10xy(y-x)(x^2+xy+y^2)$

D. None of these

21. G.C.D. of $(a+b-c)^6$ and $(a+b-c)^4$ is:

A. $(a+b-c)^6$
B. $(a+b-c)^{10}$
C. $(a+b-c)^2$
D. $(a+b-c)^4$

22. The L.C.M of x^2-4 and x^2-5x+6 is

A. $(x-2)(x+2)(x-3)$
B. $(x-2)(x+2)(x+3)$
C. $(x+3)(x-3)(x+2)$
D. $(x-2)^2(x-3)(x-4)$

23. H.C.F. of x^2-1 and x^3-1 is:

A. $(x^2-1)^2$ B. $(x-1)$
C. $x+1$ D. x^2+x+1

24. HCF of x^2-y^2 and x^3-y^3 is :

A. $x-y$
B. x^3-y^3
C. (x^2-y^2)
D. $(x+y)(x^2+xy+y^2)$

25. $(4x+3y)^2+(4x-3y)^2$ is equal to :

A. $16x^2-9y^2$ B. $32x^2+18y^2$
C. $16x^2+9y^2$ D. $32x^2+9y^2$

EXPLANATORY ANSWERS

1. D: $\because \left(x+\frac{1}{x}\right)=5$

$\therefore \quad x^2+\frac{1}{x^2} = \left(x+\frac{1}{x}\right)^2-2$

$= 25 - 2 = 23$

2. D: $\because x+\frac{1}{x} = 4$

$\therefore x^2+\frac{1}{x^2} = \left(x+\frac{1}{x}\right)^2-2x\cdot\frac{1}{x}$

$2 = 4^2 - 2 = 16 - 2 = 14$

$x^4+\frac{1}{x^4} = (14)^2 - 2$

$= 196 - 2 = 194.$

3. C: $\because x^2+\frac{1}{x^2} = 66 = 64 + 2$

$x^2+\frac{1}{x^2} - 2 = 64$

$\left(x-\frac{1}{x}\right)^2 = (8)^2$

$\therefore \quad x-\frac{1}{x} = 8$

4. B: $\because (a+b)^2+(a-b)^2 = 2a^2+2b^2 = 2(a^2+b^2)$

$(8)^2 + (4)^2 = 2(a^2 + b^2)$

$64 + 16 = 2(a^2 + b^2)$

$\Rightarrow \quad 80 = 2(a^2 + b^2)$

$\therefore \quad a^2 + b^2 = 40$

5. C: $\because x - 1$ is a factor of $x^2 + 5x - 2k$

$\therefore \quad x - 1 = 0$

$x = 1$

$(1)^2 + 5(1) - 2k = 0$

$6 - 2k = 0$

$2k = 6$

$\therefore \quad k = 3.$

6. B: $\because x^2+\frac{1}{x^2} = 7$

$x^2+\frac{1}{x^2}+2 = 7 + 2 = 9$

$\left(x+\frac{1}{x}\right)^2 = (3)^2$

$\therefore \quad x+\frac{1}{x} = 3.$

7. A: $\because x+\frac{1}{x} = 4$

$\therefore x^3+\frac{1}{x^3} = \left(x+\frac{1}{x}\right)^3 - 3\cdot x\cdot\frac{1}{x}\left(x+\frac{1}{x}\right)$

$= (4)^3 - 3(4) = 64 - 12 = 52$

8. A: $\because x + y = 8$ and $xy = 7$

$\therefore \quad x^3 + y^3 = (x + y)^3 - 3xy(x + y)$

$= (8)^3 - 3(7)(8)$

$= 512 - 168 = 344.$

9. D: $\because x - 2$ is a factor of $x^2 + 4x - 2k$

$x - 2 = 0$

$x = 2$

$(2)^2 + 4(2) - 2k = 0$

$12 = 2k$

$k = 6.$

10. A: $\because x + 1$ is a factor of $x^{100} + 2x^{99} + k$

$x + 1 = 0$

$x = -1$

$(-1)^{30} + 2(-1)^{11} + k = 0$

$1 - 2 + k = 0$

$-1 + k = 0$

$k = 1.$

11. B: $\because x - 2 = 0 \Rightarrow x = 2$

$x^2 - kx + 2 = 0 \Rightarrow 4 - k(2) + 2 = 0$

$6 - 2k = 0 \Rightarrow 2k = 6$

$k = 3.$

12. D: $\because \quad x-\frac{1}{x} = 3$

$\therefore \quad x^2-\frac{1}{x^2} = \left(x-\frac{1}{x}\right)^2 + 2x\cdot\frac{1}{x}$

$= 9 + 2 = 11.$

13. A: $\because\ x - \frac{1}{x} = 2$

$\therefore\quad x^3 - \frac{1}{x^3} = \left(x - \frac{1}{x}\right)^3 + 3x \cdot \frac{1}{x}\left(x - \frac{1}{x}\right)$

$= (2)^3 + 3(2) = 8 + 6 = 14.$

14. D: $\because\ x - 1$ is a factor of $4x^3 + 3x^2 - 4x + k$

$x - 1 = 0$

$x = 1$

$4(1)^3 + 3(1)^2 - 4(1) + k = 0$

$4 + 3 - 4 + k = 0$

$k = -3.$

15. C: $x + 2$ is a factor of $x^3 + 10x^2 + mx + n$

$x = -2$

$(-2)^3 + 10(-2)^2 + m(-2) + n = 0$

$2m - n = 32 \quad ...(i)$

Again, $\quad x - 1 = 0$

$x = 1$

$1 + 10 + m + n = 0$

$m + n = -11 \quad ...(ii)$

From (*i*) and (*ii*)

$m = 7$

$n = -18$

16. B: $f\left(-\frac{1}{2}\right) = 0$

$2\left(-\frac{1}{2}\right) + 1 = -1 + 1 = 0$

$\therefore\quad f(x) = 2x + 1$

$\therefore$ factor of $f(x) = 2x + 1.$

17. A: $\because$ One factor of $x^4 + x^2 - 20$ is $x^2 + 5$

$(x^2 + 5)(x^2 - 4) = x^4 + x^2 - 20$

$\therefore$ Other factor $= x^2 - 4.$

18. B: We know that if $a + b + c = 0$

then $a^3 + b^3 + c^3 = 3abc$

19. A: $x^8 + 1 + x^4$

$= (x^4)^2 + (1)^2 + x^4$

$= (x^4 + 1)^2 - 2x^4 + x^4$

$= (x^4 + 1)^2 - (x^2)^2 = (x^4 + 1 + x^2)(x^4 + 1 - x^2)$

$= [(x^2)^2 + (1)^2 + x^2]\,[x^4 - x^2 + 1]$

$= [(x^2 + 1)^2 - 2x^2 + x^2]\,[x^4 - x^2 + 1]$

$= [(x^2 + 1)^2 - (x)^2]\,[x^4 - x^2 + 1]$

$= (x^2 + 1 + x)(x^2 + 1 - x)(x^4 - x^2 + 1)$

$= (x^2 + x + 1)(x^2 - x + 1)(x^4 - x^2 + 1).$

20. C: Given expression

$10xy^4 - 10x^4y$

$= 10xy\,(y^3 - x^3)$

$= 10xy\,\{(y^3) - (x^3)$

$= 10xy\,(y - x)\,(x^2 + xy + y^2)$

21. D: G.C.D. is $(a + b - c)^4$ because $(a + b - c)^4$ is greatest common in $(a + b - c)^4$ and $(x + y - c)^6$.

22. A: $x^2 - 4 = (x + 2)(x - 2)$

$x^2 - 5x + 6 = x^2 - 3x - 2x - 6$

$= (x - 3)(x - 2)$

$\therefore\quad$ LCM $= (x - 2)(x + 2)(x - 3)$

23. B: $x^2 - 1 = (x + 1)(x - 1)$

$x^3 - 1 = (x - 1)(x^2 + x + 1)$

$\therefore$ H.C.F. $= (x - 1)$

24. A: $x^2 - y^2 = (x + y)(x - y)$

$x^3 - y^3 = (x - y)(x^2 + xy + y^2)$

H.C.F. $= (x - y)$

25. B: $(4x + 3y)^2 + (4x - 3y)^2 = 2(4x)^2 + 2(3y)^2$

$= 32x^2 + 18y^2$

$[\because\ (a + b)^2 + (a - b)^2 = 2a^2 + 2b^2].$

18

VOLUME AND SURFACE AREA

In mensuration we often have to deal with the problem of finding the volume of solid figure.

Cuboid : A cuboid has six faces, each one a ractangle. It has 12 edges. For example, a rectangular brick.

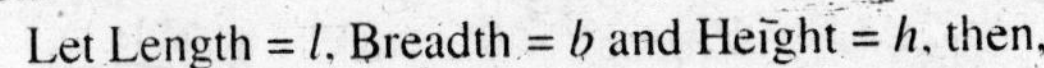

Let Length = l, Breadth = b and Height = h, then,

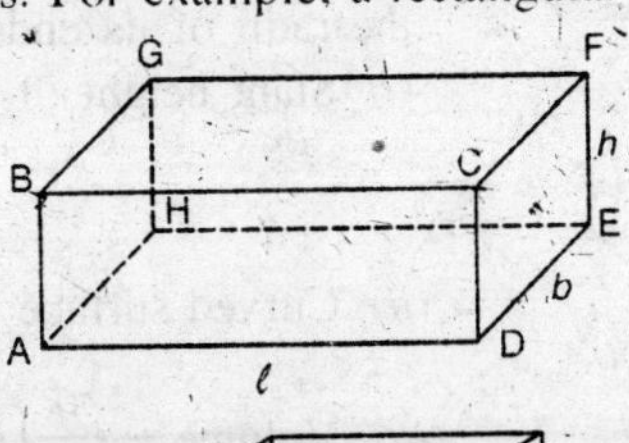

1. Volume = (Length × Breadth × Height)
2. Whole Surface Area = $2(lb + bh + lh)$
3. Diagonal = $\sqrt{l^2 + b^2 + h^2}$
4. Area of 4 walls of a room = $2 \times h\,(l + b)$

Cube : In a cube, Length = Breadth = Height

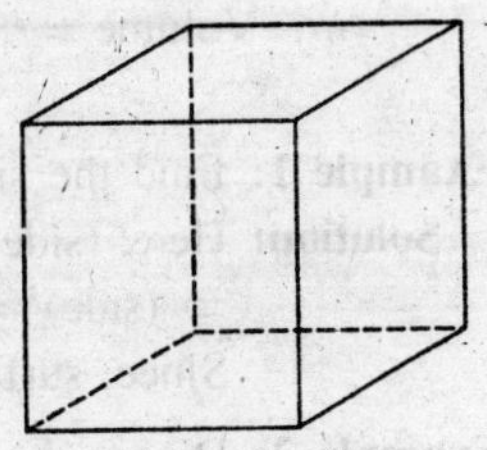

1. Volume = $(l)^3$
2. Length = $\sqrt[3]{\text{Volume}}$
3. Whole Surface Area = $6\,l^2$
4. Diagonal = $l \times \sqrt{3}$
5. Lateral Surface Area = $4\,l^2$

Cylinder :

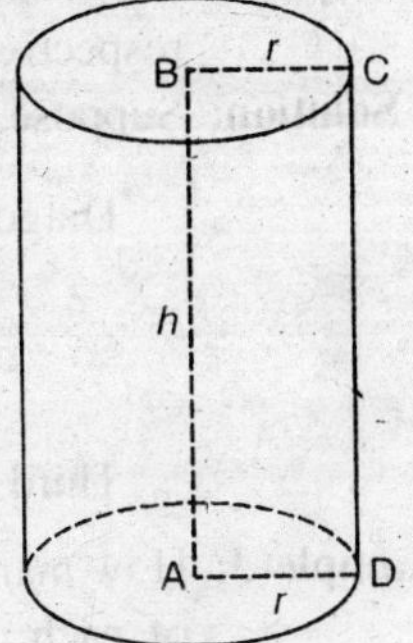

1. Volume = $\pi r^2 h$
2. Curved Surface Area = $2\pi rh$
3. Total Surface Area = $2\pi r(r + h)$
   where r = radius, h = height

Spherical Cell :

1. Volume = $\frac{4}{3}\pi\left(R^3 - r^3\right)$
2. Total Surface Area= $4\pi(R^2 - r^2)$
   where R = Outer radius
   r = Inner radius

Sphere :

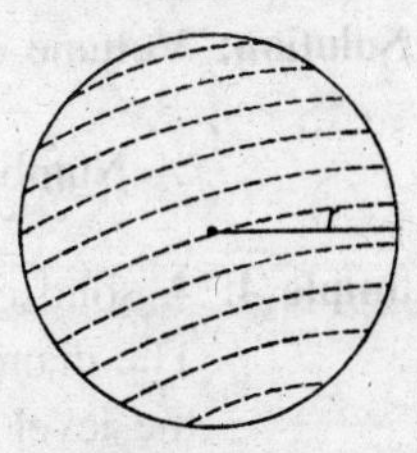

1. Volume = $\frac{4}{3}\pi r^3$
2. Surface Area = $4\pi r^2$

Semi-sphere :

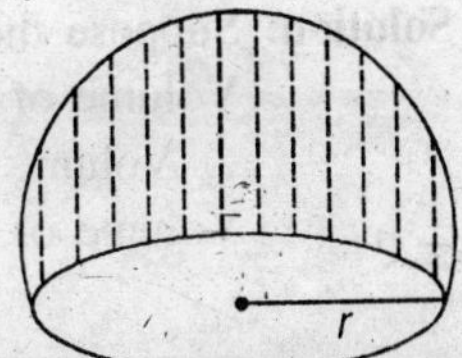

1. Volume = $\frac{2}{3}\pi r^3$
2. Curved surface area = $2\pi r^2$
3. Total surface area = $3\pi r^2$

Cone :

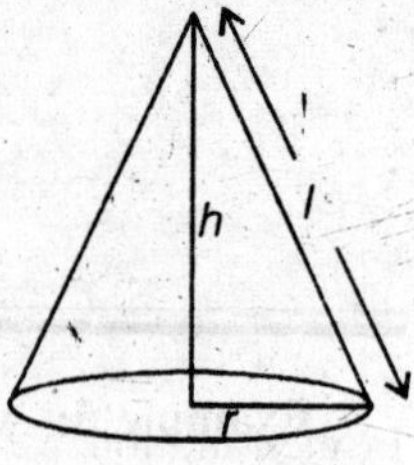

1. Slant height $(l) = \sqrt{r^2 + h^2}$

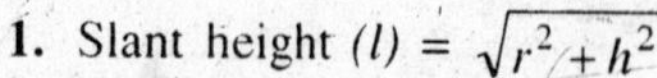

2. Volume $= \frac{1}{3}\pi r^2 h$
3. Curved surface area $= \pi r l$
4. Total surface area $= \pi r\,(l + r)$
5. If the depth of the frustum of a cone be k and the radii of its ends are r_1 and r_2, then

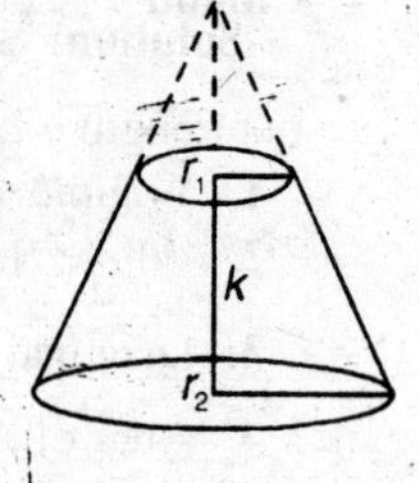

(i) Slant height of the frustum of a cone

$$= \sqrt{k^2 + (r_1 - r_2)^2}$$

(ii) Curved surface of the frustum $= \pi(r_1 + r_2)\, l$.

(iii) Volume $= \frac{\pi k}{3}\left(r_1^2 + r_1 r_2 + r_2^2\right)$

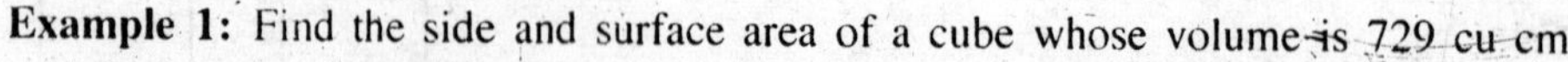

Example 1: Find the side and surface area of a cube whose volume is 729 cu cm.

Solution: Here, $(\text{side})^3 = 729$

$\Rightarrow (\text{side})^3 = (9)^3 \quad \Rightarrow \text{side} = 9$ cm

Since, surface area $= 6 \times (9)^2 = 6 \times 81 = 486$ sq. cm.

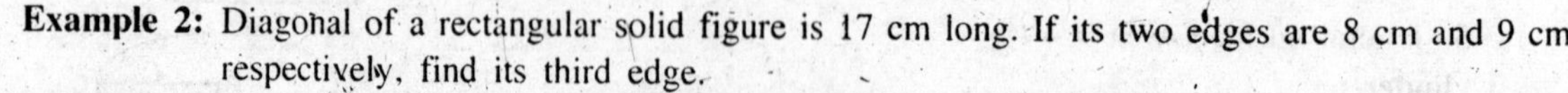

Example 2: Diagonal of a rectangular solid figure is 17 cm long. If its two edges are 8 cm and 9 cm respectively, find its third edge.

Solution: Suppose, the length of the third edge $= x$ cm

$$\text{Diagonal} = 17 = \sqrt{(8)^2 + (9)^2 + x^2} \Rightarrow (17)^2 = (8)^2 + (9)^2 + x^2$$

$$\Rightarrow \quad 289 = 64 + 81 + x^2 \Rightarrow 289 = 145 + x^2$$

$$\Rightarrow \quad x^2 = 289 - 145 = 144 \Rightarrow x = \sqrt{144} = 12$$

$\therefore$ Third edge is 12 cm long.

Example 3: How many cubical blocks can be packed in a carton of size 10 m × 6 m × 4 m, if the volume of each cubical block is 15 cu metre?

Solution: Volume of the carton $= l \times b \times h = 10 \times 6 \times 4 = 240$ cu m

$\therefore$ Number of cubical blocks that can be packed in the carton $= \frac{240}{15} = 16$

Example 4: A solid cube of side 5.5 cm is dropped into a cylindrical vessel partly filled with water. The diameter of the vessel is 11 cm. If the cube is wholly submerged, by how much will the level of the water rise?

Solution: Suppose the level of water in the cylindrical vessel is raised by h cm

Volume of the cubical solid $= (5.5)^3$ cu cm

$\therefore$ Volume of water displaced by the cubical solid $= (5.5)^3$ cu cm

Volume of water that is increased in the cylindrical vessel $= \pi r^2 h$

$$= \pi \times \left(\frac{11}{2}\right)^2 \times h = \pi \times (5.5)^2 \times h$$

$\because \pi \times (5.5)^2 \times h = (5.5)^3 \Rightarrow h = \dfrac{(5.5)^3}{\pi(5.5)^2} = \dfrac{5.5}{\pi}$

$\therefore$ Level of water raised in the cylinder $= h = \dfrac{5.5}{22/7} = \dfrac{5.5 \times 7}{22} = 1.75$ cm.

Example 5: A 1100 cu cm iron cube is to be melted and recast into a iron rod in the form of a right circular cylinder. If diameter of the rod is kept 4 cm, what will be the length of this rod?

Solution: Suppose length of the rod = h cm

Radius of the rod $= \dfrac{4}{2} = 2$ cm

Here, Volume of the rod = Volume of the iron cube

$\therefore \dfrac{22}{7} \times (2)^2 \times h = 1100$

$\Rightarrow h = \dfrac{1100 \times 7}{22 \times 4} = 87.5$ cm

$\therefore$ Rod will be 87.5 cm long.

Example 6: How many spherical bullets of radius 2 cm can be made from a metallic sphere whose radius is 8 cm?

Solution: Here, Number of bullets $= \dfrac{\text{Volume of metallic sphere}}{\text{Volume of each bullet}} = \dfrac{\frac{4}{3}\pi(8)^3}{\frac{4}{3}\pi(2)^3} = (8)^2 = 64$

Example 7: Height of a right circular cone is double the base diameter. If volume of the cone is 36π cu cm, find the height of this cone.

Solution: Suppose the height and base radius of the cone are $4r$ cm and r cm respectively.

$\because$ Volume of the cone $= \dfrac{1}{3}\pi r^2 \times 4r = \dfrac{4}{3}\pi r^3$ cu cm

$\therefore \dfrac{4}{3}\pi r^3 = 36\pi \Rightarrow r^3 = \dfrac{36\pi \times 3}{4\pi}$

$\Rightarrow r^3 = 27 \Rightarrow r = 3$ cm

$\therefore$ Height of the cone $= 4 \times r = 4 \times 3 = 12$ cm.

Example 8: If each edge of a cube is increased by 40%, then by how much per cent will the volume of the cube be increased?

Solution: Suppose each edge of the cube = a cm

$\therefore$ Volume of the cube = a^3 cu cm

Each edge of the new cube = $1.4a$ cm

Volume of the new cube = $(1.4a)^3 = 2.744a^3$ cm

$\therefore$ Increase in volume = $2.744a^3 - a^3 = 1.744a^3$ cu cm

$\therefore$ Percentage increase in volume $= \dfrac{1.744a^3}{a^3} \times 100 = 174.4\%$

EXERCISE

1. Two spheres have their surface areas in the ratio 9 : 16. Their volumes are in the ratio of
A. 64 : 27 B. 27 : 64
C. 16 : 27 D. 11 : 27

2. The length of the longest rod that can be placed in a room 12 m long, 9 m broad and 8 m high is
A. 17 m B. 18 m
C. 25 m D. 16 m

3. The radius and the height of a right circular cone are in the ratio of 3 : 5. If its volume is 120π cu m, its slant height is
A. $3\sqrt{34}$m B. $2\sqrt{28}$m
C. $2\sqrt{44}$m D. $2\sqrt{34}$m

4. Circumference of the base of a cylinder is 88 cm and height of the cylinder is 42 cm. Its volume is
A. 25872 cu cm
B. 28572 cu cm
C. 25870 cu cm
D. 22584 cu cm

5. If a solid sphere of 3 cm radius is melted and recast into a right circular cone whose base radius is same as that of the sphere, the height of the cone will be
A. 8 cm B. 12 cm
C. 6 cm D. 5 cm

6. Diameter of a roller is 2.4 m and it is 1.68 m long. If it takes 1000 complete revolutions once over to level a field, the area of the field is
A. 12672 sq. m B. 12671 sq. m
C. 12762 sq. m D. 11768 sq. m

7. If each edge of a cube is increased by 10%, then by how much per cent will the surface area of this cube be increased?
A. 21% B. 18%
C. 15% D. 20%

8. Height and base radius of a solid cylinder are 14 m and 4 m respectively. It is melted and recast into a solid cone of the same base radius as that of the cylinder, what will be the height of the cone?
A. 21 m B. 42 m
C. 48 m D. 54 m

9. Three cubes having side 2 cm, 3 cm and 4 cm respectively are melted together to form a new cube. The side of the new cube will be
A. 3.526 cm B. 4.628 cm
C. 4.626 cm D. 4.528 cm

10. If base diameter of a cylinder is increased by 50%, then by how much per cent its height must be decreased so as to keep its volume unaltered?
A. 45.56% B. 55.56%
C. 50.16% D. 62.33%

11. The surface area of a cube is 600 sq. m. Its diagonal is
A. $10\sqrt{3}$ cm B. $5\sqrt{3}$ cm
C. $4\sqrt{2}$ cm D. $10\sqrt{2}$ cm

12. The base diameter of a conical tomb is 28 m and its slant height is 50 m. Find the cost of white washing its curved surface at the rate of 80 paise per sq. m?
A. Rs. 1860 B. Rs. 1760
C. Rs. 1950 D. Rs. 1875

EXPLANATORY ANSWERS

1. B: Here, $4\pi r_1^2 : 4\pi r_2^2 = 9 : 16 \Rightarrow r_1^2 : r_2^2 = 9 : 16$

$$\Rightarrow \left(\frac{r_1}{r_2}\right)^2 = \left(\frac{3}{4}\right)^2 \qquad \Rightarrow r_1 : r_2 = 3 : 4$$

$$\Rightarrow \frac{r_1^3}{r_2^3} = \frac{27}{64} \qquad \Rightarrow r_1^3 : r_2^3 = 27 : 64.$$

Therefore, ratio of their volumes

$$= \frac{4}{3}\pi r_1^3 : \frac{4}{3}\pi r_2^3 = r_1^3 : r_2^3 = 27 : 64$$

2. A: The longest rod that can be placed in the cuboidal room = Length of the diagonal

$= \sqrt{l^2+b^2+h^2} = \sqrt{(12)^2+(9)^2+(8)^2}$

$= \sqrt{144+81+64} = \sqrt{289} = 17$ m

3. D: Suppose the base radius and the height of the right circular cone are $3x$ m and $5x$ m respectively.

∴ Volume of the cone

$= \frac{1}{3}\pi r^2 h = \frac{1}{3}\pi(3x)^2 \times 5x$ cu m

Now, $\frac{1}{3}\pi \times 9x^2 \times 5x = 120\pi \Rightarrow x^3 = \frac{120\times 3}{9\times 5}$

$\Rightarrow x^3 = 8 \Rightarrow x^3 = (2)^3 \Rightarrow x = 2$ m

∴ The radius and the height of the cone will be 3 × 2 = 6 m and 5 × 2 = 10 m respectively.

∴ Slant height of the cone

$= \sqrt{r^2+h^2} = \sqrt{(6)^2+(10)^2}$

$= \sqrt{36+100} = \sqrt{136} = 2\sqrt{34}$m.

4. A: Here, $2\pi r = 88$

$\therefore r = \frac{88}{2\pi} = \frac{88\times 7}{2\times 22} = 14$ cm

Since, volume of the cylinder = $\pi r^2 h$

$= \frac{22}{7}\times(14)^2 \times 42 = 22 \times 2 \times 14 \times 42$

= 25872 cu cm.

5. B: Volume of the cone = Volume of the sphere

$\therefore \frac{1}{3}\pi(3)^2 \times h = \frac{4}{3}\pi\times 3^3 \Rightarrow h = 12$ cm

Hence, height of the cone = 12 cm.

6. A: Surface area of the roller = $2\pi rh$

$= 2\times\frac{22}{7}\times 1.2\times 1.68 = 12.672$ sq. m

In one complete revolution, the roller covers 12.672 sq. m.

∴ It will cover in 1000 revolutions

= 12.672 × 1000 = 12672 sq. m

Hence, area of the field = 12672 sq. m.

7. A: Percentage increase in the surface area of the cube = $\left(x+y+\frac{xy}{100}\right)\%$

$= \left(10+10+\frac{10\times 10}{100}\right)\% = 21\%$.

8. B: Here,

Volume of the cone = Volume of the cylinder

$\Rightarrow \frac{1}{3}\pi r^2 \times \text{height} = \pi r^2 \times 14$

∴ Height = 14 × 3 = 42 m

Thus, height of the cone = 42 m.

9. C: Volume of the new cube = $2^3 + 3^3 + 4^3$

= 8 + 27 + 64 = 99cu cm

∴ Side of the new cube = $\sqrt[3]{99}$ = 4.626 cm.

10. B: Change in the volume of the cylinder

$= \left(x+y+(-z)+\frac{xy+y(-z)+(-zx)}{100}+\frac{xy(-z)}{100^2}\right)\%$.

Since volume of the cylinder remains unchanged.

∴ Change = 0%

Now,

$\left(50+50+(-z)+\frac{50\times 50-50z-50z}{100}+\frac{50\times 50\times(-z)}{100^2}\right)=0$

∴ $100 - z + 25 - z - .25z = 0$

$\Rightarrow 2.25z = 125 \Rightarrow z = \frac{125}{2.25} = 55.56$

∴ Height of the cylinder should be decreased by 55.56%.

11. A: Here, 6 × (side)^2 = 600

⇒ side^2 = 100 ⇒ side = $\sqrt{100}$ = 10 cm

∴ Diagonal of the cube

$= \sqrt{3}\times\text{side} = \sqrt{3}\times 10 = 10\sqrt{3}$ cm.

12. B: Area of the curved surface of the cone

$= \frac{22}{7}\times\frac{28}{2}\times 50 = 2200$ sq. m.

∴ Cost of white washing at 80 paise per sq. m

$= 2200\times\frac{80}{100} =$ ₹ 1760.

19

TRIGONOMETRICAL RATIOS

Measurement of Angles: In general, the angles are measured in degrees or in radians which are defined as follows:

(a) ***Degrees***: A right angle is divided into 90 equal parts and each part is called a degree. Thus a right angle is equal to 90 degrees. One degree is denoted by 1°.

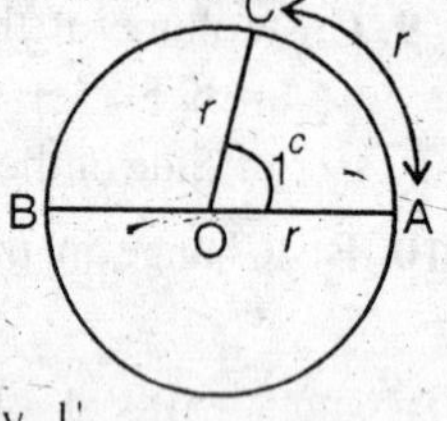

A degree is divided into sixty equal parts and each part is called a minute and is denoted by 1'.

A minute is divided into sixty equal parts and each part is called a second and is denoted by 1".

Thus, we have

1 right angle = 90° (read as 90 degrees)

1° = 60' (read as 60 minutes)

1' = 60" (read as 60 seconds)

(b) ***Radians***: A radian is the angle subtended at the centre of a circle by an arc equal in length to the radius of the circle.

In the adjacent figure OA = OC = arc AC = r = radius of the circle, then measurement of ∠ AOC is one radian and is denoted by 1^c. Thus ∠ AOC = 1^c.

Trigonometrical Ratios: In a right angled triangle ABC, if ∠ CAB = θ, then BC = side opposite to the angle θ = Perpendicular = p (say), AC = side opposite to the right angle = Hypotenuse = h (say) and AB = b (say).

The six trigonometrical ratios are given as follows:

$\sin\theta = p/h$, $\cos\theta = b/h$,

$\tan\theta = p/b$.

(Also $\tan\theta = \sin\theta/\cos\theta$,

$\operatorname{cosec}\theta = 1/\sin\theta$,

$\sec\theta = 1/\cos\theta$,

$\cot\theta = 1/\tan\theta$,)

Basic Formulae Connecting Six Trigonometrical Ratios: The formulae connecting the six trigonometrical ratios are:

(i) $\sin^2\theta + \cos^2\theta = 1$ *or* $\cos^2\theta = 1 - \sin^2\theta$ *or* $\sin^2\theta = 1 - \cos^2\theta$.

(ii) $1 + \tan^2\theta = \sec^2\theta$ *or* $\sec^2\theta - \tan^2\theta = 1$

(iii) $1 + \cot^2\theta = \operatorname{cosec}^2\theta$ *or* $\operatorname{cosec}^2\theta - \cot^2\theta = 1$.

EXERCISE

1. The angles of a triangle are in A.P. and the radian measure of the smallest to the degree measure of the mean is π : 200. The greatest angle in radians is:

A. (11/30)π　　B. π/3
C. π/2　　D. None of these

2. The moon's distance from the earth is 3,50,000 kilometres and its diameter subtends an angle of 31' at the eye of the observer. The diameter of the moon is:

A. 3157 (11/27) km　　B. 315 (11/27) km
C. 3050 (11/27) km　　D. None of these

3. If sin θ = – 3/5 and θ lies in the third quadrant, then the value of cos (θ/2) is:

A. 1/5　　B. $-1/\sqrt{10}$
C. –1/5　　D. $1/\sqrt{10}$

4. If tan θ = – 4/3, then sin θ is:

A. – 4/5 but not 4/5　　B. –4/5 or 4/5
C. 4/5 but not – 4/5　　D. None of these

5. If the angle θ is in the third quadrant and tan θ = 3, then the value of sin θ is:
A. $1/\sqrt{(10)}$
B. $-1/\sqrt{(10)}$
C. $-3/\sqrt{(10)}$
D. $3/\sqrt{(10)}$

6. If (sec α + tan α) (sec β + tan β) (sec γ + tan γ) = tan α tan β tan γ, then (sec α – tan α) (sec β – tan β) (sec γ – tan γ) = ?
A. cot α cot β cot γ
B. tan α tan β tan γ
C. cot α + cot β + cot γ
D. tan α + tan β + tan γ

7. Which of the following is correct?
A. sin 1° > sin 1
B. sin 1° < sin 1
C. sin 1° = sin 1
D. sin 1° = (π/180) sin 1

8. Which of the following is correct?
A. tan 1 > tan 2
B. tan 1 = tan 2
C. tan 1 < tan 2
D. tan 1 = 1

9. The value of log tan1° + log tan2° + ... + log tan89° is:
A. 0
B. 1
C. ∞
D. None of these

10. The value of cos105° + sin105° is:
A. 0
B. $\sqrt{(3/2)}$
C. $1/\sqrt{2}$
D. $(\sqrt{3}+1)/2$

11. The value of $\sin\left(67\frac{1}{2}^{\circ}\right)\sin\left(22\frac{1}{2}^{\circ}\right)$ is:
A. $-2\sqrt{2}$
B. $2\sqrt{2}$
C. $1/2\sqrt{2}$
D. $-1/2\sqrt{2}$

12. The value of (1 + cosπ/8) (1 + cos3π/8) (1 + cos5π/8) (1 + cos7π/8) is:
A. 1/2
B. 1/4
C. 1/8
D. 1/16

13. The value of $\sin^2\frac{2\pi}{15} - \sin^2\frac{\pi}{30}$ is:
A. $(\sqrt{5}-1)/4$
B. $(\sqrt{5}-1)/8$
C. $(\sqrt{5}+1)\sqrt{3}/2$
D. $(\sqrt{5}-1)\sqrt{3}/2$

14. The value of sin50° – sin70° + sin10° is:
A. 0
B. 1
C. 2
D. None of these

15. The value of $\left(\sqrt{3}\,\text{cosec}\,20^\circ - \sec 20^\circ\right)$ is:
A. 2
B. $2\sqrt{3}$
C. 4
D. $\sqrt{8}/2$

16. The value of tan20° tan40° tan80° is:
A. $1/\sqrt{3}$
B. $\sqrt{3}$
C. 1/8
D. $\sqrt{8}/8$

EXPLANATORY ANSWERS

1. A: Let the angles in degrees in A.P. be taken as A = θ – φ, B = θ, C = θ + φ

∴ A + B + C = 180°= 3θ ⇒ B = θ = 60°

$$\text{Now } \frac{\pi}{200} = \frac{\text{A in radian}}{\text{B in degrees}}$$

$$= \frac{(60-\phi)(\pi/180)}{60} \Rightarrow \phi = 6^\circ$$

∴ Greatest angle C = θ + φ = 66°
= 66 × (π/180) = (11/30) π radians.

2. A: Let l be the diameter of moon and a its distance from the earth. If the moon subtends an angle θ at the eye of the observer, then

$$l = a\theta = 350000 \times \left(\frac{31}{60}\times\frac{\pi}{180}\right)$$

$$= \frac{3500\times 31}{6\times 18}\times\frac{22}{7} = 3157\frac{11}{27}\text{ km.}$$

3. B: ∵ θ lies in the third quadrant
∵ cos θ is –ve
∴ sin θ = – 3/5

$\Rightarrow \cos\theta = -\sqrt{(1-\sin^2\theta)} = -4/5$

Now, $\cos^2 \frac{1}{2}\theta = \frac{1}{2}(1+\cos\theta)$

$= \frac{1}{2}(1 - 4/5) = 1/10 \Rightarrow \cos\frac{1}{2}\theta = \pm 1/\sqrt{(10)}$

But given that, $180° < \theta < 270°$

$\Rightarrow 90° < \theta/2 < 135°$

i.e., $\theta/2$ lies in the second quadrant

$\Rightarrow \cos\frac{1}{2}\theta$ is –ve

Hence, $\cos\frac{1}{2}\theta = -1/\sqrt{10}$.

4. B: $\tan\theta = -4/3$

$\Rightarrow \theta$ lies in 2nd or 4th quadrant.

$\therefore \sin\theta$ is positive or negative according as θ lie in 2nd or 4th quadrant respectively, *i.e.,* $\sin\theta$ may be positive or negative.

Now $\sin\theta = \tan\theta/\sqrt{(1+\tan^2\theta)} = 4/5$

Hence, $\sin\theta = -4/5$ or $4/5$.

5. C: $\because \theta$ is in the third quadrant,

$\because \sin\theta < 0$.

Thus, $\sin\theta = -\tan\theta/\sqrt{(1+\tan^2\theta)} = -3/\sqrt{(10)}$.

6. A: Multiplying both sides of the given expression by $(\sec\alpha - \tan\alpha).(\sec\beta - \tan\beta).(\sec\gamma - \tan\gamma)$, we get, $1.1.1 = (\sec\alpha - \tan\alpha).(\sec\beta - \tan\beta).(\sec\gamma - \tan\gamma).\tan\alpha\tan\beta\tan\gamma$

$\Rightarrow (\sec\alpha - \tan\alpha).(\sec\beta - \tan\beta).(\sec\gamma - \tan\gamma) = \cot\alpha.\cot\beta.\cot\gamma$.

7. B: 1 radian = $(180/\pi)$ Degrees = 57° (appr.)

$\therefore \sin 1° < \sin 57° \Rightarrow \sin 1° < \sin 1$.

8. A: 1 radian = 57° (appr.) which lie in first quadrant. $\therefore \tan 1 > 0$, and 2 radians = 114° (appr.), which lie in second quadrant $\therefore \tan 2 < 0$

Hence, $\tan 1 > \tan 2$.

9. A: $\log\tan 1° + \log\tan 2° + ... + \log\tan 89°$

$= \log[\tan 1°.\tan 2° ... \tan 45° ... \tan 88°.\tan 89°]$

$= \log[\tan 1°.\tan 2° ... \tan 45° ... \tan(90°-2°)\tan(90°-1°)]$

$= \tan[\tan 1°.\cot 1°.\tan 2°.\cot 2° ... 1]$

$= \log 1 = 0$

10. C: $\cos 105° + \sin 105°$

$= \cos(60°+45°) + \sin(60°+45°)$

$= \cos 60°\cos 45° - \sin 60°\sin 45° + \sin 60°\cos 45° + \cos 60°\sin 45°$

$= \frac{1}{2}.\frac{1}{\sqrt{2}} - \frac{\sqrt{3}}{2}.\frac{1}{\sqrt{2}} + \frac{\sqrt{3}}{2}.\frac{1}{\sqrt{2}} + \frac{1}{2}.\frac{1}{\sqrt{2}}$

$= \frac{2}{2\sqrt{2}} = \frac{1}{\sqrt{2}}$

11. C: $\sin\left(67\frac{1°}{2}\right)\sin\left(22\frac{1°}{2}\right)$

$= \sin\left(45° + 22\frac{1°}{2}\right)\sin\left(45° - 22\frac{1°}{2}\right)$

$= \sin^2 45° - \sin^2 22\frac{1°}{2} = \left(\frac{1}{\sqrt{2}}\right)^2 - \frac{1-\cos 45°}{2}$

$= \frac{1}{2} - \frac{1}{2}\left(1 - \frac{1}{\sqrt{2}}\right) = \frac{1}{2}\left(1 - 1 + \frac{1}{\sqrt{2}}\right)$

$= \frac{1}{2\sqrt{2}}$

12. C: $\left(1+\cos\frac{\pi}{8}\right)\left(1+\cos\frac{3\pi}{8}\right)\left(1+\cos\frac{5\pi}{8}\right)\left(1+\cos\frac{7\pi}{8}\right)$

$= (1+\cos\pi/8)(1-\cos\pi/8)(1+\cos 3\pi/8)(1-\cos 3\pi/8)$

$= \sin^2\pi/8.\sin^2 3\pi/8 = \frac{1}{4}\left(2\sin\frac{3\pi}{8}.\sin\pi/8\right)^2$

$= \frac{1}{4}\left[\cos\frac{\pi}{4} - \cos\frac{\pi}{2}\right]^2 = \frac{1}{4}\left(\frac{1}{\sqrt{2}} - 0\right)^2$

$= \frac{1}{4} \times \frac{1}{2} = \frac{1}{8}$

13. B: $\sin^2\frac{2\pi}{5} - \sin^2\frac{\pi}{30}$

$= \sin\left(\frac{2\pi}{15} + \frac{\pi}{30}\right)\sin\left(\frac{2\pi}{15} - \frac{\pi}{30}\right)$

$= \sin\frac{\pi}{6}.\sin\frac{\pi}{10} = \frac{1}{2} \times \frac{\sqrt{5}-1}{4}$

$= \frac{1}{8}\left(\sqrt{5}-1\right)$

14. A: $\sin 50° - \sin 70° + \sin 10°$

$= 2\cos 60° \sin (-10)° + \sin 10°$

$= 2 \times \frac{1}{2} \times -\sin 10° + \sin 10°$

$= -\sin 10° + \sin 10° = 0$

15. C: $\sqrt{3}\ \text{cosec}\ 20° - \sec 20°$

$= \tan 60°\ \text{cosec} 20° - \sec 20°$

$= \frac{\sin 60°}{\cos 60°}.\frac{1}{\sin 20°} - \frac{1}{\cos 20°}$

$= \frac{\sin 60° \cos 20° - \cos 60° \sin 20°}{\cos 60°.\sin 20° \cos 20°}$

$= \frac{\sin(60°-20°)}{\frac{1}{2}.\frac{1}{2}(2\sin 20° \cos 20°)} = 4.\frac{\sin 40°}{\sin 40°} = 4$

16. B: $\tan 20° + \tan 40° + \tan 80°$

$= \tan 20° + \tan (60° - 20°) \tan (60° + 20°)$

$= \tan (3 \times 20°) = \tan 60° = \sqrt{3}$

20

HEIGHT AND DISTANCE

Complementary Angles: Two angles, the sum of whose measure is 90°, are called Complementary angles.
The complement of 40° is 50°.

Supplementary Angles: Two angles, the sum of whose measure is 180°, are called Supplementary angles.
The supplement of 60° is 120°.

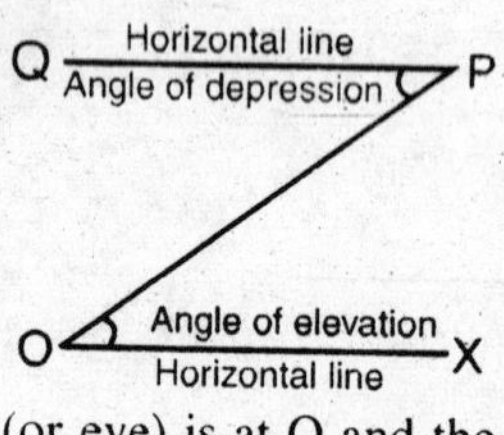

Angle of Elevation and Depression: Let O and P be two points such that P is at higher level than O. Let PQ, OX be horizontal lines through P and O, respectively. If an observer (or eye) is at O and the object is at P, then ∠XOP is called the angle of elevation of P as seen from O. This angle is also called the angular height of P from O.

If an observer (or eye) is at P and the object is at O, then ∠QPO is called the angle of depression of O as seen from P.

Example: A kite is flying with the string inclined at 60° to the horizon. What is the height of the kite above the ground, when the string is 20 m long ?

Solution: Length of string = AP = 20 m.
Height of kite = OP
= AP sin 60°
$= 20 \times \frac{\sqrt{3}}{2}$
$= 10\sqrt{3}$ m.

P
20m
60°
A
O

EXERCISE

1. A person standing on the bank of a river observes that the angle subtended by a tree on the opposite bank is 60°, when he retires 40 metres from the bank he finds the angle to be 30°. Then the breadth of the river is:
   A. 40 m B. 60 m
   C. 20 m D. 30 m

2. The angle of elevation of the top of two vertical towers as seen from the middle point of the line joining the foot of the towers are 60° and 30° respectively. The ratio of the heights of the towers is:
   A. 2 : 1 B. √3 : 1
   C. 3 : 2 D. 3 : 1

3. The angles of elevation of the top of a vertical tower from two points, distant a and b $(a > b)$ from the base and in the same straight line with it are complementary. Then the height of the tower is:
   A. $\sqrt{(ab)}$ B. $\sqrt{(a^2+b^2)}$
   C. $\sqrt{(a^2-b^2)}$ D. $\sqrt{a(a-b)}$

4. A vertical pole is 75m high. Find the angle subtended by the pole a point 75 m away from its base.
   A. 30° B. 45°
   C. 60° D. 90°

5. A person standing on the bank of river finds that the angle of elevation of the top of a tower on opposite side bank is 45°. Which of the following statement is correct?
   A. Breadth of the river is half of the height of the tower
   B. Breadth of the river and the height of the tower are equal
   C. Breadth of the river is twice the height of the tower
   D. None of these

6. An observer measures angles of elevation of two towers of equal heights from a point between the towers. If the angles of elevation are 60° and 30° and distance of nearer tower is 100 m then the height of each tower and the distance between the towers, respectively are

A. $\frac{100}{\sqrt{3}}$ m and 300m

B. $\frac{100}{\sqrt{3}}$ m and 400m

C. $100\sqrt{3}$ m and 300m

D. $100\sqrt{3}$ m and 400 m

7. On the ground level the angle of elevation of the top of a tower is 30°. On moving 20 m nearer the tower, the angle of elevation found to be 60°. The height of the tower is:

A. 10 m B. $10\sqrt{3}$ m

C. 15 m D. 20 m

8. A man on the top of a vertical towers observes a car moving at a uniform speed coming directly towards it. If it takes 12 minutes for the angle of depression to change from 30° to 45°, how soon after this will the car reach the tower?

A. 14 min 20 sec.

B. 15 min 22 sec.

C. 16 min.

D. 16 min. 23 sec.

9. From a point P on a level ground, the angle of elevation of the top of a tower is 30°. If the tower is 100 m high, find the distance of point P from the foot of the tower.

A. 100 m B. 173 m

C. 200 m D. 273 m

10. A man is observing from the top of a tower a boat speeding away from the tower. The boat makes an angle of depression of 45° with the man's eye when at a distance of 60 m from the tower. After 5 seconds, the angle of depression becomes 30°. Find the speed of the boat, assuming that it is running in still water.

A. 30 km/hr. B. 31.5 km/hr

C. 33 km/hr D. 34 km/hr

EXPLANATORY ANSWERS

1. C: Let A be the position of a person on the bank of a river and OP the tree on the opposite bank and ∠OAP = 60°. When the person retires to the position B, s.t.

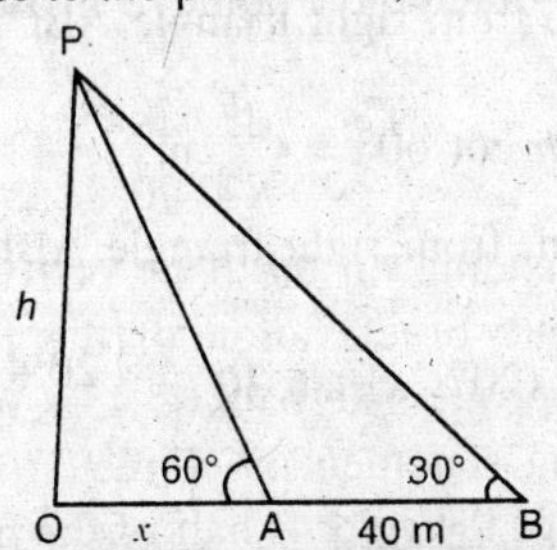

AB = 40 m, then ∠ OBP = 30°

Let OA = x m and OP = h m

In Δ OAP, OP = OA tan 60° = $x\sqrt{3}$

and in Δ OBP, OP = OB tan 30°

= $(x + 40)/\sqrt{3}$

∴ $(x + 40)/\sqrt{3} = x\sqrt{3} \Rightarrow x = 20$ m

2. D: Let AB and CD be two towers of heights h_1 and h_2 respectively and O the mid-point of the line joining the foots A and C of the towers.

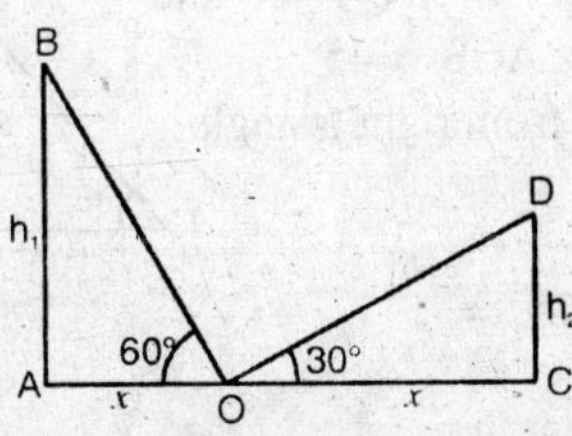

Let OA = OC = x

Then $h_1 = x \tan 60° = x\sqrt{3}$

and $h_2 = x \tan 30° = x/\sqrt{3}$

∴ $\frac{h_1}{h_2} = \frac{3}{1}$, Hence, $h_1 : h_2 = 3 : 1$.

3. A: Let CD = h unit be the height of the tower and A and B be the two points on the ground, such that DA = a; DB = b; $\angle$DAC = α and $\angle$ DBC = 90° – α

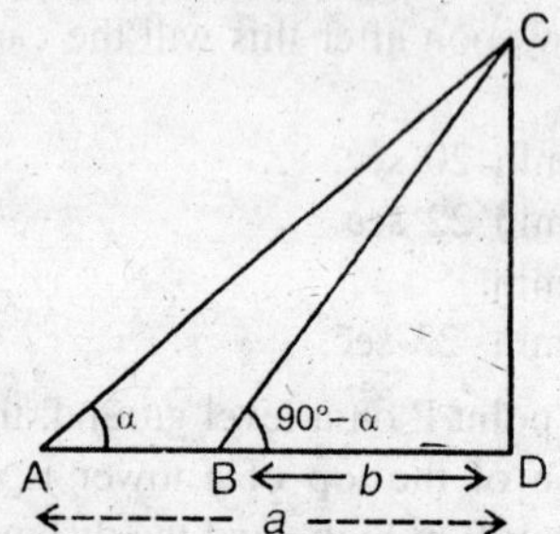

From right triangle ADC, CD = $h = a \tan\alpha$ ...(i)

From right triangle BDC, CD = $h = b \tan(90° - \alpha) = b \cot\alpha$ ...(ii)

Multiplying equations (i) and (ii), we get

$h^2 = a \tan\alpha \,.\, b\cot\alpha$

Hence, $h = \sqrt{ab}$

4. B: Let AB = 75m be the height of pole and C is a point on the ground such that BC = 75m

Now, from right triangle ABC,

$$\tan\alpha = \frac{AB}{BC} = \frac{75}{75}$$

$\Rightarrow \quad \tan\alpha = 1$

$\therefore \quad \alpha = 45°$

5. B: Let AB = h m be the height of the tower; BC = x m be the breadth of the river and also $\angle$ACB = 45°

Now from right triangle ABC

$$\tan 45° = \frac{h}{x}$$

$$\Rightarrow 1 = \frac{h}{x}$$

$\therefore x = h$

Hence, breadth of the river = height of the tower

6. D: Let AB = CD = h m be the heights of the towers. E is a point such that DE = 100m; $\angle$CED = 60° and $\angle$AEB = 30°

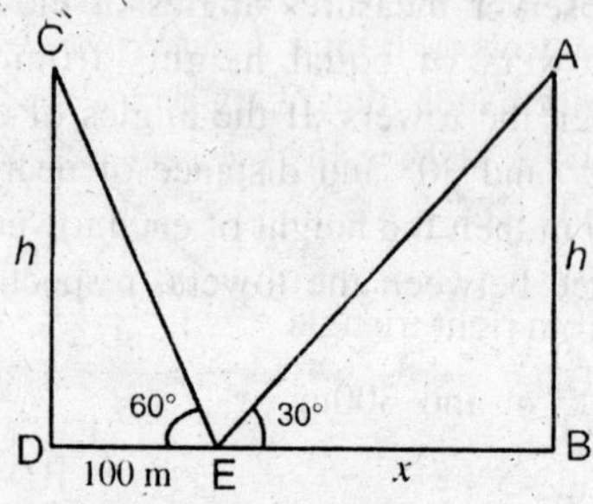

Now, BE = x m (say)

From right triangle CDE,

$h = 100 \tan 60° = 100\sqrt{3}$ m

From right triangle ABE,

$x = h \cot 30° = 100\sqrt{3} \times \sqrt{3} = 300$ m

Distance between the towers = DE + EB = 100 + 300 = 400 m

Height of the tower = $100\sqrt{3}$ m

7. B: Let AB = h m be the height of the tower; B and C are two points such that BC = 20 m;

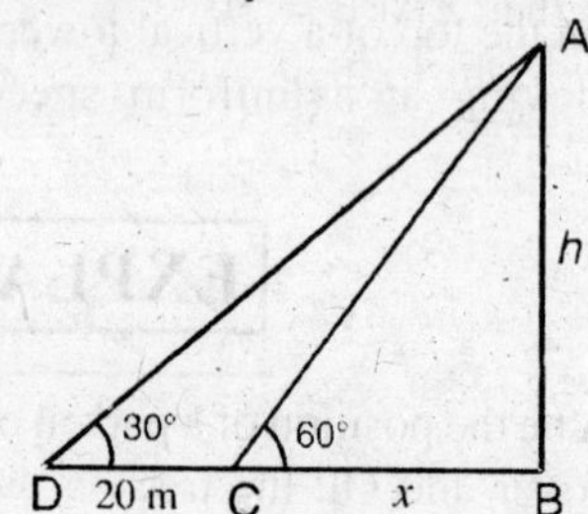

$\angle$ADB = 30° and $\angle$ACB = 60°; BC = x m (say)

Now, from right triangle ABC,

$$x = h \cot 60° = \frac{h}{\sqrt{3}} \text{ m}$$

Again, from right triangle ABD,

$$h = (20 + x) \tan 30° = \left(20 + \frac{h}{\sqrt{3}}\right) \times \frac{1}{\sqrt{3}}$$

$$\left(\because \; x = \frac{h}{\sqrt{3}} \text{ m}\right)$$

$$\Rightarrow h - \frac{h}{3} = \frac{20}{\sqrt{3}} \Rightarrow \frac{2h}{3} = \frac{20}{\sqrt{3}}$$

$$\therefore h = \frac{20 \times 3}{2\sqrt{3}} = 10\sqrt{3} \text{ m}$$

8. D: Let AB = h m be the height of the tower; B and C are two points such that $\angle ACB = 30°$; $\angle ADB = 45°$ and CD = x m (say)

From right triangle ABD,

$\tan 45° = \frac{h}{BD}$ $\therefore$ BD = h m;

Again from right triangle ABC

$\tan 30° = \frac{h}{h+x} \Rightarrow h + x = \sqrt{3}\,h$

$\therefore\ x = (1.73 - 1)h = 0.73h$

Now, 0.73h m covered in 12 min

Hence, h m covered in $\frac{12}{0.73} = \frac{1200}{73}$ min $\simeq$ 16 min 23 sec.

9. B: Let. AB = 100 m be the height of a tower, P is a point on the ground such that $\angle APB = 30°$

From right triangle ABP,

BP = 100 cot 30°

$= 100\sqrt{3}$

$= 100 \times 1.73$

= 173 m

10. B: Let AB = h m be the height of the tower; C and D are the two points on the ground such that BC = 60 m; $\angle ACB = 45°$ and $\angle ADB = 30°$

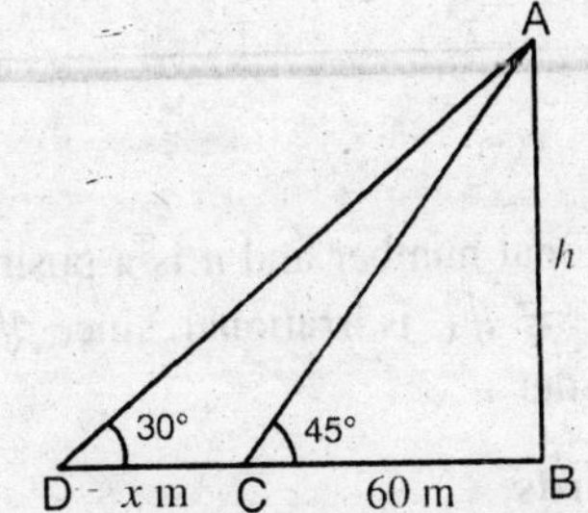

Now from right triangle ABC,

$\tan 45° = \frac{h}{60} \Rightarrow 1 = \frac{h}{60}$

$\therefore h = 60$ m;

Again from right triangle ABD;

$\tan 30° = \frac{h}{x+60} \Rightarrow \frac{1}{\sqrt{3}} = \frac{60}{x+60}$

$\Rightarrow x + 60 = 60\sqrt{3}$

$\therefore x = 60\ (1.73 - 1) = 43.8$m

Hence, speed of boat $= \frac{43.8}{5}$ m/s

$= \frac{43.8}{5} \times \frac{18}{5} \simeq 31.5$ km/hr.

21

SURDS AND INDICES

SURDS

If x is a rational number and n is a positive integer, such that $x^{1/n} = \sqrt[n]{x}$ is irrational, since $\sqrt[n]{x}$ is called a surd of order n.

Laws of Surds

(i) $\sqrt[n]{x} = x^{1/n}$

(ii) $\left(\sqrt[n]{x}\right)^m = \sqrt[n]{x^m}$

(iii) $\sqrt[m]{\sqrt[n]{x}} = \sqrt[mn]{x}$

(iv) $\left(\sqrt[n]{x}\right)^n = x$

(v) $\sqrt[n]{xy} = \sqrt[n]{x} \times \sqrt[n]{y}$

(vi) $\sqrt[n]{\frac{a}{b}} = \frac{\sqrt[n]{a}}{\sqrt[n]{b}}$

We know that $x \times x = x^2$, $x \times x \times x = x^3$, $x \times x \times x \times x = x^4$ ....., $x \times x \times x \times x \times x$ .... n times $= x^n$.

In the given quantity x^n, x is called **base** and n is called **exponent** or **index** or **power**. We read x^n as x raised to the power n or, nth power of x.

Laws of Indices

(i) $x^m \times x^n = x^{m+n}$

(ii) $x^m \div x^n = x^{m-n}$

(iii) $(x^m)^n = x^{mn}$

(iv) $(xy)^m = x^m \times y^m$

(v) $x^\circ = 1$

(1) **For unique solution:** $\frac{a_1}{a_2} \neq \frac{b_1}{b_2} = \frac{c_1}{c_2}$

(2) **For no solution:** $\frac{a_1}{a_2} = \frac{b_1}{b_2} \neq \frac{c_1}{c_2}$

(3) **For many solution:** $\frac{a_1}{a_2} = \frac{b_1}{b_2} = \frac{c_1}{c_2}$

EXERCISE

1. What is the value of $a^5 \times a^7$?

A. a^{35} B. a^2
C. a^{12} D. $a^{5/7}$

2. $(x^{2/3})^{-3/4}$ is equivalent to:

A. $\frac{1}{x}$ B. $\frac{1}{\sqrt{x}}$
C. $\frac{1}{x^2}$ D. $\frac{1}{x^{-2}}$

3. Third power of 4 is equivalent to:

A. 64 B. 81
C. 12 D. 49

4. What is the difference between the third power of 2 and the second power of 3?

A. 2 B. 5
C. 3 D. 1

5. The value of $\left(-\frac{1}{125}\right)^{-\frac{2}{3}}$ is:

A. $\frac{1}{25}$ B. 25
C. 5 D. $\frac{1}{5}$

6. The value of $(8)^{-(2^{-2})}$ is:

A. $2^{-1/4}$ B. $2^{-3/4}$
C. $2^{3/4}$ D. $2^{-\frac{1}{2}}$

7. If $\sqrt{2^n} = 64$, what will be the value of n?

A. 8 B. 4
C. 12 D. 16

8. $(100)^0$ is equivalent to:

A. 0 B. 10

C. 1 D. 100

9. If $10^{2/5} \times 10^{8/5} = 10^n$, the value of n is:

A. 2 B. 3

C. 6 D. 4

10. The value of $27^3 \times 3^4 \div 3^{10}$ is equal to:

A. 9 B. 27

C. 81 D. $\frac{1}{27}$

11. The expression $\frac{(-1)^{132}}{5^{-1}+3^{-1}}$ is equivalent to:

(a) $\frac{16}{9}$ (b) $-\frac{15}{8}$

(c) $\frac{15}{8}$ (d) $\frac{17}{8}$

12. The value of $6a^3\ b^3\ c^2 \div 2ab^2\ c$ is:

(a) $3a^2\ bc$ (b) $3a\ b^2\ c$

(c) $3a^2\ b^2\ c^2$ (d) $3a^3\ b^3\ c^3$

13. $\sqrt{\frac{1}{\left(\frac{3}{4}\right)^{-2}}}+\sqrt[3]{\frac{27}{64}}$ is equivalent to:

(a) $\frac{2}{3}$ (b) $\frac{4}{5}$

(c) $\frac{13}{12}$ (d) $\frac{3}{2}$

14. The positive exponential function of $\frac{a^{-3}\cdot a^{-4}}{a^{-5}}$ is:

(a) a^2 (b) $\frac{1}{a^3}$

(c) $\frac{1}{a^4}$ (d) $\frac{1}{a^2}$

15. $\sqrt[3]{x^6} \div \sqrt[3]{x^{12}} \times x^{-3} \times \sqrt[3]{x^9}$ is equivalent to:

(a) $2x$ (b) 1

(c) $\frac{1}{3x^2}$ (d) $\frac{1}{x}$

16. The value of $\left(\frac{2^3}{3^2}\right)^{2/3} \times \left(\frac{3^3}{2^2}\right)^{2/3}$ is:

(a) $6^{4/3}$ (b) $8^{2/3}$

(c) $6^{2/3}$ (d) $9^{\frac{1}{3}}$

17. $(16)^{-3/4} + 2^{-3} + (8)^{-2/3}$ is equivalent to:

(a) $\frac{1}{2}$ (b) $\frac{3}{2}$

(c) $\frac{9}{2}$ (d) $\frac{5}{4}$

18. The value of $12x^2y^4z^3 \div (2xy^2 \times 3yz^2)$ will be:

(a) $2xyz$ (b) xyz

(c) $\frac{1}{xyz}$ (d) $\frac{2}{xyz}$

19. $\left[\left(2a^2\right)^3\right]^3 \left[\left(3a^3\right)^2\right]^2 \div \left[\left(6a^6\right)^2\right]^2$ is equivalent to:

(a) $36a^6$ (b) $32\ a^6$

(c) $32\ a^4$ (d) $34\ a^5$

20. The value of $\frac{x^{-2}.y^{-4}}{x^{-3}.y^{-1}} \div \frac{y^{-2}}{x^{-1}}$ is:

(a) y (b) $\frac{1}{y}$

(c) xy (d) $\frac{1}{xy}$

EXPLANATORY ANSWERS

1. C: $a^5 \times a^7 = a^{5+7} = a^{12}$ $[\because x^m \times x^n = x^{m+n}]$

2. B: $\left[x^{2/3}\right]^{-\frac{3}{4}} = x^{\frac{2}{3} \times \frac{-3}{4}} = x^{-\frac{1}{2}}$

$= \frac{1}{x^{\frac{1}{2}}} = \frac{1}{\sqrt{x}}$ $\left[\because \left(x^m\right)^n = x^{mn}\right]$

3. A: Third power of 4 = $4^3 = 4 \times 4 \times 4 = 64$

4. D: Third power of 2 = $2^3 = 2 \times 2 \times 2 = 8$

And second power of 3 = $3^2 = 3 \times 3 = 9$

∴ Difference = 9 − 8 = 1

5. B: $\left(-\frac{1}{125}\right)^{-\frac{2}{3}} = \frac{1}{\left(-\frac{1}{125}\right)^{\frac{2}{3}}} = (-125)^{\frac{2}{3}}$

$= [(-125)^{1/3}]^2 = [(-5 \times -5 \times -5)^{1/3}]^2$

$= (-5)^2 = -5 \times -5 = 25$

6. B: $8^{-(2^{-2})} = 8^{-\left(\frac{1}{2^2}\right)} = 8^{-\frac{1}{4}} = \frac{1}{8^{\frac{1}{4}}}$

$= \frac{1}{(2\times2\times2)^{\frac{1}{4}}} = \frac{1}{(2)^{\frac{3}{4}}} = 2^{-\frac{3}{4}}$

7. C: $\sqrt{2^n} = 64 \Rightarrow 2^n = (64)^2$

$\Rightarrow 2^n = (2 \times 2 \times 2 \times 2 \times 2 \times 2)^2$

$\Rightarrow 2^n = (2^6)^2 \Rightarrow 2^n = 2^{6\times2} = 2^{12} \Rightarrow n = 12.$

8. C: If any given number (suppose x) is a rational number other than zero, then $x^0 = 1$.

9. A: $\because\ 10^{2/5} \times 10^{8/5} = 10^n \Rightarrow 10^{2/5+8/5} = 10^n$

$\Rightarrow 10^{10/5} = 10^n \Rightarrow 10^2 = 10^n \Rightarrow n = 2$

Hence, the value of n is 2.

10. B: $27^3 \times 3^4 \div 3^{10} = 27^3 \times \frac{3^4}{3^{10}}$

$= \frac{(3\times3\times3)^3\times3^4}{3^{10}} = \frac{(3^3)^3\times3^4}{3^{10}} = \frac{3^9\times3^4}{3^{10}}$

$= \frac{3^{9+4}}{3^{10}} = \frac{3^{13}}{3^{10}} = 3^{13-10} = 3^3 = 3\times3\times3 = 27$

11. C: $\frac{(-1)^{132}}{5^{-1}+3^{-1}} = \frac{\left((-1)^2\right)^{66}}{5^{-1}+3^{-1}} = \frac{(1)^{66}}{5^{-1}+3^{-1}}$

$= \frac{1}{\frac{1}{5}+\frac{1}{3}} = \frac{1}{\frac{3+5}{15}} = \frac{1}{\frac{8}{15}} = \frac{15}{8}$

12. A: $6a^3b^3c^2 \div 2ab^2c = \frac{6a^3b^3c^2}{2ab^2c}$

$= 3a^{3-1}b^{3-2}c^{2-1} = 3a^2bc$

13. D: $\sqrt{\frac{1}{\left(\frac{3}{4}\right)^{-2}}} + \sqrt[3]{\frac{27}{64}} = \sqrt{\left(\frac{3}{4}\right)^2} + \sqrt[3]{\frac{3\times3\times3}{4\times4\times4}}$

$= \sqrt{\left(\frac{3}{4}\right)^2} + \sqrt[3]{\left(\frac{3}{4}\right)^3} = \frac{3}{4}+\frac{3}{4} = \frac{6}{4} = \frac{3}{2}$

14. D: $\frac{a^{-3}.a^{-4}}{a^{-5}} = \frac{a^5}{a^3.a^4} = \frac{a^5}{a^7} = \frac{1}{a^{7-5}} = \frac{1}{a^2}$

Therefore, positive exponential function of $\frac{a^{-3}.a^{-4}}{a^{-5}}$ will be $\frac{1}{a^2}$.

14. B: $\sqrt[3]{x^6} \div \sqrt[6]{x^{12}} \times x^{-3} \times \sqrt[3]{x^9}$

$= \frac{(x^6)^{\frac{1}{3}}}{(x^{12})^{\frac{1}{6}}} \times x^{-3} \times (x^9)^{\frac{1}{3}}$

[According to BODMAS rule]

$= \frac{x^{6\times\frac{1}{3}} \times x^{-3} \times x^{9\times\frac{1}{3}}}{x^{12\times\frac{1}{6}}} = \frac{x^2\times x^{-3}\times x^3}{x^2} = x^0 = 1$

16. C: $\left(\frac{2^3}{3^2}\right)^{\frac{2}{3}} \times \left(\frac{3^3}{2^2}\right)^{\frac{2}{3}} = \left(\frac{2^3}{3^2}\times\frac{3^3}{2^2}\right)^{\frac{2}{3}}$

$= (2\times3)^{\frac{2}{3}} = 6^{\frac{2}{3}}$ $\quad [\because (xy)^m = x^m.y^m]$

17. A: $16^{-\frac{3}{4}} + 2^{-3} + 8^{-\frac{2}{3}}$

$= \frac{1}{(16)^{3/4}} + \frac{1}{2^3} + \frac{1}{(8)^{2/3}} = \frac{1}{(2^4)^{3/4}} + \frac{1}{2^3} + \frac{1}{(2^3)^{2/3}}$

$= \frac{1}{2^3} + \frac{1}{2^3} + \frac{1}{2^2} = \frac{1}{8} + \frac{1}{8} + \frac{1}{4} = \frac{1}{2}$

18. A: $12x^2y^4z^3 \div (2xy^2 \times 3yz^2)$

$= \frac{12x^2y^4z^3}{2xy^2\times3yz^2} = 2xyz$

19. B: $[(2a^2)^3]^3\ [(3a^3)^2]^2 \div [(6a^6)^2]^2 = (8a^6)^3.(9a^6)^2 \div (36a^{12})^2$

$= \frac{(8)^3.a^{18}.(9)^2.a^{12}}{(36)^2.a^{24}} = 32a^6$

20. B: $\frac{x^{-2}y^{-4}}{x^{-3}.y^{-1}} \div \frac{y^{-2}}{x^{-1}} = \frac{x^{-2}.y^{-4}.x^{-1}}{x^{-3}.y^{-1}.y^{-2}}$

$= x^0y^{-1} = \frac{1}{y}$

22

TRIANGLES AND ITS VARIOUS KINDS

Properties of geometrical figures:

(*i*) **Equilateral triangle:** All sides are equal.

(*ii*) **Isosceles triangle:** Two sides are equal.

(*iii*) **Rhombus:** All sides are equal and no angle is a right angle, but diagonals are at right angles and unequal.

(*iv*) **Square:** All sides are equal and each angle is right angle. The diagonals are also equal.

(*v*) **Parallelogram:** Opposite sides are parallel and equal, diagonals bisect each other.

(*vi*) **Rectangle:** Opposite sides are equal and each angle is a right angle, diagonals are equal.

Co-ordinates of standard points:

(*i*) *Centroid of a triangle:*

The point is the intersection of the medians. This point divides each median in the ratio 2 : 1, its co-ordinates are

$$G_1\left(\frac{x_1 + x_2 + x_3}{3}, \frac{y_1 + y_2 + y_3}{3}\right)$$

(*ii*) *Incentre of a triangle:*

This is the centre of the circle which touches the sides of a given triangle, it is the point of intersection of the internal bisectors of the angles of the triangle, its co-ordinates are given by the formula

$$I = (x, y) \text{ where } x = \frac{ax_1 + bx_2 + cx_3}{a + b + c}$$

$$y = \frac{ay_1 + by_2 + cy_3}{a + b + c}$$

where (*a*, *b*, *c*) are the lengths of the triangle

(*iii*) *Orthocentre of a triangle:*

The point *H* is the intersection of the altitudes.

(*iv*) The points *O*, *G*, *H* are collinear and *G* divides *OH* in the ratio 1 : 2.

EXERCISE

1. The points *A* (12, 8), *B*(–2, 6) and *C* (6, 0) are vertices of :

A. right angled triangle
B. isosceles triangle
C. equilateral triangle
D. None of these

2. The points (1, 1) (–1, –1) and ($-\sqrt{3}$, $\sqrt{3}$) are the angular points of a triangle, then the triangle is :

A. right angled B. isosceles
C. equilateral D. None of these

3. Two vertices of a triangle are the points (1, 4) and (7, 2). Its centroid is the point (5, 3), then the third vertex is :

A. (3, 7) B. (7, 3)
C. (1, 1) D. (0, 0)

4. Let the vertices of a triangle be (0, 0), (3, 0) and (0, 4), then its orthocentre is :

A. (0, 0) B. $\left(1, \frac{4}{3}\right)$
C. $\left(\frac{3}{2}, 2\right)$ D. None of these

5. Distance of (2, 3) from origin is :

A. 2 B. 5

C. –1 D. $\sqrt{13}$

6. Find the values of y for which the distance between the points P(2, –3) and Q(10, y) is 10 units.

A. 8, 2 B. –9, 3

C. –9, 5 D. –8, 2

7. The centroid of the triangle whose vertices are A(4, –6), B(3, –2) and C(5, 2) is :

A. 3, 2 B. 4, 1

C. 4, –2 D. 4, 3

8. If (7, 3), (6, 1), (8, 2) and (P, 4) are the vertices of a parallelogram taken in order then the value of P is :

A. 4 B. 6

C. 7 D. 9

9. If the vertices of rhombus are (3, 0), (4, 5), (–1, 4) and (–2, –1) taken in order then area of rhombus is :

A. 20 square units B. 24 square units

C. 22 square units D. 26 square units

10. Find the value of P for which the points A(–1, 3), B(2, P) and C(5, –1) are collinear :

A. 3 B. 1

C. 2 D. 4

EXPLANATORY ANSWERS

1. A: $BC^2 + CA^2 = AB^2$.

2. C: $BC^2 = CA^2 = AB^2$.

3. B: $5 = \frac{\Sigma x}{3}$, $3 = \frac{\Sigma y}{3}$.

4. A: The two altitudes *i.e.*, x-axis and y-axis of ΔOAB meet at origin.

5. D: A (0, 0) —— B (2, 3)

$AB = \sqrt{(2-0)^2 + (3-0)^2} = \sqrt{4+9} = \sqrt{13}$

6. B: $\because$ PQ = 10

$\Rightarrow \sqrt{(10-2)^2 + (y+3)^2} = 10$

$\sqrt{64 + y^2 + 9 + 6y} = 10$

Squaring both sides,

$y^2 + 6y - 27 = 0$

$\Rightarrow y^2 + 9y - 3y - 27 = 0$

$\Rightarrow y(y + 9) - 3(y + 9) = 0$

$\Rightarrow (y + 9)(y - 3) = 0$

$\Rightarrow y = -9, y = 3$

$\therefore y = -9, 3$

7. C:

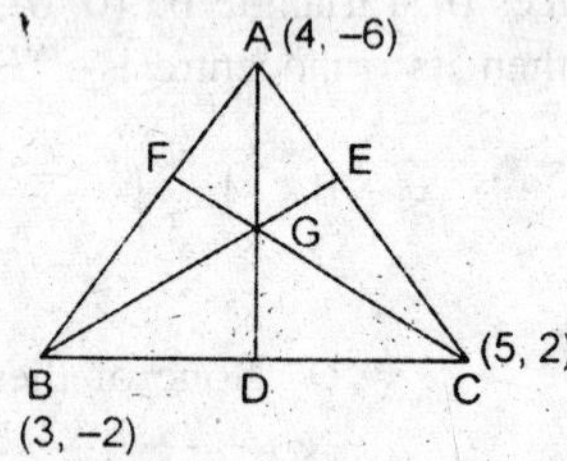

The centroid of the triangle G(x, y)

$= G\left(\frac{4+3+5}{3}, \frac{-6-2+2}{3}\right)$

$= G(4, -2)$

8. D: D(P, 4) C(8, 2) A(7, 3) B(6, 1)

We know that the diagonals of a parallelogram bisect each other.

Mid-point of AC and BD coincide.

Hence, $\left(\frac{7+8}{2}, \frac{3+2}{2}\right) = \left(\frac{6+P}{2}, \frac{1+4}{2}\right)$

$\Rightarrow \left(\frac{6+P}{2}, \frac{5}{2}\right) = \left(\frac{15}{2}, \frac{5}{2}\right)$

Equating the x-co-ordinate, we get

$\frac{6+P}{2} = \frac{15}{2} \Rightarrow P = 9$

9. B: We know that area of rhombus

$= \frac{1}{2} \times AC \times BD$

$$= \frac{1}{2} \times \sqrt{(-1-3)^2 + (4-0)^2} \times \sqrt{(-2-4)^2 + (-1-5)^2}$$

$$= \frac{1}{2}\sqrt{32} \times \sqrt{72} = \frac{1}{2} \times 4\sqrt{2} \times 6\sqrt{2}$$

$$= \frac{1}{2} \times 48 = 24 \text{ square units.}$$

10. B: Points A, B, C are collinear

$\Rightarrow$ Area of $\Delta ABC = 0$

$$\frac{1}{2}[-1\,(P+1) + 2(-1-3) + 5(3-P) = 0$$

$$\Rightarrow \frac{1}{2}[-6P + 6] = 0 \Rightarrow 3P = 3 \Rightarrow P = 1.$$

23

SIMILARITY OF TRIANGLES

Two triangles are said to be similar, if

(*i*) their corresponding angles are equal and

(*ii*) their corresponding sides are in the same ratio (*i.e.* proportional).

Also, we know that :

(*i*) If corresponding angles of two triangles are equal, then they are known as equiangular triangles.

(*ii*) Two line segments are divided proportionally when the ratio of the lengths of the segments of one of them is equal to the ratio of the lengths of the segments of the other.

EXERCISE

1. Two similar triangles have

A. equal sides B. equal areas

C. equal angles D. None of these

2. Two congruent triangles have

A. proportional sides

B. equal sides

C. equal corresponding sides

D. equal corresponding angles

3. Which of the following is false for two congruent triangles

A. Corresponding angles are equal.

B. Two sides and included angles are equal.

C. Corresponding sides are equal.

D. Two angles and one side are equal.

4. If the sides of a triangle are 8 cm, 12 cm and 15 cm then the angle is

A. Right angle B. Obtuse angle

C. Acute angle D. None of these

5. If two triangles are on the same base and between the parallel lines then they will be

A. equilaterals B. right angled

C. equal in area D. congruent

6. If the three heights of a traingle are equal then it is

A. right angled triangle

B. obtuse angled triangle

C. equilateral triangle

D. None of these

7. If two corresponding sides and the angle between them of a triangle are equal to another triangle. Then the angles are :

A. congruent but not similar

B. similar but not congruent

C. neither congruent nor similar

D. congruent and similar.

8. Ratio of areas of two similar triangles is equal to :

A. ratio of squares of the corresponding altitudes

B. ratio of squares of corresponding medians.

C. Either (A) or (B)

D. (A) and (B) both

9. If the areas of two similar triangles are equal then the triangles :

A. are congruent

B. have equal length of corresponding sides

C. (A) and (B)

D. None of these

10. Two isosceles triangles have equal vertical angles and their areas are in the ratio of 9 : 25 then the ratio between their corresponding heights is :

A. 5 : 3 B. 25 : 9

C. 3 : 5 D. 16 : 9

EXPLANATORY ANSWERS

1. C: equal angles
2. C: equal corresponding sides
3. D: Two angles and one side are equal.
4. C: Acute angle
5. C: equal in area
6. C: equilateral triangle
7. C: neither congruent nor similar
8. D: (A) and (B) both
9. C. (A) and (B)
10. C: According to equation

$\angle A = \angle D$ and $\frac{ar(\Delta ABC)}{ar(\Delta DEF)} = \frac{9}{25}$

Since, $AB = AC$ (given) ....(*i*)

$DE = DF$ (given) ....(*ii*)

Dividing (i) by (ii)

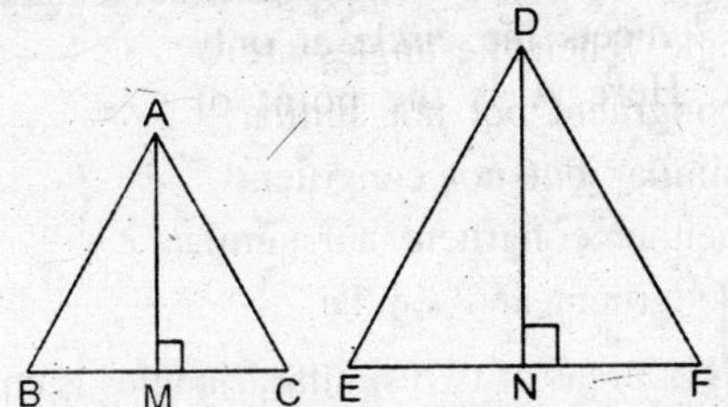

$$\frac{AB}{DE} = \frac{AC}{DF} \quad ...(iii)$$

Hence, $\Delta ABC \sim \Delta DEF$

[By SAS criterion of similar Δs]

In ΔAMC and ΔDNF,

$\angle AMC = \angle DNF = 90°$

$\angle C = \angle F$

(because $\Delta ABC \sim \Delta DEF$)

$\therefore \angle AMC \sim DNF$ (By AA criterion of similar Δs)

$$\therefore \quad \frac{AC}{DF} = \frac{AM}{DN}$$

and, $$\frac{ar(\Delta ABC)}{ar(DEF)} = \frac{AC^2}{DF^2} = \frac{AM^2}{DN^2}$$

$$\therefore \quad \frac{AM^2}{DN^2} = \frac{9}{25}$$

$$\Rightarrow \quad \frac{AM}{DN} = \frac{3}{5}$$

Hence, required ratio = 3 : 5

24

CIRCLE AND TANGENTS

A circle is a set of those points in a plane that are at a given constant distance from a given fixed point in the plane. The fixed point is called the **centre of the circle** and the constant distance of every point on the circle from its centre is called the **radius of the circle**.

The fixed point O is called its centre and the constant distance r is called the radius.

Diameter is the longest chord of the circle.

Secant

A line which interesects a circle in two distinct points is called a **secant** of the circle. In the fig. the line l intersects the circle in two distinct points A and B. The line l is a secant to the circle.

Tanget

A tangent to a circle is a line that intersects the circle at exactly one point.

The point at which it meets the circle is called its point of contact and the line (tangent) is said to touch the circle at this point. In the figure, the line l meets the circle at only point A. Here A is the point of contact.

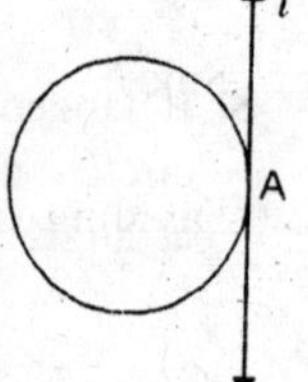

EXERCISE

1. PQ is a diameter and PQRS is a cyclic quadrilateral. If ∠PSR = 150°, then measure of ∠RPQ is :

A. 90°

B. 60°

C. 30°

D. None of these

2. Determine the value of x in the figure given below.

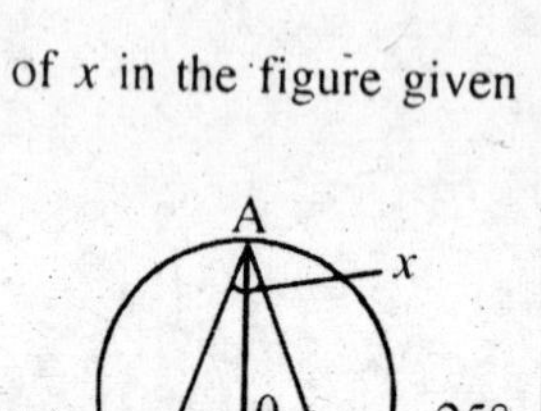

A. 35°

B. 25°

C. 30°

D. 60°

3. O is the centre of the circle. If ∠OAB = 30° and ∠OCB = 40°, find ∠AOC.

A. 120°

B. 140°

C. 110°

D. 130°

4. In fig. if ∠ACB = 40°, ∠DPB = 120°, then find y.

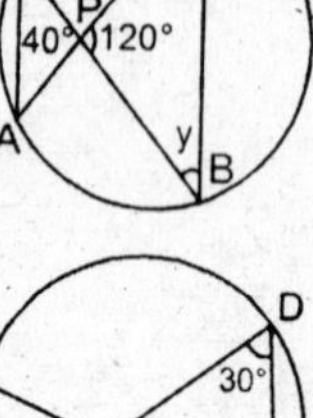

A. 10°

B. 20°

C. 15°

D. 25°

5. In the fig. if ∠BDC = 30°, ∠CBA = 110°, then find BCA.

A. 20°

B. 40°

C. 35°

D. 60°

6. From a point Q, the length of the tangent to a circle is 24 cm and the distance from the centre is 25 cm. The radius of the circle is

A. 7 cm B. 12 cm
C. 15 cm D. 24.5 cm

7. In the given figure, if TP and TQ are the two tangents to a circle with centre O and that ∠POQ = 110°, then ∠PTQ is equal to

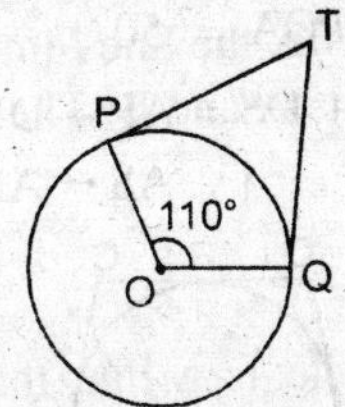

A. 60° B. 70°
C. 80° D. 90°

8. If tangents PA and PB from a point P to a circle with centre O are inclined to each other at angle of 80°, then ∠POA is equal to

A. 50° B. 60°
C. 70° D. 80°

9. A circle touches all the four sides of a quadrilateral ABCD whose sides AB = 6 cm, BC = 7 cm and CD = 4 cm. Find AD.

A. 2 cm B. 5 cm
C. 3 cm D. 4 cm

10. If AB, AC, PQ are tangents in the figure and AB = 5 cm. The perimeter of ΔAPQ is

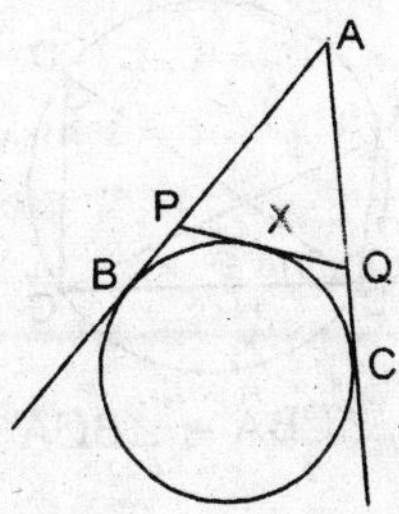

A. 8 cm B. 6 cm
C. 10 cm D. 5 cm

EXPLANATORY ANSWERS

1. B: $\angle PQR = 180° - 150° = 30°$

$\angle PRQ = 90°$ (Angle of a semicircle)

$\angle RPQ + 90° + 30° = 180°$

$\Rightarrow \angle RPQ = 60°$

2. D: $\angle OAB = \angle OBA\ (\because OA = OB)$

$\angle OAB = 35°$

Similarly, $\angle AOC = 25°$

$\therefore\ \angle x = 35° + 25° = 60°$

3. B: O is the centre of the circle,

∠OAB = 30°, ∠OCB = 40°. join OB

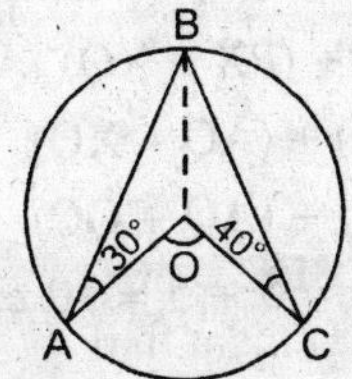

In ΔOAB,

∴ OA = OB (radii of the same circle)

∴ ∠OBA = ∠OAB = 30°

(∠s opp. to equal sides of a Δ) ...(*i*)

Similarly, ∠OBC = ∠OCB = 40° ...(*ii*)

Adding equations (*i*) and (*ii*), we get

∠OBA + ∠OBC = 30° + 40°

⇒ ∠ABC = 70°

∵ $\overset{\frown}{AC}$ subtends ∠AOC at the centre and ΔABC at any point on the circumference

∠AOC = 2 × ∠ABC

= 2 × 70° = 140°

4. B: ∠D = ∠C

[∵ ∠s in the same segment of a circle are equal]

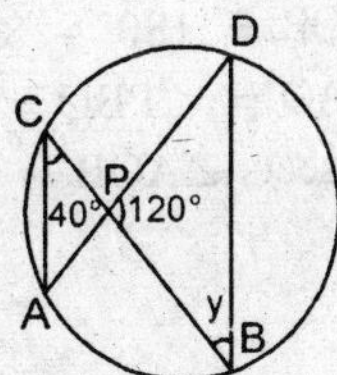

But, ∠C = 40° (Given)

∴ ∠C = 40°

In Δ BPD, we have

$\angle BPD + \angle D + \angle B = 180°$

[$\because$ sum of three $\angle s$ of $a\ \Delta = 180°$]

$\Rightarrow 120° + 40° + y = 180°$

$\Rightarrow y = 180° - 160° = 20°$.

5. B: $\angle BAC = \angle BDC$

($\angle$s in the same segment)

$= 30°$ (given)

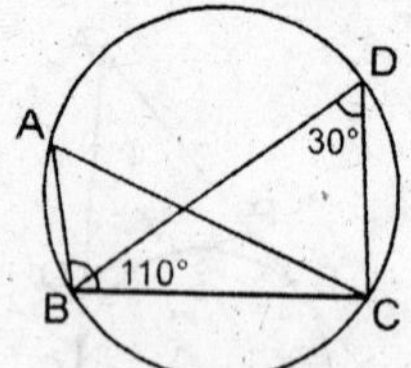

$\angle BAC + \angle CBA + \angle BCA = 180°$

($\angle$s of ΔABC)

$\Rightarrow 30° + 110° + \angle BCA = 180°$

$\Rightarrow \angle BCA = 180° - 30° - 110° = 40°$

6. A: In rt. $\angle d\ \Delta$OTQ,

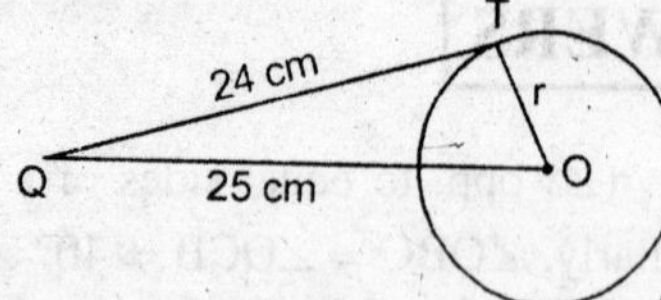

$OT = \sqrt{OQ^2 - OT^2}$

$= \sqrt{25^2 - 24^2} = \sqrt{625 - 576}$

$= \sqrt{49} = 7$ cm.

7. B: Since $\angle POQ + \angle PTQ = 180°$

[$\because \angle OPT = 90°, \angle OQT = 90°$]

$\Rightarrow 110° + \angle PTQ = 180°$

$\Rightarrow \angle PTQ = 180° - 110° = 70°$.

8. A: Since $\angle APB = 80°$

$\angle AOB = 180° - 80° = 100°$

$\angle PAO = \angle PBO = 90°$

Since OP bisects $\angle AOB$

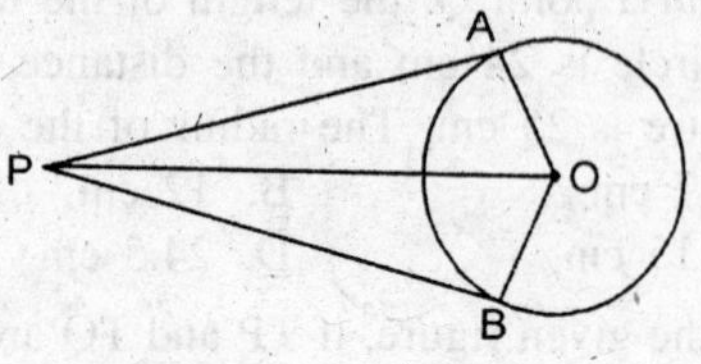

$\angle AOP = \frac{1}{2}(100°) = 50°$

i.e. $\angle POA = 50°$.

9. C: $AD = AS + DS = AP + DR$

[$\because$ AS = AP and DS = DR]

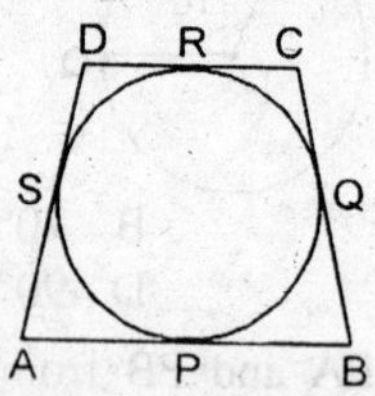

$= (AB - BP) + (CD - RC)$

$= AB + CD - (BP + RC)$

$= AB + CD - (BQ + CQ)$

[$\because$ BP = BQ, RC = CQ]

$= AB + CD - BC = 6 + 4 - 7 = 3$ cm.

10. C: Since AB and AC are the tangents from the same point A

$\therefore$ AB = AC = 5 cm

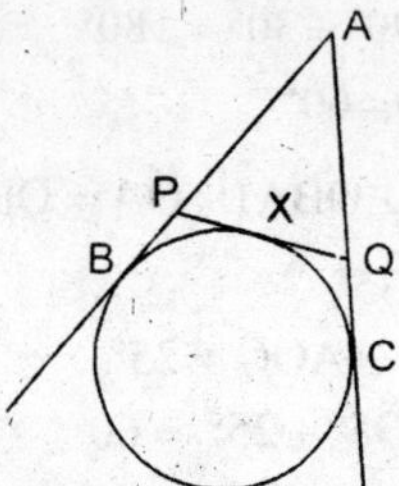

Similarly, BP = PX and XQ = QC

Perimeter of $\Delta APQ = AP + AQ + PQ$

$= AP + AQ + (PX + XQ)$

$= (AP + PX) + (AQ + XQ)$

$= (AP + BP) + (AQ + QC)$

$= AB + AC = 5 + 5 = 10$ cm.

GENERAL AWARENESS

NATIONAL SYMBOLS

STATE EMBLEM

State Emblem of India is an adaptation from the Sarnath Lion Capital of Ashoka. It was adopted by the Government of India on January 26, 1950. In the adapted form, only three lions are visible, the fourth being hidden from the view. The wheel (Dharma Chakra) appears in relief in the centre of the abacus with a bull on the right and a horse on the left.

The bell-shaped lotus has been omitted. The words "Satyameva Jayate" meaning "Truth alone triumphs" are inscribed below the Emblem in Devanagari script.

NATIONAL FLAG

The National Flag of India is a horizontal tricolour of deep saffron (Kesari), white and dark green in equal proportion. In the centre of the white band there is a wheel in navy blue colour. It has 24 spokes. The ratio of the length and the breadth of the flag is 3 : 2. Its design was adopted by the Constituent Assembly of India on July 22, 1947.

NATIONAL ANTHEM

Rabindranath Tagore's song 'Jana-gana-mana' was adopted by the Constituent Assembly as the National Anthem of India on January 24, 1950.

Jana-gan-mana-adhinayaka jaya he, Bharata-bhagya-vidhata
Punjab-Sindh-Gujarat-Maratha-Dravida-Utkala-Banga
Vindhya-Himachala-Yamuna-Ganga Uchhala-jaladhi-taranga.
Tava subha name jage, Tava subha asisa mange, Gahe tava jaya gatha,
Jana-gana-mangala-dayak, jaya he Bharata bhagya vidhata,
Jaya he, jaya he, jaya he, Jaya jaya jaya, jaya he.

NATIONAL SONG

Bankim Chandra Chatterji's 'Vande Mataram' which was a source of inspiration to the people in their struggle for freedom, has been adopted as National Song. It has an equal status with the National Anthem.

Vande Mataram
Sujalam, suphalam, malayaja-shitalam,
Shasya shyamalam, Mataram
Shubhrajyotsna,pulkita yaminim,
Phulla kusumita drumadalashobhinim,
Subhasinim sumadhura—bhashinim,
Sukhadam, Varadam, Mataram.

NATIONAL CALENDAR

It is based on the Saka era with Chaitra as its first month and a normal year of 365 days. It was adopted from March 22, 1957. Dates of the national calendar have a permanent correspondence with dates of Gregorian calendar as Chaitra I falls on March 22 in a normal year and March 21 in a leap year. In official communications, both Saka and Gregorian calendar dates are written. Months of the national calendar are Chaitra, Vaishakha, Jaishtha, Ashada, Shravan, Bhadra, Ashvina, Kartika, Margashirsha, Pausha, Magha and Phalguna.

NATIONAL ANIMAL

The magnificent tiger — Panthera tigris (Linnaeus) is the national animal of India. Tiger is found in several parts of the country and is known for its grace, strength, agility and enormous power. 'Project Tiger' was launched in 1973 to check their dwindling population in India.

NATIONAL BIRD

The Indian Peacock — Pavo Christatus (Linnaeus) is the national bird of India. It is a colourful, swan-sized bird with a fan-shaped crest of feathers on its head and a long-slander neck. The male species is more colourful with blue breast and a spectacular bronze-green train of around 200 elongated feathers.

National Flower—Lotus

National Tree—Banyan

National Fruit—Mango

National Currency—Rupee '₹'

(One Rupee = 100 Paise)

National Aquatic Animal—Dolphin

BOOKS AND AUTHORS

Name of Book	Author
Ain-e-Akbari	Abul Fazal
Anand Math	Bankim Chandra Chatterjee
An Unknown Indian	Nirad C. Chaudhuri
Arthshastra	Kautilya
Coolie	Mulk Raj Anand
Das Kapital	Karl Marx
Discovery of India	Jawaharlal Nehru
Eternal India	Mrs. Indira Gandhi
Godan	Prem Chand
Gitanjali	Rabindranath Tagore
Gora	Rabindranath Tagore
Geet Govinda	Jayadeva
Harsha Charit	Bana Bhatta
Hindu View of Life	Dr. S. Radhakrishnan
India Wins Freedom	Maulana Abul Kalam Azad
Jobs of Millions	V.V. Giri
Jungle Book	Rudyard Kipling
Kamayani	Jai Shankar Prasad
Kadambari	Bana Bhatta
Life Divine	Sri Aurobindo
Last days of Netaji	G.D. Khosla
Les Miserables	Victor Hugo
Mahabharat	Veda Vyas
Macbeth	William Shakespeare
Mein Kempf	Hitler
Meghduta	Kalidas
Mother (Maa)	Maxim Gorky
Mother India	Katherine Mayo
My Experiments with Truth	Mahatma Gandhi
My Presidential Years	R. Venkataraman
Neeti Shatak	Bhartrihari
Nehru and His Vision	Dr. K.R. Narayanan
Old Man and the Sea	Ernest Hemingway
One World	Wendell Wilkie
Panchtantra	Vishnu Sharma
Paradise Lost	John Milton
Ramayana	Valmiki (in Sanskrit)
Raghuvansham	Kalidas
Rajtarangini	Kalhan
Ram Charit Manas	Tulsi Das
Abhijnan Shakuntalam	Kalidas
Satanic Verses	Salman Rushdie
Saket	Maithili Sharan Gupta
Speed Post	Shobha De
The God of Small Things	Arundhati Roy
Treasure Island	R.L. Stevenson
Twelfth Night	William Shakespeare
Train to Pakistan	Khuswant Singh
Uttara Ram Charitra	Bhava Bhuti
Vanity Fair	W.M. Thackeray
War and Peace	Leo Tolstoy
Wealth of Nations	Adam Smith
Wake up India	Annie Besant

INVENTIONS AND DISCOVERIES

Geographical Discoveries

Discovery	Discoverer
America	Columbus
Brazil	Cabral
North Pole	Robert Peary
Everest (Conquered)	Tabie Junko
Planetary Motion	Kepler
Hawaiian Islands	Captain Cook
South Pole	Amundsen
Solar System	Copernicus

Chemistry and Physics

Discovery	Discoverer
Atom Bomb	Otto Hahn
Atomic Theory	Dalton
Atomic Numbers	Moseley
Cosmic Rays	R.S. Millikan
Dynamite	Alfred Nobel
Electrons Theory	Bohr
Electricity (current)	Volta
Electric Telegraphy (Code)	S. Morse

Discovery	Discoverer	Discovery	Discoverer
Gravitation	Newton	Microscope	Z. Jansen
Gas Light	Murdock	Printing Press	Gutenberg
Oxygen	J. Priestly	Revolver	Colt
Photography	L. Daguerre	Sewing Machine	Elias Howe
Printing for the blind	Louis Braille	Thermometer	Fahrenheit
Radium	Madame Curie	Transistor	W. Shockley
Telegraph	Samuel Morse	Typewriter	Sholes
Television	J.L. Baird	Telescope	Hans Lippershey
Telephone	Graham Bell	Tank (Military)	Swinton
Wireless	G. Marconi	**Medical**	
X-rays	W.K. Roentgen	Antiseptic Surgery	Lord Joseph Lister
Mechanical		Bacteria	Leeuwenhock
Aeroplane	Wright Brothers	Circulation of Blood	William Harvey
Bicycle	Macmillan	Homoeopathy (Discovered)	Hahnemann
Computer	Charles Babbage	Insulin	F. Banting
Dynamo	Michal Faraday	Penicillin	Alexander Flemming
Diesel Engine	Rudolf Diesel	Malaria Parasite	Dr. Ronald Ross
Engine (Railway)	Stephenson	Stethoscope	Laennec
Fountain Pen	Waterman	Vitamins	Funk
Gramophone	Edison	Anti-Rabies Treatment	Pasteur
Locomotive Power of Steam	James Watt	**General**	
Helicopter	Brequet	Nylon	Carouthers
Life Boat	Henry Greathead	Science of Geometry	Euclids

WORLD'S GEOGRAPHICAL SURNAMES

• City of Sky-scrapers—New York • City of Seven Hills—Rome • City of Dreaming Spires—Oxford • City of Golden Gate—San Francisco • City of Magnificent Buildings—Washington D.C. • City of Eternal Springs—Quito (S. America) • China's Sorrow—Hwang Ho • Cockpit of Europe—Belgium • Dark Continent—Africa • Emerald Isle—Ireland • Eternal City—Rome • Empire City—New York • Forbidden City—Lhasa (Tibet) • Garden City—Chicago • Gate of Tears—Strait of Bab-el-Mandeb • Gift of the Nile—Egypt • Granite City—Aberdeen (Scotland) • Hermit Kingdom—Korea • Herring Pond—Atlantic Ocean • Holy Land—Jerusalem • Island Continent—Australia • Islands of Cloves—Zanzibar • Isle of Pearls—Bahrein (Persian Gulf) • Key to the Mediterranean—Gibralter • Land of Cakes—Scotland • Land of Golden Fleece—Australia • Land of Maple Leaf—Canada • Land of Morning Calm—Korea • Land of Midnight Sun—Norway • Land of the Thousand Lakes—Finland • Land of the Thunderbolt—Bhutan • Land of White Elephant—Thailand • Land of Thousand Elephants—Laos • Land of Rising Sun—Japan • Loneliest Island—Tristan De Gunha (Mid-Atlantic) • Manchester of Japan—Osaka • Pillars of Hercules—Strait of Gibraltar • Pearl of the Antilles—Cuba • Playground of Europe—Switzerland • Quaker City—Philadelphia • Queen of the Adriatic—Venice • Roof of the World—The Pamirs, Central Asia • Sugar bowl of the world—Cuba • Venice of the North—Stockholm • Windy City—Chicago • Whiteman's grave—Guinea Coast of Africa • Yellow River—Huang Ho (China) • Sickman of Europe—Turkiye

CAPITALS AND CURRENCIES OF COUNTRIES

Country	Capital	Currency
Afghanistan	Kabul	Afghani
Algeria	Algiers	Dinar
Angola	Luanda	New Kwanza
Argentina	Buenos Aires	Peso
Armenia	Yeravan	Dram
Australia	Canberra	Dollar
Austria	Vienna	Euro
Azerbaijan	Baku	Manat
Bahrain	Manama	Dinar
Bangladesh	Dhaka	Taka
Barbados	Bridgetown	Dollar
Belgium	Brussels	Euro
Bhutan	Thimphu	Ngultrum
Bolivia	La paz	Boliviano
Brazil	Brasilia	Cruzeiro
Bulgaria	Sofia	Euro
Belarus	Minsk	Ruble
Cambodia	Phnom-Penh	Riel
Canada	Ottawa	Dollar
Chile	Santiago	Peso
China	Beijing	Yuan
Colombia	Bogota	Peso
Congo (Republic)	Brazzaville	Franc (CFA)
Croatia	Zagreb	Kuna
Cuba	Havana	Peso
Cyprus	Nicosia	Euro
Czech Republic	Prague	Koruna
Denmark	Copenhagen	Krone
Egypt	Cairo	Pound
Estonia	Tallinn	Euro
Ethiopia	Addis Ababa	Birr
Fiji	Suva	Dollar
Finland	Helsinki	Euro
France	Paris	Euro
Georgia	Tbilisi	Lari
Germany	Berlin	Euro
Ghana	Accra	Cedi
Greece	Athens	Euro
Guatemala	Guatemala City	Quetzal
Hong Kong	Victoria	Dollar
Hungary	Budapest	Forints
Iceland	Reykjavik	Krona
India	New Delhi	Rupee

Country	Capital	Currency
Indonesia	Jakarta	Rupiah
Iran	Teheran	Rial
Iraq	Baghdad	Dinar
Ireland	Dublin	Euro
Israel	Jerusalem	Shekel
Italy	Rome	Euro
Jamaica	Kingston	Dollar
Japan	Tokyo	Yen
Jordan	Amman	Dinar
Kazakhstan	Astana	Tenge
Kenya	Nairobi	Shilling
Korea (S)	Seoul	Won
Korea (N)	Pyongyang	Won
Kyrgyzstan	Bishkek	Som
Kuwait	Kuwait City	Dinar
Laos	Vientiane	Kip
Latvia	Riga	Euro
Lebanon	Beirut	Pound
Libya	Tripoli	Dinar
Lithuania	Vilnius	Litas
Malaysia	Kuala Lumpur	Ringgit
Maldives	Male	Rufiyya
Mauritius	Port Louis	Rupee
Moldavia	Chisinau	Leu
Mexico	Mexico City	Peso
Morocco	Rabat	Dirham
Mozambique	Maputo	Metical
Myanmar	Nay Pyi Taw	Kyat
Nepal	Kathmandu	Rupee
Netherlands	Amsterdam	Euro
New Zealand	Wellington	Dollar
Nigeria	Abuja	Naira
Norway	Oslo	Krone
Oman	Muscat	Rial
Pakistan	Islamabad	Rupee
Philippines	Manila	Peso
Poland	Warsaw	Zloty
Portugal	Lisbon	Euro
Qatar	Doha	Riyal
Romania	Bucharest	Leu
Russia	Moscow	Ruble
Saudi Arabia	Riyadh	Rial

Country	Capital	Currency
Slovakia	Bratislava	Euro
Spain	Madrid	Euro
Sri Lanka	Colombo	Rupee
Sudan	Khartoum	Dinar
Sweden	Stockholm	Krona
Switzerland	Berne	Swiss Francs
Syria	Damascus	Pound
South Africa	Capetown (Legislative) Pretoria (Administrative)	Rand
Tajikistan	Dushanbe	Somoni
Taiwan	Taipei	Dollar
Tanzania	Dodoma	Shilling
Thailand	Bangkok	Baht
Turkiye	Ankara	Turkish Lira
Turkmenistan	Ashgabat	Manat
Uganda	Kampala	Shilling
Ukraine	Kiev	Hryvna
United Arab Emirates	Abu Dhabi	Dirham
U.K.	London	Pound Sterling
U.S.A.	Washington	Dollar
Uzbekistan	Tashkent	Som
Vietnam	Hanoi	Dong
Yemen	Sana'a	Rial/Dinar
Zimbabwe	Harare	Dollar
Congo (Democratic Republic)	Kinshasa	Franc (CDF)
Zambia	Lusaka	Kwacha

INDIAN CITIES AND THEIR RIVERS

City	State	River
Agra	U.P.	Yamuna
Ahmedabad	Gujarat	Sabarmati
Alwaye	Kerala	Periyar
Kolkata	West Bengal	Hooghly
Cuttack	Odisha	Mahanadi
Delhi	Delhi	Yamuna
Haridwar	Uttarakhand	Ganga
Kanpur	Uttar Pradesh	Ganga
Ludhiana	Punjab	Sutlej
Lucknow	Uttar Pradesh	Gomati
Nasik	Maharashtra	Godavari
Patna	Bihar	Ganga
Prayagraj	U.P.	Confluence of the Ganga, Yamuna, and invisible Saraswati
Srinagar	J & K	Jhelum
Surat	Gujarat	Tapti
Tiruchirapally	Tamil Nadu	Kaveri
Ujjain	Madhya Pradesh	Shipra
Vijayawada	Andhra Pradesh	Krishna
Varanasi	Uttar Pradesh	Ganga

WONDERS OF THE WORLD

Seven Wonders of the Ancient World: (1) the Pyramids of Egypt, built in approximately 2700 BC; (2) the Hanging Gardens at Babylon; (3) the temple of Artemis at Emphesus; (4) the statue of Zeus at Olympia; (5) the tomb of Mausolus at Halicarnassus, built in nearly 350 BC; (6) the Colossus of Rhodes, built in nearly 280 BC; (7) the Pharos Lighthouse at Alexandria.

Seven Wonders of the Medieval World: (1) the Colosseum of Rome; (2) the Great Wall of China; (3) the Porcelain Tower of Nanking; (4) the Mosque at St. Sophia (Constantinople); (5) Stonehenge; (6) the Catacombs of Rome; (7) the Leaning Tower of Pisa.

Seven New Wonders of the World: (1) Taj Mahal of Agra (India); (2) Pyramid at Chichen Itza (Mexico); (3) Machu Picchu (Peru); (4) Statue of Christ The Redeemer (Brazil); (5) Great Wall of China; (6) Roman Colosseum, Italy; (7) Ruins of Petra, Jordan.

STATES & UNION TERRITORIES OF INDIA (CAPITALS, PRINCIPAL LANGUAGES)

States & Union Territories	Capitals	Principal Languages
Andhra Pradesh	Amravati	*Telgu and Urdu*
Arunachal Pradesh	Itanagar	*Monpa, Adi, Nissi etc.*
Assam	Dispur	*Assamese and Bengali*
Bihar	Patna	*Hindi and Maithili*
Chhattishgarh	Raipur	*Hindi*
Goa	Panaji	*Konkani*
Gujarat	GandhiNagar	*Gujarati*
Haryana	Chandigarh	*Hindi*
Himachal Pradesh	Shimla	*Hindi and Pahari*
Jharkhand	Ranchi	*Hindi*
Kerala	Thiruvananthpuram	*Malyalam*
Karnataka	Bengluru	*Kannada*
Madhya Pradesh	Bhopal	*Hindi*
Maharashtra	Mumbai	*Marathi*
Meghalaya	Shillong	*Khashi, Jayantia and Garo*
Manipur	Imphal	*Manipuri*
Mizoram	Aizawl	*Mizo and English*
Nagaland	Kohima	*Naga, Assamese and English*
Odisha	Bhubaneshwar	*Odiya*
Punjab	Chandigarh	*Punjabi*
Rajasthan	Jaipur	*Hindi, Rajasthani*
Sikkim	Gangtok	*Sikkimese and Gorkhali*
Tamil Nadu	Chennai	*Tamil*
Tripura	Agartala	*Bengali, Tripuri*
Uttar Pradesh	Lucknow	*Hindi*
Uttarakhand	Dehradun	*Hindi*
West Bengal	Kolkata	*Bengali*
Telangana	Hyderabad	*Telgu and Urdu*
Jammu & Kashmir	Srinagar/Jammu	*Kashmiri, Dongri, Urdu, Dardi and Pahari*
Andaman and Nicobar Islands	Shri Vijaya Puram	*Hindi, Nicobarese, Bengali, Malayalam, Tamil, Telugu*
Chandigarh	Chandigarh	*Hindi, Punjabi, English*
Dadar and Nagar Haveli and Daman and Diu	Daman	*Gujarati, Hindi*
Delhi	Delhi	*Hindi, Punjabi*
Lakshadweep	Kavaratti	*Malayalam*
Puducherry	Puducherry	*Tamil, Telugu, Malayalam, English and French*
Ladakh	Leh	*Ladakhi*

HIGH COURTS IN INDIA

Name	*Territorial Jurisdiction*	*Seat*
Allahabad	Uttar Pradesh	Prayagraj (Bench at Lucknow)
Andhra Pradesh	Andhra Pradesh	Amaravati
Bombay	Maharashtra, Goa, Dadar and Nagar Haveli and Daman and Diu	Mumbai (Benches at Nagpur, Panaji, and Aurangabad)
Calcutta	West Bengal and Andaman & Nicobar Islands	Kolkata (Circuit Benches at Port Blair and Jalpaiguri)
Chhattisgarh	Chhattisgarh	Bilaspur
Delhi	New Delhi	NCT of Delhi
Gauhati	Assam, Nagaland, Mizoram and Arunachal Pradesh	Guwahati (Benches at Kohima, Aizawl and Itanagar)
Gujarat	Gujarat	Sola (Ahmedabad)
Himachal Pradesh	Himachal Pradesh	Shimla
Jammu & Kashmir and Ladakh	Jammu & Kashmir/Ladakh	Srinagar and Jammu
Jharkhand	Jharkhand	Ranchi
Karnataka	Karnataka	Bengaluru (Circuit Benches at Dharwar and Gulbarga)
Kerala	Kerala & Lakshadweep	Kochi
Madhya Pradesh	Madhya Pradesh	Jabalpur (Benches at Gwalior and Indore)
Madras	Tamil Nadu & Puducherry	Chennai (Bench at Madurai)
Orissa	Odisha	Cuttack
Patna	Bihar	Patna
Punjab and Haryana	Punjab, Haryana and Chandigarh	Chandigarh
Rajasthan	Rajasthan	Jodhpur (Bench at Jaipur)
Sikkim	Sikkim	Gangtok
Uttarakhand	Uttarakhand	Nainital
Tripura	Tripura	Agartala
Meghalaya	Meghalaya	Shillong
Manipur	Manipur	Imphal
Telangana	Telangana	Hyderabad

FAMOUS HILL STATIONS

Hill Station	State/UT
1. Almora, Mussoorie, Nainital	Uttarakhand
2. Cherrapunji (Shillong), Khasi Hills (Shillong)	Meghalaya
3. Ooty, Kodaikanal, Yercaud	Tamil Nadu
4. Dalhousie, Kassauli	Himachal Pradesh
5. Darjeeling	West Bengal
6. Gulmarg, Srinagar	Jammu and Kashmir
7. Mahabaleshwar	Maharashtra
8. Mt. Abu	Rajasthan
9. Pachmarhi	Madhya Pradesh

FAMOUS NATIONAL PARKS

1. Corbett National Park	Nainital, Uttarakhand
2. Dudhwa National Park	Lakhimpur Kheri, Uttar Pradesh
3. Kaziranga National Park	Jorhat, Assam
4. Kanha National Park	Jabalpur, Bhedaghat
5. Gir National Park	Rajkot, Junagarh, Gujarat
6. Guindy National Park	Guindy, Chennai, Tamil Nadu
7. Nagairhole National Park	Coorg, Karnataka
8. Bandipur National Park	Mysore, Karnataka

FAMOUS NATIONAL WILDLIFE SANCTUARIES

1. Dachigam Wildlife Sanctuary	Srinagar, Jammu and Kashmir
2. Sariska	Alwar, Rajasthan
3. Hazaribagh Wildlife Sanctuary	Hazaribagh, Jharkhand
4. Tiger Project	Sawai Madhopur, Rajasthan
5. Mudhumali Wildlife Sanctuary	Mudhumalia, Nilgiri, Tamil Nadu
6. Periyar Wildlife Sanctuary	Idukki, Kottayam, Kerala

HOLY PLACES IN INDIA

1.	Amarnath	Jammu and Kashmir
2.	Ayodhya	Uttar Pradesh
3.	Badrinath	Uttarakhand
4.	Dwarka	Gujarat
5.	Haridwar	Uttarakhand
6.	Kancheepuram	Tamil Nadu
7.	Kedarnath	Uttarakhand
8.	Mathura	Uttar Pradesh
9.	Puri	Odisha
10.	Rameswaram	Tamil Nadu
11.	Tirupati	Andhra Pradesh
12.	Ujjain	Madhya Pradesh
13.	Varanasi	Uttar Pradesh
14.	Bodh Gaya	Bihar

SPORTS

Terms Associated With Sports :

Cricket : Ashes, Bye, Bodyline, Bowling, Break, Cover-point, Creases, Chinaman, Chucker, Drive, Duck, Follow on, Googly, Hit-Wicket, Hat-trick, Leg-before-wicket, Leg break, Leg-bye, Maiden over, No ball, Night-watchman, Runner, Run-out, Stumped, Silly-point, Slip.

Football : Handball, Corner kick, Dribble, Free Kick, Hat-trick, Off-side, Penalty Kick, Try, Throw in, Wembley.

Hockey : Bully, Carry, Corner kick, Corner, Penalty stroke, Off-side, Penalty, Roll in scoop, Sticks, Sudden death, Striking circle, Short Corner, Scoop, Tie-breaker, Under-cutting, Hat-trick.

Tennis : Backhand drive, Deuce, Fault, Half-volley, Net, Let, Volley, Smash, Service.

Billiards : Break, Cannons, Cue, Pot, Jigger, Scratch, In Bauk, In, Off.

Bridge : Dummy, Finesse, Grand-slam, Little Slam, Revoke, Ruff slam, Trump, Tricks, Vulnerable.

Volley Ball : Booster, Love, Service, Volley, Smasher.

Badminton : Smash, Drop, Let.

Chess : Check, Checkmate, Gambit, State-mate.

Golf : Bogy, Caddie, Hole, Links, Stymie, Tee, Put.

Polo : Chukker, Mallet, Bunder.

Baseball : Bunting, Diamond, Pitcher, Put-out, Strike, Home.

Boxing : Knockout, Punch, Upper-cut, Jab, Hook.

FAMOUS TROPHIES

Agha Khan Cup	Hockey
Beighton Cup	Hockey
Corbillion Cup	World Table Tennis (Women)
Davis Cup	Lawn Tennis
Duleep Trophy	Cricket
Durand Cup	Football
Ezra Cup	Polo
I.F.A. Shield	Football
Irani Cup	Cricket (India)
Jayalaxmi Cup	Table Tennis (Women)
Lady Rattan Tata Trophy	Hockey (Women)
Nehru Cup	Hockey (India)
Obaidullah Cup	Hockey
Ranji Trophy	Cricket (India)
Rangaswamy Cup	Hockey (India)
Rovers Cup	Football (India)
Santosh Trophy	Football (India)
Subroto Cup	Football
Thomas Cup	Badminton
Uber Cup	Badminton (Women)
Wellington Trophy	Rowing (India)

BIGGEST, LARGEST, TALLEST OF THE WORLD

Airport, *Largest*—King Fahd International Airport, Dammon (Saudi Arabia)

Animal, *Tallest*—Giraffe (Average height 6.09 m); *Largest and Heaviest*—Blue Whale (190 tonnes)

Longest recorded Animal—Boot lace Worm (55 m); *Fastest*—Cheetah (Approximately 100 km/hr)

Bay, *Largest*—Bay of Bengal

Continent, *biggest*—Asia (31,845,872 km^2); *Smallest*—Australia Mainland (Area 76,17,930 km^2)

Desert, *Largest*—Sahara (N. Africa; maximum length 5,150 km EW; maximum width 3,200 km NS)

Dome, *Largest*—Singapore National Stadium (310 m)

Fish, *Largest fresh water*—Plabeuk (China, Laos and Thailand); *Most abundant*—Bristle mouth; *Most venomous*—Stone Fish (Indo-Pacific Waters)

Fountain, *Tallest*—King Fahd's Fountain (Jeddah, Saudi Arabia)

Gulf, *Largest*—Gulf of Mexico (1,544,000 sq. km)

Island, *Biggest*—Greenland (Kalaatdlit Nunaat-2,175,000 sq km)

Lake, *Largest*—Caspian Sea (Azerbaijan, Russia, Iran border: 37.18 lakh km^2); *Deepest*—Baikal (Siberia); *Largest (fresh water)*—Superior Lake (USA---Canada border: 82,350 km^2)

Mountain, *Highest peak*—Mt. Everest (8848 m; Nepal); *Highest range*—Himalayas, Asia (upto 4200 m); *Greatest mountain range*—Himalaya-Karakoram (96 out of 109 peaks over 7315 m are here)

Museum, *Largest*—American Museum of Natural History, New York

Ocean, *Largest and Deepest*—The Pacific (Area: 166,240,000 km^2; Depth: 10,924 m)

Platform, *Longest (rail)*—Shri Siddharoodha Swamiji Railway Station, Hubballi (Karnataka; India, 1507 m. long)

Railway Station, *Largest*—Grand Central Terminal (New York City; 19 hc)

Rivers, *Longest*—(i) Nile (6650 km) (ii) Amazon (6437 km)

Star, *Brightest*—Sirius A (also called Dog Star)

Temple, *Largest*—Angkor Vat (Cambodia: 402 acres)

Tunnel, *Longest (railway)*—Gotthard Base Rail Tunnel (Switzerland; 57.1 km); *Largest (road)*—Laerdal, Norway (24.51 km)

FIRST IN INDIA

Governor General of Independent India — Lord Mountbatten

Cosmonaut — Sq. Ldr. Rakesh Sharma

Field Marshal — S.H.F.J. Manekshaw

Indian Governor General of Indian Union — C. Rajagopalachari

Indian I.C.S. Officer — Satyendra Nath Tagore

Indian to swim across English Channel — Mihir Sen

Indian Women to swim across English Channel — Miss Arti Saha

Man to climb Mount Everest — Tenzing Norgay

Man to climb Mount Everest without Oxygen — Phu Dorjee

Man to climb Mount Everest twice — Nwang Gombu

Nobel Prize Winner — Rabindra Nath Tagore

President of Indian National Congress — W.C. Banerjee

President of Indian Republic — Dr. Rajendra Prasad

Talkie Film — Alam Ara (1931)

Test Tube Baby (Documented) — Indira

Viceroy of India — Lord Canning

Woman Minister of Indian Union — Rajkumari Amrit Kaur

Woman Governor — Mrs. Sarojini Naidu

Woman President of Indian National Congress — Dr. Annie Besant

Woman Prime Minister — Mrs. Indira Gandhi

Woman Speaker of a State Assembly — Mrs. Shanno Devi

Prime Minister of India — Pt. Jawaharlal Nehru

Muslim President of Indian Union — Dr. Zakir Hussain

Speaker of Lok Sabha — G.V. Mavlankar

Women to Climb Mount Everest — Bachhendri Pal

Woman Judge in Supreme Court — Mrs. Meera Sahib Fatima Biwi

Women Chief Justice of a High Court — Smt. Leela Seth

The First Indian Weightlifter to Win bronze medal in Olympics — Karnam Malleshwari (Sydney, in 2000)

Chief of Defence Staff (CDS) —General Bipin Rawat

World Chess Champion — Vishwanathan Anand

India's First Woman Merchant Navy Officer — Sonali Banerjee

The First Woman Air Vice-Marshal — P. Bandopadhyaya

The First Indian to be appointed as United Nations Civilian Police Advisor — Ms. Kiran Bedi

The First Women to be appointed Deputy Governor of Reserve Bank of India — K.J. Udeshi

The First Indian Lady to win a medal in World Athletic Championship — Anju Bobby George

The First Sikh Prime Minister of India — Dr. Manmohan Singh

IMPORTANT DAYS

15th January — Army Day
26th January — Republic Day
30th January — Leprosy Eradication Day/ Martyr's Day
28th February — National Science Day
8th march — International Women's Day
15th March — World Consumer's Day
21st March — World Disabled Day
5th April — National Marine Day
7th April — World Health Day
18th April — World Heritage Day
22nd April — International Earth Day
Ist May — Worker's Day
3rd May — International Sun Day
21st May — Anti-Terrorism Day
24th May — Commonwealth Day
31st May — World No Tobacco Day
5th June — World Environment Day
21st June — World Yoga Day
26th June — International Day against Drug Abuse
11th July — World Population Day
15th August — Independence Day
24th August — Sanskrit Day
5th September — Teacher's Day
8th September — World Literacy Day
27th September — World Tourism Day
1st October — World Elder's Day
4th October — World Animal Day
8th October — Air Force Day
10th October — National Solidarity Day
16th October — World Food Day
24th October — U.N. Day
14th November — World Diabetes Day
14th November — Children's Day
19th November — National Integration Day
26th November — Law Day
1st December — World AIDS Day
4th December — Navy Day
7th December — Flag Day
10th December — Human Rights Day

PARLIAMENTS OF IMPORTANT COUNTRIES

Afghanistan — Shora
Britain — Parliament House of Commons, House of Lords
Denmark — Folketing
The Netherlands — States General
India — Sansad
Israel — Knesset
Iran — Majlis
Ireland — Airetann
Iceland — Althing
Japan — Diet
Norway — Storting
Russia — Supreme Soviet
Spain — Cortes
Sweden — Riksdag
U.S.A. — Congress Senate
Germany — Bundestag

MINERAL RESOURCES OF THE WORLD

Mineral	Largest Producers
Iron Ore	China, Japan, Russia
Tin	China, Indonesia, Peru
Lead	China, Australia, U.S.A.
Zinc	China, Australia, Peru
Manganese	South Africa, Brazil, Australia
Aluminium	China, Russia, Canada
Petroleum	Saudi Arabia, Russia, USA
Silver	Peru, Mexico, China
Coal	China, USA, India

WORLD'S LARGEST PRODUCERS

Articles	Producers	Articles	Producers
Carpets	Iran	Cheese	USA
Cocoa	Cote d'Ivoire	Coffee	Brazil
Copper	Chile	Cotton	China
Diamonds	Russia	Jute	India
Rice	China	Rubber	Thailand
Silk	China	Steel	China
Sugar	Brazil	Tea	China
Tin	China	Wheat	China
Wool	Australia		

TEN LARGEST COUNTRIES BY AREAS

Rank by Area	Country	Area (sq. km.)
1.	Russia	17,075,400
2.	Canada	9,976,139
3.	China	9,561,000
4.	U.S.A.	9,363,123
5.	Brazil	8,511,965
6.	Australia	7,686,848
7.	India	3,287,263
8.	Argentina	2,776,889
9.	Kazakhstan	2,724,900
10.	Algeria	2,381,741

PRESIDENT OF INDIA

He is the constitutional head of the Republic but not the real executive.

Qualifications: (1) Indian citizen; (2) age not less than 35 years; (3) should have qualifications for election to Lok Sabha; (4) should not hold any office of profit; (5) should not be a Member of Parliament or State Legislature.

Election: He is elected by the elected Members of Parliament and State Legislative Assemblies in accordance with the system of proportional representation by means of single transferable vote.

Powers: He makes appointment to all the Constitutional posts. He can address either House of Parliament and send message to them. He can summon and prorogue either House of Parliament and dissolve Lok Sabha. All Bills passed by Parliament must receive his assent to become an Act. He issues Ordinance when Parliament is not in session. No money Bill can be introduced in Lok Sabha without his recommendation. He can grant pardon, reprieve or remit punishment and he can commute death sentences. He can declare national emergency, state emergency and financial emergency.

VICE-PRESIDENT OF INDIA

The Vice-President acts as the ex-officio Chairman of Rajya Sabha and acts as the President when the latter is unable to discharge his functions due to illness, absence or any other reason, or till the election of a new President when a vacancy is caused by the death, resignation or removal of the President.

The Vice-President is elected by an electoral college consisting of the members of both Houses of Parliament in accordance with the system of proportional representation by means of the single transferable vote. He must be a citizen of India, not less than 35 years of age, and should be eligible for election as a member of the Council of States.

PRIME MINISTER OF INDIA

The Prime Minister is the leader of the majority party in the Parliament and the President cannot exercise his discretion in the appointment of the Prime Minister. He stays in office till the majority of the members of Lok Sabha has confidence in him. He occupies an important posi-tion in relation to the council of Ministers. He recommends the names of the persons to be included in the Council of Ministers. He allocates portfolios among them and can ask any minister to tender resignation. He can drop a minister while reshuffling the ministry. He coordinates the administration of various departments. He is the chief link between the President and the Council. He is the leader of the majority party and so, he has a great influence on the Parliament and the party. The Prime Minister enjoys such extensive powers as have been described as the virtual ruler of the country.

THE SOLAR SYSTEM: SOME FACTS

Number of Planets: 8—Mercury, Venus, Earth, Mars, Jupiter, Saturn, Uranus and Neptune.

Largest most

Massive planet .... Jupiter
Brightest planet .... Venus
Brightest star .... Sirius
Fastest orbiting planet .... Mercury
Longest (Synodic) day .... Mercury
Planet with largest moon .... Jupiter
Greatest average density .... Jupiter
Tallest mountain .... Earth

Strongest magnetic fields .... Jupiter
Most circular orbit .... Venus
Shortest (synodic) day .... Jupiter
Hottest planet .... Venus
No moons .... Mercury, Venus
Planet with moon with most eccentric orbit .... Neptune
Lowest average density .... Saturn
Deepest Oceans .... Jupiter
Greatest amount of liquid on the surface .... Earth

THE EARTH: FACTS AND DATA

Composition of the Earth: Aluminium (0.4%), Sulphur (2.7%), Silicon (13%), Oxygen (28%), Calcium (1.2%), Nickel (2.7%), Magnesium (17%), Iron (35%)

Surface area	: 510100500 sq km
Land Surface (29.1%)	: 148950800 sq km
Ocean Surface (70.9%)	: 361149700 sq km
Type of water	: 97% salt, 3% fresh
Total area of water	: 382672000 sq km
Equatorial diameter	: 12753 km
Equatorial Circumference	: 40066 km

Polar Circumference	: 39992 km
Polar diameter	: 12710 km
Equatorial radius	: 6376 km
Polar radius	: 6335 km
Mass (estimated weight)	: 594×10^{19} metric tons
Mean distance from the Sun	: 149407000 km

Earth's orbit speed (around sun)	: 107320 kmph	Time of Rotation (on its axis)	: 23 hrs 56 min 4.09 seconds
Period of Revolution (round the sun)	: 365 days 5 hrs 48 min. 45.51 seconds	Inclination of the axis (to the plane of the ecliptic)	: 23°27'

PRINCIPAL MOUNTAIN PEAKS OF THE WORLD

Mountains	Height in Metres	Range	Date of First Ascent
1. Mount Everest	8,848	Himalayas	May 29, 1953
2. K-2 (Godwin Austen)	8,611	Karakoram	July 31, 1954
3. Kanchenjunga	8,597	Himalayas	May 25, 1955
4. Lhotse	8,511	Himalayas	May 18, 1956
5. Makalu I	8,481	Himalayas	May 15, 1955
6. Dhaulagiri I	8,167	Himalayas	May 13, 1960
7. Mansalu I	8,156	Himalayas	May 9, 1956
8. Chollyo	8,153	Himalayas	Oct. 19, 1954
9. Nanga Parbat	8,124	Himalayas	July 3, 1953
10. Annapurna I	8,091	Himalayas	June 3, 1950
11. Gasherbrum I	8,068	Karakoram	July 5, 1958
12. Broad Peak I	8,047	Karakoram	June 9, 1957
13. Gasherbrum II	8,034	Karakoram	July 7, 1956
14. Shisha Pangma (Gosainthan)	8,014	Himalayas	May 2, 1964
15. Gasherbrum III	7,952	Karakoram	Aug. 11, 1975

POPULAR NICK NAMES OF SOME FAMOUS PERSONALITIES

Andhra Kesari	T. Prakasam	Lal, Bal, Pal	Lala Lajpat Rai, Bal Gangadhar Tilak, Bipin Chandra Pal
Anna	C.N. Anna Durai	Little Corporal	Napoleon Bonaparte
Bang Bandhu	Sheikh Mujibur Rehman	Lokmanya	Bal Gangadhar Tilak
Bapu	Mahatma Gandhi	Mahamana	Pt. Madan Mohan Malaviya
Bard of Avon	William Shakespeare	Maid of Orleans	Joan of Arc
Chachaji	Jawaharlal Nehru	Maiden Queen	Queen Elizabeth I
Desh Bandhu	C.R. Das	Missile Man	A.P.J. Abdul Kalam
Frontier Gandhi	Khan Abdul Gaffar Khan	Man of Destiny	Napoleon Bonaparte
Fuhrer	Adolf Hitler	Netaji	Subhash Chandra Bose
G.B.S.	George Bernard Shaw	Nightingale of India	Sarojini Naidu
Grand Old Man of India	Dadabhai Naoroji	Panditji	Jawaharlal Nehru
Grand Old Man of Britain	Gladstone	Punjab Kesari	Lala Lajpat Rai
Guru Dev	Rabindra Nath Tagore	Shastriji	Lal Bahadur Shastri
Guruji	M.S. Golwalkar	Uncle Ho	Ho Chi Minh
Iron Man of India	Sardar Patel	Wizard of the North	Walter Scott
Lok Nayak	Jayaprakash Narayan		
Lady with the Lamp	Florence Nightingale		

FAMOUS INTERNATIONAL ORGANISATIONS, HEADQUARTERS

International Organisations	*Headquarters*
United Nations Organisations (U.N.O.)	New York
International Monetary Fund (I.M.F.)	Washington D.C.
World Health Organisation (W.H.O.)	Geneva
Food & Agricultural Organisation (FAO)	Rome
International Labour Organisation (ILO)	Geneva
UNESCO	Paris
International Court of Justice	The Hague
Universal Postal Union (UPU)	Berne
International Civil Aviation Organisation (ICAO)	Montreal
UNIDO	Vienna
International Atomic Energy Agency (IAEA)	Vienna
International Finance Corporation (IFC)	Washington
United Nations Development Programme (UNDP)	New York
UNICEF	New York
International Maritime Organisation (IMO)	London
World Meteorological Organisation (WMO)	Geneva
International Telecommunication Union (ITU)	Geneva
Arab League	Cairo
Commonwealth of Nations	London
World Trade Organisation (WTO)	Geneva
International Development Association (IDA)	Washington D.C.
International Bank for Reconstruction and Development (IBRD)	Washington D.C.
World Intellectual Property Organisation (WIPO)	Geneva
Organisation of Islamic Conference (OIC)	Jeddah (Saudi Arabia)
European Union	Brussels
Red Cross	Geneva
Interpol	Lyons (France)
Asian Development Bank (ADB)	Manila
North Atlantic Treaty Organisation (NATO)	Brussels
Association of South East Asian Nations (ASEAN)	Jakarta

AWARDS

NOBEL PRIZES

- These Prizes were instituted in 1901 by a Swedish scientist, Dr. Alfred Nobel; the discoverer of Dynamite.
- Six prizes are awarded annually for (*i*) Chemistry, (*ii*) Physics, (*iii*) Medicine, (*iv*) Literature, (*v*) Peace and (*vi*) Economics —started since 1969.
- The following Indians so far have been awarded these prizes: (*i*) Dr. Rabindra Nath Tagore (1913) for his "Geetanjali". (*ii*) Dr. C.V. Raman for Physics in 1930, (*iii*) Mother Teresa for Peace in 1979, (*iv*) Prof. Amartya Sen in 1998 for Economics and (*v*) Kailash Satyarthi in 2014 for Peace.
- In addition, four non-resident Indians have also been awarded the Nobel Prize. They are: (*i*) Hargobind Khurana for Medicine in 1968, (*ii*) Subramanian Chandrasekhar for Physics in 1983, (*iii*) Venkatraman Ramkrishnan for Chemistry in 2009, (*iv*) Abhijit Vinayak Banerjee for Economics in 2019.

BHARAT RATNA

- Bharat Ratna is India's highest Civilian Award. It was first awarded in 1954.
- The actual award is designed in the shape of a *peepal* leaf with Bharat Ratna inscribed in Devanagri script in the Sun Figure.
- This is India's highest civilian award. It is given for exceptional work on art, literature, science and recognition of public service of the highest order.
- The emblem, the Sun and the rim are of platinum. The inscriptions are in burnished bronze.
- Government servants are not eligible for it.

ART AND CULTURE

☞ Classical Dances

Dance	*State*	*Famous Artists*
Bharat Natyam	Tamil Nadu	Yamini Krishnamurthy, Rukmini Devi Arundale, Swapna Sundari, Sonal Mansingh, Vaijanti Mala, Mrinalini Sarabhai, Chandralekha, Indrani, Ram Gopal, Bal Saraswati
Kathakali	Kerala	Gopinath, K.K. Nayar, Kunju-Kurup, T.K. Chandu
Kuchipudi	Andhra Pradesh/ Telangana	Sapna Sundari, Raja Reddy, Shobha Nayar, Radha Reddy, Vedantam Satyanarayan, Vimpanti Chinna Satyam.
Kathak	North India	Birju Maharaj, Gopi Krishna, Shambhu Maharaj, Sitara Devi, Vishnu Sharma, Durga Lal, Shobhana Narayan
Odissi	Odisha	Kelucharan Mahapatra, Indrani Rehman, Madhavi Mudgal, Pratima Bedi, Samyukta Panigrahi, Sonal Mansingh, Debudas
Manipuri	Manipur	Uday Shankar, Bipin Singh, Suryamukhi, Darohra Jhaveri

☞ Famous Folk Dances

State/UT	*Folk Dance*	*State/UT*	*Folk Dance*
Andhra Pradesh/ Telangana	Dandari, Banjara	Kerala	Mohini Attam, Padayuni
Assam	Bihu, Keli Gopal, Sataria	Madhya Pradesh	Lota Nritya, Jawara
Bihar	Chhau, Magahi, Durga dance	Maharashtra	Tamasha, Dahi Handi, Gof, Deepak Dindi
W. Bengal	Kirtan, Kalatri, Asweabadh, Brita, Kalidance	Manipur	Dhol Cholam
Chhattisgarh	Saila, Karama, Bhagoria	Meghalaya	Nongakarem
Gujarat	Garba, Rasalila, Tippani, Dandia,	Nagaland	Bamboo dance
		Odisha	Chhau, Maya Shabari, Dalachai
Haryana	Damyal, Lahoor	Punjab	Gidda, Bhangra, Panihari
Himachal Pradesh	Dussehra dance, Hikat, Notio	Rajasthan	Thumar, Kathaputali, Tera Tali
Jammu & Kashmir	Dumhal	Tamil Nadu	Terukalathu, Kabalatam, Kargam, Pulivesham
		Tripura	Hazagiri
Jharkhand	Jhau, Ghumakudia, Jadur, Sarhul, Soharai, Karama, Vaima, Loojhari, Jat-Jatin, Vidayat	Uttar Pradesh	Rasalila, Nautanki, Thali, Dhurang, Jhumela, Huraka, Bol.
		Uttarakhand	Kajari, Karan
Karnataka	Yakshagan, Dolu Kunitha	Goa	Dhode Modini

MUSIC

Main Schools of Classical Music

- There are two main schools of classical music, namely, the Hindustani and the Carnatic. The Hindustani school of classical music is in vogue in north-western India, eastern India and northern parts of the South India.

Musical Instruments

- ***They are:*** Tabla, Mridangam, Pakhawaj, Chandai, Dholak, Veena, Sitar, Sarod, Gootuvadhyam, Sarangi, Flute, Nadaswaram, Shehnai, Shringi and Turahi.

FAMOUS INTERNATIONAL AIR SERVICES

Air Service	*Name of Country*	*Air Service*	*Name of Country*
Air India	India	Lufthansa Airlines	Germany
British Overseas Airways Corporation	Britain	Iraqi Airways	Iraq
Trans World Airlines	America	National Airlines	Iran
Russian Airlines	Russia	Quantas Airlines	Australia
Japan Airlines	Japan	Hong-Kong Airlines	Hong-Kong
Pakistan International Airlines	Pakistan	Egypt Airlines	Egypt
Malaysia Airlines	Malaysia	Slovak Airlines	Slovakia
Royal Nepal Airlines	Nepal	S.I.A.	Singapore
Swiss Airways	Switzerland	Garuda Airways	Indonesia
Air France	France	Bangladesh Viman Sewa	Bangladesh
Kuwait Airways	Kuwait	Air Lanka	Sri Lanka
Pan American World Airways	America	Elitalia Airlines	Italy
K.L.M. Royal Airlines	The Netherlands (Holland)	Air Canada	Canada

FAMOUS RELIGIONS, FOUNDERS, HOLY BOOKS & PLACES OF WORSHIP

Religion	*Founder*	*Holy Books*	*Place of Worship*
Hinduism	Hinduism has no one Founder. (This religion is based upon the religion of original Aryan Settlers)	Ramayan, Vedas, Puranas and Geeta	Temple
Sikh	Guru Nanak Dev	Guru Grantha Sahib	Gurdwara
Christianity	Jesus Christ	Bible	Church
Islam	Prophet Mohammed	Koran (Quran)	Mosque
Parsi	Zoroaster	Zend Avesta	Fire Temple
Jainism	Adinath Rishavdev	Jain Granth	Jain Temple
Buddhism	Gautam Buddha	Tripitaka	Buddha Temple
Jew	Moosa	Torah	Synagogue

INTELLIGENCE AGENCIES OF SOME PROMINENT COUNTRIES

Country	*Intelligence Agency*	*Country*	*Intelligence Agency*
India	Research & Analysis Wing (RAW), Intelligence Bureau (I.B.), Central Bureau of Investigation (C.B.I.)	Russia	K.G.B. (Komitel Gosudarstvennoy Bezopasnosty) (Committee for State Security)
Pakistan	Inter Service Intelligence (I.S.I.)	Canada	Security Intelligence Service
U.S.A.	Central Intelligence Agency, Federal Bureau of Investigation	S. Africa	Bureau of State Security
		Iran	Sabak
Britain	Military Intelligence (M.I.)-5 and 6, Special Branch, Ultra, Joint Intelligence Organisation	Iraq	Al-Mukhabarat
		Australia	Australian Security and Intelligence Organisation
Israel	Mosad	France	S.D.E.C.E.
Egypt	Mukhabarat	Spain	C.E.S.I.D.
Japan	Nicho	Cuba	D.G.I.

SOME PROMINENT RACES OF THE WORLD

Races	Country/Area	Races	Country/Area	Races	Country/Area	Races	Country/Area
Veddas	Sri Lanka	Pygmy	Congo Basin	Eskimo	Canada, Tundra Region	Bushman	Kalahari Desert
Somaid	West Sıberıa	Bantu	Central and South Africa	Lapps	European Tundra	Red Indian	North America
Masai	East Africa						
Muree	New Zealand	Tartars	Siberia	Hausa	Nigeria		
Yakoot	Russian Tundra	Baddu	Arab's Desert	Kirghiz	Steppes (Russia)		
Papuans	New Guyana	Semang	Malaysia				

FAMOUS STRAITS OF THE WORLD

Strait	Between	Country
Malacca Strait	Andaman Sea and South China Sea	Indonesia
Palk Strait	Mannar and Bay of Bengal	India-Sri Lanka
Magellan Strait	Pacific and South Atlantic Ocean	Chile
Dover Strait	English Channel and North Sea	England-France
Berring Strait	Berring Sea and Chukasi Sea	Alaska-Russia
Sugaroo Strait	Japan Sea and Pacific Ocean	Japan
Sunda Strait	Java and Indian Ocean	Indonesia
Gibralter Strait	Mediterranean Sea and Atlantic Ocean	Spain
Harmuj Strait	Persia and Bay of Oman	Oman-Iran
Hudson Strait	Bay of Hudson and Atlantic Ocean	Canada

FAMOUS NEWSPAPERS OF THE WORLD

Newspaper	Place of Publishing	Language	Newspaper	Place of Publishing	Language
Daily News	New York (America)	English	Hindu, Hindustan, Times of India, Tribune, Statesman, Indian Express, Economic Times	India	English
Guardian	London (Britain)	English	Hindustan, Nav Bharat Times, Dainik Bhaskar, Dainik Jagaran, Punjab Kesari	India	Hindi
Pravada	Moscow (Russia)	Russian			
Al-Ahram	Cairo (Egypt)	Arabic			
Merdeca	Jakarta (Indonesia)	Indonesian			
Times	London (Britain)	English			
People's Daily	Beijing (China)	Chinese			
New Statesman	Britain	English			
Daily Mirror	Britain	English			

IMPORTANT BOUNDARY LINES

Boundary Line	Countries	Boundary Line	Countries
Durand Line	Pakistan and Afghanistan	17th Parallel	The line which defined the boundary between North Vietnam and South Vietnam before the two were united.
Hindenberg Line	Germany-Poland	38th Parallel	North Korea and South Korea
Maginot Line	France and Germany	49th Parallel	U.S.A. and Canada
Mannerhein Line	Russia-Finland		
Mc Mahon Line	India-China		
Order Niesse Line	Germany-Poland		
Radcliff Line	India-Pakistan		
Seigfrid Line	Germany-France		
24th Parallel	India-Pakistan		

SIGNALS/SIGNS AND MEANING

Signal/Sign	*Meaning*	*Signal/Sign*	*Meaning*
Red Triangle	Family Planning	White Flag	Treaty or Surrender
Red Cross	Medical Help	Yellow Flag	Vehicles with patients of contagious diseases
Red Light	Danger, 'Stop' for the movement of vehicles	Two Bones across with a Skull	Danger of electricity
Green Light	Go	Half mast flown Flag	National mourning
Olive Branch	Peace	Lotus and culture	Sign of civilization
White Pigeon or Dove	Peace	Wheel (Chakra)	Sign of Progress
Black Strip on Arm	(i) Opposition (ii) Sorrow	A blind folded woman with scale in hand	Sign of Justice
Black Flag	Opposition	Reversed flown	National calamity flag
Red Flag	(i) Danger (ii) Revolution		

NATIONAL EMBLEMS OF IMPORTANT COUNTRIES

Country	*National Emblem*	*Country*	*National Emblem*
America	Golden Rod	New Zealand	Kiwi, Fern Southern Cross
Australia	Kangaroo	Norway	Lion
Ireland	Shamrock	Nepal	Kukri
Italy	White Lily	Pakistan	Crescent
Israel	Candelabrum	Poland	Eagle
Iran	Rose	France	Lily
Canada	White Lily	Belgium	Lion
Great Britain	Rose	Bangladesh	Water Lily
Chile	Candor and Huemul	Mongolia	The Soyombo
Germany	Corn Flower	Russia	Double headed eagle
Japan	Chrysanthemum	Lebanon	Cedar Tree
Zimbabwe	Zimbabwe Bird	Sudan	Secretary Bird
Denmark	Beach	Syria	Eagle
Turkiye	Crescent and Star	India	Lioned Capital
The Netherlands	Lion		

THE CONTINENTS OF THE WORLD

Name	*Population (2021) (In million)*	*Per cent of the world's population*
Asia	4,584	59.1
Africa	1,375	17.4
Europe	747	9.8
North America	373	4.8
South America	651	8.4
Australia	41.66	0.5
Antarctica	NA	NA

COMPUTER

The computer is the system of that electronic device through which various informations are processed on the basis of a definite set of instructions called program and mathematical (numerical) and non-mathematical both types of informations are processed.

The first mechanical computer was composed or fabricated by Blaise Pascal in 1642 and it is called Pascalene. But in 1833, Charles Babbage first time conceived an automatic calculator or computer. Charles Babbage is called the father of modern computer. Herman made an electronic tabulating machine based on punch cards which operates automatically.

In 1937, first mechanical computer mark-I was fabricated by Howard Akeen. The most outstanding contribution in the development of modern computer goes to John Wan Newmaan who brought the 2nd revolution in the area of computer in 1951. He discovered EDVAC (Electronic Discrete Variable Automatic Computer) and utilised the stored program and the binary number system in the computer.

FUNCTIONS OF COMPUTER

1. Collection and composition (input) of datas;
2. Storage of datas.
3. Processing of datas.
4. Retrieval or output of the proccessed informations and datas.

UNITS OF COMPUTER

1. Input unit.
2. Central processing unit–CPU.
3. External Memory unit.
4. Output unit.

The CPU of the computer is called brain of the computer and sometimes CPU is also called Micro Processor of the computer. The data is entered through the input unit in the computer and through the central processing unit with the help of External Memory Unit datas are arranged and processed. Ultimately by the output unit these datas or informations are issued or released.

PARTS OF COMPUTER

- **Monitor :** The monitor of the computer is like a television in which the picture appears in the form of doted points on the screen and these are called pixcels.
- **Hard Disc and Floppy Disc :** The Hard Disc is the permanent disc in the computers while the Floppy Disc is the disc utilised when datas or informations are to be transferred from one computer to another.
- **Mouse :** The mouse of the computer is like the remote control of TV through which computer is directly regulated or controlled without utilising the key-board.
- **Printer :** The printer is a device which prints any documents or processed informations of the computer.

SOME HIGH LEVEL LANGUAGES

1. **FORTRAN :** This language was developed for solving the mathematical formulae very quickly and conveniently.
2. **COBOL :** This language was developed for the commerical purposes. For the processing of this language a group of sentences is selected called paragraph and all paragraphs composed are called a section, while all sections composed are called a division.
3. **BASIC :** In basic a definite part of the prescribed instruction is only inserted in the computer.
4. **ALGOL :** This was basically fabricated and designed for the complex algebraic calculations.
5. **PASCAL :** It is an amplified and modified form of ALGOL.
6. **COMAL :** This computer language is used for the students of secondary level.
7. **LOGO :** This language is used for children and kids for drawing Graphic line diagrams.
8. **PROLOG :** This language is developed in 1973 in France and this language is used for Artificial Intelligence which is capable and equivalent to the logical program.

9. **FORTH :** This language was invented by Charles Mure which is frequently used in all types of the works in the computer.

COMPUTER VIRUS

The computer virus is an electronic code which is used to abolish or erradicate the inclusive informations or programs of the computer. Some important computer viruses are Micheleanjalo, Dork Avangor, kilo, filip, Macmug, Scores, Casecade, Jeruslem, Date crime, Coloumbs crime, Internet virus, Pachcom, Pach EXE, COM-EXE, Marizuana, C-brain, bloody, Chenge Mungu and Desi etc.

COMPUTER NETWORKING

There are two types of networkings which are usually occur—Local Area Networking (LAN) and Wide Area Networking (WAN). By LAN all the computers of the same buildings are connected like the computers of university premises, computers of offices etc.

By WAN all the comptuers of a large area are connected like the computers of all the offices of a city or town etc. In India a very large computer network namely INDONET has been installing through which all the main towns and cities has to be interlinked.

COMPUTER TERMINOLOGY

- **Bit :** The bit is a unit of measurement of the electronic data. One bit is either 0 or 1 but not both. On composing 8 bits, 1 byte is formed.
- **Bug :** The Bug is the error in the computer program or system and its eradication is called Debug.
- **Byte :** Total eight bits compose a byte. Thus 8 bits = 1 byte.
- **CD-ROM :** A CD like of music CD in which data can be stored substantially called CD-ROM. In a CD with comparison to floppy extremely more datas can be stored but one problem in it is that one time recorded data can not be deleted or modified.
- **Chip :** It is a thin slice on which by a special mechanism a circuit is designed which is normally made from Silicon.
- **Memory System :** The place where computer data and program are temporarily kept is called Memory system. Usually memory is implied from RAM.
- **Modem :** The device which converts digital signals into analogue signals and vice-versa is called Modem.
- **RAM :** It is Random Access Memory (a place) where datas to be processed are kept temporarily and it is unstable memory.
- **ROM :** It is Read Only Memory and it is stable or Non-valatile memory which doesn't ended after power off.
- **Scanner :** It is a device through which graphic image is transformed to digital image and the scanners are of usually two types one desktop and another hand operating.

PROGRAMING

Computers perform phenomenal feats of calculation, but they do not do so in a complicated way. They actually carry out very simple operations, such as addition and subtraction. They achieve their fantastic computing power by carrying out these operations at incredible speed.

The programme, or set of instructions for operating the computer, is therefore written as a sequence of very simple steps. (See box below) Several computer languages have been developed for different applications, including BASIC, COBOL, FORTRAN and PASCAL. Writing programmes is very skilled and time-consuming work. But for most typical computer applications ready-written programmes are available, called "packages".

☞ How A Programme Works

Without a programme to tell it what to do and how to do it, a computer is unable to function. If, for example, you wanted to know how many times the word 'the' appears in this paragraph, or in the whole book, it would not be enough merely to put the text into a computer and then ask it how many times the word appears. For the computer to accomplish the calculations it has to be told what to do in simple steps. The instructions might be:

1. Scan the text until a space followed by 'T' or 't' is found.
2. If the next letter is not 'h', go back to step 1.
3. If the letter is 'h', is the next letter 'e'?
4. If not, go back to step 1. If it is, go to step 5.
5. If 'e' is followed by a space, add 1 to the total.
6. Go back to step 1.

A full computer programme for this operation would need to be broken down into even more simple steps, but a series of such programmes could enable a computer to analyse any amount of text in great detail.

DEFENCE

The Supreme Command of the Armed Forces is vested in the hands of the President of the Country. The responsibility for national defence, however, rests with the Cabinet. All important questions having a bearing on defence are decided by the Cabinet Committee on Political Affairs, which is presided over by the Prime Minister. The Defence Minister is responsible to Parliament for all matters concerning the Defence Services. All the administrative and operational control of Armed Forces are exercised by the Ministry of Defence. The three services – Army, Navy and Air Force function through their respective service headquarters headed by the chief of Staff.

COMMISSIONED RANKS IN DEFENCE SERVICES

Army	Navy	Air Force
General	Admiral	Air Chief Marshal
Lieutenant-General	Vice-Admiral	Air Marshal
Major-General	Rear-Admiral	Air Vice-Marshal
Brigadier	Commodor	Air Commodor
Colonel	Captain	Group Captain
Lieutenant-Colonel	Commander	Wing Commander
Major	Lt.Commander	Squadron Leader
Captain	Lieutenant	Flight Lieutenant
Lieutenant	Sub-Lieutenant	Flying Officer

INTERNAL SECURITY ORGANISATIONS OF INDIA

S. No	Name of Organisation	Year of Creation	Headquarters
1.	Assam Rifles (A.R.)	1835	Shillong
2.	Central Reserve Police Force (C.R.P.F.)	1939	New Delhi
3.	National Cadet Corps (N.C.C.)	1948	New Delhi
4.	Territorial Army	1948	In different States
5.	Indo-Tibetan Border Police	1962	New Delhi
6.	Home Guard	1962	In different States
7.	Coast Guard	1978	New Delhi
8.	Border Security Force (B.S.F.)	1965	New Delhi
9.	Central Industrial Security Force (C.I.S.F.)	1969	New Delhi
10.	National Security Guard	1984	New Delhi
11.	Police	—	In different States

COMMANDER-IN-CHIEFS OF INDIA

1. General Sir Rob Lockhart	Aug. 15, 1947 — Dec. 31, 1947
2. General Sir Roy Bucher	Jan. 1, 1948 — Jan. 14, 1949
3. General K. M. Kariappa	Jan. 15, 1949 — Jan. 14, 1953
4. General Maharaj Rajendra Sinhji	Jan. 15, 1953 — March 31, 1955

FIRST INDIAN CHIEFS OF STAFF OF INDIAN FORCES

1. General Maharaj Rajendra Sinhji (Army Staff)	April 1, 1955 — May 14, 1955
2. Vice Admiral R.D. Katari (Naval Staff)	April 22, 1958 — June 4, 1962
3. Air Marshal S. Mukherjee (Air Staff)	April 1, 1954 — Nov. 8, 1960

ARMY INSTITUTES

1. Sainik Schools upto +2 Level	33 places in India
2. Rashtriya Indian Military College (prepare for entrance to N.D.A)	Dehradun
3. National Defence Academy (three services)	Khadakwasla, Pune
4. Indian Military Academy (Army)	Dehradun
5. Officers Training Academy (3 services) Short Courses	Chennai
6. National Defence College	New Delhi
7. The College of Combat	Mhow
8. The College of Military Engineering	Kirkee
9. Military College of Telecommunication Engineering	Mhow
10. The armoured Corps Centre and School	Ahmed Nagar
11. The School Artillery	Deolali
12. The Infantry School	Mhow and Belgaum
13. College of Material Management	Jabalpur

AIR FORCE INSTITUTIONS

Air Force Academy	Hyderabad
Helicopter Training School	Hakimpet
Flying Instructors School	Tambaram, Chennai
The College of Air Warfare	Secunderabad
Air Force Administrative College	Coimbatore
Air Force Technical College	Jalahalli

DEFENCE PRODUCTION UNITS

1. Bharat Dynamites Ltd.	Hyderabad
2. Praga Tools	Hyderabad
3. Mishra Dattu Nigam	Hyderabad
4. Bharat Electronics Ltd.	Bangalore
5. Bharath Earthmovers Ltd.	Bangalore
6. Heavy Vehicles Ltd.	Avadi, Chennai
7. Garden Reach Ship Builders and Engineers Ltd.	Kolkata
8. Mazagaon Dock	Mumbai
9. Goa Shipyard	Marmugao
10. Hindustan Shipyard Ltd.	Vishakhapatnam
11. Hindustan Aeronautics Ltd.	Bangalore, Hyderabad, Nasik, Koraput, Kanpur, Lucknow

☞ Indian Army Commands

Command	HQ Location	Command	HQ Location
Eastern Command	Kolkata	Western Command	Chandigarh
Northern Command	Udhampur	Southern Command	Pune
Central Command	Lucknow	Training Command	Shimla
South-Western Command	Jaipur		

☞ Indian Air Force Commands

Command	HQ Location	Command	HQ Location
Western Air Command	New Delhi	South-Western Air Command	Gandhinagar
Central Air Command	Prayagraj	Eastern Air Command	Shillong
Southern Air Command	Thiruvananthapuram	Training Command	Bengaluru

☞ Indian Navy Commands

Command	HQ Location	Command	HQ Location
Eastern Naval Command	Vishakhapatnam	Western Naval Command	Mumbai
Southern Naval Command	Kochi		

☞ Missile and Other Weapons

Name	Class	Range
✶ Agni I	SRBM	850 km
✶ Agni II	MRBM	2500 km
✶ Agni III	IRBM	3500 km-5500 km
✶ Agni IV *or* Agni II Prime	IRBM	4000 km
✶ Agni V	ICBM	5000 km-6000 km
✶ Agni VI	ICBM	8000 km-10000 km
✶ Agni 3SL	ICBM	5200 km-11600 km
✶ Dhanush	SRBM	350 km
✶ Nirbhay	Subsonic Cruise Missile	1000 km

Name	Class	Range
✶ Brahmos	Supersonic Cruise Missile	290 km
✶ Brahmos 2	Hypersonic Cruise Missile	290 km
✶ Prithvi I	SRBM	150 km
✶ Prithvi III	SRBM	350 km
✶ Sagarika	SLBM	700 km-2200 km
✶ Shaurya	TBM	700 km-2200 km
✶ Astra	Air to Air Missile	80 km-100 km
✶ Barak-I	SRSAM	12 km
✶ Barak-8	SRSAM	90 km

☞ Chief of Defence Staff (CDS)

To bring in reform in higher defence management in the country, the post of Chief of Defence Staff (CDS) was created in the rank of a four-star General with salary and prerequisites equivalent to a Service Chief. The Chief of Defence Staff will also head the Department of Military Affairs (DMA), to be created within the Ministry of Defence and functions as its Secretary. Gen. Bipin Rawat was the first CDS of the country from January 1, 2020 to December 08, 2021. Gen. Anil Chauhan assumed the charge of the second CDS on September 30, 2022.

MULTIPLE CHOICE QUESTIONS

1. Match List-I with List-II and select the correct answer from the codes given below the lists:

List-I

(*a*) Napoleon Bonaparte

(*b*) Jean Jacques Rousseau

(*c*) Croce

(*d*) Madame Roland

List-II

1. 'A history is contemporary history'
2. 'Liberty what crimes are committed in thy name'
3. 'Man is born free but everywhere he is in chains.'
4. 'I am the Child of Revolution'

Codes :

	(*a*)	(*b*)	(*c*)	(*d*)
A.	1	2	3	4
B.	4	3	1	2
C.	3	4	2	1
D.	3	4	1	2

2. Abraham Lincon was elected the President of United States in:

A. 1862 B. 1860
C. 1875 D. 1855

3. Who was known as the 'Prince of Humanists'?

A. Francisco Petrarch B. Dante
C. Boccacio D. Erasmus

4. D-Day is the day when:

A. Germany declared war on Britain
B. US dropped the atom bomb on Hiroshima.
C. Allied Troops landed in Normandy
D. Germany surrendered to the allies

5. Whose teachings inspired the French Revolution?

A. Locke
B. Rousseau
C. Hegel
D. Plato

6. At a time when empires in Europe were crumbling before the might of Napoleon which one of the following Governor-Generals kept the British flag flying high in India?

A. Warren Hastings B. Lord Cornwallis
C. Lord Wellesley D. Lord Hastings

7. Which one of the following statements regarding Fascism in Italy is *not* true?

A. The Fascists came to power as a result of popular uprising
B. In 1926, all political parties except Mussolini's party were banned
C. The Fascists suppressed the Socialist movement
D. The Fascists were hostile to the Communists

8. The fall of Czar Nicholas-II is known as:

A. Bloody Sunday
B. Bolshevik Revolution
C. February Revolution
D. October Revolution

9. Industrial Revolution took place first in:

A. France B. Germany
C. United Kingdom D. Japan

10. The British Prime Minister at the outbreak of World War II was :

A. Churchill B. Baldwin
C. Attlee D. Chemberlain

11. The 'Great Depression' (1929) economic crisis was met by adopting the policy of

A. Stimulus B. Marshall Plan
C. New Deal D. Open Door

12. The slogan "No taxation without representation" was raised during the:

A. American War of Independence
B. Russian Revolution
C. French Revolution
D. Indian Freedom struggle

13. In the nineteenth century the people of Europe started moving from the villages to the cities due to the impact of :
A. Epidemics
B. War
C. Industrialisation
D. Population explosion in villages

14. The important cause of the Civil War in America was:
A. Abolition of slavery
B. Quest for freedom
C. Industrialisation
D. Rebellion by the native Americans

15. Industrial Revolution could not have come about without:
A. Merchant capitalism
B. The Enclosure Movement
C. The services of the proletariat class
D. An agricultural revolution

16. Consider the following statements :
The French Revolution came about mainly due to the :
1. Extreme poverty of the people
2. Impact of the works of great writers
3. Cruelty of the rulers
4. Impact of impulsive reaction
Which of the above statements are correct?
A. 1, 2 and 4 B. 2 and 3
C. 1, 3 and 4 D. 1, 2, 3 and 4

17. Asia's oldest and largest Buddhist monastery is situated in :
A. Tawang (Arunachal Pardesh)
B. Lhasa (Tibet)
C. Trincomallee (Sri Lanka)
D. Ulan Bator (Mongolia)

18. Who was the main architect of the Russian Revolution?
A. Karl Marx B. Lenin
C. Stalin D. Tolstoy

19. V.I. Lenin is associated with :
A. Russian Revolution of 1917
B. Chinese Revolution of 1949
C. German Revolution
D. French Revolution of 1789

20. Which one of the following statements is *not* correct?
A. Voltaire believed in Natural Religion
B. Rousseau wrote *Social Contract*
C. Montesquieu authored *The Spirit of Laws*
D. Necker believed in 'General Will'

21. 6th April, 1930 is well known in the history of India because this date is associated with..........
A. Dandi March by Mahatma Gandhi
B. Quit India Movement
C. Partition of Bengal
D. Partition of India

22. Which ruler enforced the system of 'Price Control' in India?
A. Mohammad Tughlak
B. Razia Begum
C. Alauddin Khilji
D. Sher Shah Suri

23. The concept of 'Din-e-Elahi' was founded by which king?
A. Dara Shikoh B. Akbar
C. Sher Shah Suri D. Shahjahan

24. Who are supposed to be the earliest inhabitants of India? Where did they come from?
A. Aryans from Central Asia
B. Dravidians from Mediterranean
C. Negroids from Africa
D. Bhils and the Santhals from West Asia

25. The one chief characteristic of temple architecture of the Gupta Age was :
A. Absence of dome
B. Huge size
C. Beautiful carvings
D. absence of a covered courtyard for the gathering of worshippers

26. The Rigveda consists of :
A. 1000 hymns B. 2028 hymns
C. 1028 hymns D. 1038 hymns

27. The central point in Ashoka's dharma was :
A. royalty to kings
B. peace and non-violence
C. respect to elders
D. religious tolerance

28. The social evil which was conspicuously absent during ancient India was :
A. *Sati*-System B. *Devadasi*-System
C. Polygamy D. *Purdah*-System

29. Which, among the following, can be accepted as a novelty introduced by Mughal emperors to their buildings?
A. Domes B. Minarets
C. Arches D. Attached gardens

30. The first ruler of India who defeated Muhammud of Ghur was :
A. Mularaja II of Gujarat
B. Prithviraja Chauhan of Delhi
C. Jayachand of Kannauj
D. Parmaldeva of Bundelkhand

31. What important event happened in India in 1911?
A. Bengal was partitioned
B. Non-Cooperation movement was launched
C. India's capital was shifted from Calcutta to Delhi
D. Mahatma Gandhi presided over the Congress session

32. The first phase of the Congress Party (1885-1905) was characterized by its efforts to secure:
A. limited independence
B. complete freedom
C. Indianization of services
D. constitutional reforms

33. The Muslim League demanded a separate homeland for the Indian Muslims openly for the first time at its annual session held in Lahore in the year :
A. 1931 A.D. B. 1936 A.D.
C. 1940 A.D. D. 1941 A.D.

34. Under whose governorship did the East India Company secure the Diwani Rights in Bengal, Bihar and Odisha from Emperor Shah Alam?
A. Lord Cornwallis
B. Lord William Bentinck
C. Lord Clive
D. Lord Wellesley

35. The Simon Commission was generally boycotted by the Indian political parties. What was the reason for this general non-cooperation?
A. the Commission aimed at dividing the people
B. it was an 'all white' Commission
C. it came after the Jallianwala Bagh carnage
D. it was an eye wash

36. Aligarh Muslim University was founded by :
A. Dr. Saifuddin Kitchlu
B. Mohammad Ali Jinnah
C. Sir Syed Ahmed Khan
D. Maulana Mohammad Ali

37. Ibn Batutah was an African traveller visiting India during the time of :
A. Alivardi Khan
B. Ala-ud-din Khalji
C. Iltutmish
D. Mohammad-bin-Tughlaq

38. The battle of Wandiawash was fought in :
A. 1726 B. 1760
C. 1818 D. 1857

39. The abolition of *Sati* by government regulation was at the time of :
A. Warren Hastings B. Lord Wellesley
C. Lord Bentinck D. Lord Ahmerst

40. Pick out the wrong combination :
A. Dilwara Temple : Mt. Abu
B. Pashupati Temple : Kathmandu
C. Padmanabh Temple : Bangalore
D. Minakshi Temple : Madurai

41. Match the following:
(*a*) Chanhudaro (*b*) Kalibangan
(*c*) Lothal (*d*) Surkotada
1. Alleged discovery of the skeleton of horse.
2. Bead making.
3. Traces of a dock and ship on seal.
4. Evidence of ploughing the fields.

The Correct code is :

	(*a*)	(*b*)	(*c*)	(*d*)
A.	2	4	3	1
B.	2	1	3	4
C.	1	2	3	4
D.	2	1	4	3

42. Match the Harappan settlements with the banks of rivers on which they were located :

(*a*) Harappa	1. Ravi
(*b*) Mohenjodaro	2. Indus
(*c*) Ropar	3. Sutlej
(*d*) Kalibangan	4. Ghaggar
(*e*) Lothal	5. Bhogava

Codes :

	(*a*)	(*b*)	(*c*)	(*d*)	(*e*)
A.	1	2	3	4	5
B.	1	2	3	5	4
C.	2	1	3	5	4
D.	2	1	4	3	5

43. The Goddess 'Kannagi' whose many temples were erected during the 'Sangam Age' was the goddess of :

A. Chastity B. Love
C. Prowess D. Wisdom

44. The Jain goal of life is to attain deliverance from the fetters of mudane existence, the way to which lies through three jewels. Which one of the following was not included among the 'three jewels' of Jainism?

A. Right faith B. Right action
C. Right knowledge D. Right conduct

45. The most striking feature of the Ashokan pillar is polish. Name the Ashokan pillar which is considered to be the most graceful of all Ashokan pillars.

A. Sarnath
B. Rampurva
C. Laurya-Nandangarh
D. Rummindei

46. Which are the correct statements?

1. The land grants, started in Satavahana period, paved the way for feudal developments in India.
2. Silk and spices were the Chief Indian export articles of Indo-Roman trade.
3. The Guptas issued the largest number of gold coins in ancient India.
4. The first memorial of a 'SATI' dated 510 A.D. is found at Eran in Madhya Pradesh.

A. 1 and 2 B. 1, 3, and 4
C. 1 and 4 D. 1, 2, 3 and 4

47. Who among the following patronised the 'Gandhara' (Indo-Greek style) School of Art?

A. Ashoka, the Great
B. Harsha Vardhana
C. Kanishka
D. Chandragupta Vikramaditya

48. The Sultanate of Delhi had five ruling dynasties. The dynasty having longest and shortest period were :

A. Ilbari and Khalji
B. Tughlaq and Khalji
C. Tughlaq and Sayyid
D. Ilbari and Lodis

49. Which one of the following events took place at the last during reign of Muhammad-bin-Tughlaq?

A. Introduction of token currency
B. Increase of land-revenue in Doab
C. Transfer of Capital from Delhi to Devagiri.
D. Conquest of Khurasan and Iraq

50. The most learned medieval Muslim ruler who was well versed in various branches of learning including astronomy, mathematics and medicine was :

A. Jalaluddin Khilji
B. Sikander Lodi
C. Ghiyasuddin Tughlaq
D. Muhammad-bin-Tughlaq

51. The 'Sufis' had 12 silsilas. They propounded the idea of Union with God through:

A. Love B. Rituals
C. Fasts D. Prayers

52. Match the following:

(*a*) Peshwa	1. Foreign affairs
(*b*) Panditrao	2. Audit and accounts
(*c*) Amatya	3. Providing grants to scholars
(*d*) Sumant	4. General supervision
	5. Military affairs

Select the correct code :

	(*a*)	(*b*)	(*c*)	(*d*)
A.	2	3	4	5
B.	4	1	2	3
C.	4	3	2	1
D.	3	1	4	2

53. The Regulating Act of 1773 can be regarded as the first measure to :
A. assert the right of British Parliament to legislate for India
B. separate the legislature from the executive
C. separate the judiciary from the executive
D. centralise law-making

54. What was the exact constitutional status of the Indian Republic on 26th January, 1950?
A. A Democratic Republic
B. A Sovereign, Democratic Republic
C. A Sovereign, Secular, Democratic Republic
D. A Sovereign, Socialist, Secular, Democratic Republic

55. When the British obtained the grant of Diwani of Bengal, Bihar and Odisha they acquired the right to :
A. maintain law and order in these territories
B. administer civil justice and collect revenue in these territories
C. collect revenue and establish revenue administration in these territories
D. militarily defend these territories

56. Which of the following were responsible for the growth of nationalism in India during the British rule?
1. Economic exploitation of India.
2. Impact of western education.
3. Role of the Press.
Select the correct answer using the codes given below :
Codes:
A. 1, 2 and 3 B. 1 and 2
C. 2 and 3 D. 1 and 3

57. Which one of the following nationalist leaders has been described as being radical in politics but conservative on social issues?
A. G.K. Gokhale
B. B.G. Tilak
C. Lala Lajpat Rai
D. Madan Mohan Malviya

58. Provincial Autonomy in British India was envisaged by the :
A. Act of 1909 B. Act of 1919
C. Act of 1935 D. Act of 1947

59. Dyarchy means :
A. double government
B. a government in which the centre is very powerful
C. a government based on division of power between centre and provinces
D. None of the above

60. The Indian National Congress observed 'Independence Day' for the first time on 26th January in :
A. 1920 B. 1925
C. 1930 D. 1947

61. ....is situated near the banks of Sabarmati River
A. Bhavnagar B. Aurangabad
C. Ahmedabad D. Rajkot

62. Sericulture is:
A. science of the various kinds of serum
B. artificial rearing of fish
C. art of silkworm breeding
D. study of various cultures of a community

63. The most abundant constituents of earth's crust are:
A. Igneous rocks
B. Sedimentary rocks
C. Metamorphic rocks
D. Granite

64. Indian Standard Time is based on:
A. 80°E longitude B. 82½°E longitude
C. 110°E longitude D. 25°E longitude

65. Tides in the oceans are caused by :
A. Gravitational pull of the moon on the earth's surface including sea water
B. Gravitational pull of the sun on the earth's surface only and not on the sea water
C. Gravitational pull of the moon and the sun on the earth's surface including the sea water
D. None of these

66. Nagarjunasagar Project is situated on the river:
A. Tungabhadra
B. Cauvery
C. Krishna
D. Godavari

67. The difference between the Indian Standard Time and the Greenwich Mean Time is:
A. – 3½ hours B. + 3½ hours
C. – 5½ hours D. + 5½ hours

68. Which of the following dams is not on Narmada river?
A. Indira-Sagar Project
B. Maheshwar Hydel Power Project
C. Jobat Project
D. Koyna Power Project

69. Which of the following statements is **not true** about the availability of water on the earth, the crisis for which is going to increase in the years to come?
A. About 97.5 per cent of the total volume of water available on the earth is salty
B. 80 per cent of the water available to us for use comes in bursts as monsoons
C. About 2.5 per cent of the total water available on the earth is polluted water and cannot be used for human activities
D. Possibility is that some big glaciers will melt in the coming ten-fifteen years and sea level will rise by 3-4 metres all over the earth

70. Which of the following is **not** a cash crop?
A. Jute B. Paddy
C. Cashewnut D. Sugarcane

71. Through which States does Cauvery River flow?
A. Gujarat, M.P., Tamil Nadu
B. Karnataka, Kerala, Tamil Nadu
C. Karnataka, Kerala, Andhra Pradesh
D. M.P., Maharashtra, Tamil Nadu

72. Indian Standard Time is the local time of 82½°E which passes through :
A. Guntur B. Delhi
C. Allahabad D. Kolkata

73. The 17th parallel defines the boundary between:
A. North and South Korea
B. USA and Canada
C. North and South Vietnam
D. China and Russia

74. During the period of south-west monsoon, Tamil Nadu remains dry because:
A. the winds do not reach this area
B. there are no mountains in this area
C. it lies in the rain shadow area
D. the temperature is too high to let the winds cool down

75. Which country does top in producing cocoa?
A. Cote d'Ivoire B. Brazil
C. Croatia D. Nigeria

76. The biggest reserves of thorium are in :
A. India B. China
C. The Soviet Union D. U.S.A.

77. The Girnar Hills are situated in which of the following states?
A. Gujarat B. Karnataka
C. Madhya Pradesh D. Maharashtra

78. During December 22nd the sun is vertically over:
A. Tropic of Cancer
B. Tropic of Capricorn
C. The Equator
D. None of the above

79. Photosphere is described as the :
A. Lower layer of atmosphere
B. Visible surface of the sun from which radiation emanates
C. Wavelength of solar spectrum
D. None of the above

80. Broadly, there are three layers of the earth of the crust, the mantle and the core. The crust forms what percentage of the volume of the earth?
A. 0.5% B. 2.5%
C. 7.5% D. 12.5%

81. The grassland of Argentina is known as :
A. Pampas B. Campos
C. Savanna D. None of the above

82. Different seasons are formed because :
A. Sun is moving around the earth
B. of revolution of the earth around the Sun on its orbit
C. of rotation of the earth around its axis
D. All of the above

83. Eskers and Drumlins are features formed by:
A. underground water
B. running water
C. the action of wind
D. glacial action

84. Match List-I and List-II and select the correct answer using the codes given below the Lists :

List-I *(Rivers)*	**List-II** *(Towns)*
(*a*) Ghaghara	1. Lucknow
(*b*) Brahmaputra	2. Hoshangabad
(*c*) Narmada	3. Ahmedabad
(*d*) Sabarmati	4. Guwahati
	5. Ayodhya

	(*a*)	(*b*)	(*c*)	(*d*)
A.	4	5	1	2
B.	5	4	2	3
C.	5	4	3	1
D.	3	5	2	1

85. Which of the statements as regards the consequences of the movement of the earth is not correct?
A. Revolution of the earth is the cause of the change of seasons.
B. Rotation of the earth is the cause of days and nights.
C. Rotation of the earth causes variation in the duration of days and nights.
D. Rotation of the earth effects the movement of winds and ocean currents.

86. The world is divided into :
A. 12 time zones
B. 20 time zones
C. 24 time zones
D. 36 time zones

87. The 'Kiel' canal links the :
A. Pacific and Atlantic Oceans
B. Mediterranean Sea and Red Sea
C. Mediterranean Sea and Black Sea
D. North Sea and Baltic Sea

88. Match the following :

List-I	**List-II**
(*a*) Himadri	1. Outer Himalayas
(*b*) Shivalik	2. Inner Himalayas
(*c*) Himanchal	3. Middle Himalayas
(*d*) Sahyadri	4. Western Ghats

Codes:

	(*a*)	(*b*)	(*c*)	(*d*)
A.	1	2	3	4
B.	4	2	3	1
C.	2	1	3	4
D.	1	2	3	4

89. The term 'Regur' refers to:
A. Laterite soils
B. Black Cotton soils
C. Red Soils
D. Deltaic Alluvial Soils

90. Location of sugar industry in India is shifting from north to south because of:
A. cheap labour
B. expanding regional market
C. cheap and abundant supply of power
D. high yield and high sugar content in sugarcane

91. Consider the following statements :
1. Ozone is found mostly in the Stratosphere.
2. Ozone layer lies 55-75 km above the surface of the earth.
3. Ozone absorbs ultraviolet radiation from the Sun.
4. Ozone layer has no significance for life on the earth.

Which of the above statements are correct?
A. 1 and 3 B. 2 and 4
C. 2 and 3 D. 1 and 4

92. Match List-I with List-II and select the correct answer using the codes given below the Lists :

List-I *(Crops)*	**List-II** *(Producer)*
(*a*) Banana	1. Brazil
(*b*) Cocoa	2. Cote d'Ivoire
(*c*) Coffee	3. India
(*d*) Tea	4. China

Codes :

	(*a*)	(*b*)	(*c*)	(*d*)
A.	2	3	1	4
B.	3	2	1	4
C.	3	2	4	1
D.	2	3	4	1

93. Darjeeling and Dharamsala would be the right places to visit if one wanted to get a clear view respectively of :

A. Kanchanjunga and Dhauladhar ranges
B. Nandadevi and Dhauladhar ranges
C. Kanchanjunga and Nandadevi ranges
D. Nandadevi and Nanga Parvat

94. Atmosphere exists because:

A. The Gravitational force of the Earth
B. Revolution of the Earth
C. Rotation of the Earth
D. Weight of the gases of atmosphere

95. Victoria lake is located in the continent:

A. Africa
B. Asia
C. North America
D. South America

96. The famous Lagoon Lake of India is :

A. Dal Lake B. Chilka Lake
C. Pulicat Lake D. Mansarover

97. Where are most of the earth's active volcanoes concentrated?

A. Indian Ocean B. Pacific Ocean
C. Aral Sea D. Atlantic Ocean

98. Through which of the following states does the river Chambal flow?

A. U.P., M.P., Rajasthan
B. M.P., Gujarat, U.P.
C. Rajasthan, M.P., Bihar
D. Gujarat, M.P., U.P.

99. Which country is called the sugar bowl of the world?

A. Cuba B. India
C. Argentina D. USA

100. The area covered by forest in India is about:

A. 46% B. 33%
C. 23% D. 21.76%

101. A closed economy is the one which :

A. does not permit emigration or immigration
B. permits emigration but no immigration
C. engages in no foreign trade
D. engages in no foreign and domestic trade or transit

102. In a developed economy the major share of employment originates in the :

A. primary sector B. tertiary sector
C. secondary sector D. any of the above

103. The Economic and Social Commission for Asia and Pacific (ESCAP) is located at :

A. Bangkok B. Kuala Lumpur
C. Manila D. Singapore

104. Commercial vehicles are not produced by which of the following companies in India?

A. TELCO B. Ashok Leyland
C. DCM Daewoo D. Birla Yamaha

105. In India, the Public Sector is most dominant in:

A. transport
B. steel production
C. commercial banking
D. organised term-lending financial institutions

106. The main argument advanced in favour of small scale and cottage industries in India is that:

A. cost of production is low
B. they require small capital investment
C. they advance the goal of equitable distribution of wealth
D. they generate a large volume of employment

107. The most serious economic problems of India are:

A. Poverty and unemployment
B. Stagnation, not poverty
C. Unemployment, not poverty
D. Underdevelopment, not poverty

108. Which of the following is not one of the three central problems of an economy?

A. What to produce
B. How to produce
C. When to produce
D. For whom to produce

109. If saving exceeds investment, the national income will:

A. fall B. rise
C. fluctuate D. remain constant

110. In which of the following industries in India are the maximum number of workers employed?
A. Sugar B. Jute
C. Textiles D. Iron and Steel

111. Terrace Cultivation is practiced mostly:
A. in urban areas
B. on slopes of mountains
C. on tops of hills
D. in undulating tracts

112. Which of the following is a Selective Credit Control method?
A. Bank Rate
B. RBI directives
C. Cash Reserve Ratio
D. Open market operations

113. Which of the following taxes is not shared by the Central Government with the States?
A. Union excise duties
B. Customs duty
C. Income tax
D. Estate duty

114. ICICI is the name of a:
A. Financial Institution
B. Chemical Industry
C. Cotton Industry
D. Chamber of Commerce and Industry

115. Structural Unemployment arises due to
A. Deflationary conditions
B. Heavy industry bias
C. Shortage of raw material
D. Inadequate productive capacity

116. Which Commission replaced the Planning Commission in 2015?
A. NIYAM Aayog
B. NAGRIK Aayog
C. NITI Aayog
D. Jan Aayog

117. The largest public sector bank in India is:
A. Central Bank of India
B. Punjab National Bank
C. State Bank of India
D. Indian Overseas Bank

118. Which of the following statements best explains the term contraband goods?
A. Goods produced only for exports
B. Goods produced in joint sector only
C. Goods for the trading of which licence is not required
D. Goods that are forbidden, from export, import or even possession, by law

119. Price in the market is fixed by:
A. Stock exchange rates
B. The demand and supply ruling in the market at a particular time
C. The Finance Minister
D. None of the above

120. Devaluation of currency helps to promote:
A. National Income
B. Savings
C. Imports at lower cost
D. Exports

121. Balanced economic growth can be achieved only if:
A. All the sectors of economy grow at the same rate
B. Population growth is arrested
C. All the inter dependent sectors grow in harmony
D. Basic and heavy industries are assigned highest priority

122. P.V. Sindhu is associated with which of the following sports?
A. Badminton
B. Weightlifting
C. Swimming
D. Tennis

123. 'MODVAT' stands for:
A. Modified Value Added Tax
B. Deduction of cost of inputs from the value of output
C. Reduction in import duties
D. Imposition of tax on professions

124. Who among the following is the first to receive 'Dada Saheb Phalke' award?
A. Shivaji Ganeson B. Devika Rani
C. Dr. Raj Kumar D. None of the above

125. The term 'devaluation' means:
A. Reducing the value of a currency in terms of another currency
B. Increasing the value of a currency
C. Revising the value of a currency
D. None of the above

126. Per capita net availability of pulses has shown a tendency of:
A. Increase over time
B. Decrease over time
C. Constant over time
D. First increase then decrease

127. National Income is the same as:
A. Net national product at market price
B. Net domestic product at market price
C. Net national product at factor cost
D. Net domestic product at factor cost

128. Which one of the following is not an example of indirect tax?
A. Sales tax B. Excise duty
C. Customs duty D. Expenditure tax

129. The major aim of devaluation is to:
A. encourage imports
B. encourage exports
C. encourage both exports and imports
D. discourage both exports and imports

130. Structural unemployment arises due to:
A. deflationary conditions
B. heavy industry bias
C. shortage of raw materials
D. inadequate productive capacity

131. When was the Family Planning Programme officially started in India?
A. 1950 B. 1952
C. 1956 D. 1962

132. When was the Reserve Bank of India nationalised?
A. 1947 B. 1949
C. 1950 D. 1951

133. Which of the following is *not* a feature of the Indian economy?
A. High rate of population growth
B. Disguised unemployment
C. Lowest rate of adult literacy
D. High rate of exports

134. The 'Relative Deprivation' approach for measuring poverty has been adopted by:
A. developing countries
B. developed countries
C. under-developed countries
D. None of the above

135. One of the main factors that led to rapid expansion of Indian exports is:
A. Imposition of import duties
B. Liberalisation of the economy
C. Recession in other countries
D. Diversification of exports

136. Sustainable economic development means an increase in the rate of growth of real:
A. total and per capita product
B. total and per capita product and level of literacy rate
C. total and per capita product and life expectancy at birth
D. total and per capita product, taking into account the cost of degradation of the quality of environment in this process

137. Functional unemployment occurs when:
A. unemployed have no qualification for job
B. people frequently change their job
C. people were thrown out from job due to recession
D. None of these

138. Which among the following does **not** have a 'free trade zone'?
A. Kandla B. Mumbai
C. Visakhapatnam D. Thiruvanantpuram

139. Sun Belt of USA is important for which one of the following industries?
A. Cotton textile
B. Petrochemicals
C. Hi-tech electronics
D. Food Processing

140. Commercial banking system in India is
A. unit banking B. branch banking
C. mixed banking D. None of the above

141. Who gives recognition to political parties in India?
A. Parliament

B. President
C. Supreme Court
D. Election Commission

142. The Quorum of the Legislative Council is :
A. one-fourth of its total membership
B. one-third of its membership
C. one-tenth of its membership
D. 25

143. The Indian Constitution is:
A. federal
B. unitary
C. a happy mixture of the federal and unitary
D. federal in normal times and unitary in times of emergency

144. Universal adult franchise implies a right to vote to all:
A. adult residents of the State
B. adult male citizens of the State
C. residents of the State
D. adult citizens of the State

145. When a resolution prefering a charge against the President has been passed by a specified majority in the House, it is sent to the other House for investigation. If, as a result of such an investigation, a resolution is passed through a specified majority by the other House, declaring that the charge has been sustained, the President shall leave his office. The specified special majority must not be less than :
A. two-third of the members present and voting
B. one-third of the members present and voting
C. three-fourth of the members present and voting and two-third of the total membership
D. two-third of the total membership

146. Which one of the following judicial powers of the President of India has been *wrongly* listed?
A. he appoints the Chief Justice and other judges of the Supreme Court
B. he can remove the judges of the Supreme Court on grounds of misconduct
C. he can consult the Supreme Court on any question of law or fact which is of public importance
D. he can grant pardon, reprieves and respites to persons punished under Union Law

147. The Vice-president of India can be removed from his office before the expiry of his term if :
A. the Rajya Sabha passes a resolution by a majority of its members and the Lok Sabha agrees with the resolution
B. if the Supreme Court of India recommends his removal
C. the President so desires
D. None of the above

148. The Chief Justice of a High Court in India is appointed by the :
A. Governor of the State
B. Prime Minister of India
C. Chief Justice of the Supreme Court
D. President of India

149. Which of the following statements is constitutionally not true about the passing of the Union Budgets, Railway Budgets and Finance Bill in India?
1. Under the law, Finance Bill should be adopted by both the Houses of the Parliament within 45 days of its introduction.
2. If the Finance Bill is not adopted within specified period, the government loses its authority to levy the taxes proposed in the budgets.
3. In the absence of full budget, a vote-on-account gives the power to the government to spend.
4. Government cannot raise revenues without a proper approval of the Finance Bill

A. Only 2 B. Only 3
C. Only 4 D. Only 1, 2 and 3

150. Normally, on whose advice the President's Rule is imposed in a State?
A. Chief Minister
B. Legislative Assembly
C. Governor
D. Chief Justice of High Court

151. Which Article of the Indian Constitution deals with Amendment procedure?
A. Article 368 B. Article 358
C. Article 367 D. All of these

152. Government is the agency through which the will of :
A. the state is expressed
B. the people is expressed
C. the head of the state is expressed
D. the majority is expressed

153. In a unitary system of government :
A. The centre is all powerful
B. The centre is weaker than the states
C. The centre and states stand at par
D. The states and centre are supreme in their respective spheres

154. In Cabinet System of Government the real executive authority rests with :
A. The Council of Ministers
B. The Prime Minister
C. The Constitution
D. The Parliament

155. The Head of the State under a parliamentary government:
A. is an elected representative
B. is a hereditary person
C. is a nominated person
D. may be any one of the above

156. In the event of a ministerial proposal being defeated on the floor of the legislature, under the parliamentary system :
A. the government waits for a general no-confidence motion
B. the minister concerned is taken to task by the Prime Minister
C. the minister is forced to resign
D. the whole Council of Ministers resign

157. The "due process of law" is an essential characteristic of the judicial system of:
A. UK B. France
C. USA D. India

158. Under the Constitution it is :
A. obligatory for the President to accept the advice of the Council of Ministers but is not obliged to follow it
B. obligatory for the President to accept the advice of the Council of Ministers
C. not obligatory for the President to seek or accept the advice of the Council of Ministers
D. obligatory for the President to seek the advice of the Council of Ministers if his own party is in power

159. Which one of the following statements is correct?
A. the Presiding Officer of Rajya Sabha is elected every year
B. the Presiding Officer of Rajya Sabha is elected for a term of two years at a time
C. the Presiding Officer of Rajya Sabha is elected for a term of six years
D. the Vice-President of India is the ex-officio Presiding Officer of Rajya Sabha

160. The introduction of "no confidence" motion in the Lok Sabha requires the support of at least:
A. 50 members B. 70 members
C. 60 members D. 80 members

161. The High Court comes under :
A. State List B. Union List
C. Concurrent List D. None of the above

162. Which one of the following has been wrongly listed as a Fundamental Duty of the Indian citizens?
A. to develop scientific temper, humanism and spirit of inquiry and reform
B. to work for raising the prestige of the country in the international sphere
C. to protect and improve the natural environment
D. to strive towards excellence in all spheres of individual and collective activity

163. Which one of the following is not a Fundamental Duty as outlined in Article 51A of the Constitution?
A. to abide by the Constitution and respect its ideals
B. to defend the country and render national service when called upon to do so

C. to work for the moral upliftment of the weaker sections of society
D. to preserve the rich heritage

164. The main characteristics of the Directive Principles of State Policy given in the Indian Constitution are :
A. not enforceable by any court
B. fundamental in the governance of the country
C. 'Like instruments, instructions, political manifesto and a code of moral precepts which have to guide governors of the country'
D. no law can be passed, which is opposed to these principles

165. Of the following which are true?
A. In a State, the Legislative Council is dominant with regard to non-financial bills and the Legislative Assembly with regard to financial (money) bills
B. Vidhan Parishad can virtually block legisla-tion even if the same is passed by the Vidhan Sabha
C. In case of a tie between the two Houses, the Governor is duty-bound to call a joint session of the two Houses to have the issue settled on a majority verdict
D. If a Bill is twice approved by the Vidhan Sabha, it becomes law even if rejected by the Vidhan Parishad

166. Which one of the following types of emergency can be declared by the President?
A. Emergency due to threat of war and external aggresion
B. Emergency due to break-down of constitutional machinery in a State
C. Financial emergency on account of threat to the financial credit of India
D. all the three emergencies

167. The chairman of which of the following parliamentary committees is invariably from the members of ruling party?
A. Committee on public undertakings
B. Public accounts committee
C. Estimates committee
D. Committee on delegated legislation

168. Which of the following is not a formally prescribed device available to the members of parliament?
A. Question hour
B. Zero hour
C. Half-an-hour discussion
D. Short duration discussion

169. Which of the following is not a tool of executive control over public administration?
A. Power of appointment and removal
B. Line agencies
C. Appeal to public opinion
D. Civil services code

170. If the Speaker of the State Legislative Assembly decides to resign, he should submit his resignation to the:
A. Judges of the High Court
B. Deputy Speaker
C. Chief Minister
D. Finance Minister

171. Who was the first Home Minister of Independent India?
A. Rajendra Prasad
B. Jawahar Lal Nehru
C. B.R. Ambedkar
D. Sardar Vallabh Bhai Patel

172. India is a Federal State because of:
A. dual judiciary
B. dual citizenship prevalent here
C. share of power between the Centre and the States
D. rigid Constitution

173. Residuary Subjects are those subjects which are:
A. contained in the State list
B. contained in the Union list
C. contained in the Concurrent list
D. not covered by any of the three lists

174. Which of the following writs can be issued, by the Supreme Court, to enforce Fundamental Rights?
A. Writ of Habeas Corpus
B. Writ of Mandamus
C. Writ of Quo Warranto
D. All of these

175. When the offices of both the President and the Vice-President of India are vacant, who will discharge their functions?
A. Prime Minister
B. Home Minister
C. Chief Justice of India
D. The Speaker

176. The Supreme Court tenders advice to the President of India on a matter of law or fact:
A. on its own
B. only when such advice is sought
C. only if the matter relates to some basic issue
D. only if the issue poses a threat to the unity and integrity of the country

177. Six months shall **not** intervene between two sessions of the Indian Parliament because :
A. it is the customary practice
B. it is the British convention followed in India
C. it is an obligation under the Constitution of India
D. None of the above

178. The States of the Indian Union can be recognised or their boundaries altered by:
A. the Union Parliament by a simple majority in the ordinary process of legislation
B. two-thirds majority of both the Houses of Parliament
C. two-thirds majority of both the Houses of Parliament and the consent of the legislatures of concerned States
D. an executive order of the Union government with the consent of the concerned State governments

179. The Basic Feature theory of the Constitution of India was propounded by the Supreme Court in the case of :
A. Minerva Mills Vs. Union of India
B. Golaknath Vs. State of Punjab
C. Maneka Gandhi Vs. Union of India
D. Keshavananda Vs. State of Kerala

180. Which one of the following writs is issued by a court in case of illegal detention of a person?
A. Habeas corpus B. Mandamus
C. Certiorari D. Quo-warranto

181. Name the instrument with the help of which a sailor in a submarine can see the objects on the surface of the sea.
A. Telescope B. Periscope
C. Gycroscope D. Stereoscope

182. 'HEMOPHILLIA' is the disease of ....
A. liver B. blood
C. brain D. bones

183. Vitamin A is abundantly found in ....
A. Brinjal B. Tomato
C. Carrot D. Cabbage

184. .... is not soluble in water.
A. Vitamin A B. Vitamin B
C. Vitamin C D. None of these

185. The blood vessels with the smallest diameter are called ....
A. capillaries B. arterioles
C. venules D. lymphatics

186. Out of the following .... has the greatest elasticity.
A. steel B. rubber
C. aluminium D. annealed copper

187. Cooking gas is a mixture of which of the following two gases?
A. Carbon Dioxide and Oxygen
B. Butane and Propane
C. Carbon Monoxide and Carbon Dioxide
D. Methane and Ethylene

188. The substance most commonly used as a food preservative is:
A. sodium carbonate B. tartaric acid
C. acetic acid D. benzoic acid

189. Normally, the substances that fight against diseases in human systems are known as:
A. dioxyribonucleic acids
B. carbohydrates
C. enzymes
D. antibodies

190. The SI unit of temperature is ....
A. Kelvin B. Celsius
C. Fahrenheit D. None of the above

191. One of the common fungal diseases of man is :
A. plague B. ringworm
C. cholera D. typhoid

192. A clear sky is blue because:
A. red light is scattered more than blue
B. ultraviolet light has been absorbed
C. blue light is scattered more than red
D. blue light has been absorbed

193. Jenner introduced the method of making people immune to :
A. small pox B. rabies
C. cholera D. polio

194. The largest cell in the human body is :
A. Nerve cell B. Live cell
C. Muscle cell D. Kidney cell

195. What is the device that steps up or steps down the voltage?
A. Dynamo B. Conductor
C. Inductor D. Transformer

196. The protein deficiency disease is known as :
A. Kwashiorker B. Cirrhosis
C. Eczema D. Clycoses

197. Iron deficiency causes :
A. rickets B. anaemia
C. cirrhosis D. goitre

198. Blood group of an individual is controlled by :
A. Haemoglobin B. Shape of RBC
C. Shape of WBC D. Genes

199. In a normal man the amount of blood pumped out by the heart per minute is about :
A. 1 litre B. 3 litres
C. 4 litres D. 5 litres

200. Red/green colour blindness in man is known as :
A. Protanopia
B. Deutetanopia
C. Both A and B above
D. Marfan's syndrome

201. The blue colour of the water in the sea is due to :
A. Reflection of the blue light by the impurities in sea water
B. Reflection of the blue sky by sea water and scattering of blue light by water molecules
C. Absorption of other colours by water molecules
D. None of the above

202. The image formed on the retina of the eye is:
A. upright and real
B. larger than the object
C. small and inverted
D. enlarged and real

203. Unit of loudness of sound is:
A. bel B. decibel
C. phon D. none of these

204. Oil rises up the wick in a lamp :
A. because oil is volatile
B. due to the capillary action phenomenon
C. due to the surface tension phenomenon
D. because oil is very light

205. The 'stones' formed in human kidney consist mostly of :
A. calcium oxalate
B. sodium acetate
C. magnesium sulphate
D. calcium

206. We hear the sound later, while the light is seen earlier:
A. because light's speed is more than that of sound
B. because lights travel in a straight direction while sound in a zigzag direction
C. because sound's frequency is lower than light
D. All of the above

207. Which part of an eye is transplanted?
A. Cornea B. Retina
C. Iris D. Sciera

208. The Universal donor group of blood is:
A. O B. A
C. B D. AB

209. The green colour of the leaf is due to :
A. Presence of Chloroplast
B. Presence of Chromium
C. Presence of Nicoplast
D. Presence of excess of oxygen

210. Voice of a child is more shrill than that of an elderly person because:
A. the pitch of the child's voice is higher than that of the person
B. the pitch is lower
C. the child is more energetic
D. None of the above

ANSWERS

1	**2**	**3**	**4**	**5**	**6**	**7**	**8**	**9**	**10**
B	C	D	C	B	C	A	C	C	D
11	**12**	**13**	**14**	**15**	**16**	**17**	**18**	**19**	**20**
C	A	C	A	A	D	A	B	A	D
21	**22**	**23**	**24**	**25**	**26**	**27**	**28**	**29**	**30**
A	C	B	C	D	C	B	D	D	B
31	**32**	**33**	**34**	**35**	**36**	**37**	**38**	**39**	**40**
C	D	C	C	B	C	D	B	C	C
41	**42**	**43**	**44**	**45**	**46**	**47**	**48**	**49**	**50**
A	A	A	B	C	D	C	B	B	D
51	**52**	**53**	**54**	**55**	**56**	**57**	**58**	**59**	**60**
A	C	A	B	B	A	B	C	A	C
61	**62**	**63**	**64**	**65**	**66**	**67**	**68**	**69**	**70**
C	C	B	B	C	C	D	D	D	B
71	**72**	**73**	**74**	**75**	**76**	**77**	**78**	**79**	**80**
B	C	C	C	A	A	A	B	B	A
81	**82**	**83**	**84**	**85**	**86**	**87**	**88**	**89**	**90**
A	B	D	B	C	C	D	C	B	D
91	**92**	**93**	**94**	**95**	**96**	**97**	**98**	**99**	**100**
A	B	A	A	A	B	B	A	A	D
101	**102**	**103**	**104**	**105**	**106**	**107**	**108**	**109**	**110**
C	B	D	D	D	D	A	C	B	C
111	**112**	**113**	**114**	**115**	**116**	**117**	**118**	**119**	**120**
B	B	B	A	D	C	C	B	B	D
121	**122**	**123**	**124**	**125**	**126**	**127**	**128**	**129**	**130**
C	A	A	B	A	D	C	D	B	D
131	**132**	**133**	**134**	**135**	**136**	**137**	**138**	**139**	**140**
B	B	D	A	B	D	B	D	D	C
141	**142**	**143**	**144**	**145**	**146**	**147**	**148**	**149**	**150**
D	C	D	D	D	B	A	D	C	C
151	**152**	**153**	**154**	**155**	**156**	**157**	**158**	**159**	**160**
A	B	A	A	A	D	C	B	D	A
161	**162**	**163**	**164**	**165**	**166**	**167**	**168**	**169**	**170**
B	B	C	B	D	D	C	B	B	B
171	**172**	**173**	**174**	**175**	**176**	**177**	**178**	**179**	**180**
D	C	D	D	C	B	C	A	B	A
181	**182**	**183**	**184**	**185**	**186**	**187**	**188**	**189**	**190**
B	B	C	A	A	A	B	D	D	A
191	**192**	**193**	**194**	**195**	**196**	**197**	**198**	**199**	**200**
B	C	A	A	D	A	B	D	D	A
201	**202**	**203**	**204**	**205**	**206**	**207**	**208**	**209**	**210**
B	B	B	B	A	A	A	A	A	A